A Programmer's Guide to .NET

GW00360888

A Programmer's Guide to .NET

Alexei Fedorov

Addison-Wesley

An imprint of **Pearson Education**

London · Boston · Indianapolis · New York · Mexico City · Toronto · Sydney · Tokyo · Singapore
Hong Kong · Cape Town · New Delhi · Madrid · Paris · Amsterdam · Milan · Munich · Stockholm

PEARSON EDUCATION LIMITED

Head Office:
Edinburgh Gate
Harlow CM20 2JE
Tel: +44 (0)1279 623623
Fax: +44 (0)1279 431059

London Office:
128 Long Acre
London WC2E 9AN
Tel: +44 (0)20 7447 2000
Fax: +44 (0)20 7447 2170
Websites: www.it-minds.com
          www.aw.com/cseng/

First published in Great Britain in 2002

© Pearson Education Ltd 2002

The right of Alexei Fedorov to be identified as the author of this work has been
asserted by him in accordance with the Copyright, Designs and Patents Act 1988.
Screenshots reprinted by permission from Microsoft Corporation.

ISBN 0-321-11232-6

British Library Cataloguing-in-Publication Data
A CIP catalogue record for this book can be obtained from the British Library.

Library of Congress Cataloging in Publication Data
Applied for.

10 9 8 7 6 5 4 3 2 1

Typeset by Pantek Arts Ltd, Maidstone, Kent.
Printed and bound in Great Britain by Biddles Ltd of Guildford and King's Lynn.

The Publishers' policy is to use paper manufactured from sustainable forests.

Contents

About the author

Alexei Fedorov is a developer and consultant based in Moscow. Alexei has more than 20 years' experience, including working as a Chief Technology Officer for a Swiss company, technical writing for a software magazine, creation of internet and intranet sites, providing technical support for Borland languages, development and software localization as well as writing books and articles for progammers. Alexei has coauthored such books a *Professional ASP 2.0* and *ASP 2.0 Programmer's Reference*, published by Wrox, and *Advanced Delphi Developer's Guide to ADO*, published by Wordware, and contributed several articles to such magazines as *Asp.Net Pro*, *Office Pro*, and *Delphi Informant Magazine*.

Introduction

Welcome to *A Programmer's Guide to .NET*. This book will teach you about the .NET Framework, its architecture, main components, and supported technologies. Here are brief summaries of the contents of the chapters in this book.

In *Chapter 1, .NET platform overview*, we provide an overview of the Microsoft .NET platform and discuss its main components. We discuss development tools and .NET languages, .NET enterprise servers, and provide a brief overview of the Microsoft .NET Framework. We discuss the .NET Framework class library, common language runtime, and web services. In the second part of this chapter, we learn how to install Microsoft .NET Framework SDK.

The second chapter, *Common Language Runtime*, is dedicated to the core component of the Microsoft .NET Framework – Common Language Runtime (CLR), which is the infrastructure .NET uses to execute all .NET applications – from simple console applications to web forms (ASP.NET applications) to Windows forms-based applications.

The .NET Framework class library – types and structures is Chapter 3. In this chapter we start our journey through the .NET Framework class library – a set of namespaces, classes, interfaces, and value types that are used in our .NET applications, components, and controls.

Chapter 4, More on the .NET Framework class library – streams, file system, and networking, covers classes that are implemented in two namespaces – the `System.IO` namespace and `System.Net` namespace. We start with the `System.IO` namespace and discuss such things as streams, streams readers, and writers, as well as classes that provide us with functions to work with the file system and files. After this, we move on to the `System.Net` namespace and learn about networking features implemented by the classes available in this namespace.

In *Chapter 5, The Microsoft .NET Framework class library – more goodies*, we end our tour around the .NET Framework class library that we started back in Chapter 3. Here we discuss several useful classes and other types that are available in the class library.

Chapter 6, ASP.NET and web forms, shows how to use Microsoft .NET to create web applications with the help of two technologies – Active Server Pages .NET (ASP.NET) and web forms.

ASP.NET server controls are covered in *Chapter 7*, where we learn about this set of classes, which we can use to create an ASP.NET applications user interface.

The eighth chapter focuses on *Windows forms*. Here we explore the .NET Framework library classes that allow us to create Windows applications. We discuss the "real" Windows applications that run on the desktop under Microsoft .NET. Such applications can have windows, controls, can draw graphics, and react to keyboard and mouse events.

Chapter 9, Windows forms controls, starts our two-part discussion of these controls. Here we learn about such standard controls as buttons, text controls, labels, lists, and menus. For each group, we provide a list of classes that comprise it, as well as detailed descriptions of each class, its properties and methods, as well as usage examples.

The tenth chapter is entitled *Additional Windows forms controls*. In Chapter 9 we learned how to make the most of the standard Windows controls – text boxes, buttons, check boxes, radio buttons, list boxes, and so on. The Microsoft .NET Framework class library contains controls that extend the basic set of controls found in Windows. In *Chapter 10* we learn about these additional controls, as well as how to use ActiveX controls in web forms.

In *Chapter 11, Graphical functions and GDI+*, we explore graphical functions available in the System.Drawing namespace and its secondary namespaces. We start this chapter with an overview of the graphics device interface (GDI) and its advanced version – graphics device interface plus (GDI+), then move on to a discussion of the System.Drawing namespace and its secondary namespaces. The second part of the chapter is dedicated to printing in .NET applications and the third part to talking about using graphics functionality in ASP.NET applications.

Chapter 12, Working with Data – ADO.NET, explores the ADO.NET – the data access component of the .NET Framework. As with the ASP.NET, ADO.NET is not just a new version of Microsoft ADO – it is a completely new data access architecture based on managed providers and a set of classes that we discuss in this chapter.

The thirteenth chapter, *Using data binding controls*, focuses on the data binding controls available in the ASP.NET and Windows forms. Data binding is the process of automatically setting properties of one or more controls at runtime from a structure that contains data.

The penultimate chapter, *Working with XML*, is about XML support in the Microsoft .NET Framework. XML is the universal format for data on the web. It allows developers to easily describe and deliver rich, structured data from any application in a standard, consistent way. XML is at the core of many features of the Microsoft .NET Framework – configuration management, object serialization, remoting, web services, database access, and file storage.

The last chapter, *Building and consuming web services*, provides information about web services – reusable web components that can be invoked from any platform capable of communicating over the internet. Web services expose their functionality via standard web protocols such as HTTP and XML and enable us to interconnect web applications. We can say that web services are URL-addressable resources that return requested information to a client or manipulate the data model behind the web service.

In the appendix, a list of selected web resources is provided.

All code examples in this book are provided in Visual Basic .NET, but it should not be a problem to port the code to other .NET languages – the code illustrates the usage of .NET Framework rather than the programming techniques of VB.NET.

chapter 1

.NET platform overview

- Development tools

- .NET languages

- .NET Enterprise servers

- The .NET Framework

- Installing the Microsoft.NET Framework

In this chapter we will provide an overview of the Microsoft .NET platform and discuss its main components. Microsoft .NET can be considered from different points of view. As a *platform*, it consists of the following product groups.

- **Development tools** A set of languages, including C#, VB.NET, J#, a set of development tools, including Visual Studio.NET (a suite of language-independent developer tools, a set of programming interfaces), .NET Framework (for building web and Windows applications, as well as web services), and Common Language Runtime, which is the execution engine for .NET Framework applications

- **.NET Enterprise servers** A suite of e-business infrastructure applications that run XML web services – SQL Server 2000, Exchange Server 2000, BizTalk Server 2000 and others. These servers are used to store relational data, data exchange and business-to-business (B2B) commerce

- **Web services (building block services)** A set of commercial web services, which includes customer services (.NET MyServices), authentication and identification services (.NET Passport) and communication services (.NET Alerts). Developers can use these services to build applications that require knowledge of user identity

- **.NET device software** Consisting of Windows XP, Windows Me, Windows CE, Windows Embedded, the .NET Framework and .NET Compact Framework, this software enables a new set of .NET-enabled devices – from mobile phones to PDAs and game boxes.

Figure 1.1 shows the main components of the .NET platform.

The bottom layer is the operating system, which runs on different devices, ranging from servers to smart devices. Right now .NET is implemented as an add-on on top of existing operating systems – Windows XP, Windows 2000, Windows Me and Windows CE.

The middle layer consists of .NET Enterprise servers, .NET Framework and .NET web services. .NET Enterprise servers will be used to create and manage business applications. Enterprise servers are designed using open web standards, such as extensible markup language (XML). They are also built to provide interoperability with existing infrastructure investments and for scalability to meet internet demands.

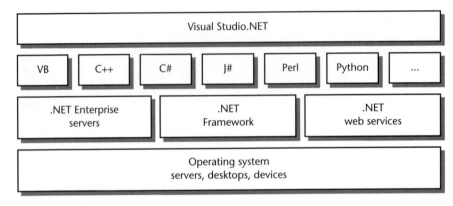

FIGURE 1.1   The main components of the .NET platform

1.1 Development tools

Microsoft Visual Studio.NET is a professional development environment that is built on top of the .NET Framework. It provides an integrated development environment that is a single, unified, fully customizable environment shared across all Visual Studio.NET languages – both languages provided by Microsoft, namely C#, C++, Visual Basic VB and J# (see below) and third-party languages. Visual Studio.NET simplifies many development tasks and allows us to quickly create .NET applications based on Windows forms and web forms as well as consume services provided by the underlying operating system (see Figure 1.2).

Visual Studio.NET comes in three editions:

- Visual Studio.NET Professional;
- Visual Studio.NET Enterprise Developer;
- Visual Studio.NET Enterprise Architect.

All three versions of Visual Studio.NET are compatible with the following versions of Windows:

- Windows XP Professional;
- Windows XP Home Edition;

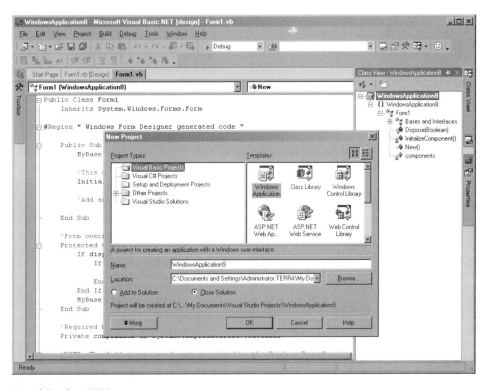

FIGURE 1.2   Visual Studio.NET in use

- Windows 2000 Professional;
- Windows 2000 Server;
- Windows 2000 Advanced Server;
- Windows 2000 Datacenter Server.

Here is the list of hardware requirements for Visual Studio.NET:

- **CPU** 450 MHz, Pentium II;
- **Memory** – 64 MB for Windows NT Workstation 4.0;
  - 96 MB for Windows 2000 Professional;
  - 192 MB for Windows 2000 Server;
  - 160 MB for Windows XP Professional;
- **Hard disk** 2.5 GB of free hard disk space, including a minimum 500 MB on the system drive.

1.2 .NET languages

As part of the initial .NET release, Microsoft will provide compilers for C#, C++, Visual Basic, and J#. Other vendors will provide .NET compilers for such languages as COBOL, Eiffel, Perl, Smalltalk, and Python. More up-to-date information on third-party languages can be found at:

http://msdn.microsoft.com/net/thirdparty/default.asp#lang

C#

C# (pronounced C sharp) is a new programming language designed for building a wide range of enterprise applications that run on the .NET Framework. An evolution of C and C++, C# is simple, modern, type safe, and object oriented. C# code is compiled as managed code, which means it benefits from the services of the Common Language Runtime. These services include language interoperability, garbage collection, enhanced security, and improved versioning support.

C# is introduced as Visual C# in the Visual Studio.NET suite. Support for Visual C# includes project templates, designers, property pages, code wizards, an object model, and other features of the development environment. The library for Visual C# programming is the .NET Framework.

C++

The .NET version of Visual C++ is called 'Managed Extensions for C++'. Managed extensions for C++ are a set of language extensions that extend the standard C++ langauge and help Microsoft Visual C++ developers write applications for Microsoft .NET. A program written with managed code using managed extensions for C++, for example, can operate with the Common Language Runtime to provide services such as memory management, cross-language integration, code access security, and automatic lifetime control of objects.

The managed extensions are useful if you:

- want to enhance developer productivity by using C++ to write .NET applications;
- want to migrate a large body of code, in stages, from unmanaged C++ to the .NET platform;
- have unmanaged C++ components that you want to use from .NET Framework applications;
- have .NET Framework components that you want to use from unmanaged C++;
- want to mix unmanaged C++ code and .NET code in the same application.

Managed extensions for C++ offer unparalleled flexibility to developers targeting the .NET platform. Traditional unmanaged C++ and managed C++ code can be mixed freely within the same application. New applications written with managed extensions can take advantage of the best of both worlds. Existing components can be wrapped easily as .NET components by using the managed extensions, preserving investment in existing code while integrating with .NET.

The extensions allow you to write managed (or .NET) classes in C++, that run under the control of the .NET Framework. (Unmanaged C++ classes run in the traditional Microsoft Windows-based environment.) A managed class is a native .NET class and can fully leverage the .NET Framework.

The managed extensions are new keywords and attributes in the Visual C++ development system. They allow the developer to decide which classes and functions to compile as managed or unmanaged code. These pieces then interoperate smoothly with each other and external libraries.

Note that we can still use the Visual Studio.NET IDE to produce unmanaged – that is, native – code.

Managed extensions are also used to express .NET types and concepts directly in C++ source code. This allows developers to write .NET applications easily and without writing extra code.

Visual Basic.NET

Visual Basic.NET – the next generation of the Visual Basic language – is designed to be a fast and easy way to create .NET applications, including web services and web applications.

Visual Basic.NET has many new and improved features, such as inheritance, interfaces, and overloading, that make it a powerful object-oriented programming language. Other new language features include free threading and structured exception handling. Visual Basic.NET fully integrates the .NET Framework and the Common Language Runtime, which together provide language interoperability, garbage collection, enhanced security, and improved versioning support.

Microsoft Visual J#.NET

Visual J#.NET is a development tool for Java-language developers who want to build applications and services on the .NET Framework. Visual J#.NET joins more than 20 previously announced languages with its ability to target the .NET Framework and first-class XML web services.

Visual J#.NET provides the easiest transition for Java developers into the world of XML web services and dramatically improves the interoperability of Java language programs with existing software written in a variety of other programming languages. Visual J#.NET enables Microsoft Visual J++ customers and other Java-language programmers to take advantage of existing investments in skills and code while fully exploiting the Microsoft platform today and into the future.

Visual J#.NET includes technology that enables customers to migrate Java language investments to the .NET Framework. Existing applications developed with Visual J++ (see note below) can be easily modified to execute on the .NET Framework, interoperate with other .NET-based languages and applications, and incorporate new .NET functionality, such as ASP.NET, ADO.NET, and Windows forms. Further, developers can use it to create entirely new .NET-based applications.

Note that Visual J#.NET supports most of the class library functionality of JDK 1.1.4, as well as Microsoft extensions (such as J/Direct and Java-COM) that shipped with Visual J++ 6.0.

Visual J#.NET provides the following.

- Full integration with Visual Studio.NET. Visual J#.NET provides programming tools support via its integration with the award-winning Visual Studio.NET integrated development environment (IDE). All the features of the IDE are easily accessible to the Visual J# developer.

- Full integration with the .NET Framework. Visual J#.NET is designed to take full advantage of the .NET Framework, including ASP.NET, ADO.NET, Windows forms, and XML web services, as well as full cross-language integration.

- Visual J++ 6.0 upgrade tools. Visual J#.NET includes tools to automatically upgrade and convert existing Visual J++ 6.0 projects and solutions to the new Visual Studio.NET format. These tools ensure that an existing Visual J++ 6.0 developer can easily move to Visual J#.NET and produce .NET-based applications and components.

Applications and services built with Visual J#.NET will run only on the .NET Framework. They will not run on any Java virtual machine as Visual J#.NET code does not compile to Java bytecode and so will not run in any current Web browser. Visual J#.NET has been independently developed by Microsoft. It is not endorsed or approved by Sun Microsystems, Inc.

Microsoft J#.NET is the first part of the Java user migration path to Microsoft.NET (JUMP to .NET) strategy. The JUMP to .NET strategy gives customers two paths for bringing their Java-language investments to the .NET platform. First, Visual J#.NET provides the easiest transition for Java developers into the world of XML web services and dramatically improves the interoperability of Java-language programs with existing software written in a variety of other programming languages. Visual J#.NET enables Microsoft Visual J++ customers and other Java-language programmers to take advantage of existing investments in skills and code while fully exploiting the .NET Framework. Second, with JUMP to .NET, Microsoft announced a tool that automatically converts existing Java source code into C#, migrating both language syntax and library calls. Any code that cannot be converted is flagged within the Visual Studio.NET integrated development environment to help developers easily find and quickly address any remaining conversion issues.

1.3 .NET Enterprise servers

.NET Enterprise servers are Microsoft's family of server applications for building, deploying, and managing scalable, integrated, web-based solutions. .NET Enterprise servers provide scalability, reliability, and manageability for the global, web-enabled enterprise. .NET Enterprise servers are based on open web standards, such as XML. The first generation of the .NET Enterprise servers allow customers to start building, deploying, and orchestrating scalable, reliable web services and applications.

.NET Enterprise servers can be divided into several functional groups, depending on the types of services it provides. This is shown in Table 1.1.

TABLE 1.1   Functional groupings for .NET Enterprise servers

Service	Description	.NET Enterprise servers
Base services	Provide basic operating system services, such as clustering and load balancing	● Windows 2000 server ● Windows XP server ● Application Center 2000
Infrastructure services	Provide storage for structured and unstructured data and basic interoperability services	● SQL Server 2000 ● Exchange Server 2000 ● Host Integration Server 2000 ● Internet Security and Acceleration Server 2000
Business integration services	Provide a rich set of servers and applications to interoperate with other business applications	● BizTalk Server 2000 ● Commerce Server 2000 ● SharePoint Portal Server 2001 ● Content Management Server 2000
Multidevice services	Extend the reach of .NET Enterprise servers, enterprise data and intranet content into the realm of the mobile user	● Mobile Information Server 2001

The core .NET Enterprise servers are as follows:

- **Application Center 2000.** Provides management for web applications. This is Microsoft's deployment and management tool for high-availability web applications built on the Microsoft Windows 2000 operating system. Application Center 2000 makes managing groups of servers as simple as managing a single computer.

- **BizTalk Server 2000.** An XML-based business process integration tool that integrates with other services in the organization or other businesses. BizTalk server 2000 offers a suite of tools and services that make building business processes and integrating applications faster. Secure, reliable trading partner relationships can be quickly implemented independent of operating system, programming model, or programming language.

- **Commerce Server 2000.** Next generation of the Site Server that allows you to quickly create e-commerce infrastructures. This server can be used to build business-to-business or business-to-consumer communication with a powerful management suite, allowing you to react very quickly to market changes.

- **Content Management Server.** Dramatically reduces the time required to build and deploy content-driven websites that deliver high scalability, reliability, and performance. A content management server empowers content providers to manage their own content and provides site users with a targeted and personalized experience tailored to their profile and browsing device.

- **Exchange Server 2000.** Delivers a reliable, scalable, and manageable infrastructure with 24×7 messaging and collaboration and low cost of ownership. It supports a wide range of collaborative activities, including group scheduling capabilities, discussion groups, and team folders. It also provides access to information across barriers of geography, organization, and technology, with features such as instant messaging, real-time data, and video conferencing.

- **Host Integration Server 2000.** This replaces an SNA server and allows mainframe systems to be integrated into the .NET world by exposing huge amounts of information stored on mainframes through web services.

- **Internet Security and Acceleration Server 2000.** This provides security and protection for the entire system. This server is an integrated firewall and web cache server that will make web-enabled enterprises safer, faster, and more manageable.

- **Mobile Information Server.** This server provides real-time access for the mobile community. Outlook users can use their pocket PCs to access their Outlook data while they are on the move.

- **SharePoint Portal Server.** This uses the power of Microsoft's robust search technologies to create an intranet site that lets you easily access key content from a broader set of enterprise information. In addition, you can rapidly deploy an out-of-the-box portal site and easily use web parts technology to customize a web-based view of your organization.

- **SQL Server 2000.** This is a complete, web-enabled database and data analysis package that opens the door to the rapid development of a new generation of enterprise-class business applications that can give your company a critical competitive advantage. An SQL server provides core support for XML and the ability to query across the internet and beyond the firewall.

Detailed discussion of .NET Enterprise servers is outside the scope of this book. For more information, see Microsoft's website at:

www.microsoft.com/servers/default.asp

Details of .NET Enterprise servers' interoperability are available in the Microsoft paper called 'Introduction to .NET Enterprise Server Interoperability', available at:

www.microsoft.com/servers/evaluation/interop.asp

The NET Framework will be discussed in more detail in the following section. For .NET web services (.NET Passport, .NET My Services, and .NET Alerts), please refer to the last section of Chapter 15.

1.4 The .NET Framework

According to the Microsoft, .NET Framework is:

> A platform for building, deploying, and running web services and applications. It provides a highly productive, standards-based, multi-language environment for integrating existing investments with next-generation applications and services as well as the ability to solve the challenges of deployment and operation of Internet-scale applications.

The Microsoft .NET Framework consists of three main parts:

- Common Language Runtime;
- .NET class library, which is sometimes called "Base Framework";
- ASP.NET.

Figure 1.3 shows the components of the Microsoft .NET Framework.

The .NET Framework class library

The .NET Framework includes classes, interfaces, and value types that are used in the development process and provide access to system functionality. To facilitate interoperability between languages, the .NET Framework types are Common Language Specification (CLS) compliant and can therefore be used from any programming language where the compiler conforms to the CLS.

The .NET Framework types are the foundation on which .NET applications, components, and controls are built. The .NET Framework includes types that perform the following functions:

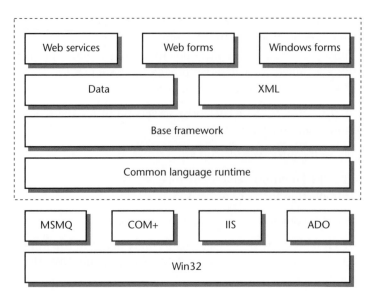

FIGURE 1.3   The components of the .NET Framework

- represent base data types and exceptions;
- encapsulate data structures;
- perform I/O operations;
- access information about loaded types via reflections;
- invoke .NET Framework security checks;
- provide data access, rich client-side GUI, and server-controlled, client-side GUI.

The .NET Framework provides a rich set of interfaces, as well as abstract and concrete (non-abstract) classes. You can use the concrete classes as is or, in many cases, derive your own classes from them, as well as from abstract classes. To use the functionality of an interface, you can either create a class that implements the interface or derive a class from one of the .NET Framework classes that implements the interface.

Microsoft, with the help of Hewlett-Packard and Intel, supplied the OS-independent subset of .NET class library to the ECMA standardization board. For more information visit:

http://msdn.microsoft.com/net/ecma

Note that there are several open source implementations of the common language environment. For example, there is the Intel Labs' C# implementation of portions of the CLI:

http://sourceforge.net/projects/ocl/

or Project Mono:

www.go-mono.com/

www.southern-storm.com.au/

We will start to learn about the .NET Framework class library in Chapter 3.

Common Language Runtime

The Common Language Runtime is the execution engine for .NET Framework applications. It provides a number of services, including the following:

- code management – loading and execution;
- application memory isolation;
- verification of type safety;
- conversion of IL (platform-independent code generated by compilers) to native, platform-dependent code;
- access to metadata, which is enhanced type information;
- managing memory for managed objects;
- enforcement of code access security;
- exception handling, including cross-language exceptions;
- interoperation between managed code, COM objects, and pre-existing DLLs (unmanaged code and data);
- automation of object layout;
- support for developer services – profiling, debugging, and so on.

Figure 1.4 dissects Common Language Runtime.

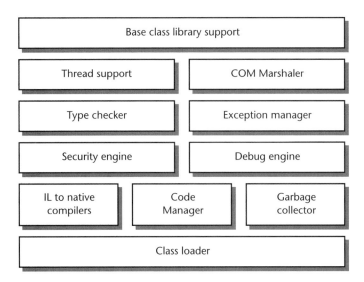

FIGURE 1.4 The constituent parts of common language runtime

We will discuss Common Language Runtime and its components in more detail in the next chapter.

Web services

Web services is a core technology provided by the .NET Framework. By using web services, companies can more easily integrate internal applications, but they can also access services exposed by other businesses. By combining web services exposed on the Internet with internally built services, companies can create a wide variety of value-added applications. For example, a company could unify banking, electronic bill payment, stock trading, and insurance services into a single, seamless financial management portal. Another possibility is the integration of inventory control, fulfilment mechanisms and purchase-order tracking into a comprehensive supply chain management system.

We will discuss web services further in Chapter 15.

1.5   Installing the Microsoft .NET Framework

The Microsoft .NET Framework comes either as part of Microsoft Visual Studio.NET or as a separate package that also includes the Microsoft .NET Framework SDK. Future versions of Microsoft Windows will include the Microsoft .NET Framework as part of the operating system.

We can install the Microsoft .NET Framework on Windows XP, Windows 2000 and NT4. Windows 95 and Windows Me/98 are not supported. The minimal requirements for hardware are:

- Intel Pentium class, 133 megahertz (MHz) or higher;
- 128 MB of RAM (256 MB or higher recommended);
- hard disk space required to install is 600 MB hard disk space, required to run – 370 MB RAM;
- display is 800 × 600, 256 colors;
- Microsoft mouse or compatible pointing device.

The Microsoft .NET Framework SDK can be downloaded from Microsoft's website. Let's look at the steps involved when we install this package, which comes as a single file called setup.exe.

If we want to run this program, it will ask us whether or not we would like to install Microsoft .NET Framework SDK.

Clicking on the "Yes" button will start the installation. The next screen welcomes us to the .NET Framework SDK and starts the setup wizard, which will guide us through the installation process (see Figure 1.5).

At the first step (see Figure 1.6), we should read and accept the license agreement. To read the whole text of the agreement, click on the "page down" button several times. Click on the "I accept the agreement" button to accept it and then click on the "Next" button.

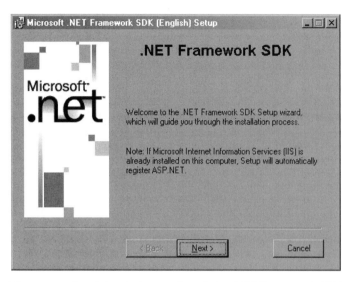

FIGURE 1.5 The setup wizard that helps you install the .NET Framework SDK

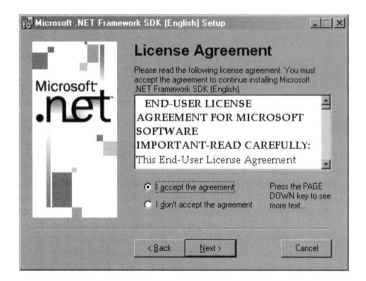

FIGURE 1.6 The first step of the installation process

On the next screen, we can choose which software components we will install (see Figure 1.7). We can select "Software Development Kit" which includes the components, tools, and samples necessary to build and run .NET applications, "SDK Samples" and "Documentation" for the SDK (this option will be available only if we uncheck the SDK option). If you want to install the entire SDK, leave this screen with the options set by default.

FIGURE 1.7   Choosing which components to install

Pressing the "Next" button moves us to the next screen. There, we can select the path for the folder where the .NET Framework SDK and samples will be installed (see Figure 1.8). By default this is the folder named:

```
C:\Program Files\Microsoft.NET\Framework SDK\
```

FIGURE 1.8   Deciding where the files for the .NET Framework will be stored

The `Register Environment Variables` option allows us to automatically set the PATH environment variable like this:

```
PATH=C:\WINNT\Microsoft.NET\Framework\v1.0.3705\;
C:\Program Files\Microsoft.NET\FrameworkSDK\Bin;
```

Clicking on the "`Next`" button once again moves us to the information screen shown in Figure 1.9.

This screen informs us on the actions currently taken by the `Setup` program. When all the required information is gathered, `Setup` starts to install components of the .NET Framework SDK: core components, product documentation, SDK, and samples.

When setup has finished copying the required files and registering components – this may take 15–30 minutes – it will produce the final message. This indicates that the installation has been completed.

The result is that the `C:\Program Files\Microsoft.NET\Framework SDK\` (assuming that you have used the default path) folder will have been created. It will contain two subfolders – `FrameworkSDK` and `Primary Interop Assemblies`. The first one contains all the SDK files and the second one several files required by .NET to interact with the underlying operating system (see Figure 1.10).

In the "`FrameworkSDK`" folder, there are several subfolders – namely the "`Bin`" folder, which contains all tools that comes with SDK (except the debugger, which is located in the "`GuiDebug`" folder). The "`Docs`" folder stores all documentation in compiled help format, the "`include`" folder contains `.h` and `.idl` files required by C++ compiler, the "`lib`" folder stores library files. The "`symbols`" folder contains PDB files, used when we debug our applications, the "`Samples`" folder stores source code for the sample programs that are part of the SDK, and the "`Tool Developers`

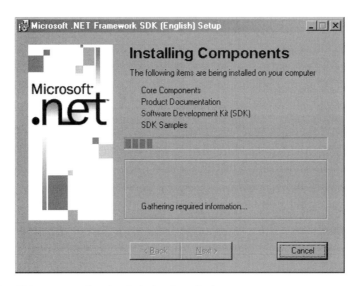

FIGURE 1.9   This screen tells what is being installed

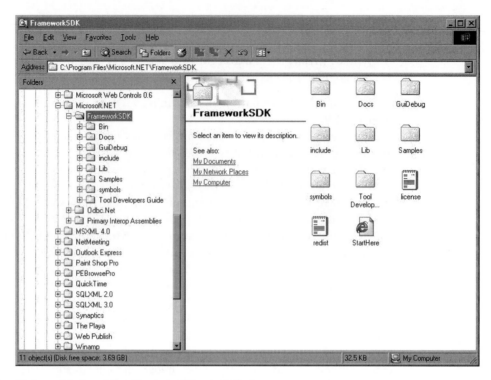

FIGURE 1.10 The result once all the files have been installed

Guide" folder contains documentation that is of interest to those who are planning to write low-level development tools, such as compilers, browsers, profilers, and debuggers that operate within the .NET Framework. Core.NET files are stored in the "WINNT\Microsoft.NET\Framework\<version>" folder (see Figure 1.11).

Note that the version number for the Beta 2 version of Microsoft .NET is v1.0.2914. The version v1.0.3215 is available with Windows .NET server Beta 3, while the version number for the final release (which comes both as part of Microsoft Visual Studio .NET and as a Web download) is v1.0.3705.

Setup also creates an entry in the Start/Programs menu called Microsft.NET Framework SDK, which provides shortcuts to the SDK documentation, as well as some explanatory files.

Now we are ready to explore the Microsoft .NET Framework. Our journey will start in the next chapter.

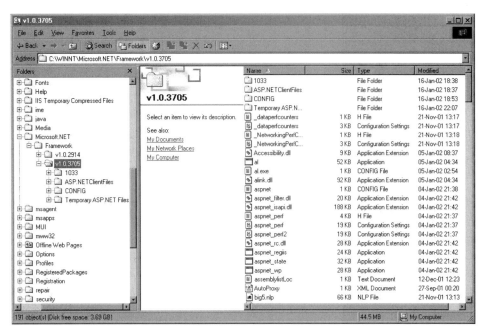

FIGURE 1.11 Core .NET files are stored here

1.6 Conclusion

In this chapter, we have learned about Microsoft .NET and its main components. We discussed development tools and .NET languages, .NET Enterprise servers, and also provided a brief overview of the Microsoft .NET Framework and discussed the .NET Framework class library, Common Language Runtime, and web services.

In the second part of this chapter we saw how to install Microsoft .NET Framework SDK.

In the next chapter, we will learn about one of the core components of Microsoft .NET Framework – Common Language Runtime.

chapter 2

Common Language Runtime

- Components of the Common Language Runtime (CLR)

- Managed code

In the previous chapter we have learned about the Microsoft .NET Framework and its role in the entire Microsoft .NET platform. We have seen that the framework consists of three main parts – Common Language Runtime, the .NET Framework class library, and ASP.NET.

This chapter is dedicated to the core component of the Microsoft .NET Framework – Common Language Runtime (CLR). This is the infrastructure that .NET uses to execute all .NET applications – from simple console applications to web forms (ASP.NET applications) to Windows forms-based applications. By infrastructure here we mean the environment, which provides a lot of functionality, such as memory management, threads and processes management, security management, and many other tasks. That's why this environment is called a managed environment.

2.1 Components of the Common Language Runtime (CLR)

A big difference between CLR and such runtimes as VBRUN/MSVBVM in Visual Basic or MSVCRT in Visual C++, is that CLR is a unified environment for all of the languages available for .NET. There is no difference if you write code in VB.NET, C#.NET or Perl.NET – your code will still be run in the same environment and have access to the common subset of classes. We can even mix and match code in different programming languages, including full multilingual object-oriented features, such as inheriting objects, created in one language from the code, written in other language. All of this is made available by Common Language Runtime.

Figure 2.1 shows the components of Common Language Runtime.

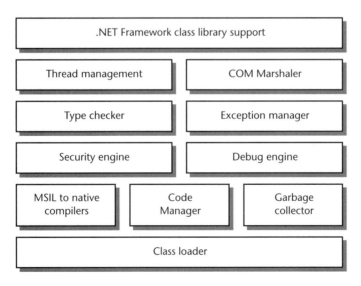

FIGURE 2.1   The components of Common Language Runtime

Let's look at the components of Common Language Runtime in more detail.

- **Class Loader** This component provides metadata management and loads classes. This is part of the execution process and involves the metadata stored within the executable file. Class Loader uses `Code Manager` to assign memory for the objects and data. It computes the layout of classes in memory and each method receives an entry in the methods table. Later, when the Just-In-Time compiler converts the MSIL code (see next point) to native code, the entry in the methods table is replaced with the pointer to the native code.

- **Microsoft Intermediate Language (MSIL) to native compilers** This component converts code in Microsoft intermediate language to native code. This can be done through either Just-in-Time (JIT) compiling or native generation using the NGEN tool that comes as part of the Microsoft .NET Framework SDK. For more information see later in this chapter.

- **Code Manager** This component manages code execution and is used by the `Class Loader` to assign memory for the objects and data.

- **Garbage collector** This component manages the allocation and release of memory for the application, and automatically reclaims unused memory. Its optimizing engine determines the best time to perform a collection in order to free some memory based on the allocations being made. When the garbage collector performs a collection, it checks for objects in the managed heap that are no longer being used by the application and performs the necessary operations to reclaim their memory. The `System.GC` class can be used to control the system garbage collector.

- **Security engine** This provides evidence-based security using information about the origin of the code as well as the user. The security engine offers the safe execution of the semi-trusted code, protects from malicious software and several kinds of attacks, and allows controlled, identity-based access to resources.

- **Debug engine** This provides support for such tools as debuggers and tracers. Several classes in the Microsoft .NET Framework class library rely on the services provided by the debug engine. For example, we can use the `Debug` and `Trace` classes found in the `System.Diagnostics` namespace.

- **Type checker** This guarantees type safety guarding us from unsafe casts and uninitialized variables. Type checking is performed at the JIT-compilation step in the process called "verification". At that point, it examines code and attempts to determine whether or not the code is type safe.

- **Exception manager** This provides structured exception handling. Exception handling is the essential part of the Common Language Runtime and is supported through the huge hierarchy of classes based on the `Exception` class and its derived classes.

- **Thread management** This supports multithreading. It includes starting and ending threads, suspending and scheduling threads, and thread pooling, as well as providing thread manipulation support at runtime. This is achieved via the `Thread` class implemented in the `System.Threading` namespace.

- **COM Marshaler** This provides marshaling to and from COM. It includes the data type conversions between COM types and .NET types and back.

- **.NET Framework class library support** This provides integration between the runtime and code via the Common Type System.

2.2 Managed code

When we compile for CLR, the resulting code is called "managed code". This code can take advantage of services provided by Common Language Runtime. This is available via the metadata, which is information about types, members, and references in the code that is created during the compilation and stored with the compiled code. Common Language Runtime uses metadata to locate classes and load them, generate platform-dependent code (also called "native code"), and provide security.

Microsoft Intermediate Language

The result of the compilation of the source code is the Microsoft Intermediate Language – a CPU-independent set of instructions that can later be converted to native code. Microsoft Intermediate Language contains instructions for loading, storing, initializing, and calling methods on objects, instructions for arithmetic and logical operations, control flow, direct memory access, exception handling, and many other operations. Let's look at how the simple console application, created for .NET platform, looks in MSIL. Here is the VB.NET source code for our application:

```
Imports System
Module Cons

  Sub Main()
    Console.WriteLine(".NET Console application")
    Console.ReadLine()
  End Sub

End Module
```

The `Imports` directive indicates that we will use the `System` namespace. In particular we will use the `Console` class and two methods: the `WriteLine` method to output a string; the `ReadLine` method to accept a line from the keyboard.

We compile our code with the call to the VB.NET command-line compiler shown in Figure 2.2.

```
C:\WINNT\System32\cmd.exe                                              _ □ ×

C:\Dot_Net>vbc conapp.vb /verbose
Microsoft (R) Visual Basic.NET Compiler version 7.00.9254
for Microsoft (R) .NET CLR version 1.00.2914.16
Copyright (C) Microsoft Corp 2001. All rights reserved.

Adding file 'C:\Dot_Net\conapp.vb'
Compiling...
Compilation successful

C:\Dot_Net>dir conapp.*
 Volume in drive C has no label.
 Volume Serial Number is 1CB3-CBE0

 Directory of C:\Dot_Net

09-11-01  18:41                 3,072 conapp.exe
09-11-01  18:33                   255 conapp.vb
               2 File(s)         3,327 bytes
               0 Dir(s)  2,687,533,056 bytes free

C:\Dot_Net>
```

FIGURE 2.2   Compiling the code to create the executable file required for CLR

The result of the compilation is an executable file that contains a standard portable executable (PE) header, as well as other data, required by Common Language Runtime (we will talk about this a little bit later). The portable executable format is the Microsoft implementation of a COFF format, which is a format in 32-bit programming for executable (image) and object files that is portable across platforms.

Now, let's use the special tool called ILDASM (Microsoft Intermediate Language Disassembler) that ships with the .NET Framework SDK. This tool produces human-readable MSIL code, as well as namespaces, types, and their interfaces. ILDASM is a great learning tool as it allows us to examine modules that come with the .NET Framework, as well as other modules and our own applications. We launch the ILDASM with the following command line:

```
>ildasm conapp.exe
```

This will open the main window of the ILDASM and show the main contents of our executable file. In Figure 2.3 we can see how the contents of the ILDASM correspond to the source code of our application.

Note that the first child node of the conapp.exe is called MANIFEST – the block of information describing this assembly. The assembly is the unit of functionality, deployment, and is the primary building block of a .NET application. We will talk about assemblies later in this chapter.

Going back to ILDASM, we can look at the MSIL source of our Sub Main by clicking to its name. Here is the disassembly:

```
.method public static void Main() cil managed
{
  .entrypoint
  .custom instance void [mscorlib]System.STAThreadAttribute::.ctor() =
  ( 01 00 00 00 )
  // Code size       17 (0x11)
  .maxstack 8
  IL_0000: ldstr        ".NET Console application"
  IL_0005: call         void [mscorlib]System.Console::WriteLine(string)
  IL_000a: call         string [mscorlib]System.Console::ReadLine()
  IL_000f: pop
  IL_0010: ret
} // end of method Cons::Main
```

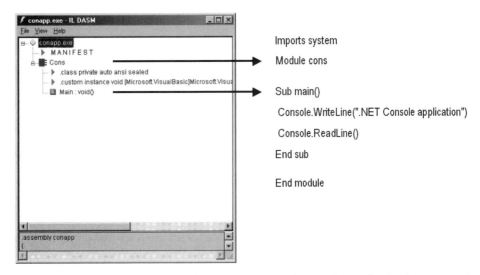

FIGURE 2.3   The main window of ILDASM and how its contents relate to the application's source code

The MSIL instruction set has about 220 instructions and we obviously will not cover them all here. It is sufficient to know that the code starts with the method declaration (.method directive) that defines our Main subroutine as public, static, and managed. The last keyword means that the code will run under CLR.

Next come the .entrypoint directive, which indicates the entry point to our subroutine, and the .custom directive which specifies the threading context of our application. The commented line (beginning with //) shows the size of our code – it takes 17 bytes of MSIL code. The .maxstack directive is used everywhere in the MSIL. As CLR is stack-based, all operands should be pushed on to a stack and, after this, operators can manipulate them. Results are pushed back on to the stack.

After this comes the main part of our application. The ldstr instruction pushes the string on to the stack. The call instruction calls the WriteLine and ReadLine methods of the static `System.Console` class. The `[mscorlib]` prefix indicates where this class is defined. The last two instructions – `pop` and `ret` – are used to get the possible results from the `ReadLine` method (allocated on the stack) and return back. In our case, this ends our application.

Let's briefly look at the common MSIL instructions.

- `ldxxx` – used to load a value on to a stack:
  - `ldarg.0` – loads argument 0;
  - `ldc.i4.2` – loads integer 4 byte (i4) constant of value 2;
  - `ldint.i4` – loads indirect, 4 bytes (i4) from address on to stack;
  - `ldstr` – loads string;
  - `ldloc` – loads local variable;
  - `ldloca` – loads address of a local variable;
  - `ldsfld` – loads static field;
- `stxxx` – used to store element from stack with pop:
  - `stloc.0` – store to local variable 0;
  - `stfld` – store to the specified field;
  - `stsfld` – store to the specified static field;
  - `stelem.i4` – store to array element (i4);
  - `stobj` – store into an object;
- `add`, `sub`, `mul`, `div` – provide basic mathematical functions that operate on the top two operands of the stack;
- `call`, `calli`, `callvirt` – used to perform call, indirect call or virtual call;
- `ret` – return from method;
- `bxxx` – branch if the element on top of the stack meets specified condition:
  - `brtrue.s` – branch if true;
  - `bge` – branch if greater than or equal to;
- `cxxx` – used to compare top arguments on stack:
  - `ceq` – compare for equality;
- `newxxx` – used to allocate objects, arrays and so on:
  - `newobj` – allocates a new object of the specified type;
  - `newarr` – allocates a new array of the specified type;
- `and`, `or`, `xor`, `not` – provides bitwise operators;
- `shl`, `shr` – used for shift operations – shift left and shift right;
- `throw` – throws an exception;
- `box`, `unbox` – convert to and from managed type;
- `conv` – performs data-type conversion.

For more information about MSIL, please refer to the document called *Common Language Infrastructure: Partition III CIL Instruction Set*, which can be found at Microsoft's website:

www.microsoft.com/net/ecma

Let's go back to our executable file. As we have mentioned above, this is the standard PE (portable executable) file with some extra headers, used by Common Language Runtime. To look at its contents, we will use the COFF/PE dumper utility (DUMP-BIN.EXE). The command line looks like this:

```
>dumpbin conapp.exe /all
```

This will produce the dump of the executable file headers – the partial result of which is shown below:

```
Microsoft (R) COFF/PE Dumper Version 7.00.9254
Copyright (C) Microsoft Corporation. All rights reserved.


Dump of file conapp.exe
PE signature found
File Type: EXECUTABLE IMAGE

FILE HEADER VALUES
     14C machine (x86)
     3 number of sections
     . . .


OPTIONAL HEADER VALUES
     10B magic # (PE32)

SECTION HEADER #1
     . . .
     Code
     Execute Read

RAW DATA #1
     . . .

clr Header:

48 cb
2.00 runtime version
205C [     294] RVA [size] of MetaData Directory
1 flags
```

```
6000001 entry point token
205C [        0] RVA [size] of Resources Directory
0    [        0] RVA [size] of StrongNameSignature Directory
0    [        0] RVA [size] of CodeManagerTable Directory
0    [        0] RVA [size] of VTableFixups Directory
0    [        0] RVA [size] of ExportAddressTableJumps Directory
Section contains the following imports:
  mscoree.dll
            402000 Import Address Table
            402318 Import Name Table
            0 time date stamp
            0 Index of first forwarder reference

            0 _CorExeMain
  . . .
```

The file dump starts with the common PE header used by all Windows programs. The optional header value indicates that this is the 32-bit Windows program (PE32). The CLR-specific data can be found in the data section #1 (not shown) – note that this section has code and execute read attributes – that shows the loader that this section contains code (MSIL code) that will be executed by the Common Language Runtime.

In the CLR Header we will find the exported function named _CorExeMain, which came from the mscoree.dll – the main module of the CLR. This is the entry point into the CLR. The new loader, used under Windows 98, Windows Me, Windows 2000 and Windows XP, checks if there are CLR headers in the executable file and jumps to this entry point. The rest (like calling our Main() function) is done by the CLR itself.

All of the information about the executable is available to the Common Language Runtime at the program loading, Just-In-Time (JIT) compiling, and execution phases.

Just-In-Time compiler (JIT)

The MSIL code rests in the executable file until we execute this file. At the time when the CLR receives control, the MSIL code is converted into the native code. This conversion is performed by the special compiler, called the Just-In-Time compiler. In theory, this JIT compiler should be the only platform-dependent component of .NET, but in real life, the majority of the .NET Framework class library and some of the other components are tied to the Windows platform. Here is a partial list:

- mscorlib;
- System;
- System.Design;
- System.Drawing;
- System.Windows.Forms.

The Just-In-Time compiler compiles MSIL down to native code on a per-method basis. Here are the main steps in this process.

1 Program is loaded and a function table is initialized with pointers referencing the MSIL code.

2 The `Main` method is JIT-compiled into native code and this code is executed. Calls to functions get compiled into indirect calls via the function table.

3 When another method is called, the CLR looks at the function table to see if it points into JIT-compiled code. If it does, the control flow continues. If not, the method is JIT-compiled and the table is updated.

4 As they are called, more and more methods are compiled into native code and more entries in the function table point into native code.

5 As the program continues to run, the JIT is called less and less often until everything is compiled.

6 A method is not compiled until it is called and it is never compiled again during the execution of the program.

The Just-in-Time compiler is fast and generates good, optimized code. Here is a list of some of the optimizations performed by the JIT.

- **constant folding** Calculates constant values at compile time.

- **constant and copy propagation** Substitutes backwards to free variables earlier on.

- **method inlining** Replaces arguments with values passed at calltime and eliminates the call – currently only small methods (MSIL code size under 32 bytes) are inlined.

- **code hoisting and dominators** Removes code from inside loops if it is duplicated outside.

- **loop unrolling** The overhead of incrementing counters and performing the test can be removed and the code of the loop can be repeated.

- **common sub-expression elimination** If a live variable still contains the information being recalculated, it uses that instead.

- **enregistration** Possible use of registers to store local variables instead of placing them on the stack.

To avoid the delay caused by JIT compilation at runtime, we can precompile our applications using the special tool `NGEN – CLR Native Image Generator`, which runs the JIT compiler over the whole program once and saves the native code result on disk.

Figure 2.4 illustrates the whole process of the .NET application lifetime.

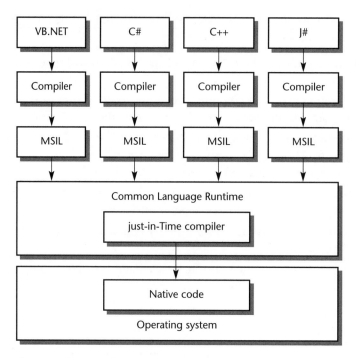

FIGURE 2.4   The complete .NET application process

Assemblies

We have defined "assembly" as the unit of functionality and primary building block of a .NET application. Each assembly consists of all physical files that make up the functional unit – any managed modules, resource, and data files, such as graphics and binary data. There are two types of assemblies:

- **Static** assemblies are stored on the disk;
- **Dynamic** assemblies are created during the program execution and usually are not stored on disk.

Each assembly contains metadata that is called the "manifest". In the manifest we can find information about classes, types, and references to other assemblies.

Let's go back to the ILDASM and explore the MANIFEST portion of the disassembly. Here it is:

```
.assembly extern mscorlib
{
  .publickeytoken = (B7 7A 5C 56 19 34 E0 89 ) // .z\V.4..
  .ver 1:0:2411:0
}
```

```
.assembly extern Microsoft.VisualBasic
{
  .publickeytoken = (B0 3F 5F 7F 11 D5 0A 3A ) // .?_....:
  .ver 7:0:0:0
}
.assembly conapp
{
  .hash algorithm 0x00008004
  .ver 0:0:0:0
}
.module conapp.exe
// MVID: {73932607-DC82-4B1A-B73B-88E336EE6E43}
.imagebase 0x00400000
.subsystem 0x00000003
.file alignment 512
.corflags 0x00000001
// Image base: 0x034b0000
```

This manifest describes the elements in the assembly. It is the place where the meta-data is stored. In the example of the manifest shown above, we will find the following information.

- **referenced assemblies** Here we use mscorlib and Microsoft.VisualBasic. The .publickeytoken directive indicates the token of the actual key of the referenced assembly, where the .versionnumber directive indicates the version number of the referenced assembly.
- **assembly name** Conapp in our example.
- **assembly version number** 0:0:0:0 in our example.
- **assembly hash algorithm**.
- **the name of the modules that make up the assembly** In our example, this is the only file – conapp.exe.
- **.imagebase**.
- **.subsystem** Indicates what kind of application environment is required for the program. In this example, the value 3 indicates that this executable is run from a console.
- **.file alignment** Indicates the file alignment in the executable file.
- **.corflags** This is the reserved field.

Assemblies can contain more than one class – Microsoft .NET class library itself consists of a dozen assemblies, each of them holding hundreds of classes. Figure 2.5 shows assemblies that contain single and multiple files.

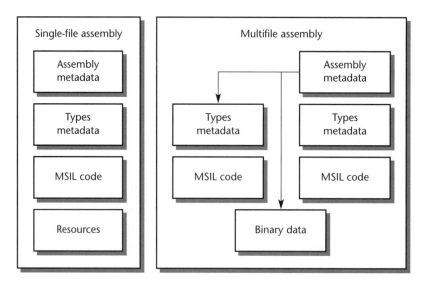

FIGURE 2.5   Assemblies with single and multiple files

Besides the standard fields that we have seen in the MANIFEST dump earlier, it can contain additional fields defined by programmers or special tools used to create assemblies. Using assemblies and version numbers allows the compatibility problem that arises between different versions of DLLs – known as "DLL hell" – to be solved. Now .NET applications look for assemblies in the local directory, which allows us to simultaneously use different versions of the same assembly without any problems.

For more in-depth information about assemblies and metadata, please refer to the document *Common Language Infrastructure: Partition II Metadata Definition and Semantics*, which can be found at the Microsoft website:

www.microsoft.com/net/ecma

Global assembly cache

If more than one .NET application uses the same assembly, it should be stored somewhere. A good example of this is the Microsoft .NET Framework library, which consists of the set of assemblies used by all .NET applications. Common language runtime supports two types of assembly storages:

● download cache;
● global assembly cache (GAC).

Assemblies used by more than one .NET application are stored in the machine-wide assembly cache called the **global assembly cache**. This cache makes assemblies available independently of where the application is located. If the assembly cannot be located in the application directory or in the GAC, Common Language Runtime tries to read the application configuration file. It is possible to specify the location of the assembly (`code base` parameter), in which case runtime will load the assembly and save it in the download cache.

To view the contents of the global assembly cache, we can use the special utility called `GACUtil`. Here is the partial list of the contents of the global assembly cache provided by the `GACUtil`, called with the following command line:

```
>gacutil /l
Microsoft (R) .NET Global Assembly Cache Utility. Version 1.0.2914.16
Copyright (C) Microsoft Corp. 1998-2001. All rights reserved.


The Global Assembly Cache contains the following assemblies:
    Accessibility, Version=1.0.2411.0, Culture=neutral,
      PublicKeyToken=b03f5f7f11d50a3a, Custom=null
    ADODB, Version=2.7.0.0, Culture=neutral,
      PublicKeyToken=b03f5f7f11d50a3a, Custom=null


 . . .


    Microsoft.JScript, Version=7.0.0.0, Culture=neutral,
     PublicKeyToken=b03f5f7f11d50a3a, Custom=null
    Microsoft.VisualBasic, Version=7.0.0.0, Culture=neutral,
     PublicKeyToken=b03f5f7f11d50a3a, Custom=null


 . . .


    System, Version=1.0.2411.0, Culture=neutral,
     PublicKeyToken=b77a5c561934e089, Custom=null
    System.Data, Version=1.0.2411.0, Culture=neutral,
     PublicKeyToken=b77a5c561934e089, Custom=null
    System.DirectoryServices, Version=1.0.2411.0, Culture=neutral,
     PublicKeyToken=b03f5f7f11d50a3a, Custom=null
    System.Drawing, Version=1.0.2411.0, Culture=neutral,
     PublicKeyToken=b03f5f7f11d50a3a, Custom=null
    System.EnterpriseServices, Version=1.0.2411.0, Culture=neutral,
     PublicKeyToken=b03f5f7f11d50a3a, Custom=null
    System.Management, Version=1.0.2411.0, Culture=neutral,
     PublicKeyToken=b03f5f7f11d50a3a, Custom=null
    System.Messaging, Version=1.0.2411.0, Culture=neutral,
     PublicKeyToken=b03f5f7f11d50a3a, Custom=null
    System.Web, Version=1.0.2411.0, Culture=neutral,
     PublicKeyToken=b03f5f7f11d50a3a, Custom=null
```

```
    System.Windows.Forms, Version=1.0.2411.0, Culture=neutral,
    PublicKeyToken=b77a5c561934e089, Custom=null
    System.Xml, Version=1.0.2411.0, Culture=neutral,
    PublicKeyToken=b77a5c561934e089, Custom=null


The cache of ngen files contains the following entries:
    conapp, Version=0.0.0.0, Culture=neutral,
    PublicKeyToken=null, Custom=5a00410050002d004e0035002e0030002
    d00380046002d0030003000450042003400340031003600000
    Microsoft.VisualStudio, Version=1.0.2411.0, Culture=neutral,
    PublicKeyToken=b03f5f7f11d50a3a,
    Custom=5a00410050002d004e0035002e0030002
    d00380046002d0030003000340041003300410044003500000
    mscorlib, Version=1.0.2411.0, Culture=neutral,
    PublicKeyToken=b77a5c561934e089,
    Custom=5a00410050002d004e0035002e0030002
    d003800460053002d003000300030003800340037004400380000000
    System, Version=1.0.2411.0, Culture=neutral,
    PublicKeyToken=b77a5c561934e089,
    Custom=5a00410050002d004e0035002e0030002
    d00380046002d003000300030003800320037004200300000000


    ...


Number of items = 62
```

The ngen files cache is used to store files created with the help of the NGEN utility described above.

The GACUtil can be also used to check the contents of the download cache. Just use the following command line:

```
>gacutil /ldl
```

to install and remove assemblies and delete the contents of the download cache. Note that the global assembly cache is the specialized directory and it can be found in C:\WINNT\assembly (see Figure 2.6).

The assembly directory contains several subdirectories – one for the global assembly cache, one for the download cache, and so on. Each subdirectory consists of more subdirectories – one or more per assembly. For example, the download cache is the subdirectory of the global assembly cache and it contains subdirectories for each downloaded assembly. Such a subdirectory contains the assembly itself and its description, stored in the __fusion__.info file.

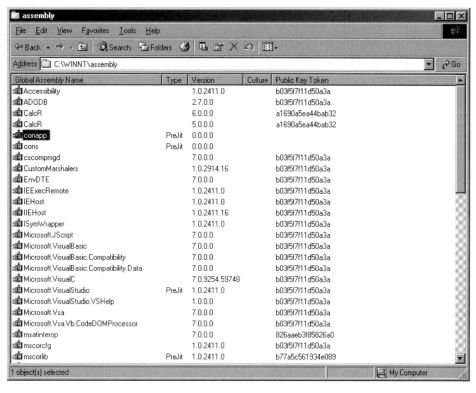

FIGURE 2.6   Looking at the directory of the global assembly cache

Common Type System

The Common Type System (CTS) is the component of the Common Language Runtime that specifies the types supported by the CLR. There are two groups of types – value types and reference types. We will talk about these types in the next chapter.

The purpose of the CTS is to set out the rules for the language compilers. It defines how types are declared, used, and managed in the runtime and provides support for cross-language integration and type safety. It also provides an object-oriented model that supports the complete implementation of many programming languages.

2.3   Conclusion

In this chapter we have discussed the Common Language Runtime. We have learned about the components of the Common Language Runtime and discussed the concept of managed code, which includes compiler-generated code in Microsoft Intermediate Language, metadata, as well as Just-in-Time compiling into the native, platform-dependent code.

We have also discussed assemblies and the global assembly cache, and we have seen the role of both under .NET. At the end of the chapter we briefly touched on the topic of the Common Type System and said that it is used to specify the types supported by the Common Language Runtime.

In the next chapter, we will start our journey through the .NET Framework class library – a set of namespaces, classes, interfaces, and value types that we will use in our .NET applications, components, and controls. One of the topics discussed in that chapter is types.

chapter 3

The .NET Framework class library – types and structures

- Console class and applications

- System namespace

- Object class

- Type class and Reflection namespace

- Types

- Conversions with the System.Convert Class

- Reference types

- Arrays

- Collections

- Strings

- System.Text namespace

- Formatting

In this chapter we will start our journey through the .NET Framework class library – a set of namespaces, classes, interfaces, and value types that are used in our .NET applications, components, and controls. Contrary to class libraries such as Microsoft Foundation Classes (MFC) or Borland Visual Class Library (VCL), the .NET Framework class library is language-independent. This means it can be used from any programming language, such as Visual Basic.NET, C#.NET, C++ with managed extensions, J#.NET, or any third-party language that conforms to the Common Language Specification (CLS).

The .NET Framework class library includes classes that support the following functions:

- base and user-defined data types;
- support for handling exceptions;
- input/output and stream operations;
- communications with the underlying system;
- access to data;
- ability to create Windows–based GUI applications;
- ability to create web–client and server applications;
- support for creating web services.

All classes implemented in the .NET class library are organized into namespaces. Each namespace contains classes and other types that are related to the specific task or set of tasks – input/output operations, web applications creation, working with data and XML, and so on. Table 3.1 shows the most important namespaces in the .NET class library.

TABLE 3.1 The main namespaces in the .NET class library

Namespace	Description
System	Contains fundamental classes and base classes that define common value and reference data types, events and event handlers, interfaces, processing exceptions, data conversion, mathematics, as well as garbage collection and application environment management. Some of the classes defined in the namespace are covered in this chapter and also in Chapters 4 and 5.
System.IO	Provides classes that support asynchronous and synchronous reading from and writing to data streams and files. Contains classes like FileStream, MemoryStream, Path, and Directory. We will learn about this namespace and its classes in the next chapter.
System.Collections	Contains interfaces and classes that define various collections of objects, such as lists, arrays, hash tables, stacks, queues, and dictionaries. The classes defined in this namespace are covered in this chapter.
System.Threading	Provides classes and interfaces that support multithreaded programming. Contains classes such as Thread, ThreadPool, Mutex, and AutoResetEvent.

TABLE 3.1   Continued

Namespace	Description
System.Reflection	Contains classes that provide dynamic binding and a managed view of loaded types, methods, and fields. Contains classes such as `Assembly`, `Module`, and `MethodInfo`.
System.Security	Implements a security system, including base classes for permissions. Includes classes of the likes of `SecurityManager`, `PermissionSet`, and `CodeAccessPermission`.
System.Net	Provides support for network programming. Includes, for example, the classes `HttpWebRequest`, `IPAddress`, `Dns`, and `Connection`. We will learn about this namespace and its classes in the next chapter.
System.Data	Contains classes that implement ADO.NET. Child namespaces include OLEDB, and `SqlClient`. This namespace will be discussed in Chapter 12.
System.XML	The System.XML namespace provides support for processing XML documents. Child namespaces include Schema, XSL, and XPath. We will discuss this namespace and its secondary namespaces in Chapter 14.
System.Web	Serves as a base for ASP.NET applications. Contains such classes as HTTPRequest, HTTPResponse, and HTTPServerUtility. Child namespaces include Caching, Configuration, Security, and UI. We will discuss this namespace and its secondary namespaces in Chapters 6 and 7.
System.Web.Services	Enables us to build and use web services. Secondary namespaces include Description, Discovery, and Protocols. We will discuss this namespace and its secondary namespaces in Chapter 15.
System.Windows.Forms	Contains classes used to create form-based Windows applications. We will discuss this namespace in Chapters 8, 9, and 10
System.Drawing	Provides access to the graphics functionality of GDI+. Contains secondary namespaces such as Design, Drawing2D, Imaging, Printing, and Text. We will discuss this namespace and its secondary namespaces in Chapter 11.
System.Globalization System.Resources	Contains classes that define culture-related information – language, country/region, calendar, and so on. Classes from the Resources namespace are used to create localized Windows and web applications.

After this brief overview of most of the chapters in the book, we are ready to start our journey through the .NET Framework class library. Main namespaces are shown in Figure 3.1. Our first stop is a little bit unusual – instead of covering the `Object` class – that is, the ultimate ancestor for all of the classes in the .NET Framework class library – we will discuss the `Console` class. The following section will explain why we do this.

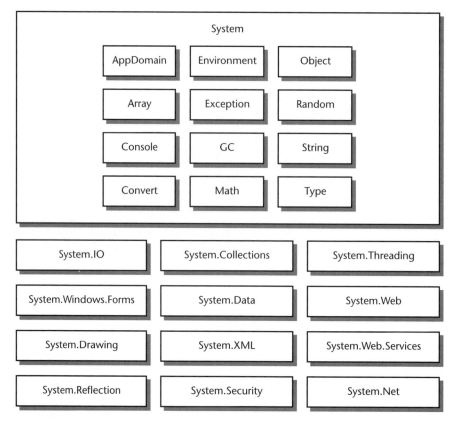

FIGURE 3.1   Main namespaces in the .NET framework class library

3.1 Console class and applications

Using the System.Console class, we can implement the simplest .NET application –
a console application that runs in a system-supplied window and does not require a
graphical user interface. Since in this and several other chapters of this book we will
use the console applications heavily, we will start this chapter with an overview of the
Console class.

The Console class represents the standard input, output, and error streams.
Applications built on this class can read characters from the standard input stream and
write characters to the standard output stream. Errors are written to the standard error
output stream. These three streams are automatically associated with the console on
which the application starts and we can obtain them via the In, Out, and Error properties of the Console class. By default, the standard input stream is a System.IO.
TextReader object, the output and output error streams are System.IO.TextWriter
objects. If we need it, we can associate input and output streams with different streams –
file streams, network streams, memory streams, and so on.

In Visual Basic.NET, we create a console application by creating a new module that contains one subroutine called `Main` – this is the entry point into our console application (see Figure 3.2):

```
'--------------------------------------
' .NET Console Application
'--------------------------------------
Imports System
Module Cons

  Sub Main()

    Console.WriteLine(".NET Console application")
    Console.ReadLine()

  End Sub

End Module
```

The `Read` and `ReadLine` methods allow us to read a character or new line character from the standard input, while `Write` and `WriteLine` perform the output.

The `SetIn`, `SetOut`, and `SetError` methods allows us to specify different input, output, and error output streams. These methods take a parameter of `TextWriter` type that specifies the output stream.

Now we are ready to start to learn about the Microsoft .NET class library. We will start with an overview of the `System` namespace.

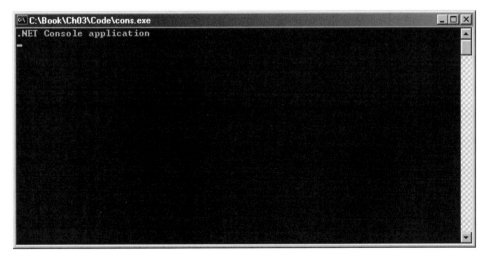

FIGURE 3.2   Console application in action

3.2   System namespace

The System namespace is the root namespace that contains the fundamental types of the .NET Framework. This namespace contains the Object class that is the root of the inheritance hierarchy, primitive and extended types, and many other classes. Indeed, there are almost 100 classes to handle exceptions, support runtime execution, application domains, garbage collection, and so on.

3.3   Object class

The System.Object class serves as a base class for all of the classes in the Microsoft .NET Framework class library. Figure 3.3 shows the methods implemented in the Object class.

Here is a brief outline of these methods.

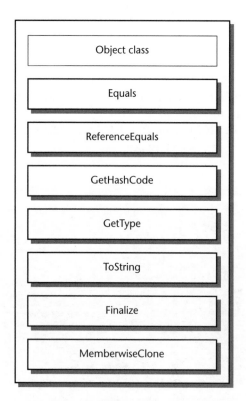

FIGURE 3.3   The methods implemented in the Object class

- **Equals(*Object*)** or **Equals(*Object*, *Object*)** This method is used to test if an object is the same instance as another object. For value types, this method is over-ridden (in the `ValueType` class) to test for value identity. Note the difference – when we compare two reference types, this method checks if both instances refer to the same object instance; for value types, the `Equals` method also checks if the two objects contain the same value.

- **ReferenceEquals(*Object*, *Object*)** This method determines if two objects are of the same instance or both are null references.

- **Finalize()** By default, this method is empty – it does nothing. It can be overridden in the derived classes to perform some cleanup before the garbage collector reclaims the object.

- **GetHashCode()** This method generates a hash value (of `Integer` type) that can be used to store the `object` in a hash table.

- **MemberwiseClone()** This method creates an exact clone of the object and returns it as an `Object` type.

- **ToString()** This method returns a text representation of the object (`String` type). In most cases it returns the fully qualified name of the class.

- **GetType()** This method returns the `Type` class for this instance of the class. We will look at this class in the next section.

3.4 Type class and Reflection namespace

The `Type` class is our entry point into the `Reflection` namespace and its members. Reflection, in .NET terms, is the ability to examine the capabilities of classes at run-time. By using `Reflection`, we can take a class and examine its methods, properties, constructors, fields, events, and other members – that is, the metadata associated with a class.

The `Type` class contains methods such as `GetMethods` and `GetProperties` that are used to return member information. By using the classes inside the `Reflection` namespace, we can go deeper and examine, for example, parameters of the methods (using `System.Reflection.MethodInfo` class) and even call methods via the `Invoke` method.

The following example can be used as a starting point into the reflection. It shows how to use the `GetType` method to get the `Type` object and some of the properties of this object (see also Figure 3.4):

```
Name      = Int32
Module    = CommonLanguageRuntimeLibrary
Namespace = System
```

FIGURE 3.4 The GetType method demo output

```
'-----------------------------------------
' .NET GetType Method Demo
'-----------------------------------------
Imports System
Imports System.Reflection

Module Cons

  Sub Main()

    Dim I As Integer
    Dim T As Type

    T = I.GetType()
    Console.WriteLine("Name      = " & T.Name)
    Console.WriteLine("Module    = " & T.Module.ToString())
    Console.WriteLine("Namespace = " & T.Namespace)

  End Sub

End Module
```

The whole topic of reflections really deserves its own chapter, but here we will briefly focus on the main features of the Reflection namespace.

- We can use the Assembly class to define and load assemblies, load modules from the assembly manifest, locate types, defined in this assembly, and create instances of it.

- We use the Module class to find classes in the module as well as all global methods and other non-global methods defined in the module.

- The ConstructorInfo class can be used to discover the name, parameters, access modifiers, and implementation details of a constructor. To invoke a specific constructor we can use the GetConstructors or GetConstructor methods of a Type object.

- We use the MethodInfo class to find the name, return type, parameters, access modifiers, and implementation details of a method. To invoke a method we can use the GetMethods or GetMethod methods of a Type object.

- To find the information about the fields – name, access modifiers, and implementation details – we use the FieldInfo class. Using this class we can also get and set field values.

- We use the EventInfo class to discover the name, event handler data type, custom attributes, declaring type, and reflected type of an event. Using this class we can also add and remove event handlers.

● The `PropertyInfo` class helps us to find the name, data type, declaring type, reflected type, and status of a property. We can also get and set property values.

● To find information about parameters – name, data type, input or output, and its position – we use the `ParameterInfo` class.

The following example shows how to get a list of types defined in the module:

```
'----------------------------------------
' .NET Reflections Demo
'----------------------------------------
Imports System
Imports System.Reflection

Module Cons

  Sub Main()

    Dim I As Integer
    Dim T As Type
    Dim Types() As Type
    Dim M As [Module]

    T = I.GetType()
    M = T.Module
    Types = M.GetTypes()
    For Each T In Types
     Console.WriteLine(T.FullName)
    Next

  End Sub


End Module
```

The partial output of this code is shown in Figure 3.5.

As we can see from the list in Figure 3.5, the whole concept of reflections resembles the `ITypeLibrary` API found in Win32 API, but the .NET version is more complete, easier to use, and more "friendly" to different programming languages.

```
C:\Documents and Settings\Administrator\My Documents\Visual Studio Projects\ConsoleApplication...
System.Runtime.Remoting.Contexts.ContextTransitionFrame
System.Convert
Microsoft.Win32.Win32Native
Microsoft.Win32.Win32Native+OSVERSIONINFO
Microsoft.Win32.Win32Native+SECURITY_ATTRIBUTES
Microsoft.Win32.Win32Native+WIN32_FILE_ATTRIBUTE_DATA
Microsoft.Win32.Win32Native+WIN32_FIND_DATA
Microsoft.Win32.Win32Native+USEROBJECTFLAGS
System.Runtime.InteropServices.COMException
System.ResolveEventArgs
System.AssemblyLoadEventArgs
System.ResolveEventHandler
System.AssemblyLoadEventHandler
System._AppDomain
System.AppDomain
System.AppDomain+EvidenceCollection
System.CrossAppDomainDelegate
System.UnloadWorker
System.UnloadThreadWorker
System.Security.Permissions.PublisherIdentityPermission
System.Security.Policy.NetCodeGroup
System.Byte
System.Runtime.Serialization.Formatters.Binary.BinaryFormatter
System.IO.DirectoryInfo
System.Reflection.AssemblyNameProxy
System.Reflection.Emit.OperandType
System.Collections.Stack
System.Collections.Stack+SyncStack
System.Collections.Stack+StackEnumerator
System.Reflection.TargetException
System.Security.Principal.PrincipalPolicy
System.IAppDomainSetup
System.AppDomainSetup
System.AppDomainSetup+LoaderInformation
System.AppDomainSetup+Mapping
```

FIGURE 3.5 Part of the output when using the Reflection namespace

3.5 Types

The .NET Framework class library supports two groups of types:

● value types;
● reference types.

The major distinction between these two groups is that value types are allocated on the stack, while reference types are stored in the heap.

Value types cannot be null and must always contain data. That's why for each value type there is always a default value. Value types are always passed by value – that is, in our functions, we always deal with the copy of the value, leaving the original value unchanged. Most of the value types are not more than 12 to 16 bytes in size – as they are located in the stack, they should not consume much memory.

Reference types are used to represent data structures that may consume significant memory resources. Reference types can be thought of as a combination of location (reference) and a sequence of bytes. As reference types are pointers plus data, stored in the heap, they can be null. Figure 3.6 shows various value and reference types in the .NET Framework.

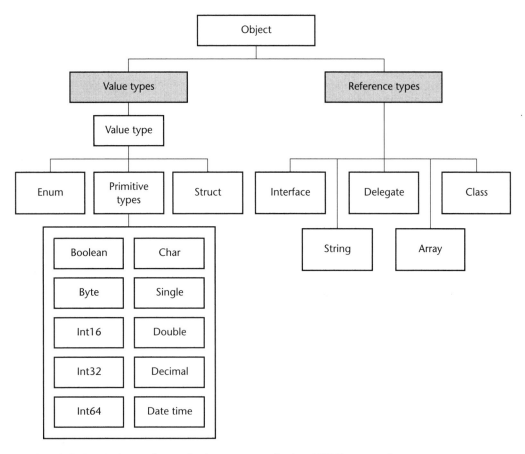

FIGURE 3.6 Various value and reference types in the .NET Framework

Our discussion of the types supported in the .NET Framework will start with value types.

Value types

There are several groups of basic value data types, which are sometimes called primitive data types. They are integers, floating point types, logical types, and other types. We will cover them in the following sections. All of the value types are based on the `ValueType` class that overrides the virtual methods of its parent class – the `Object` class – and provides more appropriate implementations of these methods for value types.

We will start our discussion of value types with the primitive ones, then we will describe enumerations and structures.

Table 3.2 shows the main integers, while Table 3.3 shows additional integer types that are not Common Language Specification (CLS)-compliant.

TABLE 3.2   The main integers

Class name	Description
Byte	An 8-bit unsigned integer with values ranging from 0 to 255. Default value is 0.
Int16	A 16-bit signed integer with values ranging from –32768 through to +32767. Default value is 0.
Int32	A 32-bit signed integer with values ranging from –2,147,483,648 through to +2,147,483,647. Default value is 0.
Int64	A 64-bit signed integer with values ranging from –9,223,372,036,854,775,808 through to +9,223,372,036,854,775,807. Default value is 0.

TABLE 3.3   Additional integers

Class name	Description
SByte	An 8-bit signed integer with values ranging from –128 to +127. This type is not CLS-compliant. Use Int16 type as a CLS-complaint alternative. Default value is 0.
UInt16	A 16-bit unsigned integer with values ranging from 0 to 65535. This type is not CLS-compliant. Use Int16 type as a CLS-complaint alternative. Default value is 0.
UInt32	A 32-bit unsigned integer with values ranging from 0 to 4,294,967,295. This type is not CLS-compliant. Use Int32 type as a CLS-compliant alternative. The default value is 0.
UInt64	A 64-bit unsigned integer with values ranging from 0 to 18,446,744,073,709,551,615. This type is not CLS-compliant. Use Int64 type as a CLS-compliant alternative. Default value is 0.

Note that all integer types implement interfaces IComparable, IFormattable, and IConvertible. We will discuss interfaces later in this chapter.

TABLE 3.4 Floating point

Class Name	Description
Single	A single-precision (32-bit) floating point number with values ranging from -3402823×10^{38} to $+3.402823 \times 10^{38}$. Its values also include positive and negative zero, PositiveInfinity, NegativeInfinity and Not-a-Number (NaN). The default value is 0.0.
Double	A double-precision (64-bit) floating point number with values ranging from $-1.79769313486232 \times 10^{308}$ to $+1.79769313486232 \times 10^{308}$. Its values also include positive and negative zero, PositiveInfinity, NegativeInfinity, and Not-a-Number (NaN). The default value is 0.0. This type conforms to standard IEC 60559:1989, Binary Floating point Arithmetic for Microprocessor Systems.

Note that all floating point types implement interfaces IComparable, IFormattable, and IConvertible.

TABLE 3.5 Logical

Class name	Description
Boolean	A Boolean value – true or false. The default value is false.

Note that a logical type implements interfaces IComparable and IConvertible.

TABLE 3.6 Other types

Class name	Description
Char	A Unicode (16-bit) character with values ranging from hexadecimal 0 x 0000 to 0 x FFFF. The default value is ChrW(0) .
Decimal	A 96-bit decimal value ranging from $-79,228,162,514,264,337,593,543,950,335$ to $+ 79,228,162,514,264,337,593,543,950,335$. The default value is 0.0.
IntPtr	A signed integer with platform-dependent size. This type can be used by languages that provide pointer support. This type is not CLS-compliant.
UintPtr	An unsigned integer with platform-dependent size. This type can be used by languages that provide pointer support. This type is not CLS-compliant.

Note that a `Char` type implements interfaces `IComparable` and `IConvertible`, while a `Decimal` type implements interfaces `IComparable`, `IFormattable`, and `IConvertible`. `IntPtr` and `UintPtr` types can implement an `ISerializable` interface that allows an object to control its own serialization and deserialization.

The .NET Framework class library supports conversion between data types. The following section explains the basic rules of conversions, as well as the `System.Convert` class that performs them.

3.6 Conversions with the System.Convert class

The `System.Convert` class is used to perform various conversions. Using this class we can perform narrow conversions and conversions to unrelated data types. The following is a list of supported conversions:

- we can convert between `Byte`, `SByte`, `Int16`, `Int32`, `Int64`, `UInt16`, `UInt32`, `UInt64`, `Single`, `Double`, `Decimal`, `String`, and `Object`;
- we can convert from `Char` to `Int32`, `UInt32`, `String`, and `Object`;
- `Byte`, `SByte`, `Int16`, `Int32`, `UInt16`, `UInt32`, and `String` can be converted to `Char`;
- we can convert from `Boolean` to `Byte`, `Char`, `Int16`, `Int32`, `Int64`, `UInt16`, `UInt32`, `UInt64`, `String`, and `Object`;
- `Byte`, `SByte`, `Int16`, `Int32`, `Int64`, `UInt16`, `UInt32`, `UInt64`, and `String` can be converted to `Boolean`;
- `DateTime` can be converted to and from `String`.

Conversions can be widening conversions and narrowing conversions. For widening conversions, the following rules apply:

- enumerations widen to underlying type;
- there can be widening from a type to one of its base classes;
- there can be widening from a type to an interface it implements;
- there can be widening from `Char` to `String`;
- there can be widening from any array of x to array of y if x and y are reference types and x widens to y.

Some of the conversions of a numeric type result in a loss of precision – some of the least significant digits may be lost. These are called "narrowing conversions". For narrowing conversions, the following rules apply. Narrowing occurs:

- in numeric conversions that may overflow – for example, when converting a Double into an Integer value results in a narrowing conversion and the value will be rounded;
- when converting Boolean to numeric and numeric to Boolean;
- when converting from a numeric type to an enumerated type;
- when converting to a class type from an interface or a non-deriving class;
- when converting to an interface from a non-deriving class;
- when converting from string to numeric and numeric to string;
- when converting from String to Char;
- when converting from Char() to String.

Conversion methods implemented by the System.Convert class have names that indicate the type of conversion performed; for example, ToBoolean, ToInt16, and so on. To perform conversions we use the following code:

```
'----------------------------------------
' .NET Conversions Demo
'----------------------------------------
Imports System

Module Module1

 Sub Main()

  Dim S As String
  Dim I As Integer
  S = "1024"
  I = System.Convert.ToInt16(S)

 End Sub

End Module
```

Note that if a conversion cannot be performed, the InvalidCastException will be thrown.

Besides the primitive data types, the .NET Framework supports other value types. Among them are enumerations and structures, which are covered in the following sections.

Enumerations

Enumerations represent a set of values of one of the primitive integral types except Char. Enumerations are based on the System.Enum class, which provides methods to compare instances of this class, convert the value of an instance to String, convert the String representation of a number to an instance, and create an instance of a specified enumeration and value.

Like all value types, the System.Enum class inherits from the ValueType class. It implements such interfaces as IComparable, IFormattable, and IConvertible. The System.Enum class contains the following methods, which are available to us:

- **Format(*Type*, *Object*, *String*) method** Performs the conversion of a value to a String according to the specified format. Supported formats are general, hex, and decimal.

- **GetName(*Type*, *Object*) method** Returns the name of the enumeration value.

- **GetNames(*Type*)** Returns a String array of names in the enumeration.

- **GetUnderlyingType(*Type*)** Returns the underlying type of the enumeration.

- **GetValues(*Type*) method** Returns an array of values in the enumeration.

- **IsDefined(*Type*, *Object*) method** Checks that a specified value exists in the enumeration.

- **Parse(Type, String)** or **Parse (Type, String, Boolean) method** Used to convert the String into one or more enumeration values. The Boolean parameter specifies whether or not the operation is case-sensitive.

- **ToObject(Type, Object) method** Returns an Object of the specified enumeration type set to the specified value. The second parameter of this method can be of type Byte, Short, Integer, Long, Object, SByte, UInt16, UInt32, or UInt64.

The following example shows how to create and use enumerations (see also Figure 3.7):

```
'----------------------------------------
' .NET Enumerations Demo
'----------------------------------------
Imports System


Module Module1


    '
    ' Geometric Shapes
    '
```

```
Public Enum Shapes
    None        = 0
    Circle      = 1
    Rectangle   = 2
    Ellipse     = 3
    Triangle    = 4

End Enum

Sub Main()

    Dim GeoShapes As New Shapes()
    Dim Names As String()
    Dim Values() As Integer
    Dim I As Integer
    Console.WriteLine(GeoShapes.GetType)
    Names   = GeoShapes.GetNames(GeoShapes.GetType)
    Values = GeoShapes.GetValues(GeoShapes.GetType)
    For I = 0 To Names.GetUpperBound(0)
        Console.WriteLine(ControlChars.Tab & Names(I) & "=" & _
          CType(Values(I), Integer).ToString("G"))
    Next
    Console.Write(ControlChars.CrLf & "Underlying Type: ")
    Console.WriteLine(GeoShapes.GetUnderlyingType _
      (GeoShapes.GetType))
End Sub
End Module
```

```
ConsoleApplication11.Module1+Shapes

        None=0
        Circle=1
        Rectangle=2
        Ellipse=3
        Triangle=4

Underlying Type: System.Int32
```

FIGURE 3.7   Creating and using enumerations

Note that the .NET Framework class library contains many enumerations. These predefined enumerations range from FileAttributes to DisplayMode and OleDbType.

In the next section we will discuss the last value type – structure.

Structures

Structures are used to store data members and function members. Structures are similar to classes, but they are value types and are allocated on the stack. Let's look at the following example where we declare a TPoint structure with two integer members (see also Figure 3.8):

```
'-----------------------------------------
' .NET Structures Demo
'-----------------------------------------
Imports System

Module Module1

'
' TPoint Structure contains two Integer members
'

    Structure TPoint
        Public X As Integer
        Public Y As Integer
    End Structure

    Sub Main()

    Dim MyPoint As TPoint

    MyPoint.X = 100
    MyPoint.Y = 150

    Console.WriteLine(" X should be 100" & " X=" & MyPoint.X)
    Console.WriteLine(" Y should be 150" & " Y=" & MyPoint.Y)

    End Sub

End Module
```

```
X should be 100 X=100
Y should be 150 Y=150
```

FIGURE 3.8   The two integer numbers of a TPoint structure

Now, let's copy our structure to a variable and change its fields. Because we change the contents of the *copy* of our structure, the original values will not be changed (see also Figure 3.9):

```
'---------------------------------------
' .NET Structures Demo
'---------------------------------------
Imports System

Module Module1

Sub Main()

 Dim MyPoint As TPoint
 Dim NewPoint

 MyPoint.X = 100
 MyPoint.Y = 150

 NewPoint = MyPoint

 NewPoint.X = 200
 NewPoint.Y = 50

 Console.WriteLine("NewPoint X, Y=" & NewPoint.X & ", " & NewPoint.Y)
 Console.WriteLine("MyPoint  X, Y=" & MyPoint.X  & ", " & MyPoint.Y)

 End Sub

 End Module
```

This ends our overview of value types. In the next section, we will discuss reference types – classes, methods, events, delegates, and interfaces.

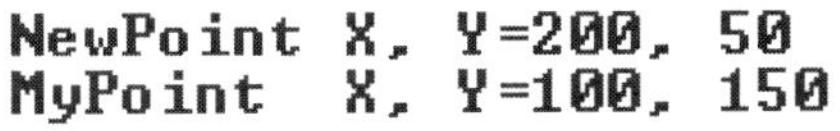

```
NewPoint X, Y=200, 50
MyPoint  X, Y=100, 150
```

FIGURE 3.9   Changing the contents of a copy of the TPoint structure

3.7 Reference types

Reference types got their name because they contain references to the objects allocated on the heap. Such types can contain null references and are always passed by
reference. This means that an address of the object, not the object itself, is passed to a
procedure or function, meaning that changes will be made to the object, not its copy,
as we have seen in the previous example for structures. The main reference type is a
class – we will learn about this type in the next section.

Classes

By definition, a "class" is a data structure that may contain data members (constants,
variables, and events), function members (methods, properties, indexers, operators,
and constructors), and nested types. One important note about classes is that they
support inheritance. They can thus serve as a base for derived classes that extend the
basic functionality provided by the base class.

Let's take the structure created in the previous example and rewrite it as a class.
How to do this is shown below:

```
'----------------------------------------
' .NET Class Demo
'----------------------------------------

Imports System

Module Module1

    '
    ' TPoint class contains two integer members
    '

    Public Class TPoint
        Dim ptX As Integer     ' X
        Dim ptY As Integer     ' Y
    '
    ' Get and Set for ptX property
    '

        Public Property X() As Integer

            Get
                Return ptX
            End Get

            Set(ByVal Value As Integer)
                ptX = Value
            End Set

        End Property
```

```vbnet
'
' Get and Set for ptY property
'

        Public Property Y() As Integer

            Get
                Return ptY
            End Get

            Set(ByVal Value As Integer)
                ptY = Value
            End Set

        End Property
'
' Constructor
'

        Public Sub New()

            ptX = 0
            ptY = 0

        End Sub

    End Class

    Sub Main()
        Dim MyPoint As New TPoint()
'
' Object initialization
'

        MyPoint.X = 100
        MyPoint.Y = 150

        Console.WriteLine(" X should be 100" & " X=" & MyPoint.X)
        Console.WriteLine(" Y should be 150" & " Y=" & MyPoint.Y)

    End Sub

End Module
```

The main change here, when compared to the structure, is not the declaration, but the treatment of members. Now we have two special sections that describe each property and specify the mechanisms to get and set their values. Note that the "internal" names of properties (ptX and ptY in our example) must be different from the "external" property names (X and Y in our example).

Methods

Methods are used to implement a class's functionality. Let's have an example that illustrates this. We will extend our TPoint class and implement the SetXY method that can be used to set the new values of the X and Y properties.

To do this, we need to add the following code to our class declaration:

```
Public Sub SetXY(ByVal newX As Integer, ByVal newY As Integer)


    X = newX
    Y = newY


End Sub
```

Now, let's change the code of our main program like this:

```
Sub Main()
   Dim MyPoint As New TPoint()
'
' Object initialization
'


    MyPoint.SetXY(100, 150)


    Console.WriteLine(" X should be 100" & " X=" & MyPoint.X)
    Console.WriteLine(" Y should be 150" & " Y=" & MyPoint.Y)


End Sub
```

Events

Events are asynchronous actions that can be responded to by our applications. The source of an event can be a user action – pressing a key or clicking the mouse, program code or system. The applications that contain code that responds to events are called "event-driven applications". The code that responds to the particular event is called an "event handler".

Let's look at our TPoint class. The possible event here is the change of the value of the X or Y property. The code inside the TPoint class can generate the PTChanged event that will indicate that the value of the X or Y property (or both) is set.

Let's implement this in our code. In Visual Basic.NET, we use the Event keyword to describe an event. For the code of the event we should use the RaiseEvent keyword and the event name – this will raise an event. All of this is shown in the following example:

```
Public Class TPoint
    Dim ptX As Integer  ' X
    Dim ptY As Integer  ' Y

    '
    ' Declare new event
    '

    Event PTChanged()

    '
    ' Get and Set for ptX property
    '

    Public Property X() As Integer

        Get
            Return ptX
        End Get

        Set(ByVal Value As Integer)
            ptX = Value
            RaiseEvent PTChanged()
        End Set

    End Property

    '
    ' Get and Set for ptX property
    '

    Public Property Y() As Integer

        Get
            Return ptY
        End Get

        Set(ByVal Value As Integer)
            ptY = Value
            RaiseEvent PTChanged()
        End Set

    End Property
```

```
'
' Constructor
'

    Public Sub New()

    ptX = 0
    ptY = 0

    End Sub
    Public Sub SetXY(ByVal newX As Integer, ByVal newY As Integer)

     X = newX
     Y = newY

    End Sub
End Class
```

Now, let's test how our event works. To do this we will create a simple Windows application that will contain the Button, List, and Panel controls. We will talk about Windows applications in detail in Chapter 6, but for now, let's just follow the code of our example.

Every time we click the mouse on the panel, the SetXY method of our TPoint class is called, which generates two events that are handled by our client application. Here is the code for our client application. Our class is now implemented in the separate class library:

```
Imports ClassLibrary1
Public Class Form1
    Inherits System.Windows.Forms.Form


    Dim WithEvents MyPoint As TPoint

    Private Sub Button1_Click(ByVal sender As System.Object, _
     ByVal e As System.EventArgs) Handles Button1.Click
        MyPoint = New TPoint()
    End Sub

    Private Sub Panel1_MouseDown(ByVal sender As Object, _
     ByVal e As System.Windows.Forms.MouseEventArgs) _
    Handles Panel1.MouseDown
        MyPoint.SetXY(e.X, e.Y)
    End Sub
```

```
'
' Handle PTChanged event, generated by TPoint class
'

    Private Sub MyPoint_PTChanged() Handles MyPoint.PTChanged

        ListBox1.Items.Add(MyPoint.X & ", " & MyPoint.Y)
    End Sub

End Class
```

Note that now an instance of MyPoint of the TPoint type is declared with the WithEvents keyword. This means that our class supports events and we can create event handlers for them. The screenshot in Figure 3.10 shows our client application in action.

If we look at the results – logged in the ListBox control (the box on the left side of the screen) – we can see the paired coordinates –X, Y, X, Y1, X1, Y1 and so on. The cause of this is that, in our class' code, the PTChanged event is raised both when we change the X coordinate and the Y coordinate. This means that when we changed both coordinates, we got two events. To change our event generation logic, we must remove the event generation code from the properties descriptions and move it to the SetXY method. The new version of the class is shown overleaf.

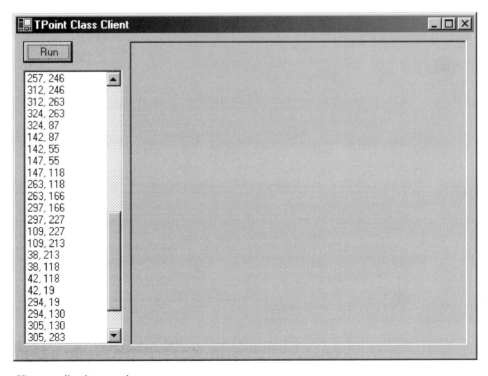

FIGURE 3.10   Client application running

```
Public Class TPoint
    Dim ptX As Integer   ' X
    Dim ptY As Integer   ' Y


'
' Declare new event
'

    Event PTChanged()


'
' Get and Set for ptX property
'

    Public Property X() As Integer

        Get
            Return ptX
        End Get

        Set(ByVal Value As Integer)
            ptX = Value
        End Set


    End Property


'
' Get and Set for ptX property
'

    Public Property Y() As Integer

        Get
            Return ptY
        End Get

        Set(ByVal Value As Integer)
            ptY = Value
        End Set

    End Property


'
' Constructor
'
```

```
      Public Sub New()

      ptX = 0
      ptY = 0

      End Sub

      Public Sub SetXY(ByVal newX As Integer, ByVal newY As Integer)

       X = newX
       Y = newY
       RaiseEvent PTChanged()

      End Sub
   End Class
```

Delegates

Talking about events, we should mention delegates – the mechanism used to bind events to the methods used to handle them. Delegates are classes based on the System.Delegate class, and they contain pointers to methods. Let's look at how we can change the code of our example to be able to specify the event handler at runtime.

```
   Dim MyPoint As TPoint

   Private Sub Button1_Click(ByVal sender As System.Object, _
     ByVal e As System.EventArgs) Handles Button1.Click
         MyPoint = New TPoint()
         AddHandler MyPoint.PTChanged, AddressOf MyPoint_PTChanged
   End Sub

   Private Sub Panel1_MouseDown(ByVal sender As Object, _
     ByVal e As System.Windows.Forms.MouseEventArgs) _
     Handles Panel1.MouseDown
       MyPoint.SetXY(e.X, e.Y)
   End Sub

   Private Sub MyPoint_PTChanged()
       ListBox1.Items.Add(MyPoint.X & ", " & MyPoint.Y)
   End Sub
```

In the Button1_Click method (which itself handles the Click event generated by the Button control), we dynamically added the handler (AddHandler keyword) for MyPoint.PTChanged event. This event handler is implemented by the MyPoint_ PTChanged method, the address being specified with the AddressOf keyword.

Using delegates, we can create event handlers for more than one event, dynamically change and even switch off event handlers, as well as perform other operations.

Interfaces

Interfaces are reference types that are used to specify features for the classes that implement them. In this section, we will discuss some of the most important interfaces defined in the `System` namespace. Later in this chapter we will extend our knowledge of standard interfaces and describe interfaces implemented in the `System.Collections` namespace.

- **The `IComparable` interface** Defines a generalized comparison method. This method is used to implement a type-specific comparison method – `CompareTo` – for the particular data type. This interface is implemented by `Enum`, `String`, and `Version` classes.

- **The `IFormattable` interface** Provides functionality to format the value of an object via the implementation of the `ToString` method. This interface is implemented by the `Enum` class.

- **The `ICloneable` interface** Can be used to provide a `Clone` method to create a new instance of a class with the same value as an existing instance. This interface is implemented by many classes, including `Array`, `ArrayList`, `BitArray`, `Queue`, `Stack`, and so on.

- **The `IConvertible` interface** Describes generalized type conversion and appropriate methods that are used to implement type-specific conversion methods. The `IConvertible` interface specifies such methods as `ToBoolean`, `ToByte`, `ToChar`, and so on. This interface is implemented by `DBNull`, `Enum`, and `String` classes. For more information about conversions see the next section.

We have now finished our discussion of basic value and reference types. In the following sections we will learn about arrays, collections, and strings.

3.8 Arrays

The `System.Array` class contains methods to manipulate arrays. The elements of an `Array` can be of any type, as everything in .NET is an object and derives directly or indirectly from the `System.Object`, `Array`, stores `System.Object` elements. To find the type of array declaration, we use the `GetType` method. The `Length` property specifies the total number of its elements or the number of elements it can contain. The `Rank` property returns the number of dimensions in the array. To find out whether or not the array has a fixed size, we use the `IsFixedSize` property. Fixed size arrays do not allow us to add and remove elements. Such arrays only support the modification of existing elements. Arrays may be read only. To find this out, we should check the value of the `IsReadOnly` property.

THE .NET FRAMEWORK CLASS LIBRARY – TYPES AND STRUCTURES

- **IndexOf(*Array*, *Object*) and LastIndexOf(*Array*, *Object*) methods** Can be used to find the index of the first and last occurrence of a value in a one-dimensional array.

- **Clear(*Array*, *Integer*, *Integer*) method** Sets a range of elements in the array to zero (for value-type elements) or to a null reference (for reference-type elements).

- **Initialize() method** Calls the default constructor for each value-type element in the array, thus initializing its contents.

- **GetLowerBound(*Integer*) and GetUpperBound(*Integer*) methods** Used to find the lower and upper bounds of the specified dimension in the array. It is always wise to use both methods when you iterate a dimension of the array. For example:

```
For I = Chars.GetLowerBound(0) to Chars.GetUpperBound(0)
    '
    ' Perform operations on elements – Chars(I)
    '
Next
```

- **GetLength(*Integer*) method** Returns the number of elements in the specified dimension in the array.

- **Reverse(*Array*) or Reverse(*Array*, *Integer*, *Integer*) method** Used to reverse the order of elements in a one-dimensional array.

- **Sort(*Array*) method** Sorts the elements in a one-dimensional array. The following example shows how to use the Sort and Reverse methods (see also Figure 3.11):

```
'----------------------------------------
' .NET Array Demo
'----------------------------------------
Imports System
Imports System.Array

Module Module1

  Sub Main()
    Dim Langs() As String = _
      {"VB.NET", "C#", "J#", "C++", "JScript .NET", "Perl .NET"}
    ShowArray(Langs, "Original Array")
    Array.Sort(Langs)
    ShowArray(Langs, "Sorted Array")
    Array.Reverse(Langs)
    ShowArray(Langs, "Reversed Array")
  End Sub
```

```
Sub ShowArray(ByVal A As Object, ByVal Title As String)
  Dim I As Integer
  Console.WriteLine(Title)
  For I = A.GetLowerBound(0) To A.GetUpperBound(0)
    Console.WriteLine(I & ControlChars.Tab & A(I))
  Next
  Console.WriteLine()
End Sub


End Module
```

```
Original Array
0      UB.NET
1      C#
2      J#
3      C++
4      JScript .NET
5      Perl .NET

Sorted Array
0      C#
1      C++
2      J#
3      JScript .NET
4      Perl .NET
5      UB.NET

Reversed Array
0      UB.NET
1      Perl .NET
2      JScript .NET
3      J#
4      C++
5      C#
```

FIGURE 3.11   The results of the different ways of arranging an array

- **GetValue(*Integer*) method** Gets a value of an element with a specified index. The plain old ( ) access method maps on to this.
- **SetValue(*Object*, *Integer*) method** Sets a value. The following example shows how to use these methods. Note that the plain old ( ) access method maps on to GetValue/SetValue, as we have seen in the example above (see also Figure 3.12).

```
'-------------------------------------
' .NET Array GetValue/SetValue Demo
'-------------------------------------
Imports System
Imports System.Array

Module Module1

 Sub Main()

  Dim I As Integer
  Dim A() As Integer = {0, 1, 2, 3, 4, 5, 6, 7, 8, 9}
  With A

  Console.WriteLine("Original Array:")
   For I = .GetLowerBound(0) To .GetUpperBound(0)
    Console.WriteLine("Array(" & I & ")" & " = " & .GetValue(I))
    .SetValue(.GetValue(I) * 10, I)
  Next

  Console.WriteLine("Modified Array:")
  For I = .GetLowerBound(0) To .GetUpperBound(0)
   Console.WriteLine("Array(" & I & ")" & " = " & .GetValue(I))
  Next

  End With

 End Sub

End Module
```

- **Copy**(*Array*, *Array*, *Integer*) **method** Used to copy a section of one array to another array. The CopyTo(*Array*, *Integer*) method copies all the elements of the current one-dimensional array to the specified one-dimensional array starting at the specified destination array index.

The Array class implements ICloneable, IList, ICollection, and IEnumerable interfaces.

```
Original Array:
Array(0) = 0
Array(1) = 1
Array(2) = 2
Array(3) = 3
Array(4) = 4
Array(5) = 5
Array(6) = 6
Array(7) = 7
Array(8) = 8
Array(9) = 9

Modified Array:
Array(0) = 0
Array(1) = 10
Array(2) = 20
Array(3) = 30
Array(4) = 40
Array(5) = 50
Array(6) = 60
Array(7) = 70
Array(8) = 80
Array(9) = 90
```

FIGURE 3.12   The results of `GetValue()` and `SetValue()` methods

3.9 Collections

Collections in the Microsoft .NET Framework class library are implemented in the `System.Collections` namespace. Here we will find various collections of objects, such as lists, queues, hash tables, and dictionaries. Also, this namespace contains several interfaces used to define some basic functionality for collections. The partial contents of the `System.Collections` namespace are shown in Figure 3.13.

We will start with a brief overview of the interfaces, then we will discuss various collections. As we remember, interfaces are used to define some functionality without its realization – classes that implement interfaces are required to implement methods, declared in interfaces.

IEnumerable interface

The `IEnumerable` interface exposes the enumerator, which supports a simple iteration over a collection. It specifies only one method – `GetEnumerator` – that returns the `IEnumerator` – the enumerator used in iterations. The `Current` property of the `Object` type returns the current element in the collection. The `MoveNext()` method moves to the next element of the collection. The `Reset()` method sets the enumerator to its initial position, before the first element in the collection.

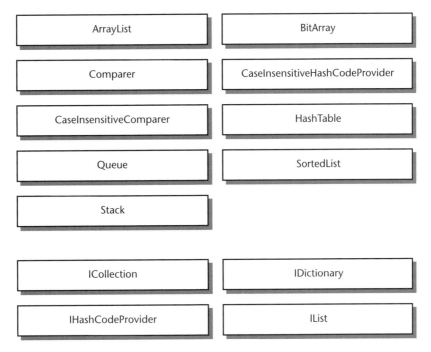

FIGURE 3.13   Partial contents of the System.Collections namespace

ICollection interface

This interface inherits the IEnumerable one and is the basic collection interface – all classes in the System.Collections namespace implement this interface. The ICollection interface defines a set of methods common to all collections, such as size, enumerators, and synchronization. The most important are the Count property of Integer type, which returns the number of elements contained in the collection, and the CopyTo(*Array*, *Integer*) method, which copies the elements of the collection to a one-dimensional Array, starting at a particular Array index.

IDictionary interface

This interface extends the ICollection interface and is an implementation of key/value pairs. The IDictionary interface allows the contained keys and values to be enumerated. Implementations of this interface can be read only (dictionary cannot be modified), fixed size (addition and removal of elements is not allowed), and variable size (addition, removal and modification of elements is allowed).

- The `IsFixedSize` and `IsReadOnly` are Boolean properties that can be used to find if the dictionary is fixed size or read only.
- The `Item(Object)` property gives us access to the element with the specified key.
- The `Keys` property of the `ICollection` type returns the collection of keys in the dictionary.
- The `Values` property of the `ICollection` type returns the collection of values in the dictionary.
- We use the `Add(Object, Object)` method to add an entry (key and value) to the dictionary.
- To remove all entries we use the `Clear()` method.
- To remove the entry with the specified key we use the `Remove(Object)` method.
- To find if an entry with the specified key exists in the dictionary, we use the `Contains(Object)` method.
- The `GetEnumerator()` method returns an `IDictionaryEnumerator` for the dictionary.

IList interface

This interface is inherited from the `ICollection` and `IEnumerable` interfaces and defines a collection of values that can be sorted and the members of which can be accessed by index. The `IList` interface is a basic list container interface – a base class for all lists. The `Add(Object)` and `Remove(Object)` methods are used to add and remove items to/from the list. The `Contains(Object)` method lets us check whether or not the list contains a certain value. The `Clear()` method removes all items from the list.

Now we know the basic functionality of collections, let's look at which collections are available in the `System.Collections` namespace.

ArrayList class

This class is a dynamic array that implements the `IList` interface. Unlike the `Array` class discussed above, the `ArrayList` can grow and shrink in size, and we can dynamically add or remove elements from a list.

If we need a fixed-size array – which means that elements can be modified but not added to or removed – we should use the `FixedSize(ArrayList or IList)` method, which returns a list wrapper with a fixed size. For read-only arrays we should use the `ReadOnly(ArrayList or IList)` method. It returns a list wrapper that allows read-only access. To get a thread-safe array we should use the wrapper returned by the `Synchronized(ArrayList or IList)` method. The `Capacity` property of the `Integer` type specifies the number of elements the array can hold. The `Count` property of the `Integer` type returns the actual number of elements in the array and the `Item(Integer)` property of the `Object` type provides access to the element with the specified index.

The following example shows how to use the ArrayList class:

```
'---------------------------------------
' .NET ArrayList Demo
'---------------------------------------
Imports System
Imports System.Collections

Module Module1


  Sub Main()
   Dim AList As New ArrayList()
   Dim E As IEnumerator
    With AList
     .Add("Microsoft ")
     .Add(".NET ")
     .Add("Platform")
     Console.WriteLine(.Capacity)
     Console.WriteLine(.Count)
     E = .GetEnumerator
     While E.MoveNext()
      Console.WriteLine(E.Current)
     End While
    End With
  End Sub


  End Module
```

Note that in this example we have used the IEnumerator interface to iterate elements of the array – the same can be done with the For/Next construction:

```
For I = 0 To .Count – 1
 Console.WriteLine(ControlChars.Tab & .Item(I))
Next
```

BitArray class

This class is an array of bits. Each bit value is expressed as a Boolean value – that is, if a single bit is turned on/off, its value is "true/false". The BitArray class supports such operations as Not, Or, and Xor.

● **And(*BitArray*) method** Performs the bitwise AND operation on the elements in the current array against the corresponding elements in the specified array and returns the resulting BitArray.

- **Not()** **method** Inverts all the bit values in the current array and returns the resulting BitArray.

- **Or(*BitArray*)** **method** Performs the bitwise OR operation on the elements in the current array against the corresponding elements in the specified array and returns the resulting BitArray.

- **Xor(*BitArra*)** **method** Performs the bitwise exclusive OR operation on the elements in the current array against the corresponding elements in the specified array and returns the resulting BitArray.

- **Set(Integer, Boolean)** **method** Sets the bit at a specific position in the array to the specified value.

- **SetAll(Boolean)** **method** Sets all bits in the array to the specified value.

The following example shows how to perform some operations on bit arrays (see Figure 3.14):

```
'----------------------------------------
' .NET BitArray Demo
'----------------------------------------
Imports System
Imports System.Collections

Module Module1

 Sub Main()

  Dim Bools() As Boolean = {True, False, True, False, _
                            True, False, True, False}
  Dim BA As New BitArray(Bools)
  Dim BA2 As New BitArray(8, False)

  ShowArray("Original Array:", BA)
  ShowArray("After NOT:", BA.Not)
  BA = New BitArray(Bools)
  ShowArray("After AND:", BA.And(BA2))
  BA = New BitArray(Bools)
  ShowArray("After OR:", BA.Or(BA2))
  BA = New BitArray(Bools)
  ShowArray("After XOR:", BA.Xor(BA2))

 End Sub


 Sub ShowArray(ByVal Header As String, ByVal A As IEnumerable)
```

```
    Dim E As IEnumerator
    E = A.GetEnumerator
    Console.WriteLine(ControlChars.NewLine & Header)
    Console.WriteLine("+-----+-----+-----+-----+" & _
                      "-----+-----+-----+-----+")
    While E.MoveNext()
     Console.Write("|")
     Console.Write(CType(E.Current, String).PadLeft(5))
    End While
    Console.WriteLine("|")
    Console.WriteLine("+-----+-----+-----+-----+" & _
                      "-----+-----+-----+-----+")


  End Sub


  End Module
```

```
Original Array:
+-----+-----+-----+-----+-----+-----+-----+-----+
| True|False| True|False| True|False| True|False|
+-----+-----+-----+-----+-----+-----+-----+-----+

After NOT:
+-----+-----+-----+-----+-----+-----+-----+-----+
|False| True|False| True|False| True|False| True|
+-----+-----+-----+-----+-----+-----+-----+-----+

After AND:
+-----+-----+-----+-----+-----+-----+-----+-----+
|False|False|False|False|False|False|False|False|
+-----+-----+-----+-----+-----+-----+-----+-----+

After OR:
+-----+-----+-----+-----+-----+-----+-----+-----+
| True|False| True|False| True|False| True|False|
+-----+-----+-----+-----+-----+-----+-----+-----+

After XOR:
+-----+-----+-----+-----+-----+-----+-----+-----+
| True|False| True|False| True|False| True|False|
+-----+-----+-----+-----+-----+-----+-----+-----+
```

FIGURE 3.14   Operations have been performed on this bit array

HashTable class

This class is a fast hash table that implements the IDictionary interface. It represents a collection of key and value pairs that are organized in a hash table using the hash value of the key. We can use the HashTable class if we want to work with key and value pair collections.

The following example shows how to use the HashTable class (see also Figure 3.15).

```vb
'----------------------------------------
' .NET HashTable Demo
'----------------------------------------
Imports System
Imports System.Collections

Module Module1


  Sub Main()

   Dim HT As New Hashtable()
   With HT
'
' Build hashtable with IDD country codes
'

     .Add("Austria", "+43")
     .Add("France", "+33")
     .Add("Germany", "+49")
     .Add("Italy", "+39")
     .Add("Spain", "+34")
     .Add("Switzerland", "+41")
     ShowTable("Original Table", HT)
'
' Remove Switzerland if we have it in the table
'
     If .Contains("Switzerland") Then
       .Remove("Switzerland")
     End If
     ShowTable("Modified Table", HT)
   End With

  End Sub

  Sub ShowTable(ByVal Header As String, ByVal T As Hashtable)

   Dim E As IDictionaryEnumerator
   E = T.GetEnumerator
   Console.WriteLine(ControlChars.NewLine & Header)
   While E.MoveNext()
    Console.WriteLine(E.Key & "=" & E.Value)
   End While

  End Sub

End Module
```

```
Original Table
France=+33
Switzerland=+41
Italy=+39
Spain=+34
Germany=+49
Austria=+43

Modified Table
France=+33
Italy=+39
Spain=+34
Germany=+49
Austria=+43
```

FIGURE 3.15 Using the HashTable class

SortedList class

Like the HashTable class discussed above, this class also implements the IDictionary interface. The SortedList class organizes the key and value pair collection using the key, not a hash value like the HashTable class. Items can be accessed either by key or index.

The following example shows how to use the SortedList class (see also Figure 3.16):

```
'-------------------------------------
' .NET SortedList Demo
'-------------------------------------
Imports System
Imports System.Collections

Module Module1

 Sub Main()

  Dim SL As New SortedList()
  With SL
 '
 ' Build sorted list with IDD country codes
 '
    .Add("Austria", "+43")
    .Add("France", "+33")
    .Add("Germany", "+49")
    .Add("Italy", "+39")
    .Add("Spain", "+34")
    .Add("Switzerland", "+41")
    ShowTable("Original Table", SL)
```

```
'
' Remove Switzerland if we have it in the table
'
   If .Contains("Switzerland") Then
     .Remove("Switzerland")
   End If
   ShowTable2("Modified Table", SL)
   End With

End Sub


Sub ShowTable(ByVal Header As String, ByVal L As SortedList)

  Dim E As IDictionaryEnumerator
  E = L.GetEnumerator
  Console.WriteLine(ControlChars.NewLine & Header)
  While E.MoveNext()
    Console.WriteLine(E.Key & "=" & E.Value)
  End While

End Sub


Sub ShowTable2(ByVal Header As String, ByVal L As SortedList)

  Dim I As Integer
  Console.WriteLine(ControlChars.NewLine & Header)
  For I = 0 To L.Count - 1
    Console.WriteLine(L.GetKey(I) & "=" & L.GetByIndex(I))
  Next

End Sub


End Module
```

Comparing the above to the previous example, here we have items sorted by the key value, not by hash value like in the HashTable class. Also take a look at the ShowTable2 method – it shows how to access the items of the SortedList class by index and find its keys (GetKey(Integer) method) and values (GetByIndex(Integer) method).

```
Original Table
Austria=+43
France=+33
Germany=+49
Italy=+39
Spain=+34
Switzerland=+41

Modified Table
Austria=+43
France=+33
Germany=+49
Italy=+39
Spain=+34
```

FIGURE 3.16   Using the SortedList class

Stack class

This class implements a simple queue (last-in-first-out, or LIFO, collection) of objects. It is a stack implementation with such methods as Push and Pop to insert and remove objects at the top of the stack. The Peek method returns the top item without removing it from the stack. To copy elements of the stack to a new array we can use the ToArray method.

The Stack class also provides the GetEnumerator method to get an enumerator of the stack. The Stack is implemented as a circular buffer.

The following example shows how to use the Stack class (see also Figure 3.17):

```
'-------------------------------------
' .NET Stack Demo
'-------------------------------------
Imports System
Imports System.Collections

Module Module1


  Sub Main()
    Dim S As New Stack()

    With S
'
' Push 3 items
'
      .Push("Item0")
      .Push("Item1")
      .Push("Item2")
      ShowStack("Original Stack", S)
```

```
        '
        ' Remove top item
        '

          .Pop()
          ShowStack("Modified Stack", S)
        '
        ' Push one item
        '

          .Push("Item3")
        '
        ' Show top item and preserve it
        '

          ShowStack("Modified Stack", S)
          Console.WriteLine("Top item: " & .Peek())
        End With

    End Sub

    Sub ShowStack(ByVal Header As String, ByVal S As IEnumerable)

      Dim E As IEnumerator
      E = S.GetEnumerator
      Console.WriteLine(ControlChars.NewLine & Header)
      While E.MoveNext()
        Console.WriteLine(E.Current)
      End While

    End Sub

  End Module


Original Stack
Item2
Item1
Item0

Modified Stack
Item1
Item0

Modified Stack
Item3
Item1
Item0
Top item: Item3
```

FIGURE 3.17   Using the Stack class

Queue class

This class implements a first-in-first-out (FIFO) form of collection. To add and remove objects from the queue, we use the Dequeue() and Enqueue(*Object*) methods. The Dequeue() method removes an object at the beginning of the queue, while the Enqueue(*Object*) method adds an object to the end of the queue. To copy elements of the queue to a new array, we can use the ToArray() method.

The following example shows how to use the **Queue** class (see Figure 3.18).

```
'----------------------------------------
' .NET Queue Demo
'----------------------------------------
Imports System
Imports System.Collections

Module Module1


 Sub Main()
  Dim Q As New Queue()

  With Q
'
' Add 3 items
'
    .Enqueue("Item0")
    .Enqueue("Item1")
    .Enqueue("Item2")
    ShowQueue("Original Queue", Q)
'
' Remove top item
'
    .Dequeue()
    ShowQueue("Modified Queue", Q)
'
' Add one item
'
    .Enqueue("Item3")
    ShowQueue("Modified Queue", Q)
'
' Show top item and preserve it
'
```

```
      Console.WriteLine("Top item: " & .Peek())
    End With

  End Sub

  Sub ShowQueue(ByVal Header As String, ByVal Q As IEnumerable)

    Dim E As IEnumerator
    E = Q.GetEnumerator
    Console.WriteLine(ControlChars.NewLine & Header)
    While E.MoveNext()
      Console.WriteLine(E.Current)
    End While

  End Sub

End Module
```

Note that the Peek() method plays the same role as in the Stack class – it returns the top element without removing it.

The System.Collections.Specialized namespace contains specialized and strongly typed collections. Among them is the HybridDictionary class, used to create hybrid dictionaries, the ListDictionary class, which implements a single-linked list, the NameValueCollection class, which is a sorted collection of associated string keys and string values, the StringCollection class, which implements a collection of strings, the StringDictionary class, a hash table with the key strongly typed to be a string rather than an object, and the StringEnumerator class, which supports iteration over a StringCollection.

```
Original Queue
Item0
Item1
Item2

Modified Queue
Item1
Item2

Modified Queue
Item1
Item2
Item3
Top item: Item1
```

FIGURE 3.18   Using the Queue class

3.10 Strings

The System.String class contains methods to manipulate strings. Using methods of this class, we can determine a string's length, search for substrings, change the case of a string, compare two strings, split strings, and perform other string-related operations. Once created, an instance of a String class cannot be changed – all methods that modify a string return a new instance that contains the modification. The StringBuilder class in the System.Text namespace should be used to create strings, the content of which can be modified. In Microsoft .NET, strings are zero-based, that is, the first character in a string has the index zero.

The String class implements IComparable, ICloneable, IConvertible, and IEnumerable interfaces.

The String class contains two properties – the Chars(Integer) property, which returns the character at a specified position, and the Length property, which returns the number of characters in the string.

The following example shows how to use these properties to print the contents of the string, one character per line.

```
'----------------------------------------
' .NET String Demo
'----------------------------------------
Imports System
Imports System.String

Module Module1

 Sub Main()

  Dim Str As String
  Dim I As Integer

   Str = "Microsoft .NET"

  While I <= Str.Length - 1
   Console.WriteLine(Str.Chars(I))
    I += 1
  End While
 End Sub

End Module
```

The IndexOf(Char) method is used to find the first instance of a substring within a string. It returns the starting position of the substring if it is found or –1 if the substring is not found. The overloaded versions of the IndexOf method allow us to use a parameter of type Char, String or an array of type Char. Here is an example of this functionality:

```
'----------------------------------------
' .NET Strings Demo
'----------------------------------------
Imports System
Imports System.String


Module Module1


  Sub Main()
   Dim Str As String
   Dim Ch As Char
   Dim Chars As Char() = {".", "N", "E", "T"}
   Str = "Microsoft .NET"
   Ch = "."
   Console.WriteLine(Str.IndexOf(".NET"))      'returns 10
   Console.WriteLine(Str.IndexOf(Ch))          'returns 10
   Console.WriteLine(Str.IndexOf(Chars))       'returns 10
   End Sub


End Module
```

The IndexOf() method has two optional parameters that allow us to limit the search by specifying the starting and ending positions within the string to search.

The LastIndexOf() method also performs the substring searching, but it searches the last instance of a substring.

To change the case of a string into all uppercase or all lowercase, we use the ToUpper() and ToLower() methods respectively.

To compare two strings we use one of the overloaded versions of the Compare method. It returns 0 if the strings are equal, a negative number if the first string is less than the second, or a positive number if the first string is greater than the second. By default, the comparison is case-sensitive. To ignore the case, we can set an optional third parameter of the Compare method to True.

For example, the following two comparisons return different results:

```
Str = "Microsoft .NET"
Console.WriteLine(Str.Compare(Str.ToUpper, Str.ToLower))          ' 1
Console.WriteLine(Str.Compare(Str.ToUpper, Str.ToLower, True))      ' 0
```

To convert a string into an array of substrings, we use the Split(*ParamArray Char()*) method. This method expects a separator character of type Char that it will use to split the strings. The following example illustrates the use of the Split method:

```
'-------------------------------------
' .NET Strings Demo
'-------------------------------------
Imports System
Imports System.String

Module Module1

  Sub Main()
    Dim Str As String
    Dim Words() As String
    Dim I As Integer
    Str = "Microsoft .NET Platform"
    Words = Str.Split(" ")
    For I = 0 To Words.GetUpperBound(0)
      Console.WriteLine(I & " : " & Words(I))
    Next
  End Sub

End Module
```

The Join(String, String()) method does the opposite job. It is used to concatenate elements of a String array into a string.

Let's briefly look at some other methods available in the String class.

● **StartsWith(*String*) and EndsWith(*String*) methods** Can be used to find if
the start or end of this string matches the specified string. For example, the following code:

```
Str = "** Microsoft .NET Platform **"
Console.WriteLine(Str.StartsWith("**") & " " & Str.EndsWith("**"))
```

returns true because there is matching at both ends of the string.

● **Replace(Char, Char) or Replace(String, String) method** Use this method
to replace all occurrences of a specified character with another character. This
returns a resulting String. To replace each format specification in a string with
the textual equivalent, we use one of the overloaded Format method. For example,
the following code:

```
Str = "Microsoft .NET Platform"
Console.WriteLine(Str.Replace(" ", "_"))
```

returns "Microsoft_.NET_Platform".

The following example shows how to use the Format method:

```
Str = "Amount to pay: {0:C}"
Console.WriteLine(Str.Format(Str, 12.34))
```

The result of this code will be "Amount to pay: $12.34".

- **Concat method** To concatenate one or more strings use one of the overloaded versions of this method. For example, the following code concatenates "Microsoft", ".NET", and "Platform" strings into one:

```
Dim Str1, Str2, Str3 As String
 Str1 = "Microsoft "
 Str2 = ".NET "
 Str3 = "Platform"
 Console.WriteLine(Str1.Concat(Str1, Str2, Str3))
```

- **PadLeft(*Integer*, *Char*) and PadRight(*Integer*, *Char*) methods** Used to right- or left-align the characters in a string by padding on the left or on the right with spaces or other specified characters. For example, the following code:

```
Str = "Microsoft .NET Platform"
Console.WriteLine(Str.PadLeft(Str.Length + 5, "*"))
```

returns "*****Microsoft .NET Platform".

The following code, though:

```
Str = "Microsoft .NET Platform"
Console.WriteLine(Str.PadRight(Str.Length + 5, "*"))
```

returns "Microsoft .NET Platform*****".

- **TrimStart(*Char*()) and TrimEnd(*Char*()) methods** These do the opposite job – they remove all occurrences of a set of specified characters from the beginning or from the end of the string.

- **Remove(*Integer*, *Integer*) method** Removes a specified number of characters from the string, beginning at a specified position. For example, the following code converts the original string into "Microsoft Platform":

```
Str = "Microsoft .NET Platform"
Console.WriteLine(Str.Remove(Str.IndexOf(".NET"), ".NET".Length + 1))
```

- **Insert(Integer, String) method** Inserts a string at a specified index position. For example, the following code adds the string "Platform" at the end of the original string:

```
Str = "Microsoft .NET"
Console.WriteLine(Str.Insert(Str.Length, " Platform"))
```

- **Substring(Integer, Integer)** Use this **method** to get a substring from a string. For example, the following code returns ".NET":

```
Str = "Microsoft .NET Platform"
Console.WriteLine(Str.Substring(Str.IndexOf(".NET"), ".NET".Length))
```

Note that in the example above we have used the Length property of the String class with a string literal. This is another way to use the String class without creating instances of it.

3.11 System.Text namespace

The System.Text namespace contains classes representing various character encoding and conversions, as well as providing helper classes for manipulating and formatting String objects.

The StringBuilder class can be used in conjunction with the String class to manipulate a string. This class is useful in situations when we need to modify a contents of a String – insert, replace, or remove characters – without creating a new string.

To perform the desired operations we use the Insert, Replace, and Remove methods of the StringBuilder class. Access to the character in the String is provided by the Chars property, which allows us to manipulate strings on a per character basis.

The System.Text namespace also contains several decoders – classes that represent and support character encoding and conversions, including ASCII (ASCIIEncoding class), UTF-7 (UTF7Encoding class), UTF-8 (UTF8Encoding class), Uncode (UnicodeEncoding class), and Windows code pages.

- The ASCIIEncoding class encodes Unicode characters (U+0000 to U+007F) as single 7-bit ASCII characters.

- The UnicodeEncoding class encodes each Unicode character as two consecutive bytes.

- The UTF7Encoding class encodes Unicode characters using UCS transformation format, 7-bit form. All unicode characters are supported.

- The UTF8Encoding class encodes Unicode characters using UCS transformation format, 8-bit form. All unicode characters are supported.

All of these classes are derived from the Encoding class (see Figure 3.19), which provides some basic functionality.

- The GetDecoder() and GetEncoder() methods return Decoder and Encoder objects for this Encoding object. The Decoder object is used to decode a sequence of bytes into characters, and the Encoder object performs the reverse operation – it encodes a sequence of characters into bytes.

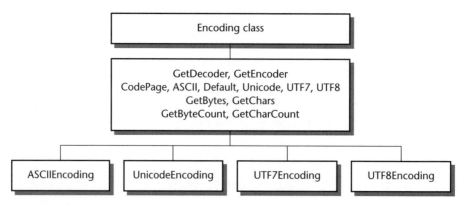

FIGURE 3.19   The `Encoding` class and derived classes

- The `CodePage` property of the `Integer` type contains the code page for the partic-
  ular encoding.
- The `ASCII` property of the `Encoding` type returns the encoding for the 7-bit ASCII
  character set.
- The `Default` property of the `Encoding` type returns the encoding for the current
  ANSI code page.
- The `Unicode` property of the `Encoding` type returns the encoding for the Unicode
  format in the little-endian byte order (which specifies that the least significant byte
  is stored in the lowest-memory address).
- The `UTF7` property of the `Encoding` type returns the encoding for the
  UTF7 format.
- The `UTF8` property of the `Encoding` type returns the encoding for the
  UTF8 format.
- The `GetByteCount(Char())` and `GetCharCount(Byte())` methods are used to
  compute the size of the result of a particular conversion.

We have spent a good deal of time discussing arrays, collections, and strings. The rest
of this chapter will be dedicated to formatting.

3.12 Formatting

As we already know from our discussion of the `Object` class, every class in the .NET
Framework class library has the `ToString()` method. Implementations of this
method vary from class to class, but for the value types, especially for the primitive
ones, we can use this method to output their values. In the following sections we will
see how to use various formatting specifiers to format the values as currency, decimal,
exponential, hexadecimal, and so on.

Default formatting

By default, when we use the `Console.WriteLine()`, or any other method that implicitly converts the value to a `String`, it is the `ToString()` method that performs the action. For example, the following code:

```
'----------------------------------------
' .NET Formatting Demo
'----------------------------------------
Imports System

Module Module1

  Sub Main()

    Dim Amount As Decimal = 123.45
    Console.WriteLine(Amount)

  End Sub

End Module
```

will produce what we expect: `123.45`. This is fine for output, but to display the value of the `Amount` as a currency or in any other format, we need some more sophisticated tools. That's where the formatting strings can be very handy. Let's look at what is available to us.

Currency formatting

To format the value as a currency, we use the `C` (or `c`) format specifier, as shown in the following example:

```
'----------------------------------------
' .NET Formatting Demo
'----------------------------------------
Imports System

Module Module1

  Sub Main()

    Dim Amount As Decimal = 123.45
    Dim Saldo  As Decimal = 94.20

    Console.WriteLine("Amount: {0:C}, Saldo: {1:C}", Amount, Saldo)
  End Sub

End Module
```

This will produce Amount: €123.45, Saldo: €94.20. If we now change the country information:

```
'----------------------------------------
' .NET Formatting Demo
'----------------------------------------


Imports System.Globalization
Imports System.Threading

Module Formatting

    Sub Main()
        Dim Cult As CultureInfo
        Dim Cults() As String = {"FR-FR", "EN-GB", "FR-CH"}
        Dim I As Integer

        Dim Amount As Decimal = 123.45
        Dim Saldo As Decimal = 94.2

        For I = 0 To Cults.GetUpperBound(0)

         Cult = New CultureInfo(Cults(I))
         Thread.CurrentThread.CurrentCulture = Cult
         Console.WriteLine("Amount: {0:C}, Saldo: {1:C}", _
          Amount, Saldo)
         Cult = Nothing

        Next

    End Sub

End Module
```

we will get the output that shows a country-specific currency symbol – the euro for France, pounds for the United Kingdom, and Swiss Francs for Switzerland (see Figure 3.20).

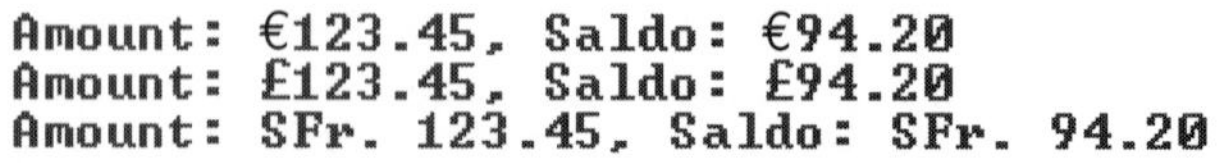

```
Amount: €123.45, Saldo: €94.20
Amount: £123.45, Saldo: £94.20
Amount: SFr. 123.45, Saldo: SFr. 94.20
```

FIGURE 3.20   The countries' currency symbols have appeared

Decimal format

The decimal format (D or d format specifier) is used to format integer values. Using the precision specifier, we can also specify the minimum number of decimal digits to display. For example, the following code:

```
'---------------------------------------
' .NET Formatting Demo
'---------------------------------------
Imports System

Module Module1

  Sub Main()
    Dim Formats() As String = {"D", "D4", "D6"}
    Dim I As Integer

    Dim Value As Integer = 123

      For I = 0 To Formats.GetUpperBound(0)
        Console.WriteLine("Value:  {0:" & Formats(I) & "}", Value)
      Next

  End Sub

  End Module
```

will produce the output shown in Figure 3.21.

```
Value:   123
Value:   0123
Value:   000123
```

FIGURE 3.21   Using the decimal format, the number of digits can be specified

Exponential format

We use this format (also called engineering format, E or e format specifier) to convert the values into the exponential representation. Using the precision specifier, we can also specify the number of digits after the decimal point. For example, the following code:

```
'---------------------------------------
' .NET Formatting Demo
'---------------------------------------
Imports System
```

```
Module Module1

  Sub Main()
    Dim Formats() As String = {"E", "E2", "E3"}
    Dim I As Integer

    Dim Value As Integer = 123456

    For I = 0 To Formats.GetUpperBound(0)
      Console.WriteLine("Value: {0:" & Formats(I) & "}", Value)
    Next

  End Sub

End Module
```

will produce the output shown in Figure 3.22.

```
Value:    1.234560E+005
Value:    1.23E+005
Value:    1.235E+005
```

FIGURE 3.22   Using the exponential format, we can specify how many decimal places will be displayed

Note that if we use the lowercase format specifier, such as e:

```
Dim Formats() As String = {"e", "e2", "e3"}
```

we will receive the result shown in Figure 3.23:

```
Value:    1.234560e+005
Value:    1.23e+005
Value:    1.235e+005
```

FIGURE 3.23   The exponential 'E' is now lowercase

Fixed point format

The fixed point format (F or f format specifier) is used to represent a decimal number as a non-decimal by inserting the specified number of zeros (the default is two) after the decimal point. For example, the following code:

```
'----------------------------------------
' .NET Formatting Demo
'----------------------------------------
Imports System
```

```
Module Module1

  Sub Main()
    Dim Formats() As String = {"F", "F3", "F5"}
    Dim I As Integer

    Dim Value As Integer = 123

    For I = 0 To Formats.GetUpperBound(0)
      Console.WriteLine("Value:  {0:" & Formats(I) & "}", Value)
    Next

  End Sub

End Module
```

will produce the output shown in Figure 3.24.

```
Value:   123.00
Value:   123.000
Value:   123.00000
```

FIGURE 3.24   The fixed point format inserts a specified number of zeros for integers

General format

This format (G or g format specifier) can be used to convert a value to either the fixed point or scientific format. The maximum precision value for the Double type is 17, while the default precision is 15. To specify a precision, we use the precision specifier. For example, the following code:

```
'---------------------------------------
' .NET Formatting Demo
'---------------------------------------
Imports System

Module Module1

  Sub Main()
    Dim Formats() As String = {"G", "G3", "G17"}
    Dim I As Integer

    Dim Value As Double = 123456789123456789
```

```
For I = 0 To Formats.GetUpperBound(0)
  Console.WriteLine("Value:  {0:" & Formats(I) & "}", Value)
Next

End Sub


End Module
```

will produce the output shown in Figure 3.25:

```
Value:   1.23456789123457E+17
Value:   1.23E+17
Value:   1.2345678912345678E+17
```

FIGURE 3.25   Using the general format, the precision specifier here has been set to maximum (17)

Number format

This format (N or n format specifier) is used to convert a value to the form [-]d,ddd,ddd.dd. The following example shows how the formatting is performed (see also Figure 3.26):

```
'---------------------------------------
' .NET Formatting Demo
'---------------------------------------
Imports System

Module Module1

  Sub Main()
   Dim Formats() As String = {"N", "N3", "N5"}
   Dim I As Integer

   Dim Value As Integer = 123456

   For I = 0 To Formats.GetUpperBound(0)
    Console.WriteLine("Value:  {0:" & Formats(I) & "}", Value)
   Next

  End Sub


End Module
```

```
Value:  123,456.00
Value:  123,456.000
Value:  123,456.00000
```

FIGURE 3.26   The number format sets numbers out in hundreds and with a decimal point

Percent format

We use this format (P or p format specifier) to convert a numeric value to the percent format. The following example shows how the formatting is performed (see also Figure 3.27):

```
'---------------------------------------
' .NET Formatting Demo
'---------------------------------------
Imports System

Module Module1

  Sub Main()
    Dim Formats() As String = {"P", "P3", "P5"}
    Dim I As Integer

    Dim Value As Decimal = 0.12345

    For I = 0 To Formats.GetUpperBound(0)
      Console.WriteLine("Value:  {0:" & Formats(I) & "}", Value)
    Next

  End Sub

End Module
```

```
Value:  12.35 %
Value:  12.345 %
Value:  12.34500 %
```

FIGURE 3.27   The percent format converts values into this format

Round-trip format

This format (R or r format specifier) is used when we need to ensure that the string representation of an integer value can be parsed back to the same value.

Hexadecimal format

This format (X or x) is useful when we need to set out hexadecimal representations of values. The following example shows how the formatting is performed (see also Figure 3.28):

```
'----------------------------------------
' .NET Formatting Demo
'----------------------------------------
Imports System

Module Module1

  Sub Main()
    Dim Formats() As String = {"X", "X3", "X5"}
    Dim I As Integer

    Dim Value As Byte = 128

    For I = 0 To Formats.GetUpperBound(0)
      Console.WriteLine("Value:  0x{0:" & Formats(I) & "}", Value)
    Next

    Console.WriteLine()

  End Sub

End Module
```

```
Value:   0x80
Value:   0x080
Value:   0x00080
```

FIGURE 3.28   Values converted to hexadecimal format

Picture numeric format

We have already used picture formats to display the values when we have discussed various format specifiers. They are in a form of {0:xy}, where x is one of the available formats and y the precision specifier. Besides this simple picture format, we can use other formatting symbols. This is shown in the following example (see also Figure 3.29).

```
'-------------------------------------
' .NET Formatting Demo
'-------------------------------------
Imports System

Module Module1

 Sub Main()
   Dim Formats() As String = {" {0:0.##}", " {0:##.###}", _
    "{0:%#.##}", "{0:##.##E+0}", "{0:{{##.##}}}", _
    "{0:\###.##\#}"}

   Dim I As Integer
   Dim Value As Double = 1.23456

   For I = 0 To Formats.GetUpperBound(0)
    Console.WriteLine("Value:   " & Formats(I), Value)
   Next

 End Sub

End Module
```

```
Value:   1.23
Value:   1.235
Value:   %123.46
Value:   12.35E-1
Value:   {1.23}
Value:   #1.23#
```

FIGURE 3.29   Various formatting symbols can be used and here are some picture numeric ones

We can use the G, F, D, and X format specifiers (or their lowercase equivalents) to convert the names of members of enumerations into their string equivalents. The following example shows how to do this (see also Figure 3.30):

```
'-------------------------------------
' .NET Formatting Demo
'-------------------------------------
Imports System

Module Module1

 Sub Main()
```

```
    Dim Formats() As String = {"{0:G}", "{0:F}", "{0:D}", "{0:X}"}

    Dim I As Integer
    Dim Value As FileAttributes = FileAttributes.Directory

    For I = 0 To Formats.GetUpperBound(0)
     Console.WriteLine("Value:  " & Formats(I), Value)
    Next

  End Sub

  End Module
```

```
Value:   Directory
Value:   Directory
Value:   16
Value:   00000010
```

FIGURE 3.30 Names of members of enumerations can be converted into their string equivalents

Note that the Microsoft .NET Framework class library also supports various formatting options for date and time values. This topic will be covered in Chapter 5.

3.13 Conclusion

In this chapter we discussed several basic classes included in the .NET Framework class library. We started with an overview of the namespaces and their purpose in the library. After this, we learned how to create console applications that serve as a base type of the applications we use in several chapters to provide examples. Then, we learned about the System namespace and the Object class. After this we briefly discussed the Type class and the Reflection namespace. Then we started to discuss the types in the .NET Framework class library and looked at an overview of value and reference types. The next topic we discussed in this chapter was arrays. Then we moved on to an overview of collections, interfaces that they are based on, and various types of collections available in the library. Having discussed these, we moved our attention to strings and discussed this type, as well as the System.Text namespace and formatting options available for developers.

In the next chapter we will continue our study of the .NET Framework class library. We will learn about streams, file system support, networking, and several other related namespaces and classes.

chapter 4

More on the .NET Framework class library – streams, the file system, and networking

- The System.IO namespace – streams and file system access

- Working with the file system

- Environment.SpecialFolder enumeration

- The System.Net namespace – internet programming under .NET

- Helper classes

In this chapter, we will discuss classes that are implemented in two namespaces – System.IO and System.Net. We will start with the System.IO namespace, and discuss such things as streams, stream readers and writers, as well as classes that provide functions to work with the file system and files. After this, we will move on to the System.Net namespace and learn about networking features implemented by the classes available in this namespace.

4.1 System.IO namespace – streams and file system access

This namespace contains classes and other types used to work (synchronous and asynchronous reading and writing) with data streams and files. The System.IO namespace consists of classes that implement streams, streams readers, and writers, as well as classes used to work with the file system. Figure 4.1 shows most of the classes in the System.IO namespace.

Streams

The Stream class is an abstract view of a sequence of bytes. Derived classes provide more specific functionality – working with files (FileStream class), memory (MemoryStream class), and the network (NetworkStream class). In general, streams support reading, writing, and seeking operations. Note that the seeking operation requires definition of the current position, which may be not available for the particular type of stream – for example, a network stream. To check the capabilities of the particular type of stream, we use the CanRead, CanWrite, and CanSeek Boolean properties.

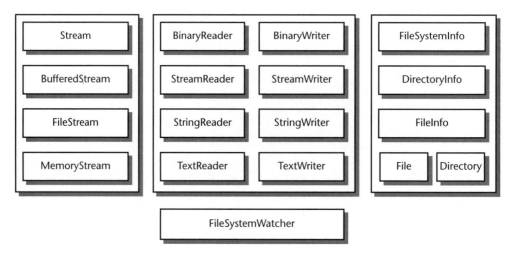

FIGURE 4.1   The main classes in the System.IO namespace

The `Length` property is used to find the length of the stream, which is the number of bytes the stream contains as a `Long` value. To find the current position within the stream or to change it, we use the `Position` property, which returns a `Long` value.

The `Stream` class contains several methods that define the basic functionality of all streams.

- `BeginRead(Byte(), Integer, Integer, AsyncCallback, Object)`,`ReadByte()`, `Read(Byte(), Integer, Integer)` and `EndRead(IAsyncResult)` methods Used to begin and end asynchronous reading operations and read a byte or a sequence of bytes from the current position in the stream.
- `BeginWrite(Byte(), Integer, Integer, AsyncCallback, Object)`, `WriteByte(Byte)`, `Write(Byte(), Integer, Integer)` and `EndWrite (IAsyncResult)` methods Used to begin and end asynchronous writing operations and write a byte or a sequence of bytes to the current position in the stream.
- `Seek(Long, SeekOrigin)` method Used to change the current position in the stream.
- `SetLength` method Changes the length of the current stream.
- `Flush()` method Causes all buffered data to be written to the underlying device.
- `Close()` method Closes the current stream.

Table 4.1 shows when you cannot use some of the properties and methods of the classes derived from the `Stream` class.

TABLE 4.1 When you cannot use the properties and methods of the `Stream` class

If this property is false	We cannot use these properties and methods
`CanRead = False`	`Read, ReadByte, BeginRead, EndRead, Peek`
`CanSeek = False`	`Length, SetLength, Position, Seek`
`CanWrite = False`	`SetLength, Write, BeginWrite, EndWrite, WriteByte`

The `Stream` class serves as a base class for several types of streams. Figure 4.2 shows the classes derived from the abstract `Stream` class.

Note that the `NetworkStream` and `CryptoStream` classes are implemented in seperate namespaces – in `System.Net.Sockets` and `System.Security.Cryptography` namespaces respectively.

BufferedStream Class

The `BufferedStream` class is used to buffer read or write operations – but not both simultaneously – to another stream. This class creates a memory buffer (a default buffer size is 4 Kbytes, but this value can be changed by using the overloaded con-

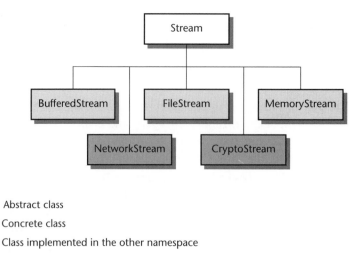

FIGURE 4.2   Classes derived from the `Stream` class

structor) which is used to cache data, thus improving the performance of read and write operations by reducing the number of calls to the operating system.

To create a buffer for an existing stream, we use the `BufferedStream` class's constructor and specify the existing stream as an input parameter. Further operations are performed via the methods of the `BufferedStream` class, and we can save all changes in the buffer to the stream by calling its `Flush` method.

FileStream Class

The `FileStream` class is used to read from and write to files. We can use this class to read and write bytes, characters, strings, and other types from and to a file. The `FileStream` class supports both synchronous and asynchronous file opening, synchronous reading and writing (`Read` and `Write` methods), as well as asynchronous reading and writing (`BeginRead` and `BeginWrite` methods).

Asynchronous operations are ended by a call to `EndRead` and `EndWrite` methods respectively. The default mode is synchronous – to check the mode we use the `IsAsync` property. Asynchronous operations use the `WaitHandle` object. The `Seek` method is used for random access to files.

The `Position` property allows us to get or set the current position in the stream. The `Lock` and `Unlock` methods are used to prevent access to all or part of a file and to allow access to a file that was previously locked. The `Length` property returns the length of the stream in bytes, while `SetLength` is used to specify the length of the stream. The `ReadByte` and `WriteByte` methods are used to read and write a single byte. For other primitive data types we should use the `BinaryReader` and `BinaryWriter` classes.

Derived from the `FileStream` class, the `IsolatedStorageFileSystem` class is used to read, write, and create files in isolated storage. Such storage exposes a virtual file system that allows us to read and write data that is not accessible to less trusted code. Isolated storage provides data isolation by current user, by assembly or application domain (a unit of processing that the common language runtime uses to provide isolation between applications).

MemoryStream class

The MemoryStream class can be used to create a stream that stores its contents in memory instead of on a disk or network. This class uses an unsigned byte array that can be of a resizable or fixed size. In the first case, we can change the size of the byte array, read from and write into it. Non-resizable streams can only be written to.

To find the number of bytes allocated for the memory stream, we use the Capacity property, which returns an Integer value. The Length property returns the actual number of bytes in the stream as a Long value. The GetBuffer() method returns the array of unsigned bytes where the stream data resides. To save the entire stream contents to a byte array, we use the ToArray() method. The WriteTo(Stream) method is used to copy the entire contents of the memory stream into another stream.

The following example shows how to use the MemoryStream class to create a new memory stream, set its contents, then save it in a file.

```
'----------------------------------------
' .NET MemoryStream Class usage example
'----------------------------------------

Imports System
Imports System.IO

Module Module1

 Sub Main()

  Dim Bytes() As Byte = New Byte(10) {}
  Dim I As Integer
  Dim MemStr As New MemoryStream()
  Dim FileStr As New FileStream("c:\temp\bytes.bin", _
   FileMode.CreateNew)

  Dim Rand As System.Random = New System.Random()

  For I = 0 To 9
   Bytes(I) = Rand.Next(0, 100)
  Next
```

```
MemStr.Write(Bytes, 0, I)
MemStr.WriteTo(FileStr)

MemStr.Close()
FileStr.Close()

End Sub

End Module
```

The last two streams we will briefly cover in this section are not implemented in the System.IO namespace, but are based on the generic Stream class.

NetworkStream class

This class implements a stream that is used to send data across the network. The NetworkStream class provides a stream that does not support seeking – we cannot use the Position property and the Seek method with this type of stream.

We will discuss networking under Microsoft .NET in greater detail later in this chapter.

CryptoStream class

This class implements a stream that links data streams to cryptographic transformations. The CryptoStream class is implemented in the System.Security.Cryptography namespace.

To encrypt and decrypt streams, we should select encryption and decryption providers. Currently we can choose between symmetrical algorithms such as the Data Encryption Standard (DES), RC2, Triple Data Encryption Standard (TripleDES) and Rijndael/AES, and asymmetrical algorithms (also known as public key algorithms) such as RSA, DSA, and hash algorithms (MD5, SHA1, SHA256, SHA384, SHA512). The System.Security.Cryptography.X509 namespace also contains minimal support for public certificates.

Classes that implement support of the W3C standard for digitally signing XML are located in the System.Security.Cryptography.XML namespace. Most of the algorithms in the System.Security.Cryptography namespace are implemented as managed wrappers on top of Microsoft CryptoAPI implementations. Some of the crypto algorithms – SHA256, SHA384, SHA512, and Rijndael/AES – are not currently available in CryptoAPI.

Next, we use the appropriate provider – DESCryptoServiceProvider, RC2CryptoServiceProvider, TripleDESCryptoServiceProvider and so on – with the specified key and initialization vector to encrypt or decrypt a specified stream.

The last step is to save encrypted or decrypted streams to the file. The following example shows how to encrypt an array of bytes, save it to a file, then decrypt it using the DES algorithm. In this example, we use the default constructor that populates the algorithm parameters with strong defaults (see also Figure 4.3):

```vb
'----------------------------------------
' .NET CryptoStream Class usage example
'----------------------------------------

Imports System
Imports System.IO
Imports System.Security.Cryptography

Module Module1

 Sub Main()

  Dim Bytes() As Byte = {65, 66, 67, 68, 69, 70, 71, 72, 73, 74}
  Dim EncBytes() As Byte = New Byte(15) {}
  Dim DecBytes() As Byte = New Byte(10) {}

  Dim FileName As String = "c:\temp\text.enc"
  Dim EncFile As New FileStream(FileName, FileMode.Create, _
   FileAccess.Write)
  Dim DES As New DESCryptoServiceProvider()
  Dim DESEncrypt As ICryptoTransform = DES.CreateEncryptor()
  Dim CryptoStreamEnc As New CryptoStream(EncFile, DESEncrypt, _
   CryptoStreamMode.Write)

  Console.WriteLine("Original Data")
  ToHexArray(Bytes)

  CryptoStreamEnc.Write(Bytes, 0, Bytes.Length)
  CryptoStreamEnc.Close()
  EncFile.Close()

  EncFile = New FileStream(FileName, FileMode.Open, FileAccess.Read)
  EncFile.Read(EncBytes, 0, EncFile.Length)
  EncFile.Close()

  Console.WriteLine("Encrypted Data")
  ToHexArray(EncBytes)
  Console.WriteLine()

  Dim DecFile As New FileStream(FileName, FileMode.Open, _
   FileAccess.Read)
  Dim DESDecrypt As ICryptoTransform = DES.CreateDecryptor()
```

```
Dim CryptoStreamDec As New CryptoStream(DecFile, DESDecrypt, _
 CryptoStreamMode.Read)
Dim Reader As New BinaryReader(CryptoStreamDec)

Console.WriteLine("Decrypted Data")
DecBytes = Reader.ReadBytes(10)
ToHexArray(DecBytes)

End Sub


Sub ToHexArray(ByVal A As Byte())

 Dim I As Integer

 For I = 0 To A.GetUpperBound(0)
  Console.Write("0x{0:x2} ", A(I))
  If I = 7 Then
   Console.WriteLine()
  End If
 Next

 End Sub


 End Module


Original Data
0x41 0x42 0x43 0x44 0x45 0x46 0x47 0x48
0x49 0x4a

Encrypted Data
0xae 0x30 0xc0 0xe4 0x24 0x58 0x57 0x30
0xaf 0x7c 0x6a 0x2d 0xa3 0xaa 0xcb 0x92

Decrypted Data
0x41 0x42 0x43 0x44 0x45 0x46 0x47 0x48
0x49 0x4a
```

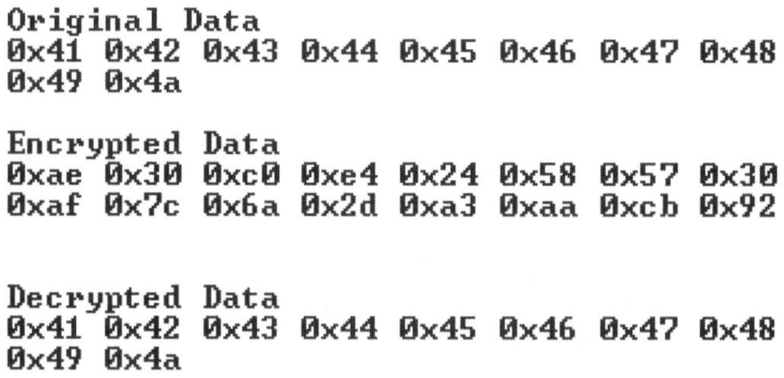

FIGURE 4.3 An array of bytes has been encrypted, saved to a file, then decrypted with a DES algorithm

The use of "strong" key length is supported in all encryption algorithms, but for algorithms that are implemented on top of CryptoAPI, we need to install a High Encryption Pack, which is part of the Windows 2000 Service Pack, Windows NT 4.0 Service Pack 6a or Internet Explorer 5.5 for Windows Me, Windows 98 and Windows 95 users.

Stream readers and writers

The System.IO namespace contains four pairs of readers and writers – classes that are used to read or write a sequential series of bytes or characters. There are BinaryReader and BinaryWriter classes that deal with all primitive data types defined in the common type system as well as classes to read and write sequences of characters – TextReader and TextWriter; strings – StringReader and StringWriter; and streams – StreamReader and StreamWriter.

BinaryReader

The BinaryReader class provides mechanisms for reading primitive data types as binary values. It contains methods to read each type defined in the common type system – ReadBoolean, ReadByte (ReadBytes), ReadChar (ReadChars), ReadDecimal, ReadDouble, and so on.

To get the stream associated with the BinaryReader, which is always done in the constructor, we can use the BaseStream property of the Stream type. The PeekChar() method returns the next character from the stream, but does not advance the position. This means that we can use this method to check if there are more characters to read before actually reading them. The Read(*Byte*(), *Integer*, *Integer*) or Read(*Char*(), *Integer*, *Integer*) methods are used to read specified numbers of characters or bytes from the stream. These are generic methods that can be used instead of specific methods that read other primitive types.

The following example shows how to use the BinaryReader class to implement a simple hex dump utility (see also Figure 4.4):

```
'----------------------------------------
' .NET BinaryReader Class usage example
'----------------------------------------

Imports System
Imports System.IO

Module Module1

 Sub Main()

  Dim Bytes As Byte()
  Dim I As Integer
  Dim Reader As BinaryReader
  Reader = New BinaryReader(File.OpenRead("c:\demo.exe"))

  While Reader.PeekChar() > -1
   Bytes = Reader.ReadBytes(16)
```

```
    For I = 0 To Bytes.GetUpperBound(0)
     Console.Write("0x{0:X2}|", Bytes(I))
    Next
    Console.WriteLine()
   End While

  End Sub

 End Module
```

```
0x6C|0x00|0x4E|0x00|0x61|0x00|0x6D|0x00|0x65|0x00|0x00|0x00|0x43|0x00|0x6F|0x00|
0x6E|0x00|0x73|0x00|0x6F|0x00|0x6C|0x00|0x65|0x00|0x41|0x00|0x70|0x00|0x70|0x00|
0x6C|0x00|0x69|0x00|0x63|0x00|0x61|0x00|0x74|0x00|0x69|0x00|0x6F|0x00|0x6E|0x00|
0x31|0x00|0x33|0x00|0x2E|0x00|0x65|0x00|0x78|0x00|0x65|0x00|0x00|0x00|0x00|0x00|
0x28|0x00|0x02|0x00|0x01|0x00|0x4C|0x00|0x65|0x00|0x67|0x00|0x61|0x00|0x6C|0x00|
0x43|0x00|0x6F|0x00|0x70|0x00|0x79|0x00|0x72|0x00|0x69|0x00|0x67|0x00|0x68|0x00|
0x74|0x00|0x00|0x00|0x20|0x00|0x00|0x00|0x2C|0x00|0x02|0x00|0x01|0x00|0x4C|0x00|
0x65|0x00|0x67|0x00|0x61|0x00|0x6C|0x00|0x54|0x00|0x72|0x00|0x61|0x00|0x64|0x00|
0x65|0x00|0x6D|0x00|0x61|0x00|0x72|0x00|0x6B|0x00|0x73|0x00|0x00|0x00|0x00|0x00|
0x20|0x00|0x00|0x00|0x5C|0x00|0x19|0x00|0x01|0x00|0x4F|0x00|0x72|0x00|0x69|0x00|
0x67|0x00|0x69|0x00|0x6E|0x00|0x61|0x00|0x6C|0x00|0x46|0x00|0x69|0x00|0x6C|0x00|
0x65|0x00|0x6E|0x00|0x61|0x00|0x6D|0x00|0x65|0x00|0x00|0x00|0x43|0x00|0x6F|0x00|
0x6E|0x00|0x73|0x00|0x6F|0x00|0x6C|0x00|0x65|0x00|0x41|0x00|0x70|0x00|0x70|0x00|
```

FIGURE 4.4 Using the `BinaryReader` class to implement a hex dump utility

BinaryWriter class

We use the `BinaryWriter` class to write primitive data types to an associated stream. This class contains the `Write()` method that is overloaded to handle writing values of different types to the current stream.

By combining methods from both `BinaryReader` and `BinaryWriter` classes, we can write code that performs copy operations, like the one shown in the example below:

```
'---------------------------------------
' .NET BinaryWriter Class usage example
'---------------------------------------


Imports System
Imports System.IO


Module Module1
```

```
Sub Main()

  Dim Bytes As Byte()

  Dim Reader As BinaryReader
  Dim Writer As BinaryWriter

  Reader = New BinaryReader(File.OpenRead("c:\demo.exe"))
  Writer = New BinaryWriter(File.Create("c:\demo_copy.exe"))

  While Reader.PeekChar() > -1
   Bytes = Reader.ReadBytes(1024)
   Writer.Write(Bytes)
  End While

  Reader.Close()
  Writer.Flush()
  Writer.Close()

 End Sub
End Module
```

TextReader class

The TextReader class is a reader that is used to read a sequence of characters from an associated stream. This class serves as a base type for two more readers – StreamReader and StringReader – that will be discussed later in this chapter (see Figure 4.5).

The TextReader class has the following methods that we can use in our code.

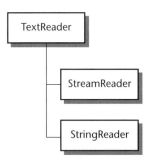

FIGURE 4.5   The TextReader class is the basis of two more readers

- **Peek() method** Returns the next character (as an Integer value) from the stream, but does not advance the position.

- **Read() or Read(*Char()*, *Integer*, *Integer*) methods** Read the specified numbers of characters (as Integer value(s)) from the stream.

- **ReadBlock(*Char()*, *Integer*, *Integer*) method** Reads the specified number of characters to the buffer.

- **ReadLine() method** Reads a line of characters (as a String value) from the stream.

- **ReadToEnd() method** Reads all characters from the current position to the end of the stream as one string.

As the TextReader class is an abstract class, it cannot be used directly – we should use either the StreamReader or StringReader classes.

StreamReader class

We use the StreamReader class to read a sequence of characters from the specified file or stream. The following example shows how to read from the text file line by line and as one string:

```
'----------------------------------------
' .NET StreamReader Class usage example
'----------------------------------------

Imports System
Imports System.IO

Module Module1

 Sub Main()

  Dim FileName As String = _
   "C:\Program Files\Microsoft.NET\FrameworkSDK\include\corsym.h"
  Dim Reader As TextReader
  Dim I As Int32

  Reader = New StreamReader(FileName)

  While Reader.Peek() > -1
   Console.WriteLine(Reader.ReadLine)
   I += 1
  End While
```

```
    Console.WriteLine("Read {0:G} lines", I)
    Reader.Close()


  End Sub


End Module
```

If we do not care about the number of lines we have read and we know the file isn't huge, we can use the ReadToEnd method, as shown in the example below:

```
'----------------------------------------
' .NET StreamReader Class usage example
'----------------------------------------


Imports System
Imports System.IO


Module Module1

  Sub Main()

   Dim FileName As String = _
     "C:\Program Files\Microsoft.NET\FrameworkSDK\include\corsym.h"
   Dim Reader As TextReader
   Dim I As Int32


   Reader = New StreamReader(FileName)


   Console.WriteLine(Reader.ReadToEnd)


   Reader.Close()


  End Sub


  Module1
```

StringReader class

The StringReader class is used to read characters from strings. The following example shows how to use the StreamReader and StringReader classes to read a string from a text file and then read characters from it, as this string is a stream:

```
'-----------------------------------------
' .NET StringReader Class usage example
'-----------------------------------------


Imports System
Imports System.IO

Module Module1

  Sub Main()

    Dim FileName As String = _
     "C:\Program Files\Microsoft.NET\FrameworkSDK\include\corsym.h"
    Dim Reader As TextReader
    Dim S As String

    Reader = New StreamReader(FileName)

    S = Reader.ReadLine

    Dim SReader As New StringReader(S)

     While SReader.Peek > -1
      Console.WriteLine(Chr(SReader.Read))
     End While

    Reader.Close()

  End Sub

End Module
```

TextWriter class

The TextWriter class is a writer that is used to write a sequence of characters. For byte output, we should use the Stream class; to write the primitive types in binary, we should use the BinaryWriter class.

The TextWriter class is an abstract class – it serves as a base for several text writer classes, such as StreamWriter and StringWriter, which are implemented in the System.IO namespace, IntendedTextWriter, implemented in the System.CodeDom. Complier namespace, and HTTPWriter and HTMLWriter, implemented in the System.Web and System.Web.UI namespaces respectively (see Figure 4.6).

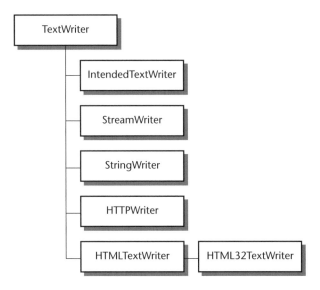

FIGURE 4.6   The TextWriter class provides the basis for several other text writer classes

StreamWriter class

The StreamWriter class is used to output a sequence of characters in a particular encoding. By default, it uses an instance of UTF8Encoding class to write Unicode UTF-8 characters. There are several overloaded constructors that allow us to specify the stream, default encoding, specific encoding, buffer size, and file operation (whether an existing file should be overwritten or appended to).

The AutoFlush Boolean property is used to specify whether or not the buffer will be flushed to the underlying stream after every call to Write or WriteLine methods.

StringWriter class

The StringWriter class writes to a string, which is stored in an underlying StringBuilder class, that is implemented in the System.Text namespace.

Other TextWriter-based classes

As mentioned above, in the .NET Framework class library there are several other writer classes that are based on the abstract TextWriter class.

- *IndentedTextWriter* (**System.CodeDom.Complier namespace**) This class is used as a text writer that can indent new lines by a tab string token.
- *HTTPWriter* (**System.Web namespace**) A writer that is accessed via the HTTPRequest object – its Write method makes calls to the HTTPWriter object.

- *HTMLTextWriter* (**System.Web.UI namespace**) This writer is used by ASP.NET server controls to render HTML content to clients.
- *HTML32TextWriter* (**System.Web.UI namespace**) This writer extends the HTMLTextWriter and provides support for rendering HTML 3.2.

This ends our discussion of streams, stream readers, and writers. The next topic in this chapter is the classes in the System.IO namespace that are used to work with files and directories. In the following section we will learn about the FileSystemInfo, FileInfo, DirectoryInfo, File, and Path classes.

4.2 Working with the file system

The System.IO namespace contains several classes used to work with the file system. The FileSystemInfo class serves as a base class for the FileInfo and DirectoryInfo classes. There is also a File class that allows us to work with files and a Directory class for directory manipulations. Figure 4.7 shows these classes.

Note the difference between the classes mentioned above. The FileInfo class provides instance methods for the creation, copying, deletion, moving, and opening of files – it aids in the creation of FileStream objects. The File class provides static methods – to use them we do not need to create an instance of the class. The same is true for the DirectoryInfo and Directory classes. The FileInfo and DirectoryInfo are sealed classes – we can create instances of these classes, but we cannot derive from them.

FileSystemInfo class

This class provides basic functionality for its derived classes – the FileInfo and DirectoryInfo classes. It contains properties and methods that are common to both

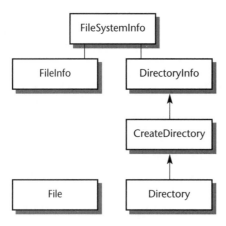

FIGURE 4.7 The File and Directory classes

files and directories. Following is a list of properties and methods of the `FileSystemInfo` class.

- **Attributes** Used to get or set the attributes of the file. This property is of the `FileAttributes` enumeration type, which supports a bitwise combination of its member values. The following list shows members of `FileAttributes` enumeration.

  - **Archive** If this attribute is set, a file is ready for backup or removal.
  - **Compressed** If this attribute is set, a file is compressed.
  - **Device** This attribute is reserved for the future versions of the operating system.
  - **Directory** This attribute indicates that a file is a directory.
  - **Encrypted** If this attribute is set, a file is encrypted.
  - **Hidden** If this attribute is set, a file is hidden and it is not visible in an ordinary directory listing.
  - **Normal** If this attribute is set, a file has no other attributes set.
  - **NotContentIndexed** If this attribute is set, a file is not indexed by Windows indexing system.
  - **Offline** If this attribute is set, a file's content is not accessible.
  - **ReadOnly** If this attribute is set, a file's content cannot be modified.
  - **ReparsePoint** If this attribute is set, a file contains a reparse point – a block of user-defined data associated with a file or a directory.
  - **SparsePoint** If this attribute is set, a file is a sparse file – typically a large file containing mostly zero data.
  - **System** If this attribute is set, a file is a system file – part of the operating system or used exclusively by the operating system.
  - **Temporary** If this attribute is set, a file is a temporary file, created either by the operating system or user application.

- **CreationTime** Used to get or set the creation time of the file. This property is of `DateTime` type.
- **Exists** We use this Boolean property to find whether or not the file or directory exists.
- **Extension** Returns the string containing the file name extension.
- **FullName** We use this property to find the full path of the directory or file.
- **LastAccessTime and LastWriteTime** These two properties of `DateTime` type are used to find when the file or directory was last accessed or written to respectively.
- **Name** We use this property to find the name of the file or the name of the last directory in the hierarchy.
- **Delete()** This method is used to delete a file or directory.

These properties and methods are available in the classes derived from the `FileSystemInfo` class – the `FileInfo` and `DirectoryInfo` classes.

FileInfo class

This class acts as a wrapper for a file path and extends the `FileSystemInfo` class by providing additional properties and methods used to manipulate files. The `FileInfo` class adds the following properties and methods.

- **Directory** This property returns the `DirectoryInfo` object that contains information about the parent directory.
- **DirectoryName** This property returns the file's full path.
- **Length** This property returns the size of the current file as a Long value.
- **AppendText()** This method creates a `StreamWriter` object that appends text to a file.
- **CopyTo(*String*) or CopyTo(*String,Boolean*)** Use this method to copy an existing file to a new file.
- **Create()** Use this method to create a file – this method returns a `FileStream` object.
- **CreateText()** This method creates a `StreamWriter` object that writes a new text file.
- **MoveTo(*String*)** Use this method to rename a file or to move a file to a new location.
- **Open(*FileMode*) or Open(*FileMode, FileAccess*)or Open(*FileMode, FileAccess, FileShare*)** These methods open a file, returning a `FileStream` object.

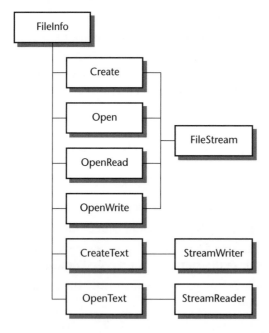

FIGURE 4.8 The relationship between the `FileInfo` class and other stream classes

- **OpenRead()** Use this method to create a read-only `FileStream` object.
- **OpenText()** This method creates a `StreamReader` object with UTF8 encoding that reads from an existing text file.
- **OpenWrite()** Use this method to create a read/write `FileStream` object.

Figure 4.8 shows how methods of the `FileInfo` class relate to other stream classes.

The following example shows how to use the `FileInfo` class to show file length and attributes for the files in the directory (see also Figure 4.9):

```
'----------------------------------------
' .NET FileInfo Class usage example
'----------------------------------------


Imports System
Imports System.IO


Module Module1


 Sub Main()


  Dim Path As String = GetPersonalFolder() & "\MyText"
  Dim DirInfo As New DirectoryInfo(Path)
  Dim Files As FileInfo() = DirInfo.GetFiles("*.TXT")
  Dim I As Integer
  Console.WriteLine(Path & ControlChars.CrLf)
  For I = Files.GetLowerBound(0) To Files.GetUpperBound(0)
   Console.Write((Files(I).Name.PadRight(15)) & _
    (Files(I).Length).ToString.PadRight(15))
   Console.Write(ControlChars.Tab)
   Console.WriteLine(ShowAttribs(Files(I)))
  Next


 End Sub


 Function GetPersonalFolder() As String


  Dim E As Environment
  Return E.GetFolderPath(Environment.SpecialFolder.Personal)


 End Function


 Function ShowAttribs(ByVal F As FileInfo) As String
```

```
Dim S As String
With F
  If .Attributes And FileAttributes.Archive Then
    S = "A"
  Else
    S = "-"
  End If
  If .Attributes And FileAttributes.Hidden Then
    S += "H"
  Else
    S += "-"
  End If
  If .Attributes And FileAttributes.Normal Then
    S += "N"
  Else
    S += "-"
  End If
  If .Attributes And FileAttributes.ReadOnly Then
    S += "R"
  Else
    S += "-"
  End If
End With
Return S

End Function


End Module
```

```
C:\Documents and Settings\Administrator\My Documents\MyText

MyText01.txt    0              A--R
MyText02.txt    0              A---
MyText03.txt    0              -H-R
MyText04.txt    0              A---
MyText05.txt    0              A---
```

FIGURE 4.9   The FileInfo class shows file length and attributes for files in the directory

Let's have another example. The following code uses the CreateText method to create a StreamWriter object that writes a new text file:

```
'----------------------------------------
' .NET FileInfo Class usage example
'----------------------------------------

Imports System
Imports System.IO

Module Module1

  Sub Main()
    Dim FileName As String = "c:\temp\mytext01.txt"
    Dim Writer As StreamWriter
    Dim MyFile As New FileInfo(FileName)

    Writer = MyFile.CreateText()

    Writer.WriteLine("Created by " & MyFile.GetType.ToString)
    Writer.WriteLine("Written by " & Writer.ToString)

    Writer.Close()

  End Sub

  End Module
```

This will produce the text file shown in Figure 4.10.

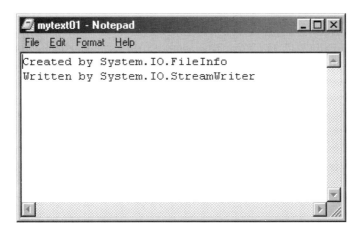

FIGURE 4.10   Using the CreateText method to write a new text file

For examples of how to use some other methods of the `FileInfo` class, see the section below headed `File` class.

DirectoryInfo class

This class allows us to create and move directories as well as enumerate their contents and subdirectories. The `DirectoryInfo` class has the following properties:

- **Parent** returns the parent directory of a subdirectory – this property is of the `DirectoryInfo` type;
- **Root** returns the root of the path as a `DirectoryInfo` type.

The following example shows how to use the **Parent** and **Root** properties to retrace a directory to the root directory (see also Figure 4.11):

```
'----------------------------------------
' .NET DirectoryInfo Class usage example
'----------------------------------------

Imports System
Imports System.IO

Module Module1

 Sub Main()

  Dim Path As String = GetPersonalFolder() & "\MyText"
  Dim DirInfo As New DirectoryInfo(Path)
  Dim Parent As String

  Console.WriteLine("Initial Directory : " & DirInfo.FullName)
  Parent = DirInfo.Parent.FullName
  While Parent <> DirInfo.Root.FullName
    Console.WriteLine("Parent Directory  : " & _
    DirInfo.Parent.FullName)
   Parent = DirInfo.Parent.FullName
   DirInfo = New DirectoryInfo(Parent)
  End While

 End Sub


 Function GetPersonalFolder() As String
```

```
        Dim E As Environment
        Return E.GetFolderPath(Environment.SpecialFolder.Personal)


    End Function


End Module
```

```
Initial Directory : C:\Documents and Settings\Administrator\My Documents\MyText
Parent Directory  : C:\Documents and Settings\Administrator\My Documents
Parent Directory  : C:\Documents and Settings\Administrator
Parent Directory  : C:\Documents and Settings
Parent Directory  : C:\
```

FIGURE 4.11   Retracing a directory to its root directory

The following list shows the methods available in the `DirectoryInfo` class.

- **Create() method** Used to create a directory.
- **CreateSubDirectory(*String*) method** Used to create a subdirectory. It returns the `DirectoryInfo` object for the newly created directory. The following example shows how to use the `Create` and `CreateSubDirectory` methods:

```
'---------------------------------------
' .NET DirectoryInfo Class usage example
'---------------------------------------


Imports System
Imports System.IO


Module Module1

  Sub Main()

    Dim Path As String = "c:\temp\demos"
    Dim DirInfo As New DirectoryInfo(Path)
    DirInfo.Create()
    DirInfo.CreateSubdirectory("ch04")

  End Sub


End Module
```

- **GetDirectories() method** Returns the subdirectories of the current directory as an array of `DirectoryInfo`-type items. The following example shows how to use the `GetDirectories` method to get a list of all top-level directories in the `C:\` drive (see also Figure 4.12):

```vb
'-----------------------------------------
' .NET DirectoryInfo Class usage example
'-----------------------------------------

Imports System
Imports System.IO

Module Module1

  Sub Main()

    Dim Path As String = "c:\"
    Dim DirInfo As New DirectoryInfo(Path)
    Dim Dirs() As DirectoryInfo
    Dim I As Integer

    Console.WriteLine("Initial Directory : " & DirInfo.FullName)
    Dirs = DirInfo.GetDirectories
    For I = 0 To Dirs.GetUpperBound(0)
     Console.WriteLine(Dirs(I).FullName)
    Next

  End Sub

End Module
```

```
Initial Directory : c:\
c:\Alex
c:\ASP
c:\Book
c:\Documents and Settings
c:\Dot_Net
c:\IIS
c:\Inetpub
c:\Program Files
c:\RECYCLER
c:\Reference
c:\Software
c:\SQLServer
c:\System Volume Information
c:\Temp
c:\USResources
c:\WINNT
c:\Work
c:\XML
```

FIGURE 4.12   Using the GetDirectories method returns a list of top directories in the C drive

- **GetFiles() method** Returns an array of `FileInfo` items for the files in the current directory. We have already seen how to use this method in the previous section when we discussed the `FileInfo` class.

- **GetFileSystemInfos() method** Returns an array of `FileSystemInfo` items for the files in the current directory.

- **MoveTo(String) method** Moves a directory and its contents to a new path.

4.3   Environment.SpecialFolder enumeration

This enumeration can be used to obtain directory paths to the system's special folders, such as program files, programs, system, startup, and so on. The following is a list of members of the `SpecialFolder` enumeration.

- **ApplicationData** Returns the path to the directory that is used as a common repository for application-specific data.

- **CommonApplicationData** Returns the path to the directory that is used as a common repository for application-specific data used by all users.

- **CommonProgramFiles** Returns the path to the directory for components shared across applications.

- **Cookies** Returns the path to the directory that is used to store internet cookies.

- **DesktopDirectory** Returns the path to the directory that stores files and objects on the desktop.

- **Favorites** Returns the path to the directory that is used to store the user's favorites.

- **History** Returns the path to the directory that is used to store internet history items.

- **InternetCache** Returns the path to the directory that is used to store temporary internet files.

- **LocalApplicationData** Returns the path to the directory that is used to store application-specific data.

- **Personal** Returns the path to the directory that is used to store documents.

- **ProgramFiles** Returns the path to the directory that is used to store program files.

- **Programs** Returns the path to the directory that is used to store the user's program groups.

- **Recent** Returns the path to the directory that stores the user's most recently used documents.

- **SendTo** Returns the path to the directory that stores "Send To" menu items.

- **StartMenu** Returns the path to the directory that stores the "Start" menu items.
- **Startup** Returns the path to the directory that stores the user's "Startup" program group.
- **System** Returns the path to the "System" directory.
- **Templates** Returns the path to the directory that stores document templates.

The following example shows typical names of the paths to the system's special folders under Windows 2000 (see also Figure 4.13):

```
'-------------------------------------------------
' .NET Environment.SpecialFolder usage example
'-------------------------------------------------

Imports System
Imports System.Environment

Module Module1

  Sub Main()
    Dim E As Environment
    Dim Names As String()
    Dim Values() As Integer
    Dim I As Integer

    Console.WriteLine("SpecialFolder Enumeration")
    Names  = SpecialFolder.System.GetNames(SpecialFolder.System.GetType)
    Values = SpecialFolder.GetValues(SpecialFolder.System.GetType)

    For I = 0 To Names.GetUpperBound(0)
      Console.WriteLine(ControlChars.Tab & Names(I) & "=" & _
        E.GetFolderPath(Values(I)))
    Next

  End Sub

End Module
```

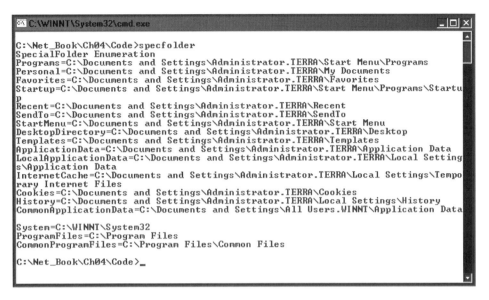

```
C:\WINNT\System32\cmd.exe                                              _ □ ×
C:\Net_Book\Ch04\Code>specfolder
SpecialFolder Enumeration
Programs=C:\Documents and Settings\Administrator.TERRA\Start Menu\Programs
Personal=C:\Documents and Settings\Administrator.TERRA\My Documents
Favorites=C:\Documents and Settings\Administrator.TERRA\Favorites
Startup=C:\Documents and Settings\Administrator.TERRA\Start Menu\Programs\Startu
p
Recent=C:\Documents and Settings\Administrator.TERRA\Recent
SendTo=C:\Documents and Settings\Administrator.TERRA\SendTo
StartMenu=C:\Documents and Settings\Administrator.TERRA\Start Menu
DesktopDirectory=C:\Documents and Settings\Administrator.TERRA\Desktop
Templates=C:\Documents and Settings\Administrator.TERRA\Templates
ApplicationData=C:\Documents and Settings\Administrator.TERRA\Application Data
LocalApplicationData=C:\Documents and Settings\Administrator.TERRA\Local Setting
s\Application Data
InternetCache=C:\Documents and Settings\Administrator.TERRA\Local Settings\Tempo
rary Internet Files
Cookies=C:\Documents and Settings\Administrator.TERRA\Cookies
History=C:\Documents and Settings\Administrator.TERRA\Local Settings\History
CommonApplicationData=C:\Documents and Settings\All Users.WINNT\Application Data

System=C:\WINNT\System32
ProgramFiles=C:\Program Files
CommonProgramFiles=C:\Program Files\Common Files

C:\Net_Book\Ch04\Code>_
```

FIGURE 4.13   The result of a search for special folders in Windows 2000

File class

This class provides a set of static methods that can be used to create, copy, delete, move, and open files. Some of the methods available in the `File` class create `StreamWriter` and `FileStream` objects.

The `Create(String)` or `Create(String, Integer)` method is used to create a file in the specified fully qualified path with the specified buffer size. This method returns the `FileStream` object. The `CreateText(String)` method creates a `StreamWriter` object that writes a new text file on the specified fully qualified path. Use the `AppendText(String)` method to create a `StreamWriter` object that appends text to an existing file or creates a new one. To check if a file already exists, use the `Exists(String)` method.

The `Open(String, FileMode)` or `Open(String, FileMode, FileAccess)` or `Open(String, FileMode, FileAccess, FileShare)` methods open a `FileStream` object on a specified file. The `OpenRead(String)` method creates a `FileStream` object that reads from an existing file. The `OpenWrite(String)` method creates a read/write `FileStream` object on the specified file. The `OpenText(String)` method creates a `StreamReader` object that is used to read from a file.

Figure 4.14 shows how methods of the `File` class relate to other stream classes.

The `Copy(String, String)` or `Copy(String, String, Boolean)` method is used to copy an existing file to a new one with overwriting enabled or disabled. To delete a file, use the `Delete(String)` method, and to move a specified file to a new location and, optionally, change the file name, use the `Move(String, String)` method.

The File class has four pairs of Get/Set methods to manipulate with attributes, creation time, last access time, and last write time. These are shown in Table 4.2.

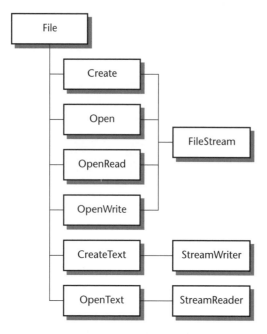

FIGURE 4.14   How the File class relates to other stream classes

TABLE 4.2 The File class' Get/Set methods

GetAttributes(*String*) : FileAttributes	SetAttributes(*String*, *FileAttributes*) : FileAttributes	Use these methods to get or set the FileAttributes of the specified file.
GetCreationTime	SetCreationTime	Use these methods to get or set the date and time the specified file was created.
GetLastAccessTime	SetLastAccessTime	Use these methods to get or set the date and time the specified file was last accessed.
GetLastWriteTime	SetLastWriteTime	Use these methods to get or set the date and time the specified file was last written to.

The following example shows how to use the Open method to open a FileStream on a specified file:

```
'---------------------------------------
' .NET File Class usage example
'---------------------------------------

Imports System
Imports System.IO

Module Module1

 Sub Main()
  Dim MyFile As String = "c:\temp\mytext\mytext01.txt"
  Dim FS As FileStream
  Dim Reader As StreamReader

  FS = File.Open(MyFile, FileMode.Open)
  Reader = New StreamReader(FS)

  While Reader.Peek() > -1
    Console.WriteLine(Reader.ReadLine())
  End While
  Reader.Close()
  FS.Close()

 End Sub

 End Module
```

Note that in the call to the Open method of the File object, we have specified the file access type. The possible values for file access are available through the FileMode enumeration and are shown below.

● **Append** This mode specifies that a file should be opened to append data. In this mode it is not possible to read from a file.

● **Create** This mode specifies that a new file should be created by the operating system. If the file already exists, it will be overwritten.

● **CreateNew** This mode specifies that a new file should be created by the operating system.

● **Open** This mode specifies that an existing file should be opened.

● **OpenOrCreate** This mode specifies that an existing file should be opened. If a file does not exist, the operating system creates a new file.

● **Truncate** This mode specifies that an existing file should be opened and its size should be truncated to zero bytes.

The following example shows how to read a specified file using the `OpenFile` method and the `StreamReader` class:

```
'----------------------------------------
' .NET File Class usage example
'----------------------------------------


Imports System
Imports System.IO

Module Module1

 Sub Main()

  Dim MyFile As String = "c:\temp\mytext\mytext01.txt"
  Dim Reader As StreamReader

  Reader = File.OpenText(MyFile)
  While Reader.Peek() > -1
   Console.WriteLine(Reader.ReadLine())
  End While
  Reader.Close()

 End Sub

End Module
```

The following example shows how to use the `GetXXX` methods on a specified file (see also Figure 4.15):

```
'----------------------------------------
' .NET File Class usage example
'----------------------------------------


Imports System
Imports System.IO

Module Module1

 Sub Main()
  Dim MyFile As String = "c:\temp\mytext\mytext01.txt"
```

```
    Console.WriteLine()
    Console.WriteLine(MyFile)
    Console.WriteLine("Attributes      : " & _
     ShowAttribs(File.GetAttributes(MyFile)))
    Console.WriteLine("Creation time   : " & _
     File.GetCreationTime(MyFile))
    Console.WriteLine("Last access time : " & _
     File.GetLastAccessTime(MyFile))
    Console.WriteLine("Last write time  : " & _
     File.GetLastWriteTime(MyFile))

End Sub

Function ShowAttribs(ByVal Attributes As FileAttributes) As String

 Dim S As String

      If Attributes And FileAttributes.Archive Then
          S = "A"
      Else
          S = "-"
      End If
      If Attributes And FileAttributes.Hidden Then
          S += "H"
      Else
          S += "-"
      End If
      If Attributes And FileAttributes.Normal Then
          S += "N"
      Else
          S += "-"
      End If
      If Attributes And FileAttributes.ReadOnly Then
          S += "R"
      Else
          S += "-"
      End If

 Return S

 End Function

End Module
```

```
c:\temp\mytext\mytext01.txt
Attributes        : -H-R
Creation time     : 22-Oct-01 22:34:43
Last access time  : 29-Oct-01 20:50:58
Last write time   : 29-Oct-01 20:43:39
```

FIGURE 4.15   Using GetXXX methods on a specific file

The last example shows how to use the OpenWrite method to open a FileStream on a specified file and write into it:

```
'----------------------------------------
' .NET File Class usage example
'----------------------------------------

Imports System
Imports System.IO

Module Module1

  Sub Main()
    Dim MyFile As String = "c:\temp\mytext\mytext01.txt"
    Dim FS As FileStream
    Dim Writer As StreamWriter

    FS = File.OpenWrite(MyFile)
    Writer = New StreamWriter(FS)
    FS.Seek(0, SeekOrigin.End)
    Writer.WriteLine("One more line")
    Writer.Flush()
    Writer.Close()
    FS.Close()

  End Sub

End Module
```

Path class

The Path class provides a set of static methods used to parse and process directory strings. The methods implemented in this class are as follows.

- **ChangeExtension(*String*, *String*) method** Changes a file name extension and returns a result as String.

- **Combine(*String*, *String*) method** Combines two file paths and returns a result as String.

- **GetDirectoryName(*String*) method** Gets the directory path of the file as a `String`.
- **GetExtension(*String*) method** Gets the extension of the path as a `String`.
- **GetFileName(*String*) method** Gets the file name as a `String`.
- **GetFileNameWithoutExtension(*String*) method** Gets the file name extension as a `String`.
- **GetFullPath(*String*) method** Expands the path to a fully qualified path and returns a result as `String`.
- **GetPathRoot(*String*) method** Returns the root of the path and returns a result as `String`.
- **GetTempFileName() method** Returns a unique temporary file name as `String` and creates a zero-byte file with this name.
- **GetTempPath() method** Returns the path to the system's temporary folder as a `String`.
- **HasExtension(*String*) method** Allows you to check if a path includes a file name extension.
- **IsPathRooted(*String*) method** Allows you to check if a path includes the root.

The following example shows how to use methods of the `Path` class (see also Figure 4.16):

```
'----------------------------------------
' .NET Path Class usage example
'----------------------------------------

Imports System
Imports System.IO

Module Module1

 Sub Main()
  Dim FullPath As String    = "c:\book\ch04\ch04.doc"
  Dim FullPathExt As String = "c:\book\ch04.old\ch04.doc"
  Dim Partial1 As String    = "c:\book"
  Dim Partial2 As String    = "ch04"

  Console.WriteLine("ChangeExtension            : " & _
   Path.ChangeExtension(FullPath, ".bak"))
  Console.WriteLine("Combine                    : " & _
   Path.Combine(Partial1, Partial2))
  Console.WriteLine("GetDirectoryName           : " & _
   Path.GetDirectoryName(FullPath))
  Console.WriteLine("GetExtension               : " & _
   Path.GetExtension(FullPathExt))
```

```
        Console.WriteLine("GetFileName                 : " & _
          Path.GetFileName(FullPath))
        Console.WriteLine("GetFileNameWithoutExtension : " & _
          Path.GetFileNameWithoutExtension(FullPath))
        Console.WriteLine("GetFullPath                 : " & _
          Path.GetFullPath(FullPath))
        Console.WriteLine("GetPathRoot                 : " & _
          Path.GetPathRoot(FullPath))
        Console.WriteLine("GetTempFileName             : " & _
          Path.GetTempFileName)
        Console.WriteLine("GetTempPath                 : " & _
          Path.GetTempPath)
        Console.WriteLine("HasExtension                : " & _
          Path.HasExtension(FullPathExt))
        Console.WriteLine("IsPathRooted                : " & _
          Path.IsPathRooted(Partial2))

    End Sub


End Module


ChangeExtension                 : c:\book\ch04\ch04.bak
Combine                         : c:\book\ch04
GetDirectoryName                : c:\book\ch04
GetExtension                    : .doc
GetFileName                     : ch04.doc
GetFileNameWithoutExtension     : ch04
GetFullPath                     : c:\book\ch04\ch04.doc
GetPathRoot                     : c:\
GetTempFileName                 : C:\DOCUME~1\ADMINI~1\LOCALS~1\Temp\tmp10A.tmp
GetTempPath                     : C:\DOCUME~1\ADMINI~1\LOCALS~1\Temp\
HasExtension                    : True
IsPathRooted                    : False
```

FIGURE 4.16   Using the methods of the Path class

The five properties of the Path class contain platform-specific characters that allow us to use this class on different platforms.

- AltDirectorySeparatorChar Alternate directory separator char.
- DirectorySeparatorChar Directory separator char.
- InvalidPathChars List of invalid characters in a path.
- PathSeparator Directory path separator char.
- VolumeSeparatorChar Volume separator char.

The following example shows the value of these properties for the Microsoft Windows platform (see also Figure 4.17):

```
'----------------------------------------
' .NET Path Class usage example
'----------------------------------------


Imports System
Imports System.IO

Module Module1

 Sub Main()

  Console.WriteLine("AltDirectorySeparatorChar : " _
   & Path.AltDirectorySeparatorChar)
  Console.WriteLine("DirectorySeparatorChar    : " _
   & Path.DirectorySeparatorChar)
  Console.WriteLine("InvalidPathChars          : " _
   & Path.InvalidPathChars)
  Console.WriteLine("PathSeparator             : " _
   & Path.PathSeparator)
  Console.WriteLine("VolumeSeparatorChar       : " _
   & Path.VolumeSeparatorChar)

 End Sub

End Module


AltDirectorySeparatorChar : /
DirectorySeparatorChar     : \
InvalidPathChars           : "<>¦
PathSeparator              : ;
VolumeSeparatorChar        : :
```

FIGURE 4.17   The values for the five platform-dependent properties of the Windows platform

We have now come to the end of our discussion of the System.IO namespace and most of its classes that are used to read from and write to streams and manipulate directories and files in a file system. The rest of this chapter will be dedicated to networking – classes that are implemented in the System.Net namespace.

4.4   The `System.Net` namespace – internet programming under .NET

The `System.Net` namespace contains classes (net classes) that provide support for building applications that use internet protocols to send and receive data. These classes allow us to build different types of applications depending on our needs – from sockets-based communications to simple request/response programs.

The net classes provide us with the implementation of the HTTP protocol. These classes support most of the HTTP 1.1 protocol features. Beside the advanced features there are pipelining, chunking, authentication, pre-authentication, encryption, proxy support, server certificate validation, connection management, and HTTP extensions.

The Net classes use universal resource identifiers (URIs) to identify internet resources. URIs consist of the parts shown in Figure 4.18.

The `System` namespace contains two helper classes that can be used to manipulate a URI and its parts – the `Uri` and `UriBuilder` classes.

Also, the `HTTPUtility` class in the `System.Web` namespace can be used to perform URI encoding and decoding.

The `WebRequest` and `WebResponse` classes are the base classes that implement so-called "pluggable protocols" – network services that hide specific protocol details from developers. The classes derived from the `WebRequest` and `WebResponse` classes are `HTTPWebRequest`, `FileWebRequest`, `HTTPWebResponse`, and `FileWebResponse` classes. They implement the `http://`, `https://`, and `file://` schemes to request remote and local resources.

The following is a list of other classes included in the `System.Net` namespace.

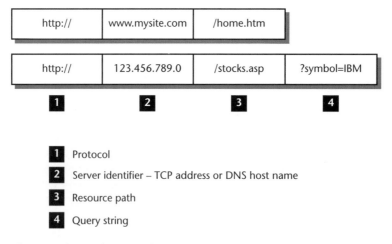

1 Protocol
2 Server identifier – TCP address or DNS host name
3 Resource path
4 Query string

FIGURE 4.18   The parts that make up a URI

- **AuthentificationManager and Authorization classes** Used to authorize user access to the internet server.

- **NetworkCredential class** Provides credentials for password-based authentication schemes – basic, digest, NTLM, Kerberos, and so on.

- **Cookie, CookieCollection, CookieContainer, CookieException class** Provides us with all of the methods we need to deal with cookies.

- **Dns, DnsPermission and DnsPermissionAttribute classes** Used to work with domain name resolution functions and control rights to access domain name system (DNS) servers.

- **WebClient class** Contains methods for sending data to and receiving data from local and remote resources.

- **WehHeaderCollecton class** Used to access protocol headers associated with a request or response.

- **WebPermission and WebPermissionAttributes classes** Control rights to access an internet resource.

- **WebProxy class** Contains HTTP proxy settings associated with the WebRequest.

- **WebException class** Contains the exception thrown when there is an error while accessing the network.

- **IPAddress, IPEndPoint and IPHostEntry classes** Represent an internet protocol (IP) address, a network endpoint as an IP address and port numbers, and provide a container for internet host address information.

- **ServicePoint and ServicePointManager classes** Implement connection management for HTTP connections.

- **SocketAddress, SocketPermisison, SocketPermissionAttribute classes, EndPoint and EndPointPermission classes**, as well as the classes implemented in the **System.Net.Sockets** namespace Support all sockets-based communications.

- **Socket, TCPClient, TCPListener, and UDPClient classes** The System.Net. Sockets namespace contains classes that implement the Windows sockets interface, the socket class being the main one, while the ICPClient, TCPListener, and UDPClient classes encapsulate the details of creating TCP and UDP connections over the internet.

As noted above, the two classes WebRequest and WebResponse are the base classes that implement HTTP protocol. In the following section, we will look at the basic functionality provided by these classes.

WebRequest class

The WebRequest class is the abstract class that makes a request to a resource, defined by the URI. This is the base class for the request/response model that allows applications to request data over the internet without knowing protocol-specific details.

Applications work with instances of the `WebRequest` class while its descendants implement protocol-specific details. The following code snippet shows how to create an `HTTPWebRequest`:

```
Dim Request As HttpWebRequest = _
    CType(WebRequest.Create("http://localhost/home.htm"), _
    HttpWebRequest)
```

Note that we create a `WebRequest` class instance, not a `HTTPWebRequest` class instance, and cast it to the `HTTPWebRequest` class type.

When errors occur while accessing an internet resource, an exception of the `WebException` type is thrown. The `WebException.Status` property indicates the source of the error.

The `WebRequest` class contains the following important properties and methods:

- **ContentLength** This property of a `Long` type is used to get or set the content length of the request data to be sent.

- **ContentType** This property of a `String` type is used to specify the content type of the request data to be sent.

- **Credentials** Contains the network credentials used for authentication. This property is of the `ICredentials` type.

- **Headers** Contains the collection of header name and value pairs for this request as a `WebHeadersCollection` type.

- **Method** This property of a `String` type specifies the protocol method for this request. For the HTTP 1.1 protocol, this can be GET, HEAD, POST, PUT, DELETE, TRACE, or OPTIONS.

- **PreAuthenticate** This Boolean property indicates whether or not to preauthenticate the request.

- **Proxy** Specifies the network proxy for this request. This property is of the `IWebProxy` type.

- **RequestUri** Specifies the internet resource URI (as a `Uri` type) to send the request to.

- **Timeout** Specifies the length of time before the request times out as an `Integer` value.

- **Abort() method** Use to cancel an asynchronous request.

- **BeginGetRequestStream(*AsyncCallback*, *Object*), EndGetRequestStream(*IAsyncResult*) methods** Provide an asynchronous version of the `GetRequestStream()` method and a `Stream` for writing data to the internet resource.

- **BeginGetResponse(*AsyncCallback*, Object), EndGetResponse(*IAsyncResult*) methods** Start an asynchronous request and return a `WebResponse`.

- **GetRequestStream() method** Returns a `Stream` for writing data to the internet resource.

- **GetResponse() method** Returns a response (`WebResponse`) to an internet request.

The `WebRequest` class serves as the base class for the classes that implement the `http://`, `https://`, and `file://` protocols to request remote and local resources (see Figure 4.19).

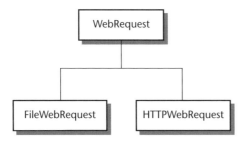

FIGURE 4.19   WebRequest is the base class for implementing internet protocols

HTTPWebRequest class

This class implements `http://` and `https://` requests to internet resources. The `HTTPWebRequest` class extends its base `WebRequest` class by overriding some of its methods and providing new properties and methods.

The properties listed in Table 4.3 are used to get or set the values of the appropriate HTTP headers.

TABLE 4.3   The properties used to get or set values of HTTP headers

Property	HTTP header	Default value
Accept	Accept	Null.
Connection	Connection	Null. If KeepAlive property is true, the value of the Connection property will be set to "Keep-alive".
ContentLength	Content-length	–1.
ContentType	Content-type	Null.
Expect	Expect	"100-continue".
IfModifiedSince	If-Modified-Since	Current date and time.
Referrer	Referrer	Null.
TransferEncoding	Transfer-Encoding	Null. If SendChunked property is set to true, the value of the TransferEncoding property is set to "Chunked".
UserAgent	User-agent	Null.

Other HTTP headers are accessible via the **Headers** collection. For more information about the HTTP headers as well as the HTTP protocol itself, please refer to the RFC 2616.

- **Address** Returns the URI (a **Uri** type) of the internet resource that provided the response after all redirections are complete.
- **AllowAutoRedirect** Indicates whether or not the request should follow redirection responses.
- **AllowWriteStreamBuffering** Indicates whether or not to buffer the data sent to the URI.
- **ClientCertificates** Contains the collection of security certificates for the request (an **X509CertificateCollection** type).
- **CookieContainer** Contains the cookies associated with the request as an object of a **CookieContainer** type.
- **HaveResponse** Indicates whether or not you have a response from the internet resource.
- **KeepAlive** Indicates whether or not to make a persistent connection to the internet resource. The keep-alive feature allows a client to reuse an existing TCP connection to the server without closing it and reopening it for each new request.
- **Pipelined** Indicates whether or not to pipeline the request. Pipelining is an HTTP 1.1 feature that allows you to send multiple HTTP requests over a persistent connection without waiting for a response from the server before the next request is sent. Pipelined connections are made only when the **KeepAlive** property is set to "True".
- **ProtocolVersion** Indicates the version of HTTP to use for this request. This property can be set to **HTTPVersion.Version11** (this is the default value) or to **HTTPVersion.Version10**.
- **SendChunked** Indicates whether or not to send data in chunks to the internet resource. Chunking is useful when an application needs to send data, the exact size of which is not known at the time of the request. You can use this property only with servers that accept chunked data – servers that are HTTP/1.1 (or greater)-compliant. If the server does not accept chunked data, you must buffer all data to be written and send a HTTP **Content-Length** header with the buffered data.

The other class derived from the **WebRequest** class is the **FileWebRequest** class – this is discussed next.

FileWebRequest class

This class provides a file system implementation (**file://** scheme) of the **WebRequest** class. We use the **FileWebRequest** class to request local files. This class overrides several methods of the **WebRequest** class to provide the desired functionality. It relies on the **File** class for error handling and code access security.

The WebRequest counterpart class is the WebResponse class, which provides basic functionality to manage responses from the internet or local resources.

WebResponse class

This class returns a response from the resource specified by the URI. This is the base class for a request/response model that allows applications to receive data over the internet without knowing protocol-specific details. Applications work with instances of the WebResponse class while its descendants implement protocol-specific details. The following code snippet shows how to create an HTTPWebResponse:

```
Dim Response As HttpWebResponse = _
    CType(Request.GetResponse(), HttpWebResponse)
```

The WebResponse class contains several properties and methods that are outlined below.

- **ContentLength** This property of a Long type indicates the content length of the received data.
- **ContentType** This property of a String type indicates the content type of the received data.
- **Headers** Contains the collection of header value and name pairs associated with this response (WebHeaderCollection type).
- **ResponseUri** Indicates the URI of the response (a Uri type) – the address of the resource that actually responded to the request.
- **Close()** Use this method to close the response stream.
- **GetResponseStream()** This method returns the data stream (of Stream type) from the Internet resource.

The WebResponse class serves as a base class for the classes that implement the http://, https://, and file:// protocols to get the response from remote and local resources (see Figure 4.20).

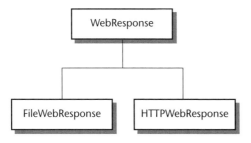

FIGURE 4.20   The WebResponse class is the basis for classes implementing internet protocols

HTTPWebResponse class

The HTTPWebResponse class is the HTTP-specific implementation of the WebResponse class. The Headers property (of WebHeaderCollection type) contains most of the HTTP headers set by the internet server. Other header information is exposed via the properties of the HTTPWebResponse class. The contents of the response are returned as a Stream instance, accessible by the GetResponseStream() method. The most important properties and methods of the HTTPWebResponse class are listed below.

- **CharacterSet** This String property indicates the character set of the response.
- **LastModified** This DateTime property contains the last date and time (DateTime type) that the contents of the response were modified.
- **Server** This String property contains the name of the server that sent the response.
- **StatusCode** This property contains the status of the response. This is one of the HTTPStatusCode enumeration values. The successful request sets this property value to 200.
- **StatusDescription** This String property contains the status description of the response.
- **Close() method** Closes the response stream.
- **GetResponseHeader(*String*) method** Returns a specified header value as a String.
- **GetResponseStream() method** Gets the body of the response as a Stream instance.

A response from the FileWebRequest class is available via the FileWebResponse class, which is described below.

FileWebResponse class

The FileWebResponse class is a file system implementation of the WebResponse class. The Headers property (of WebHeaderCollection type) contains two name and value pairs that are also exposed by the ContentLength and ContentType properties. The contents of the response are returned as a Stream instance, accessible by using the GetResponseStream method.

Practice

To show the HTTPWebRequest and HTTPWebResponse classes in action, let's create a small HTML page, place it in the root of the web server, and request it. While some controls in System.Windows or System.Web namespaces are more suitable for displaying HTML pages, for the purposes of our example, we will use a simple console application.

We start with the creation of two objects – one that is based on the HTTPWebRequest class, which will issue an HTTP request to a web server, and one that is based on the HTTPWebResponse class, which will receive the response from the web server. To get the contents of the response, we need a Stream – that's why we will use the StreamReader object discussed in the first part of this chapter.

Here is the HTML code for our HTML page:

```
<html>
<head>
<title>Home Page</title>
</head>
<body>
 <h1 align="center">Welcome</h1>
</body>
</html>
```

Now, the console program that sends an HTTP request to the web server receives the answer and shows it on screen (see Figure 4.21).

```
'----------------------------------------------------------------
' .NET HTTPWebRequest and HTTPWebResponse Classes usage example
'----------------------------------------------------------------

Imports System
Imports System.Net
Imports System.IO

Module Module1

 Sub Main()

  Dim Request As HttpWebRequest = _
   CType(WebRequest.Create("http://localhost/home.htm"), _
   HttpWebRequest)

  Dim Response As HttpWebResponse = _
   CType(Request.GetResponse(), HttpWebResponse)

  Dim WebStream As StreamReader
  WebStream = New StreamReader(Response.GetResponseStream)

  Console.WriteLine(WebStream.ReadToEnd)

  Console.ReadLine()

 End Sub

End Module
```

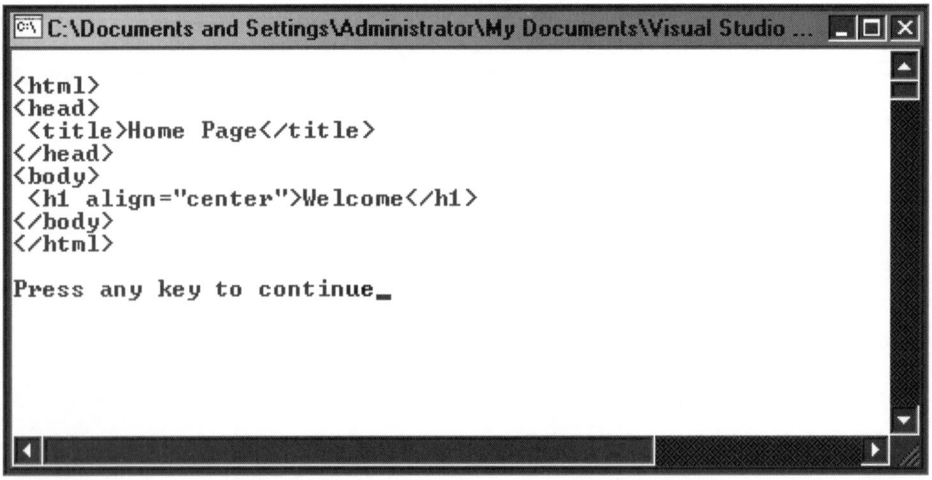

```
C:\Documents and Settings\Administrator\My Documents\Visual Studio ...

<html>
<head>
 <title>Home Page</title>
</head>
<body>
 <h1 align="center">Welcome</h1>
</body>
</html>

Press any key to continue_
```

FIGURE 4.21   The console program shows the answer to the web request

Next, let's look at the interaction between the HTTP client (which is our console application) and web server.

By setting some of the properties of the HTTPWebRequest instance, we can set the values of the HTTP headers that will be sent to the server. For example, to turn off the HTTP keep-alive behavior, we set the KeepAlive property to False. If we want to follow redirects in our application other than doing this automatically, we need to set the AllowAutoRedirect value to False and handle redirects as HTTP protocol errors. To handle protocol errors, we need to catch any exceptions of the WebException type with the Status property set to WebExceptionStatus.ProtocolError.

The following code shows how to get and set some of the properties of the HTTPWebRequest instance:

```
'-----------------------------------------------------------------
' .NET HTTPWebRequest Class usage example
'-----------------------------------------------------------------

Imports System
Imports System.Net
Imports System.IO

Module Module1

 Sub Main()

  Dim Request As HttpWebRequest = _
   CType(WebRequest.Create("http://localhost/home.htm"), _
   HttpWebRequest)
```

```
      Request.UserAgent = ".NET Console Client"

      With Request
        Console.WriteLine("IfModifiedSince  : " & .IfModifiedSince)
        Console.WriteLine("Pipelined        : " & .Pipelined)
        Console.WriteLine("SendChunked      : " & .SendChunked)
        Console.WriteLine("Timeout          : " & .Timeout)

      End With

    ' ... Make request here

    End Sub

  End Module
```

The following program shows how to display HTTP response headers that are exposed by various properties of the **HTTPWebResponse** class (see also Figure 4.22):

```
    '-----------------------------------------------------------------
    ' .NET HTTPWebResponse Class usage example
    '-----------------------------------------------------------------

    Imports System
    Imports System.Net
    Imports System.IO

  Module Module1

    Sub Main()

      Dim Request As HttpWebRequest = _
        CType(WebRequest.Create("http://localhost/home.htm"), _
        HttpWebRequest)

      Dim Response As HttpWebResponse = _
      CType(Request.GetResponse(), HttpWebResponse)

      With Response

        Console.WriteLine("CharacterSet     : " & .CharacterSet.ToString)
        Console.WriteLine("ContentEncoding  : " & .ContentEncoding)
        Console.WriteLine("ContentLength    : " & .ContentLength)
        Console.WriteLine("ContentType      : " & .ContentType)
        Console.WriteLine("HTTP Headers")
        PrintHeaders(.Headers)
        Console.WriteLine("LastModified     : " & .LastModified)
```

```
        Console.WriteLine("Method            : " & .Method)
        Console.WriteLine("ProtocolVersion   : " & _
          .ProtocolVersion.ToString)
        Console.WriteLine("Server            : " & .Server)
        Console.WriteLine("StatusCode        : " & .StatusCode)
        Console.WriteLine("StatusDescription : " & .StatusDescription)

    End With

  End Sub

  Sub PrintHeaders(ByVal H As WebHeaderCollection)

    Dim E As IEnumerator
    E = H.GetEnumerator
    Console.WriteLine()

    While E.MoveNext
      Console.WriteLine(ControlChars.Tab & _
        CType(E.Current, String).PadRight(20) & _
        H.Item(E.Current))
    End While

    Console.WriteLine()

  End Sub

End Module
```

```
CharacterSet      :
ContentEncoding   :
ContentLength     : 185
ContentType       : text/html
HTTP Headers

        Server            Microsoft-IIS/5.0
        Date              Fri, 02 Nov 2001 21:13:32 GMT
        Content-Type      text/html
        Accept-Ranges     bytes
        Last-Modified     Fri, 02 Nov 2001 21:07:19 GMT
        ETag              "b0d9cb5be263c11:89f"
        Content-Length    185

LastModified      : 02-Nov-01 22:07:19
Method            : GET
ProtocolVersion   : 1.1
Server            : Microsoft-IIS/5.0
StatusCode        : 200
StatusDescription : OK
```

FIGURE 4.22   Displaying HTTP response headers exposed by the HTTPWebResponse class

By default, we use the GET method to send a request to the internet server specified by the URI. To make a POST request, we set the Method property of the HTTPWebRequest instance to "POST" and the value of the ContentType property to "application/x-www-form-urlencoded". The contents of the request should be URI encoded and stored in the Stream, obtained by using the GetRequestStream method. The following example shows how to do this. Suppose we have a very simple ASP code that receives a POST request and shows its contents:

```
<%

Response.Write "FirstName = " & Request.Form("FirstName")
Response.Write "<BR>"
Response.Write "LastName = " & Request.Form("LastName")

%>
```

When called as an action attribute of the FORM tag, this code shows what it received (see Figure 4.23):

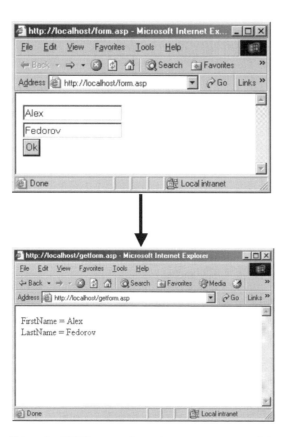

FIGURE 4.23   Using the FORM tag to show the name content of the URI requested

```
<form method="POST" action="getform.asp">
 <input type="text" name="FirstName">
 <br>
 <input type="text" name="LastName">
 <br>
 <input type="submit" value="Ok">
</form>
```

Now, let's simulate sending the form with our code. To do this we need to "pack" the data as a string, i.e.

```
"FirstName=Alexei&LastName=Fedorov"
```

specify the type of the content we are sending to the server:

```
"application/x-www-form-urlencoded"
```

and send the data through the output stream. The following example shows how to do this, and how to receive the response from the server (see also Figure 4.24):

```
'-------------------------------------------------------------
' .NET Net Class usage example
'-------------------------------------------------------------

Imports System
Imports System.Net
Imports System.IO

Module Module1

 Sub Main()
  Try
   Dim Request As HttpWebRequest
   Dim Response As HttpWebResponse

   Dim WebStream As StreamReader
   Dim RequestStream As Stream
   Dim Bytes() As Byte
   Dim Data As String

   Request = CType(WebRequest.Create("http://localhost/getform.asp"), _
    HttpWebRequest)

   Data = "FirstName=Alexei&LastName=Fedorov"
   Bytes = Text.Encoding.ASCII.GetBytes(Data)
```

```
      Request.ContentLength = Bytes.Length
      Request.Method = "POST"
      Request.ContentType = "application/x-www-form-urlencoded"

      RequestStream = Request.GetRequestStream()
      RequestStream.Write(Bytes, 0, Bytes.Length)
      RequestStream.Close()

      Response = CType(Request.GetResponse(), HttpWebResponse)
      WebStream = New StreamReader(Response.GetResponseStream)
      Console.WriteLine(WebStream.ReadToEnd)

      Catch E As WebException
       Console.WriteLine(E.Response)
      End If

    End Try

   End Sub

  End Module


FirstName = Alexei<BR>LastName = Fedorov

Press any key to continue
```

FIGURE 4.24   Simulate sending a form, specifying the content, then send it through the output stream

Note that in the last example we wrapped all our code in the Try/Catch block. This was done to handle the exceptions of the WebException type. This type of exception is thrown when an error occurs while accessing the Internet resource through WebRequest and WebResponse descendants.

The Message property contains the error message text, the Status property (the code of the response) and the Response property contains the response (WebResponse class instance) sent by the server.

The Status property is of the WebExceptionStatus enumeration type, and it may have one of the following values.

● **ConnectFailure** The remote service point could not be contacted at the transport level.

● **ConnectionClosed** The connection was prematurely closed.

● **KeepAliveFailure** The connection for a request that specifies the keep alive header was closed unexpectedly.

- **NameResolutionFailure** The name resolver service could not resolve the host name.
- **Pending** An internal asynchronous request is pending.
- **ProtocolError** The response received from the server was complete but indicated a protocol-level error.
- **ProxyNameResolutionFailure** The name resolver service could not resolve the proxy host name.
- **ReceiveFailure** A complete response was not received from the remote server.
- **RequestCanceled** The request was canceled or the WebRequest.Abort method was called.
- **SecureChannelFailure** An error occurred in a secure channel link.
- **SendFailure** A complete request could not be sent to the remote server.
- **Success** No error was encountered. This is the default value for the Status property.
- **Timeout** No response was received during the timeout period for a request.
- **TrustFailure** A server certificate could not be validated.

If the value of the Status property is set to ProtocolError, it indicates that an HTTP error has occurred, and we can examine the Request property to get more information. The following example shows how to do this (see also Figure 4.25):

```
'-----------------------------------------------------------------
' .NET HTTPWebRequest and HTTPWebResponse Classes usage example
'-----------------------------------------------------------------


Imports System
Imports System.Net
Imports System.IO


Module Module1


 Sub Main()


  Try
   Dim Request As HttpWebRequest
   Dim Response As HttpWebResponse
   Dim WebStream As StreamReader

   Request = CType(WebRequest.Create("http://localhost/nopage.htm"), _
    HttpWebRequest)

   Response = CType(Request.GetResponse(), HttpWebResponse)
   WebStream = New StreamReader(Response.GetResponseStream)
   Console.WriteLine(WebStream.ReadToEnd)
```

```
        Catch E As WebException
         If E.Status = WebExceptionStatus.ProtocolError Then

            Console.WriteLine(" Error Message : " & E.Message)
            Console.WriteLine(" Status Code   : " & _
             CType(E.Response, HttpWebResponse).StatusCode)

         End If

       End Try

     End Sub

   End Module


Error Message : The remote server returned an error: (404) Not Found.
Status Code   : 404
```

FIGURE 4.25   Examining HTTPWebRequest error information

In the above example, we requested a page that does not exist and have received an appropriate message from the server. By casting the Response property of the WebException to the HTTPWebResponse type, we have access to the StatusCode property that contains the status code of the request and allows us to create more sophisticated error handlers. The Status property is of the HTTPStatusCode enumeration type and it contains the values of the status codes of the HTTP 1.1 protocol set out in Table 4.4.

TABLE 4.4   HTTPStatusCode enumeration values and what they mean

Enumeration member	Code	Description
Continue	100	Indicates that the client may continue with request.
SwitchingProtocols	101	Indicates that the protocol version or protocol is being changed.
OK	200	Indicates that the request succeeded and the requested information is in the response. This is the most common status code received.
Created	201	Indicates that the request resulted in a new resource created before the response was sent.

Enumeration member	Code	Description
Accepted	202	Indicates that the request has been accepted for further processing.
NonAuthoritativeInformation	203	Indicates that the returned metainformation is from a cached copy instead of the original server and therefore may be incorrect.
NoContent	204	Indicates that the request has been successfully processed and that the response is intentionally blank.
ResetContent	205	Indicates that the client should reset (not reload) the current resource.
PartialContent	206	Indicates that the response is a partial response as requested by a GET request that includes a byte range.
Ambiguous	300	Indicates that the requested information has multiple representations. We usually treat this result as a redirect and follow the contents of the location header associated with this response. This is a synonym for MultipleChoices (see below).
MultipleChoices	300	Indicates that the requested information has multiple representations. We should treat this status as a redirect and follow the contents of the location header associated with this response. This is a synonym for Ambiguous (see above).
Moved	301	Indicates that the requested information has been moved to the URI specified in the location header. When this status is received, we should follow the location header associated with the response. When the original request method was POST, the redirected request will use the GET method.
MovedPermanently	301	Indicates that the requested information has been moved to the URI specified in the location header. When this status is received we should follow the location header associated with the response. This is a synonym for Moved (see above).
Found	302	Indicates that the requested information is located at the URI specified in the location header. When this status is received we should follow the location header associated with the response. When the orig inal request method was POST, the redirected request will use the GET method. This is a synonym for Redirect (see below).

TABLE 4.4 Continued

Enumeration member	Code	Description
Redirect	302	Indicates that the requested information is located at the URI specified in the location header. When this status is received we should follow the location header associated with the response. When the original request method was POST, the redirected request will use the GET method. This is a synonym for Found (see above).
RedirectMethod	303	Automatically redirects the client to the URI specified in the location header as the result of a POST. The request to the resource specified by the location header will be made with a GET. This is a synonym for SeeOther (see below).
SeeOther	303	Automatically redirects the client to the URI specified in the location header as the result of a POST. The request to the resource specified by the location header will be made with a GET. This is a synonym for RedirectMethod.
NotModified	304	Indicates that the client's cached copy is up to date. The contents of the resource are not transferred.
UseProxy	305	Indicates that the request should use the proxy server at the URI specified in the location header.
Unused	306	This is a proposed extension to the HTTP 1.1 specification that is not fully specified.
RedirectKeepVerb	307	Indicates that the requested information is located at the URI specified in the location header. When this status is received, we should follow the location header associated with the response. When the original request method was POST, the redirected request will also use the POST method. This is a synonym for TemporaryRedirect (see below).
TemporaryRedirect	307	Indicates that the requested information is located at the URI specified in the location header. When this status is received, we should follow the location header associated with the response. When the original request method was POST, the redirected request will also use the POST method. This is a synonym for RedirectKeepVerb (see above).

Enumeration member	Code	Description
BadRequest	400	Indicates that the request could not be understood by the server. This code is sent when no other error is applicable or if the exact error is unknown or does not have its own error code.
Unauthorized	401	Indicates that the requested resource requires authentication. The "WWW-Authenticate" header contains the details of how to perform the authentication.
PaymentRequired	402	This code is reserved for future use.
Forbidden	403	Indicates that the server refuses to fulfill the request.
NotFound	404	Indicates that the requested resource does not exist on the server.
MethodNotAllowed	405	Indicates that the request method (POST or GET) is not allowed on the requested resource.
NotAcceptable	406	Indicates that the client has indicated with "Accept" headers that it will not accept any of the available representations of the resource.
ProxyAuthenticationRequired	407	Indicates that the requested proxy requires authentication. The "Proxy-Authenticate" header contains the details of how to perform the authentication.
RequestTimeout	408	Indicates that the client did not send a request within the time the server was expecting the request.
Conflict	409	Indicates that the request could not be carried out due to a conflict on the server.
Gone	410	Indicates that the requested resource is no longer available.
LengthRequired	411	Indicates that the required "Content-length" header is missing.
PreconditionFailed	412	Indicates that a condition set for this request failed and so the request cannot be carried out. Conditions are set with conditional request headers such as "If-Match", "If-None-Match" or "If-Unmodified-Since".
RequestEntityTooLarge	413	Indicates that the request is too large for the server to process.
RequestUriTooLong	414	Indicates that the URI is too long.
UnsupportedMediaType	415	Indicates that the request is of an unsupported type.

TABLE 4.4   Continued

Enumeration member	Code	Description
RequestedRangeNotSatisfiable	416	Indicates that the range of data requested from the resource cannot be returned, either because the beginning of the range is before the beginning of the resource or the end of the range is after the end of the resource.
ExpectationFailed	417	Indicates that an expectation given in an "Expect" header could not be met by the server.
InternalServerError	500	Indicates that a generic error has occurred on the server.
NotImplemented	501	Indicates that the server does not support the requested function.
BadGateway	502	Indicates that an intermediate proxy server received a bad response from another proxy of the server of origin.
ServiceUnavailable	503	Indicates that the server is temporarily unavailable, usually due to high load or maintenance.
GatewayTimeout	504	Indicates that an intermediate proxy server timed out while waiting for a response from another proxy or the origin server.
HttpVersionNotSupported	505	Indicates that the requested HTTP version is not supported by the server.

4.5   Helper classes

The `System` namespace contains two helper classes – the `Uri` and `UriBuilder` classes. These can be used to manipulate the contents of URIs. The `Uri` class provides easy access to the parts of the URI. The properties of the `Uri` class are read only – to modify a `Uri` class instance we should use the `UriBuilder` class.

The `Uri` class contains the following read-only `String`-type fields that specify the characters and schemes.

- **SchemeDelimiter** Specifies the characters that separate the communication protocol scheme from the address portion of the URI.
- **UriSchemeFile** Specifies that the URI is a pointer to a file.
- **UriSchemeFtp** Specifies that the URI is accessed via the file transfer protocol (FTP).
- **UriSchemeGopher** Specifies that the URI is accessed via the Gopher protocol.

- **UriSchemeHttp** Specifies that the URI is accessed via the hypertext transfer Protocol (HTTP).

- **UriSchemeHttps** Specifies that the URI is accessed via the secure hypertext transfer Protocol (HTTPS).

- **UriSchemeMailto** Specifies that the URI is an e-mail address and is accessed via the simple network mail protocol (SNMP).

- **UriSchemeNews** Specifies that the URI is an internet newsgroup accessed via the network news transport protocol (NNTP).

- **UriSchemeNntp** Specifies that the URI is an internet newsgroup accessed via the network news transport protocol (NNTP).

The following example shows the contents of these properties (see also Figure 4.26):

```
'----------------------------------------------------------------
' .NET Uri Class usage example
'----------------------------------------------------------------


Imports System
Imports System.Net
Imports System.IO


Module Module1

 Sub Main()

  Dim MainURI As New Uri("http://www.mysite.com/stocks.asp?symbol=IBM")

  With MainURI

   Console.WriteLine("SchemeDelimiter  = " & .SchemeDelimiter)
   Console.WriteLine("UriSchemeFile    = " & .UriSchemeFile)
   Console.WriteLine("UriSchemeFtp     = " & .UriSchemeFtp)
   Console.WriteLine("UriSchemeGopher  = " & .UriSchemeGopher)
   Console.WriteLine("UriSchemeHTTP    = " & .UriSchemeHttp)
   Console.WriteLine("UriSchemeHTTPS   = " & .UriSchemeHttps)
   Console.WriteLine("UriSchemeMailto  = " & .UriSchemeMailto)
   Console.WriteLine("UriSchemeNews    = " & .UriSchemeNews)
   Console.WriteLine("UriSchemeNntp    = " & .UriSchemeNntp)

  End With

 End Sub


End Module
```

```
UriSchemeFile   = file
UriSchemeFtp    = ftp
UriSchemeGopher = gopher
UriSchemeHTTP   = http
UriSchemeHTTPS  = https
UriSchemeMailto = mailto
UriSchemeNews   = news
UriSchemeNntp   = nntp
```

FIGURE 4.26   The properties of the `Uri` class

The `Uri` class contains the following properties and methods:

- **AbsolutePath** This `String` property contains the absolute path of the URI.
- **AbsoluteURI** This `String` property contains the absolute URI.
- **Authority** This `String` property contains the DNS host name or IP address of the server and the port number.
- **Fragment** This `String` property contains the escaped fragment.
- **Host** This `String` property contains the DNS host name or the IP address of the server.
- **HostNameType** This `UriNameType` property contains the type of the host name.
- **IsDefaultPort** This `Boolean` property indicates whether or not the port value is the default port for this scheme.
- **IsFile** This `Boolean` property indicates whether or not the URI is a file URI.
- **IsLoopBack** This `Boolean` property indicates whether or not the URI references the local host.
- **IsUnc** This `Boolean` property indicates whether or not the URI is a universal naming convention (UNC) path.
- **LocalPath** This `String` property contains a local OS representation of a file name.
- **PathAndQuery** This `String` property contains the `AbsolutePath` and `Query` properties separated by a question mark (?).
- **Port** This `Integer` property contains the port number for the URI.
- **Query** This `String` property contains a query part of the URI.
- **Scheme** This `String` property contains the protocol of the URI.
- **Segments** This `String()` property contains an array of segments for the URI.
- **UserEscaped** Indicates that the URI string escaped before the `Uri` instance was created.
- **UserInfo** This `String` property contains the user name, password, and other user-specific information associated with the URI.

The following example shows how to use some of these properties (see also Figure 4.27):

```
'-------------------------------------------------------------
' .NET Uri Class usage example
'-------------------------------------------------------------

Imports System
Imports System.Net
Imports System.IO

Module Module1

Sub Main()

 Dim MainURI As New Uri("http://www.mysite.com/stocks.asp?symbol=IBM")
 Dim I

  With MainURI

    Console.WriteLine("AbsolutePath  = " & .AbsolutePath)
    Console.WriteLine("AbsoluteUri   = " & .AbsoluteUri)
    Console.WriteLine("Authority     = " & .Authority)
    Console.WriteLine("Host          = " & .Host)
    Console.WriteLine("IsDefaultPort = " & .IsDefaultPort)
    Console.WriteLine("IsUnc         = " & .IsUnc)
    Console.WriteLine("Port          = " & .Port)
    Console.WriteLine("Query         = " & .Query)
    Console.WriteLine("Scheme        = " & .Scheme)
    Console.WriteLine("Segments")

    For I = 0 To .Segments.GetUpperBound(0)
     Console.WriteLine(ControlChars.Tab & I & _
      ControlChars.Tab & .Segments(I))
    Next

  End With

End Sub

End Module
```

```
AbsolutePath   = /stocks.asp
AbsoluteUri    = http://www.mysite.com/stocks.asp?symbol=IBM
Authority      = www.mysite.com
Host           = www.mysite.com
IsDefaultPort  = True
IsUnc          = False
Port           = 80
Query          = ?symbol=IBM
Scheme         = http
Segments
         0          /
         1          stocks.asp
```

FIGURE 4.27   Using some of the properties of the Uri class

The following is a list of methods of the Uri class.

- **CheckHostName(*String*) method** Use this to determine whether or not the specified host name is valid, but it does not provide a host name lookup to find out if the specified host exists. This method returns one of the host name types, defined in the URIHostNameType enumeration:
  - Basic The host is set, but the type cannot be determined;
  - Dns The host name is a domain name system (DNS)-style host name;
  - IPv4 The host name is an internet protocol (IP) version 4 host address;
  - IPv6 The host name is an internet protocol (IP) version 6 host address;
  - Unknown The type of the host name is not supplied.
- **CheckSchemeName(*String*) method** Determines whether or not the specified scheme is valid according to RFC 2396. The scheme name must begin with a letter, and must contain only letters, digits, and the characters ".", "+" or "-".
- **FromHex(*Char*) method** Converts the hexadecimal digit (0–9, a–f, A–F) to the decimal value (0–15).
- **GetLeftPart(*UriPartial*) method** Returns the specified path of a URI. In this method we specify one of the UriPartial values and it will return the result. The following UriPartial values can be used:
  - Scheme has the scheme delimiter added;
  - Authority does not have the path delimiter added;
  - Path includes any delimiters in the original URI up to the query or fragment delimiter.

The following example shows how to use the GetLeftPart method (see also Figure 4.28):

```
'-----------------------------------------------------------
' .NET Uri Class usage example
'-----------------------------------------------------------

Imports System
Imports System.Net
Imports System.IO
```

```
Module Module1


  Sub Main()

    Dim Path As String = "http://www.mysite.com/stocks.asp?symbol=IBM"
    Dim MainURI As New Uri(Path)

    With MainURI

      Console.WriteLine("Scheme    = " _
        & .GetLeftPart(UriPartial.Scheme))
      Console.WriteLine("Path      = " _
        & .GetLeftPart(UriPartial.Path))
      Console.WriteLine("Authority = " _
        & .GetLeftPart(UriPartial.Authority))

    End With

  End Sub

End Module
```

```
Scheme    = http://
Path      = http://www.mysite.com/stocks.asp
Authority = http://www.mysite.com
```

FIGURE 4.28 Using the GetLeftPart method

- **HexEscape(*Char*) method** Converts a specified character into its hexadecimal equivalent.
- **HexUnescape(*String*, *Integer*) method** Converts a specified hexadecimal representation of a character to the character.
- **IsHexDigit(Char) methods** Checks whether or not a specified character is a valid hexadecimal digit.
- **MakeRelative(*Uri*) method** Finds the difference between two Uri instances.

The UriBuilder class is used to modify a Uri class instance. It provides access to the following properties of the URI.

- **Fragment** Used to get or set the fragment portion of the URI.
- **Host** Used to get or set the domain name system (DNS) host name or IP address of a server.
- **Password** Used to get or set the password associated with the user accessing the URI.
- **Path** Used to get or set the path to the resource referenced by the URI.

- **Port** Used to get or set the port number of the URI.
- **Query** Used to get or set any query information included in the URI.
- **Scheme** Used to get or set the scheme name of the URI.
- **Uri** Used to get the Uri instance constructed by the specified UriBuilder instance.
- **UserName** Used to get or set the user name associated with the user accessing the URI.

To create an instance of the UriBuilder from the existing instance of the Uri, we use the following constructor:

```
'----------------------------------------------------------------
' .NET Uri Class usage example
'----------------------------------------------------------------


Imports System
Imports System.Net
Imports System.IO


Module Module1


Sub Main()


 Dim Path As String = "http://www.mysite.com/stocks.asp?symbol=IBM"
 Dim MainURI As New Uri(Path)
 Dim Builder As New UriBuilder(MainURI)


  With Builder


 '
 '    ...
 '


   End With


 End Sub


End Module
```

Talking about helper classes, we should also mention the HTTPUtility class implemented in the System.Web namespace. It provides methods for URI encoding and decoding when processing web requests.

4.6 Conclusion

In this chapter we have covered three major topics – streams, file system access, and networking functions. We have learned about two namespaces – the `System.IO` namespace, which provides us with streams and file system access, and the `System.Net` namespace, which contains classes used to create client and server applications that use internet-based data exchange. Then we discussed streams and related classes – `BufferedStream`, `FileStream`, `MemoryStream`, `NetworkStream`, and `CryptoStream`. After this we introduced the concept of readers and writers and learned about `Binary`, `Text`, `Stream`, and `String` readers and writers.

Next, we switched our attention to file system access and discussed the main classes used to access files and directories – `FileSystemInfo`, `FileInfo`, `DirectoryInfo`, `File`, and `Path`.

In the second part of the chapter, we spent time discussing the network functionality available in the .NET Framework class library. We have seen the different classes that comprise the `System.Net` namespace and their purposes. We provided detailed information about the `WebRequest` and `WebResponse` classes and their descendants and created many examples that illustrate how to use them. We finished this chapter with a discussion of the helper classes that can be used to manipulate the contents of URIs – the `Uri` and `UriBuilder` classes.

In the next chapter, we will finish our tour around the .NET Framework class library started in Chapter 3. We will discuss several useful classes and other types that are available in the class library.

chapter 5

The Microsoft .NET Framework class library – more goodies

- System.Math class
- System.Random class
- Date and time support
- Formatting date and time values
- Access to the environment

In this chapter, we will end our tour around the .NET Framework class library, started back in Chapter 3. Here we will discuss several useful classes and other types that are available in the class library. We will discuss the following topics.

- The `System.Math` class, which provides constants and static methods for trigonometric, logarithmic, and other common mathematical functions.
- The `System.Random` class, which serves as a pseudo-random number generator.
- Date and time support in the .NET class library, which is available by means of the `System.DateTime`, `System.TimeSpan`, and `System.TimeZone` structures.
- Formatting date and time values.
- The `System.Environment` class, which provides information about the current environment and platform.
- The `OperatingSystem` class, which is used to obtain version and platform information for the platform on which the process is running.
- Accessing the registry.
- Getting information about processes using the `System.Diagnostics` namespace.
- The `System.GUID` structure.

We will start with the `System.Math` class and its constants and methods used for mathematical operations.

5.1 System.Math class

The `System.Math` class provides constants and static methods for trigonometric, logarithmic, and other common mathematical functions. Beside the constants, there is one that specifies the natural logarithmic base – E – and one that specifies the ratio of the circumference of a circle to its diameter – PI.

The following are the common mathematical functions implemented in the `Math` class:

- **Abs()** Returns the absolute value of a specified number. There are overloaded methods for `Decimal`, `Double`, `Short`, `Integer`, `Long`, `SByte`, and `Single` arguments.
- **Ceiling(*Double*)** Returns the smallest whole number that is greater than or equal to the specified number. The rounding performed by this method is called rounding towards positive infinity.
- **Exp(*Double*)** Returns e raised to the specified power. To calculate powers of other bases, we should use the Pow method.
- **Floor(*Double*)** Returns the largest whole number that is less than or equal to the specified number. The rounding performed by this method is called rounding towards negative infinity.

- **Max()** Returns the larger of two specified numbers. There are overloaded methods for `Byte`, `Decimal`, `Double`, `Short`, `Integer`, `Long`, `SByte`, `Single`, `UInt16`, `UInt32`, and `UInt64` arguments.

- **Min()** Returns the smaller of two specified numbers. There are overloaded methods for `Byte`, `Decimal`, `Double`, `Short`, `Integer`, `Long`, `SByte`, `Single`, `UInt16`, `UInt32`, and `UInt64` arguments.

- **Pow(*Double*, *Double*)** Raises a specified number to the specified power.

- **Round()** Returns the number nearest the specified value. Using the overloaded methods we can also specify the level of precision.

- **Sign()** Returns the sign of a number. There are overloaded versions for `Decimal`, `Double`, `Short`, `Integer`, `Long`, `SByte`, and `Single` arguments.

- **Sqrt(*Double*)** Returns the square root of a specified number.

The following example shows how to use some of the mathematical functions defined in the `Math` class:

```
'----------------------------------------
' .NET Math Class usage example
'----------------------------------------
Imports System
Imports System.Math

Module Module1

  Sub Main()

    Console.WriteLine(Math.Sqrt(81))        ' returns 9
    Console.WriteLine(Math.Abs(-3.14))      ' returns 3.14
    Console.WriteLine(Math.Round(Math.PI))  ' returns 3
    Console.WriteLine(Math.Ceiling(-3.4567)) ' returns -3
    Console.WriteLine(Math.Floor(3.4567))   ' returns 3

  End Sub

End Module
```

Here is the list of trigonometric functions defined in the `Math` class:

- **Acos(*Double*)** Returns an angle (as a *Double* value), the cosine of which is a specified number. Multiply the return value by `180/Math.PI` to convert from radians to degrees.

- **Asin(*Double*)** Returns an angle (as a *Double* value), the sine of which is a specified number. Multiply the return value by `180/Math.PI` to convert from radians to degrees.

- **Atan(*Double*)** Returns an angle (as a *Double* value), the tangent of which is a specified number. Multiply the return value by 180/Math.PI to convert from radians to degrees.
- **Atan2(*Double*, *Double*)** Returns an angle (as a *Double* value), the tangent of which is the quotient of two specified numbers.
- **Cos(*Double*)** Returns the cosine (as a *Double* value) for the specified angle. Multiply by Math.PI/180 to convert degrees to radians.
- **Cosh(*Double*)** Returns the hyperbolic cosine (as a *Double* value) for the specified number. Multiply by Math.PI/180 to convert degrees to radians.
- **Sin(*Double*)** Returns the sine (as a *Double* value) for the specified angle. Multiply by Math.PI/180 to convert degrees to radians.
- **Sinh(*Double*)** Returns the hyperbolic cosine (as a *Double* value) for the specified number. Multiply by Math.PI/180 to convert degrees to radians.
- **Tan(*Double*)** Returns the tangent (as a *Double* value) for the specified number. Multiply by Math.PI/180 to convert degrees to radians.
- **Tanh(*Double*)** Returns the hyperbolic tangent (as a *Double* value) for the specified number. Multiply by Math.PI/180 to convert degrees to radians.

```
'----------------------------------------
' .NET Math Class usage example
'----------------------------------------

Imports System
Imports System.Math

Module Module1

 Sub Main()

  Console.WriteLine(Math.Asin(0.5) * 180 / Math.PI) ' returns 30
  Console.WriteLine(Math.Acos(0.5) * 180 / Math.PI) ' returns 60
  Console.WriteLine(Math.Sin(45 * Math.PI / 180))    ' returns 0.707
  Console.WriteLine(Math.Tan(45 * Math.PI / 180))    ' 1

 End Sub

End Module
```

There are also two logarithmic functions in the Math class. The Log(*Double*) or Log(*Double*, *Double*) function returns the logarithm of a specified number, while the Log10(*Double*) function returns the base 10 logarithm of a specified number.

To generate pseudo-random numbers we can use methods implemented in the System.Random class – this is the topic of our next section.

5.2 System.Random class

The System.Random class serves as a pseudo-random number generator. We can use this class to get a random number – either decimal or whole random numbers. To generate such numbers we can use the Next() method to return a random number, NextDouble() to return a Double random number between 0.0 and 1.0 (the number will be greater than or equal to 0.0 and less than 1.0), or NextBytes(*Byte()*) to fill the elements of a specified array of bytes with random numbers. The following example illustrates how to use these methods to generate random numbers – both Double and Integers:

```
'----------------------------------------
' .NET System.Random Class Demo
'----------------------------------------

Imports System

Module Cons

 Sub Main()

    Dim I As Integer
    Dim Rand As System.Random = New System.Random

    Console.WriteLine("Next(0-99)" & Constants.vbTab _
      & "NextDouble")
    For I=0 to 9

     Console.WriteLine(Rand.Next(0,100) & Constants.vbTab _
      & Constants.vbTab & Rand.NextDouble)

    Next

    Console.ReadLine()

  End Sub

 End Module
```

This program generates the output shown in Figure 5.1.

```
Next(0-100)     NextDouble
16              0.861726166616066
62              0.307511231539543
21              0.88650934206625
2               0.150887788343657
27              0.0439550066571473
9               0.991797787599171
40              0.63503196539126
96              0.0869611958446732
14              0.0847616051718414
2               0.422731975290334
```

FIGURE 5.1   Using Next() and NextDouble() methods to generate random numbers

5.3 Date and time support

The .NET Framework class library provides extensive support for dates and times by means of the following structures.

- **System.DateTime Structure** Used to represent a date and time of day.
- **System.TimeSpan Structure** Used to represent arbitrary time spans.
- **System.TimeZone Structure** Provides support for multiple time zones and includes support for daylight saving time.

In the following sections we will look at these structures in more detail.

DateTime structure

This structure (value type) can be used to represent a date and time of day. It contains a number of methods to work with DateTime values. The DateTime represents dates and times that range between MinValue and MaxValue constants. The MinValue constant is 00:00:00 (12:00:00 AM, 1/1/0001 Common Era) and the MaxValue constant is 9999-12-31 23:59:59.

To get the current date and time, we use the Now property, while the Today property contains the current date. The following code shows how to use these properties:

```
'----------------------------------------
' .NET DateTime usage example
'----------------------------------------

Imports System

Module Module1

Sub Main()

Dim DT As DateTime
```

```
      Console.WriteLine(DT.Now & Constants.vbCRLF & DT.Today)
      Console.ReadLine()

   End Sub

 End Module
```

To split a `DateTime` value into its parts, we use the properties, which have self-explanatory names such as `Year`, `Month`, `Day`, `DayOfWeek`, `DayOfYear`, `Hour`, `Minute`, `Second`, and so on. The following example shows how to use these properties:

```
'----------------------------------------
' .NET DateTime usage example
'----------------------------------------

Imports System

Module Module1

 Sub Main()

  Dim DT As DateTime

  DT = Now

  Console.WriteLine(Constants.vbCRLF & DT & Constants.vbCRLF)

  With DT
   ShowOneLine("Year      ", .Year)
   ShowOneLine("Month     ", .Month)
   ShowOneLine("Day       ", .Day)
   ShowOneLine("DayOfWeek ", .DayOfWeek)
   ShowOneLine("DayOfYear ", .DayOfYear)
   ShowOneLine("Hour      ", .Hour)
   ShowOneLine("Minute    ", .Minute)
   ShowOneLine("Second    ", .Second)
  End With
  Console.ReadLine()

 End Sub

 Sub ShowOneLine(Part1 As String, Part2 As String)

   Console.WriteLine(Part1 & Constants.vbTab & Part2)

 End Sub

End Module
```

```
2001-08-16 11:12:11

Year          2001
Month         8
Day           16
DayOfWeek     4
DayOfYear     228
Hour          11
Minute        12
Second        11
```

FIGURE 5.2   The DateTime values split into parts

Figure 5.2 shows the output, which has the whole DateTime value as well as its parts.

The DateTime values are culture-dependent. Here is an example of how different cultures affects the formatting of date (see also Figure 5.3):

```
'----------------------------------------
' .NET DateTime usage example
'----------------------------------------

Imports System.Globalization
Imports System.Threading

Module Module1

Sub Main()

  Dim DT      As DateTime
  Dim Cult    As CultureInfo
  Dim Cults() As String = {"EN-US", "EN-GB", "FR-CH"}
  Dim I       As Integer

  DT = Today

  For I=0 to Cults.GetUpperBound(0)

  Cult = New CultureInfo(Cults(I))
  Thread.CurrentThread.CurrentCulture = Cult
  Console.WriteLine(Cults(I) & " : " & Constants.vbTab & DT)
  Cult = Nothing

  Next

  Console.ReadLine()

 End Sub

End Module
```

```
EN-US :        2001-08-16
EN-GB :        16/08/2001
FR-CH :        16.08.2001
```

FIGURE 5.3   Different cultures represent dates in different ways and DateTime values reflect this

The DaysInMonth(*Integer*, *Integer*) method returns the number of days in the specified month of the specified year. The IsLeapYear(*Integer*) method allows us to find out if the specified year is a leap year. For a leap year, the value returned for the second month (February) will be 29, while it will be 28 for the ordinal year.

The DateTime structure supports several AddXXX methods shown below.

- **Add(*TimeSpan*)** Adds the value of the TimeSpan instance to the DateTime instance.
- **AddYears(*Integer*)** Adds the specified number of years to the DateTime instance.
- **AddMonths(*Integer*)** Adds the specified number of months to the DateTime instance.
- **AddDays(*Double*)** Adds the specified number of days to the DateTime instance.
- **AddHours(*Double*)** Adds the specified number of hours to the DateTime instance.
- **AddMinutes(*Double*)** Adds the specified number of minutes to the DateTime instance.
- **AddSeconds(*Double*)** Adds the specified number of seconds to the DateTime instance.
- **AddMilliseconds(*Double*)** Adds the specified number of milliseconds to the DateTime instance.
- **AddTicks(*Long*)** Adds the specified number of ticks to the DateTime instance.

The following example shows how to use the AddYears methods and IsLeapYear method to get a list of all leap years in XX century (see also Figure 5.4):

```
'----------------------------------------
' .NET DateTime usage example
'----------------------------------------

Imports System

Module Module 1

  Sub Main()
```

```
Dim DT As DateTime
Dim I As Integer
DT = "01/01/1900"
Console.WriteLine("Leap years in XX century")
For I = 1 To 100
  If DT.IsLeapYear(DT.Year) Then
   Console.WriteLine(DT.Year)
  End If
  DT = DT.AddYears(1)
Next


End Sub


End Module
```

```
Leap years in XX century
          1904
          1908
          1912
          1916
          1920
          1924
          1928
          1932
          1936
          1940
          1944
          1948
          1952
          1956
          1960
          1964
          1968
          1972
          1976
          1980
          1984
          1988
          1992
          1996
```

FIGURE 5.4   A list of leap years can be produced by means of the AddYear and IsLeapYear methods

Several ToXXX methods provide conversions of the DateTime value into different formats.

- **ToFileFormat()** Converts the DateTime value to the format of the local system file time.

- **ToLocalTime()** Converts the DateTime value to the local time.

- **ToLongDateString()** Converts the DateTime value to the long date string format.

- **ToLongTimeString()** Converts the DateTime value to the long time string format.

- **ToOADate()** Converts the DateTime value to the format for the OLE automation.

- **ToShortDateString()** Converts the DateTime value to the short date string format.

- **ToShortTimeString()** Converts the DateTime value to the short time string format.

- **ToUniversalTime()** Converts the DateTime value to UTC time.

The following example shows how the ToXXX methods affect date and time formatting (see also Figure 5.5).

```
'----------------------------------------
' .NET DateTime usage example
'----------------------------------------

Imports System

Module Module1

  Sub Main()

    Dim DT As DateTime
    DT = Now
    Console.WriteLine("   ToFileTime  = " & DT.ToFileTime)
    Console.WriteLine("   ToLocalTime = " & DT.ToLocalTime)
    Console.WriteLine("   ToLongDate  = " & DT.ToLongDateString)
    Console.WriteLine("   ToLongTime  = " & DT.ToLongTimeString)
    Console.WriteLine("   ToString    = " & DT.ToString)
    Console.WriteLine("   ToShortDate = " & DT.ToShortDateString)
    Console.WriteLine("   ToShortTime = " & DT.ToShortTimeString)
    Console.WriteLine("   ToUTCTime   = " & DT.ToUniversalTime)
    Console.WriteLine()

  End Sub

End Module
```

```
ToFileTime  = 126480746372834176
ToLocalTime = 20-Oct-01 22:03:57
ToLongDate  = 20 October, 2001
ToLongTime  = 20:03:57
ToString    = 20-Oct-01 20:03:57
ToShortDate = 20-Oct-01
ToShortTime = 8:03 PM
ToUTCTime   = 20-Oct-01 18:03:57
```

FIGURE 5.5 ToXXX methods affect date and time formats in different ways

The DateTime structure implements the IComparable, IFormattable, and IConvertible interfaces.

System.TimeSpan structure

The System.TimeSpan structure is used to represent arbitrary time spans. The value stored in an instance of this structure is the number of "ticks" contained in the instance. Each tick is equal to 100 nanoseconds – the smallest unit of time that can be specified.

This structure contains properties and methods that can be used in our time manipulation code. To convert from different values to a TimeSpan type, we can use the following FromXXX methods.

- **FromDays(*Double*)** Converts the number of days to TimeSpan type.
- **FromHours(*Double*)** Converts the number of hours to TimeSpan type.
- **FromMilliseconds(*Double*)** Converts the number of milliseconds to TimeSpan type.
- **FromMinutes(*Double*)** Converts the number of minutes to TimeSpan type.
- **FromSeconds(*Double*)** Converts the number of seconds to TimeSpan type.
- **FromTicks(*Long*)** Converts the number of ticks to TimeSpan type.

Several methods in the System.TimeSpan structure allow us to get the number of days, hours, and so on stored in the TimeSpan type:

- **Days** Returns the number of whole days stored the TimeSpan type. To get the number of whole and fractional days, use the TotalDays method.
- **Hours** Returns the number of whole hours stored in the TimeSpan type. To get the number of whole and fractional hours, use the TotalHours method.
- **Milliseconds** Returns the number of whole milliseconds stored in the TimeSpan type. To get the number of whole and fractional milliseconds, use the TotalMilliseconds method.
- **Minutes** Returns the number of whole minutes stored in the TimeSpan type. To get the number of whole and fractional minutes, use the TotalMinutes method.

- **Seconds** Returns the number of whole seconds stored in the TimeSpan type. To get the number of whole and fractional seconds, use the TotalSeconds method.
- **Ticks** Returns the number of ticks stored in the TimeSpan type.

The following example shows how to find the number of hours in the specified number of days:

```
'----------------------------------------
' .NET TimeSpan usage example
'----------------------------------------

Imports System

Module Module1

Sub Main()

  Dim TS As TimeSpan
  TS = TimeSpan.FromDays(10)
  Console.WriteLine(TS.TotalHours)   ' 240

End Sub

End Module
```

The TimeSpan structure implements the IComparable interface.

System.TimeZone structure

The System.TimeZone structure provides support for multiple time zones and includes support for daylight saving time. To get a current time zone, we use the CurrentTimeZone property. The DaylightName property contains the daylight saving time zone name, such as "W. Europe Daylight Time". The StandardName property contains the standard time zone name, such as "W. Europe Standard Time". The GetDaylightChanges(*Integer*) method returns an array that contains the daylight saving time periods in a given year. This array contains elements of DaylightTime type. Here is an example of how to use this method to find the period of daylight changes for the year 2001 (see also Figure 5.6):

```
'----------------------------------------
' .NET TimeZone usage example
'----------------------------------------

Imports System
Imports System.Globalization

Module Module1
```

```
Sub Main()

  Dim DLT As DaylightTime
  Dim TZ As TimeZone
  TZ = TimeZone.CurrentTimeZone
  DLT = TZ.GetDaylightChanges(2001)
  Console.WriteLine(DLT.Start & ":" & DLT.End)

End Sub

End Nodule
```

25-Mar-01 02:00:00<-->28-Oct-01 03:00:00

FIGURE 5.6　Finding daylight changing time using `DaylightTime`

The `IsDaylightSavingTime(`*DateTime*`)` or `IsDaylightSavingTime(`*DateTime*, *DaylightTime*`)` method allows us to find if a specified time is within a daylight saving period.

5.4　Formatting date and time values

In Chapter 3, we saw how to use the various formatting specifiers to produce the string representation of values in different formats. Here we will look at how to use the date and time format strings to represent the `DateTime` data type in various formats. Without providing much reference information about the format specifiers available, let's look at an example that shows how to use each format specifier available – its output shows you exactly what to expect in each case (see also Figure 5.7):

```
'----------------------------------------
' .NET DateTime formatting example
'----------------------------------------

Imports System

Module Module1

Sub Main()

    Dim Formats() As String = _
      {"Short date              : {0:d}", _
       "Long  date              : {0:D}", _
       "Long  date/Short time    : {0:f}", _
```

```
                "Long  date/Long  time      : {0:F}", _
                "Short date/Short time       : {0:g}", _
                "Short date/Long  time       : {0:G}", _
                "Month day                   : {0:M}", _
                "RFC1123 format              : {0:R}", _
                "Sortable date/time          : {0:s}", _
                "Short time                  : {0:t}", _
                "Long  time                  : {0:T}", _
                "Sortable date/universal time : {0:u}", _
                "Sortable universal date/time : {0:U}", _
                "Year/month                  : {0:Y}"}

           Dim I As Integer

           Dim Value As New DateTime()
           Value = Now

           For I = 0 To Formats.GetUpperBound(0)
            Console.WriteLine(Formats(I), Value)
           Next

        End Sub

     End Module


Short date                  : 26-Oct-01
Long   date                 : 26 October, 2001
Long   date/Short time      : 26 October, 2001 11:12 PM
Long   date/Long  time      : 26 October, 2001 23:12:45
Short date/Short time       : 26-Oct-01 11:12 PM
Short date/Long   time      : 26-Oct-01 23:12:45
Month day                   : October 26
RFC1123 format              : Fri, 26 Oct 2001 23:12:45 GMT
Sortable date/time          : 2001-10-26T23:12:45
Short time                  : 11:12 PM
Long   time                 : 23:12:45
Sortable date/universal time : 2001-10-26 23:12:45Z
Sortable universal date/time : 26 October, 2001 21:12:45
Year/month                  : October, 2001
```

FIGURE 5.7 Using different DateTime format specifiers

If the formats provided by the standard format specifiers are not enough, we can create our own patterns to format the DateTime data type.

The following example shows various customized date and time format patterns (see also Figure 5.8):

```
'---------------------------------------
' .NET DateTime formatting example
'---------------------------------------

Imports System

Module Module1

Sub Main()

  Dim Formats() As String = _
   {"{0:dd-MMMM-yy}", _
    "{0:dddd, dd-MMM}", _
    "{0:yyyy, gg}", _
    "{0:hh.mm.ss tt}", _
    "{0:HH.mm.ss.ff}", _
    "{0:HH.mm.ss zzzz}"}

  Dim I As Integer

  Dim Value As New DateTime()
  Value = Now

  For I = 0 To Formats.GetUpperBound(0)
    Console.WriteLine(Formats(I), Value)
  Next

 End Sub

 End Module


26-October-01
Friday, 26-Oct
2001, A.D.
11.24.32 PM
23.24.32.75
23.24.32 +02:00
```

FIGURE 5.8 Using customized date and time formats

The last class that we will discuss in this chapter is the System.Environment class.

5.5 Access to the environment

The `System.Environment` class provides information about the current environment and platform. It contains the following properties and methods, which can be used in our applications:

- **CommandLine** This property returns the `String` that contains the command line supplied for this process.
- **CurrentDirectory** Indicates the directory (`String` type) from which this process was started.
- **ExitCode** Specifies the exit code for this process as an `Integer` value.
- **MachineName** Contains the `String` with the name of the computer you are using.
- **NewLine** Contains the new line `String` for this environment.
- **OSVersion** Contains an `OperatingSystem` object.
- **StackTrace** This property returns the current stack trace information as a `String`.
- **SystemDirectory** This property is a `String` that contains the fully qualified path of the system directory – for example, `C:\WINNT\System32`.
- **TickCount** This property returns the number of milliseconds that have elapsed since the system started, as an `Integer` value.
- **UserDomainName** This property contains the name of the application domain for the current user (`String` type).
- **UserInteractive** This property indicates whether or not the current process is running in user interactive mode. This property contains `false` if the process is running as a service process or from inside a web application.
- **Version** This property returns the `Version` object for this assembly – this is the version of .NET Framework.
- **WorkingSet** This property returns the amount of physical memory mapped to the process context, as a Long value.
- **Exit(*Integer*) method** Terminates the process with the specified exit code.
- **ExpandEnvironmentVariables(*String*) method** Returns the names of specified environment variables as a `String`.
- **GetCommandLineArgs() method** Returns a string array of the command line arguments.
- **GetEnvironmentVariable(String) method** Returns the value of the specified environment variable as a `String`.
- **GetEnvironmentVariables() method** Returns all environment variables and their values as an `IDictionary` object.
- **GetFolderPath(Environment.SpecialFolder) method** Returns the path to the specified special system folder as a `String`.
- **GetLogicalDrives() method** Returns a string array that contains the names of the logical drives for your computer.

The following example shows how to use the Environment class (see also Figure 5.9):

```
'----------------------------------------
' .NET Environment Class usage example
'----------------------------------------


Imports System
Imports System.Collections

Module Module1

Sub Main()

  Dim E As Environment
  Dim I As Integer
  Dim DEnum As IDictionaryEnumerator


  With E

'--------------------------------------------
' Return platform and version information
'--------------------------------------------
    With .OSVersion
      Console.WriteLine(.ToString())
      Console.WriteLine(.Platform)
      Console.WriteLine(.Version.Major & "." & .Version.Minor)
    End With
'--------------------------------------------
' Get list of logical drives
'--------------------------------------------
    For I = 0 to .GetLogicalDrives.GetUpperBound(0)
      Console.WriteLine(.GetLogicalDrives(I))
    Next
'--------------------------------------------
' Get command line arguments
' Args[0] is the name of the exe-file
' --------------------------------------------
    For I = 0 to .GetCommandLineArgs.GetUpperBound(0)
      Console.WriteLine(.GetCommandLineArgs(I))
    Next
'--------------------------------------------
' Show Environment Variables
'--------------------------------------------
```

```
DEnum = .GetEnvironmentVariables.GetEnumerator
While DEnum.MoveNext()
  Console.WriteLine(DEnum.Key & "=" & DEnum.Value)
End While

  End With

  End Sub

End Module
```

```
C:\WINNT\System32\cmd.exe                                          _ □ ×
C:\Net_Book\Ch05\Code>env
Microsoft Windows NT 5.0.2195.0
2
5.0
A:\
C:\
D:\
env
SystemDrive=C:
USERPROFILE=C:\Documents and Settings\Administrator.TERRA
INCLUDE=C:\Program Files\Microsoft.NET\FrameworkSDK\include\;C:\Program Files\Mi
crosoft Visual Studio.NET\Vc7\include\;C:\Program Files\Microsoft.NET\FrameworkS
DK\include\
Path=C:\Program Files\Microsoft.NET\FrameworkSDK\Bin\;C:\Program Files\Microsoft
 Visual Studio.NET\Vc7\bin\;C:\Program Files\Microsoft Visual Studio.NET\Common7
\IDE\;C:\WINNT\Microsoft.NET\Framework\v1.0.2914\;C:\Program Files\Microsoft Vis
ual Studio.NET\Vc7\bin\;C:\Program Files\Microsoft Visual Studio.NET\Common7\IDE
\;C:\WINNT\system32;C:\WINNT;C:\WINNT\System32\Wbem;C:\Program Files\Microsoft S
QL Server\80\Tools\BINN;C:\WINNT\Microsoft.NET\Framework\v1.0.2914\;C:\Program F
iles\Microsoft.NET\FrameworkSDK\Bin;
PROMPT=$P$G
Os2LibPath=C:\WINNT\system32\os2\dll;
LOGONSERVER=\\THERION
PROCESSOR_REVISION=0806
ProgramFiles=C:\Program Files
NUMBER_OF_PROCESSORS=1
CommonProgramFiles=C:\Program Files\Common Files
TMP=C:\DOCUME~1\ADMINI~1.TER\LOCALS~1\Temp
APPDATA=C:\Documents and Settings\Administrator.TERRA\Application Data
ComSpec=C:\WINNT\system32\cmd.exe
PROCESSOR_IDENTIFIER=x86 Family 6 Model 8 Stepping 6, GenuineIntel
HOMEDRIVE=C:
COMPUTERNAME=THERION
OANOCACHE=1
PROCESSOR_LEVEL=6
OS=Windows_NT
SystemRoot=C:\WINNT
windir=C:\WINNT
ALLUSERSPROFILE=C:\Documents and Settings\All Users.WINNT
USERNAME=Administrator
PATHEXT=.COM;.EXE;.BAT;.CMD;.VBS;.VBE;.JS;.JSE;.WSF;.WSH
USERDOMAIN=THERION
HOMEPATH=\
PROCESSOR_ARCHITECTURE=x86
```

FIGURE 5.9   Using the Environment class

OperatingSystem class

This class is used to obtain version and platform information for the platform on which the process is running. The platform is stored in the Platform property and it is a PlatformID value that indicates the operating system. The following list shows platform identifiers that are defined in the System.PlatformID enumeration.

- **Win32NT** Indicates that the operating system is Windows NT or later. In general, this `PlatformID` indicates the server operating system.

- **Win32S** Indicates that the operating system is the 16-bit version of Windows with a Win32s extension layer. In general, this `PlatformID` indicates an unsupported operating system, and cannot be obtained by the .NET code.

- **Win32Windows** Indicates that the operating system is Windows 95 or later. In general, this `PlatformID` indicates the desktop operating system.

The version information is available via the `Version` property, which is of `Version` type. This object contains major and minor version numbers, as well as the platform revision and build number.

Accessing the registry

The `Microsoft.Win32` namespace provides two classes – the `Registry` and `RegistryKey` classes – that can be used to access the system registry. The `Registry` class is a set of `RegistryKey` type objects that are used to access the different parts of the system registry. The following list shows properties of the `Registry` class and explains how they map to the parts of the registry. All properties are of the `RegistryKey` types:

- **ClassesRoot** Maps to the HKEY_CLASSES_ROOT registry key. This area of the system registry is used to store information about classes and their properties.

- **CurrentConfig** Maps to the HKEY_CURRENT_CONFIG registry key. This area of the system registry is used to store non-user-specific hardware information.

- **CurrentUser** Maps to the HKEY_CURRENT_USER registry key. This area of the system registry is used to store information about user preferences.

- **LocalMachine** Maps to the HKEY_LOCAL_MACHINE registry key. This area of the system registry is used to store information about the local machine.

- **Users** Maps to the HKEY_USERS registry key. This area of the system registry is used to store information about the default user configuration.

- **PerfomanceData** Maps to the HKEY_PERFOMANCE_DATA registry key. This area of the system registry is used to store performance information for software components. This key is available only on the Windows NT platform.

- **DynData** Maps to the HKEY_DYN_DATA registry key. This area of the system registry is used to store dynamic data. This key is available only on the Windows NT platform.

The `RegistryKey` class represents a key-level node in the system registry and implements a set of methods to manipulate the contents of the registry. Figure 5.10 shows the system registry.

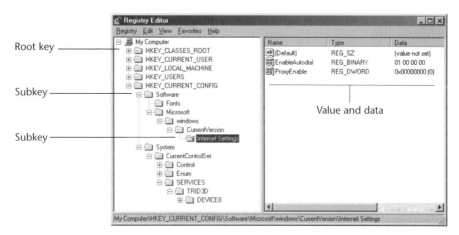

FIGURE 5.10   The system registry

Here are the properties of the RegistryKey class:

- **Name** Returns the name of the key as a String.
- **SubKeyCount** Returns the Integer number of subkeys one level deeper from the current key.
- **ValueCount** Returns the Integer number of values for this key.

Several methods of the RegistryKey class allow us to perform various operations on the system registry.

- **Close() method** Closes the key and saves its contents if it has been modified.
- **OpenSubKey(*String*) or OpenSubKey(*String*, *Boolean*) method** Opens a specified subkey with read-only or read/write access.
- **CreateSubKey(*Subkey*) method** Creates a new subkey or opens an existing one.
- **DeleteSubKey(String) or DeleteSubKey(String, Boolean) method** Deletes the specified subkey.
- **DeleteSubKeyTree(*String*) method** Deletes the specified subkey and all of its child subkeys.
- **GetSubKeyNames() method** Returns an array of Strings filled with the value names associated with this key.
- **GetValueNames() method** Returns an array of Strings that contain all the value names associated with this key.
- **SetValue(*String*, *Object*) method** Sets the specified value.
- **GetValue(*String*) or GetValue(*String*, *Object*) method** Retrieves the specified value.
- **DeleteValue(*String*) or DeleteValue(*String*, *Boolean*) method** Deletes the specified value from this key.
- **Flush() method** Writes all changes to the specified key into the registry.

The following example shows how to use the **GetSubKeyNames** method to retrieve all first-level subkeys from the **HKEY_CURRENT_USER** registry key (see also Figure 5.11).

```
'----------------------------------------
' .NET Registry class usage example
'----------------------------------------

Imports Microsoft.Win32
Imports System

Module Module1

Sub Main()

  Dim RegKey As RegistryKey = Registry.CurrentUser
  Dim SubKeys As String() = RegKey.GetSubKeyNames
  Dim I As Integer

  Console.WriteLine("Root Key : " & RegKey.Name)

  For I = 0 To SubKeys.GetUpperBound(0)
   Console.WriteLine("SubKey : " & SubKeys(I))
  Next

 End Sub

End Module
```

```
Root Key : HKEY_CURRENT_USER
        SubKey : AppEvents
        SubKey : Console
        SubKey : Control Panel
        SubKey : Environment
        SubKey : Identities
        SubKey : Keyboard Layout
        SubKey : Printers
        SubKey : RemoteAccess
        SubKey : Software
        SubKey : UNICODE Program Groups
        SubKey : Volatile Environment
```

FIGURE 5.11　Using the GetSubkeyNames method to find the first-level subkeys

The following example shows how to create a new subkey in the HKEY_CURRENT_USER\Software key and set two values of this newly created subkey (see also Figures 5.12 and 5.13):

```
'---------------------------------------
' .NET RegistryKey Class usage example
'---------------------------------------

Imports Microsoft.Win32
Imports System

 Module Module1

 Sub Main()

  Dim RegKey As RegistryKey = _
   Registry.CurrentUser.OpenSubKey("Software", True)
  Dim SubKey As String = "DotNetSoftware"
  Dim NewSubKey As RegistryKey

  With RegKey

   Console.WriteLine("Key : " & .Name)
    .CreateSubKey(SubKey)
   NewSubKey = .OpenSubKey(SubKey, True)
   Console.WriteLine("SubKey : " & NewSubKey.Name)
   NewSubKey.SetValue("Version", 1)
   NewSubKey.SetValue("Author", "Alex Fedorov")
   Console.WriteLine("Version = " & NewSubKey.GetValue("Version"))
   Console.WriteLine("Author  = " & NewSubKey.GetValue("Author"))
   NewSubKey.Close()
   .Close()

  End With

 End Sub

 End Module
```

```
Key : HKEY_CURRENT_USER\Software
SubKey : HKEY_CURRENT_USER\Software\DotNetSoftware
Version = 1
Author  = Alex Fedorov
```

FIGURE 5.12   Creating a new subkey

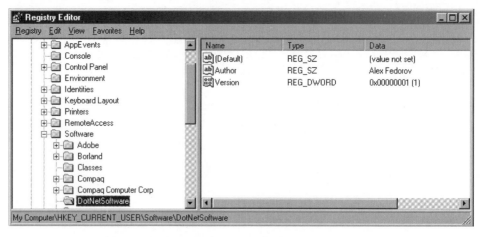

FIGURE 5.13   Creating a new subkey in the HKEY_CURRENT_USER software key and two values in it

If you need to read the values stored in your subkey, use the following code:

```
'----------------------------------------
' .NET RegistryKey Class usage example
'----------------------------------------

Imports Microsoft.Win32
Imports System

Module Module1

Sub Main()

  Dim RegKey As RegistryKey = _
    Registry.CurrentUser.OpenSubKey("Software\DotNetSoftware", True)

  With RegKey
   Console.WriteLine("Version = " & .GetValue("Version"))
   Console.WriteLine("Author  = " & .GetValue("Author"))
   .Close()

  End With

 End Sub

End Module
```

Getting information about processes

The `System.Diagnostics` namespace contains classes that are used to debug applications, trace execution of the code, and get information about the current process, as well as other processes running on the computer. In this section, we will learn how to get this information.

To get information about the current process, we use the `Process` class. This class provides access to information about the running application. Using its methods, we can start, stop, control, and monitor processes. We can also obtain such information as the set of threads, loaded modules, and amount of memory used by the process. Below is a list of the most important methods in the `Process` class.

- **`GetCurrentProcess()` method** Returns the `Process` class for the currently active process.
- **`GetProcessById(*Integer*)` or `GetProcessById(*Integer*, *String*)` method** Returns the `Process` class for the process specified by the process identificator.
- **`GetProcessByName(*String*)` or `GetProcessByName(*String*, *String*)` method** Returns the `Process` class for the process specified by its name.
- **`GetProcesses()` or `GetProcesses(String)` method** Returns an `Array` of the `Process` classes for each process that runs on the system.
- **`Start()` method** Starts the process. Overloaded versions of this method accept the `ProcessStartInfo` or application name as an argument.
- **`Kill()` method** Stops the process.
- **`CloseMainWindow()` method** Sends the close message to the process's main window.
- **`Refresh()`**. Refreshes the contents of the `Process` class.

The following properties contain information about the process:

- **`BasePriority`** Returns the base priority for the process as an `Integer` value. This can be one of the `PriorityClass` values – namely `PriorityClass.Idle`, `PriorityClass.Normal`, `PriorityClass.High`, and `PriorityClass.RealTime`.
- **`ExitCode`** Returns the value of the process's exit code when it terminates as an `Integer` value.
- **`ExitTime`** Returns the time that the process exited as a `DateTime` value.
- **`Handle`** Returns the process's handle as an `IntPtr` value.
- **`HandleCount`** Returns the number of handles opened by this process as an `Integer` value.
- **`ID`** Returns the unique identifier for the process as an `Integer` value.
- **`MainModule`** Returns the `ProcessModule` class that contains the information about the main module for this process.
- **`MainWindowHandle`** Returns the window handle for the process's main window as an `IntPtr` value.

- **MainWindowTitle** Returns the captions of the process's main window as a `String`.
- **MinWorkingSet** Used to get or set the minimum allowable working set size for the process as an `IntPtr` value.
- **MaxWorkingSet** Used to get or set the maximum allowable working set size for the process as an `IntPtr` value.
- **Modules** Returns the modules loaded by the process as a `ProcessModule Collection`.
- **NonPagedSystemMemorySize** Returns the non-paged system memory size for the process as an `Integer` value.
- **PagedMemorySize** Returns the paged memory size for the process as an `Integer` value.
- **PagedSystemMemorySize** Returns the paged system memory size for the process as an `Integer` value.
- **PeakPagedMemorySize** Returns the peak paged memory size as an `Integer` value.
- **PeakVirtualMemorySize** Returns the peak virtual memory size as an `Integer` value.
- **PeakWorkingSet** Returns the peak working set size as an `Integer` value.
- **PriorityBoostEnabled** Used to get or set a value that indicates whether or not the process priority can be boosted when its main window has the focus.
- **PriorityClass** Used to get or set the priority for the process. This can be `PriorityClass.Idle`, `PriorityClass.Normal`, `PriorityClass.High`, or `PriorityClass.RealTime`.
- **PrivateMemorySize** Returns the private memory size for the process as an `Integer` value.
- **PrivilegedProcessorTime** Returns the privileged processor time for the process as a `TimeSpan` value.
- **ProcessName** Returns the name of the process as a `String`.
- **Responding** Indicates whether or not the user interface of the process is responding.
- **StandardError** Returns an error stream for the process as a `StreamReader` object.
- **StandardInput** Returns an input stream for the process as a `StreamWriter` object.
- **StandardOutput** Returns an output stream for the process as a `StreamReader` object.
- **StartInfo** Used to get or set properties for the `Start` method – this property is of the `ProcessStartInfo` type.
- **StartTime** Returns the time when the process was started as a `DateTime` value.
- **Threads** Returns the set threads that are running in the process as a `Process ThreadCollection` object.

- **TotalProcessorTime** Returns the total processor time for this process as a TimeSpan value.
- **UserProcessorTime** Returns the user processor time for this process as a TimeSpan value.
- **VirtualMemorySize** Returns the size of the virtual memory for this process as an Integer value.
- **WorkingSet** Returns the working set for this process as an Integer value. The working set is the total amount of physical memory used by the process.

Figure 5.14 shows how some of the properties and methods of the Process class refer to other process-related classes in the System.Diagnostics namespace.

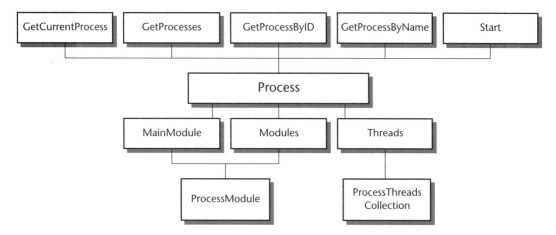

FIGURE 5.14   How some of the properties and methods of the Process class relate to process-related classes in the System.Diagnostics namespace

Now, let's look at how we can get information about the process currently running our application. Here is the code that shows how to use some of the properties we have just discussed (see also Figure 5.15):

```
'---------------------------------------
' .NET Process Class usage example
'---------------------------------------

Imports System
Imports System.Diagnostics

Module Module1

Sub Main()
```

```
Dim ThisProcess As Process
ThisProcess = Process.GetCurrentProcess()
Dim S As String

Console.WriteLine("Process ID        : " & ThisProcess.Id)
Console.WriteLine("Process Name      : " & ThisProcess.ProcessName)
Console.WriteLine("Main Module       : " & _
 ThisProcess.MainModule.ModuleName)
Console.WriteLine("Main Window Title : " & _
 ThisProcess.MainWindowTitle)
Console.WriteLine("Working set       : " & ThisProcess.WorkingSet)

S = "Base Priority    : "

Select Case ThisProcess.BasePriority
 Case 4
  S += "Idle"
 Case 8
  S += "Normal"
 Case 13
  S += "High"
 Case 24
  S += "RealTime"
End Select
S += " (" & ThisProcess.BasePriority & ")"
Console.WriteLine(S)

Console.WriteLine("Start time        : " & "{0:t}", _
 ThisProcess.StartTime)
Console.WriteLine("Total CPU time    : " & _
 ThisProcess.TotalProcessorTime.TotalSeconds.ToString)

 End Sub

 End Module
```

```
Process ID       : 1380
Process Name     : ProcessInfo
Main Module      : ProcessInfo.exe
Main Window Title :
Working set      : 10706944
Base Priority    : Normal (8)"
Start time       : 9:39 AM
Total CPU time   : 0.3204608
```

FIGURE 5.15 Using the Process class to look at information about an application that is running

As we learned above, the GetProcess method returns an Array of Process classes for each process that runs on the system. The following example shows how to get information about all of the processes (see also Figure 5.16):

```
'----------------------------------------
' .NET Process Class usage example
'----------------------------------------


Imports System
Imports System.Diagnostics

Module Module1

Sub Main()

 Dim P As Process
 Dim Processes As Process()
 Dim I As Integer
 Processes = P.GetProcesses
 For I = 0 To Processes.GetUpperBound(0)

  With Processes(I)
   Try
     Console.WriteLine(.Id.ToString.PadRight(10) & _
      .MainModule.ModuleName.PadRight(30) & _
      .ProcessName)

   Catch e As SystemException     ' if we have no access rights
                                  ' we just skip this process

   End Try
  End With

 Next

 End Sub

End Module
```

Note that in the example above we handle the System exception. We need to do this to avoid errors when we are trying to get information on some system processes that we don't have access rights to.

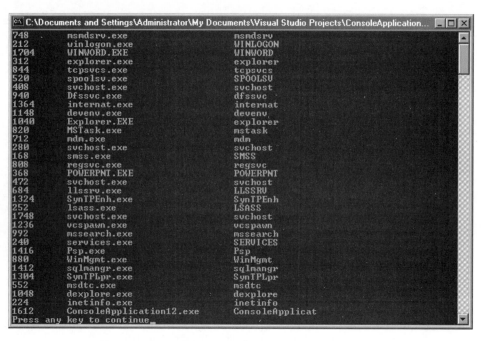

FIGURE 5.16   The information about all of the processes retrieved using the GetProcess method

Let's have another example. Here we start a new process by launching NotePad.exe and then opening a text file in it (see also Figure 5.17):

```
'----------------------------------------
' .NET Process Class usage example
'----------------------------------------


Imports System
Imports System.Diagnostics


Module Module1


  Sub Main()


    Dim NotePadProc As New Process()
    NotePadProc.EnableRaisingEvents = False
    NotePadProc.Start("notepad.exe", "c:\demo.txt")


  End Sub


End Module
```

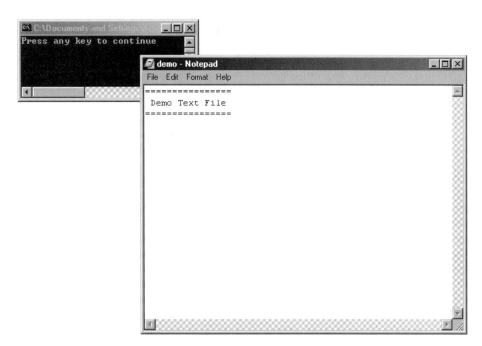

FIGURE 5.17   Using NotePad.exe and opening a text file

Using the StartInfo property of the ProcessStartInfo type, we can specify many startup parameters for the process about to be launched – arguments, window style, working directory, and so on.

The ProcessInfo class implemented in the System.Web namespace can be used to track information about processes from ASP.NET applications. The main process of interest here is the aspnet_wp.exe process, which is responsible for handling calls to ASP.NET pages (.ASPX files). The other useful class is the ProcessModel Info class, which can be used, for example, to get information about current (GetCurrentProcessInfo method) and past instances (the GetHistory method returns an array of ProcessInfo type objects) of the process.

System.GUID structure

This structure of the value type represents a globally unique indentifier (GUID) – a 128-bit integer value that can be used in cases when we need a unique identifier. The software algorithms used to generate the GUID guarantee that this value has a very low probability of being duplicated.

The following code snippet shows how to generate a new GUID value:

```
Console.WriteLine(Guid.NewGuid)
```

If we create an instance of the GUID structure, we will get an empty GUID (see also Figure 5.18):

```
'----------------------------------------
' .NET GUID Structure usage example
'----------------------------------------


Imports System

Module Module1

Sub Main()

 Dim EmptyGUID As New Guid()

  Console.WriteLine(EmptyGUID.ToString)
  Console.WriteLine(Guid.NewGuid.ToString)

End Sub

End Module
```

```
00000000-0000-0000-0000-000000000000
2f8afa64-3368-49a5-a61a-b7b7aac0f6fe
```

FIGURE 5.18   A new, empty GUID structure

To create a GUID based on user-supplied values, we can use one of its overloaded constructors:

● we can specify an array of bytes containing values that will be used to initialize the GUID;
● we can specify a string that contains a new value of the GUID;
● we can use the sequence of Integer, Short, Short, and Byte array;
● we can specify the sequence of Integer, Short, Short, and 8 Byte values;
● we can use the non-CLS-compliant constructor to specify the sequence of UInt32, UInt16, UInt16, and 8 Byte values.

The following example shows how to create a GUID value (see also Figure 5.19):

```
'----------------------------------------
' .NET GUID Structure usage example
'----------------------------------------

Imports System

Module Module1

Sub Main()

  Dim NewGUID As New Guid(128, 96, 64, 9, 8, 7, 6, 5, 4, 3, 2)
  Console.WriteLine(NewGUID.ToString)

End Sub

End Module
```

00000080-0060-0040-0908-070605040302

FIGURE 5.19 A GUID value has been created

The ToByteArray method is used to unpack the value of the GUID into a 16-element byte array. The following example shows how to use this method (see also Figure 5.20):

```
'----------------------------------------
' .NET GUID Structure usage example
'----------------------------------------

Imports System

Module Module1

Sub Main()

  Dim NewGUID As New Guid(128, 96, 64, 9, 8, 7, 6, 5, 4, 3, 2)
  Dim GUIDArray As Byte()
  Dim I As Integer

  Console.WriteLine("Original : " & NewGUID.ToString)

  Console.WriteLine("Unpacked :")
  GUIDArray = NewGUID.ToByteArray
```

```
For I = 0 To GUIDArray.GetUpperBound(0)
  Console.WriteLine(Chr(65 + I) & " : " & "0x{0:x}", GUIDArray(I))
Next

NewGUID = New Guid(GUIDArray)

Console.WriteLine("Repacked : " & NewGUID.ToString)

  End Sub

End Module
```

```
Original : 00000080-0060-0040-0908-070605040302
Unpacked :
        A : 0x80
        B : 0x0
        C : 0x0
        D : 0x0
        E : 0x60
        F : 0x0
        G : 0x40
        H : 0x0
        I : 0x9
        J : 0x8
        K : 0x7
        L : 0x6
        M : 0x5
        N : 0x4
        O : 0x3
        P : 0x2
Repacked : 00000080-0060-0040-0908-070605040302
```

FIGURE 5.20   Unpacking the GUID into a byte array using the `ToByteArray` method

5.6 Conclusion

In this chapter we discussed several useful classes and other types that are available in the .NET Framework class library.

- We learned how to use the constant and static methods of the `System.Math` class to perform trigonometric, logarithmic, and other common mathematical functions.

- We discussed how to use the pseudo-random number generator implemented in the `System.Random` class.

- We learned about date and time support in the .NET class library and discussed the `System.DateTime`, `System.TimeSpan`, and `System.TimeZone` structures.

- After this we considered an overview of how we can use standard and customized formats for formatting date and time values.

- We discussed how to use the `System.Environment` class, which provides information about the current environment and platform, and the `OperatingSystem` class, which is used to obtain version and platform information for the platform on which the process is running.
- We learned about the two classes in the `Microsoft.Win32` namespace – the `Registry` and `RegistryKey` classes – that can be used to access the system registry.
- We discussed how to get information about the current process and other processes running in the system and how to launch processes using the classes provided by the `System.Diagnostics` namespace.
- We learned how to manage GUIDs using the `System.GUID` structure.

This chapter ends our tour around the .NET Framework class library. We have a lot of information with which to start to create Windows and web applications. In the next chapter, we will begin to learn about the ASP.NET and web forms – two technologies that enable web application development under .NET.

chapter 6

ASP.NET and web forms

- How ASP.NET works

- System.Web namespace

- ASP.NET applications

- ASP applications configuration files

- Web forms pages

- Control class

- Page class

- Practice

- Web forms' internals

In this chapter we will learn how to use Microsoft .NET to create web applications with the help of two technologies – Active Server Pages .NET (ASP.NET) and web forms. Microsoft Active Server Pages is a very popular and widely used technology to create dynamic websites. Currently ASP provides a very simple object model with limited access to the underlying operating system. Every time we need to do something, we either struggle with existing COM objects or create our own, and the server-side code that we put on ASP pages is interpreted.

ASP.NET is not just the new version of ASP – it is a completely re-architectured technology for creating dynamic, web-based applications. ASP.NET pages use the .ASPX extension, contrary to the .ASP extension used by ASP pages. We can use ASP and ASP.NET pages on the same website. This simplifies development and migration and allows us to use some of the existing code without rewriting.

ASP.NET contains a host of new features – the following list shows only the main ones:

- **Multiple languages support** We are no longer limited to VBScript and JScript to create our server code. Now, ASP.NET provides a true language-neutral compiled environment. To create our ASP.NET pages, we can use Visual Basic, C#, C++, and JScript.NET, as well as .NET languages provided by third-party vendors.

- **Increased performance** ASP.NET code is compiled. When you request a web page for the first time, the CLR compiles the code inside it and stores a cached copy of the compiled result. This copy is used in subsequent requests to this page.

- **Powerful object model** ASP.NET contains a huge object model (found in the System.Web namespace and its secondary namespaces) that includes classes that envelope the HTTP request and response, used to access the server-side utilities and processes, as well as classes for cookies manipulation, output cache control, file transfer, and so on. Also, in ASP.NET code we can use thousands of classes from the Microsoft .NET Framework class library – most of the classes described in the previous three chapters.

- **Server controls** ASP.NET provides server controls that simplify the creation of web pages. Server controls automatically maintain their state and expose object models that allow us to manipulate them from our ASP.NET code.

- **Improved security** ASP.NET provides several methods of authentication – Windows (this is the only type of authentication available in ASP), basic, digest, or integrated Windows authentication, passport, forms and client certificates, as well as enabling account impersonation.

- **Greater scalability** Session state in ASP.NET can be maintained in a separate process on a separate machine or database. This allows cross-server sessions to occur, which solves the problems associated with web farms when we need to add more web servers as our traffic grows.

- **Cookieless sessions** ASP.NET supports a session state even when browsers have disabled cookie support. In this case, the session ID is passed as part of the URL.

● **Easy configuration and deployment** All configuration information for ASP.NET applications is stored in the XML-based `web.config` file. All web application-related files are stored under the site's root folder. The configuration file is in the root folder, while DLLs are in the `/bin` folder. This means that we can deploy our web application by simply copying its root folder by either using file copy commands like XCOPY, or FTP protocol.

6.1 How ASP.NET works

Figure 6.1 shows how a client's HTTP request for an `.ASPX` page is processed on the Internet Information Server (IIS).

The HTTP request arrives at the IIS (`INETINFO.EXE`) and, as this request is for an `.ASPX` page, it is passed to the ISAPI filter (`ASPNET_ISAPI.DLL`) provided by ASP.NET. This works the same way for "normal" ASP pages – only the ISAPI DLL is different. The ISAPI filter redirects the request to the ASP.NET worker process (`ASPNET_WP.EXE`) via the named pipe. ASP.NET checks if the requested page is already compiled and, if it is, loads it from the cache and sends back to the client. If this is the first request to this page, ASP.NET automatically compiles this page and stores the generated assembly in the `Temporary ASP.NET Files` directory that can be found at the following path on the server machine:

```
WINNT\Microsoft.NET\Framework\v.<version>\
```

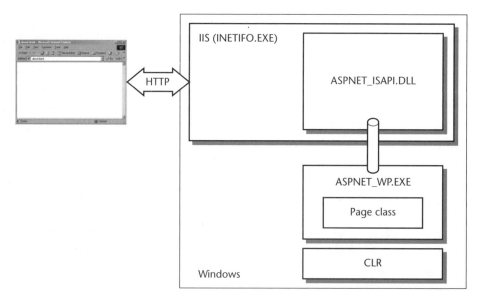

FIGURE 6.1   How a client's request is processed on the server

ASP.NET automatically references all assemblies in the \bin directory and several assemblies in the global assembly cache (see below).

The most important class in this process is the Page class. The .ASPX page is transformed into a derived class, while all static HTML content, as well as render blocks in ASP.NET code, goes to the Render method. The Page class also serves as a base for web forms and server controls. We will talk about this class later in this chapter.

Here is a command line generated by ASP.NET to invoke the Visual Basic.NET compiler to compile the requested page (where xxx replaces the .NET Framework version-dependent information that is not essential for this example):

```
C:\WINNT\system32> "c:\winnt\microsoft.net\framework\xxx\vbc.exe"
 /t:library
 /utf8output
 /R:"c:\winnt\assembly\gac\system.drawing\xxx\system.drawing.dll"
 /R:"c:\winnt\assembly\gac\system.data\xxx\system.data.dll"
 /R:"c:\winnt\assembly\gac\system.web.services\xxx\
  system.web.services.dll"
 /R:"c:\winnt\assembly\gac\system.web\xxx\system.web.dll"
 /R:"c:\winnt\assembly\gac\system\xxx\system.dll"
 /R:"c:\winnt\assembly\gac\system.xml\xxx\system.xml.dll"
 /out:"C:\WINNT\Microsoft.NET\Framework\xxx\
 Temporary ASP.NET Files\root\fa7064c6\2014c0f1\o7xveyt-.dll"
 /debug-  "C:\WINNT\Microsoft.NET\Framework\xxx\
 Temporary ASP.NET Files\root\fa7064c6\2014c0f1\o7xveyt-.0.vb"
```

From this we can learn that our page is stored as a library (dll-file). In our code, we can refer to the following namespaces:

● System (mscorlib)
● System.Web
● System.Web.Services
● System.XML
● System.Data
● System.Drawing

without the need to specify the reference to them. We have also proved here that the Temporary ASP.NET Files directory is used to store the compiled ASP.NET pages.

As mentioned above, the ASP.NET object model is available in the System.Web namespace and its secondary namespaces. This is the topic of the next section.

6.2   System.Web namespace

The `System.Web` namespace (found in the `System.Web.dll` and `System.Web.Services.dll` assemblies) contains classes, interfaces, delegates, and enumerations that are used to enable communication between the web browser and server. Besides the classes, included in this namespace are the `HTTPRequest` class, which envelopes the HTTP request and contains information about it, and the `HTTPResponse` class, which sends the server's output to the client, and the `HTTPServerUtility` object, which can be used to access the server-side utilities and processes. There are also classes for cookies manipulation, output cache control, file transfer, and so on. The following list shows the main classes included in the `System.Web` namespace.

- **HTTPApplication** This class defines common attributes for all application objects within an ASP.NET application. An ASP.NET application is the collection of all the files, pages, handlers, modules, and code within the scope of the virtual directory and its subdirectories on a single web server. The `HTTPApplication` provides such properties as `Application`, `Context` (see `HTTPContext` class below), `Modules` (collection of `IHTTPModule` objects), `Request` (see `HTTPRequest` class below), `Response` (see `HTTPResponse` class below), `Server` (see `HTTPServerUtility` class below), `Session`, `Site`, and `User`.

- **HTTPApplicationState** This class allows us to share information across sessions and requests, but only within the same process. This means that an application state is not shared across applications hosted across multiple machines (a web farm) or across multiple processes on the same machine (a web garden). An instance of this class is created the first time a client requests any URL from an ASP.NET application's virtual directory. This instance is later exposed via the `Application` object.

- **HTTPBrowserCapabilities** This class allows us to find out information about the client browser and its capabilities. For more information about the `HTTPBrowserCapabilities`, see under the heading *Getting information about the client browser* later in this chapter.

- **HTTPCachePolicy** Used to manipulate cache-specific HTTP 1.1 headers and ASP.NET output cache.

- **HTTPCacheVaryByHeaders and HTTPCacheVaryByParams** classes These are used to specify that a cache should contain multiple representations of a particular URI.

- **HTTPClientCertificate** Represents a collection of certificate fields retrieved from a web browser request. These fields are specified in the X.509 standard and sent by the browser in the response to the server request when we use the SSL3.0/PCT1 protocol to connect to the server.

- **HTTPContext** Contains all the HTTP-specific information about an HTTP request.

- **HTTPCookie** and **HTTPCookieCollection** Used to manage HTTP cookies.

- **HTTPException** Used to generate HTTP exceptions.

- **HTTPFileCollection** Allows us to access files uploaded by a client. The HTTPPostedFile class allows us to access individual files uploaded by a client.

- **HTTPRequest** Represents the HTTP request sent by a web client. The HTTPResponse class represents an HTTP response from a web server.

- **HTTPRuntime** Provides access to ASP.NET runtime services, including properties to find the application identifier, path, path to /bin directory, CodeGen directory, and so on.

- **HTTPServerUtility** Contains several helper methods for processing web requests, such as HTMLDecode, HTMLEncode, MapPath, Transfer, URLEncode, URLDecode and URLPathEncode.

- **HTTPStaticObjectsCollection** Represents a collection of StaticObjects. Static objects are objects declared with the <object runat=server>... </object> tag within the ASP.NET application.

- **HTTPUtility** Contains methods for URL encoding and decoding – URLDecode, URLDecodeToBytes, URLEncode, URLEncodeToBytes, URLEncodeUnicode, and URLEncodeToBytes.

- **HTTPWriter** Represents a TextWriter descendant that is used to write through the HTTPResponse object stream.

The System.Web namespace contains several secondary namespaces shown in Figure 6.2. We will briefly discuss these namespaces in the next section.

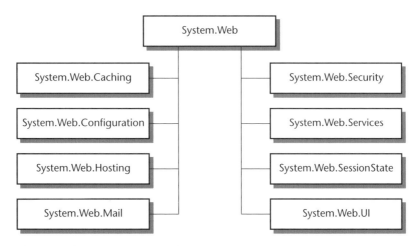

FIGURE 6.2   The secondary namespaces in the System.Web namespace

System.Web.Caching namespace

The System.Web.Caching namespace provides classes for caching frequently used resources, such as ASP.NET pages, web services, and user controls on the server. The Cache class implements the cache and the CacheDependency class is used to track cache dependencies – files, directories or keys to other objects in an application's cache. For more information see the *Using a cache* section later in this chapter.

System.Web.Configuration namespace

The System.Web.Configuration namespace contains classes and enumerations that are used to set up an ASP.NET configuration. For more information see under the heading *ASP applications configuration files* later in this chapter.

System.Web.Hosting namespace

The System.Web.Hosting namespace contains classes that provide the hosting environment for ASP.NET applications. This includes classes for the creation of application domains, ASP.NET worker process support, access to ISAPI runtime, and several others.

System.Web.Mail namespace

We use the classes implemented in the System.Web.Mail namespace to send an e-mail attachment using the SMTP mail service built in to Microsoft Windows 2000. This namespace includes such classes as MailAttachment, MailMessage, and SmtpMail. For more information see the **Sending e-mail** section later in this chapter.

System.Web.Security namespace

This namespace provides classes that are used to implement ASP.NET security in web server applications. This includes such classes as:

● DefaultAuthenticationModule;
● FileAuthorizationModule;
● FormsAuthentication;
● FormsAuthenticationModule;
● PassportAuthenticationModule;
● URLAuthorizationModule;
● WindowsAuthenticationModule.

The word Module in the name of the class indicates that this class implements an HttpModule interface. To find out how these modules correspond to the authentication types, check the `<httpModules>` section of the `machine.config` configuration file. We will discuss security in more detail in the *Applications security* section later in this chapter.

System.Web.Services namespace

This namespace includes classes that are used to build and consume web services. The main class is the `WebService` class, which provides access to the common ASP.NET objects. This namespace contains the following secondary namespaces:

- `System.Web.Services.Description`;
- `System.Web.Services.Discovery`;
- `System.Web.Services.Protocols`.

We will cover web services in more detail in Chapter 15.

System.Web.SessionState namespace

Classes implemented in this namespace provide support for the `Session` state:

- `HTTPSessionState`;
- `SessionStateModule`;
- `SessionStateSectionHeader`;
- `StateRuntime`.

For more information see under the heading *Maintaining state* later in this chapter.

System.Web.UI namespace

The `System.Web.UI` namespace provides classes that are used to create the user interface parts of a web application. This includes the `Control` class (the base class for HTML, web, and user controls), the `Page` class that represents an HTML page, and several other classes. In this chapter, we will learn about the `Control` and `Page` classes. HTML, web, and user controls will be discussed in the next chapter.

6.3 ASP.NET applications

The ASP.NET application is the collection of all files, pages, handlers, modules, and code within the scope of the virtual directory and its subdirectories on a single web server. In this section, we will look at the main classes that comprise the ASP.NET application – the `HTTPApplication`, `HTTPContext`, `HTTPRequest`, `HTTPResponse`, and `HTTPServerUtility` classes. We will start with the `HTTPApplication` class, which defines the basic attributes of the ASP.NET application.

HTTPApplication class

The HTTPApplication class is the direct descendant of the Object class. It implements four interfaces – IHttpAsyncHandler, IHttpHandler, IComponent, and IDisposable.

The IHttpAsyncHandler interface declares two methods that should be implemented by the class – BeginProcessRequest and EndProcessRequest. These methods are used to initiate an asynchronous call to the handler and finalize this call. The handler is based on the IHttpHandler interface that defines the ProcessRequest method used to process HTTP web requests. Note that we can create our own custom HTTPHandler code to process web requests. The IComponent interface is required by all components and it defines the Site property of ISite type that is used to communicate between the component and its container. The IDisposable interface defines the Dispose method that is used to release all resources of the object.

Here is a list of the properties of the HTTPApplication class.

- **Application** Returns a reference to a state bag instance of an HTTPApplication. A state bag is used to manage the view state of all ASP.NET server controls, including pages.
- **Context** Returns the HTTPContext object that provides access to additional pipeline module-exposed objects.
- **Modules** Contains the collection of IHTTPModule objects for the current application.
- **Request** Provides access to incoming HttpRequest data.
- **Response** Allows you to transmit HttpResponse data to a client.
- **Server** Returns the HttpServerUtility object.
- **Session** Returns the HttpSessionState object that provides access to session data.
- **Site** Returns the ISite object that is used to communicate between the component and its container.
- **User** Returns the IPrincipal object used to access the data about this application user.

Besides the methods of the HTTPApplication class, we should mention the Init method. This is used to initialize HttpModule instance variables and register event handlers with the hosting Application. Other methods of the HTTPApplication class include AddXXX methods, which are used to add appropriate event handlers.

HTTPContext class

This class provides access to all HTTP-specific information about an individual HTTP request. The following is a list of the properties of the HTTPContext class.

- **AllErrors** Contains an array of errors that occurred during the process of an HTTP request. The **AddError** method can be used to add an error to this array; **ClearError** clears the contents of this array.

- **Application** Contains the **HttpApplicationState** object for the current request. This object enables the sharing of global information across multiple sessions and requests within an ASP.NET application.

- **ApplicationInstance** Indicates the **HttpApplication** object for the current request.

- **Cache** Contains the **Cache** object for the current HTTP request.

- **Current** This property returns the **HttpContext** object for the current HTTP request.

- **Error** Returns the first error that occurred during the process of an HTTP request.

- **Handler** Specifies the **IHttpHandler** object for the current HTTP request.

- **IsCustomErrorEnabled** Indicates whether or not the customized errors are enabled for the current HTTP request.

- **IsDebuggingEnabled** Indicates whether or not you are running in debug mode.

- **Items** Returns a key/value collection used to share data between an **IHttpModule** and an **IHttpHandler** during the current request.

- **Request** Contains the **HttpRequest** object for the current request.

- **Response** Contains the **HttpResponse** object for the current request.

- **Server** Contains the **HttpServerUtility** object for the current request.

- **Session** Contains the **SessionState** object for the current HTTP request.

- **SkipAuthorization** Indicates whether or not the **URLAuthorization** module will skip the authorization check for the current request.

- **Timestamp** Returns the timestamp of the current HTTP request.

- **Trace** Returns the **TraceContext** object used to output the trace information for the current request.

- **User** Specifies the security information for the current HTTP request.

We have already mentioned the **AddError** and **ClearError** methods, but there are other methods in the **HTTPContext** class.

- **GetAppConfig method** Returns configuraton information for the current application. The application settings are stored in the WEB.CONFIG file in the <appSettings> section. For more information, see under the *ASP applications configuration files* section below.

- **GetConfig method** Returns the configuration information from the user-defined section of the WEB.CONFIG file for the current request. For more information see the *ASP applications configuration files* section below.

- **RewritePath method** Returns the current internal rewrite path.

HTTPRequest class

This class is used to get the HTTP values sent by a client during a web request. It contains several properties and methods, as discussed below.

Here is a list of properties of the HTTPRequest class:

- **AcceptTypes** Returns a string array of MIME types accepted by the client browser. The following example shows how to use this property:

```
Private Sub Page_Load(ByVal sender As System.Object,
 ByVal e As System.EventArgs) Handles MyBase.Load

 Dim MIME() As String
 Dim I As Integer

 MIME = Request.AcceptTypes
 For I = 0 To MIME.GetUpperBound(0)
  Response.Write("Accept Type " & MIME(I) & "<br>")
 Next I

 End Sub
```

The value */* means that all standard MIME types are accepted by the browser. Note that this property returns the same information as the call to the Request.Headers("Accept"). Some examples of MIME types are:

- "text/HTML";
- "image/GIF";
- "image/JPEG";
- "text/plain";
- "Application/msword";
- "Application/x-msexcel".

For more informtaion on MIME types, see RFC 822 and RFC 1521, which can be found at:

www.faqs.org/rfcs/index.htm

or www.ietf.org/rfc

- **ApplicationPath** Returns the application root path. For example, if we call the following page:

http://localhost/WebApplication1/WebForm1.aspx

this property will return:

/WebApplication1

- **Browser** Contains the HttpBrowserCapabilities object, which represents the capabilities of the client browser that make a request. For more information about browser capabilities, see the discussion of the `HttpBrowserCapabilities` class below under the heading *Getting information about the client browser*.

- **ClientCertificate** Returns the client security certificate.
- **ContentEncoding** Returns the character set for the request. For example, this can be Unicode (UTF-8), represented by the `System.Text.UTF8Encoding` type. By default, UTF-8 encoding is used for both request and response.
- **ContentLength** Indicates the number of bytes sent by the client.
- **ContentType** Indicates the MIME content type of request.
- **Cookies** Contains the collection of cookies sent by the client.
- **FilePath** Returns the virtual path of the current request.
- **Files** Contains the collection of files uploaded by the client. This property is of the `HttpFileCollection` type, which will be discussed later in this chapter.
- **Form** Contains the collection of form variables.
- **Headers** Contains the collection of HTTP headers.
- **HttpMethod** Indicates the HTTP method used by the client. This can be GET, POST, or HEAD.
- **InputStream** Specifies the `Stream` object representing the contents of the incoming HTTP content body.
- **IsAuthenticated** Indicates whether or not the user has been authenticated.
- **IsSecureConnection** Indicates whether or not we use an HTTP connection or HTTPS connection (HTTP over secure sockets).
- **Params** Contains the collection of `QueryString`, `Form`, `ServerVariables`, and `Cookies` items.
- **Path** Returns the virtual path of the current request.
- **PathInfo** Returns additional path information for the current request.
- **PhysicalApplicationPath** Returns the file system path of the current application's root directory.
- **PhysicalPath** Returns the file system path of the current request. The following example shows the difference between the `Path`, `PathInfo`, `PhysicalApplicationPath`, and `PhysicalPath` properties:

```
<script runat="server">
 Sub Page_Load
  Response.Write(Request.Path & "<br>")
  Response.Write(Request.PathInfo & "<br>")
  Response.Write(Request.PhysicalApplicationPath & "<br>")
  Response.Write(Request.PhysicalPath & "<br>")
 End Sub
</script>
```

For a request like this:

http://therion/asp_net/path.aspx/extra%20info

we will get the following values of the properties:

- **Path**   /asp_net/path.aspx/extra info;
- **PathInfo**   /extra info;
- **PhysicalApplicationPath**   c:\inetpub\wwwroot\;
- **PhysicalPath**   c:\inetpub\wwwroot\asp_net\path.aspx.

● **QueryString** Contains the collection of HTTP query string variables. For example, the following request:

```
http://therion/asp_net/query.aspx?FirstName=Alex&
 LastName=Fedorov&City=Lausanne&Canton=Vaud
```

can be processed with the following code:

```
<script runat="server">

 Sub Page_Load

  Dim Coll As System.Collections.Specialized.NameValueCollection
  Dim En As IEnumerator

  Coll = Request.QueryString
  En = Coll.GetEnumerator
  Response.Write("<TABLE BORDER='1'>")

  While En.MoveNext()

   Response.Write("<TR><TD>" & En.Current & "</TD>")
   Response.Write("<TD>")
   If Coll.Item(En.Current) <> "" Then
    Response.Write(Coll.Item(En.Current))
   Else
    Response.Write(" ")
   End If
   Response.Write("</TD></TR>")

  End While

  Response.Write("</TABLE>")


 End Sub

</script>
```

which will display the result shown in Figure 6.3.

FirstName	Alex
LastName	Fedorov
City	Lausanne
Canton	Vaud

FIGURE 6.3   `QueryString` results set out as a table

- **RawUrl** Returns the raw URL of the current request. For the request like this:

  ```
  http://therion/asp_net/path.aspx/extra%20info
  ```

  the property will contain the following value:

  ```
  /asp_net/path.aspx/extra info
  ```

- **RequestType** Indicates the HTTP data transfer method used by the client – either GET or POST.

- **ServerVariables** Returns a collection of server variables. The following example shows how to display the contents of this property (see also Figure 6.4):

```
Imports System.Collections.Specialized

...

 Private Sub Page_Load(ByVal sender As System.Object, _
   ByVal e As System.EventArgs) Handles MyBase.Load

   Dim Coll As NameValueCollection
   Dim En As IEnumerator

   Coll = Request.ServerVariables
   En = Coll.GetEnumerator
   Response.Write("<TABLE BORDER='1'>")

   While En.MoveNext()

    Response.Write("<TR><TD>" & En.Current & "</TD>")
    Response.Write("<TD>")
    If Coll.Item(En.Current) <> "" Then
     Response.Write(Coll.Item(En.Current))
```

```
   Else
    Response.Write(" ")
   End If
   Response.Write("</TD></TR>")


 End While


 Response.Write("</TABLE>")


End Sub
```

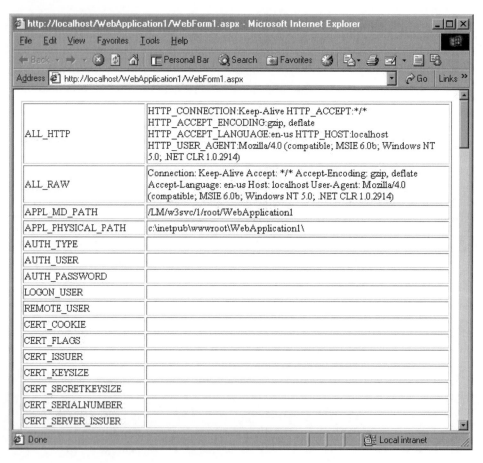

FIGURE 6.4 The contents of the ServerVariables property

To get a value of a particular variable, use the following syntax:

```
Response.Write(Request.ServerVariables("ALL_RAW"))
```

- **TotalBytes** Returns the number of bytes in the current input stream.
- **Url** Returns the Uri object that contains information about the URL of the current request. For more information about the Uri class, see Chapter 4.
- **UrlReferrer** Returns the Uri object that contains information about the URL of the client's previous request linked to the current URL.
- **UserAgent** Returns the User-Agent HTTP header. For example, if the client browser is Microsoft Internet Explorer 6.0, this property will contain:

```
Mozilla/4.0 (compatible; MSIE 6.0b; Windows NT 5.0; .NET CLR 1.0.2914)
```

See also the Browser property and the discussion of the HttpBrowserCapabilities class below.

- **UserHostAddress** Returns the IP address of the client.
- **UserHostName** Returns the DNS name of the client.
- **UserLanguages** Returns the weighted array of client language preferences. "Weighted" means that if the user has specified more than one language, the first one will be the default language while others will have numeric weights indicating how far the particular language is from the default one. The following example shows how to use this property (see also Figure 6.5):

```
Sub Page_Load(ByVal sender As Object, _
 ByVal e As EventArgs)

 Dim UserLangs() As String
 Dim Count As Integer
 Dim Pos As Integer
 Dim Lang As String
 Dim Weight As String

 UserLangs = Request.UserLanguages
 Response.Write("<TABLE BORDER='2' WIDTH='50%'>")

 For Count = 0 To UserLangs.GetUpperBound(0)

  Pos = InStr(1, UserLangs(Count), ";")
  If Pos > 0 Then
   Lang = Left(UserLangs(Count).ToUpper, Pos - 1)
   Weight = Right(UserLangs(Count).ToUpper, _
    UserLangs(Count).Length - InStr(1, UserLangs(Count), "="))
```

```
 Else
  '
  ' Default language
  '
   Lang = UserLangs(Count).ToUpper
   Weight = "1.0"
  End If
  Response.Write("<TR><TD>" & Lang & _
   "</TD><TD>" & Weight & "</TD></TR>")
 Next Count

 Response.Write("</TABLE>")

End Sub
```

EN-US	1.0
FR-CH	0.8
DE-CH	0.5
IT-CH	0.3

FIGURE 6.5   A weighted array of a client's language preferences set in the `UserLanguage` property

This property is your entry point into localization. Using the language with the weight `"1.0"`, we can select the default language for the user interface.

The `HTTPRequest` class contains the following methods.

- **BinaryRead method** Reads a specified number of bytes from the current input stream into a byte array.
- **MapImageCoordinates method** Maps an incoming image field form parameter to appropriate x/y coordinate values.
- **MapPath method** Maps the virtual path in the requested URL to a physical path on the server for the current request.
- **SaveAs method** Allows us to save the HTTP request to the specified disk file, either with HTTP headers or without them. For example, we might issue the following request:

```
http://therion/asp_net/query.aspx?FirstName=Alex&
 LastName=Fedorov&City=Lausanne&Canton=Vaud
```

and then save it to disk using the `SaveAs` method. We will end up with a text file that contains the following information:

```
GET /asp_net/query.aspx?FirstName=Alex&
 LastName=Fedorov&City=Lausanne&Canton=Vaud HTTP/1.1
Connection: Keep-Alive
Accept: */*
Accept-Encoding: gzip, deflate
Accept-Language: en-us,fr-ch;q=0.8,de-ch;q=0.5,it-ch;q=0.3
Host: therion
User-Agent: Mozilla/4.0 (compatible; MSIE 6.0b; Windows NT 5.0;
 .NET CLR 1.0.2914)
```

This method can be useful for debugging our ASP.NET applications.

HTTPResponse class

This class represents HTTP response information in the ASP.NET application. It contains several properties and methods discussed below.

Here is a list of properties of the HTTPResponse class.

- **Buffer** Indicates whether or not to buffer the output and send it after the entire response has finished processing. This property exists only to provide compatibility with the ASP code. In ASP.NET applications we should use the BufferOutput property.

- **BufferOutput** Indicates whether or not to buffer output and send it after the entire page has finished processing.

- **Cache** Specifies the HttpCachePolicy object that contains the caching policy (expiration time, privacy, vary clauses) of a web page.

- **CacheControl** Used to set the cache control HTTP header. Possible values are "Private" and "Public". This property, as well as properties such as Expires and ExpiresAbsolete, exists only to provide compatibility with the ASP code. In ASP.NET applications we should use the Cache property.

- **Charset** Specifies the character set for the output stream.

- **ContentEncoding** Specifies the Encoding object that contains the character set for the output stream.

- **ContentType** Specifies the MIME content type for the output stream. The default value is "text/html".

- **Cookies** Specifies the HttpCookieCollection object that represents the response cookie collecton.

- **Expires** Specifies when the page expires. This property exists only to provide compatibility with the ASP code. In ASP.NET applications we should use the Cache property.

- **ExpiresAbsolute** Specifies the absolute date and time at which to remove cached information from the cache. This property exists only to provide compatibility with the ASP code. In ASP.NET applications we should use the Cache property.

- **Filter** Specifies the `Stream` object that acts as a filter for the output stream.
- **IsClientConnected** Allows us to check whether or not the client is still connected to the server before processing with the response.
- **Output** Specifies the `TextWriter` object that creates customized output to the client.
- **OutputStream** Specifies the `Stream` object that represents the raw contents of the outgoing HTTP content body.
- **Status** Indicates the `Status` line to be returned to the client. The default value is `"200 OK"`. This property exists only to provide compatibility with the ASP code. In ASP.NET applications we should use the `StatusDescription` property.
- **StatusCode** Indicates the HTTP status code to be returned to the client. The default value is 200.
- **StatusDescription** Indicates the HTTP status string to be returned to the client. The default value is `"OK"`.
- **SuppressContent** Indicates whether or not to send HTTP content to the client.

The HTTPResponse class contains the following methods.

- **AddFileDependencies and AddFileDependency methods** Used to add a group of file names or a single file name to the collection of file names on which the current response is dependent.
- **AddHeader method** Adds an HTTP header to the output stream. It exists only to provide compatibility with the ASP code. In ASP.NET applications we should use the AppendHeader method.
- **AppendToLog method** Writes information to the IIS log file.
- **BinaryWrite method** Writes a string of binary characters to the HTTP output stream. The following example shows how to write the graphics to the client:

```
Sub Page_Load

  Dim Stream As System.IO.FileStream
  Dim FileSize As Long

   Stream = New System.IO.FileStream( _
    Server.MapPath("sample.jpg"), System.IO.FileMode.Open)
   Dim Buffer(CInt(FileSize)) As Byte
   Stream.Read(Buffer, 0, CInt(FileSize))
   Stream.Close()

   Response.ContentType = "image/jpeg"
   Response.BinaryWrite(Buffer)


  End Sub
```

- **Clear method** Clears the current buffer stream.
- **ClearContent method** Clears all content output from the buffer stream.
- **ClearHeaders method** Clears all headers from the buffer stream. Headers should be cleared before the HTTP headers have been sent to the client.
- **Close method** Closes the connection to a client.
- **End method** Stops execution of the page, sends buffered output to the client, fires the Application_EndRequest event, and closes the connection.
- **Flush method** Sends all currently buffered output to the client.
- **Pics method** Appends a PICS-Label HTTP header to the output stream. PICS stands for platform for internet content selection and it defines ratings that can be applied to your site. For more information on PICS, see www.rsac.org
- **Redirect method** Redirects execution to another page and internally calls the Response.End method. The overloaded version of this method allows us to suppress the internal call to Response.End method.
- **Write method** Writes information to an output stream.
- **WriteFile method** Writes the specified file directly to an output stream. The following example shows how to send the XML file to the client:

```
Sub Page_Load()

  Response.ContentType = "text/xml"
  Response.WriteFile("nw.xml")

End Sub
```

HTTPServerUtility class

This class contains several properties and methods that can be used to process web requests. The HttpServerUtility class is exposed by means of the Server object. Here is a list of properties of the HttpServerUtility class.

- **MachineName** Contains the server machine name.
- **ScriptTimeout** Specifies the number of seconds before the request is automatically timed-out. The default value is 90 seconds – this is specified in the executionTimeout attribute of the <httpRuntime> header in the machine.config file.

The HttpServerUtility class contains the following methods.

- **ClearError method** Clears the previous exception.
- **CreateObject and CreateObjectFromClsid methods** Used to create a server instance of a COM object from a specified programmatic identifier or class identifier.
- **Execute method** Executes a request to another page. After execution of the specified page has been completed, the Execute method continues execution of the original page. To completely transfer execution to another page, use the Transfer

method. We can use the overloaded version of this method to include the output from another page in the resulting output. To do this we create an object of the `StringWriter` type and save the output in it. Later, when our page gets back control, we use the `Response.Write` method to produce the combined output.

- **GetLastError method** Returns the previous exception.
- **HtmlDecode method** Decodes an encoded string to eliminate illegal HTML characters.
- **HtmlEncode method** Encodes a string.
- **MapPath method** Gets the physical path for the specified virtual path.
- **Transfer method** Terminates execution of the current page and begins execution of a specified page. This method internally calls the `Response.End` method. To suppress this functionality, use the `Execute` method.
- **UrlDecode method** Decodes an encoded string.
- **UrlEncode method** Encodes a string.
- **UrlPathEncode method** Encodes the path portion of a URL.

Application and session lifetime

In this section we will learn about the events that occur during the application and session lifetime. We will also discuss how and when to create event handlers in the `GLOBAL.ASAX` file.

ASP.NET applications are created the first time a request is made to the server. At this time the pool of `HttpApplication` class instances (each instance is available as the `Application` object) is created and the `Start` event occurs. After this, instances of `HttpApplication` class process requests until the last instance exits, then the End event occurs. Each instance of the `HttpApplication` class may rise in `Init` and `Dispose` methods that occur more than once between the application's `Start` and End events.

Every time a new user accesses an .ASPX page, this initiates a session. ASP.NET creates a `Session` object that exists until the user disconnects from the site or a timeout occurs. When a session starts, the session's `Start` event occurs; at the end of the session, the session's `End` event occurs. For each request issued to an ASP.NET application, events occur, in the order shown in Figure 6.6:

- Application.BeginRequest
- Application.AuthenticateRequest
- Application.ResolveRequestCache
- Session.Start
- Application.PreRequestHandlerExecute

  - Page.Init
  - Page.Load
  - Page.PreRender

- Application.PostRequestHandlerExecute
- Application.UpdateRequestCache
- Application.EndRequest

FIGURE 6.6   The events that occur for each request to an ASP.NET application

Note that there are application-level, session-level, and page-level events. Fgure 6.6 shows deterministic events that usually occur in the order shown. Such application-level events as `Error`, `PreSendRequestContent`, and `PreSendRequestHeaders` are non-deterministic – they are not guaranteed to occur and the order is not predefined. Let's look at application-level events in more detail.

- **BeginRequest** This event indicates that the request has been started. If we need to do something at the beginning of the request, we should place the code in the event handler for the `BeginRequest` event.

- **AuthenticateRequest** We should use the event handler for this event if we want to plug in our own customized authentication scheme.

- **AuthorizeRequest** This event is used internally to implement authorization mechanisms. There is no reason to create an event handler for it.

- **ResolveRequestCache** This event is used to determine if a page can be served from the output cache. If we want to implement our own caching module, we put the code in the event handler for the `ResolveRequestCache` event.

- **AcquireRequestState** This event indicates that the session state is retrieved from the state store. In the event handler we can implement our own state management algorigthms.

- **PreRequestHandlerExecute** This event occurs just before the HTTP handler is executed.

- **PostRequestHandlerExecute** This event occurs just after the HTTP handler has been executed.

- **ReleaseRequestState** This event indicates that the session state is stored back in the state store. In the event handler, we can implement our own state management algorithms.

- **UpdateRequestCache** This event occurs when the output is written back to the output cache. If we want to implement our own caching module, we put the code in the event handler for the `UpdateRequestCache` event.

- **EndRequest** This event indicates that a request has been completed.

For ASP.NET applications, the `global.asax` file plays the same role as a `global.asa` file for classical ASP applications. This file is used to provide application and session startup and cleanup code as well as to set some options for the ASP.NET application. The `global.asax` file can be used for:

- creation of event handlers for application and session events – usually we create event handlers for `Application_Start` and `Session_Start` events where we add some initialization code. Event handlers for `Application_End` and `Session_End` events are used to perform cleanup;

- creation of event handlers for custom HTTP modules;

- importation of several namespaces that can then be used in any code of our application (@ `Imports` directive) – for example, if we want to use classes from the `System.IO` namespace in our ASP.NET pages, we may add the following @ `Imports` directive:

```
<%@ Imports Namespace = "System.IO" %>
```

- registration of assemblies (@ `Assembly` directive);
- creation of server-side COM objects or .NET components (`<object runat="server" />` tag) – for example:

```
'
' Create an instance of .NET component
'
<object id="ds" class="System.Data.DatatSet" runat="server" />
'
' Create and instance of COM objects
'
<object id="pdf" progID="Adobe.Acrobat.Reader" runat="server" />
```

Note that any COM objects we create with the `<object runat="server" />` tag should be multithreaded. Objects created in the `global.asax` file can be found later in the `HTTPStaticObjectsCollection` collection.

6.4 ASP applications configuration files

ASP.NET uses several XML-based configuration files that we will cover in this section. The root configuration file is named `machine.config` and it provides ASP.NET configuration for the entire web server. This file can be found in the following directory:

```
WINNT\Microsoft.NET\Framework\v.<version>\Config
```

The second configuration file is `web.config`, which contains configuration settings for the particular ASP.NET application. When a request for an ASPX page is made, the configuration files are compiled in the following way:

- the `web.config` file in the current directory overrides the configuration sesstings stored in a `web.config` file in an application directory, which overrides settings at the website level and global settings in the `machine.config` file;
- after the configuration settings have been compiled, they are cached and used in future requests until one of the configuration files is modified.

This is shown in Figure 6.7.

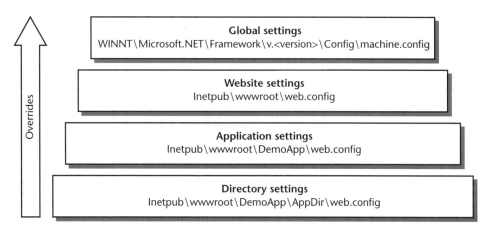

FIGURE 6.7 The hierarchy of configuration files

A web.config file at any level is optional, but a machine.config file is required.

Let's briefly look at the configuration sections available in the configuration files. These sections are contained in the <system.web> section within the <configuration> tag:

```
<configuration>

 <system.web>

  <appSettings></appSettings>

  ...

  <webServices></webServices>

 </system.web>

</configuration>
```

Table 6.1 lists all the configuration sections and their purposes.

TABLE 6.1 The configuration sections and what they do

Section	Description
<appSettings>	Used to create customized settings for an application. This tag contains two attributes – key and value: <add key="key" value="value" />

Section	Description
`<authentication>`	This section contains authentication and security-related settings. The authentication section contains a single attribute mode that specifies which type of authentication to use. Possible values are Forms, None, Passport, and Windows. To specify anonymous access, use mode attribute set to None: `<authentication mode="None" />` The default value is "Windows".

`<authorization>`	This section allows us to specify which users are allowed to visit a website. There are two subtags – allow and deny – each with three attributes: users, roles, and verbs. For example, to allow only users with "Admins" oles, we use the following configuration settings (* means all users):
	
	`<authorization>`
	`  <allow roles="Admins" />`
	`  <deny users="*" />`
	`</authorization>`
	
	The default value allows all users:
	
	`<allow users="*" />`

`<browserCaps>`	This section is used to configure settings for the HttpBrowserCapabilities class.
`<compilation>`	This section is used to configure compilation settings for ASP.NET applications. We can specify whether or not to insert debugging symbols (.pdb information) into the compiled page (debug attribute), default language (defaultLanguage attribute), turn on or off the explicit option (explicit attribute), turn on or off the strict compile option (strict attribute), and so on.
`<customErrors>`	This section is used to provide information about customized error messages for an ASP.NET application. The defaultRedirect tag specifies the URL to redirect a browser if any unexpected error occurs. The subtag `<error>` is used to specify error codes and pages to redirect for a specific error code, such as 404.

`<globalization>`	This section is used to configure the globalization settings of an application. For example:
	
	`<globalization`
	`  requestEncoding="UTF-8"`
	`  responseEncoding="UTF-8"`
	`/>`

`<httpHandlers>`	This section is used to map incoming URL requests to the IHttpHandler classes. This section also sets the types of files that will not be downloaded.
`<httpModules>`	This section is used to add, remove, or clear HTTP modules within an application.
`<httpRuntime>`	This section is used to configure ASP.NET HTTP runtime settings.

TABLE 6.1   Continued

Section	Description
`<identity>`	This section is used to control the application identity of the web application. If the `impersonate` attribute is set to `True`, client impersonation is used on each request to the web server.
`<machineKey>`	This section is used to configure keys for encryption and decryption of forms authentication cookie data.
`<pages>`	This section is used to specify page-specific configuration settings. The `Buffer` attribute specifies whether resources are buffered or not – it can have values `On`, `Off`, and `Readonly`. To enable or disable the session state, we use the `enableSessionState` attribute, which can be either `True` or `False`. To specify the code-behind class that an .ASPX page inherits, we use the `pageBaseType` attribute. The `userControlBaseType` attribute specifies a code-behind class that user controls inherit. To enable or disable any event firing in the page, we use the `autoEventWireup`, which takes either `True` or `False` values.
`<processModel>`	This section is used to configure the ASP.NET process model settings on an IIS web server. This tag can be used only in the `machine.config` file.
`<securityPolicy>`	This section is used to define valid mappings of named security levels to policy levels.

`<sessionState>`	This section is used to configure the session state module. We specify where to store the session settings. The mode attribute can be set to `Off`, `InProc`, `StateServer`, or `SqlServer`. We can also specify if we use cookies to store session settings (`cookieless` attribute) and session timeout (`timeout` attribute). The default values are:
	
	`<sessionState>`
	`  mode="InProc"`
	`  stateConnectionString="tcpip=127.0.0.1:42424"`
	`  sqlConnectionString="data source=127.0.0.1;`
	`   user id=sa;password="`
	`  cookieless="false"`
	`  timeout="20"`
	`/>`

`<trace>`	In this section, we can enable or disable the ASP.NET trace service that can be used on an application or page base. Tracing is useful when we debug our aplications. In this section, we can specify the number of traces stored in memory (`requestLimit` attribute) and indicate whether we want to see the trace output in page or in file (`pageOutput` attribute). The trace file is called `trace.axd`. The default values are:

Section	Description

	``
	<trace>
	  enabled="false"
	  requestLimit="10"
	  pageOutput="false"
	  traceMode="SortByTime"
	  localOnly="true"
	/>
	``

`<trust>`	This section is used to configure the set of code access security permissions that is used to run a particular application. The attributes are `level` and `originUrl`. The `level` corresponds to the `trustLevel` attribute in the `<securityPolicy>` section and maps to one of the following files, which contain detailed information: ● `web_hightrust.config;` ● `web_lowtrust.config;` ● `web_notrust.config;` that can be found in the directory: `WINNT\Microsoft.NET\Framework\v.<version>\Config.`
`<webServices>`	This section is used to configure the settings of ASP.NET web services.

Later in this chapter, in the section headed *Dealing with configuration*, we will see how to use customized settings stored in the `<appSettings>` section.

6.5 Web forms pages

Web forms is the technology that allows us to create programmable web pages that comprise the ASP.NET application. A web form – commonly referred to as an ASP.NET or ASPX page – consists of two components: visual elements and code. With ASP.NET we have two ways to create our pages. We can continue to work the "ASP way" – to mix our code and HTML code – or completely separate them. The latter is called the code-behind technique and it works in the following way:

● we create a `.VB` or `.CS` file that contains all the code;
● this code can be compiled and placed in the `\bin` directory;
● we can force the compilation on demand by using the `src` attribute of the @ Page directive.

Let's look at an example. Suppose we want to partition our page into user interface syntax and logic. To do so, we should create two files. The first one will contain code that will be used in our web forms page. The second file will contain only HTML.

Here is the code for the `cblib.vb` file which contains the **NFUtils** class containing one method – ShowDateTime:

```
'----------------------------------------
' CBLIB.VB - general utilities
'----------------------------------------
Imports System.Globalization
Imports System.Threading

Namespace Netface
 Public Class NFUtils

  Function ShowDateTime() As String

   Dim Cult As CultureInfo

   Cult = New CultureInfo("FR-CH")
   Thread.CurrentThread.CurrentCulture = Cult
   Dim DT As DateTime
   Return DT.Now

  End Function

 End Class
End Namespace
```

Here is how we refer to the code behind in our ASPX page (see also Figure 6.8 for the finished result):

```
<%-- Code-behind demo --%>
<%@ Page Language="VB" src="cblib.vb" %>
<%@ Import Namespace="Netface" %>

<html>
 <body>
  <h3 align="center">

  <%
   Dim Utils As New NFUtils
   Response.Write(Utils.ShowDateTime())
  %>

  </h3>
 </body>
</html>
```

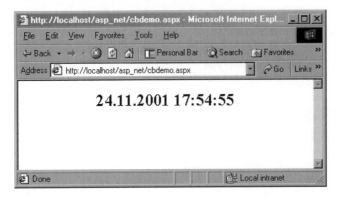

FIGURE 6.8 The finished result of code used to set up an ASPX page

The special type of web forms files are files that contain user controls. Such files have the .ASCX extension, which distinguishes them from ordinal ASPX files. We will discuss user controls in the next chapter.

Elements of the web forms page

A web forms page may contain the following elements.

- **Directives** Page-level directives allow us to control how the compiler will process the ASP.NET web forms page. Directives has the following syntax:

```
<%@ directive attribute="value" [...]%>
```

The @ Page directive defines page-specific attributes that are used by the ASP.NET page parser and compiler. For example, we can set the language attribute to specify the language that will be used to write the code on the page (code that is included in <% %> and <%= %> blocks). Only one @ Page directive is allowed per ASPX file. Table 6.2 shows the most commonly used @ Page directive attributes.

TABLE 6.2 The most commonly used @ Page directive attributes

Attribute	Description
Buffer	Enables or disables HTTP response buffering. By default response buffering is enabled.
ClientTarget	Indicates the type of target for which the ASP.NET server controls should render content.
CodePage	Indicates the code page for the response.
CompilerOptions	Allows us to specify compiler options.
ContentType	Indicates MIME content type for the response.
Debug	Enables or disables compiling with debug symbols.

TABLE 6.2   Continued

Attribute	Description
EnableSessionState	Enables or disables session state. By default session state is enabled.
EnableViewState	Enables or disables view state maintenance across page requests. By default, view state is enabled.
ErrorPage	Specifies the URL for redirection if an unhandled page exception occurs.
Explicit	Enables or disables Option Explicit mode. By default this mode is enabled.
Inherits	Indicates base class for the page to inherit. This can be any class derived from the Page class.
Language	Specifies the language for the code in this page. The default language is Visual Basic (synonyms: vb, visualbasic, vbscript). We can also specify C (synonyms: c#, cs, csharp), JScript (synonyms: js, jscript, javascript) or any other third-party .NET-compatible language.
Src	Indicates the source file for code behind. For Visual Basic, the code file name extension should be .vb, for C# code .cs and for JScript .js.
Strict	Enables or disables the Option Strict mode. By default this mode is disabled.
Trace	Enables or disables tracing. When tracing is enabled, the TraceMode attribute indicates how trace messages are displayed.

The following example shows the @ Page directive:

```
<%@ Page Language="VB" Buffer="True" Strict="True" %>
```

Other directives that may appear in ASPX and ASCX files include the following.

- @ Control. Used to specify control-specific attributes. This directive can only be included in ASCX files – the files that contain user controls.
- @ Import. Used to import a namespace.
- @ Implements. Used to declare the interface, implemented by page or user control.
- @ Register. Used to associate aliases with namespaces and class names.
- @ Assembly. Used to declare assembly, linked to the page or control.
- @ OutputCache. Used to control the output cache of a page or user control.
- @ Reference Used to declare the link between a page or user control and the current page or user control.

● **Code declaration blocks** These blocks contain ASP.NET code, written on the language, specified by the language attribute in the @ Page directive or with the language attribute within the block – the default language is Visual basic. A web forms page can contain more than one code declaration block, but the programming language must be the same in all blocks on a page. A code declaration block has the following structure:

```
<script runat="server" [language = ...]>

    [lines of code]

</script>
```

All code that is included within the `<script>...</script>` tags, except global statements such as variables declarations, must be encapsulated within procedures and functions.

● **Code render blocks**. These blocks include code enclosed within `<% ... %>` tags. For example:

```
<BODY>

  <% =Now()%>

</BODY>
```

Note that while such blocks are processed when the page is parsed and compiled, unlike in ASP, there is no notion of "first `<% ... %>` block" that will be executed as soon as the page is loaded. In ASP.NET, we must include such code in the `Page_Load` event handler – this event is fired immediately after the ASP.NET engine loads the page.

● **HTML server controls**. In ASP.NET, HTML controls are classes that expose an object model that maps very loosely to the HTML elements they render. Server controls are represented by common HTML form-type tags, but with the `runat="server"` attribute:

```
<input

  id="FirstName"
  type="text"
  size="40"
  runnat="server"

>
```

HTML controls are defined in the classes found in the `System.Web.UI.ASPControls` namespace.

● **Web server controls** In ASP.NET, Web controls extend the basic set of HTML controls and provide such controls as a calendar. Web controls are more abstract than HTML controls and their object models do not necessarily reflect HTML syntax. For example:

```
<asp:Button

 id="Button1"
 Text="Submit"
 OnClick="SubmitBtn_Click"
 runat="server"


/>
```

Web controls are defined in the classes found in `System.Web.UI. WebControls`.

- **Validation controls** Validation controls are server controls that validate user input. Such controls include attributes that attach them to other controls (`ControlToValidate`), specify the error message, its inner contents, and display behavior. Validation controls use the `<asp:Control ... />` syntax:

```
<asp:RequiredFieldValidator

 id="NotEmptyChecker"
 runat="server"
 ControlToValidate="FirstName"
 InitialValue=""
 ErrorMessage="You must enter the first name "
 ForeColor="Red" BackColor="DarkGrey">


</asp:RequiredFieldValidator>
```

Validation controls are defined in the classes found in `System.Web.UI. WebControls`.

- **User controls** These are user-defined controls stored in ASCX files and used in ASP.NET web pages.

- **Server-side objects** The `<object>` tag specifies an object (either a COM or .NET one) that can be instantiated on the server. The syntax for this tag is:

```
<object id="id" runat="server" identifier="idName">
```

  - `class` attribute – used to specify the .NET Framework class;
  - `progID` attribute – specifies the COM component using the programmatic identifier;
  - `classID` attribute – specifies the COM component using the class identifier.

- **Server-side includes** The `#include` directive can be used to insert the contents of a specified file anywhere within an ASP.NET page. It is possible to specify the physical file names (for files located in the same directory as the ASP.NET page or in a subdirectory) or virtual file names. For example:

```
<!-- #include file=".shared\pagetop.inc" -->
```

- **Server-side comments** The <%-- and --%> tags are used to specify the block of comments – ASP.NET code or literal text that will be ignored by the compiler. Inside the <script runat="server"> ... </script> and <% ... %> blocks we can also use language-specific comments, for example:

```
<script runat="server" language="C#">

// This is a single-line comment in C#

/*

    Multi-line comment in C#

*/

</script>
```

or

```
<script runat="server" language="VB">

' This is a single-line comment in VB

REM This is a single-line comment in VB ("old-fashioned")

</script>
```

- **HTML content** The last, but not the least, element of the web forms page is static HTML content. In ASP.NET, HTML content – HTML tags and text inside them – is also compiled. During the page processing, ASP.NET creates an object of the `LiteralControl` class type for each static HTML code. Then this object is included into the `Controls` collection of the **Page** object that represents the whole page. At runtime, we have access to all static HTML content via the collection mentioned above. Suppose, as in the following example, at the page load we turn all static content within the page to uppercase (see also Figure 6.9):

```
<%@ Page Language="VB" %>
<script runat="server">

    Sub Page_Load

        Dim HTML As LiteralControl
        For Each HTML In Page.Controls
```

```
        HTML.Text = HTML.Text.ToUpper()
     Next

     End Sub

</script>
<html>
<body>
 <h1>header level 1</h1>
 <h2>header level 2</h2>
 <h3>header level 3</h3>
</body>
</html>
```

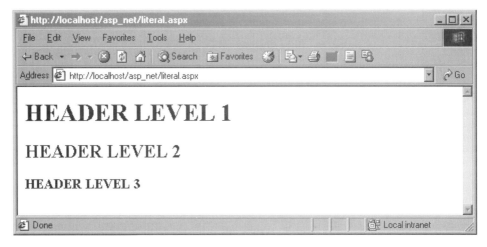

FIGURE 6.9 Changing the HTML content to uppercase

Page lifetime events

In ASP.NET, a web forms page raises several events that indicate different stages of the page processing. The following example shows event handlers for four main events – Init, Load, PreRender, and Unload (see also Figure 6.10):

```
<%-- Page Events Demo --%>
<%@ Page Language="VB" %>
<html>
 <body>
  <h2 align="center">Page Events</h2>
  <ul>
```

```
<script runat="server">
 Dim Msg As String

 Sub Page_Init
   Msg = "<li>Init</li>"
 End Sub

 Sub Page_Load
   Msg += "<li>Load</li>"
 End Sub

 Sub Page_PreRender
   Msg += "<li>PreRender</li>"
 End Sub

 Sub Page_Unload
   Msg += "<li>Unload</li>"
 End Sub

</script>
<% Response.Write(Msg) %>
</ul>
</body>
</html>
```

FIGURE 6.10   The outcome of entering the four main event handlers

Note that in the screenshot shown in Figure 6.10 there is no message from the Unload event handler. This is because this event occurs after all of the contents have been rendered to the page.

The Init event indicates the first step in the page lifecycle. This starts the page and its controls initialization. The Load event occurs when the page content is loaded into the Page object. At this time, we can initialize any of the variables and the state of any controls on the page. At this step, we can also check the IsPostBack property to find whether or not this is the first time that the page has been processed. The PreRender is the last event that occurs within the page before it is rendered. The last event that occurs in the page lifecycle is the Disposed event – this indicates that the page is released from memory.

Note that if we enable the Trace option in the @ Page directive, we can also see the sequence of events for that page (see the Trace Information section in the screenshot shown in Figure 6.11).

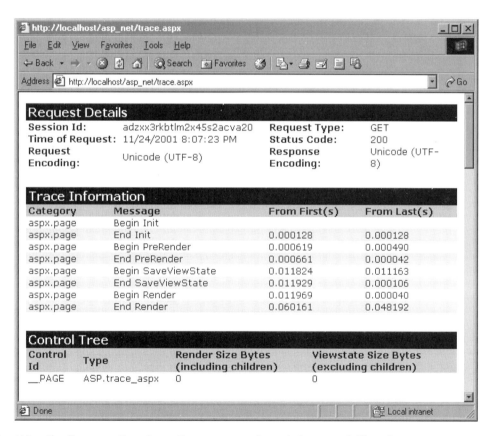

FIGURE 6.11   Using the Trace option shows the sequence of events in a page's lifecycle

We have discussed several topics concerning web forms pages and ASP.NET applications. Now is a good time to learn about two major classes in the System.Web namespace – the Control class and the Page class.

6.6 Control class

This class defines properties, methods, and events for all ASP.NET server controls – either controls that have a user interface or controls without one. Web forms pages are server controls and are based on the Page class, which we will discuss below.

The Control class has the following properties.

- **ClientID** Contains the server control identifier generated by ASP.NET.
- **Controls** Contains the ControlCollection object, which is a collection of all child controls for this server control.
- **EnableViewState** Indicates whether or not the server control maintains its view state and the view state of any of its child controls.
- **ID** Specifies the server control's programmatic identifier.
- **Page** Indicates the Page object that contains this server control.
- **Parent** Indicates the server control's parent control.
- **TemplateSourceDirectory** Specifies the virtual directory of the Page or UserControl for this server control.
- **UniqueID** Contains the unique identifier for this server control.
- **Visible** Indicates whether or not a server control is rendered.

The Control class contains several methods that are available for all derived classes that implement server-side controls. These methods are as follows.

- **DataBind method** Used to bind a data source to the server control and all of its child controls. Data binding will be discussed in more detail in Chapter 13.
- **FindControl method** Used to search for the specified server controls in the current container.
- **HasControls method** Checks if the server control has any child controls.
- **RenderControl method** Outputs server control content to a provided HtmlTextWriter object. If tracing is enabled, outputs trace information for this control.
- **ResolveUrl method** Resolves a relative URL to the absolute URL.
- **SetRenderMethodDelegate method** Specifies an event handler delegate that will render the server control to its parent control.

We have already seen some important events raised by the Page class, which is a descendant of the Control class. There is one more event that may be raised by the Control class. This is the DataBinding event, which occurs when the server control binds to a data source.

6.7   Page class

As we already know, the Page object is created by ASP.NET in response to a web page request. In this section, we will learn about the main properties of the Page class. They are the following.

- **Application** Contains the Application object for the current request.
- **Cache** Contains the Cache object that is used to store the page for subsequent requests.
- **ClientTarget** Allows us to specify how a page renders for particular browsers.
- **ErrorPage** Indicates the page to which the request browser should be redirected in the event of an unhandled page exception.
- **IsPostBack** Indicates whether or not the page is being loaded and accessed for the first time.
- **IsValid** Indicates whether or not page validation has succeeded.
- **Request** Contains the Request object that allows us to access data from the HTTP request.
- **Response** Contains the Response object that is used to send HTTP response data back to a browser.
- **Server** Contains an instance of the HttpServerUtility class.
- **Session** Contains the current SessionState object.
- **SmartNavigation** Enables or disables smart navigation. Smart navigation eliminates browser flicker/scrolling.
- **Trace** Contains the TraceContext object for the current request.
- **User** Contains information about the user.
- **Validators** Contains a collection of all validation controls (ValidatorCollection) for the current page. For more information on validation controls, see the next chapter.

6.8   Practice

In this section we will discuss the following topics:

- getting information about the client browser;
- getting and setting cookies;
- using a cache;
- dealing with configuration;
- applications security;
- sending e-mail;
- maintaining state.

Getting information about the client browser

The `HttpBrowserCapabilities` class represents the capabilities of the client browser that make a request. An object of the `HttpBrowserCapabilities` type is accessible via the `Browser` property of the `Request` object. The `HttpBrowserCapabilities` class contains the following properties.

- **ActiveXControls** Indicates whether or not the client browser supports ActiveX controls.
- **AOL** Indicates whether or not the client browser is an America Online (AOL) browser.
- **BackgroundSounds** Indicates whether or not the client browser supports background sounds.
- **Beta** Indicates whether or not the client browser is a beta release.
- **Browser** Contains the browser string from the HTTP user agent header.
- **CDF** Indicates whether or not the client browser supports channel definition format, used for webcasting.
- **ClrVersion** Indicates the version of common language runtime installed on the client computer.
- **Cookies** Indicates whether or not the client browser supports cookies.
- **Crawler** Indicates whether or not the client browser is a web crawler search engine.
- **EcmaScriptVersion** Indicates the version of ECMA script supported by the client browser.
- **Frames** Indicates whether or not the client browser supports frames.
- **JavaApplets** Indicates whether or not the client browser supports Java applets.
- **JavaScript** Indicates whether or not the client browser supports JavaScript.
- **MajorVersion** Returns the major version of the client browser.
- **MinorVersion** Returns the minor version of the client browser.
- **MSDomVersion** Returns the version of Microsoft XML DOM supported by the client browser.
- **Platform** Returns the name of the client's platform.
- **Tables** Indicates whether or not the client browser supports tables.
- **Type** Returns the name and major version of the client browser.
- **VBScript** Indicates whether or not the client browser supports VBScript.
- **Version** Returns the full version of the client browser.
- **W3CDomVersion** Returns the version of World Wide Web Consortium XML DOM supported by the client browser.
- **Win16** Indicates whether or not the client runs under 16-bit Windows.
- **Win32** Indicates whether or not the client runs under 32-bit Windows.

The following example shows how to extract properties of the `HttpBrowserCapabilities` object:

```
Private Sub Page_Load(ByVal sender As System.Object,
 ByVal e As System.EventArgs) Handles MyBase.Load

  Response.Write("<TABLE BORDER='1' WIDTH='60%'>")
  With Request.Browser

   Response.Write("<TR><TD>ActiveXControls</TD><TD>" & _
     .ActiveXControls & "</TD></TR>")
   Response.Write("<TR><TD>AOL</TD><TD>" & _
     .AOL & "</TD></TR>")
   Response.Write("<TR><TD>BackgroundSounds</TD><TD>" & _
     .BackgroundSounds & "</TD></TR>")
   Response.Write("<TR><TD>Beta</TD><TD>" & _
     .Beta & "</TD></TR>")
   Response.Write("<TR><TD>Browser</TD><TD>" & _
     .Browser & "</TD></TR>")
   Response.Write("<TR><TD>CDF</TD><TD>" & _
     .CDF & "</TD></TR>")
   Response.Write("<TR><TD>CLRVersion</TD><TD>" & _
     .ClrVersion.ToString & "</TD></TR>")
   Response.Write("<TR><TD>Cookies</TD><TD>" & _
     .Cookies & "</TD></TR>")
   Response.Write("<TR><TD>Crawler</TD><TD>" & _
     .Crawler & "</TD></TR>")
   Response.Write("<TR><TD>EcmaScriptVersion</TD><TD>" & _
     .EcmaScriptVersion.ToString & "</TD></TR>")
   Response.Write("<TR><TD>Frames</TD><TD>" & _
     .Frames & "</TD></TR>")
   Response.Write("<TR><TD>JavaApplets</TD><TD>" & _
     .JavaApplets & "</TD></TR>")
   Response.Write("<TR><TD>JavaScript</TD><TD>" & _
     .JavaScript & "</TD></TR>")
   Response.Write("<TR><TD>MajorVersion</TD><TD>" & _
     .MajorVersion & "</TD></TR>")
   Response.Write("<TR><TD>MinorVersion</TD><TD>" & _
     .MinorVersion & "</TD></TR>")
   Response.Write("<TR><TD>MSDomVersion</TD><TD>" & _
     .MSDomVersion.ToString & "</TD></TR>")
   Response.Write("<TR><TD>Platform</TD><TD>" & _
     .Platform & "</TD></TR>")
```

```
Response.Write("<TR><TD>Tables</TD><TD>" & _
  .Tables & "</TD></TR>")
Response.Write("<TR><TD>Type</TD><TD>" & _
  .Type & "</TD></TR>")
Response.Write("<TR><TD>VBScript</TD><TD>" & _
  .VBScript & "</TD></TR>")
Response.Write("<TR><TD>Version</TD><TD>" & _
  .Version & "</TD></TR>")
Response.Write("<TR><TD>W3CDomVersion</TD><TD>" & _
  .W3CDomVersion.ToString & "</TD></TR>")
Response.Write("<TR><TD>Win16</TD><TD>" & _
  .Win16 & "</TD></TR>")
Response.Write("<TR><TD>Win32</TD><TD>" & _
  .Win32 & "</TD></TR>")

    End With

  End Sub
```

Figure 6.12 shows the output of the above produced for Microsoft Internet Explorer 6.0, running under Microsoft Windows 2000.

Note that "raw" information about the client browser can be obtained by querying the user agent header:

```
Response.Write(Request.Headers("User-Agent"))
```

which returns:

```
Mozilla/4.0 (compatible; MSIE 6.0b; Windows NT 5.0; .NET CLR 1.0.2914)
```

for the same configuration. This string provides enough information for ASP.NET to fill other properties of the HttpBrowserCapabilities object. The browser capabilities are described in the <browserCaps> section of the machine.config file. Updated browser data can be found at cyScape, Inc. Visit their website at:

www.cyscape.com/browsercaps

Getting and setting cookies

In ASP.NET, two classes – HTTPCookie and HTTPCookieCollection – are used to get and set cookies on the client's computer. To set a cookie, we include information in an HttpResponse object (in the Set-Cookie header), which tells the browser to save a cookie on the client's computer. Future HTTP requests will send this cookie back to the server.

ActiveXControls	True
AOL	False
BackgroundSounds	True
Beta	True
Browser	IE
CDF	False
CLRVersion	1.0.2914
Cookies	True
Crawler	False
EcmaScriptVersion	1.2
Frames	True
JavaApplets	True
JavaScript	True
MajorVersion	6
MinorVersion	0
MSDomVersion	6.0
Platform	WinNT
Tables	True
Type	IE6
VBScript	True
Version	6.0b
W3CDomVersion	1.0
Win16	False
Win32	True

FIGURE 6.12   The properties of the `HttpBrowserCapabilities` object have been extracted

To create a cookie we use the following code:

```
Dim CookieColl as New HttpCookieCollection()
Dim Cookie As New HttpCookie("LastVisit")

Cookie.Value = DateTime.Now().ToString()
CookieCollection.Add(Cookie)
```

To read a cookie we use the following code:

```
Response.Write(Request.Cookies("LastVisit").Value)
```

In order to iterate the `HTTPCookieCollection` collection, we use the following code:

```
Dim Cookies As New HttpCookieCollection()
Cookies = Request.Cookies
Dim En As IEnumerator
En = Cookies.GetEnumerator

Response.Write("<TABLE BORDER='1'>")

While En.MoveNext()

 Response.Write("<TR><TD>" & En.Current & "</TD>")
 Response.Write("<TD>")
 Response.Write(Cookies.Item(En.Current).Value)
 Response.Write("</TD></TR>")


 End While
```

To find out if the client's cookies are enabled, check the `HTTPCookieCollection` collection for the presence of a `"ASP.NET_SessionId"` cookie – this is the ASP.NET session identifier cookie.

While debugging your applications, you may also want to turn on tracing (`<%@ Page Trace="True" %>`). The `Cookies` and `Headers` collections will show you the cookies you receive from the client (see Figure 6.13).

Cookies Collection

Name	Value	Size
ASP.NET_SessionId	y4hdag55zx4jb1yfbdav2n45	42

Headers Collection

Name	Value
Connection	Keep-Alive
Accept	*/*
Accept-Encoding	gzip, deflate
Accept-Language	en-us,fr-ch;q=0.8,de-ch;q=0.5,it-ch;q=0.3
Cookie	ASP.NET_SessionId=y4hdag55zx4jb1yfbdav2n45
Host	localhost
User-Agent	Mozilla/4.0 (compatible; MSIE 6.0b; Windows NT 5.0; .NET CLR 1.0.2914)

FIGURE 6.13   Using tracing to find cookies received from a client

Using a cache

ASP.NET provides a general-purpose cache facility for web applications. Classes for caching frequently used resources – ASP.NET pages, web services, and user controls on the server – can be found in the `System.Web.Caching` namespace.

There are two types of caching supported in ASP.NET – output cache and fragment cache. Output caching can be used to store the results of dynamic page generation. In this case, the subsequent request output will be loaded from the cached output rather than from dymanically executed page code.

To enable the output cache, we use the @ OutputCache Page-level directive. For example, the following directive caches the page output for 30 seconds:

```
<%@ OutputCache  Duration="30" VaryByParam="*" %>


<script runat="server">


    . . .


</script>
```

We can also use the Response.Cache object to specify expiration time, vary clauses, and other cache-related information. For example:

```
Response.Cache.SetExpires(DateTime.Now.AddSeconds(30))
```

When we use the page cache, the response page is saved in the cache when the first request for this page is made. Subsequent requests refer to the cache until the cache expires.

A cache can be located on a server, client, or proxy server. To specify the cache location we use the Location attribute of the @ OutputCache Page-level directive. This attribute can be set to Client, Downstream (proxy server cache), Server, or None (no cache). To set the cache location in code, we use the SetCacheability method, which may receive one of the following arguments:

- **HttpCacheability.NoCache** indicates that there is no cache;
- **HttpCacheability.Private** indicates that there is a client cache – this is the default value;
- **HttpCacheability.Public** indicates that there is a proxy server cache;
- **HttpCacheability.Server** indicates that there is a server cache.

To cache multiple versions of a page – create a cache based on a query string or form contents – we use the VaryByParam attribute of the @ OutputCache Page-level directive. For example:

```
<%@ OutputCache  Duration="60" VaryByParam="SectionID;SubSectionID" %>
```

In this case, the first time the page is requested, it is stored in the cache. If, within 60 seconds, the page is requested with the same values for SectionID and SubSectionID, its cached version will be returned to the client.

To cache pages based on the HTTP header, we use the VaryByHeader attribute of the @ OutputCache Page-level directive. For example:

```
<%@ OutputCache  Duration="60" VaryByHeader="Referer" %>
```

In this example, the first time the page is requested, it is stored in the cache. If, within 60 seconds, the page is requested from the same link, its cached version will be returned to the client.

A fragment cache can be used for caching portions of an ASP.NET page. Good candidates for fragment caching are navigation bars, headers, and footers. To implement fragment caching, we should create web forms user controls for the portions of the page we want to cache and include the @ OutputCache directive in the user control ASCX file.

Dealing with configuration

We already know that the <appSettings> section of the web.config file can be used to store customized settings for an application. For example, we can store the connection string there, as is shown in the following example:

```
<appSettings>

<add
  key="ConnectionString"
  value="server=(local);database=swiss;Trusted_Connection=yes"
/>

</appSettings>
```

In our code we refer to this "application variable" as shown in the following example:

```
Dim Conn As SqlConnection

...

Conn =  New SqlConnection(ConfigurationSettings.AppSettings
 ("ConnectionString"))

...
```

Note that, below, we have used the ConfigurationSettings class to access the key/value pair stored in the <appSettings> section of the web.config file.

We can also add our own configuration sections. Suppose we want to store our "application variable" in a <CustomSettings> section:

```
<?xml version="1.0" encoding="utf-8" ?>
<configuration>

<configSections>
```

```
<section
 name="CustomSettings"
 type="System.Configuration.NameValueSectionHandler, System"
/>

</configSections>

<CustomSettings>
  <add
   key="ConnectionString"
   value="server=(local);database=swiss;Trusted_Connection=yes"
  />
</CustomSettings>

</configuration>
```

To read the value, we use the following code:

```
Dim Conn As SqlConnection
...


Conn =  New SqlConnection(ConfigurationSettings.GetConfig
  ("CustomSettings")("ConnectionString"))


...
```

The GetConfig method used above takes the name of the customized configuration section as an argument, and the name of the key we have specified in our section is used as a property of this section.

Applications security

In this section, we will provide a brief overview of ASP.NET applications security. ASP.NET security works in conjunction with Microsoft's internet information server security and includes authentication (establishing identity) and authorization (granting or denying identity privileges) services to implement the ASP.NET security model.

ASP.NET also includes a role-based security feature that we can implement for both Microsoft Windows and non-Windows user accounts.

When a client makes a request, the following events occur:

● a client requests an .ASPX page from an IIS server;
● the client's credentials are passed to IIS;

- IIS authenticates the client and forwards the authenticated token along with the client's request to the ASP.NET worker process;
- based on the authenticated token and the configuration settings for the Web application, ASP.NET decides whether or not to impersonate a user on the thread that is processing the request.

Configuration

While IIS maintains security-related configuration settings in the IIS metabase, ASP.NET uses the XML-based `web.config` file. This file contains seveal sections related to ASP.NET security:

- `<authentication>`;
- `<authorization>`;
- `<identity>`;
- `<machineKey>`.

For more information on the purpose and contents of these sections, see our discussion of configuration files earlier in this chapter.

Authentication

ASP.NET supports the following four types of authentication.

- **Forms authentication** Refers to a system in which unauthenticated requests are redirected to an HTML form in which users enter their credentials. After the user submits the form and the application authenticates the request, the system issues an authorization ticket in the form of a cookie. This cookie contains the credentials or a key to reacquire the identity. Subsequent requests from the browser automatically include the cookie. To enable forms authentication, set the following `<authentication>` section attribute of the `web.config` file:

  ```
  <authentication mode="Forms" >
  ```

  We also need to specify the URL for the login page as a child node of the `<authentication>` node:

  ```
  <forms redirectUrl='inc/login.aspx' />
  ```

- **Windows authentication** IIS performs the authentication and the token is forwarded to the ASP.NET worker process. This type of authentication requires minimal coding. To enable Windows authentication, set the following `<authentication>` section attribute of the `web.config` file:

  ```
  <authentication mode="Windows" />
  ```

- **Passport authentication** This is based on the Passport centralized authentication service provided by Microsoft. It offers a single logon and core profile services for member sites. This type of authentication is used when we need single logon capabilities across multiple domains. To enable passport authentication, set the following `<authentication>` section attribute of the `web.config` file:

```
<authentication mode="Passport" />
```

- **Default authentication** This is used when we do not want any security on our web application or when we want to use our own customized security module. To enable this mode, set the following `<authentication>` section attribute of the `web.config` file:

```
<authentication mode="None" />
```

Authorization

ASP.NET supports the following types of authorization.

- **File authorization** We use the `FileAuthorizationModule` class to perform file authorization, and this type of authorization is active when we use Windows authentication. The `FileAuthorization` class is responsible for performing checks on Windows access control lists (ACLs) to find whether or not a user should have access.

- **URL authorization** We use the `UrlAuthorizationModule` class to perform URL authorization – authorization based on the URI namespace. This namespace can be quite different from the physical folder and file paths that NTFS permissions use. The `UrlAuthorizationModule` class implements both positive and negative authorization assertions. You can use this module to selectively allow or deny access to arbitrary parts of the URI namespace for users, roles, and verbs, such as `POST` and `GET`.

Role-based security

Role-based security in ASP.NET is not limited to Windows accounts and groups. For example, if we use Windows authentication and impersonation, the identity of the user is a Windows identity:

```
User.IdentityName  = "Domain\User"
```

To check identities for membership or in specific roles, and restrict access accordingly, we can use the following code:

```
If User.IsInRole("BUILTIN\Administrators") Then
  Response.Write("Admins are allowed")
Else If User.IsInRole("BUILTIN\Users") Then
```

```
  Response.Write("Users are not allowed")
Else
  Response.Write("You are not allowed")
End If
```

If we use forms authentication, roles are not assigned to the authenticated user – we must do this programmatically. To do this we create an event handler for the OnAuthenticate event and create a new GenericPrincipal object that is later assigned to the User property of the HttpContext object:

```
Sub Application_AuthenticateRequest
  If (Not(HttpContext.Current.User Is Nothing) Then
    If HttpContext.Current.User.Identity.AuthenticationType = _
      "Forms" Then

      Dim ID as System.Web.Security.FormsIdentity = _
        HttpContext.Current.User.Identity

      Dim Roles(4) As String

      Roles(0) = "admins"
      Roles(1) = "managers"
      Roles(2) = "testers"
      Roles(3) = "developers"

      HttpContext.Current.User = New _
        System.Security.Principal.GenericPrincipal(ID, Roles)

    End If
  End If
End Sub
```

To check if the user is in a specific role and restrict access accordingly, we use the following code:

```
If User.IsInRole("admins") Then
  Response.Write("Admins are allowed")
Else If User.IsInRole("developers") Then
  Response.Write("developers are not allowed")
Else
  Response.Write("You are not allowed")
End If
```

Sending e-mail

As we already know, classes implemented in the `System.Web.Mail` namespace can be used to send an e-mail attachment using the SMTP mail service built in to Microsoft Windows 2000. This namespace includes such classes as `MailAttachment`, `MailMessage`, and `SmtpMail`.

The simplest way to send an e-mail is to use the `MailMessage` class to construct a new message and use the `Send` method of the `SmtpMail` class to send the message. Let's look at the properties of the `MailMessage` class – they should be familiar to those who have used the CDONTS (colaborative data object for NT server) component to send e-mails from ASP code.

- **Attachments** This property specifies the list of attachments (`IList` collection) for this message.

- **Bcc** Specifies the semicolon-delimited list of e-mail addresses of blind carbon copy (BCC) recipients of this e-mail message.

- **Body** Specifies the body (main content) of this e-mail message.

- **BodyEncoding** Specifies the encoding type for this e-mail message. This property is of the `Encoding` type and contains such properties as `CodePage`, `ASCII`, `Unicode`, and so on. There are several predefined encodings, such as `ASCIIEncoding`, `UnicodeEncoding`, `UTF7Encoding`, and `UTF8Encoding`. For more information, see under `System.Text` namespace in Chapter 3.

- **BodyFormat** Specifies the content type of the e-mail body. This property can contain either a `MailFormat.Html` or `MailFormat.Text` value. The latter indicates a plain-text message.

- **Cc** Specifies the semicolon-delimited list of e-mail addresses of carbon copy (CC) recipients of this e-mail message.

- **From** Specifies the e-mail address of the sender of this message.

- **Headers** Allows us to specify the customized headers that will be transmitted with this e-mail message. For example, we can specify the `Reply-To` header to specify the e-mail address to reply to.

- **Priority** Indicates the priority of this e-mail message. Possible values for this property include `MailPriority.Low`, `MailPriority.Normal` (this is the default value, and `MailPriority.High`.

- **Subject** Specifies the subject line for this e-mail message.

- **To** Specifies the recipient's e-mail address.

- **UrlContentBase** Specifies the URL base for all relative URLs that are contained in the mail body.

- **UrlContentLocation** Specifies the URL of the mail body content location.

The following example shows how to use the `MailMessage` class.

```
<%@ Import Namespace="System.Web.Mail" %>

<script runat="server">

 Sub SendMail

  Dim EMail As New MailMessage

  With EMail

    .BodyFormat = MailFormat.Text
    .To         = "test@netface.ch (Test message recipient)"
    .From       = "fedorov@netface.ch (Alexei Fedorov)"
    .Subject    = "ASP.NET Email Test"
    .Body       = " ASP.NET Email Test Message"

  End With

  SmtpMail.Send(EMail)

 End Sub

</script>
```

The `SmtpMail` class has only one method – `Send` – that expects the object of `MailMessage` type. Note that the overloaded `Send` method can be used to send simple messages. This method takes four `String` parameters: `From`, `To`, `Subject`, and `MessageText`.

To create a mail attachment, we use the `MailAttachment` class, the constructor of which accepts file name and `Encoding` parameters. By default, `UUEncode` encoding is used. We can change this to `MailEncoding.Base64` if necessary.

Maintaining state

HTTP protocol does not maintain state across requests from clients – each request is serviced as it comes and, after the request has been processed, all of the data is discarded. This is called a "stateless" protocol. To maintain the application and session state in ASP.NET applications, we can use application and session variables.

Application variables are global variables defined for each ASP.NET application. To set these variables, we use the `Application_Start` event handler and then we can access and modify these variables in individual ASP.NET pages. The lifetime of application variables is the same as the lifetime of the whole ASP.NET aplication.

The following example shows how to set the application variable:

```
Application("StartedAt") = Date.Now
```

We can also add name/value pairs to the `Application` object. This object is an instance of the `HttpApplicationState` class, which contains several properties and methods used to manipulate the application state.

Here is the list of properties of the `HttpApplicationState` class.

- **AllKeys** Returns the access keys in the collection.
- **Contents** Returns a reference to the `HttpApplicationState` object.
- **Count** Returns the number of objects in the collection.
- **Item** Returns a specified object in the collection – we can access an item either by name or numerical index.
- **Keys** Returns all keys in the collection.
- **StaticObjects** Returns all objects declared with the `<object runat="server">...` `</object>` tag.

The `HttpApplicationState` class has the following methods.

- **Add method** Use to add a new object to the collection.
- **Clear method** Removes all objects from a collection.
- **Get method** Returns an object by name or index.
- **GetKey method** Returns an object name by index.
- **Lock method** Locks access to a collection to facilitate access synchronization and prevent other sessions from changing the value of the application variables.
- **Remove method** Removes the specified object from a collection.
- **RemoveAll method** Removes all objects from a collection. This is an internal call to `Clear` method.
- **RemoveAt method** Removes an object with the specified index.
- **Set method** Updates the value of an object specified by name.
- **Unlock method** Unlocks access to a collection. If the unlock method is not called, ASP.NET will unlock the collection when the request ends, times out or encounters an unhandled error.

To store variables that needed to be persistent for the duration of a user's session, we use session variables. These variables are unique to each user session and can be accessed in any ASP.NET page within an application.

To set the session variable, we can use the following code:

```
Session("CreatedAt") = Date.Now
```

To retrieve the session variable, we use the following code:

```
If Not (Session("CreatedAt") Is Nothing) Then

 Response.Write(Session("CreatedAt"))

 End If
```

In the previous example, we checked the session variable against Nothing – we needed to do this to avoid a runtime error. In an ASP.NET session variables are objects and they should exist before we try to access them.

Session variables exist during the session lifetime and are automatically discarded when the session is timed out or explicitly abandoned in the code.

When a session is initiated on first request, the server issues a unique session ID to the client. By default, this session ID is stored as an in-memory cookie or embedded within the request URL after the ASP.NET application name. This can be configured by the cookieless parameter in the web.config file.

```
<?xml version="1.0" encoding="utf-8" ?>
<configuration>

  <system.web>
   <sessionState cookieless="true" />
  </system.web>


</configuration>
```

Here is how a session ID is stored within the URL:

```
http://localhost/asp_net/(jhj4noumsqcrot5550ln3w21)/test.aspx
```

Note that the server automatically inserts the session ID in the relative URLs only. An absolute URL is not modified, even if it points to the same ASP.NET application, which can cause the loss of session variables.

We can also specify the mode of the session state. it can be either InProc, StateServer, or SqlServer.

- **InProc** Values are stored in the memory of the ASP.NET worker process. This is the fastest way to store and access the session values, but they will be lost when the ASP.NET worker process recycles.

- **StateServer** Values are stored in a standalone Microsoft Windows service that is independent of the Microsoft internet information server and can be run on a separate server. This mode can be used as a load-balancing solution – multiple web servers can share session variables. In this mode, session variables are not lost when we restart IIS, but performance can be impacted when we cross process boundaries. In this case, we need to add one extra attribute to the cookieless parameter in the web.config file – stateConnectionString. The default value is "tcpip=127.0.0.1:42424".

- **SqlServer** Values are stored in the Microsoft SQL Server. This allows us to use a state store that is located out of the IIS process and can be located on the local or remote server. In this case, we need to add one extra attribute to the cookieless parameter in the web.config file – sqlConnectionString. The default value is "data source=127.0.0.1;user id=sa;password=". You may also want to look at the source in the `InstallSqlState.sql` file, which contains the Transact-SQL script used to create databases and tables used to store session states. This file is located in the directory:

```
WINNT\Microsoft.NET\Framework\v.<version>\
```

All three modes can be used with a cookie or cookieless session ID persistence.

6.9 Web forms' internals

In this section we will look at how the web form is created by ASP.NET. Let's create a simple form that contains two fields and a button (see Figure 6.14). The code for this form is shown below.

```
<html>
<body>
<form id="login" runat="server">
 <center>
 <table width="50%">
  <tr>
   <td>User name</td>
   <td>
    <input type="text" runat="server" id="uname">
   </td>
  </tr>
  <tr>
   <td>Password</td>
   <td>
    <input type="password" runat="server" id="pass">
   </td>
  </tr>
  <tr>
   <td colspan="2" align="right">
    <input type="submit" value="Ok" id="ok" runat="server">
   </td>
  </tr>
 </table>
 </center>
</form>
</body>
</html>
```

Note that here we have four server-side controls – form, input box, password input box, and button.

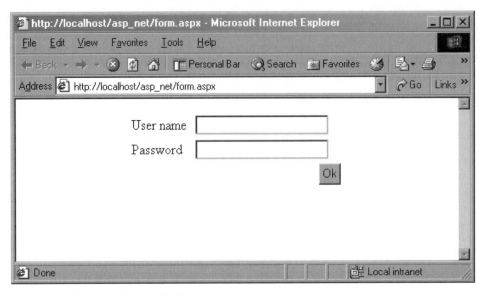

FIGURE 6.14   A simple web form with two fields and a button

ASP.NET starts with the creation of an assembly with a random name, such as 0v8jvl62. It also creates an XML file that contains the name of the assembly, its type, hash code, and path to the source:

```
<preserve assem="0v8jvl62" type="ASP.form_aspx" hash="1bec63da53d">
  <filedep name="c:\inetpub\wwwroot\asp_net\form.aspx" />
</preserve>
```

If we look into the assembly, we will find that it consists of an ASP namespace and one class, named form_aspx. This class extends the System.Web.UI.Page class and implements the System.Web.SessionState.IRequiresSessionState interface.

What is interesting is that for each server-side control, we have a field of an appropriate type – the field name is taken from the id attribute of the HTML tag, as shown in Table 6.3.

The main task of the constructor is to create an array of file dependencies, which is later used to track source files for the page.

TABLE 6.3   For each server control there is a field with matching type

Field	Type
login	System.Web.UI.HtmlControls.HtmlForm
ok	System.Web.UI.HtmlControls.HtmlInputButton
pass	System.Web.UI.HtmlControls.HtmlInputText
uname	System.Web.UI.HtmlControls.HtmlInputText

The `BuildControlTree` method is used to iterate all controls in the web form and add them to the `Controls` collection (by means of the call to the `IParserAccessor.AddParsedSubObject` method). For our code, it does the following:

- creates a new `LiteralControl` object with the following content:

  `"<html>\r\n<body>\r\n"`

- creates a new `HtmlForm` object with the name `login` by calling the `__BuildControllogin()` method;

- creates a new `LiteralControl` object with the following content:

  `"\r\n</body>\r\n</html>"`

Note that all static HTML is converted into server-side objects which become part of the `Page` object `Controls` collection (see Figure 6.15).

```
<html>                                                          LiteralControl
<body>

<form id="login" runat="server" border="1">
 <center>
 <table width="50%">
  <tr>
   <td>User name</td>
   <td>
    <input type="text" runat="server" id="uname">
   </td>
  </tr>
  <tr>
   <td>Password</td>
   <td>                                                         HTMLForml
    <input type="password" runat="server" id="pass">
   </td>
  </tr>
  <tr>
   <td colspan="2" align="right">
    <input type="submit" value="Ok" id="ok" runat="server">
   </td>
  </tr>
 </table>
 </center>
</form>

</body>                                                         LiteralControl
</html>
```

FIGURE 6.15 Static HTML is turned into server-side objects that become part of the `Controls` collection

```
<form id="login" runat="server" border="1">

  <center>
  <table width="50%">                                           LiteralControl
    <tr>
     <td>User name</td>
     <td>
       <input type="text" runat="server" id="uname">          HTMLInputText
     </td>
    </tr>                                                        LiteralControl
    <tr>
     <td>Password</td>
     <td>                                                                              HTMLForml
       <input type="password" runat="server" id="pass">       HTMLInputText
     </td>
    </tr>                                                        LiteralControl
    <tr>
     <td colspan="2" align="right">
       <input type="submit" value="Ok" id="ok" runat="server"> HTMLInputButton
     </td>
    </tr>                                                        LiteralControl
  </table>
  </center>
</form>
```

FIGURE 6.16   Form HTML code is separated into a set of controls

A form acts as a container for other controls. The __BuildControllogin() method used to create a new HtmlForm object performs the following tasks:

- creates a new HtmlForm object and sets its ID property to "login" by using the set_ID("login") method;
- for each HTML text within the form, it creates a separate LiteralControl object;
- calls __BuildControluname(), __BuildControlpass(), and __BuildControlok() methods to create child controls.

Figure 6.16 shows how the form HTML code is separated into a set of controls.

Each child control is created with the appropriate method. For example, a button is created with the call to the __BuildControlok() method:

```
IAttributeAccessor::SetAttribute("type", "submit")
HtmlInputControl::set_Value("Ok")
Control::set_ID("ok")
```

Input boxes are created by calls to the __BuildControluname() and __BuildControlpass() methods:

```
__BuildControlpass()

IAttributeAccessor::SetAttribute("type", "password")
System.Web.UI.Control::set_ID("pass")
```

```
__BuildControluname()


IAttributeAccessor::SetAttribute("type", "text")
System.Web.UI.Control::set_ID("uname")
```

At the end of this process, we will have the tree of server-side controls shown in Figure 6.17.

Control Id	Type
__PAGE	ASP.form_aspx
ctrl0	System.Web.UI.LiteralControl
login	System.Web.UI.HtmlControls.HtmlForm
ctrl1	System.Web.UI.LiteralControl
uname	System.Web.UI.HtmlControls.HtmlInputText
ctrl2	System.Web.UI.LiteralControl
pass	System.Web.UI.HtmlControls.HtmlInputText
ctrl3	System.Web.UI.LiteralControl
ok	System.Web.UI.HtmlControls.HtmlInputButton
ctrl4	System.Web.UI.LiteralControl
ctrl5	System.Web.UI.LiteralControl

FIGURE 6.17   Tree of server-side controls

Our Page object is ready to render. This is done by the RenderControl method, which iterates the Controls collection and calls the RenderControl method for each element. The output is sent to the client.

6.10   Conclusion

In this chapter, we learned how to use Microsoft .NET to create web applications with the help of two technologies – active server pages .NET (ASP.NET) and web forms.

We learned a lot about the ASP.NET-related namespace, its main classes, and its secondary namespaces, web applications infrastructure, and the main features provided by ASP.NET. We also discussed how to use ASP.NET to get information about a client browser, how to get and set cookies, use a cache, deal with configuration, application security, send e-mails, and maintain the state of ASP applications. We ended this chapter with a discussion of the internals of web forms.

In the next chapter, we will learn about ASP.NET server controls – a set of classes used to create an ASP.NET application's user interface.

chapter 7

ASP.NET server controls

- Types of server controls

- Server controls

- HTML server controls

- Web server controls

- Validation controls

- Validation controls and page validation

In the previous chapter we discussed ASP.NET applications and web form pages. We have learned a lot about the ASP.NET-related namespace and main classes, about web applications infrastructure, and the main features of ASP.NET. Here we will learn about ASP.NET server controls – a set of classes used to create an ASP.NET applications user interface.

ASP.NET includes a number of built-in server controls that are designed to provide a more structured programming model for the web than has previously been available. Here is a list of the main features provided by server controls:

- automatic state management;
- simple access to object values without having to use the `Request` object;
- ability to react to events in server-side code to create better, structured applications;
- common approach to building user interfaces for web pages;
- output is automatically customized, based on the capabilities of the browser.

We can also create our own user and customized controls. Such controls can enhance and extend existing controls to build a much richer user interface than has been possible before.

Server controls are declared within an `.aspx` file using customized tags that contain a `runat="server"` attribute value. This attribute enables server-side events and view state management for controls. A server control declaration must follow XML syntax rules – that is, a tag that declares a control should be closed with `/>` or using a separate closing tag. Also note that server controls work only within a `<form runat="server">...</form>` container tag, which is the "heart" of the web forms page. The following example shows how to use server controls to create a form with two input boxes and a button (see also Figure 7.1):

```
<%@ Page Language="VB" %>
<html>
<body>
<form id="login" runat="server">
 <center>
 <table width="70%">
  <tr>
   <td>User name</td>
   <td>
    <input type="text" runat="server" id="uname" />
   </td>
  </tr>
  <tr>
   <td>Password</td>
   <td>
    <input type="password" runat="server" id="pass" />
   </td>
  </tr>
```

```
    <tr>
     <td colspan="2" align="right">
      <input type="submit" value="Ok" id="ok" runat="server" />
     </td>
    </tr>
   </table>
   </center>
  </form>
  </body>
  </html>
```

FIGURE 7.1   Server controls have been used to create this form with two input boxes and a button

Let's look at the code in more detail. The first thing we note is that we have a server-side form that acts as a container for other controls:

```
<form id="login" runat="server">


    . . .


</form>
```

Note, too, that we have not specified the method and action attributes for the form tag. In ASP.NET, by default method is defined as POST and action is the name of the page.

Next, we use three server controls that are no more than usual HTML controls, but with the runat="server" attribute value:

```
<input type="text" runat="server" id="uname" />
...
<input type="password" runat="server" id="pass" />
...
<input type="submit" value="Ok" id="ok" runat="server" />
```

If we enter some values in the fields and press the "OK" button, the form's data will be sent to our page, but the difference here is that the entered values will be preserved (see Figure 7.2).

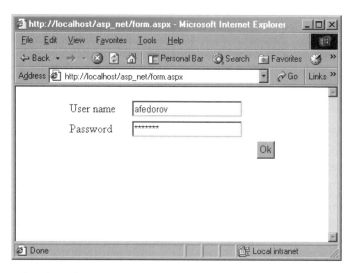

FIGURE 7.2   Values have been entered in the fields and these will be preserved once sent to our page

If we look at the source of the page (right-click on the page and select "View Source" command), we will find one extra field that has been added by the ASP.NET. This is a hidden field named "__VIEWSTATE" that is used to store the form's data between the requests:

```
<html>
<body>
<form name="login" method="post" action="form.aspx" id="login">
<input type="hidden" name="__VIEWSTATE"
 value="dDwtODkzMTQ3NzM1Ozs+" />

 <center>
 <table width="70%">
  <tr>
   <td>User name</td>
   <td>
```

```
      <input name="uname" id="uname" type="text" value="afedorov" />
     </td>
    </tr>
    <tr>
     <td>Password</td>
     <td>
      <input name="pass" id="pass" type="password" />
     </td>
    </tr>
    <tr>
     <td colspan="2" align="right">
      <input name="ok" id="ok" type="submit" value="Ok" />
     </td>
    </tr>
   </table>
   </center>
  </form>
  </body>
  </html>
```

Also note the other bold text in the above code – ASP.NET has added some attributes that we omitted.

The server controls provide properties, methods, and events for use in our code. The controls are programmable in our server code, allowing us to interact with those controls and their data. For example, to access the contents of a text box, we use the following code:

```
<script runat="server">

  Sub Page_Load()

    If IsPostBack Then
      Response.Write("Hello, " & uname.Value & "<BR>")
    End If

  End Sub

</script>
```

The IsPostBack is a Page object property that allows us to find out whether the page is being loaded in response to a client postback, or loaded and accessed for the first time.

7.1 Types of server controls

When we create web forms, we can use the following types of controls.

- **HTML server controls** Such controls expose an object model that maps very closely to the HTML elements they render. All HTML server controls can be bound to a data source. Table 7.1 shows some of the HTML server controls available in ASP.NET.

TABLE 7.1   Some of the HTML server controls found in ASP.NET

HTML control	Description
HtmlAnchor	Used to create web navigation links.
HtmlButton	Used to create a button – an element that can be clicked on in order to perform an assigned task. This control can contain any type of HTML code, which makes it very flexible.
HtmlForm	Used to define an HTML form. When the form is submitted, the values of controls within the form are posted to the server.
HtmlInputText	Used to display text entered at design time that can be edited by users at runtime or changed programmatically. Can also be used to create password input boxes.
HtmlTextArea	Used to enter or edit multiline text.

- **Web server controls** Such controls include not only form-type controls, such as buttons and text boxes, but also special-purpose controls, such as a calendar. Web server controls are more abstract than HTML server controls – the object model does not necessarily reflect HTML syntax. All Web server controls can be bound to a data source. Table 7.2 shows some of the Web server controls available in ASP.NET.

- **Validation controls** Used along with an input control to test what the user enters. Validation controls can check for a required field, test against a specific value or pattern of characters, and so on. Table 7.3 shows the validation server controls available in ASP.NET.

- **User controls** This type of control is created by us. We create user controls as web forms pages and embed them in other web forms pages – this is the easy way to implement menus, toolbars, headers, footers, and other reusable elements.

TABLE 7.2 Some of the web server controls found in ASP.NET

Web control	Description
AdRotator	Used to display a sequence (predefined or random) of images.
Calendar	Used to display a graphic calendar on which users can select a date.
CheckBoxList	Used to display a group of check boxes.
DataGrid	Used to display data-bound information in tabular form with columns. Supports editing and sorting.
DataList	Used instead of Repeater when we need more formatting and layout options.
DropDownList	Used to allow users to select one option from a list or enter text.
HyperLink	Used to create web navigation links.
Image	Used to display an image.
ImageButton	Used instead of a Button control – incorporates displays of an image instead of text.
Label	Used to display text that cannot be directly edited. Text can be changed programmatically.
LinkButton	Used instead of a Button control – has the appearance of a hyperlink.
ListBox	Used to display a list of choices and allow multiple selections.
Panel	Used to create a borderless container for other controls.
RadioButton	Used to display a single button that users click to enable or disable the control.
Repeater	Used to display information from a data set using a set of HTML elements and controls we specify, repeating elements once for each record in the data set.
Table	Used to create a table.
TextBox	Used to display text entered at design time that can be edited by users at runtime or changed programmatically.

Now we have an idea of ASP.NET server controls, let's learn about them in more detail. We will start with discussion of the ASP.NET classes that serve as a base for server controls, then we will learn about the functionality provided by particular controls – HTML server, web server, and validation controls. We will end this chapter with an overview of how we can create user controls. Data-bound features of controls, as well as controls used to display data-bound information, will be covered in Chapter 13, Using data binding controls.

TABLE 7.3 Validation server controls found in ASP.NET

Validation control	Description
CompareValidator	Performs comparison with a value. Compares a user's entry against a constant value or a property value of another control using a comparison operator (less than, equal to, greater than, and so on).
CustomValidator	Performs user-defined validation. Check the user's entry using validation logic that you code yourself. This type of validation allows you to check for values derived at runtime.
RangeValidator	Performs range checking. Verifies that a user's entry is between specified lower and upper boundaries. We can check ranges within pairs of numbers, alphabet characters, and dates.
RegularExpressionValidator	Performs pattern matching. Checks that the entry matches a pattern defined by a regular expression.
RequiredFieldValidator	Performs required entry validation. Ensures that the user does not skip a required entry.

7.2 Server controls

Server controls are implemented in the `System.Web.UI` namespace – which can be found in the `system.web.dll` assembly – and its secondary namespaces – `System.Web.UI.HtmlControls` and `System.Web.UI.WebControls`. All server controls are indirectly based on the `Control` class, which we covered in the previous chapter when we discussed web forms pages.

Let's just briefly refresh our memories about the main properties of the `Control` class.

- **ID** Used to identify a control.
- **Controls** Indicates a collection of child controls.
- **Page** Specifies the `Page` object that contains the control.
- **Parent** Specifies the control to which this control belongs.
- **ViewState** Used for persisting data across round trips between client and server.
- **UniqueID** Contains a unique identifier assigned to the control by ASP.NET.
- **Visible** Indicates whether or not a control is visible.

Figure 7.3 shows classes derived from the `Control` class.

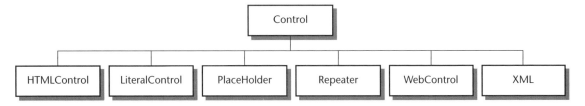

FIGURE 7.3 Classes derived from the `Control` class

Let's look at these derived classes briefly.

- **HTMLControl class** Provides common properties inherited by all HTML server control classes within the System.Web.UI.HTMLControls namespace.

- **LiteralControl class** Represents HTML elements, text, and any other strings in an ASP.NET page. These do not require processing on the server.

- **PlaceHolder class** Used to store added server controls dynamically on the web page.

- **Repeater class** Data-bound list control that allows customization of layout by repeating a specified template for each item displayed in the list.

- **WebControl class** Defines methods, properties, and events common to all controls within the System.Web.UI.WebControls namespace.

- **XML class** Used to display the contents of an XML document or the results of an XSL Transform.

We will start our journey through server controls with HTML controls that are derived from the HTMLControl class.

7.3 HTML server controls

The HTMLControl class provides common properties inherited by all HTML server control classes within the System.Web.UI.HTMLControls namespace. The HTMLControl class adds its own properties to those inherited from the Control class.

- **Attributes** This property returns a collection of all attribute name and value pairs in the server control tag.

- **Disabled** Indicates whether or not the HTML server control is disabled.

- **Style** Returns a collection of all CSS properties applied to an HTML control.

- **TagName** Returns the element name of a control.

The HTMLControl class does not add any of its own methods and events – all are inherited from the Control class.

This class serves as a base for three derived classes – HTMLContainerControl, HTMLInputControl, and HTMLImage. The first two have their own derived classes, which are shown in Figure 7.4.

The HTMLContainerControl class defines methods, properties, and events available to all HTML server controls that must have a closing tag, such as <form>, <table>, <tr>, <td>, <a>, and <span> elements. It adds two properties available in the derived classes – the InnerHtml property, which specifies the content found between the opening and closing tags of the control, and the InnerText property, which specifies the text found between the opening and closing tags of the control.

The HtmlImage class provides properties to programmatically access the HTML <img> element on the server.

The HtmlInputControl class defines methods, properties, and events common to all HTML input controls, such as <input type=text>, <input type=submit>, and <input type=file> elements.

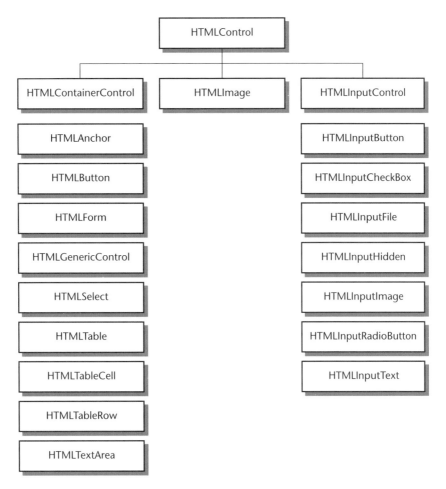

FIGURE 7.4 The Control class is the basis of a host of other classes

HTMLForm control

One of the most important server controls in the whole web forms architecture is the HtmlForm control. It serves as a container for all the other server controls we place on the web forms page. It contains the following properties, which correspond to the attributes of the <form> HTML element.

- **EncType** Specifies the encoding type used when posting the form's data to the server. The default value is "application/x-www-form-urlencoded". Other possible values include "multipart/form-data" (used to upload files on the server), "text/plain", and "image/jpeg".

- **Method** Specifies how the form's data will be sent to the server. The default value is POST, while we can also specify the GET method. We should not change the value of this property (or specify another value for the `method` attribute of the `<form>` HTML element) if we want to use the "post back" and "state management" capabilities of the web forms.

● **Name** Specifies the identifier for the `HtmlForm` control.

● **Target** Specifies where the rendered results will be posted. Possible values include `_blank` (new window), `_parent` (immediate frameset parent), `_self` (the frame with focus) or `_top` (unframed window). We can also specify a frame name – if no such frame exists, a window will be created.

The following example shows the `HtmlForm` control with most of the properties set to its default values:

```
<form id="login" runat="server">

  . . .

</form>
```

Here is how ASP.NET fills the values of the default properties for the same control when it renders it on the client:

```
<form id="login" method="post" action="form.aspx" id="login">

  . . .

</form>
```

HTMLGeneric control

This control represents HTML elements that do not map to a specific HTML server control – `<span>`, `<body>`, `<div>`, `<font>`, and several others. We use this control to dynamically change the inner content of the HTML element.

In most cases, we use the `<span>` or `<div>` elements to dynamically display text generated by event-handler code. For example:

```
<script runat="server">

 Sub ButtonClick(sender As Object, e As System.EventArgs)

   Msg.InnerText = "Button was clicked"

 End Sub

</script>
```

```
<form id="main" runat="server">

<button runat="server" OnServerClick="ButtonClick">Ok</button>
<span id="Msg" runat="server"></span>

</form>
```

HTMLAnchor control

This control represents an HTML <a> element used to create hyperlinks. Using this control, we can dynamically modify the attributes and properties of the <a> element and control events to generate HTMLAnchor controls dynamically.

The Target property is used to specify the location to display the hyperlink – it can be a name of a window or some special value, such as _blank, _self, _parent, or _top.

The HRef property specifies the URL target of the link and the Title property specifies the title that the browser displays for a web page.

The ServerClick event occurs on the server when a user clicks the HTMLAnchor control on the browser.

The following example shows how to use the HTMLAnchor server control:

```
<script runat="server">

  Sub AnchorClick(sender As Object, e As System.EventArgs)

    Response.Redirect("http://www.microsoft.com")

  End Sub

</script>


<form id="main" runat="server">

<a OnServerClick = "AnchorClick" runat="server">Click here</a>

</form>
```

HTMLButton control

This control represents an HTML <button> element (defined in the HTML 4.0 specification) used to create buttons. To specify the action performed when the control is clicked, we use the ServerClick event. The CausesValidation property indicates whether or not validation is performed when the control is clicked.

The following example shows how to use the **HTMLButton** server control:

```
<script runat="server">
Sub ButtonClick(sender As Object, e As System.EventArgs)
'
' Add your button-click processing code here
'
 End Sub
</script>


<form id="main" runat="server">

<button runat="server" OnServerClick="ButtonClick">Ok</button>

</form>
```

HTMLImage control

This control represents an HTML <img> element and provides programmatic access to its attributes, including the src, width, height, border, alt, and align attributes.

The following example shows how to dynamically change images using the HTMLImage control (see also Figure 7.5).

```
<%@ Import Namespace = "System.IO" %>

<script runat="server">

 Sub Page_Load()

  If Not IsPostBack Then
   Dim Path As String = Server.MapPath("Images\")
   Dim DirInfo As New DirectoryInfo(Path)
   Dim Files As FileInfo() = DirInfo.GetFiles("*.BMP")
   List.DataSource=Files
   List.DataBind
  End If

 End Sub

 Sub ShowImage(sender As Object, e As System.EventArgs)
```

```
      Img.Src = Server.MapPath("Images\" & List.Value)
      Img.Height = 120
      Img.Width  = 120


   End Sub


</script>


<form id="main" runat="server">
 <select id="list" runat="server" />
 <button OnServerClick="ShowImage" runat="server">Show</button>
 <p align="center">
  <img id="img" runat="server" />
 </p>
</form>
```

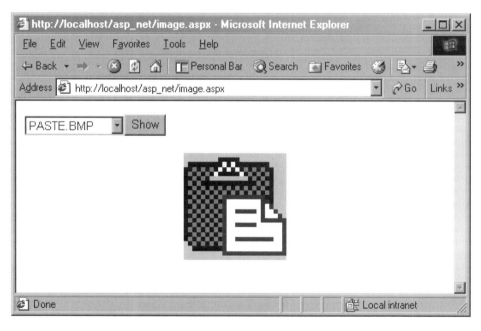

FIGURE 7.5   Using the HTMLImage control, we can change images

In our web forms page, we have three server-side controls: select (discussed later in this chapter), button, and image. When we load our page for the first time, the code in the Page_Load event creates a list of .BMP files in the Images subdirectory of our application directory and attaches it to the select control. Now, we can select an

image and click on the "Show" button to look at it. The event handler for the button
`ServerClick` event changes the SRC attribute of the image control to the name of
the image, currently selected in the list box.

HTMLInputButton control

This control represents HTML `<input type=button>`, `<input type=submit>`, and
`<input type=reset>` elements and provides a `ServerClick` event that is fired
when a user clicks on the button. The `Type` property indicates the type of the button.
It can be either `"button"`, `"submit"`, or `"reset"`.

HTMLInputCheckBox control

This control represents an HTML `<input type=checkbox>` element and provides a
`Checked` property that indicates the state of the control. This control does not fire
any events of its own. We should use it with the `HTMLInputButton` control to determine whether or not a check box is selected. The following example shows how to do
this (see also Figure 7.6):

```
<script runat="server">

Sub ChooseClick(sender As Object, e As System.EventArgs)

  Dim Langs As String
  If (CS.Checked = true) Then
   Langs += " CSharp "
  End If
  If (VB.Checked = true) Then
   Langs += " VB.NET "
  End If
  If (CP.Checked = true) Then
   Langs += " C++ .NET "
  End If

  Lang.InnerText = Langs

End Sub

</script>

<form id="main" runat="server">
 <h3>Please choose languages:</h3>
  <input id="CS" checked type=checkbox runat="server"> CSharp.NET
```

```
<input id="VB" type=checkbox runat="server"> Visual Basic.NET
<input id="CP" type=checkbox
  runat="server"> C++ with Managed Extensions
<input type=button value="Choose"
  OnServerClick="ChooseClick" runat="server">
<p align="center">
 <span id="Lang" runat="server" />
</p>

</form>
```

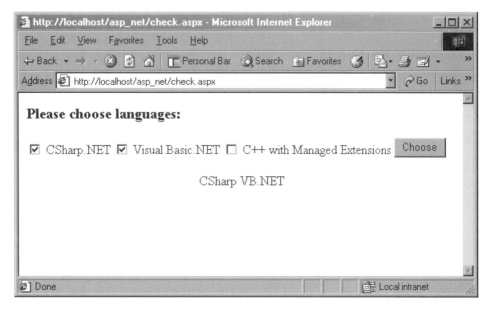

FIGURE 7.6   Using the HTMLInputCheckBox control

HTMLInputFile control

This control represents an HTML <input type=file> element and provides several properties to programmatically manage this element.

- **Accept** Specifies a comma-separated list of MIME encodings used to constrain the file types the user can select.
- **MaxLength** Specifies the maximum length of the file path for the file to upload from the client machine.
- **PostedFile** Provides access to the uploaded file.
- **Size** Specifies the width of the text box used to enter the file path.

In order to implement the file uploading functionality, we must specify the encoding type of our form control as `"multipart/form-data"`. The following example shows how to use this control (see also Figure 7.7).

```
<%@ Import Namespace = "System.IO" %>

<script runat="server">

 Sub Upload(Source As Object, e As EventArgs)

 Dim FileName as String

  If Not (FileUp.PostedFile Is Nothing) Then
   Try
    FileName = Server.MapPath("Images\") + _
     Path.GetFileName(FileUp.PostedFile.FileName)
    FileUp.PostedFile.SaveAs(FileName)
    Img.Src = FileName
   Catch ex As Exception
    '
    ' Do something with exceptions here
    '
   End Try
  End If

 End Sub

</script>

<form enctype="multipart/form-data" runat="server">

 <h3>Please Select File to Upload: </h3>
  <input
   id="FileUp"
   type="file"
   runat="server">
  <input
   type=button
   id="UpBtn"
   value="Upload"
   OnServerClick="Upload"
   runat="server">
 <p align="center">
  <img id="img" width=120 height=120 runat="server" />
 </p>

</form>
```

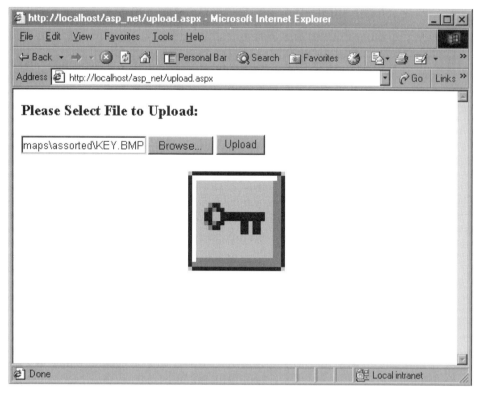

FIGURE 7.7   The `HTMInputFile` control implements the file uploading functionality

In the example above, we used input file control, button control, and image control. The `"Browse"` button is part of the input file control. We use the `"Browse"` button to select a file to upload and, when we have selected one, we press the `"Upload"` button, which calls the server-side code that does the job.

In the `"Upload"` button's `Click` event handler, we check if we have received something and then create a full name to store the file. We use the `Images` subdirectory of the current application directory to do this. Having done this, we save the uploaded file with its new name and assign this name to the `src` property of an image server-side control.

The `PostedFile` property we have used in our example is of the `HttpPostedFile` type, which contains all the information about the file we have just uploaded. It contains such properties as `ContentLength` (it returns the size of an uploaded file in bytes), `ContentType` (it returns the MIME content type for the file), `FileName` (it returns the full file name on the client's computer), and `InputStream` (it returns a `Stream` object that points to the uploaded file). We have used the `SaveAs` method to save an uploaded file to a specified directory on the server.

HTMLInputHidden control

This control represents an HTML <input type=hidden> element, which can be used to store non-visual information within the web form.

HTMLInputImage control

This control represents an HTML <input type=image> element that can be used as a button that displays an image. The HTMLInputImage control is more compatible with the previous versions of browsers than the HTMLButton control we learned about above.

The HTMLInputImage control provides programmatic access to the following attributes of HTML control: src, width, height, border, alt, and align.

The event handler for the ServerClick event receives an ImageClickEventArgs argument, which contains X and Y properties, which allows us to use the HTMLInputImage control to create very simple image maps. The following example shows how to use the HTMLInputImage control (see also Figure 7.8).

```
<script runat="server">

Sub OnClick(ByVal Source As Object, ByVal E as ImageClickEventArgs)

  Msg.InnerText = String.Format("Button was clicked at {0}, {1}", _
  E.X, E.Y)

 End Sub

</script>

<form id="main" runat="server">

 <input
   type="image"
   src="balloon.bmp"
   OnServerClick="OnClick"
   runat="server">

 <h3><span id="Msg" runat=server></span></h3>

 </form>
```

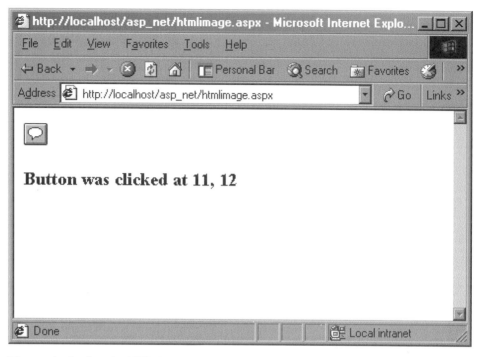

FIGURE 7.8   The result of using the HTMLInputImage control

HTMLInputRadioButton control

This control represents an HTML `<input type=radio>` element that is a button and can have two states – checked and unchecked. Radio buttons are usually used in a group to provide mutually exclusive options. To create a group, we specify the common value of the `Name` property for each control. In this case only one radio button in the group can be selected at a time.

The following example shows how to use the `HTMLInputRadioButton` control. Here we have a group of three `HTMLInputRadioButton` controls with the same `Name` property and different `ID` and `Value` attributes (see also Figure 7.9):

```
<script runat="server">

Sub Server_Change(Source As Object, e As EventArgs)

  If Radio1.Checked = True Then
   Msg.InnerText = "Radio1 is checked"
   Msg.Style("background") = Radio1.Value
   Else
     If Radio2.Checked = True Then
       Msg.InnerText = "Radio2 is checked"
```

```
        Msg.Style("background") = Radio2.Value
        Else
         If Radio3.Checked = True Then
          Msg.InnerText = "Radio3 is checked"
          Msg.Style("background") = Radio3.Value
         End If
        End If
      End If


   End Sub

</script>

<form id="main" runat="server">
 <h3>Please choose a color</h3>

  <input type="radio" id="radio1"
    OnServerChange="Server_Change"
    name="color" value="red" runat="server">Red
  <input type="radio" id="radio2"
    OnServerChange="Server_Change"
    name="color" value="green" runat="server">Green
  <input type="radio" id="radio3"
    OnServerChange="Server_Change"
    name="color" value="blue" runat="server">Blue

  <p align="center">
   <input type=submit id="Btn1"
     value="Enter"
     runat="server">

  <h3><span id="Msg" runat=server></span></h3>
  </p>
 </form>
```

The HTMLButton server control is used to send the contents of the form to the server, where the ServerChange event occurs when the radio button's state is changed. In the event handler for this event we show which radio button was checked and change the background color of the <span> element to the Value attribute of the checked radio button.

FIGURE 7.9   These buttons have been created using the HTMLInputRadioButton control

HTMLInputText control

This control represents HTML <input type=text> and <input type=password> elements, which can be used to enter text and passwords. The HTMLInputText control provides such properties as MaxLength (used to specify the maximum number of characters that can be entered in the text box), Size (used to specify the width of the text box), and Value (contains the entered text).

HTMLTextArea control

This control represents an HTML <textarea> element and provides programmatic access to its properties. The HTMLTextArea control is used to create a multiline text box, the width of which is specified by the Cols property and its height by the Rows property.

HTMLSelect control

This control represents an HTML <select> element and provides programmatic access to its <option> elements via the Items property. Other properties include Multiple (indicates whether multiple option items can be selected from the list), SelectedIndex (indicates the index of the selected item), and Size (indicates the number of visible items).

The following example shows how to dynamically add elements to the HTMLSelect control (see also Figure 7.10):

```
<script runat="server">

 Sub AddItem(Source As Object, e As EventArgs)

  Colors.Items.Add(Color.Value)

 End Sub

</script>

<form id="main" runat="server">

 <h3>Please add items</h3>

 <input type="text" id="Color" runat="server">
 <input type="button" runat="server"
   value="Add" onServerClick="AddItem">

 <select id="Colors" runat="server">

 </select>

</form>
```

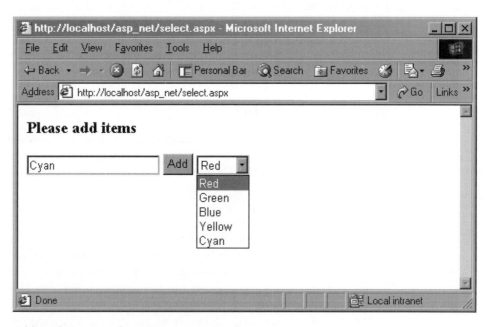

FIGURE 7.10   Adding elements to the HTMLSelect control

Note that the Items.Add method creates an <option> element with the value attribute and text set to the specified argument. For example:

```
<option value="Green">Green</option>
```

HTMLTable control

This control represents an HTML <table> element and provides programmatic access to its contents, including rows and cells, via the HTMLTableRowCollection and HTMLTableCellCollection properties respectively. Other properties of the HTMLTable control include the following.

- **Align** Specifies the alignment of the table contents.
- **BgColor** Specifies the background color of the table.
- **Border** Specifies the width of the border as an integer value.
- **BorderColor** Specifies the color of the border.
- **CellPadding** Specifies the cell padding in pixels.
- **CellSpacing** Specifies the cell spacing in pixels.
- **Height** Specifies the height of the table.
- **Rows** Returns the collection of rows in the table. Each element of this collection is an HTMLTableRow control.
- **Width** Specifies the width of the table.

The following example shows how to programmatically access the <table> element and its contents (see also Figure 7.11):

```
<script runat="server">

  Sub Show(Source As Object, e As EventArgs)

    Dim I As Integer
    Dim J As Integer
    Dim Row As HTMLTableRow

     For I = 0 to Tbl.Rows.Count-1
      Row = Tbl.Rows(I)
      For J = 0 to Row.Cells.Count-1
        Msg.InnerHTML += Row.Cells(J).InnerHTML & "<br>"
      Next
     Next

   End Sub

 </script>
```

```
<form id="main" runat="server">

  <table id="tbl" border="2" runat="server">
   <tr>
    <td>Cell 1.1</td>
    <td>Cell 1.2</td>
   </tr>
   <tr>
    <td>Cell 2.1</td>
    <td>Cell 2.2</td>
   </tr>
  </table>

  <br>
  <input type="button" runat="server"
    value="Show" onServerClick="Show">
  <p align="center">
   <h3><span id="Msg" runat=server></span></h3>
  </p>

</form>
```

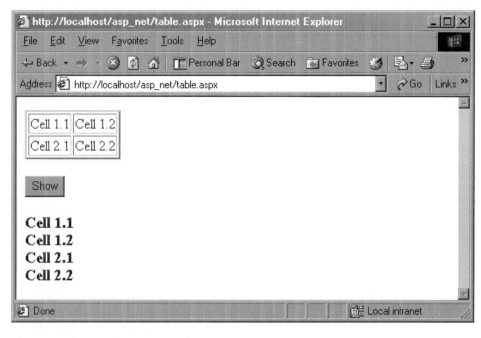

FIGURE 7.11   The result of using the <table> element

HTMLTableRow control

This control represents one row in a table and corresponds to the `<tr>` HTML element. Its properties include `VAlign` (specifies the vertical alignment of the cells contained in this row), `Align` (specifies the horizontal alignment of the cells contained in this row), `BgColor` (specifies the background color of the row), `BorderColor` (specifies the border color of the row), and a collection of `cells`, accessible via the `Cells` property. Each element of the Cells collection is an HTMLTableCell control.

HTMLTableCell control

This control represents one cell within a table row and corresponds to the `<td>` and `<th>` HTML elements. Its properties include `VAlign`, `Align`, `BgColor`, `BorderColor` (which all work in the same way as described for the previous control), `ColSpan` (specifies the number of columns that the cell spans), `NoWrap` (indicates whether or not the text within a cell should be wrapped), and `RowSpan` (specifies the number of rows that the cell spans).

The following example shows how to generate a table dynamically (see also Figure 7.12):

```
<script runat="server">

  Sub AddRow(Table As HTMLTable, Item As String, Value As String)

    Dim Row   As New HTMLTableRow()
    Dim Cell  As New HTMLTableCell()

    Cell = New HTMLTableCell()
    Cell.InnerText = Item
    Row.Cells.Add(Cell)
    Cell = New HTMLTableCell()
    Cell.InnerText = Value
    Row.Cells.Add(Cell)
    Table.Rows.Add(Row)

  End Sub

  Sub Generate(Source As Object, e As EventArgs)

   Dim I As Integer
   For I=0 to 5
    AddRow(Tbl, I+65, Chr(I+65))
   Next

  End Sub
```

```
</script>

<form id="main" runat="server">

   <table id="tbl" Align="center"
    CellPadding = 10
    Border = 2
    Runat="Server"
   />

 <br>
 <input type="button" runat="server"
   value="DoIt!" onServerClick="Generate">

</form>
```

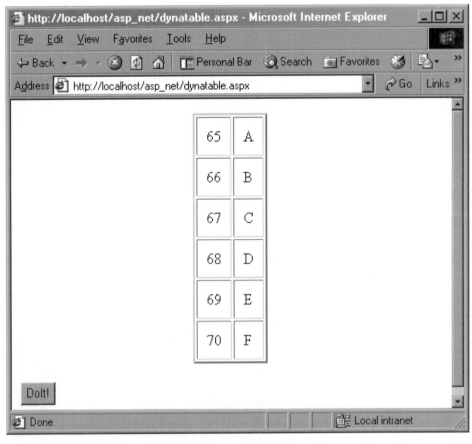

FIGURE 7.12   Using the HTMLTableCell control to generate a table

In this example, we use the `AddRow` subroutine which adds one row to the specified table. Each row contains two cells, the contents of which are passed through `Item` and `Value` arguments. The `AddRow` subroutine can be useful for showing various item/value pairs in situations when we don't know exactly how many rows we will have. To allow multiple cells, we can specify the row contents as an `Array` – each item will hold the contents of one cell.

This ends our tour around the set of HTML server controls provided by ASP.NET. Our next topic is web server controls.

7.4 Web server controls

The web server controls included in ASP.NET provide a more consistent object model and a higher level of abstraction than the HTML controls we have discussed above. The following list shows the main features of the web controls.

- The web controls represent most HTML elements.
- The web controls extend the set of HTML elements with more high-level controls, such as `Calendar` or `Ad Rotator`, than those discussed earlier.
- The web controls version of HTML elements typically has a more consistent interface than is available using the other controls.
- Web controls may render themselves differently based on client browser capabilities.
- Web controls are based on the `WebControl` class implemented in the `System.Web.UI.WebControls` namespace.

Figure 7.13 shows the web controls and related classes available in ASP.NET.

We will start learning about web controls with a brief overview of the `WebControl` class that serves as a base for all ASP.NET web controls.

WebControl Class

This class defines the basic set of properties, methods, and events shared by all ASP.NET web controls. Here is the list of the properties of the `WebControl` class.

- **AccessKey** Specifies the keyboard shortcut key used to set the focus of this web control. This property may contain only a single character that specifies that the shortcut key will be `ALT+Character`. For example, if this property is set to `"A"`, then we can press ALT+A to set the focus to this control. This property will work only with Microsoft Internet Explorer 4.0 or higher.
- **Attributes** Returns the collection of attributes (name/value pairs) that do not correspond to properties on the control. We use this collection to specify, for example, the JavaScript client-side code for certain client-side control events.

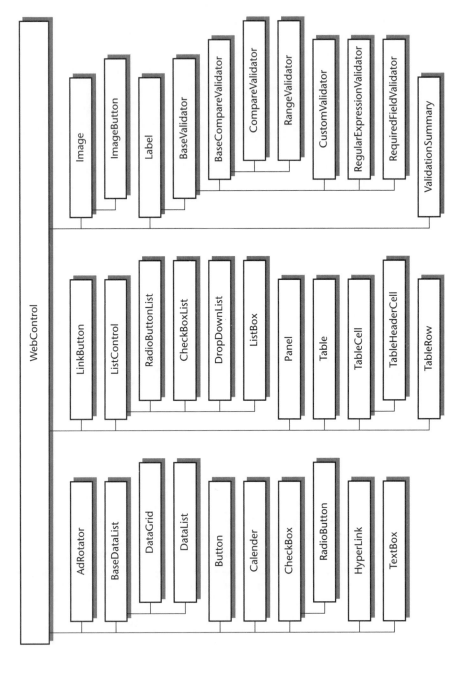

FIGURE 7.13   The web controls and related classes

- **BackColor** Specifies the background color of the control. This property is of a `System.Drawing.Color` type and can contain either the predefined colors, such as `System.Drawing.Color.Red`, or the color defined by its ARGB values. For more information see Chapter 11 – Graphical functions and GDI+. This property is not compatible with HTML 3.2 – only controls based on the `<table>` HTML element will support this property for down-level browsers.

- **BorderColor** Specifies the color of the border for this web control. This property is of a `System.Drawing.Color` type. It is supported in Netscape Navigator 4.0 or higher and Microsoft Internet Explorer 3.0 or higher, and in other browsers that support the `bordercolor` attribute.

- **BorderStyle** Specifies the style of the border for this web control. Possible values for this property – `Double`, `Inset`, and `Solid`, for example – are defined in the `BorderStyle` enumeration.

- **BorderWidth** Specifies the width of the border for this web control. This property is of a `Unit` type, which can be used to specify the value in percent, pixels, or points.

- **CssClass** Specifies the CSS class to be used for this web control.

- **Enabled** Indicates whether or not this web control is enabled.

- **Font** Returns the font information for this web control. This property is of a `FontInfo` type and encapsulates the font properties for text – `Bold`, `Italic`, `Name`, `Names`, `Strikeout`, `Underline`, `Overline`, and `Size`.

- **ForeColor** Specifies the foreground color for this web control. This property is of a `System.Drawing.Color` type.

- **Height** Specifies the height of the web control. This property is of a `Unit` type.

- **Style** Returns the collection that represents the HTML style attribute to render on the outer tag of the web control.

- **TabIndex** Specifies the tab index for this web control.

- **ToolTip** Specifies the tool tip text for this web control. Tool tips are displayed when the mouse cursor is moved over the control.

- **Width** Specifies the width of the web control. This property is of a `Unit` type.

The following example shows three ways in which to set the properties of the web control – statically (during the control definition), dynamically (in the event handler), and via the CSS:

```
<head>
 <style>

  .labelStyle {

     font-weight : bold;
     text-align  : center;
  }
```

```
  </style>
  </head>
<script runat="server">

  Sub Page_Load

    Label1.Font.Size = FontUnit.Medium
    Label1.Font.Name = "Arial Narrow"
    Label1.CssClass  = "labelStyle"

  End Sub

</script>

<form runat="server">

  <asp:Label
    id         = "Label1"
    BackColor  = "#b0c0d0"
    ForeColor  = "White"
    BorderStyle = "Outset"
    Width      = 100%
    Text       = "Label Web Control"
    runat      = "server"
  />

</form>
```

This web control will be rendered in Microsoft Internet Explorer 6.0 as the following:

```
<span
 id="Label1"
 class="labelStyle"
 style="color:White; background-color:#B0C0D0;
   border-style:Outset; font-family:Arial Narrow;
   font-size:Medium; width:100%;">
Label Web Control</span>
```

Note how all of the properties we have specified on the server side have been mapped to the appropriate in-line CSS attributes.

Most of the methods of the WebControl class are of interest to customized control developers and are not covered here. The WebControl class does not introduce its own events – all of the events are inherited from the Control class discussed in the previous chapter.

Now let's look at the web controls available in ASP.NET. We will start with the simple ones, then discuss the more sophisticated web controls, such as Ad Rotator, Calendar, and XML. After this we will learn about validation controls and will end this chapter with an overview of how we can create our own controls.

Button control

This control is used to create either a command or a submit button. The Button class introduces four new properties and two events.

- **CausesValidation** Indicates whether or not to perform validation when the Button is clicked.
- **CommandArgument** Specifies an additional parameter that is passed to the Command event along with the CommandName.
- **CommandName** Specifies the name of the command associated with the Button. The value of this property is passed to the Command event.
- **Text** Specifies the text to be displayed on the Button.

The Click event is raised when the Button is clicked. We usually handle this event for submit buttons that do not have a command name associated with them.

To handle command buttons, we use the Command event. The event handler for this event receives the data associated with the Button (CommandArgument and CommandName) via an argument of the type CommandEventArgs.

The following example shows how to implement two submit buttons:

```
<script runat="server">

 Sub Ok_Btn_Click(Sender As Object, E As EventArgs)

  Response.Write("Ok Clicked")

 End Sub

 Sub Cancel_Btn_Click(Sender As Object, E As EventArgs)

  Response.Write("Cancel Clicked")

 End Sub


</script>

<form runat="server">
```

```
<asp:Button
 id = "btn1"
 text = "Ok"
 OnClick = "Ok_Btn_Click"
 runat="server"
/>
<asp:Button
 id = "btn2"
 text = "Cancel"
 OnClick = "Cancel_Btn_Click"
 runat="server"
/>
</form>
```

The resulting HTML code will look like this:

```
<input type="submit" name="btn1" value="Ok"     id="btn1" />
<input type="submit" name="btn2" value="Cancel" id="btn2" />
```

To implement command buttons we need to specify the CommandName property and optional CommandArgument property. The event handler is for the Command event, not for the Click event, as it was for the submit button. Here is an example of how to do this:

```
<script runat=server>

 Sub OnCommand(sender As Object, E As CommandEventArgs)

   Response.Write(E.CommandName & " " & E.CommandArgument)

 End Sub
</script>

<form runat="server">

 <asp:Button
   id="Button1"
   Text="Command 1"
   CommandName="Cmd1"
   CommandArgument="Params_1"
   OnCommand="OnCommand"
   runat="server"
 />
```

```
<asp:Button
 id="Button2"
 Text="Command 2"
 CommandName="Cmd2"
 CommandArgument="Params_2"
 OnCommand="OnCommand"
 runat="server"
/>

</form>
```

Note that in the example above, we have used the same event handler for both buttons. This can be useful in situations when several buttons are processed with the same logic. In this case, it is better to create a single event handler for such buttons and use the CASE statement to distinguish between the buttons. This will allow us to keep the logic in one place and not split it between several event handlers.

CheckBox and CheckBoxList controls

The CheckBox control implements a check box that allows the user to select a state – checked or unchecked. This control has the following properties.

- **AutoPostBack** Indicates whether or not the control's state automatically posts back to the server when clicked.
- **Checked** Indicates whether or not the control is checked. When this property is changed the CheckedChanged event occurs.
- **Text** Specifies the text label for the control.
- **TextAlign** Specifies the alignment of the text label.

The following code shows how to create two check boxes:

```
<form runat="server">

 <asp:CheckBox
  id="CheckBox1"
  Text = "CheckBox1"
  TextAlign="left"
  runat="server"
 />

 <asp:CheckBox
  id="CheckBox2"
  Text = "CheckBox2"
  TextAlign="right"
  runat="server"
 />

</form>
```

Here is the code generated by ASP.NET for Internet Explorer 6.0:

```
<label for="CheckBox1">CheckBox1</label>
<input id="CheckBox1" type="checkbox" name="CheckBox1" />

<input id="CheckBox2" type="checkbox" name="CheckBox2" />
<label for="CheckBox2">CheckBox2</label>
```

The check boxes above do not generate any events. To do this we need to set the AutoPostBack property to "True" and specify the event handler for the CheckedChanged event. Here is how to do this:

```
<script runat=server>

  Sub OnCheck(sender As Object, E As EventArgs)

    Dim CheckBox As New CheckBox
    CheckBox = Sender
    Response.Write(CheckBox.id)

  End Sub
</script>

<form runat="server">

  <asp:CheckBox
    id="CheckBox1"
    Text = "CheckBox1"
    TextAlign="left"
    AutoPostBack="True"
    OnCheckedChanged="OnCheck"
    runat="server"
  />

  <asp:CheckBox
    id="CheckBox2"
    Text = "CheckBox2"
    TextAlign="right"
    AutoPostBack="True"
    OnCheckedChanged="OnCheck"
    runat="server"
  />

</form>
```

Note that in the example above, we use the same event handler for both check boxes – we can distinguish between them using the ID property.

The CheckBoxList control is used to create a group (not a list as its name suggests!) of check boxes. The main purpose of this control is to allow us to generate a group of controls from the data source, but it can be used without data binding as well.

The Items collection contains individual items in the group. Once the individual check box has been checked, its Selected property is set to "True". The RepeatLayout and RepeatDirection properties are used to control the display of the group. The default value of the RepeatLayout property is RepeatLayout.Table – this means that the group of check boxes will be rendered within a table. If we set the value of this property to RepeatLayout.Flow, the group will be rendered without any table structure. The RepeatDirection property can be set to either RepeatDirection.Vertical – this is the default value – or RepeatDirection.Horizontal.

Other properties of the CheckBoxList control include the following.

- **CellPadding** Specifies the number of pixels between the border and contents of the cell.

- **CellSpacing** Specifies the number of pixels between cells.

- **RepeatColumns** Indicates the number of columns to display.

- **TextAlign** Specifies the text alignment of the check boxes in a group.

Let's look at an example of how we can create a group of check boxes using the CheckBoxList control. We start with an empty control and define its main properties:

```
<form runat="server">

  <asp:CheckBoxList
    id="CheckBoxList1"
    AutoPostBack="True"
    RepeatColumns="3"
    RepeatDirection="Horizontal"
    RepeatLayout="Flow"
    TextAlign="Right"
    OnSelectedIndexChanged="Check_Clicked"
    runat="server"
  />

</form>
```

Then, in the Page.Load event handler, we fill the control with the elements:

```
Sub Page_Load()

  Dim I As Integer

  If Not IsPostBack Then
   For I=1 to 12
    CheckBoxList1.Items.Add("Item " & I.ToString("00"))
   Next
  End If


  End Sub
```

This produces the group of check boxes shown in Figure 7.14:

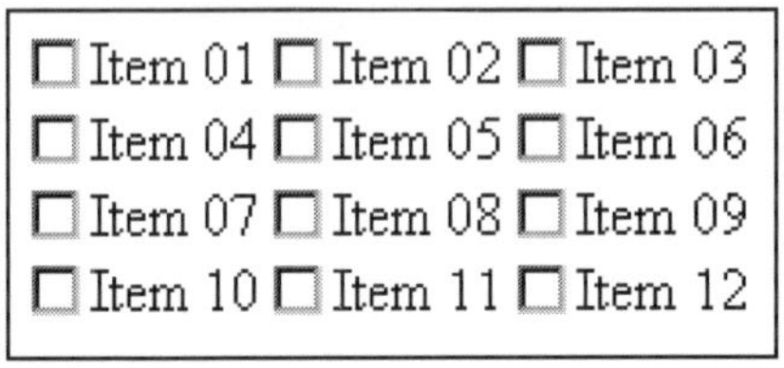

FIGURE 7.14   Once the elements have been entered in the Page.Load event handler, a group of check boxes is produced

ASP.NET generates the following code for this group:

```
<span id="CheckBoxList1">
 <input id="CheckBoxList1_0" type="checkbox" name="CheckBoxList1:0"
  onclick="__doPostBack('CheckBoxList1:0','')" language="javascript" />
<label for="CheckBoxList1_0">Item 01</label>
<input id="CheckBoxList1_1" type="checkbox" name="CheckBoxList1:1"
  onclick="__doPostBack('CheckBoxList1:1','')" language="javascript" />
<label for="CheckBoxList1_1">Item 02</label>
<input id="CheckBoxList1_2" type="checkbox" name="CheckBoxList1:2"
  onclick="__doPostBack('CheckBoxList1:2','')" language="javascript" />

 . . .

 <input id="CheckBoxList1_11" type="checkbox" name="CheckBoxList1:11"
 onclick="__doPostBack('CheckBoxList1:11','')" language="javascript" />
 <label for="CheckBoxList1_11">Item 12</label>
<br>
</span>
```

Now, let's set the `RepeatLayout` property to `RepeatLayout.Table`. ASP.NET will use the `<table>` element to lay out the check boxes:

```
<table id="CheckBoxList1" cellspacing="5" cellpadding="5" border="0">

<tr>
<td>
<input id="CheckBoxList1_0" type="checkbox" name="CheckBoxList1:0"
 onclick="__doPostBack('CheckBoxList1:0','')" language="javascript" />
<label for="CheckBoxList1_0">Item 01</label>
</td>
<td>
<input id="CheckBoxList1_1" type="checkbox" name="CheckBoxList1:1"
 onclick="__doPostBack('CheckBoxList1:1','')" language="javascript" />
<label for="CheckBoxList1_1">Item 02</label>
</td>

...

<td>
<input id="CheckBoxList1_11" type="checkbox" name="CheckBoxList1:11"
 onclick="__doPostBack('CheckBoxList1:11','')" language="javascript" />
<label for="CheckBoxList1_11">Item 12</label>
</td>
/tr>

</table>
```

In this case, we can use the `CellPadding` and `CellSpacing` properties as shown below (see also Figure 7.15):

```
<asp:CheckBoxList
  id="CheckBoxList1"
  AutoPostBack="True"
  CellPadding="5"
  CellSpacing="5"
  RepeatColumns="3"
  RepeatDirection="Horizontal"
  RepeatLayout="Table"
  TextAlign="Right"
  OnSelectedIndexChanged="Check_Clicked"
  runat="server"
  />
```

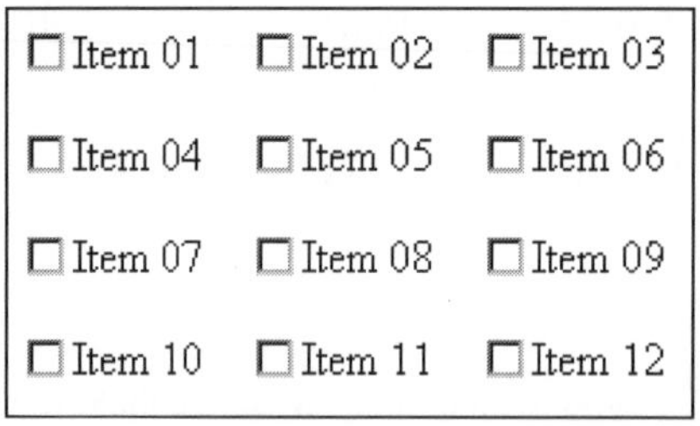

☐ Item 01	☐ Item 02	☐ Item 03
☐ Item 04	☐ Item 05	☐ Item 06
☐ Item 07	☐ Item 08	☐ Item 09
☐ Item 10	☐ Item 11	☐ Item 12

FIGURE 7.15   The results of using `CellPadding` and `CellSpacing` properties on our check boxes group

In both our examples we defined the event handler for the `SelectedIndexChanged` event:

```
OnSelectedIndexChanged="Check_Clicked"
```

Here is the code for the event handler, that is invoked every time we check or uncheck one of the check boxes (see also Figure 7.16). This is possible because we have set the `AutoPostBack` property to `"True"`:

```
Sub Check_Clicked(Sender As Object, E As EventArgs)

  Dim I As Integer
  Dim Msg As String = ""

   For I=0 To CheckBoxList1.Items.Count - 1
    If CheckBoxList1.Items(I).Selected Then
     Msg += " " & CheckBoxList1.Items(I).Text
    End If
   Next

  Response.Write(Msg)

 End Sub
```

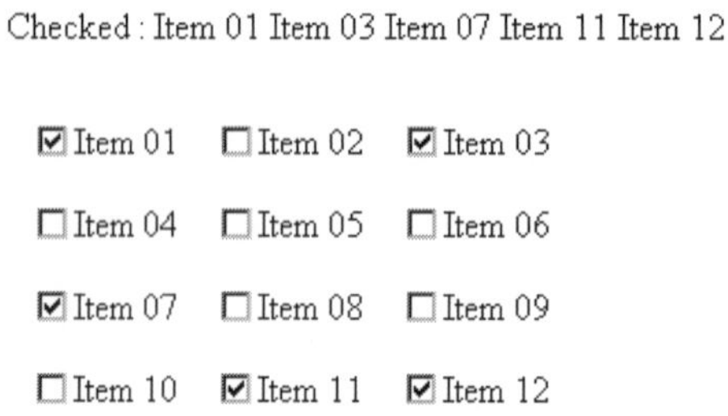

Checked : Item 01 Item 03 Item 07 Item 11 Item 12

☑ Item 01	☐ Item 02	☑ Item 03
☐ Item 04	☐ Item 05	☐ Item 06
☑ Item 07	☐ Item 08	☐ Item 09
☐ Item 10	☑ Item 11	☑ Item 12

FIGURE 7.16   Setting the `AutoPostBack` property to `"True"` notifies us which boxes have been checked

RadioButton and RadioButtonList controls

The RadioButton control implements a radio button that allows the user to select a state – checked or unchecked. This control introduces one property – GroupName, which allows us to specify the name of the group that the control belongs to. Using this property, we can create groups of radio buttons to allow users to select one of the mutually exclusive options.

The following example shows how to create a group of radio buttons (see also Figure 7.17):

```
<form runat="server">
 <h4>Please choose a language:</h4>

  <asp:RadioButton
    id=Radio1
    Text="English"
    Checked="True"
    GroupName="Languages"
    runat="server"
  />
  <br>
  <asp:RadioButton
    id=Radio2
    Text="French"
    GroupName="Languages"
    runat="server"
  />
  <br>
  <asp:RadioButton
    id=Radio3
    Text="German"
    GroupName="Languages"
    runat="server"
  /><br>

</form>
```

Please choose a language:

⊙ English
○ French
○ German

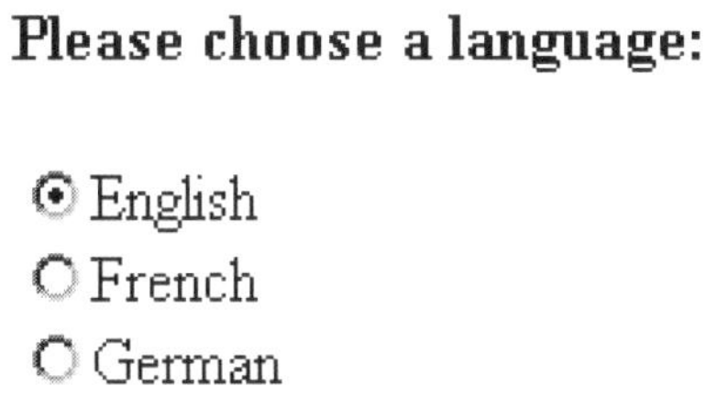

FIGURE 7.17   The group of radio buttons created using RadioButton and GroupName

As all three radio buttons belong to the same group (the GroupName property is set to Languages), users can select only one language from this group.

ASP.NET generates the following code for this group:

```
<input id="Radio1" type="radio" name="Languages"
 value="Radio1" checked="checked" />
<label for="Radio1">English</label>
<br>
<input id="Radio2" type="radio" name="Languages"
 value="Radio2" />
<label for="Radio2">French</label>
<br>
<input id="Radio3" type="radio" name="Languages"
 value="Radio3" />
<label for="Radio3">German</label><br>
```

We will be able to react to the changes required by the users' selections by adding the OnCheckedChanged="Check_Clicked" and AutoPostBack="True" properties and implementing the following event handler (see also Figure 7.18):

```
<script runat="server">

  Sub Check_Clicked(Sender As Object, E As EventArgs)
  Dim Radio As New RadioButton

   Radio = Sender
   Response.Write(Radio.id & " was changed")

  End Sub

</script>
```

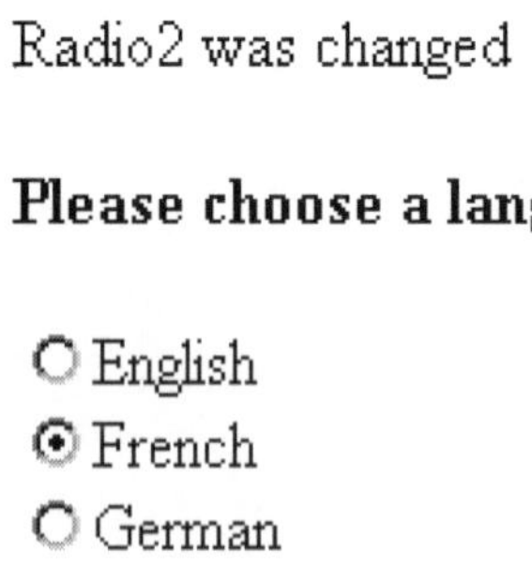

Radio2 was changed

Please choose a language:

○ English
◉ French
○ German

FIGURE 7.18 Reacting to user's actions

Just as the `CheckBoxList` control discussed above can be used to create a group of check box controls, the `RadioButtonList` control can serve to create a group of radio buttons. The main purpose of this control is to allow us to generate a group of controls from the data source, but it can be used without data binding as well.

The `Items` collection contains individual items in the group. Once the individual radio button has been selected, its `SelectedItem` property is set to `"True"`. The `RadioButtonList` control supports the same properties as the `CheckBoxList` control – `RepeatLayout` and `RepeatDirection`, to specify the rendering options. For more information, see the section dedicated to the `CheckBoxList` control above.

The following example shows how to dynamically create a group of radio buttons and how to use the `Items` collection (see also Figure 7.19):

```
<script runat="server">

  Sub Page_Load()

   Dim I As Integer

   If Not IsPostBack Then
    For I=1 to 12
     RBList.Items.Add("Option " & I.ToString("00"))
    Next
   End If

  End Sub

  Sub Check_Clicked(Sender As Object, E As EventArgs)

   Dim RadioList As New RadioButtonList
   Dim I As Integer

   RadioList = Sender
   For I = 0 To RadioList.Items.Count - 1
    If RadioList.Items(I).Selected Then
     Response.Write(RadioList.Items(I).Text)
    End If
   Next

  End Sub

</script>

<form runat="server">
 <h4>Please choose an option:</h4>
```

```
<asp:RadioButtonList
  id=RBList
  AutoPostBack="True"
  RepeatLayout = "Table"
  RepeatDirection = "Vertical"
  RepeatColumns="3"
  OnSelectedIndexChanged = "Check_Clicked"
  runat="server"
/>
</form>
```

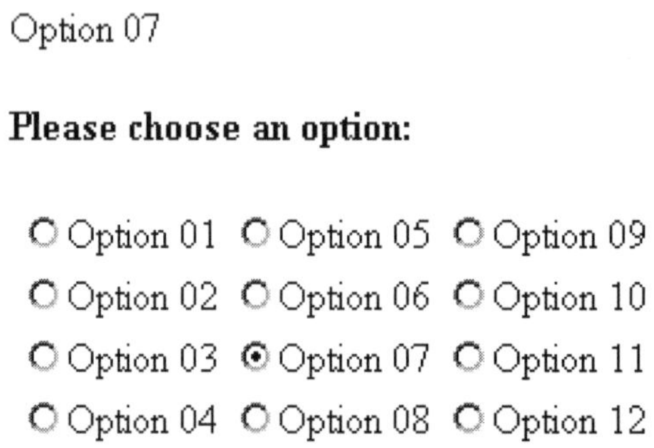

Option 07

Please choose an option:

○ Option 01   ○ Option 05   ○ Option 09
○ Option 02   ○ Option 06   ○ Option 10
○ Option 03   ⦿ Option 07   ○ Option 11
○ Option 04   ○ Option 08   ○ Option 12

FIGURE 7.19   Creating a group of radio buttons with RadioButtonList

In the example above, we start with an empty RadioButtonList control and add several items into it at the first request to the page. The event handler for the SelectedIndexChanged event iterates through the Items collection and displays the text of the currently selected item.

ASP.NET generates the following code for the group of radio buttons:

```
<table id="RBList" border="0">
<tr>
<td>
  <span value="Option 01">
  <input id="RBList_0" type="radio" name="RBList"
   value="Option 01"
   onclick="__doPostBack('RBList_0','')" language="javascript" />
   <label for="RBList_0">Option 01</label>
  </span>
</td>
```

```
<td>
 <span value="Option 05">
 <input id="RBList_4" type="radio" name="RBList"
  value="Option 05"
  onclick="__doPostBack('RBList_4','')" language="javascript" />
  <label for="RBList_4">Option 05</label>
 </span>
</td>
<td>
 <span value="Option 09">
 <input id="RBList_8" type="radio" name="RBList"
  value="Option 09"
  onclick="__doPostBack('RBList_8','')" language="javascript" />
  <label for="RBList_8">Option 09</label>
 </span>
 </td>
</tr>

...

</table>
```

DropDownList control

This control is used to create a single selection dropdown list. The `SelectedIndex` property indicates the index of the selected item and the `SelectedItem` property – the selected item itself. Each item in the `DropDownList` control is a `ListItem` object. When the selection on the list changes, the `SelectedIndexChanged` event occurs.

We can use the `BorderColor`, `BorderStyle`, and `BorderWidth` properties to change the appearance of the control.

The following example shows how to create the `DropDownList` control and handle its `SelectedIndexChanged` event to find out which item has been selected by the user (see also Figure 7.20):

```
<script runat="server">
 Sub ItemChanged(Sender As Object, E As EventArgs)

  Dim List As New DropDownList

  List = Sender
  Response.Write(List.SelectedItem.Text)

 End Sub
```

```
</script>

<form runat="server">

 <h4>Please select an item from the list</h4>
  <asp:DropDownList
   id="DropDownList1"
   AutoPostBack="True"
   OnSelectedIndexChanged = "ItemChanged"
   runat="server">

   <asp:ListItem>Item 1</asp:ListItem>
   <asp:ListItem>Item 2</asp:ListItem>
   <asp:ListItem>Item 3</asp:ListItem>
   <asp:ListItem>Item 4</asp:ListItem>

  </asp:DropDownList>

 </form>
```

Item 2

Please select an item from the list

FIGURE 7.20 A dropdown list with its SelectedIndexChanged event handled to show a user's selection

ASP.NET generated the following code for the **DropDownList** control:

```
<select name="DropDownList1" id="DropDownList1"
 onchange="__doPostBack('DropDownList1','')" language="javascript">

<option value="Item 1">Item 1</option>
<option Value="Item 2">Item 2</option>
<option value="Item 3">Item 3</option>
<option value="Item 4">Item 4</option>

</select>
```

The BorderColor, BorderStyle, and BorderWidth properties are implemented as in-line CSS attributes:

```
<select name="DropDownList1" id="DropDownList1"
 style="border-color:Red;border-width:4px;border-style:Outset;">

  ...

</select>
```

HyperLink control

This control is used to create links on a Web page. It provides programming access to the link properties from the server-side code and allows us to dynamically change these properties.

There are four main properties that define the behavior of the HyperLink control.

● **ImageUrl** Specifies the path of an image to display on this control. If both ImageUrl and Text properties are set, the ImageUrl property takes precedence.

● **NavigateUrl** Specifies the URL to navigate when the control is clicked.

● **Target** Specifies the target window or frame in which to display the content of the web page. Possible values include _blank, _parent, _self, and _top.

● **Text** Specifies the text caption for the control.

The HyperLink control does not raise an event in server code when it is clicked – it simply navigates to the resource specified by the NavigateUrl property.

The following example shows how to use a HyperLink web server control (see also Figure 7.21):

```
<form runat="server">
 <center>
 <h3>Where do you want to go today?</h3>

  <asp:HyperLink
   id="hyperlink1"
   ImageUrl="../logo.bmp"
   NavigateUrl="http://www.gotdotnet.com"
   Text="Everything about .NET"
   Target="_new"
   runat="server"
  />

 </center>
</form>
```

FIGURE 7.21 Using a hyperlink server-side control

ASP.NET generated the following code for the HyperLink web server control:

```
<a id="hyperlink1" href="http://www.gotdotnet.com" target="_new">
 <img src="/asp_net/logo.bmp" alt="Everything about .NET" border="0" />
</a>
```

Image control

We use this control to display images that can be manipulated from the server-side code. The ImageUrl property specifies the path to the image to be displayed, the text to display in case the image is not available is specified by the AlternateText property, and the ImageAlign property is used to set the alignment of the image in relation to other elements on the web page. Possible values for the ImageAlign property include those listed in Table 7.4.

The Image web server control does not support any events. To create an interactive image, use the ImageButton web server control.

The following example shows how we can use the Image web server control and dynamically change its ImageAlign property (see also Figure 7.22):

TABLE 7.4   Values for the `ImageAlign` property

Value	Meaning
NotSet	This is the default value for this property – it indicates that the alignment is not set.
Left	The image is aligned on the left edge of the web page. Text is wrapped on the right.
Right	The image is aligned on the right edge of the web page. Text is wrapped on the left.
Baseline	The lower edge of the image is aligned with the lower edge of the first line of text.
Top	The upper edge of the image is aligned with the upper edge of the highest element on the same line.
Middle	The middle of the image is aligned with the lower edge of the first line of text.
Bottom	The lower edge of the image is aligned with the lower edge of the first line of text.
AbsBottom	The lower edge of the image is aligned with the lower edge of the largest element on the same line.
AbsMiddle	The middle of the image is aligned with the middle of the largest element on the same line.
TextTop	The upper edge of the image is aligned with the upper edge of the highest text on the same line.

```
<script runat="server">

  Sub Page_Load()

    Dim Names As String()
    Dim I As Integer
    Dim IL As New ImageAlign()

    If Not IsPostBack Then
     Names  = IL.GetNames(IL.GetType)
     For I=0 to Names.GetUpperBound(0)
      RBList.Items.Add(Names(I))
     Next
    End If

  End Sub

  Sub Check_Clicked(Sender As Object, E As EventArgs)

    Dim RadioList As New RadioButtonList
    Dim I As Integer
```

```
    RadioList = Sender
    For I = 0 To RadioList.Items.Count - 1
     If RadioList.Items(I).Selected Then
      Img1.ImageAlign = I
     End If
    Next

   End Sub

</script>

<form runat="server">
  The .NET Framework is a new computing platform designed to
  simplify application development in the highly distributed
  environment of the internet. The .NET Framework has two main
  components: the common language runtime and the .NET
  Framework class library.

 <asp:Image
  id="Img1"
  AlternateText="DotNet Logo"
  ImageAlign="NotSet"
  ImageUrl="../logo.bmp"
  runat="server"
 />
 <p />

 <h4>Please choose an alignment:</h4>

 <asp:RadioButtonList
   id=RBList
   AutoPostBack="True"
   RepeatLayout = "Table"
   RepeatDirection = "Vertical"
   RepeatColumns="5"
   OnSelectedIndexChanged = "Check_Clicked"
   runat="server"
  />

</form>
```

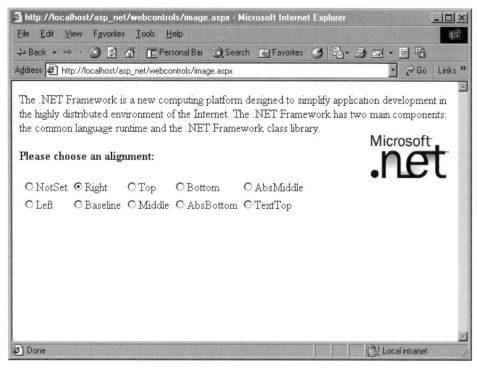

FIGURE 7.22   Using the Image web server control and changing the alignment of text

In the example above, we have generated a group of radio buttons (RadioButtonList control) based on the values of the ImageAlign enumeration. Then, each click on the particular radio button causes the ImageAlign property value to change to the appropriate value of the ImageAlign enumeration.

Using the data binding features, we can change the Page_Load code to the following:

```
Sub Page_Load()

  Dim Names As String()
  Dim IL As New ImageAlign()

  If Not IsPostBack Then
   Names  = IL.GetNames(IL.GetType)
   RBList.DataSource = Names
   RBList.DataBind
  End If

End Sub
```

ASP.NET generates the following code for the `ImageButton` web server control:

```
<img id="Img1" src="/asp_net/logo.bmp" alt="DotNet Logo" border="0" />
```

Label control

We use this control to display text on a web forms page and programmatically change the control's `Text` property from the server-side code. Here is how to add the `Label` control to the previous example to show the image alignment currently selected. To do this, we need to add a `Label` web server control to the web forms page:

```
<asp:Label
 id="Current"
 Text=""
 runat="server"
/>
```

and change the code of the `SelectedIndexChanged` event handler (see also Figure 7.23):

```
Sub Check_Clicked(Sender As Object, E As EventArgs)

    Dim RadioList As New RadioButtonList
    Dim I As Integer
    Dim IL As New ImageAlign()
    Dim Names As String()

    RadioList = Sender
    Names    = IL.GetNames(IL.GetType)

    For I = 0 To RadioList.Items.Count - 1
     If RadioList.Items(I).Selected Then
      Image1.ImageAlign = I
      Current.Text = "ImageAlign = " & Names(I)
     End If
    Next

    End Sub
```

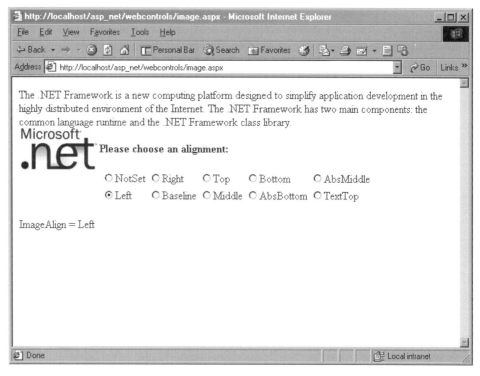

FIGURE 7.23 Using the Label control, text can be displayed on a web forms page

ASP.NET generates the following code for the Label control:

```
<span id="Current">ImageAlign = Left</span>
```

ListBox control

This web server control is used to create a list box with single or multiple item selection. To specify if a user can select a single or multiple items, we set the value of the SelectionMode property to either ListSelectionMode.Single or List SelectionMode.Multiple. The height of the ListBox control is specified by the Rows property. The Items property contains individual items displayed in the list box – each item is of the ListItem type. The SelectedIndex property indicates the lowest ordinal index of the selected items in the list and the SelectedItem property indicates the selected item with the lowest index in the list.

Other properties of the ListBox control include the BorderColor, BorderStyle, and BorderWidth properties to change the appearance of the control and properties inherited from the WebControl class.

The following example shows how to create and use the ListBox control (see also Figure 7.24):

```
<script runat="server">
 Sub ItemChanged(Sender As Object, E As EventArgs)

  Dim List As New ListBox

  List = Sender
  Response.Write(List.SelectedItem.Text)

 End Sub
</script>

<form runat="server">

 <h4>Please select an item from the list</h4>
  <asp:ListBox
   id="ListBox1"
   AutoPostBack="True"
   OnSelectedIndexChanged = "ItemChanged"
   runat="server">

   <asp:ListItem>Item 1</asp:ListItem>
   <asp:ListItem>Item 2</asp:ListItem>
   <asp:ListItem>Item 3</asp:ListItem>
   <asp:ListItem>Item 4</asp:ListItem>

  </asp:ListBox>

 </form>
```

Item 2

Please select an item from the list

FIGURE 7.24　Using the ListBox control

In case multiple selections are allowed, we need to change our event handler to handle them (see also Figure 7.25):

```
Sub ItemChanged(Sender As Object, E As EventArgs)

  Dim I As Integer
  Dim Text As String
  Dim List As New ListBox

  List = Sender
  For I=0 to List.Items.Count-1
   If List.Items(I).Selected Then
    Text += " " & List.Items(I).Text
   End If
  Next
  Response.Write(Text)

 End Sub
```

ASP.NET generates the following code for the ListBox control:

```
<select name="ListBox1" id="ListBox1" size="10" multiple="multiple"
  onchange="__doPostBack('ListBox1','')" language="javascript">

 <option selected="selected" value="Item 1">Item 1</option>
 <option value="Item 2">Item 2</option>
 <option selected="selected" value="Item 3">Item 3</option>
 <option value="Item 4">Item 4</option>
 <option selected="selected" value="Item 5">Item 5</option>
 <option value="Item 6">Item 6</option>
 <option selected="selected" value="Item 7">Item 7</option>

 </select>
```

Item 1 Item 3 Item 5 Item 7

Please select an item from the list

FIGURE 7.25   The event handler has been changed to allow multiple selections

Panel control

The Panel web server control is used as a container for other controls within a web forms page. We can use this control to manage a group of controls placed on the panel (show or hide them), to create controls dynamically, and separate web forms page into areas.

The Panel web server control can display a background image specified by the BackImageUrl property. To specify the background color for the panel, we use the BackColor property.

The HorizontalAlign property specifies how the child controls are aligned within the panel (left, right, centered, or justified) and the Wrap property indicates whether content that is too wide for the panel is wrapped to the next line or truncated at the panel's edge.

The following example shows that two panels and their background colors have been specified (see also Figure 7.26):

```
<asp:Panel
 id="Panel1"
 Height=200
 Width=300
 BorderStyle = "Outset"
 BorderWidth = 4
 BackColor="#e0e0e0"
 Wrap="True"
 HorizontalAlign="Right"
 runat="server"
/>
<asp:Panel
 id="Panel2"
 Height=200
 Width=300
 BorderStyle = "Inset"
 BorderWidth = 4
 BackColor="#e0e0e0"
 Wrap="True"
 HorizontalAlign="Left"
 runat="server"
/>
```

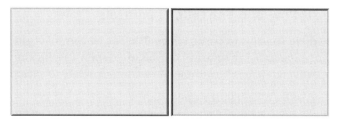

FIGURE 7.26   The Panel control with two horizontally aligned panels and a background color specified

ASP.NET generates the following code for the panels:

```
<div id="Panel1" align="Right"
 style="background-color:Silver;border-width:4px;
 border-style:Outset;height:200px;width:300px;"
>
     <span>Label in the Panel1</span>
</div>

. . .

<div id="Panel2" align="Left"
 style="background-color:#E0E0E0;border-width:4px;
 border-style:Inset;height:200px;width:300px;"
 >
     <span>Label in the Panel2</span>
</div>
```

To dynamically add controls to the panel, we use the `Controls.Add` method as shown below:

```
Sub Page_Load(sender As Object, e As EventArgs)

  Dim Msg1 As New Label()
  Dim Msg2 As New Label()

  Msg1.Text = "Label in the Panel1"
  Panel1.Controls.Add(Msg1)

  Msg2.Text = "Label in the Panel2"
  Panel2.Controls.Add(Msg2)

  End Sub
```

To show or hide panels, we can use the `Visible` property.

Table, TableRow, and TableCell controls

We use these three controls to create tables. The `Table` control creates the table itself, while the `TableRow` and `TableCell` controls are responsible for the creation of rows and cells respectively. Here is how these three controls relate to each other.

● The `Table` control describes the table itself.

● Its Rows property contains a collection of `TableRow` controls – each control defines one row.

● Each `TableRow` control has a `Cells` collection of `TableCell` controls – each control defines a cell within a row of a table.

Let's start with the properties of the `Table` control, which are the following.

● **CellPadding** Specifies the number of pixels between the border and the contents of the table cell.

● **CellSpacing** Specifies the number of pixels between table cells.

● **GridLines** Specifies the gridlines of the table. This property can have the following values: `Both` (both horizontal and vertical gridlines will be shown), `Horizontal` (only horizontal gridlines will be shown), `None` (no gridlines will be shown), or `Vertical` (only vertical lines will be shown).

● **Rows** Contains the collection of rows (TableRow controls) within the table.

The `TableRow` control is used to create rows within a table. It has the following properties.

● **Cells** Contains the collection of cells (TableCell controls) within a row.

● **HorizontalAlign** Specifies the horizontal alignment of the contents in the row. This property may have the values `NotSet`, `Left` (the content is justified left), `Center` (the content is centered), `Right` (the content is justified right), and `Justify` (the content is aligned with both left and right margins and uniformly spread out).

● **VerticalAlign** Specifies the vertical alignment of the contents in the row. This property may have the values `NotSet`, `Top` (the content is aligned with the top of the row), `Middle` (the content is aligned with the middle of the row), and `Bottom` (the content is aligned with the top of the row).

The `TableCell` control creates one cell within a table row. It has the following properties.

● **ColumnSpan** Specifies the number of columns that the cell spans.

● **HorizontalAlign** Specifies the horizontal alignment of the contents in the cell.

● **RowSpan** Specifies the number of rows that the cell spans.

● **Text** Specifies the text contents of the cell.

● **VerticalAlign** Specifies the horizontal alignment of the contents in the cell.

● **Wrap** Indicates whether or not the content of the cell wraps in the cell.

Let's look at an example of creating a table dynamically in the server-side code (see also Figure 7.27):

```
<script runat="server">
 Sub Page_Load()

   Dim Row  As TableRow
   Dim Cell As TableCell
   Dim I, J As Integer

   For I=0 to 5
    Row = New TableRow
    For J=0 to 3
     Cell = New TableCell
     Cell.Text = I & ", " & J
     Row.Cells.Add(Cell)
    Next
    Table1.Rows.Add(Row)
   Next

 End Sub
</script>

<form runat="server">

<asp:Table
 id="Table1"
 CellPadding=10
 GridLines="Both"
 HorizontalAlign="Center"
 runat="server"
 />

</form>
```

0, 0	0, 1	0, 2	0, 3
1, 0	1, 1	1, 2	1, 3
2, 0	2, 1	2, 2	2, 3
3, 0	3, 1	3, 2	3, 3
4, 0	4, 1	4, 2	4, 3
5, 0	5, 1	5, 2	5, 3

FIGURE 7.27   Using the properties of the `TableCell` control to create a table

Here is how to add one extra row to the table:

```
Sub OnCommand(sender As Object, E As CommandEventArgs)

    Dim Row  As TableRow
    Dim Cell As TableCell
    Dim I As Integer

    Row = New TableRow

    For I=0 to 3

     Cell = New TableCell
     Cell.Text = Table1.Rows.Count & ", " & I
     Row.Cells.Add(Cell)

    Next

    Table1.Rows.Add(Row)

    End Sub
```

TextBox control

The TextBox control can be used to input textual information for a web form. This control can be of three different types, depending on the value of the TextMode property. It can be single-line, multiline or password. In single-line mode, users can enter only a single line and we can also limit the number of characters that the TextBox control will accept. In multiline mode, there is a text box instead of a single line and in this mode the TextBox control supports text wrapping. The password mode is used to enter the information that should not be visible to others. In this case, all characters entered in a single line appear as asterisks.

When a user leaves the TextBox control, the TextChanged event is raised. This event is the only way to receive the indication that the contents of the TextBox control have been changed. In order to make the TextBox control raise this event immediately after a user leaves the control, set its AutoPostBack property to "True".

Here is a list of the main properties of the TextBox control:

● **Text** This property sets or gets the value contained in the TextBox control.

● **Height** Indicates the height of the TextBox control in pixels, used only in multiline mode.

- **Rows** Indicates the number of rows.
- **Width** Indicates the width of the TextBox control in pixels.
- **Columns** Specifies the number of characters to display.
- **MaxLength** Used to limit the number of characters – only for single-line mode.
- **Wrap** If set to "True", a horizontal scroll bar will be displayed in the TextBox control.

The following example shows how to create TextBox controls (see also Figure 7.28):

```
<form runat="server">

  <asp:TextBox
    ID="TextBox1"
    Columns="60"
    runat="server"
  />

  <asp:TextBox
   ID="TextBox2"
   Columns="47"
   Rows="10"
   TextMode="MultiLine"
   runat="server"
  />

  <asp:TextBox
   ID="TextBox3"
   Columns="60"
   TextMode="Password"
   runat="server"
  />

  </form>
```

If we look at the code that comes to the browser, the TextBox control is represented with HTML tags, as shown below:

```
<input name="TextBox1" type="text" size="60" id="TextBox1" />

<textarea name="TextBox2" rows="10"
  cols="47" id="TextBox2">
</textarea>

<input name="TextBox3" type="password" size="60" id="TextBox3" />
```

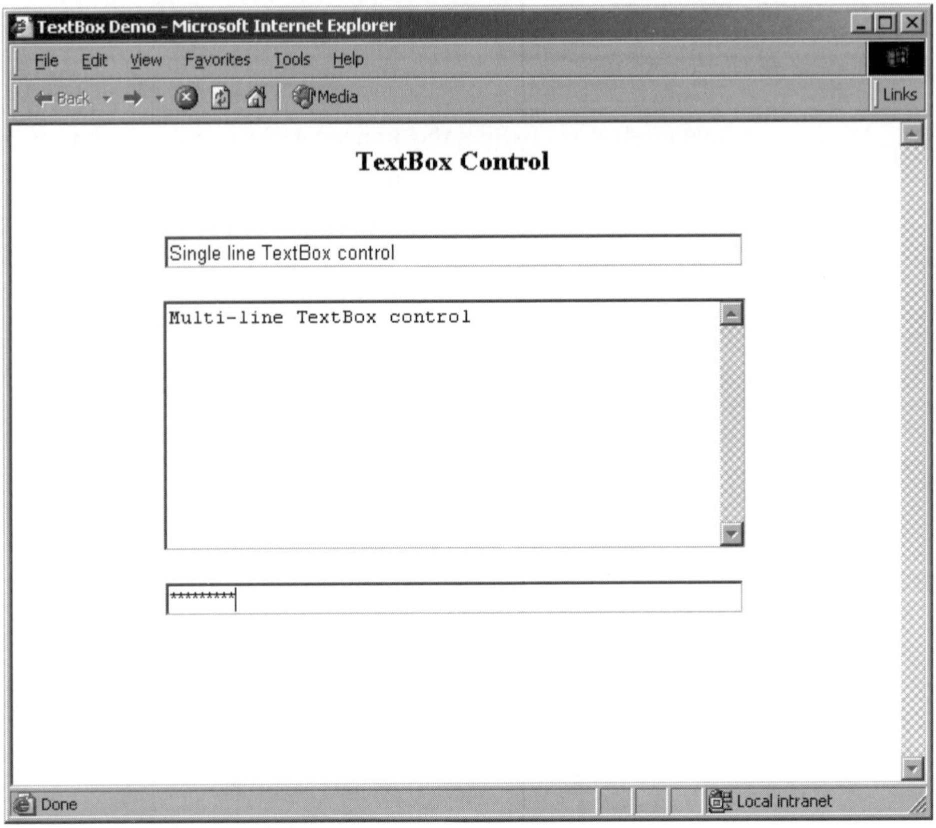

FIGURE 7.28   The result of setting up the TextBox controls

Note that the Width and Height properties are implemented in in-line CSS style. For example, the following TextBox control:

```
<asp:TextBox
 ID="TextBox4"
 Width="400"
 Height="200"
 TextMode="MultiLine"
 runat="server"
/>
```

has been created with the following in-line CSS style:

```
<textarea name="TextBox4" id="TextBox1"
  style="height:200px;width:400px;">
</textarea>
```

We have now finished our discussion of basic web server controls. The next three web server controls described that are available in ASP.NET – AdRotator, Calendar, and XML control – are at a higher level and do not have the corresponding HTML elements. We will learn about these controls in the next sections.

AdRotator control

We use this control to display randomly selected advertisement banners on the web page. Each time the page refreshes, the advertisement displayed is changed. The advertisements are stored in an XML file, which has the following structure:

```
<Advertisements>
  <Ad>
    <ImageUrl>banner.jpg</ImageUrl>
    <NavigateUrl>http://www.abc.com</NavigateUrl>
    <AlternateText>Go to ABC, Inc.</AlternateText>
    <Impressions>80</Impressions>
    <Keyword>Main</Keyword>
  </Ad>
  <Ad>
    <ImageUrl>banner2.jpg</ImageUrl>
    <NavigateUrl>http://www.xyz.com</NavigateUrl>
    <AlternateText>Go to XYZ, Ltd</AlternateText>
    <Impressions>80</Impressions>
    <Keyword>Sub1</Keyword>
  </Ad>
</Advertisements>
```

Table 7.5 explains the purposes of subnodes within the <Ad> node describing one advertisement. All subnodes except the ImageUrl are optional.

We can also use our own subnodes – the values specified in such customized subnodes will be placed in the adProperties dictionary, which can be accessed programmatically.

TABLE 7.5 The purposes of the subnodes within the <Ad> node

Subnode	Purpose
ImageUrl	Specifies the location of the image to display this advertisement.
NavigateUrl	Specifies the page to navigate when the advertisement is clicked.
AlternateText	Specifies the text to display if the image is not available.
Keyword	Specifies the category of the advertisement. The AdRotator control can use this data to filter the list of advertisements for a specific category.
Impressions	Specifies how often an advertisement is displayed in relation to other advertisements in this XML file.

The XML file that contains all advertisements is referred via the `AdvertisementFile` property of the `AdRotator` control.

The `KeywordFilter` property can be used to specify a category keyword to filter for specific types of advertisements in the XML advertisement file. The `Target` property specifies the name of the browser window or frame where the contents of the selected page will be displayed.

We use the `AdRotator` control by specifying the following code in the web forms page (see also Figure 7.29).

```
<form runat="server">

 <asp:AdRotator
  id="AdRotator1"
  Target="_self"
  AdvertisementFile="Ads.xml"
  runat="server"
 />

</form>
```

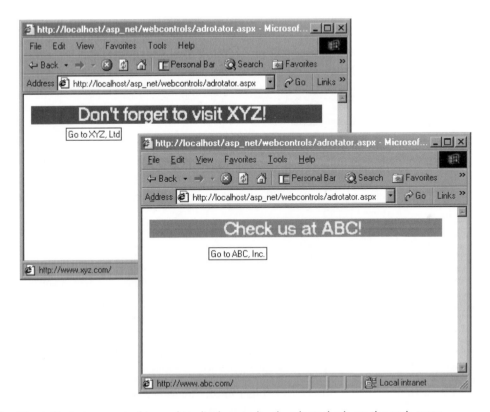

FIGURE 7.29   The AdRotator control is used to display randomly selected ads on the web page

Each time the new advertisement is selected, the AdCreated event is fired. We can write an event handler for this event to track how many times users have clicked on a particular banner. To do so, change the NavigateUrl property to point to the code that will log the information, and then navigate to the initial URL.

Calendar control

This control provides us with a one-month calendar that allows users to select dates and navigate between the months. The Calendar control contains many properties that can be manipulated from our server-side code.

The SelectionMode property specifies whether the user can select a single day, a week or a month. We can also disable date selection entirely. The SelectionMode property can have the values Day, DayWeek, DayWeekMonth, or None.

The set of xxxStyle properties is used to customize the appearance of the Calendar control and its different parts.

- **DayHeaderStyle** Specifies the style of the section where the names of the days are displayed.
- **DayStyle** Specifies the style for the days.
- **NextPrevStyle** Specifies the style for the sections where the navigation controls are displayed.
- **OtherMonthDayStyle** Specifies how to display the days for the previous and next month in the current month.
- **SelectedDayStyle** Specifies how to display the selected date.
- **SelectorStyle** Specifies how to display links for selecting a week or the entire month.
- **TitleStyle** Specifies how to display the title bar.
- **TodayDayStyle** Specifies how to display the current date.
- **WeekendDayStyle** Specifies how to display weekend days.

To show or hide different parts of the Calendar control, we can use the following properties.

- **ShowDayHeader** Indicates whether or not to display the days of the week.
- **ShowGridLines** Indicates whether or not to display gridlines between the days of the month.
- **ShowNextPrevMonth** Indicates whether or not to display navigation controls to the next or previous month.
- **ShowTitle** Indicates whether or not to show the title.

To specify the format of the name of the day, navigation controls, and title, we use the following properties.

- **DayNameFormat** Specifies the date format. This property can contain the values `FirstLetter`, `FirstTwoLetters`, `Full`, or `Short`.

- **NextPrevFormat** Specifies the format of navigation controls. This property can contain the values `CustomText` (we can programmatically specify the text for navigation controls), `FullMonth`, or `ShortMonth`.

- **TitleFormat** Specifies the title format, which can be either `Month` (only the month name is displayed in the title) or `MonthYear` (month name and year are displayed in the title).

The following properties can be used to specify the displayed text.

- **NextMonthText** Specifies the text for the next month navigation control.
- **PrevMonthText** Specifies the text for the previous month navigation control.
- **SelectMonthText** Specifies the text for the month selection.
- **SelectWeekText** Specifies the text for the week selection.

The `Calendar` control fires the `DayRender` event when each date cell in the `Calendar` control is created. In the event handler for this event, we can control the contents and formatting of date cells.

The following example shows how to use the `Calendar` control with all the properties set to their default values (see also Figure 7.30).

```
<form runat="server">
 <asp:Calendar
  id=Calendar1
  runat="server"
 />
</form>
```

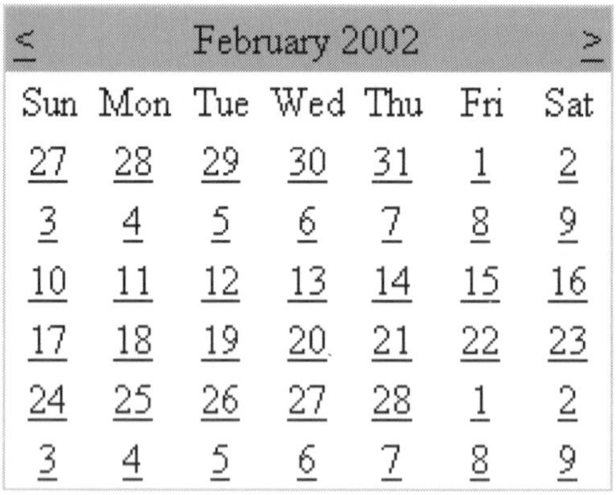

FIGURE 7.30 The `Calendar` control with all the properties set to default values

Now, let's add an event handler for the SelectionChanged event. This will allow us to find what users have selected in the Calendar control (see also Figure 7.31).

```
<script runat="server">
Sub Date_Selected(sender as Object, e As EventArgs)

   Msg.InnerText = "The selected date is " & _
     Calendar1.SelectedDate.ToShortDateString

End Sub
</script>

<asp:Calendar
  id=Calendar1
  OnSelectionChanged = "Date_Selected"
  runat="server"
/>
```

We can use the SelectedDates property of the control to find out how many days have been selected and if the user has selected a day (SelectedDates.Count = 1), a week (SelectedDates.Count = 7) or a month (SelectedDates.Count > 7). The SelectedDate property indicates either the selected date (if the user has selected a single date) or the first date in the range.

We can use the following code to find the first and last date selected and calculate how many days were selected (TimeSpan object):

```
Dim StartDate As Date = SelectedDates.Item(0).Date
Dim EndDate As Date =  SelectedDates.Item(SelectedDates.Count-1).Date
Dim DaysSelected As Integer
DaysSelected = EndDate.Substract(FirstDate).Days + 1
```

The selected date is 12/21/2001

<	December 2001					>
Sun	Mon	Tue	Wed	Thu	Fri	Sat
25	26	27	28	29	30	1
2	3	4	5	6	7	8
9	10	11	12	13	14	15
16	17	18	19	20	21	22
23	24	25	26	27	28	29
30	31	1	2	3	4	5

FIGURE 7.31   With an event handler for the SelectionChanged event we can see what users have selected

To programmatically select dates in the control, we use the `SelectedDates` property and input the required dates (as new `Date` objects) into it. To specify the selected date, we set the value of the `SelectedDate` property. To clear the selection, we either set the `SelectedDate` property to `DateTime.Empty` or call the `SelectedDates.Clear` method.

XML control

This web server control is used to display an XML document or the results of XSL transformation. There are several specific properties of the XML control.

- **Document** Specifies the `System.Xml.XmlDocument` object that contains the XML document to display.

- **DocumentContent** Specifies the string with XML contents.

- **DocumentSource** Specifies the file that contains the XML document to display.

- **Transform** Specifies the `System.Xml.Xsl.XslTransform` object that contains the XSL transform document used to format the XML document.

- **TransformSource** Specifies the file that contains the XSL transform document used to format the XML document.

Let's look at several examples of how we can use the XML control. Suppose we have the XML document shown in Figure 7.32, which contains data about employees.

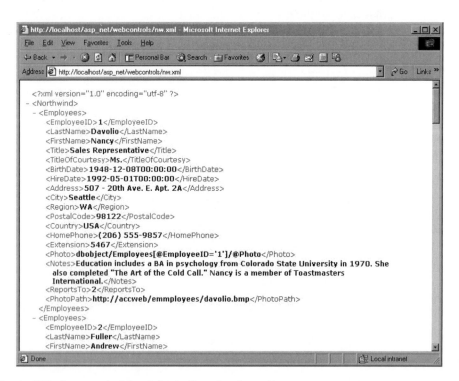

FIGURE 7.32 An XML document giving information about employees

To display this document within a web forms page, we use the XML control with the following properties.

```
<html>
<body>
    <h3>Employees</font></h3>
    <form runat=server>
     <asp:Xml
       id="xml1"
       DocumentSource="nw.xml"
       runat="server"
     />
    </form>
</body>
</html>
```

This gives us display shown in Figure 7.33.

To provide more meaningful results, we can apply an XSL style sheet to format our XML document as an HTML document:

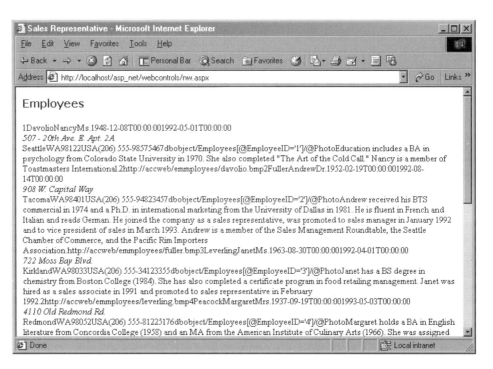

FIGURE 7.33   The XML document displayed within a web forms page

```
<xsl:stylesheet version="1.0"
 xmlns:xsl="http://www.w3.org/1999/XSL/Transform">
<xsl:template match="/">
<HTML>
<BODY>
 <TABLE BORDER="2">
       <TR>
                <TD>First Name</TD>
                <TD>Last Name</TD>
                <TD>Title</TD>
                <TD>Address</TD>
       </TR>
       <xsl:for-each select="Northwind/Employees">
       <TR>
       <TD><xsl:value-of select="FirstName"/></TD>
       <TD><xsl:value-of select="LastName"/> </TD>
       <TD><xsl:value-of select="Title"/>    </TD>
       <TD><xsl:value-of select="Address"/>  </TD>
       </TR>
                </xsl:for-each>
 </TABLE>
</BODY>
</HTML>
</xsl:template>
</xsl:stylesheet>
```

We specify this XSL file as a value of the TransformSource property of the XML control:

```
<html>
<body>
   <h3>Employees</font></h3>
   <form runat=server>
    <asp:Xml
      id="xml1"
      DocumentSource="nw.xml"
      TransformSource="nw.xsl"
      runat="server"
    />
   </form>
</body>
</html>
```

Now the XML control applies the XSL transformation to the XML document and includes the results of this transformation in the web forms page (see Figure 7.34).

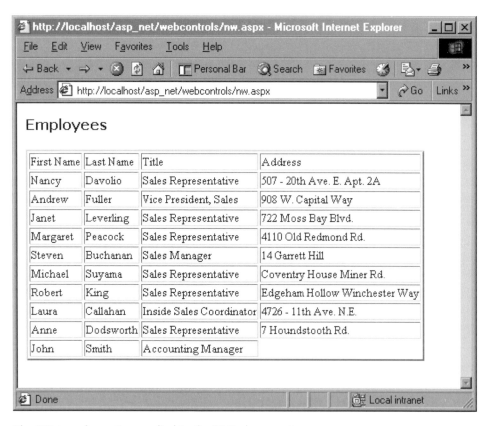

FIGURE 7.34 The XSL transformation applied to the XML document

As was noted above, we can use the XML control with the `XmlDocument` and `XslTransform` objects as sources of the XML document and XSL transformation. The following example shows how to use the XML control in this case:

```
<%@ Import Namespace="System.Xml" %>
<%@ Import Namespace="System.Xml.Xsl" %>

<html>
 <script runat="server">

 Sub Page_Load(sender As Object, e As EventArgs)

   Dim XMLDoc As XmlDocument  = New XmlDocument()
   Dim XSLDoc As XslTransform = New XslTransform()

   XMLDoc.Load(Server.MapPath("nw.xml"))
   XSLDoc.Load(Server.MapPath("nw.xsl")
```

```
xml1.Document  = XMLDoc
xml1.Transform = XSLDoc


End Sub


</script>


<body>
 <h3>Employees</font></h3>
  <form runat=server>

      <asp:Xml
        id="xml1"
        runat="server"
      />


    </form>
  </body>
```

This completes our discussion of web server controls. The rest of this chapter is dedicated to validation controls.

7.5 Validation controls

Validation controls are used along with an input control to test what the user enters for that input control. Validation controls can check for a required field, test against a specific value pattern of characters, and so on.

Only a subset of HTML and web server controls can work with validation controls. Before using the control, check if it has a `ValidationPropertyAttribute`. The following controls can be used with validation controls:

- `HTMLInputText;`
- `HTMLTextArea;`
- `HTMLSelect;`
- `HTMLInputFile;`
- `TextBox;`
- `DropDownList;`
- `ListBox;`
- `RadioButtonList.`

All validation controls have a set of common properties defined by the ancestor class `BaseValidator`. These properties are listed overleaf.

- **ControlToValidate** Specifies the ID of the input control to be evaluated by the validation control.
- **IsValid** Indicates whether or not the evaluated control is valid.
- **ErrorMessage** Specifies the error message to display if the control is not valid.
- **Display** Specifies how the validation control will be displayed. Possible values include None (the validation control is never displayed, the error message will be shown in the ValidationSummary control), Static (the page layout does not change when the validation control's contents are displayed), and Dynamic (several validation controls can occupy the same location on the page).
- **Text** Specifies the text to be displayed by the control.

Now let's look at the validation controls. We will start with the simple one – the RequiredFieldValidator control, which ensures that the user does not skip a required entry.

RequiredFieldValidator control

This control performs the required entry validation – each field that has this control attached will become a required field. If the field value does not change from the value specified by the InitialValue property, the input control fails validation.

The following example shows how to use the RequiredFieldValidator control (see also Figure 7.35):

```
<form runat="server">

  <asp:Label
    Text = "First Name"
    runat="server"
  />

  <asp:TextBox
    id="FirstName"
    runat="server"
  />

  <asp:RequiredFieldValidator
    id="ReqField1"
    ControlToValidate="FirstName"
    Type="String"
    ErrorMessage="You must enter the first name"
    InitialValue = ""
    Display="Static"
    runat="server"
  />

  <br>
```

```
<asp:Label
 Text = "Last Name"
 runat="server"
/>

<asp:TextBox
 id="LastName"
 runat="server"
/>

<asp:RequiredFieldValidator
 id="ReqField2"
 ControlToValidate="LastName"
 Type="String"
 ErrorMessage="You must enter the last name"
 InitialValue = ""
 Display="Static"
 runat="server"
/>

<br>

<asp:Button id="Button1"
 Text="Submit"
 runat="server"
/>

</form>
```

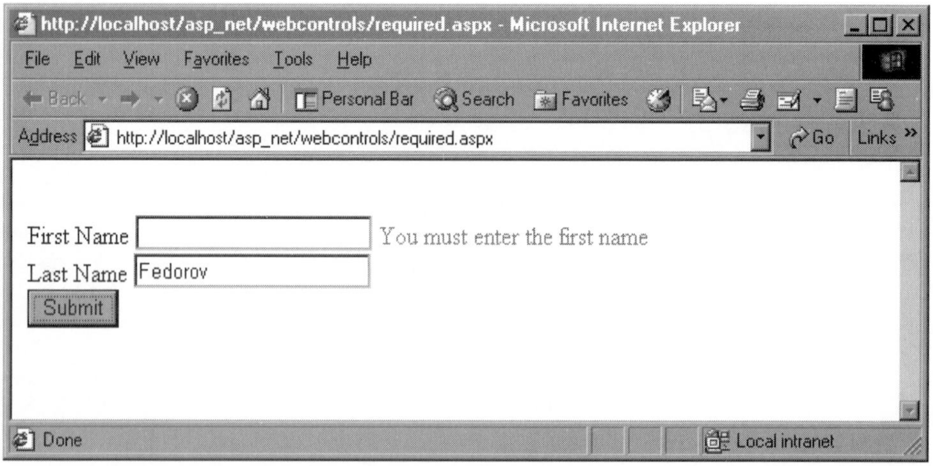

FIGURE 7.35   Using the RequiredFieldValidator control

In this example we have two fields that cannot be empty. We use the `Required FieldValidator` control with each field to ensure that the user cannot skip the required entry. ASP.NET uses client JavaScript code to check the required fields. This code can be found in the following library (`[version]` specifies the version number of CLR):

```
/aspnet_client/system_web/[version] /WebUIValidation.js"
```

If you are interested in how the client-side code works, study the source code for the web forms page and the source of this library.

To disable generation of the client-side code, set the following @ `Page` directive:

```
<%@ Page ClientTarget = "DownLevel" %>
```

CompareValidator control

This control performs comparison to a value. It compares a user's entry against a constant value or a property value of another control using a comparison operator (less than, equal to, greater than, and so on).

We specify the control to validate as a value of the `ControlToValidate` property. If we want to compare input in one control against another, we set the `ControlToCompare` property to specify the control we want it to compare with. If there is no other control to compare values with, we use a constant value that is specified in the `ValueToCompare` property. The `Operator` property specifies the comparison operation. It can take the values set out in Table 7.6.

The `Type` property is used to specify the data type to check if the `DataTypeCheck` operator is specified. It can have one of the values `String`, `Integer`, `Double`, `Date`, or `Currency`.

The following example shows how to use the `CompareValidator` control (see also Figure 7.36):

TABLE 7.6 The meaning of values in the `Operator` property

Value	Meaning
Equal	A comparison for equality will be performed between the two values.
NotEqual	A comparison for inequality will be performed between the two the values.
GreaterThan	A comparison for greater than will be performed between the two values.
GreaterThanEqual	A comparison for greater than or equal to will be performed between the two values.
LessThan	A comparison for less than will be performed between the two values.
LessThanEqual	A comparison for less than or equal to will be performed between the two values.
DataTypeCheck	A data type comparison will be performed between the input value and the value of the Type property.

```
<form runat="server">

 <asp:Label
  Text = "Name"
  runat="server"
 />

 <asp:TextBox
  id="Name"
  runat="server"
 />

 <br>

 <asp:Label
  Text = "Age "
  runat="server"
 />

 <asp:TextBox
  id="Age"
  runat="server"
 />

 <asp:CompareValidator
  ControlToValidate="Age"
  ValueToCompare="60"
  Type="Integer"
  Operator="GreaterThan"
  ErrorMessage="You must be over 60 to enter the senior's club"
  Runat="Server"
 />
 <br><br>

 <asp:Button id="Button1"
  Text="Submit"
  runat="server"
 />

</form>
```

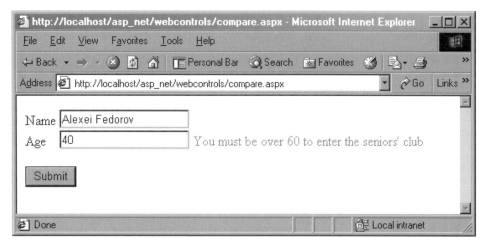

FIGURE 7.36   Using the CompareValidator control

RangeValidator control

This control performs range checking. It verifies that a user's entry is within a specified range – that is, between specified lower and upper boundaries. We can check ranges within pairs of numbers, alphabetic characters, and dates.

There are three key properties of the RangeValidator control. As with all validation controls, we specify the control to validate data as a value of the ControlToValidate property. To specify the minimum and maximum values of what is valid, we use the MinimumValue and MaximumValue properties.

The Type property is used to specify the data type to check. It can have one of the following values – String, Integer, Double, Date, or Currency.

The following example shows how to use the RangeValidator control (see also Figue 7.37):

```
<form runat="server">

  <asp:Label
   Text = "Enter number (20-80)"
   runat="server"
  />

  <asp:TextBox
   id="Num"
   width = 40
   runat="server"
  />
```

```
<asp:RangeValidator
 ControlToValidate="Num"
 Type="Integer"
 MinimumValue = 20
 MaximumValue = 80
 ErrorMessage="Number should be between 20 and 80"
 Runat="Server"
/>

<br><br>

<asp:Button id="Button1"
 Text="Submit"
 runat="server"
/>

</form>
```

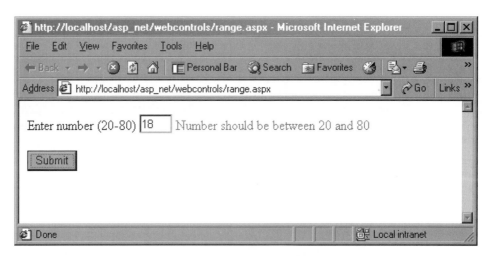

FIGURE 7.37 Using the RangeValidator control, we can set lower and upper boundaries for validation

RegularExpressionValidator control

This control performs pattern matching. It checks that the entry matches a pattern defined by a regular expression. The RegularExpressionValidator control can be used to check any input that can expressed as a pattern – e-mail addresses, phone numbers, ZIP and postcodes, and so on.

As with all validation controls, we specify the control to validate as a value of the `ControlToValidate` property. The `ValidationExpression` property specifies the regular expression used to validate an input.

Let's create an example where the `RegularExpressionValidator` control will be used to check if the user has entered his e-mail address in the valid format. For our example the valid e-mail address should contain:

● one or more characters, numbers, and the underscore symbol;

● the @ symbol;

● domain name – one or more characters, numbers, and the underscore symbol;

● the . symbol;

● one or more characters, numbers, and the underscore symbol.

This can be expressed with the following pattern:

```
^\w+@\w+\.\w+$
```

Here is a brief explanation of this regular expression pattern:

● the ^ symbol specifies that the match must occur at the beginning of the string or line;

● the \w indicates that we are looking for any word character match (`[a-zA-Z_0-9]`);

● the + symbol specifies one or more matches;

● the $ symbol specifies that the match must occur at the end of the string or before the \ at the end of the string or line.

For more information on regular expressions see the following websites:

● regular expressions how to:
  http://py-howto.sourceforge.net/regex/regex.html

● regular expressions reference:
  www.zvon.org/other/reReference/Output/

● a tao of regular expressions:
  http://sitescooper.org/tao_regexps.html

● learning to use regular expressions by example
  www.phpbuilder.com/columns/dario19990616.php3

Here is an example of how to use the `RegularExpressionValidator` control (see also Figure 7.38):

```
<form runat="server">
 <asp:Label
  Text = "E-mail please"
  runat="server"
 />
```

```
<asp:TextBox
 id="email"
 runat="server"
/>

<asp:RegularExpressionValidator
 ControlToValidate="email"
 ValidationExpression="^\w+@\w+\.\w+$"
 ErrorMessage="Your e-mail format is invalid"
 Runat="Server"
/>
<br><br>

<asp:Button id="Button1"
 Text="Submit"
 runat="server"
/>

</form>
```

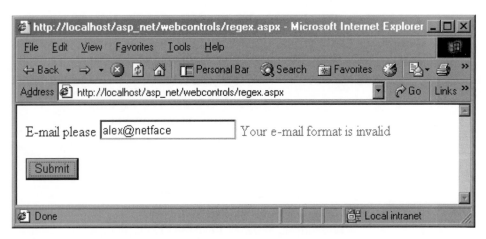

FIGURE 7.38   Using the user's e-mail address for validation with the RegularExpressionValidation control

ValidationSummary Control

This control can be used to display the error messages from all validation controls in a single location. The DisplayMode property specifies how the information is displayed – as a list, bulleted list, single paragraph, or other. For each validation control, the error message – specified by the ErrorMessage property – is displayed. If this

property is not set, the contents of the Text property will be used. The following
example shows how to use the ValidationSummary control (see also Figure 7.30):

```
<form runat="server">
 <table>
  <tr>
   <td>
    <asp:Label
     Text = "First Name"
     runat="server"
    />
   </td>
   <td>
    <asp:TextBox
     id="FirstName"
     runat="server"
    />
    <asp:RequiredFieldValidator
     id="ReqField1"
     ControlToValidate="FirstName"
     Type="String"
     ErrorMessage="You must enter the first name"
     InitialValue = ""
     Display="None"
     runat="server"
    />
   </td>
  </tr>
  <tr>
   <td>
    <asp:Label
     Text = "Last Name"
     runat="server"
    />
   </td>
   <td>
    <asp:TextBox
     id="LastName"
     runat="server"
    />
    <asp:RequiredFieldValidator
     id="ReqField2"
     ControlToValidate="LastName"
```

```
    Type="String"
    ErrorMessage="You must enter the last name"
    InitialValue = ""
    Display="None"
    runat="server"
  />
 </td>
</tr>
<tr>
 <td>
  <asp:Label
   Text = "E-mail"
   runat="server"
  />
 </td>
 <td>
  <asp:TextBox
   id="email"
   runat="server"
  />
  <asp:RegularExpressionValidator
   ControlToValidate="email"
   ValidationExpression="^\w+@\w+\.\w+$"
   ErrorMessage="Your e-mail format is invalid"
   Display="None"
   Runat="Server"
  />
 </td>
</tr>
<tr>
 <td colspan="2" align="right">
  <asp:Button id="Button1"
   Text="Submit"
   runat="server"
  />
 </td>
</tr>
<tr>
 <td colspan="2" align="center">
  <asp:ValidationSummary
   id="valSum"
   DisplayMode="BulletList"
```

```
         ShowSummary="True"
         HeaderText="Please check the following fields:"
         runat="server"
     />
     </td>
    </tr>


   </table>


 </form>
```

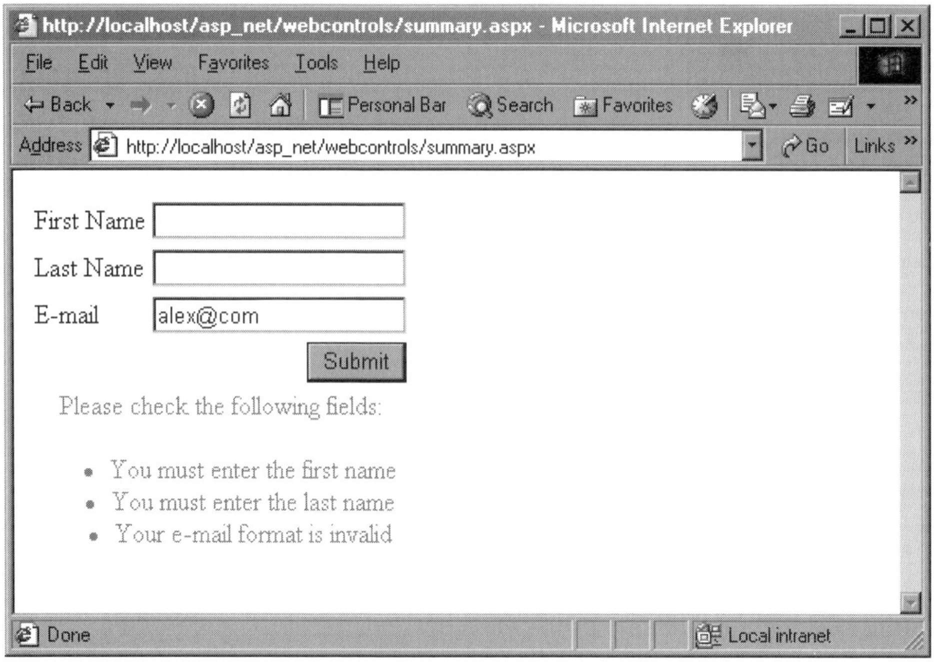

FIGURE 7.39   An example of the ValidationSummary control in use

Note that in the example above we have set the Display property of all validation controls to "None" – this tells the control to display its error message only inside the ValidationSummary control.

7.6 Validation controls and page validation

We have discussed the Page class in the previous chapter so shall only mention it briefly here. It is worth knowing that it has a Boolean property called IsValid. This property indicates whether or not the page validation has succeeded. By checking this property, we can find out programmatically if the user input has passed all validation rules defined by the validation controls on this page. Here is how it works.

The `Page` class maintains a list of all validation controls contained in the page in the `Validators` collection. This collection is an array of `IValidator` interfaces that are implemented by each validation control. The `IValidator` interface defines the `Validate` method and two properties – namely, `ErrorMessage` and `IsValid`. The `Page` class' `Validate` method iterates the list of validation controls and calls each control's `Validate` method. This process takes place during the page post-back. Validation occurs just after the `Page_Load` event before the server-side controls start to fire their own events.

7.7 Conclusion

In this chapter, we have learned about HTML and the web server controls provided by ASP.NET. We started with a discussion of HTML server controls. We learned about the `Control` class, which defines the basic functionality of all server controls, and then covered all the major properties of each control available in ASP.NET. After this we learned about web server controls, which provide more unified object models and more functionality than HTML server controls. At the end of this chapter, we discussed validation controls and provided several examples of how to use them.

This chapter ends our tour around the ASP.NET applications and server-side controls. In the next chapter, we will start to learn about another type of application we can create with Microsoft.NET – Windows forms-based applications.

chapter 8

Windows forms

- Windows forms – an introduction
- `System.Windows.Forms` namespace
- Windows forms and events
- Dialog boxes
- Message boxes
- Creating MDI windows applications

In this chapter, we will explore the .NET Framework library classes that allow us to create Windows applications. So far, we have seen two types of applications. We started with the console applications and, in the two previous chapters, discussed web applications. Here we will learn about the "real" Windows applications that run on the desktop under Microsoft .NET. Such applications can have windows, controls, can draw graphics, and can react to keyboard and mouse events.

All classes required to create the GUI aspect of a Windows application can be found in the `System.Windows.Forms` namespace. The name itself may be a little bit misleading. It implies that the concept of forms, known to users of Visual Basic, is now available as a basic concept used to create Windows applications, but it is, in fact, based on the idea of classes, is hugely borrowed from the Windows foundation classes (WFC) library, originally created for Microsoft Visual J++.

Figure 8.1 shows how Windows applications were created in pre- .NET days, when each language had its own library – Visual Basic forms in Visual Basic, Microsoft foundation classes in Visual C++, and so on. The right panel shows how things changed with the arrival of .NET. Now, every .NET-compliant language – and these include not only those that have been developed by Microsoft, but more than 15 third-party languages such as Perl and COBOL – use the same library, called Windows forms.

In this chapter, we will learn about the `System.Windows.Forms` namespace and several basic classes it is comprised of. In the following chapters, we will discuss Windows forms controls.

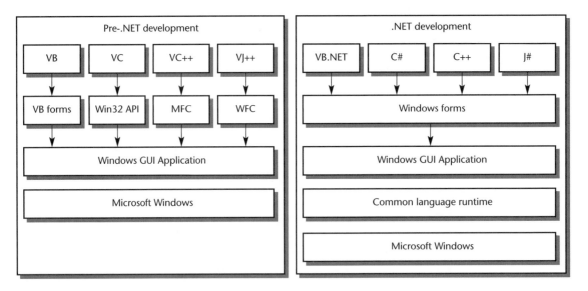

FIGURE 8.1   How Windows applications were created before and with .NET

8.1 Windows forms – an introduction

Let's start our discussion by creating a simple example of a Windows application that will run under Microsoft .NET. Here is the code:

```
'-----------------------------------------
' WinMin – Minimal .NET Windows Application
'-----------------------------------------
Imports System
Imports System.Windows.Forms

 Public Class MyForm
  Inherits System.Windows.Forms.Form

  Shared Sub Main()
   System.Windows.Forms.Application.Run(New MyForm())
  End Sub

  Public Sub New()
   MyBase.New()
  End Sub
 End Class
```

We compile this code with the following command line:

```
> vbc WinMin.vb /t:WinExe /r:system.dll /r:system.windows.forms.dll
```

where:

- vbc is the Visual Basic.NET command-line compiler;
- WinMin.vb is the name of the source file;
- /t:WinExe indicates that we are creating a Windows executable file;
- /r:system.dll and /r:system.windows.forms.dll specify the namespaces we reference in our application – system.dll containing the System namespace and system.windows.forms.dll containing the System.Windows.Forms namespace.

Readers who are familiar with creating Windows applications using Microsoft Win32 SDK will note the absence of such familiar parts as Window procedure (WndProc), message loops, and so on. Certainly, everything is here, but these "low-level" things are now hidden inside the Form and Application classes.

8.2 System.Windows.Forms namespace

The System.Windows.Forms namespace, which is in the System.Windows.Forms.dll assembly, provides developers with classes and structures for building Windows-

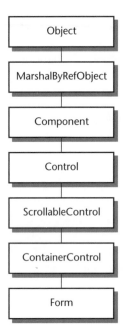

FIGURE 8.2 The hierarchy of the Form class

based applications for the Microsoft Windows operating system. There are too many classes defined within this namespace to be listed in just one table. We will start with the basic classes and then move on to the classes that add extra functionality to the Windows applications.

The main class used to create Windows applications is the Form class – it is the main window of the application. Before we discuss this class, however, we need to go up the class library hierarchy and look at some of its parent classes – the Control, ScrollableControl, and ContainerControl classes. These will help us to understand the basic functionality available in Windows forms. Figure 8.2 shows the class hierarchy of the Form class.

We are already familiar with the Object class from Chapter 3, where we discussed the .NET class library. Thus we will start our investigation of the Form class parent classes with the Component class.

Component class

This class provides the base implementation of the IComponent interface and enables object sharing between applications. All components in the System.Windows.Forms namespace are based on this class. The main features implemented by the Component class are the ability to contain other objects (see the Container property of the IContainer type), to be hosted by any object that implements the IContainer interface, and to supply the site for the component (the Site property) it contains. Also, we should mention the ability to query and get services (one or mode "service"

objects that provide customized support for other objects) from its container (see the
`GetService` method, which implements the `IServiceProvider` interface). The list
of event handlers attached to the component is available via the `Events` property of
the `EventHandlerList` type.

One of the main derived classes of the `Component` class is the `Control` class,
which is used as a base class for all Windows controls.

Control class

By definition, control is a component that has a visual representation. This class provides handling of user input via the keyboard and pointing device, it handles most of
the common Windows messages (`WM_xxx` messages), provides a window handle
(`HWND`) by implementing the `IWin32Window` interface, and defines the bounds (position and size) of a control.

Additionally, the `Control` class defines the boundaries of a control – its position
and size, foreground and background colors, drag and drop functionality, and much
more. Some of the properties of the `Control` class are already familiar to Visual Basic
programmers, but there is some new functionality, such as anchoring (a property that
determines which side of the container a control is bound to) and docking, MFC-like
input handling, handling of child controls, and the transformation of client and
screen coordinates.

Let's take a brief look at some of the properties, methods, and events of the
`Control` class.

Visual characteristics of the control are defined by the following properties.

- **DefaultBackColor** This read-only property of a `Color` type specifies the default
  background color for the control. The default value is `SystemColors.Control`. To
  change the background color of the control, use the `BackColor` property of a
  `Color` type. When the background color is changed, the `BackColorChanged`
  event occurs. To reset the `BackColor` property to its default value, use the
  `ResetBackColor()` method.

- **DefaultForeColor** This read-only property of a `Color` type specifies the default
  foreground color for the control. The default value is `SystemColors.`
  `ControlText`. To change the foreground color of the control, use the `ForeColor`
  property of a `Color` type. When the foreground color is changed, the
  `ForeColorChanged` event occurs. To reset the `ForeColor` property to its default
  value, use the `ResetForeColor()` method.

- **BackgroundImage** This property of an `Image` type specifies the background image
  displayed in the control. When the background image is changed, the
  `BackgroundImageChanged` event occurs.

- **DefaultFont** This read-only property of a `Font` type specifies the default font for
  the control. The default value is the Tahoma 8-point font or one of the following if
  Tahoma is not installed on the computer – CordiaUPC, MS PGothic, SimSun,
  Gulim, MingLiU or Arial. To change the default font, use the `Font` property. When
  the control's font is changed, the `FontChanged` event occurs. To reset the `Font`
  property to its default value, use the `ResetFont()` method.

The visual state of the control is controlled by the following properties.

- **Enabled** This `Boolean` property indicates whether or not the control is enabled. When the value of this property is changed, the `EnabledChanged` event occurs. Enabled controls can receive focus and process input from the keyboard and pointing device.

- **Focused** This `Boolean` property indicates whether or not the control has input focus. The read-only `CanFocus Boolean` property indicates if the control can receive focus. A control can receive focus only if it has a handle associated with it and its `Visible` and `Enabled Boolean` properties are both set to "True". The `ContainsFocus Boolean` property indicates whether or not the control or one of its child controls currently has an input focus. When the control receives focus (either programmatically or as a result of user actions) the `GotFocus` event occurs. The `LostFocus` event indicates that the control no longer has a focus. The `Focus()` method is used to set focus to the control.

- **Visible** This `Boolean` property manipulates the visibility state of the control. When its visible state is changed, the `VisibleChanged` event occurs. The `Show()` and `Hide()` methods can be used to change the value of the `Visible` property.

- **CanSelect** This read-only `Boolean` property indicates whether or not the control can be selected and activated. A control can be selected if its style is set to `ControlStyles.Selectable`, it is contained in another control, and all of its parent controls are visible and enabled. The `Select()` method is used to select the control.

The location and size of the control are controlled by the following properties.

- **Left, Top, Right, Bottom** These `Integer` properties indicate the x and y coordinates of the control, as well as its position within the container.

- **Width, Height, Size** These properties indicate width (`Right-Left`) and height (`Top-Bottom`) of the control. The `Size` property contains the control's size. As a `Size` structure, it stores the height and width of the control, as well as providing several methods that can be used to manipulate these values. When the value of the `Size` property is changed, the `SizeChanged` event occurs.

- **ClientSize** This property (of the `Size` type) contains the width and height of the client area of the control. The client area is the area available for drawing on the surface of the control.

- **ClientRectange** This property – of a `Rectangle` type – contains the rectangle that represents the client area of the control. The `DisplayRectangle` property (of the `Rectangle` type) contains the same value as the `ClientRectangle` property, but this can be changed in the controls derived from the base `Control` class.

- **Location** This property – of the `Point` type – is used to change the coordinates of the upper-left corner of the control. The data stored in this property is relative to the upper-left corner of the control's container.

- When the control is resized, the `Resize` event occurs.

Several properties, methods, and events are used to construct hierarchies of controls.

- **Controls** This property – of a `Control.ControlCollection` type – lists all child controls contained within the control. When a child control is added to this control, the `ControlAdded` event occurs. The `ControlRemoved` event occurs when a child control is removed from this control.

- **Parent** This property – of a `Control` type – indicates the parent container of this control. Setting this property to null removes this control from the children list of its parent control. The `TopLevelControl` property – of a `Control` type – indicates the top-level container for this control. To find out if the control is the top-level control, we use the `GetTopLevel()` method.

- **Container** To find the container (`IContainer` interface) for the control we can use this property. The `GetContainerControl()` method returns the next `ContainerControl` (`IContainerControl` type) in the chain of the control's parent controls.

- **HasChildren** To find out if the control has child controls, we use this property. The value of this property is "True" if the `Controls.Count` is greater than zero.

- **FindForm()** This method allows us to find the `Form` that contains this control. This is not always the same as the control's parent control.

- **Contains(Control)** To find a specified child control, use this method. The `GetChildAtPoint(Point)` method returns a child control that is located at the specified point (x and y coordinates).

When describing the `Control` class features, we have mentioned its ability to handle user input via the keyboard and pointing device. The following properties and events are involved in this process.

- **ModifierKeys** This is a read-only property of a `Keys` type and it contains the current state of SHIFT, CTRL, and ALT keys.

- **MouseButtons** This read-only property of a `MouseButtons` type contains the current state of the left, right, and middle mouse buttons.

- **MousePosition** This read-only property of a `Point` type indicates the position of the mouse in screen coordinates.

- **KeyDown**, **KeyUp**, and **KeyPress** These are the keyboard events.

- **Click**, **DoubleClick**, **MouseDown**, **MouseUp**, **MouseMove**, **MouseWheel** These are the mouse events.

For more information on handling events, see the Windows forms and events section below.

The manipulation of graphics and painting are provided by means of the following methods and events.

- **CreateGraphics() method** Returns the `Graphics` object for the control. For more information on the `Graphics` object and its relationship to the underlying graphics engine, see Chapter 11.

- **Invalidate() method** Causes the paint message to be sent to the control.
- **Refresh() method** Can be used to force the control to invalidate its client area, thus causing an immediate repainting of itself and its child controls.
- **Update() method** Forces the control to paint any currently invalid areas.
- **Paint event** Occurs every time a control (or its area) needs to be drawn or redrawn.

The Cursor property (of a Cursor type) is used to get or set the mouse cursor. Every time the value of this property is changed, the CursorChanged event occurs. To restore the default value of the Cursor property, we use the ResetCursor() method. To change the value of the Cursor property, we either select one of the pre-defined cursors from the Cursors class or create one from a file by assigning the Cursor.Current property to the new object of the Cursor type. Please note that the Cursor class does not support animated cursors.

The Text property (of a String type) is used to get or set the text for the control. When the value of this property is changed, the TextChanged event occurs. To change the text to the original value, use the ResetText() method.

The Anchor property (of the AnchorStyles type) is used to specify how the control is anchored to the edges of its container. Possible values for this property (None, Left, Right, Top, and Bottom) can be found in the AnchorStyles enumeration. Figure 8.3 shows several possible anchor values.

When a control is anchored to an edge of its container, the distance between the control and the specific edge remains constant when the containing control resizes.

To convert client coordinates to screen coordinates and back, we can use the PointToClient(*Point*) and PointToScreen(*Point*) methods, which that return the Point object or, if we are converting the rectangle, the RectangleToClient (*Rectangle*) and RectangleToScreen(*Rectangle*) methods return the Rectangle object.

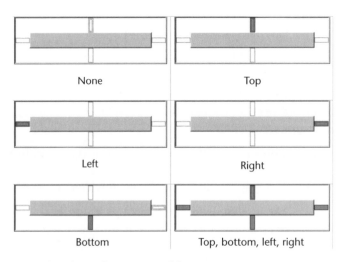

FIGURE 8.3 Several anchor values are possible

In this section, we have covered most of the functionality provided by the Control class. Before we go on to discuss the extra functionality added by its derived classes – the ScrollableControl and ContainerControl classes – let's briefly look inside the Control class to find out how it relates to the things Windows programmers are familiar with – Windows handles (HWND), Windows procedures (WndProc) message queues, and so on.

Inside *Control*

The Control class implements the IWin32Window interface to expose Win32 HWND handles. Handles are available in the Handle property, which is read only. To check if we have a handle associated with the control, we query the value of the IsHandleCreated Boolean property, which is "True" for controls with associated handles. Handle lifetime is supported by two events. When the handle is created, the HandleCreated event occurs; when it is destroyed, the HandleDestroyed event occurs.

The WndProc(*Message*) method implements the Windows procedure. It is used to process messages that come from the Windows system and dispatch them to appropriate message handlers. If we look at the IL source of the method, we find that it is implemented as a big Switch operator that performs the dispatching functions as it directs messages to WmXXX methods of the Control class.

Each WmXXX method starts with a call to a default Windows procedure (Control.DefWndProc) and, after this, performs the specific tasks. Each WmXXX method ends with a call to the appropriate OnXXX method, which should be overwritten to provide the functionality required by our application. Later in this chaper, in the section entitled Windows forms and events, we will see how to implement our own event handlers for some of the Windows messages.

The Control class also implements the many IOLExxx interfaces, such as IOleControl, IOleObject, IOleWindow, and so on. This allows it to be the OLE drag and drop host, as well as to perform in-place activation of OLE objects.

Now we know the basic functionality provided by the Control class. Let's look next at the extra functionality added by its derived classes – the ScrollableControl and ContainerControl classes.

ScrollableControl class

This class adds autoscrolling functionality to controls. The AutoScroll Boolean property is used to turn scrolling on and off and allows us to show scrollbars as needed. The VScroll and HScroll Boolean properties are used to specify which scrollbars are needed. The AutoScrollPosition property (of the Point type) gets or sets the position within the scrollable area. The AutoScrollMargin property (of the Size type) gets or sets the autoscroll margin – the distance of the child controls from the edges of the scrollable control. To set the size (its width and height) of the autoscroll margin, we use the SetAutoScrollMargin(*Integer*, *Integer*) method.

The `AutoScrollMinSize` property (of the `Size` type) is used to get or set the minimum size of the auto-scroll.

The `ScrollableControl` class is the ancestor of the three classes found in the `System.Windows.Forms` namespace – the `ComponentTray` class (which provides the component tray UI for the form designer), the `Panel` class (used to group collections of controls), and the `ContainerControl` class, which we will discuss below.

ContainerControl class

This class extends controls based on the `Control` and `ScrollableControl` classes and adds the ability to contain other controls that are called child controls. Let's look at some of the major properties and methods of the `ContainerControl` class.

- **ActiveControl property** Required by the `IContainerControl` interface, it points to the currently active child control – the child control that has the focus. This property is of a `Control` type.

- **ParentForm property** Of a `Form` type, it gets or sets the form that a container control is assigned to.

- **ProcessTabKey(Boolean) method** Allows us to iterate child controls by pressing the TAB key and activate them according to the tab order. Only controls with the `TabStop` property set to "True" can be selected and activated by the TAB key.

The `ContainerControl` class is the ancestor of the `Form` (discussed in the next section) and `UserControl` classes. The latter serves as a base for user-defined controls.

Form class

The `Form` class serves as a basis for Windows forms (windows and dialog boxes) and it inherits all of the properties, methods, and events discussed above. We use the `Form` class to create standard, tool, borderless, and floating windows. This class can also be useful when we need to create dialog boxes or multidocument interface (MDI) forms. Properties of the `Form` class allow us to determine the appearance, size, color, and window management features of the window or dialog box. Most of the methods of this class are also used to manipulate a form. To respond to actions performed in the form, we use events of the `Form` class.

Now, let's look at the properties and methods available in the `Form` class. Here we will discuss only properties and methods implemented in this class; for properies and methods inherited from the parent classes, see `Component`, `Control`, and related classes above.

Instead of providing a long list of properties and methods, let's group them by functionality or roles the form can play in Windows applications.

Form as a window

Let's look at a typical window in a Microsoft Windows application (see Figure 8.4). It consists of two main parts – the caption and the client area. The caption is used to display the name of the window, as well as to host the buttons – control box, minimize box, maximize box, and close box. The client area is where all other form controls are displayed.

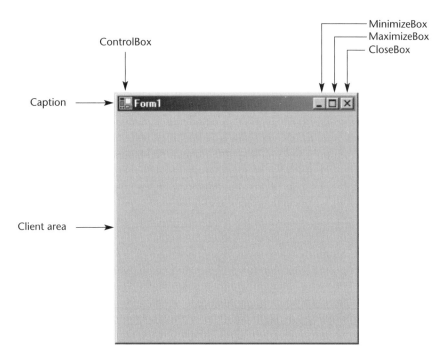

FIGURE 8.4   The parts of a typical Windows window

To control these attributes of a form, we use the appropriate properties. The `Text` property (of a `String` type) contains the form's caption text, the `ControlBox`, `MinimizeBox`, and `MaximizeBox` `Boolean` properties indicate whether or not to show the `ControlBox`, `MinimizeBox`, and `MaximizeBox` in the caption. There is no property to remove the `CloseBox` button from the caption. Forms can have borders and this is specifed by means of the `FormBorderStyle` property, which can have the following values.

- **Fixed3D** A fixed, three-dimensional border.
- **FixedDialog** A thick, fixed dialog-style border.
- **FixedSingle** A fixed, single-line border.
- **FixedToolWindow** A tool window, not resizeable border.

- **None** No border.
- **Sizeable** A resizeable border.
- **SizeableToolWindow** A resizeable tool window border.

The effects of the various values of the FormBorderStyle property are shown in Figure 8.5.

To control the minimum and maximim size of the window – that is, to limit its resized size – we use the MinimumSize and MaximumSize properties of the Size type. This type provides such properties as Height and Width, which allow us to specify the size of the form in the minimized and maximized state. By default, these properties are set to 0, 0.

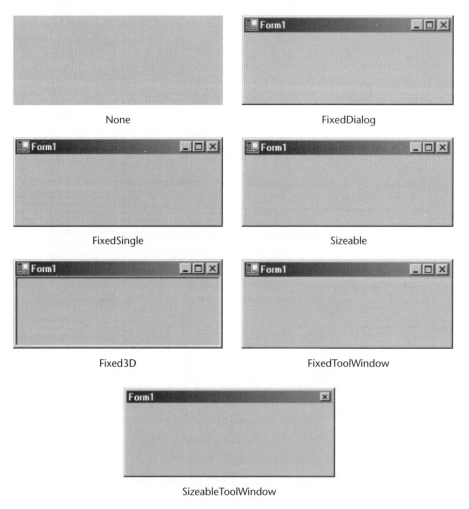

FIGURE 8.5 The effects created by the values of FormBorderStyle

The size grip is displayed in the lower right-hand corner of the form and is used to change the size of the form. The SizeGripStyle property (of the SizeGripStyle type) is used to change the style of the size grip. The value of this property can be SizeGripStyle.Auto – show size grip when needed – SizeGripStyle.Hide – never show size grip – or SizeGripStyle.Show – always show size grip. A form with the size grip turned on is shown in Figure 8.6.

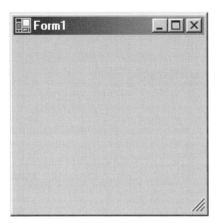

FIGURE 8.6   A form with the size grip option turned on

To get or set the size of the client area of the form, we use the ClientSize property (of a Size type). The size of the client area of the form is the size of the form excluding the borders and title bar. The client area of a form is that where controls can be placed.

To change the size and location of the form on the Windows desktop, we use the DesktopBounds property. Desktop coordinates are based on the working area of the screen, which excludes the taskbar. The coordinate system of the desktop is pixel based. The DesktopBounds property is of a Rectangle type, which represents a rectangle defined by its width, height, and upper left-hand corner.

The DesktopLocation property (of a Point type) can be used to change the location of the form on the Windows desktop.

The StartPosition property (of a FormStartPosition type) specifies the starting position of the form at runtime. It can have one of the following values.

- **CenterParent** The form is centered within the bounds of its parent form.
- **CenterScreen** The form is centered on the current display and has the dimensions specified in the form's Size property.
- **Manual** The location and size of the form will determine its starting position.
- **WindowsDefaultBounds** The form is positioned at the Windows default location and has its bounds determined by Windows default.
- **WindowsDefaultLocation** The form is positioned at the Windows default location and has its dimensions specified in the form's Size property.

The `Menu` property is used to specify the main menu (`MainMenu` type component) that is displayed in the form. A form with a main menu and two commands is shown in Figure 8.7.

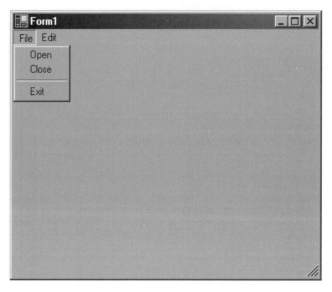

FIGURE 8.7 A form with a menu and commands

The `Icon` property of the `Icon` type specifies the icon for the form. If we don't change this value, the default icon will be used. The `ShowInTaskBar Boolean` property allows us to show or hide the form in the Windows taskbar. How our form looks with the default icon in the taskbar is shown in Figure 8.8.

FIGURE 8.8 Taskbar of a form with default icon

The `Opacity` property (of a `Double` type) is used to specify the opacity level of the form. The default value of this property is 100.00. We use this property with the `TransparencyKey` property (of a `Color` type), which specifies the color that will represent transparent areas of the form. If the value of the `Opacity` property is set to 0.00, it makes the form completely invisible. We can increase the transparency level of the form by changing the value from 1.00 (100 percent) to 0.00. Note that this feature is supported only on Windows 2000 and Windows XP platforms. Figure 8.9 shows what a window with 50 percent opacity looks like.

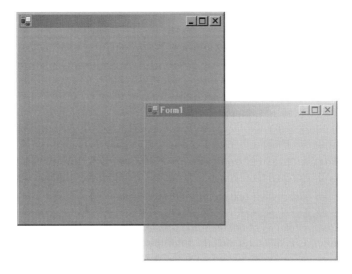

FIGURE 8.9   A form with opacity set to 50 percent

To find the form's window state, we use the `WindowState` property (of the `FormWindowState` type). The window state can be maximized, minimized or normal.

We use the `SetDesktopBounds(Integer, Integer, Integer, Integer)` method to specify the bounds of the form in desktop coordinates and the `SetDesktopLocation(Integer, Integer)` method to specify the location of the form in this way.

Form as a dialog box

Several properties and methods are used when we create a form that should act as a dialog box.

- **Show() method** Shows the form modeless.
- **ShowDialog() method** Shows the form modally.
- **DialogResult property** Specifies one of the `DialogResult` values that will be returned to the calling code to indicate how the dialog box was closed.
- **Modal property** This `Boolean` property indicates whether or not the form is displayed modally.

We will discuss dialog boxes in more detail later in this chapter.

Form as a container

A form can serve as a container for different controls – buttons, list boxes, text boxes, and so on. In this section, we will look at the properties that allow us to control the container behavior of the form.

- **AutoScroll** This `Boolean` property indicates whether or not the form implements autoscrolling.

- **AutoScale** This `Boolean` property indicates whether or not the form adjusts its size and scales its controls to fit the height of the font used on the form.

- **ActiveControl** Indicates the control that is currently active in the form. This property returns the `Control` object.

- **Controls** Specifies the collection of controls (`Control.ControlCollection` type) within the form.

- **HasChildren** This `Boolean` property indicates whether or not the control contains one or more child controls.

Form as a drawing surface

A form can act as a drawing surface for the various graphics functions found in the `System.Drawing` namespace and its secondary namespaces. Normally, we use the `OnPaint` event handler to obtain the graphics object that represents the form's surface. To create a `Graphics` object, we can also use the `CreateGraphics()` method of the `Form` class. For more information on graphical functions, see Chapter 11.

Form as an MDI container

A form can act as a multiple document interface (MDI) container. It can contain other forms that are called MDI child forms. While working with MDI forms, we use the following properties and methods.

- **ActiveMDIChild property** Indicates the active MDI child window as a `Form` object.

- **IsMDIChild property** This is a `Boolean` property and indicates whether or not the form is a MDI child form.

- **IsMDIContainer property** This `Boolean` property indicates whether or not the form acts as a container for MDI child forms.

- **MDIChildren property** Contains an array of forms that represent the MDI child forms parented to this form.

- **MDIParent property** Specifies the current MDI parent form of this form as a `Form` object.

The `LayoutMDI(MdiLayout)` method is used to arrange the MDI child forms within the MDI parent form. We will cover MDI forms in more detail later in this chapter.

8.3 Windows forms and events

Windows forms applications are event-based. This means that each user or system action, such as pressing a button, selecting an item in a list box, or repainting a window or its area causes an event. In order to intercept these events, we create event handlers – subroutines that contain pieces of code that are executed when the particular events occur. All Windows forms events are based on a feature of the common language runtime called "delegates". We can think of delegates as type-safe, secure function pointers. For more information on events and delegates, see Chapter 3.

Each event defined in the Control class has an event delegate with a signature that looks like **EventName**EventHandler. For example, the Click event for the button has an event delegate EventHandler. To handle this event, we create an event handler that has the signature of EventHandler. This type is defined like this:

```
Public Delegate Sub EventHandler( _
   ByVal sender As Object, _
   ByVal e As EventArgs _
)
```

where sender defines the source of the event and e is an object of the EventArgs type, which contains the event data. The EventArgs class contains an Empty property, which represents an event with no event data.

Let's look at the events of the Form class. These events can be divided into three big groups:

● events caused by a property change;

● events caused by user activity;

● a form's lifetime events.

Table 8.1 shows events caused by property changes.

TABLE 8.1 Events caused by changes to properties

Event	Property
BackColorChanged	BackColor
BackgroundImageChanged	BackgroundImage
BindingContextChanged	BindingContext
CausesValidationChanged	CausesValidation
ContextMenuChanged	ContextMenu
CursorChanged	Cursor
DockChanged	Dock
EnabledChanged	Enabled
FontChanged	Font
ForeColorChanged	ForeColor
ImeModeChanged	ImeMode
LocationChanged	Location

Event	Property
ParentChanged	Parent
RightToLeftChanged	RightToLeft
SizeChanged	Size
StyleChanged	Style
TabIndexChanged	TabIndex
TabStopChanged	TabStop
TextChanged	Text
VisibleChanged	Visible

Several events raised in a form are caused by user activity – clicking on controls, moving the mouse, using menus, and so on. These events are:

- **Click** Occurs when a control on a form is clicked.
- **DoubleClick** Occurs when a control on a form is double-clicked.
- **DragDrop** Occurs when a drag-and-drop operation has been completed.
- **DragEnter** Occurs when an object is dragged into the control's bounds.
- **DragLeave** Occurs when an object has been dragged out of the control's bounds.
- **DragOver** Occurs when an object has been dragged over the control's bounds.
- **Enter** Occurs when the control is entered.
- **GiveFeedback** Occurs during the drag operation.
- **GotFocus** Occurs when the control receives focus.
- **HelpRequested** Occurs when the user requests Help for a control.
- **KeyDown** Occurs when a key is held down while the control has focus.
- **KeyPress** Occurs when a key is pressed while the control has focus.
- **KeyUp** Occurs when a key is released while the control has focus.
- **Leave** Occurs when the control is left – that is, when, for example, the control loses focus.
- **LostFocus** Occurs when the control loses focus.
- **MouseDown** Occurs when the mouse pointer is over the control and a mouse button is pressed.
- **MouseEnter** Occurs when the mouse pointer enters the control.
- **MouseHover** Occurs when the mouse pointer hovers over the control.
- **MouseLeave** Occurs when the mouse pointer leaves the control.
- **MouseMove** Occurs when the mouse pointer is moved over the control.

- **MouseUp** Occurs when the mouse pointer is over the control and a mouse button is released.

- **MouseWheel** Occurs when the mouse wheel moves while the control has focus.

Several events raised in a form occur during the control's and form's lifetime.

- **Activated** Occurs when a form becomes active.

- **ChangeUICues** Occurs when the focus or keyboard or both cues have changed. User interface cues indicate the state of the user interface. For example, when the ALT key is pressed, the keyboard shortcuts on the menu are displayed by underlining the appropriate character. The event handler receives an argument of type `UICuesEventArgs` that contains data for this event. Here are properties of this argument type:

  - **Changed** The state of the focus cues and keyboard cues has changed.

  - **ChangeFocus** The state of the focus cues has changed.

  - **ChangeKeyboard** The state of the keyboard cues has changed.

  - **ShowFocus** Focus rectangles are displayed after the change.

  - **ShowKeyboard** Focus rectangles are displayed and keyboard cues are underlined after the change.

- **ControlAdded** Occurs when a new control is added. The event handler receives an argument of a `ControlEventArgs` type and the `Control` property indicates the `Control` used by this event.

- **ControlRemoved** Occurs when a control is removed. The event handler receives an argument of a `ControlEventArgs` type and the `Control` property indicates the `Control` used by this event.

- **HandleCreated** Occurs when a handle is created.

- **HandleDestroyed** Occurs when the handle is destroyed.

- **Invalidated** Occurs when a display is updated. The event handler receives an argument of the type `InvalidateEventArgs` and the `InvalidRect` property specifies the `Rectangle` that contains the invalidated window area.

- **Layout** Occurs when a form has to lay out its child controls. The event handler receives an argument of type `LayoutEventArgs` and the `AffectedControl` property specifies the child control affected by the change and the `AffectedProperty` property specifies the property affected by the change.

- **Move** Occurs when a form is moved.

- **Paint** Occurs when a form is redrawn. The event handler receives an argument of the type `PaintEventArgs`, the `ClipRectangle` property indicates the rectangle in which to paint, and the `Graphics` property indicates the `Graphics` object used to paint.

- **Resize** When a form is resized.
- **SystemColorsChanged** When the system colors have changed.
- **Validated** When the control has finished validating.
- **Validating** When the control is validating.

Let's look at how we can create event handlers for the most common types of events – mouse and keyboard events. Then we will learn how to handle system events.

Handling mouse events

Windows applications can handle three types of mouse events – clicks, presses, and moves. In general, mouse-related events occur in the order shown in Table 8.2.

TABLE 8.2   The order in which mouse events occur

Order	Event	Occurs when
1	MouseEnter	Mouse pointer enters the control.
2	MouseMove	Mouse pointer is moved over the control.
3	MouseHover	Mouse pointer hovers over the control.
4	MouseDown	A mouse button is pressed while the mouse pointer is over the control.
5	MouseUp	A mouse button is released while the mouse pointer is over the control.
6	MouseLeave	Mouse pointer leaves the control.

Let's create a sample application that will track several mouse events for the Panel component and store information about them in a list box (see Figure 8.10).

Here is the code for mouse events handlers:

```
'
'  Mouse pointer enters the control
'
Private Sub Panel1_MouseEnter(ByVal sender As Object,
    ByVal e As System.EventArgs) Handles Panel1.MouseEnter

    ListBox1.Items.Add("Mouse is inside window")

End Sub
'
' Mouse pointer leaves the control
'
```

```
Private Sub Panel1_MouseLeave(ByVal sender As Object,
    ByVal e As System.EventArgs) Handles Panel1.MouseLeave

    ListBox1.Items.Add("Mouse is outside window")

End Sub
'
' A mouse button is pressed while the mouse pointer is over the control
'
Private Sub Panel1_MouseDown(ByVal sender As Object,
    ByVal e As System.Windows.Forms.MouseEventArgs)
    Handles Panel1.MouseDown

    ListBox1.Items.Add("Clicked at " & e.X & " ," & e.Y)

End Sub
'
' A mouse button is released while the mouse pointer is over the
' control
'
Private Sub Panel1_MouseUp(ByVal sender As Object,
    ByVal e As System.Windows.Forms.MouseEventArgs)
    Handles Panel1.MouseUp

    ListBox1.Items.Add("Released at " & e.X & " ," & e.Y)

End Sub
'
' Mouse pointer is moved over the control
'
Private Sub Panel1_MouseMove(ByVal sender As Object,
    ByVal e As System.Windows.Forms.MouseEventArgs)
    Handles Panel1.MouseMove

    ListBox1.Items.Add("Moved at " & e.X & " ," & e.Y)

End Sub
```

Note that there are two types of mouse events. The MouseEnter and MouseLeave events simply notify us about the event without providing further information, while the MouseDown, MouseUp, and MouseMove events contain additional information packed inside the MouseEventArgs structure. This structure contains properties that hold information specific to the mouse event.

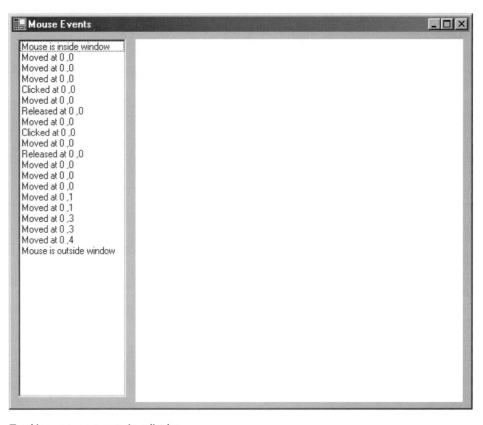

FIGURE 8.10   Tracking mouse events in a list box

- **Button** Specifies which mouse button was pressed. The MouseButtons structure specifies constants for standard mouse buttons – Left, Middle, None, Right – as well as the buttons for Microsoft IntelliMouse Explorer – XButton1 and XButton2.
- **Clicks** Contains the number of times the mouse button was pressed and released.
- **Delta** Contains the number of rotations of the mouse wheel.
- **X** Contains the x coordinate of a mouse when its button was clicked.
- **Y** Contains the y coordinate of a mouse when its button was clicked.

Using the Button property, we can extend our MouseDown event handler to show exactly which button was pressed:

```
Private Sub Panel1_MouseDown(ByVal sender As Object,
  ByVal e As System.Windows.Forms.MouseEventArgs)
  Handles Panel1.MouseDown

  Dim AtXY As String
```

```
      AtXY = " clicked at " & e.X & " ," & e.Y

    Select Case e.Button

    Case MouseButtons.Left
       ListBox1.Items.Add("Left button" & AtXY)

     Case MouseButtons.Middle
       ListBox1.Items.Add("Middle button" & AtXY)

     Case MouseButtons.None
       ListBox1.Items.Add("None button" & AtXY)

     Case MouseButtons.Right
       ListBox1.Items.Add("Right button" & AtXY)

    End Select

  End Sub
```

The other input device we can handle in our Windows applications is the keyboard. We will look at how to handle keyboard events in the next section.

Handling keyboard events

Keyboard events are generated when keys on the keyboard are pressed and released. To handle keyboard events we can create event handlers for `KeyPress` events that allow us to find the character that corresponds to the key that was pressed. To get information about modifier keys – `Shift`, `Alt`, and `Ctrl` – we must handle the `KeyUp` and `KeyDown` events.

Let's create a sample application that will track keyboard events for the `TextBox` component and store information about them in a list box (see also Figure 8.11):

```
  '
  ' Keyboard key was pressed
  '
  Private Sub TextBox1_KeyDown(ByVal sender As Object,
    ByVal e As System.Windows.Forms.KeyEventArgs)
    Handles TextBox1.KeyDown

    ListBox1.Items.Add("Alt=" & e.Alt & " Shift=" & e.Shift & _
      " Ctrl=" & e.Control & " KeyCode=" & e.KeyCode & _
      " KeyValue=" & e.KeyValue)

  End Sub
```

```
'
' Keyboard key was pressed
'
 Private Sub TextBox1_KeyPress(ByVal sender As Object,
  ByVal e As System.Windows.Forms.KeyPressEventArgs)
  Handles TextBox1.KeyPress

    ListBox1.Items.Add("Key pressed " & e.KeyChar)

 End Sub
'
' Keyboard key was released
'
 Private Sub TextBox1_KeyUp(ByVal sender As Object,
  ByVal e As System.Windows.Forms.KeyEventArgs)
  Handles TextBox1.KeyUp

    ListBox1.Items.Add("Key released " & e.KeyCode)

 End Sub
```

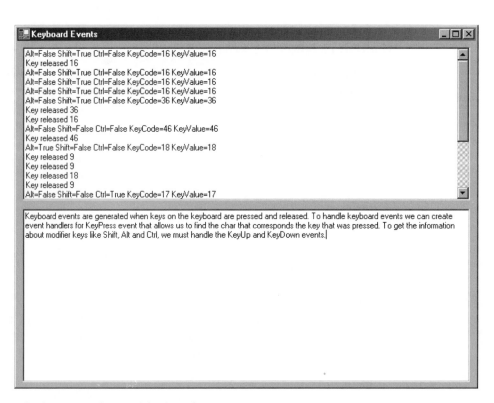

FIGURE 8.11   A list box created to track keyboard events

Handling system events

To be able to handle system events such as the display of resolution changes or low system memory, we can use the `SystemEvents` class implemented in the `Microsoft.Win32` namespace. This class provides notifications about the following events.

- **DisplaySettingsChanged** This event occurs when the user changes the display settings.
- **EventsThreadShutdown** This event occurs before the thread that listens for system events is terminated.
- **InstalledFontChanged** This event occurs when the user adds fonts to or removes fonts from the system.
- **LowMemory** This event occurs when the system is running out of available memory.
- **PaletteChanged** This event occurs when the user switches to an application that uses a different palette.
- **PowerModeChanged** This event occurs when the user suspends or resumes the system. Data for this event are provided by the `PowerModeChangedEventArgs` class. The `Mode` property contains the power mode. This property is of the `PowerModes` type and it can contain one of the following values.
  - **Resume** The operating system is about to resume.
  - **StatusChange** The power mode status of the operating system has changed.
  - **Suspend** The operating system is about to be suspended.
- **SessionEnded** This event occurs when the user is logging off or shutting down the system. Data for this event are provided by the `SessionEndedEventArgs` class. The `Reason` of the `SessionEndReasons` type indicates how the session ended and it can have one of the following values.
  - **Logoff** The user who started this application is logging off.
  - **SystemShutdown** The operating system is shutting down.
- **SessionEnding** This event occurs when the user is trying to log off or shut down the system. Data for this event are provided by the `SessionEndingEventArgs` class. The `Cancel` property indicates whether or not to cancel the user request to end the session and the `Reason` property indicates the reason for the session ending.
- **TimeChanged** This event occurs when the user changes the time on the system clock.
- **TimerElapsed** This event occurs when a window's timer interval has expired. Data for this event are provided by the `TimerElapsedEventArgs` class. The `TimerID` property contains the ID number for the timer.
- **UserPreferenceChanged** This event occurs when a user preference has changed. Data for this event are provided by the `UserPreferenceChangedEventArgs` class.

The `Category` property of the `UserPreferenceCategory` type contains the category of user preferences that has changed. This property may have one of the following values.

- **Accessibility** Indicates that user preferences associated with accessibility of the system for users with disabilities have changed.
- **Color** Indicates that user preferences associated with system colors – such as the default color of windows or menus – have changed.
- **Desktop** Indicates that user preferences associated with the system desktop – such as desktop background images or desktop layout – have changed.
- **General** Indicates that user preferences not associated with any other category have changed.
- **Icon** Indicates that user preferences for icon settings, such as icon height and spacing, have changed.
- **Keyboard** Indicates that user preferences for keyboard settings, such as the keyboard repeat rate, have changed.
- **Locale** Indicates that input locale or international settings have changed.
- **Menu** Indicates that user preferences for menu settings, such as menu delays and text alignment, have changed.
- **Mouse** Indicates that user preferences for mouse settings – such as double-click time and mouse sensitivity – have changed.
- **Policy** Indicates that user preferences for policy settings – such as user rights and access levels – have changed.
- **Power** Indicates that user preferences for system power settings, such as the time required for the system to automatically enter low power mode, have changed.
- **Screensaver** Indicates that user preferences associated with the screensaver have changed.
- **Window** Indicates that user preferences associated with the dimensions and characteristics of windows on the system have changed.

The following example shows how to create an event handler for the `SystemEvents.TimeChanged` event:

```
Imports Microsoft.Win32

...

Private Sub Button1_Click(ByVal sender As System.Object, _
ByVal e As System.EventArgs) Handles Button1.Click

AddHandler SystemEvents.TimeChanged, AddressOf TimeChanged

End Sub
```

```
Public Sub TimeChanged(ByVal sender As Object, ByVal e As EventArgs)

  MsgBox("System Time Changed")

End Sub

Private Sub Button2_Click(ByVal sender As System.Object, _
  ByVal e As System.EventArgs) Handles Button2.Click

  RemoveHandler SystemEvents.TimeChanged, AddressOf TimeChanged

End Sub
```

8.4 Dialog boxes

Windows forms can act as dialog boxes that are used to interact with users and retrieve information. To construct our own dialog box we create a new form, and set its FormBorderStyle property to FixedDialog or FixedToolWindow – this automatically removes unnecessary minimize, maximize, and system menu buttons. After this, we place the necessary controls and buttons on the form. Usually, we have Ok, Cancel, or Abort buttons in the dialog box. By associating the DialogResult property of each button with the appropriate DialogResult value, such as Ok, Cancel, and so on, we can specify the resulting action of the dialog box. This allows us to let the calling code know how it was closed.

Dialog boxes can be displayed either modally or modeless. The first type prevents users from performing tasks outside the dialog box. To display the modal dialog box, we use the ShowDialog method of the dialog box. The Show method displays it modeless.

Let's create a simple dialog box that will accept a user's first and last name and contain two buttons – Ok to confirm the input and Cancel to cancel it (see Figure 8.12).

We have set the following properties for the buttons:

```
Button1.DialogResult = System.Windows.Forms.DialogResult.OK
Button2.DialogResult = System.Windows.Forms.DialogResult.Cancel
```

and specified the following border style for the form:

```
FormBorderStyle = System.Windows.Forms.FormBorderStyle.FixedToolWindow
```

Now, on our main form, we can call the dialog box like this:

```
Private Sub Button1_Click(ByVal sender As System.Object, _
  ByVal e As System.EventArgs) Handles Button1.Click

  Dim UserName As New DialogBox()
```

```
If UserName.ShowDialog() <> DialogResult.Cancel Then

    MsgBox(String.Format("Hello, {0} {1}", UserName.TextBox1.Text, _
    UserName.TextBox2.Text))

    End If

    End Sub
```

Note that:

- we treat our dialog box as a class and create an instance of it;
- we call the ShowDialog() method to modally display our dialog box;
- we check which button on the dialog box causes it to close and, if it was the Ok button, we proceed with the data entered into it;
- all controls in the dialog box are accessible to our code – we retrieve the information entered by the user by accessing the Text properties of both the TextBox controls.

FIGURE 8.12   A simple dialog box with two buttons

The System.Windows.Forms namespace contains several controls that implement standard common dialog boxes – Color Dialog Box, Font Dialog Box, Open File Dialog Box, and Save File Dialog Box, as well as several other dialog boxes used to print. We will learn about these controls in Chapter 9.

It is not necessary to create our own dialog boxes just to display messages, warnings or confirmations. We can do this with a set of predefined dialog boxes called message boxes. We will learn how to use these in the next section.

8.5 Message boxes

To display a predefined dialog box, we use the static MessageBox class. This class has only one method – the Show method. It is used to display a message box and its properties are used to determine the title, message, buttons, and icons shown in it. Table 8.3 shows different overloaded versions of the Show method and explains when to use each of them.

TABLE 8.3   What the various parameters of Show are used for

Parameters	Used to
String	Display a message box with the specified text.
String, String	Display a message box with the specified text and caption.
String, String, MessageBoxButtons	Display a message box with the specified text, caption, and buttons
String, String, MessageBoxButtons, MessageBoxIcon	Display a message box with the specified text, caption, buttons, and icon.
String, String, MessageBoxButtons, MessageBoxIcon, MessageBoxDefaultButton	Display a message box with the specified text, caption, buttons, icon, and default button.
String, String, String, String, MessageBoxButtons, MessageBoxIcon, MessageBoxDefaultButton, MessageBoxOptions	Display a message box with the specified text, caption, buttons, icon, default button, and options.

Each version of the Show method shown below has a version that can be used to display a message box in front of the specified object. In this case, we need to specify the IWin32Window-type parameter as the first parameter of the Show method.

The MessageBoxButtons parameter is used to specify which buttons to display in a message box. Figure 8.13 shows the possible values of this parameter.

The MessageBoxIcon parameter is used to specify which information symbol to display. Figure 8.14 shows the possible values of this parameter.

The MessageBoxDefaultButton parameter is used to define the default button in a message box. There can be a first, second or third message box button that is the default button.

The MessageBoxOptions parameter specifies some of the options of the message box. Besides these options are ones to show the message box on the active desktop, the message box right-aligned, and right to left reading order of the message box contents.

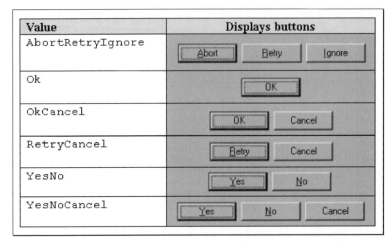

Value	Displays buttons
AbortRetryIgnore	Abort Retry Ignore
Ok	OK
OkCancel	OK Cancel
RetryCancel	Retry Cancel
YesNo	Yes No
YesNoCancel	Yes No Cancel

FIGURE 8.13   The values of the MessageBoxButtons parameter and their displayed buttons

Value	Displays
Asterisk	(i)
Error	(X)
Exclamation	(!)
Hand	(X)
Information	(i)
None	
Question	(?)
Stop	(X)
Warning	(!)

FIGURE 8.14   The values of the MessageBoxIcon parameter and their buttons

Each of the Show methods returns a DialogResult enumeration that indicates the return value of the dialog box. This can be one of the following values.

● **Abort** The Abort button was pressed.

● **Cancel** The Cancel button was pressed.

● **Ignore** The Ignore button was pressed.

- **No** The No button was pressed.
- **None** No button has been pressed yet; message box continues to run.
- **OK** The Ok button was pressed.
- **Retry** The Retry button was pressed.
- **Yes** The Yes button was pressed.

The following example shows how to use the MessageBox class. The following event handler handles the OnClosing event of the form and asks the user if they really want to close the application. The message box contains the Ok and Cancel buttons. If the Ok button is pressed, the application terminates; otherwise the event is cancelled.

```
'-----------------------------------------------------------
' MessageBox demo
'-----------------------------------------------------------


Protected Overrides Sub OnClosing(
  ByVal e As System.ComponentModel.CancelEventArgs)

  If MessageBox.Show("Close application?", "Confirmation", _
   MessageBoxButtons.YesNo, MessageBoxIcon.None) = DialogResult.Yes
  Then
   Application.Exit()
  Else
   e.Cancel = True
  End If


End Sub
```

Below is the shorter version of the same event handler.

```
'-----------------------------------------------------------
' MessageBox demo
'-----------------------------------------------------------


  Protected Overrides Sub OnClosing(
  ByVal e As System.ComponentModel.CancelEventArgs)

  e.Cancel = MessageBox.Show("Close application?", "Confirmation", _
            MessageBoxButtons.YesNo, MessageBoxIcon.None) = _
  DialogResult.No


  End Sub
```

Application class

The Application class plays an invisible, but significant, role in the lifetime of the Windows forms application. It provides a set of static methods and properties used to manage an application. Beside these methods are those that start and stop an application and threads, process Windows messages, and properties used to get information about an application.

The following is a list of the Application class properties.

- **AllowQuit property** This Boolean property indicates whether or not the caller can quit this application.
- **MessageLoop property** This Boolean property indicates whether or not a message loop exists on this thread.
- **CurrentCulture** Indicates the culture information for the current thread as a CultureInfo object.
- **CurrentInputLanguage** Indicates the current input language for the current thread as an InputLanguage object.
- **ExecutablePath** Returns the path for the executable file that started the application as a String.
- **StartupPath** Returns the path for the executable file that started the application as a String.
- **LocalUserAppDataPath** Returns the path for the application data of a local user as a String.
- **CompanyName** Returns the name of the company specified for the application as a String.
- **ProductName** Returns the product name specified for this application as a String.
- **ProductVersion** Returns the product version specified for this application as a String.
- **CommonAppDataPath** Specifies the path for the application data that is shared among all users as a String.
- **CommonAppDataRegistry** Specifies the registry key for the application data that is shared among all users as a RegistryKey object.
- **UserAppDataPath** Returns the path for the application data of a roaming user as a String.
- **UserAppDataRegistry** Returns the registry key of the application data specific to the roaming user as a RegistryKey object.

Earlier in this chapter, we have seen the code of the simple Windows forms application. In it we have used the following call or the Application.Run method:

```
System.Windows.Forms.Application.Run(New MyForm())
```

This method starts an application message loop (by virtue of the call from the RunMessageLoop method) and makes a form visible. To stop the message loop, we use the Exit() or ExitThread() methods.

To process messages while our program is in a loop, we use the DoEvents() method. This method is useful in situations when we need to allow our application to handle other messages while we proceed with the current one.

To filter messages that come to our application message loop, we can use the AddMessageFilter(IMessageFilter) method. This method accepts a parameter of IMessageFilter type, which defines one method that we should implement in the class – the PreFilterMessage.

8.6 Creating MDI windows applications

We create MDI applications when we need to provide our users with an interface that can have more than one window at the same time. Normally such applications are word processors, spreadsheets, and graphics editors. In all these applications, users can work simultaneously with more than one document.

MDI applications consist of one or more parent windows, each containing an MDI client area where the MDI child windows are displayed (see Figure 8.15).

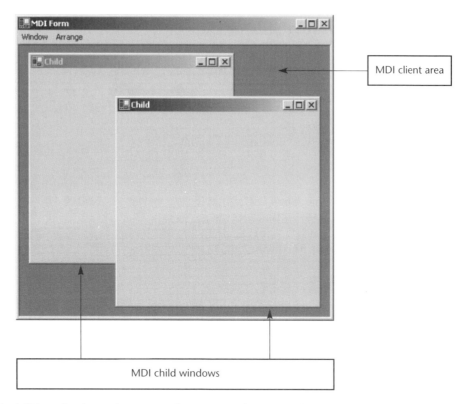

FIGURE 8.15 MDI applications where more than one window is needed

To create an MDI application, we perform several simple steps.

- In the main form of our application – the one that will play the role of MDI container and contain our MDI child windows – we set the `IsMDIContainer` property to "True".
- We create one or more child forms – classes derived from the `Form` class.
- To display the child window, we just use five lines of code:

```
Dim MDIChild As Form = New Form2()
With MDIChild

 .MdiParent = Me
 .Show()

End With
```

- To arrange child windows inside the MDI container, we use the `LayoutMDI`(*MdiLayout*) method with an appropriate argument. The following example shows how to implement the layout menu:

```
Private Sub MenuItem4_Click(ByVal sender As System.Object, _
 ByVal e As System.EventArgs) Handles MenuItem4.Click

   Me.LayoutMdi(MdiLayout.Cascade)

End Sub

Private Sub MenuItem5_Click(ByVal sender As System.Object, _
 ByVal e As System.EventArgs) Handles MenuItem5.Click

   Me.LayoutMdi(MdiLayout.TileHorizontal)

End Sub

Private Sub MenuItem6_Click(ByVal sender As System.Object, _
 ByVal e As System.EventArgs) Handles MenuItem6.Click

   Me.LayoutMdi(MdiLayout.TileVertical)

End Sub

Private Sub MenuItem7_Click(ByVal sender As System.Object, _
 ByVal e As System.EventArgs) Handles MenuItem7.Click

      Me.LayoutMdi(MdiLayout.ArrangeIcons)

End Sub
```

To center MDI child windows within the container, we should set the StartPosition property to CenterParent value.

To be able to keep track of the child windows we create, we can add a windows list to the menu (see Figure 8.16). To do so, we set the MDIList property of the menu item to "True".

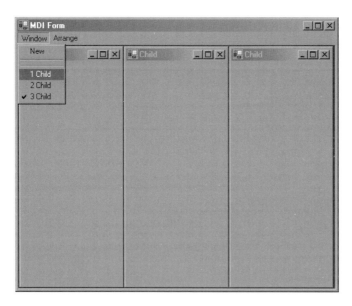

FIGURE 8.16   Using the MDList property to keep track of child windows

To find the currently active MDI child window (the one that has focus), we use the ActiveMDIChild property of the main form. This property is of the Form type, meaning that we can use the following code:

```
Dim ActiveChild As Form = Me.ActiveMDIChild
```

Note that when we maximize the MDI child, its caption is added to the MDI parent's caption. For example, if the parent has the MDI Form caption and the child has the Child caption, these combined will read MDI Form – [Child] (see Figure 8.17).

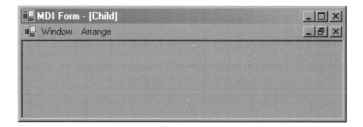

FIGURE 8.17   Parent and child captions combined

In order to differentiate between child windows, we can create a unique caption for each of them. To do so, we need a variable that will be used as a counter. Change the code that creates a new MDI child window to the following (see also Figure 8.18):

```
Private Sub MenuItem2_Click(ByVal sender As System.Object, _
ByVal e As System.EventArgs) Handles MenuItem2.Click

Static Num As Integer
Dim MDIChild As Form = New Form2()

Num += 1
With MDIChild

 .MdiParent = Me
 .Text = .Text & String.Format(" {0}", Num)
 .Show()

End With

End Sub
```

In the code above we use the static variable Num to keep track of the child forms. "Static" means that its value will be preserved between the code invocations.

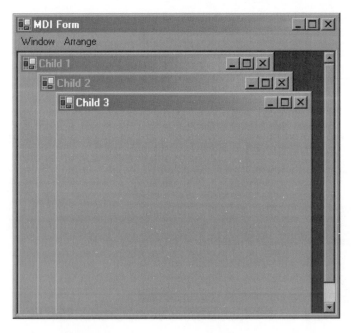

FIGURE 8.18 Unique captions can be created for each child

8.7 Conclusion

In this chapter we have learned about Windows forms and several classes included in the `System.Windows.Forms` namespace.

We started this chapter with a discussion of the minimal Windows forms application and then we covered such basic classes as `Component`, `Control`, `Scrollable Control`, and `ContainerControl`, from which the `Form` class is derived. Then we learned about the `Form` class, which serves as a base class for windows, and discussed the different roles it can play in applications.

We have seen the different events that occur during a Windows form's lifetime, caused by a user's actions. We discussed how to handle mouse, keyboard, and system events.

Next, we discussed dialog and message boxes.

We learned about the `Application` class and its role in Windows forms applications. We ended this chapter by looking at how we can create MDI applications.

In the next chapter, we will start our two-part discussion of Windows forms controls – classes that implement such windows controls as `ComboBox`, `TreeView`, and `ListView`. Like everything else, these controls are available in the .NET Framework via classes. These classes are derived from the `Control` class and share many common functions, while each of the controls provides some unique features.

chapter 9

Windows forms controls

- Windows controls
- Buttons
- Text controls
- Labels
- List controls
- Menus

This chapter starts our two-part discussion of Windows forms controls. Here we will learn about standard controls such as buttons, text controls, labels, lists, and menus. For each group, we will provide a list of classes that comprise it, as well as detailed descriptions of each class, its properties and methods, plus usage examples.

We will continue learning about Windows forms controls in the next chapter, where we will discuss controls that extend the basic set of controls found in Windows.

9.1 Windows controls

Windows offers a huge set of various controls – Button, TextBox, ComboBox, TreeView, ListView, and so on – that are used to provide a user interface to our application. They give users the ability to enter the information and see the response from the application.

Like everything else, these user interface controls are implemented in the .NET Framework as various classes. These classes are derived from the Control class and share many common functions, but each of the controls provides some unique features as well.

In the following sections we will look at some of the Windows controls that come with the Microsoft .NET Framework, their properties, methods, and events, and provide examples of their usage. In particular, we will learn about the following.

● **Button controls** This group of controls includes buttons, check boxes, radio buttons, and group boxes (see Figure 9.1).

FIGURE 9.1 Button controls

● **Text controls** This group of controls includes text boxes and rich text boxes (see Figure 9.2).

FIGURE 9.2 Text controls

● **Label controls** This group of controls includes labels and link labels (see Figure 9.3).

FIGURE 9.3 Label controls

● **List controls** This group of controls includes list boxes, combo boxes, checked list boxes, list views, tree views, and image lists (see Figure 9.4).

FIGURE 9.4 List controls

● **Menu controls** This group of controls includes main and context menus (see Figure 9.5).

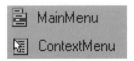

FIGURE 9.5 Menu controls

We will start with buttons – a group of controls that includes push buttons, check boxes, radio buttons, and group boxes.

9.2 Buttons

The ButtonBase class is the equivalent of the BUTTON class used in Windows API to create push buttons, check boxes, radio buttons, and group boxes. The ButtonBase class in the .NET framework is an abstract class – only derived classes, such as Button, CheckBox, and RadioButton can be instantiated. This is shown in Figure 9.6.

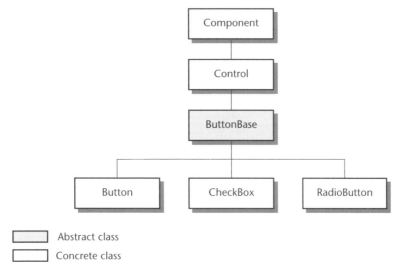

FIGURE 9.6 The different types of classes linked to create button controls

As a base class for the three types of button, the ButtonBase class offers very basic functionality. Let's look at some of the properties and methods of this class.

To display an image on a control, we can use the Image property (of an Image type), ImageList (of an ImageList type), and ImageIndex (of an Integer type) properties. In the first case, we specify the object of the Image type, but when dealing with image lists, we indicate the index of the image in the list and give a reference to the ImageList object. These properties are mutually exclusive – that is, we can either have an Image based on the Image object or based on the ImageList object. ImageList objects are used for sharing images between controls.

The ImageAlign property (of a ContentAlignment type) specifies how the image will be aligned on the button control. This property may have the same set of values as the TextAlign property used to align the text displayed on the button. The default value is MiddleCenter. Note that the ImageAlign and TextAlign properties are of the ContentAlignment enumeration type, which is defined in the System.Drawing namespace. The following list shows possible values for ImageAlign and TextAlign properties.

- **BottomCenter** Vertically aligned at the bottom, centered horizontally.
- **BottomLeft** Vertically aligned at the bottom, aligned left horizontally.
- **BottomRight** Vertically aligned at the bottom, aligned right horizontally.
- **MiddleCenter** Vertically aligned in the middle, centered horizontally.
- **MiddleLeft** Vertically aligned in the middle, aligned left horizontally.
- **MiddleRight** Vertically aligned in the middle, aligned right horizontally.
- **TopCenter** Vertically aligned at the top, centered horizontally.
- **TopLeft** Vertically aligned at the top, aligned left horizontally.
- **TopRight** Vertically aligned at the top, aligned right horizontally.

Figure 9.7 shows the various alignment options.

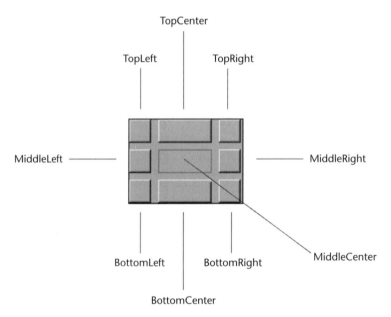

FIGURE 9.7   Where text or an image is put when various alignment properties are chosen

The FlatStyle property is used to specify the style and appearance of the control. If this property is set to FlatStyle.System, then it is up to the operating system to determine the appearance of the button. Other possible values for this property are Flat, meaning that the control will be drawn flat, and Popup, which means that the control will appear three-dimensional only when the mouse pointer moves over it. The Standard flat style specifies the default appearance of the control.

The screenshot in Figure 9.8 shows three buttons with different values of the FlatStyle property – Flat, Popup, and Standard.

FIGURE 9.8   The flat, popup, and standard styles of button

Button class

This class represents a Windows button control. Such a control may be clicked by mouse or by pressing the Enter key when the button has focus. The AcceptButton and CancelButton properties (of the IButtonControl type) of the Form class can be associated with the button. In this case, users can click a button by pressing the Enter or Esc keys even if the button does not have focus. Note that only one button can have such a style set per form and it's very unusual to set both on the same button.

The DialogResult property of a button can be used to specify the return result of a form displayed with the ShowDialog method. Possible values are contained in the DialogResult enumeration.

The PerformClick() method generates a Click event when the button is clicked by mouse or key. Here is an example of the OnClick event handler:

```
'-------------------------------------------------
' OnClick event handler for the Button control
'-------------------------------------------------

Private Sub Button1_Click(ByVal sender As System.Object, _
  ByVal e As System.EventArgs) Handles Button1.Click


  . . .


End Sub
```

There are two more types of buttons – check box and radio button. We will cover them in the next two sections.

CheckBox class

This class represents a Windows control that is used to give a user an option, such as true/false or yes/no. It is possible to display these in a check box as text or an image or both. We use the Appearance property (of an Appearance type) to specify how the check box should be displayed. A typical check box will have the value of the property set to Appearance.Normal, while a button will have its value set to Appearance.Button. The unchecked and checked states of check boxes of two types – normal and button – are shown in Figure 9.9.

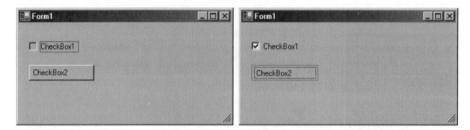

FIGURE 9.9 Using Appearance.Normal and Appearance.Button to set the look of check boxes

To allow check boxes to support three states, we use the ThreeState Boolean property. If a check box supports only two states, these are checked and unchecked. We use the Checked Boolean property to find the current state of the check box. The third state is the intermediate state. In this case, the check box may have the CheckState.Indeterminate state. In this case, when we set the ThreeState property, the Checked property will return "True" for either a checked or indeterminate state.

As with the buttons described below, check boxes can be flat. This is specified by means of the FlatStyle property.

To align the text of the check box, we use the CheckAlign property of the ContentAlignment type. While this property supports different values, the most usable are CheckAlign.MiddleLeft and CheckAlign.MiddleRight, shown in Figure 9.10.

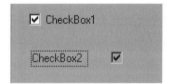

FIGURE 9.10 The text of a check box can be aligned to the right or left

The default event for the check box is the CheckedChanged event and its handler looks like this:

```
'-----------------------------------------------------------
' OnCheckedChanged event handler for the CheckBox control
'-----------------------------------------------------------

Private Sub CheckBox1_CheckedChanged(ByVal sender As System.Object, _
    ByVal e As System.EventArgs) Handles CheckBox1.CheckedChanged

...

End Sub
```

We use this event handler to immediately react to the changes in check box status. When we use check boxes to specify some options, we iterate the set of check boxes and collect its values.

The last button type control is the radio button. It has similar functionality to the CheckBox control covered in this section. However, CheckBox controls let users pick a combination of options, whereas RadioButton controls allow users to choose from mutually exclusive options.

RadioButton class

This class represents a Windows control that is used to allow a user to choose from mutually exclusive options. Normally, we use a RadioButton control in a group. Thus, the default group is the Form itself, but we can use the GroupBox or Panel controls. The Checked Boolean property indicates the current state of a radio button. To change the appearance of the control, we use the Appearance property (of the Appearance type). Here we can specify either a standard radio button (with the value of the property set to Appearance.Normal) or a toggle-style button (with the value of the property set to Appearance.Button) (see Figure 9.11).

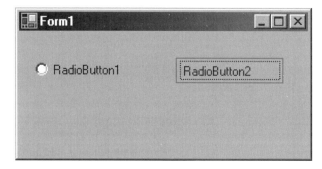

FIGURE 9.11   Standard and toggle styles of button, created using Appearance.Normal and Appearance.Button properties

As with the check box controls, to align the text of a radio button, we use the CheckAlign property (of a ContentAlignment type). While this property supports different values, the most usable are CheckAlign.MiddleLeft and CheckAlign.MiddleRight.

The default event for the radio button is the CheckedChanged event. Its handler looks like this:

```
'------------------------------------------------------
' OnCheckedChanged event handler for the Button control
'------------------------------------------------------


Private Sub RadioButton1_CheckedChanged(ByVal sender As _
  System.Object, ByVal e As System.EventArgs) _
  Handles RadioButton1.CheckedChanged


...


End Sub
```

We create an event handler if we need to react to the changes of the radio button value immediately.

GroupBox class

This class represents Windows forms' GroupBox control, which is used to create groups of other controls. We use group boxes to divide interface elements by function, usually grouping radio buttons that provide mutually exclusive options. The GroupBox control displays a frame around a group of controls and can have a caption defined by its Text property (of a String type). To add controls to the GroupBox control, we use the Add method of its Controls collection (of the Control.ControlCollection type).

The following example shows how to create a GroupBox control with three RadioButton controls in it (see also Figure 9.12).

```
Dim GroupBox1 As New GroupBox()
Dim RadioButton1 As New RadioButton()
Dim RadioButton2 As New RadioButton()
Dim RadioButton3 As New RadioButton()

GroupBox1.Location = New System.Drawing.Point(8, 48)
GroupBox1.Size = New System.Drawing.Size(272, 216)
GroupBox1.Text = "Alignment"

RadioButton1.Text = "Left"
RadioButton1.Location = New System.Drawing.Point(8, 24)
GroupBox1.Controls.Add(RadioButton1)
```

```
RadioButton2.Text = "Right"
RadioButton2.Location = New System.Drawing.Point(8, 56)
GroupBox1.Controls.Add(RadioButton2)

RadioButton3.Text = "Center"
RadioButton3.Location = New System.Drawing.Point(8, 88)
GroupBox1.Controls.Add(RadioButton3)

Controls.Add(GroupBox1)
```

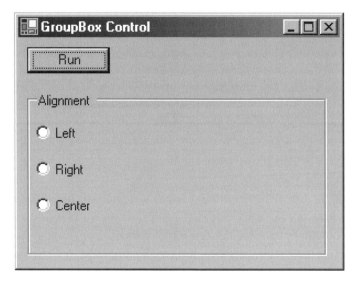

FIGURE 9.12   Using the GroupBox control to contain three radio buttons

To group controls, we can also use the Panel control, discussed in the next chapter. The difference between the GroupBox and Panel controls is that the GroupBox control can have a caption, while the Panel control has scrollable content.

9.3 Text controls

The TextBoxBase class serves as a base class for two Windows controls – TextBox and RichTextBox (see Figure 9.13). This class implements the basic functionality for the text controls, including text selection, clipboard functionality, multiline text control support, and events.

Let's look at the major properties of the TextBoxBase class.

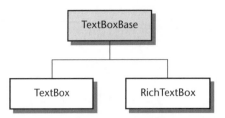

FIGURE 9.13   The TextBoxBase class is the source of two other useful controls

- **AcceptsTab** This Boolean property specifies whether the TAB key in a multiline text box control acts as a key to input a TAB character in the control or just moves the focus to the next control in the tab order.

- **AcceptsReturn** This Boolean property specifies whether the ENTER key in a multiline text box control creates a new line of text in the control or activates the default button for the form. If this property is set to "False", if we want to enter a new line we must press the CTRL+ENTER key combination.

- **AutoSize** We use this Boolean property to indicate whether or not the height of the control automatically adjusts when the font assigned to the control is changed.

- **BorderStyle** This property (of the BorderStyle type) specifies the border type of the control.

- **CanUndo** Indicates whether or not the user can undo the most recent edit operation.

- **HideSelection** Indicates whether or not the selected text in the text box control remains highlighted when the control loses focus.

- **Lines** This property is a String array that contains the lines of text in a text box control.

- **MaxLength** Use this Integer property to specify the maximum number of characters the user can enter into the text box control.

- **Modified** If set, this Boolean property indicates that the text box control has been modified by the user since the control was created or its contents were last set.

- **Multiline** If set, this Boolean property specifies that this is a multiline text box control.

- **PreferredHeight** This Integer property contains the preferred height for a single-line text box control. Preferred height is based on the font height and border style of the text box.

- **ReadOnly** If set, this Boolean property indicates that text in the text box cannot be changed.

- **SelectedText** This String property contains the currently selected text in the text box control.

- **SelectionLength** This Integer property contains the number of characters selected in the text box control.

- **SelectionStart** This `Integer` property contains the starting point of text selected in the text box control.

- **Text** Use this `String` property to get or set the current text displayed in the text box control.

- **TextLength** Use this `Integer` property to find the length of text in the control.

- **WordWrap** If set, this `Boolean` property indicates that a multiline text box control will automatically wrap words to the beginning of the next line when necessary.

Here are the most important methods of the `TextBoxBase` class.

- **AppendText(*String*) method** Appends text to the current text in the text box control.

- **Clear() method** Clears the contents of the text box control.

- **ClearUndo() method** Clears information about the most recent operation from the undo buffer of the text box control.

- **Copy() method** Copies the current selection in the text box control to the clipboard.

- **Cut() method** Moves the current selection in the text box control to the clipboard.

- **Paste() method** Replaces the current selection in the text box control with the contents of the clipboard.

- **ScrollToCaret() method** Scrolls the contents of the text box control to the current caret (insertion) position.

- **Select(*Integer*, *Integer*) method** Selects text in the text box control.

- **SelectAll() method** Selects all contents of the text box control.

- **Undo() method** Undoes the last edit operation.

As was noted above, the `TextBoxBase` class serves as a base class for two text box controls – `TextBox` and `RichTextBox`. In the following sections we will see how to use some of the properties and methods defined by the `TextBoxBase` class in its descendants. We will start with the `TextBox` class.

TextBox class

This class represents a Windows `TextBox` control. It is used to provide users with the ability to enter text in an application. This implementation of the Windows `TextBox` control provides extra functionality, including multiline editing and password character masking. By default, the `TextBox` control represents a control to input a single line of text (see Figure 9.14).

To enable multiple lines of text to be displayed or entered, we use the `Multiline` and `ScrollBars` properties (see Figure 9.15):

```
TextBox1.Multiline = True
TextBox1.ScrollBars = System.Windows.Forms.ScrollBars.Both
```

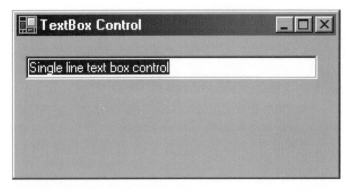

FIGURE 9.14   The default action of the TextBox control is to allow the input of a single line of text

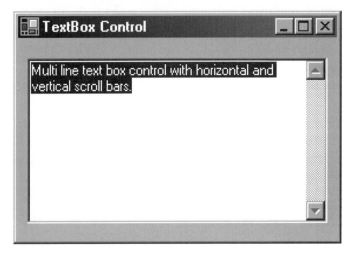

FIGURE 9.15   Using the Multiline and ScrollBars properties of TextBox to enter more than one line of text

The ScrollBars property is of the ScrollBars type and it may have the values ScrollBars.Both, ScrollBars.Horizontal, ScrollBars.Vertical, or ScrollBars.None.

The third type of TextBox control is the single-line control with password character masking. To create such a control, we take the standard single-line TextBox control and specify the PasswordChar property of the Char type (see Figure 9.16):

```
TextBox1.PasswordChar = "?"
```

We use the MaxLength Integer property to limit the amount of text that can be entered into a TextBox control. To disable text input, we use the ReadOnly Boolean property. To filter characters entered in the TextBox control, we create an event handler for the KeyDown event.

The TextBox class adds two properties of its own.

FIGURE 9.16 Creating a password character by using the TextBox control and choosing the PasswordChar property

- **CharacterCasing** This property (of a CharacterCasing type) indicates whether or not the TextBox control modifies the case of characters as they are typed. It can have the values CharacterCasing.Lower, CharacterCasing.Normal, or CharacterCasing.Upper.

- **TextAlign** Specifies how text is aligned in a TextBox control. Possible values are HorizontalAlignment.Left (this is the default value), HorizontalAlignment.Center, or HorizontalAlignment.Right.

The following example shows how to use some of the methods of the TextBox control to copy its contents to another TextBox control via the clipboard (see Figure 9.17).

```
'-------------------------------------------------
' TextBox control demo - using clipboard
'-------------------------------------------------


Dim InClipboard As Boolean = False
  ...


'
' Copy button
'


  Private Sub Button1_Click(ByVal sender As System.Object, _
    ByVal e As System.EventArgs) Handles Button1.Click
```

```
        With TextBox1
            If .SelectedText.Length <> 0 Then
                .Copy()
                Button2.Enabled = False
                InClipboard = True
            End If
        End With



End Sub


'
' Cut button
'


Private Sub Button2_Click(ByVal sender As System.Object, _
  ByVal e As System.EventArgs) Handles Button2.Click

        With TextBox1
            If .SelectedText.Length <> 0 Then
                .Cut()
                Button1.Enabled = False
                InClipboard = True
            End If
        End With
End Sub


'
' Paste button
'


Private Sub Button3_Click(ByVal sender As System.Object, _
  ByVal e As System.EventArgs) Handles Button3.Click
        If InClipboard Then
            TextBox2.Paste()
            InClipboard = False
            Button1.Enabled = True
            Button2.Enabled = True
        End If
End Sub
```

```
'
' Undo button
'

 Private Sub Button4_Click(ByVal sender As System.Object, _
   ByVal e As System.EventArgs) Handles Button4.Click
        With TextBox1
            If .CanUndo Then
                .Undo()
                .ClearUndo()
            End If
        End With

 End Sub
```

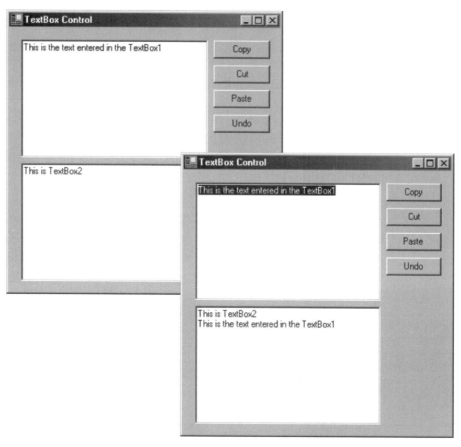

FIGURE 9.17   Using TextBox control methods to copy text from one to another

In this example we have seen how to use the `Copy`, `Cut`, and `Paste` methods of the `TextBox` class, as well as how to use the `Undo` method to undo the last edit operation.

The next `TextBox` control – the `RichTextBox` – provides extended functionality.

RichTextBox class

This class represents a Windows `RichTextBox` control. This control allows users to enter and edit text and provides advanced formatting features not found in the standard `TextBox` control. For example, text can be assigned directly to the control (as with the `TextBox` control), and can be loaded from a plain text file or from a rich text format (RTF) file. The `RichTextBox` control supports character and paragraph formatting, we can change colors, fonts, indents, create bulleted lists, and so on. Edited text can be saved in a file or stream.

The following list shows the major properties of the `RichTextBox` control.

- **AutoWordSelection** If set, this `Boolean` property enables automatic word selection.
- **BulletIndent** Specifies the indentation (`Integer` value) used in the `RichTextBox` control when the bullet style is applied to the text.
- **CanRedo** If set to "True", actions that have occurred within the `RichTextBox` can be reapplied.
- **DetectUrls** If set, the `RichTextBox` control will automatically format a uniform resource locator (URL) when it is typed into the control.
- **RedoActionName** Returns the name (`String` type) of the action that can be reapplied to the control when the `Redo` method is called.
- **RightMargin** Specifies the size (`Integer` value) of a single line of text within the `RichTextBox` control.
- **Rtf** Contains the text in RTF format as a `String` object.
- **SelectedRtf** Contains the selected text in RTF format as a `String` object.
- **SelectionAlignment** Specifies the alignment (`HorizontalAlignment` type) to apply to the current selection or insertion point.
- **SelectionBullet** If set, the bullet style is applied to the current selection or insertion point.
- **SelectionCharOffset** Specifies whether text in the control appears on the baseline, or as superscript or subscript as an `Integer` value.
- **SelectionColor** Specifies the text color (as a `Color` type) of the current text selection or insertion point.
- **SelectionFont** Specifies the font (as a `Font` type) of the current text selection or insertion point.
- **SelectionHangingIndent** Specifies the distance between the left edge of the first line of text in the selected paragraph and the left edge of subsequent lines in the same paragraph as an `Integer` value.

- **SelectionIndent** Specifies the distance in pixels between the left edge of the RichTextBox control and the left edge of the current text selection or text added after the insertion point as an Integer value.

- **SelectionProtected** Indicates whether or not the current text selection is protected. This property is used to prevent the user from modifying sections of text within the control.

- **SelectionRightIndent** Specifies the distance (in pixels) between the right edge of the RichTextBox control and the right edge of the text that is selected or added at the current insertion point as an Integer value.

- **SelectionTabs** Contains the absolute tab stop positions (array of Integers) in a RichTextBox control.

- **SelectionType** Contains the selection type within the control. This property is of the RichTextBoxSelectionTypes enumeration and can contain the following values.

  - **Empty** This value means that no text is selected in the current selection.

  - **MultiChar** This value means that more than one character is selected.

  - **MultiObject** This value means that more than one OLE object has been selected.

  - **Object** This value means that at least one OLE object has been selected.

  - **Text** This value means that the current selection contains only text.

- **ShowSelectionMargin** Indicates whether or not a selection margin is displayed in the RichTextBox control.

- **UndoActionName** Contains the name (a String type) of the action that can be undone in the control when the Undo method is called.

- **ZoomFactor** Contains the current zoom level of the RichTextBox control. The value 1.0 indicates that no zoom is applied to the control. The range of possible values of this property is between 0.64 and 64.0.

The RichTextBox class contains several methods that implement its extended editing and formatting functionality.

- **CanPaste(*DataFormats.Format*) method** Finds whether or not you can paste information from the clipboard in the specified data format.

- **Find() method and its overloaded versions** Searches for text within the contents of the RichTextBox control.

- **GetCharFromPosition(*Point*) method** Returns the character that is closest to the specified location within the control.

- **GetCharIndexFromPosition(*Point*) method** Returns the index of the character nearest to the specified location.

- **GetLineFromCharIndex(*Integer*) method** Returns the line number from the specified character position within the text of the RichTextBox control.

- **GetPositionFromCharIndex(*Integer*) method** Returns the location within the control at the specified character index.
- **LoadFile(*String*) or LoadFile(*Stream*, *RichTextBoxStreamType*) method** Loads the contents of a file into the RichTextBox control.
- **Redo() method** Reapplies the last operation that was undone in the control.
- **SaveFile(*String*) or SaveFile(*Stream*, *RichTextBoxStreamType*) method** Saves the contents of the RichTextBox control to a file or stream.

The following example shows how to use some of the features of the RichTextBox class. See how to make selected text bold or italic, set different colors and fonts, how to zoom the contents of the control, and how to load and save the text inside it (see also Figure 9.18):

```vb
'-------------------------------------------------
' RichTextBox control demo
'-------------------------------------------------


'
' Bold button
'
 Private Sub Button1_Click(ByVal sender As System.Object, -_
   ByVal e As System.EventArgs) Handles Button1.Click

   Dim F As Font
   F = New Font(RichTextBox1.SelectionFont, FontStyle.Bold)
   RichTextBox1.SelectionFont = F

 End Sub


'
' Italic button
'
 Private Sub Button2_Click(ByVal sender As System.Object, _
   ByVal e As System.EventArgs) Handles Button2.Click

   Dim F As Font
   F = New Font(RichTextBox1.SelectionFont, FontStyle.Italic)
   RichTextBox1.SelectionFont = F

 End Sub
```

```
'
' Red button
'
Private Sub Button3_Click(ByVal sender As System.Object, _
  ByVal e As System.EventArgs) Handles Button3.Click

  RichTextBox1.SelectionColor = Color.Red

End Sub


'
' Arial button
'
Private Sub Button4_Click(ByVal sender As System.Object, _
  ByVal e As System.EventArgs) Handles Button4.Click

  RichTextBox1.SelectionFont = New Font("Arial", 12, FontStyle.Regular)

End Sub


'
' 200% button
'
Private Sub Button5_Click(ByVal sender As System.Object, _
  ByVal e As System.EventArgs) Handles Button5.Click

   RichTextBox1.ZoomFactor = 2

End Sub


'
' 100% button
'
Private Sub Button6_Click(ByVal sender As System.Object, _
  ByVal e As System.EventArgs) Handles Button6.Click

   RichTextBox1.ZoomFactor = 1

End Sub
```

```
'
' Load button
'
Private Sub Button7_Click(ByVal sender As System.Object, _
    ByVal e As System.EventArgs) Handles Button7.Click

    RichTextBox1.LoadFile("c:\demotext.rtf")

End Sub


'
' Save button
'
Private Sub Button8_Click(ByVal sender As System.Object, _
    ByVal e As System.EventArgs) Handles Button8.Click

    RichTextBox1.SaveFile("c:\demotext.rtf")

End Sub
```

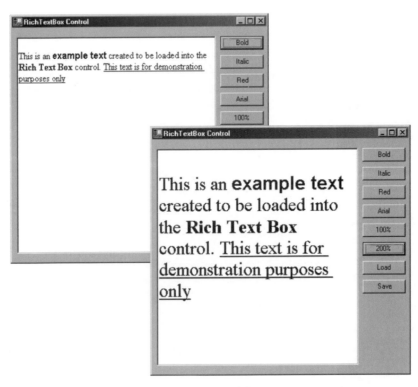

FIGURE 9.18   Some of the effects possible using features of the RichTextBox class

Note that, in this example, when we set the bold attribute for the font, we do not check other attributes such as italic. In this case, when we set the font to bold, we lose the italic attribute. Try extending this example as an exercise – all you need to do is implement the logic that will provide the Boolean operations when you set the font attributes (this will also allow you to toggle bold and italic attributes). Other improvements may include preservation of the current font size when you change the font family ("Arial" button).

We have learned about two controls that allow us to edit and change text. In the next section we will look at the non-editable controls called labels.

9.4 Labels

The Microsoft .NET Framework class library contains two classes that represent labels – the Label class, which represents a standard Windows label, and the derived LinkLabel class, which is a special version of a Windows label control that can display hyperlinks.

Label class

This class represents a standard Windows label control that is typically used to provide descriptive text for another control. The most common example is using a Label control with the TextBox or ListBox controls to provide the user with an idea as to what kind of information is expected to be entered or selected. Another example is to use a Label control to provide the main header (but not the caption or title bar) for the Form or dialog box.

The following list gives the main properties of the Label control.

- **AutoSize** This Boolean property indicates whether or not the control is automatically resized to display its entire contents.

- **BorderStyle** Specifies the border style. This property is of the BorderStyle type and contains the values Fixed3D, FixedSingle, and None (the default value). The different border styles are shown in Figure 9.19.

- **FlatStyle** Indicates whether or not the label control appears flat. This property (of a FlatStyle type) was discussed earlier in this chapter.

- **Image** Specifies the image (Image object type) that is displayed on a label control.

- **ImageAlign** Sets the alignment of an image that is displayed on a label control. This property is of a ContentAlignment type, which we discussed earlier in this chapter.

- **ImageIndex** Specifies the index of the image (an Integer value), which is taken from the ImageList control and defined by the ImageList property.

- **PreferredHeight** Returns the preferred height of the control as an Integer value.

- **PreferredWidth** Returns the preferred width of the control as an Integer value.

- **UseMnemonic** Indicates if the control interprets an ampersand character (&) in the Text property as an access key prefix character.

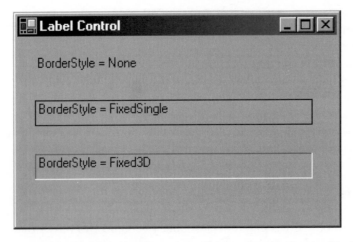

FIGURE 9.19　The different kinds of border style available using the BorderStyle property

The UseMnemonic property allows us to select the control that follows the Label in the tab order by pressing ALT+ the mnemonic character. Then, the Label works as a shortcut key for the control.

LinkLabel class

Based on the Label class, the LinkLabel class is a special version of a Windows label control that can display hyperlinks. This allows us to display web-style links on Windows forms.

● **ActiveLinkColor** Specifies the color (a Color type) used to display an active link.

● **DisabledLinkColor** Specifies the color (a Color type) used to display a disabled link.

● **LinkColor** Specifies the color (a Color type) used to display a normal link.

● **VisitedLinkColor** Specifies the color (a Color type) used to display a link that has been previously visited.

● **LinkArea** Specifies the range of text to treat as a link. This property is of the LinkArea type and provides such properties as Length and Start.

● **LinkBehavior** Specifies the behavior of a link. This property is of the LinkBehaviour type and can have one of the following values.

　– **AlwaysUnderline** The text of the link is always underlined.

　– **HoverUnderline** The text of the link is underlined only when the mouse is hovered over the link text.

　– **NeverUnderline** The text of the link is never underlined.

　– **SystemDefault** The text of the link is displayed using the system default method for displaying links.

- **Links** Contains a collection of links (LinkLabel.LinkCollection type) within the LinkLabel.

- **LinkVisited** Indicates if a link should be displayed as though it were visited – using the color specified by the VisitedLinkColor property.

To specify which part of the text will be a link – by default this is the whole text – we use the LinkArea property. For example, if the Text property contains the following text:

```
"For more information visit the Microsoft web site"
```

we may specify that the link be attached to the "Microsoft web site" part of the text (see also Figure 9.20):

```
LinkLabel1.LinkArea = New System.Windows.Forms.LinkArea(27, 18)
```

In the constructor of the LinkArea class, we specify the starting position and the length of the link text.

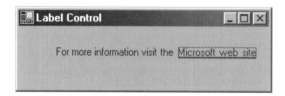

FIGURE 9.20   Using the LinkArea property to specify a link to a certain part of the text

The next step is to define the URL associated with the link. To do so, we use the Links collection, as shown in the following example:

```
LinkLabel1.Links.Add(27, 18, "http://www.microsoft.com")
```

The specified URL will be accessible later via the Link.LinkData property. For example, we can do this in the OnClick event handler:

```
'-----------------------------------------------------
' LinkLabel control demo – LinkClicked event handler
'-----------------------------------------------------

Private Sub LinkLabel1_LinkClicked(ByVal sender As System.Object, _
  ByVal e As System.Windows.Forms.LinkLabelLinkClickedEventArgs) _
  Handles LinkLabel1.LinkClicked

  MsgBox(e.Link.LinkData)

End Sub
```

To "execute" a link we use the `Start` method of the `Process` class, defined in the `System.Diagnostics` namespace. The following example shows how to do this:

```
'-----------------------------------------------
' LinkLabel control demo - opening URL
'-----------------------------------------------


Private Sub LinkLabel1_LinkClicked(ByVal sender As System.Object, _
  ByVal e As System.Windows.Forms.LinkLabelLinkClickedEventArgs) _
  Handles LinkLabel1.LinkClicked


      Dim P As System.Diagnostics.Process
      P = New System.Diagnostics.Process()
'
' This call ensures that we will open our URL with MS IE
'
      P.Start("IExplore.exe", e.Link.LinkData.ToString())
'
' To use the default browser:
'
      P.Start(e.Link.LinkData.ToString())



End Sub
```

The next group of controls we will cover in this chapter is list controls – list boxes and combo boxes.

9.5 List controls

The `ListControl` class serves as a base class for two Windows controls – `ListBox` and `ComboBox`. Figure 9.21 shows the `ListControl` class and its derived classes (`CheckedlistBox` will be covered later in this chapter as an extension of this class of controls).

Let's look briefly at the main properties, methods, and events of the `ListControl` class:

● **DisplayMember** This `String` property indicates which property of the object to show if the list control contains objects that support properties.

● **SelectedIndex** This `Integer` property indicates the zero-based index of the selected item.

● **SelectedValue** This property (of an `Object` type) indicates the value currently selected in the list box or combo box.

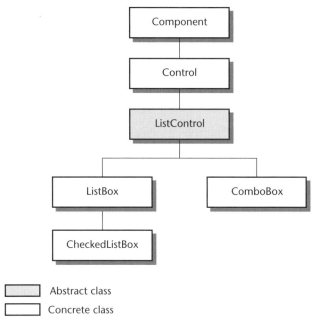

Abstract class
Concrete class

FIGURE 9.21   The `ListControl` class is the basis of two controls

- **ValueMember** This `String` property indicates the value of the selected property if the list control contains objects that support properties.
- **GetItemText(*Object*) method** Returns the text of the specified item.
- **DisplayMemberChanged** This event is fired when a selected property of the object is changed.
- **SelectedValueChanged** This event is fired when the selected value is changed.

Now let's look at the classes derived from the `ListControl`, `ListBox`, and `ComboBox` classes.

ListBox class

This class implements the standard Windows `ListBox` control. The `ListBox` control displays a list of items that can be selected by clicking on them. The `SelectionMode` property defines if it is possible to select single or multiple items. This property is of the `SelectionMode` type and it may have the values `SelectionMode.MultiExtended`, `SelectionMode.MultiSimple`, `SelectionMode.None`, or `SelectionMode.One`.

To display items in columns, we use the `MultiColumn Boolean` property. Figure 9.22 shows two `ListBox` controls, each with 100 items. The left one displays items in one column, the right one in multicolumn format.

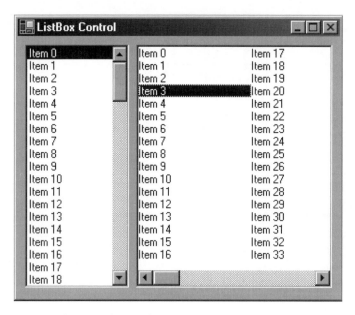

FIGURE 9.22   You can choose to lay out lists in single or several columns

To add a large number of items without causing the `ListBox` control to be repainted each time we add one, we use the `BeginUpdate()` and `EndUpdate()` methods, as shown in the example below:

```
'----------------------------------------------------
' ListBox control demo – BeginUpdate/EndUpdate usage
'----------------------------------------------------

With ListBox1
  .BeginUpdate()
  For I = 0 To 99
    .Items.Add("Item " & I.ToString)
  Next
  .EndUpdate()
End With
```

The `FindString(String)` and `FindStringExact(String)` methods are used to search for the specified string among the items in the list.

The `ListBox` control uses three collections to store all items, selected items, and selected indices. These are the `ObjectCollection`, `SelectedObjectCollection`, and `SelectedIndexCollection`. Each collection is accessible via an appropriate property – namely `Items`, `SelectedItems`, and `SelectedIndices`.

The `IntegralHeight Boolean` property specifies if the control should resize to avoid showing partial items (see Figure 9.23).

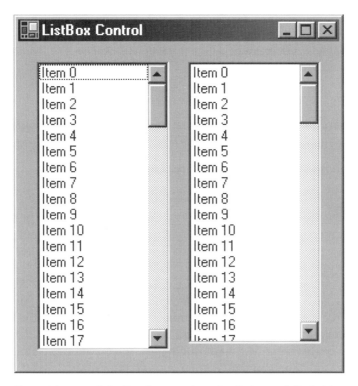

FIGURE 9.23 To avoid parts of the list disappearing, the Integral Height property can be activated

We use the Add(*Object*) method to add items to the ListBox – into the ObjectCollection collection. As the ListBox can contain any Object class descendants, the ToString() method is used to display the text for the object or, if we defined the DisplayMember property, an appropriate class member.

The following example shows how to find the selected item and display its contents. We place this code in the SelectedIndexChanged event handler:

```
'-------------------------------------------------
' ListBox control usage demo – get selected items
'-------------------------------------------------

Private Sub ListBox1_SelectedIndexChanged(ByVal sender As Object, _
    ByVal e As System.EventArgs) Handles ListBox1.SelectedIndexChanged
        With ListBox1
            TextBox1.Text = .Items(.SelectedIndex)
        End With
End Sub
```

Despite its name, the data source need not be a database table at all – any type that implements the IList interface – Array, for example – can also be a source of data for the ListBox. For example, define the following Array:

```
Dim Langs() As String = _
    {"VB.NET", "C#", "J#", "C++", "JScript .NET", "Perl .NET"}
```

and then assign its contents to the list:

```
ListBox1.DataSource = Langs
```

The second type of list control is the ComboBox control.

ComboBox class

This class represents a Windows ComboBox control. It consists of an editing field combined with a ListBox. This allows users to select a predefined value from the list or enter new data. To specify how the ComboBox control will look on screen, we use the DropDownStyle property (of the ComboBoxStyle type). It may have three values – Simple, DropDown, and DropDownList. The differences between the three types are that, in the first two modes, the user can enter the text in the editing field, while in the DropDownList mode, the edit portion is read-only. Figure 9.24 shows the three different modes of the ComboBox control – Simple, DropDown, and DropDownList – from left to right.

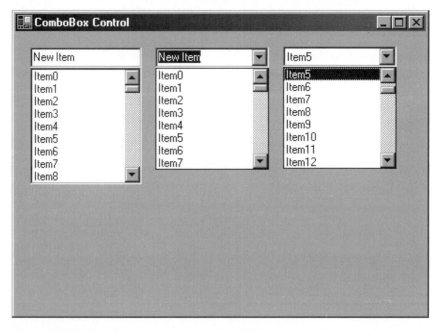

FIGURE 9.24   You have a choice of three looks for your ComboBox – Simple, DropDown, or DropDownList

The Text property is used to specify the string displayed in the editing field and, as with the ListBox control, the SelectedIndex property contains the index of the currently selected item (an Integer value) and the SelectedItem property, which is the item itself (an Object type). Here are some other interesting properties of the ComboBox control.

- **DropDownWidth** Specifies the width of the dropdown portion of a combo box control as an Integer value. Figure 9.25 shows two ComboBox controls – the left one has the default value of DropDownWidth property, while the right one has the customized value.

- **DroppedDown** Specifies whether or not the combo box is displaying its dropdown portion.

- **IntegralHeight** Specifies if the control should resize to avoid showing partial items.

The third list control is CheckedListBox, which is derived from the CheckedListBox class.

CheckedListBox class

This class provides an extended version of the Windows ListBox control. The difference between the two is that the CheckedListBox control can display a check mark next to items in the list. The other difference is that the CheckedListBox control can only be displayed in the Normal mode and it can have only one or no items selected.

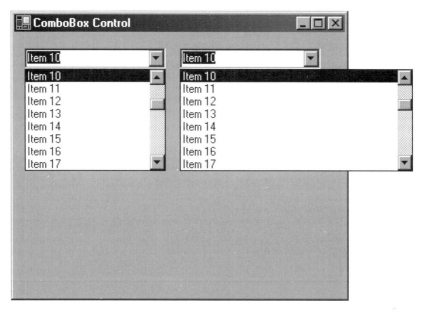

FIGURE 9.25   Default and customized widths for combo boxes

The following list shows the main properties of the CheckedListBox control.

- **CheckedIndices** Contains the checked indices in the CheckedListBox control as a CheckedListBox.CheckedIndexCollection object.
- **CheckedItems** Contains the checked items in the CheckedListBox control as a CheckedListBox.CheckedItemCollection object.
- **CheckOnClick** If set, the check box will be toggled when an item is selected.
- **SelectionMode** Specifies the selection mode (SelectionMode type). For the CheckedListBox control, this can be either None or One.
- **ThreeDCheckBoxes** Indicates how to display check boxes. Possible values are Flat and Normal.

There are several methods available in the CheckedListBox control that can be used to manipulate check boxes.

- **GetItemChecked(*Integer*)** Indicates whether or not the specified item is checked.
- **SetItemChecked(*Integer*, *Boolean*)** Sets the checked status of the specified item to Checked.
- **GetItemCheckState(*Integer*)** Indicates the check state of the current item.
- **SetItemCheckState(*Integer*, *CheckState*)** Sets the check state of the specified item.

Let's have an example of how to use the check boxes in the CheckedListBox control. The following code in the Click event handler for the Button creates a list of currently checked items in the CheckedListBox control (see also Figure 9.26):

```
'-------------------------------------------------
' CheckedListBox control demo - get checked items
'-------------------------------------------------


Private Sub Button1_Click(ByVal sender As System.Object, _
  ByVal e As System.EventArgs) Handles Button1.Click

   Dim En As IEnumerator
   Dim I As Integer
   En = CheckedListBox1.CheckedIndices.GetEnumerator()
   TextBox2.Clear()
    While En.MoveNext() <> False
      TextBox2.Text = TextBox2.Text & _
      CheckedListBox1.Items(En.Current) & ControlChars.CrLf
    End While


   End Sub
```

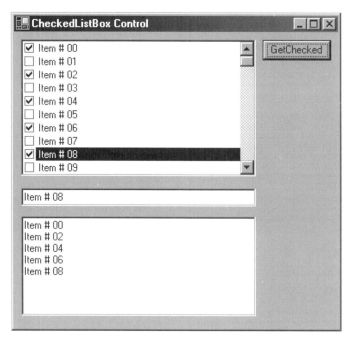

FIGURE 9.26 Using the `Click` event handler for the `Button` shows which items have been clicked in the `CheckedListBox` control

In the next section, we, will look at the more advanced list controls – the `ListView`, `TreeView`, and `ImageList` controls.

ListView class

This class implements the Windows `ListView` control, which is used to display a list of items with icons. This control has four view modes (specified by the `View` property of a `View` type):

● `View.LargeIcon;`
● `View.SmallIcon;`
● `View.List;`
● `View.Details.`

The `LargeIcon` mode displays large icons next to the item text, the items appearing in multiple columns if the control is large enough. The `SmallIcon` mode is the same except that, naturally, it displays small icons. The `List` mode displays small icons but they are always in a single column. The `Details` mode displays items in multiple columns.

All four possible modes of the `ListView` control are shown in Figure 9.27.

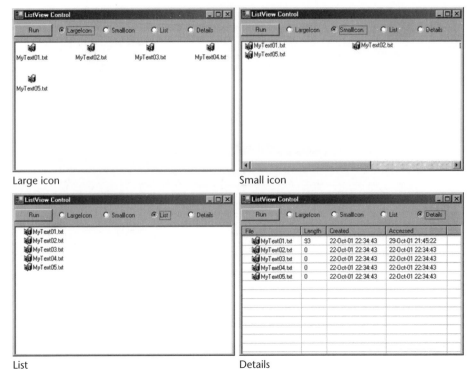

FIGURE 9.27   The four modes of the ListView control

Information displayed in the ListView control is stored in the Items collection (each item is of the ListViewItem type). Selected items are stored in the SelectedItems collection. To allow users to select more than one item, we should set the MultiSelect property to "True". To display check boxes next to the items, we should set the CheckBoxes property to "True".

The following list shows the main properties of the ListView control.

- **Activation** This property (of a ItemActivation type) determines what type of action the user must take to activate an item in the list: the options are Standard, OneClick, and TwoClick.

- **AllowColumnReorder** This Boolean property indicates whether or not the user can drag column headers to other column positions, thus changing the order of displayed columns.

- **AutoArrange** This Boolean property indicates whether or not items are automatically arranged according to the alignment property.

- **CheckedIndices** This property (of a ListView.CheckedIndexCollection type) contains indices of the currently checked list items.

- **CheckedItems** This property (of a `ListView.CheckedListViewItemCollection` type) contains the currently checked list items.
- **Columns** This is a collection of columns (of a `ListView.ColumnHeaderCollection` type).
- **FocusedItem** This property (of the `ListViewItem` type) contains the item that has the user focus.
- **FullRowSelect** This `Boolean` property indicates whether clicking on an item will select the item or entire row.
- **GridLines** This `Boolean` property indicates whether or not the gridlines are visible.
- **HeaderStyle** Specifies the column header style. This property (of a `ColumnHeaderStyle` type) can have the following values:
  - **Clickable** Column headers can be clicked to perform some actions;
  - **Nonclickable** Column headers do not respond to mouse clicks;
  - **None** Column headers are not shown.
- **HideSelection** This `Boolean` property indicates whether or not selected items are hidden when focus is removed from the control.
- **HoverSelection** This `Boolean` property indicates whether or not items can be selected by hovering over them with the mouse.
- **LabelEdit** This `Boolean` property indicates whether or not labels of items are editable.
- **LabelWrap** This `Boolean` property indicates whether or not item labels wrap in icon view.
- **Scrollable** This `Boolean` property indicates whether or not scroll bars are visible.
- **SelectedIndices** Contains the indices of the currently selected list of items (this property is of `ListView.SelectedIndexCollection` type).
- **SelectedItems** Contains the currently selected list of items (this property is of a `ListView.SelectedListViewItemCollection` type).
- **Sorting** Specifies the sort order of items (this property is of a `SortOrder` type). It may have the following values: `SortOrder.Ascending`, `SortOrder.Descending`, or `SortOrder.None`.

The last three properties above are used to specify icons associated with items (they are of an `ImageList` type).

- **LargeImageList** Indicates that the `ImageList` contains icons used in `LargeIcon` mode.
- **SmallImageList** Indicates that the `ImageList` contains icons used in `SmallIcon` mode.
- **StateImageList** Indicates that the `ImageList` contains icons used to show the state of the item.

Let's look at several methods of the `ListView` control.

● **ArrangeIcons(*ListViewAlignment*) method** Arranges items in `LargeIcon` or `SmallIcon` view according to a given behavior. The possible values of the arrangement are:

   – **ListViewAlignment.Default** aligns items according to the current alignment style;

   – **ListViewAlignment.AlignLeft** aligns items with the left edge of the window;

   – **ListViewAlignment.AlignTop** aligns items with the top edge of the window;

   – **ListViewAlignment.SnapToGrid** snaps all icons to the nearest grid position.

● **BeginUpdate()** and **EndUpdate() methods** Prevent the `ListView` from redrawing itself.

● **Clear() method** Removes all items and columns from the component.

● **EnsureVisible(*Integer*) method** Ensures that the specified item is visible, scrolling the view as necessary.

● **GetItemAt(*Integer*, *Integer*) method** Returns the item at the given x, y coordinate.

We have enough information about the `ListView` control to create an example that will show some of its features. In this example, we show the contents of the directory in four columns – file name, size, creation date, and last access time. We will start with the definition of columns.

```
ListView1.Columns.Add("File",      100, HorizontalAlignment.Left)
ListView1.Columns.Add("Length",    100, HorizontalAlignment.Left)
ListView1.Columns.Add("Created",   100, HorizontalAlignment.Left)
ListView1.Columns.Add("Accessed", 100, HorizontalAlignment.Left)
```

The next step is to create all the required objects that will be used to extract the information:

```
Dim Path As String = "C:\Temp\MyText"
Dim DirInfo As New DirectoryInfo(Path)
Dim Files As FileInfo() = DirInfo.GetFiles("*.*")
Dim I As Integer
Dim Item As ListViewItem
```

As we, already know, `ListView` items are stored in the `Items` collection. By adding an item, we define the content of the column furthest to the left. To specify the content of other columns, we should add the items to the `SubItems` collection of a given `Item`, as shown below (see also Figure 9.28):

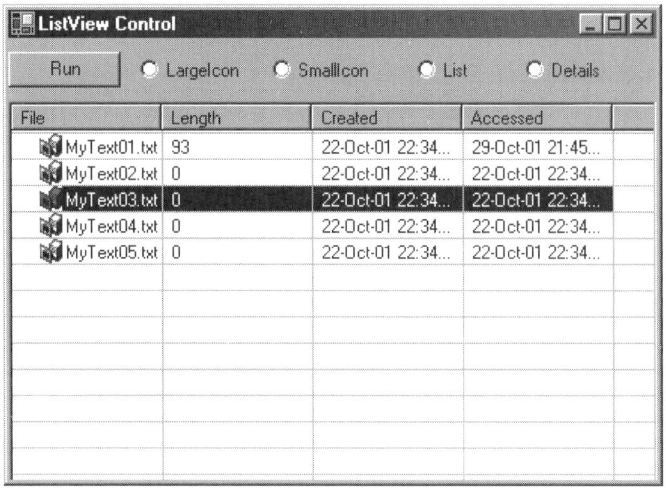

FIGURE 9.28 Creating the content of various columns by using the SubItems part of a given Item

```
For I = Files.GetLowerBound(0) To Files.GetUpperBound(0)

    Item = ListView1.Items.Add(Files(I).Name, 0)
    Item.SubItems.Add(Files(I).Length)
    Item.SubItems.Add(Files(I).CreationTime)
    Item.SubItems.Add(Files(I).LastAccessTime)

Next
```

The screenshot in Figure 9.28 shows our application as well as some extra features, such as the ability to change the view mode and icons displayed for each item. To change the view mode, we use four radio buttons – one per mode – and, in the event handler for the click event, we set this mode as shown below:

```
'------------------------------------------------
' ListView control demo – change View property
'------------------------------------------------

Private Sub RadioButton1_CheckedChanged(ByVal sender As _
    System.Object, ByVal e As System.EventArgs) _
    Handles RadioButton1.CheckedChanged

        ListView1.View = View.LargeIcon

End Sub
```

```
Private Sub RadioButton2_CheckedChanged(ByVal sender As _
System.Object, ByVal e As System.EventArgs) _
Handles RadioButton2.CheckedChanged

    ListView1.View = View.SmallIcon

End Sub

Private Sub RadioButton3_CheckedChanged(ByVal sender As _
System.Object, ByVal e As System.EventArgs) _
Handles RadioButton3.CheckedChanged

    ListView1.View = View.List

End Sub

Private Sub RadioButton4_CheckedChanged(ByVal sender As _
System.Object, ByVal e As System.EventArgs) _
Handles RadioButton4.CheckedChanged

    ListView1.View = View.Details

End Sub
```

To specify icons – for reasons of simplicity we use the same image for three types of images (large icon, small icons, and state) – we write the following code:

```
. . .

ImageList1 = New System.Windows.Forms.ImageList()

. . .

ListView1.LargeImageList = ImageList1
ListView1.SmallImageList = ImageList1
ListView1.StateImageList = ImageList1
```

The last parameter in the call to the `Items.Add` method is:

```
Item = ListView1.Items.Add(Files(I).Name, 0)
```

This specifies the index of the `Image` in the `ImageList` to be displayed with this item. The next list-type control we will learn about in this chapter is the `TreeView` control.

TreeView class

This class implements the Windows `TreeView` control, which is used to display a hierarchy of items. The contents of the `TreeView` control are stored in the `Nodes` collection, which holds all the `TreeNode` objects. Each `TreeNode` can contain a collection of other `TreeNode` objects, and so on. This produces the hierarchical structure of root and child nodes.

Each `TreeNode` object can have an associated `Image` displayed next to it. To do this, we assign the `ImageList` object to the `ImageList` property of the `TreeView` control and specify an index of the appropriate `Image` in the `ImageIndex` property of the `TreeNode` object.

Here is a list of the main properties of the `TreeView` class:

- **CheckBoxes** This `Boolean` property indicates whether or not check boxes are displayed next to the tree nodes.

- **HideSelection** This `Boolean` property indicates whether or not the selected tree node remains highlighted even when the tree view has lost the focus.

- **HotTracking** This `Boolean` property indicates whether or not a tree node label should look like a hyperlink as the mouse pointer passes over it.

- **Indent** Specifies the distances to the indents of each of the child tree node levels as an `Integer` value.

- **ItemHeight** Specifies the height of each tree node as an `Integer` value.

- **LabelEdit** This `Boolean` property indicates whether or not the label text of the tree nodes is editable.

- **PathSeparator** Specifies the delimiter string used by the tree node path.

- **Scrollable** This `Boolean` property indicates whether or not the tree view control displays scroll bars when necessary.

- **SelectedNode** Specifies the currently selected node as a `TreeNode` object.

- **ShowLines** If set, this `Boolean` property indicates that lines will be drawn between tree nodes.

- **ShowPlusMinus** If set, this `Boolean` property indicates that plus and minus signs will be displayed next to tree nodes that have child nodes.

- **ShowRootLines** If set, this `Boolean` property indicates that lines will be drawn between the tree nodes that are at the root of the tree view.

- **Sorted** If set, this `Boolean` property indicates that tree nodes will be sorted.

- **TopNode** Specifies the first fully visible node as a `TreeNode` object.

- **VisibleCount** Returns the number of tree nodes that can be fully visible.

Here are the methods of the `TreeView` class.

- **`CollapseAll()` method** Collapses all the tree nodes.
- **`ExpandAll()` method** Expands all the tree nodes.
- **`GetNodeAt(*Point*)` or `GetNodeAt(*Integer*, *Integer*)` method** Returns the node at the specified location.
- **`GetNodeCount(*Boolean*)` method** Finds the number of nodes and, optionally, the number of subnodes.

Let's try the `TreeView` class in action. The following example shows how to fill the `TreeView` control with the names of directories in the root of the C:\ drive (see also Figure 9.29):

```
'------------------------------------------------
' TreeView control demo - show directories on C:\
'------------------------------------------------

    Dim E As Environment
    Dim I As Byte
    Dim Dirs() As DirectoryInfo
    Dim DirInfo As DirectoryInfo
    Dim Nodes As TreeNodeCollection

    With E

      TreeView1.Nodes.Add(New TreeNode(.MachineName))
      TreeView1.Nodes(0).Nodes.Add(New TreeNode("c:\"))
      DirInfo = New DirectoryInfo("c:\")
      Dirs = DirInfo.GetDirectories

      For I = 0 To Dirs.GetUpperBound(0)

       Nodes = TreeView1.Nodes(0).Nodes(0).Nodes
       Nodes.Add(New TreeNode(Dirs(I).Name))

      Next

    End With
```

Now, let's extend our example by adding an event handler that will show the text of the selected node (see also Figure 9.30):

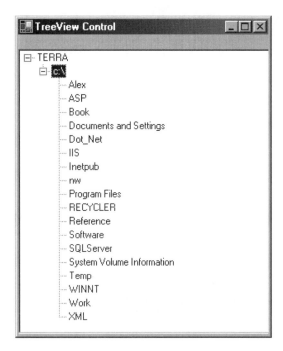

FIGURE 9.29   The names of directories in a C:\ drive shown in a TreeView control

FIGURE 9.30   Adding an event handler shows the selected node

```
'-------------------------------------------------
' TreeView control demo - show selected node
'-------------------------------------------------

Private Sub TreeView1_AfterSelect(ByVal sender As System.Object, _
  ByVal e As System.Windows.Forms.TreeViewEventArgs) _
  Handles TreeView1.AfterSelect

  TextBox1.Text = TreeView1.SelectedNode.Text

End Sub
```

Note that in the example above, we have used the Text property. To get the full node text – that is, text that includes the text of all a node's parent nodes – we can use the FullPath property.

The last list-type control we will cover in this chapter is the ImageList control, which is used to store images used by other controls. We have already seen how we can use this control with ListView and TreeView controls. In the next section, we will look at the properties and methods of the ImageList control.

ImageList class

This class is used to manage a collection of Image objects programmatically. As we have seen above, the ImageList class is used by other controls – ListView and TreeView. The ToolBar control, discussed in the next chapter, also uses this class.

The Images collection contains all Image objects currently stored in the ImageList. The ColorDepth, ImageSize, and TransparentColor properties are used to specify the depth of color of the images in the list, the size of the images, and the color to treat as transparent.

The Handle property (of the IntPtr type) returns the handle of the image list object. The HandleCreated property indicates whether or not the underlying Win32 handle has been created. The ImageStream property returns the ImageListStreamer associated with this list.

The Draw method is used to draw the specified image. It has several overloaded versions that accept the following parameters.

● Draw(*Graphics, Point, Integer*) Draws the image indicated by the specified index on the specified Graphics object at the given location.

● Draw(*Graphics, Integer, Integer, Integer*) Draws the image indicated by the given index on the specified Graphics object at the specified location.

● Draw(*Graphics, Integer, Integer, Integer, Integer, Integer*) Draws the image indicated by the given index using the specified location, size, and raster op code (which defines how the graphics device interface (GDI) combines the bits from the selected pen with the bits in the destination bitmap).

The following example shows how to use the **ImageList** control to store icons found in the subdirectory and then show its contents in the **ListView** control. We start by filling up the **ImageList** control with icons:

```
'------------------------------------------------
' ImageList control demo - load icons
'------------------------------------------------

  Private Sub Button1_Click(ByVal sender As System.Object, _
    ByVal e As System.EventArgs) Handles Button1.Click

    Dim DirInfo As DirectoryInfo
    Dim Files() As FileInfo
    Dim I As Byte
    DirInfo = New DirectoryInfo("C:\Program Files\Microsoft Visual " & _
      "Studio.NET\Common7\Graphics\icons\Computer")

    Files = DirInfo.GetFiles("*.ico")
    ImageList1.ImageSize = New Size(32, 32)

    For I = 0 To Files.GetUpperBound(0)

      ImageList1.Images.Add(Image.FromFile(Files(I).FullName))

    Next

  End Sub
```

Next, we need to associate our **ListView** control with the **ImageList**:

```
ListView1.LargeImageList = ImageList1
ListView1.SmallImageList = ImageList1
ListView1.StateImageList = ImageList1
```

Now, we are ready to show images in the **ListView** control (see also Figure 9.31):

```
'------------------------------------------------
' ImageList and ListView controls demo - show icons
'------------------------------------------------

  Private Sub Button2_Click(ByVal sender As System.Object,
    ByVal e As System.EventArgs) Handles Button2.Click
```

```
Dim En As IEnumerator
Dim Item As ListViewItem
Dim I As Byte

ListView1.Columns.Add("Image", 40, HorizontalAlignment.Center)
ListView1.Columns.Add("Item", 10, HorizontalAlignment.Center)

En = ImageList1.Images.GetEnumerator

While Not En.MoveNext()

  Item = ListView1.Items.Add("", I)
  Item.SubItems.Add("Item #" & I)
  I += 1

End While

End Sub
```

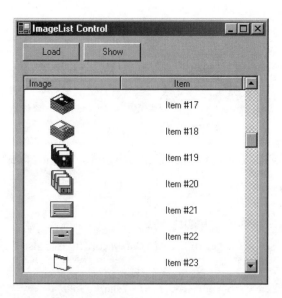

FIGURE 9.31   Linking icons with lists

Now, let's slightly improve our example. We will combine actions in two event handlers and change the View property of the ListView to LargeIcon (see also Figure 9.32):

```
'----------------------------------------------------
' ImageList and ListView controls demo - show icons.
' Imporved version
'----------------------------------------------------

Private Sub Button1_Click(ByVal sender As System.Object, _
ByVal e As System.EventArgs) Handles Button1.Click

  Dim DirInfo As DirectoryInfo
  Dim Files() As FileInfo
  Dim I As Byte
  Dim Item As ListViewItem

  DirInfo = New DirectoryInfo("C:\Program Files\Microsoft Visual " & _
   "Studio.NET\Common7\Graphics\icons\Computer")

  Files = DirInfo.GetFiles("*.ico")
  ImageList1.ImageSize = New Size(32, 32)
  ListView1.Columns.Add("Image", 40, HorizontalAlignment.Center)

   For I = 0 To Files.GetUpperBound(0)

    ImageList1.Images.Add(Image.FromFile(Files(I).FullName))
    Item = ListView1.Items.Add(Files(I).Name, I)

   Next

  End Sub
```

FIGURE 9.32   Here, two event handlers have been combined and large icons introduced

The last section of this chapter is dedicated to menus. In the following sections, we will discuss such classes as the `MainMenu`, `MenuItem`, and `ContextMenu`.

9.6 Menus

In Windows applications, menus are used to provide a list of commands available for users to execute in the application. Typical examples are the `File` menu, which may contain such commands as `New`, `Open`, `Close`, `Save`, and `SaveAs`, the `Edit` menu, with commands such as `Copy`, `Cut`, and `Paste`, the `Print` menu, which may provide such commands as `PrintPreview`, `PageSetup`, and `Print`, and so on.

To create menus in Windows forms applications, we use classes derived from the `Menu` class that provide the base functionality for all menus. The `Menu` class serves as a base class for three further classes – the `ContextMenu` class, used to create shortcut menus, the `MainMenu` class, used as a container for the menu structure of a form, and the `MenuItem` class, which represents an individual item displayed within the `MainMenu` or `ContextMenu` (see Figure 9.33).

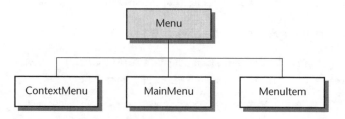

FIGURE 9.33   The `Menu` class is the basis of other menu-related classes

Menu class

Menus are hierarchical structures comprised of `MenuItem` objects. These objects can contain other `MenuItem` objects, which represent submenu items. The `MenuItem` objects can be used with the `MainMenu` object to represent an entire menu structure for a form or in a `ContextMenu` to display shortcut menus.

The `Menu` class provides the following properties and methods.

- **Handle** This property (of an `IntPtr` type) represents the window handler for the menu.

- **IsParent** This `Boolean` property indicates if this menu contains any menu items – that is, if it acts as a parent menu for other menus and menu items.

- **MDIListItem** This property returns the `MenuItem` that is used to display a list of MDI child forms.

- **MenuItems** This property contains the collection of `MenuItem` objects (of the `MenuItemCollection` type) associated with the menu.

- **GetContextMenu() method** Gets the `ContextMenu` that contains this menu.

- **GetMainMenu() method** Gets the `MainMenu` that contains this menu.
- **MergeMenu(*Menu*) method** Merges the `MenuItem` objects of the specified menu with the current menu.

Now let's look at the classes derived from the `Menu` class. We will start with the `MainMenu` class.

MainMenu class

The `MainMenu` class represents a container for the menu structure of a form. Each menu item is a `MenuItem` object that can be either a command or a parent menu for other menu items. The `Menu` property of the `Form` object is used to bind the `MainMenu` to the form. This gives us an ability to switch menus during the form's lifetime. If we need to have a copy of the menu structure, we use the `CloneMenu()` method to do this. The following example shows how to programmatically create a main menu for the form (see also Figure 9.34):

```
'-------------------------------------------------
' MainMenu control demo - create menu menu
'-------------------------------------------------

Private Sub Button1_Click(ByVal sender As System.Object, _
  ByVal e As System.EventArgs) Handles Button1.Click

  Dim Menu As New MainMenu()
  Dim FileMenu As New MenuItem()
  Dim EditMenu As New MenuItem()

  With FileMenu
   .Text = "File"
   .MenuItems.Add("New")
   .MenuItems.Add("Open")
   .MenuItems.Add("Close")
  End With

  Menu.MenuItems.Add(FileMenu)

  With EditMenu
   .Text = "Edit"
   .MenuItems.Add("Copy")
   .MenuItems.Add("Cut")
   .MenuItems.Add("Paste")
  End With

  Menu.MenuItems.Add(EditMenu)

  Me.Menu = Menu

End Sub
```

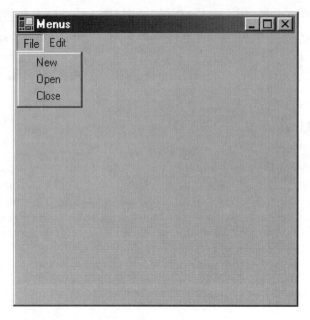

FIGURE 9.34   A main menu has been created for the form

In the example above, we created two menu items, each with three subitems. Our code specified only the names of the menu items – there was no information about commands that these items can invoke, shortcut keys and so on. To be able to supply this information, we need to learn about the `MenuItem` class. Then we will extend our example with all the required features.

MenuItem class

The `MenuItem` class represents an item in a `MainMenu` or `ContextMenu`. While these classes only serve to store the structure of the menu, the `MenuItem` class does all of the job. It represents the menu item, menu with submenus, and separators – a special type of item that does not have associated commands and serves to separate items in the menu.

Let's look at the properties of the `MenuItem` class.

- **BarBreak** This `Boolean` property indicates whether the `MenuItem` will be placed on a new line or in a new column. The first option is for a menu item to be added to a `MainMenu`; the second is for a menu item to be added to a `ContextMenu`.

- **Break** This `Boolean` property indicates whether the item will be placed on a new line or in a new column. The first option is for a menu item to be added to a `MainMenu`, the second is for a menu item to be added to a `ContextMenu`.

- **Checked** If set, a check mark appears next to the text of the menu item.

- **DefaultItem** This `Boolean` property indicates whether or not the menu item is the default menu item.

- **Enabled** This `Boolean` property indicates whether or not the menu item is enabled.

- **Index** Indicates the position of the menu item in its parent menu as an `Integer` value.

- **IsParent** If set, the menu item contains child menu items.

- **MenuItems** Contains the collection of `MenuItem` objects (`Menu.MenuItemCollection` type) for this item.

- **Mnemonic** Indicates the mnemonic character that is associated with this menu item.

- **Parent** Indicates the parent menu (of `Menu` type) – the menu that contains this menu item.

- **RadioCheck** If set, this indicates that, for checked menu items, there will be radio buttons displayed instead of check marks.

- **Shortcut** Specifies the shortcut key associated with the menu item. This property is of the `Shortcut` type.

- **ShowShortCut** This `Boolean` property indicates whether or not the shortcut key that is associated with the menu item is displayed next to the menu item caption.

- **Text** Specifies the text (caption) that will be displayed on the menu item.

- **Visible** If set, the menu item is visible.

In our previous example (see the previous section on the `MainMenu` class), we used the simplest form of `MenuItem` constructor – the one that takes a string to specify the menu item caption. In order to create a more functional menu, we should use the constructor that takes three parameters – text for the caption, pointer to event handler, and the shortcut key. Now let's extend our example:

```
'----------------------------------------------------
' MainMenu and MenuItem controls demo - create menu
'----------------------------------------------------


Private Sub Button1_Click(ByVal sender As System.Object, _
ByVal e As System.EventArgs) Handles Button1.Click

Dim Menu As New MainMenu()
Dim FileMenu As New MenuItem()
Dim EditMenu As New MenuItem()
Dim Item As MenuItem

With FileMenu

  .Text = "File"
  Item = New MenuItem("&New", AddressOf File_New_Click, _
   Shortcut.CtrlN)
  .MenuItems.Add(Item)
```

```
      Item = New MenuItem("Open", AddressOf File_Open_Click, _
        Shortcut.Ctrl0)
      .MenuItems.Add(Item)
      Item = New MenuItem("Close", AddressOf File_Close_Click, _
        Shortcut.CtrlF4)
      .MenuItems.Add(Item)

    End With

    With EditMenu

      .Text = "Edit"
      Item = New MenuItem("Copy", AddressOf Edit_Copy_Click, _
        Shortcut.CtrlC)
      .MenuItems.Add(Item)
      Item = New MenuItem("Cut", AddressOf Edit_Cut_Click, Shortcut.CtrlT)
      .MenuItems.Add(Item)
      Item = New MenuItem("Paste", AddressOf Edit_Paste_Click, _
        Shortcut.CtrlP)
      .MenuItems.Add(Item)

    End With

    Menu.MenuItems.Add(FileMenu)
    Menu.MenuItems.Add(EditMenu)

    Me.Menu = Menu

  End Sub

  Private Sub File_New_Click(ByVal sender As System.Object, _
    ByVal e As System.EventArgs)

    MsgBox("File|New")

  End Sub

  Private Sub File_Open_Click(ByVal sender As System.Object, _
    ByVal e As System.EventArgs)

    MsgBox("File|Open")

  End Sub
```

```
Private Sub File_Close_Click(ByVal sender As System.Object, _
 ByVal e As System.EventArgs)

   MsgBox("File|Close")

End Sub

Private Sub Edit_Copy_Click(ByVal sender As System.Object, _
 ByVal e As System.EventArgs)

   MsgBox("Edit|Copy")

End Sub

Private Sub Edit_Cut_Click(ByVal sender As System.Object, _
 ByVal e As System.EventArgs)

   MsgBox("Edit|Cut")

End Sub

Private Sub Edit_Paste_Click(ByVal sender As System.Object, _
 ByVal e As System.EventArgs)

   MsgBox("Edit|Paste")

End Sub
```

As a result, we have a menu with items, accessible by shortcuts, and each item now has an associated command (see Figure 9.35).

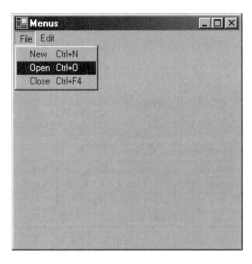

FIGURE 9.35   Using a more functional constructor, the menu now has shortcuts and each item has its own command

There are two events of the `MenuItem` class that are of interest for us. The `Popup` event occurs before a menu item's list of menu items is displayed. In the event handler for this event we can, for example, check if all of the menu items should be enabled or visible depending on the particular state of our application.

The `Select` event occurs when the user places the cursor over a menu item. The handler for this event is a good place to provide a detailed explanation of the actions performed by this menu command. Usually we use the `StatusBar` control discussed in the next chapter to display such information.

The last type of menu-related class is the `ContextMenu` class, which we will discuss in the next section.

ContextMenu class

Context menus (also called shortcut menus) are associated with other controls. If a control has a context menu, we can call it by clicking the right mouse button on the control. All visible controls and forms have a `ContextMenu` property that is used to bind the `ContextMenu` to the control or `Form`. The `SourceControl` property (of a `Control` type) allows us to find the control that called the `ContextMenu`. This is useful when we have one `ContextMenu` for several controls.

Earlier in this chapter we discussed the `ListView` control. In the example of its usage, we used four radio buttons to provide a way to change the `View` property of the `ListView` control. Let's implement this functionality by means of the `ContextMenu` (see Figure 9.36). Here is the complete code for the new version of the example (the new code is in bold so you can see more easily what has happened):

```
'------------------------------------------------------------------
' ContextMenu control demo - context menu for the ListView control
'------------------------------------------------------------------


Private Sub Button1_Click(ByVal sender As System.Object, _
    ByVal e As System.EventArgs) Handles Button1.Click

    Dim Path As String = "C:\Temp\MyText"
    Dim DirInfo As New DirectoryInfo(Path)
    Dim Files As FileInfo() = DirInfo.GetFiles("*.*")
    Dim I As Integer
    Dim Item As ListViewItem

    Dim CtxMenu As New ContextMenu()
    Dim CtxItem As MenuItem

    ListView1.Columns.Add("File",     100, HorizontalAlignment.Left)
    ListView1.Columns.Add("Length",   100, HorizontalAlignment.Left)
    ListView1.Columns.Add("Created",  100, HorizontalAlignment.Left)
    ListView1.Columns.Add("Accessed", 100, HorizontalAlignment.Left)
```

```
  For I = Files.GetLowerBound(0) To Files.GetUpperBound(0)

    Item = ListView1.Items.Add(Files(I).Name, 0)
    Item.SubItems.Add(Files(I).Length)
    Item.SubItems.Add(Files(I).CreationTime)
    Item.SubItems.Add(Files(I).LastAccessTime)

  Next

  With CtxMenu
    CtxItem = New MenuItem("LargeIcon", AddressOf Set_LargeIcon)
    .MenuItems.Add(CtxItem)
    CtxItem = New MenuItem("SmallIcon", AddressOf Set_SmallIcon)
    .MenuItems.Add(CtxItem)
    CtxItem = New MenuItem("List", AddressOf Set_List)
    .MenuItems.Add(CtxItem)
    CtxItem = New MenuItem("Details", AddressOf Set_Details)
    .MenuItems.Add(CtxItem)
  End With
  ListView1.ContextMenu = CtxMenu

End Sub

Private Sub Set_LargeIcon(ByVal sender As System.Object, _
 ByVal e As System.EventArgs)

  ListView1.View = View.LargeIcon

End Sub

Private Sub Set_SmallIcon(ByVal sender As System.Object, _
 ByVal e As System.EventArgs)

  ListView1.View = View.SmallIcon

End Sub

Private Sub Set_List(ByVal sender As System.Object, _
 ByVal e As System.EventArgs)

  ListView1.View = View.List

End Sub
```

```
Private Sub Set_Details(ByVal sender As System.Object, _
    ByVal e As System.EventArgs)

    ListView1.View = View.Details

End Sub
```

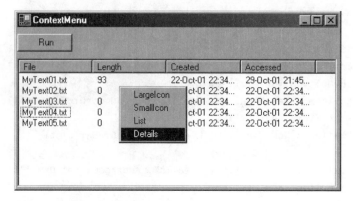

FIGURE 9.36   Increased functionality has been achieved by adding radio buttons using the `ContextMenu` class

9.7 Conclusion

In this chapter, we have learned about the Windows forms controls that we can use to provide a user interface in our Windows forms applications. We have discussed several groups of controls, such as buttons, text controls, labels, lists, and menus. For each group, we have provided a list of classes that comprise it, as well as detailed descriptions of each class, its properties and methods, and usage examples.

We will continue learning about Windows forms controls in the next chapter, where we will discuss controls that extend the basic set of controls found in Windows. In the next chapter, we will learn about these additional controls, as well as how to use ActiveX controls in Web forms.

chapter 10

Additional Windows forms controls

- Additional controls

- Toolbars

- Common dialog boxes

- Using ActiveX controls

In the previous chapter, we saw how to make the most of the standard Windows controls – text boxes, buttons, check boxes, radio buttons, list boxes, and so on. The Microsoft .NET Framework class library contains controls that extend the basic set of controls found in Windows.

In this chapter, we will learn about these additional controls, as well as how to use ActiveX controls in Web forms.

10.1 Additional controls

The additional controls discussed in this chapter are used to provide extended user-interface functionality. Such controls include the following.

- **Panels** Used to group other controls.

- **Splitters** Used to resize docked controls at runtime.

- **Tab Controls and Tab Pages** Controls that display multiple tabs can contain other controls.

- **ToolBars** This control is used as a container to display a row of bitmapped buttons and dropdown menus.

- **Status Bars** Used to implement Windows status bars, these are rectangular areas at the bottom of a form used to display status information.

- **Scroll Bars** Used with container controls that do not have their own scroll bars to implement scrolling functionality. Another way to use scroll bars is to key the numeric data, though a `TrackBar` control might be better for this.

- **Month Calendar** Allows users to visually select a date.

- **Date-time picker** This allows users to select a date from a list of dates and times.

- **UpDown controls** Provide a control that consists of a text box and a small vertical "scroll bar" (actually, this is a pair of button-like areas that look like the ends of a scroll bar) usually called a spinner control.

- **Progress Bar controls** Used to indicate the progress of an action.

- **TrackBar controls** Used to provide a way to change values visually.

- **Picture Box controls** Used to display graphics in bitmap, GIF, JPEG, icon, or metafile formats.

- **Timers** Used to implement a timer that raises an event at user-defined intervals.

- **HelpProvider control** Provides pop-up or online help for other controls.

- **ErrorProvider** Provides a way to associate an error message with the control.

- **ToolTip** Used to display a short descriptive text when the user points at other controls.

- **NotifyIcon** Provides an icon in the status area of the Windows taskbar for processes that run in the background and do not have user interfaces.

- **Common Dialog Boxes** Implement such standard dialog boxes as:
  - **Color Dialog Box** used to select colors;
  - **Font Dialog Box** used to select fonts and attributes;
  - **Open File Dialog Box** used to select a file to open;
  - **Save File Dialog Box** used to select a file to save;
  - **Print Dialog Box** used to print a file;
  - **Page Setup Dialog Box** used to set up page attributes for printing;
  - **Print Preview Dialog Box** used to preview a page that is about to be printed.

If this is not enough, we can use hundreds of ActiveX controls available on the marker or create our own, specialized controls. Note that all major producers of ActiveX controls now offer .NET components. We will talk about how to use ActiveX controls in Windows forms applications at the end of this chapter.

We will start our discussion of additional Windows forms controls with the Panel control, which is used to group other controls.

Panel Class

Like the GroupBox controls discussed in the previous chapter, Panel controls are used to create groups of other controls. The BorderStyle property (of a BorderStyle type) controls the appearance of the Panel control's border. By adding the border, we can easily distinguish the area of the panel from other areas on the form. The possible values of the BorderStyle property are BorderStyle.None (no visible border), BorderStyle.FixedSingle (a plain line), and BorderStyle.Fixed3D (a shadowed line).

If we set the AutoScroll property to "True", any control located outside the Panel control's visible region can be scrolled with the scroll bars provided.

The following example shows how to programmatically create the Panel control with three radio buttons within it (see also Figure 10.1):

```
Dim Panel1 As New Panel()
Dim RadioButton1 As New RadioButton()
Dim RadioButton2 As New RadioButton()
Dim RadioButton3 As New RadioButton()

Panel1.Location = New System.Drawing.Point(8, 48)
Panel1.Size = New System.Drawing.Size(272, 216)
Panel1.BorderStyle = System.Windows.Forms.BorderStyle.Fixed3D

RadioButton1.Text = "Left"
RadioButton1.Location = New System.Drawing.Point(8, 24)
Panel1.Controls.Add(RadioButton1)
```

```
RadioButton2.Text = "Right"
RadioButton2.Location = New System.Drawing.Point(8, 56)
Panel1.Controls.Add(RadioButton2)

RadioButton3.Text = "Center"
RadioButton3.Location = New System.Drawing.Point(8, 88)
Panel1.Controls.Add(RadioButton3)

Controls.Add(Panel1)
```

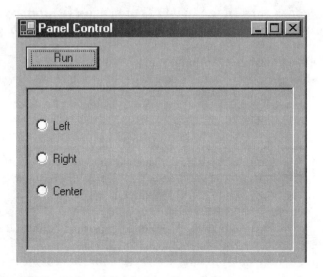

FIGURE 10.1 The Panel control with three buttons in it

In the example above, our panel has enough space to accommodate all three radio buttons. If we change its size and set the AutoScroll property to "True":

```
...

Panel1.Size = New System.Drawing.Size(272, 64)
Panel1.AutoScroll = True

...
```

we will create the Panel control with a vertical scroll bar (see Figure 10.2).

To group controls we can also use the GroupBox control discussed in the previous chapter. The difference between the GroupBox and Panel controls is that GroupBox can have a caption, while Panel can have scrollable content.

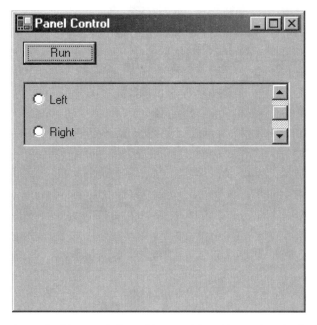

FIGURE 10.2 A panel with a vertical scroll bar – achieved by setting the AutoScroll property to "True"

Splitter class

This class implements the Windows forms Splitter control, which is used to resize docked controls at runtime. To use this control, we create two or more Panel controls and, for example, with two panels, we set the Dock property of the left panel to Left and the Dock property of the right panel to Fill. The Dock property is of the DockStyle type and it may have the following values.

- **Bottom** Specifies that the control's bottom edge is docked to the bottom of its containing control.
- **Fill** Specifies that all the control's edges are docked to all the edges of its containing control and sized appropriately.
- **Left** Specifies that the control's left edge is docked to the left edge of its containing control.
- **None** Specifies that the control is not docked. This is the default value.
- **Right** Specifies that the control's right edge is docked to the right edge of its containing control.
- **Top** Specifies that the control's top edge is docked to the top of its containing control.

Next, we place the Splitter control, which will automatically resize both Panels when we drag the edge of the Panel (see Figure 10.3).

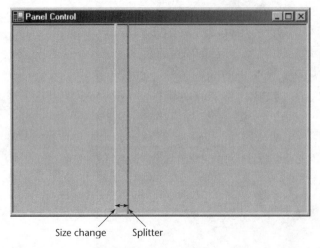

Size change   Splitter

FIGURE 10.3   The Splitter control resizes the panels when we drag the edge

Note that resizing a control using the Splitter can only be done using the mouse. It is not possible to access the Splitter using the keyboard.

TabControl and TabPage classes

The TabControl class represents the Windows forms TabControl – the control that displays multiple tabs which can contain other controls. Usually we use the TabControl to create multipage dialog boxes, like some of the dialog boxes used by Windows itself.

Each tab in the TabControl is represented by the TabPage object. The TabPages collection (of the TabControl.TabPageCollection type) contains all the tabs for the TabControl. When a tab is clicked, it raises the Click event for that TabPage object.

First, let's look at the TabControl class, then we will talk about the TabPage class. Following is a list of properties of the TabControl class.

- **Alignment** Specifies the area where the tabs are aligned (see Figure 10.4). This property is of the TabAlignment type and it can have the following values.
    - **Bottom** The tabs are located across the bottom of the control.
    - **Left** The tabs are located along the left edge of the control.
    - **Right** The tabs are located along the right edge of the control.
    - **Top** The tabs are located across the top of the control.
- **Appearance** Specifies the visual appearance of the tabs (see Figure 10.5). This property is of the TabAppearance type and it can have the following values.
    - **Buttons** The tabs look like three-dimensional buttons.
    - **FlatButtons** The tabs look like flat buttons.
    - **Normal** The tabs look like standard tabs.

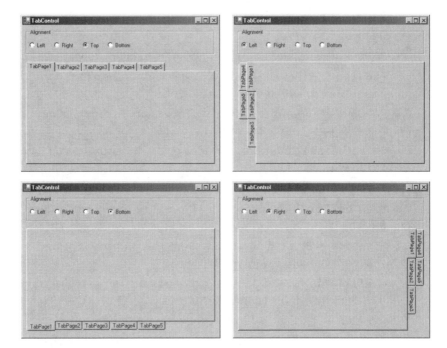

FIGURE 10.4   The different values of the Alignment property

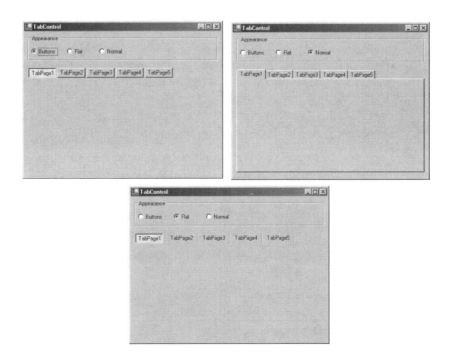

FIGURE 10.5   The Appearance property has different values to change the look of the tabs

- **HotTrack** If set, the tabs will change in appearance when the mouse passes over them.
- **Multiline** Indicates whether or not more than one row of tabs can be displayed.
- **Padding** Specifies the amount of space around each item on the control's tab pages. This property is of the `Point` type.
- **RowCount** Contains the number of rows (an `Integer` value) that are currently being displayed in the tab strip.
- **SelectedIndex** Indicates the index of the currently selected tab page. This is an `Integer` value.
- **SelectedTab** Indicates the currently selected tab page as a `TabPage` object.
- **ShowToolTips** If set, a tab's `ToolTip` will be shown when the mouse passes over the tab.
- **SizeMode** Indicates how tabs are sized. This property is of the `TabSizeMode` type and it can contains the following values.
  - **FillToRight** The width of each tab is sized so that each row of tabs fills the entire width of the container control.
  - **Fixed** All tabs in a control are the same width.
  - **Normal** The width of each tab is sized to accommodate what is displayed on the tab and the size of tabs in a row are not adjusted to fill the entire width of the container control.
- **TabCount** Returns the number of tabs as an `Integer` value.

The `TabPage` class represents one page inside the `TabControl`. It contains two properties that are now inherited from its parent `Panel` class – the `Text` property, which specifies the text to display on the tab, and the `ToolTipText` property, which specifies the tool tip text for the tab.

Let's create a `TabControl` with several tabs inside it. For each `TabPage` object, we should specify its location, size, name, and text (see Figure 10.6):

```
Private Sub Button1_Click(ByVal sender As System.Object, _
  ByVal e As System.EventArgs) Handles Button1.Click


  Dim TabControl1 As TabControl
  Dim TabPage1 As TabPage
  Dim TabPage2 As TabPage
  Dim TabPage3 As TabPage
  Dim TabPage4 As TabPage
  Dim TabPage5 As TabPage


  TabControl1 = New TabControl()
```

```
With TabControl1
  .Location = New System.Drawing.Point(8, 60)
  .Name = "TabControl1"
  .Size = New System.Drawing.Size(430, 220)
  .ShowToolTips = True
End With


TabPage1 = New TabPage()


With TabPage1
  .Location = New System.Drawing.Point(4, 22)
  .Size = New System.Drawing.Size(400, 200)
  .Name = "TabPage1"
  .Text = "TabPage1"
  .ToolTipText = .Text
End With


TabPage2 = New TabPage()


With TabPage2
  .Location = New System.Drawing.Point(4, 22)
  .Size = New System.Drawing.Size(400, 200)
  .Name = "TabPage2"
  .Text = "TabPage2"
  .ToolTipText = .Text
End With


TabPage3 = New TabPage()


With TabPage3
  .Location = New System.Drawing.Point(4, 22)
  .Size = New System.Drawing.Size(400, 200)
  .Name = "TabPage3"
  .Text = "TabPage3"
  .ToolTipText = .Text
End With


TabPage4 = New TabPage()
```

```
With TabPage4
  .Location = New System.Drawing.Point(4, 22)
  .Size = New System.Drawing.Size(400, 200)
  .Name = "TabPage4"
  .Text = "TabPage4"
  .ToolTipText = .Text
End With


TabPage5 = New TabPage()


With TabPage5
  .Location = New System.Drawing.Point(4, 22)
  .Size = New System.Drawing.Size(400, 200)
  .Name = "TabPage5"
  .Text = "TabPage5"
  .ToolTipText = .Text
End With


TabControl1.Controls.AddRange(New Control() {TabPage1, TabPage2, _
  TabPage3, TabPage4, TabPage5})


Controls.Add(TabControl1)


End Sub
```

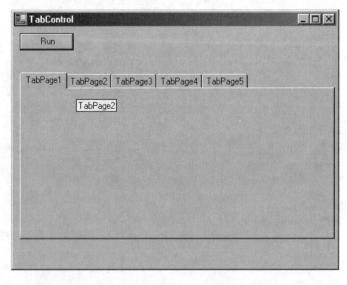

FIGURE 10.6   The TabControl set up with several tabs

Once we have created the `TabControl`, we can add and remove pages according to the needs of users. For example, we can show a limited number of pages if the program's advanced options are not activated and add pages later, if needed. To add controls to the `TabPage`, we use the `Controls` collection of this object. This collection also allows us to manipulate the controls on the particular page.

10.2 Toolbars

The `ToolBar` control is used as a container that displays a row of bitmapped buttons and dropdown menus. Clicking a toolbar button is usually equivalent to choosing a menu command, providing quick access to an application's most frequently used functions and commands. There are four types of buttons that can appear on the `ToolBar` – push buttons, dropdown buttons, toggle buttons, and separators.

Let's look at the properties defined for the `ToolBar` class (see Figure 10.7 for an example of a toolbar).

- **Appearance** Specifies the appearance of a toolbar control and its buttons. This property is of the `ToolBarAppearance` type and can be either `Flat` or `Normal`. The default value is `ToolBarAppearance.Normal`.

- **AutoSize** This `Boolean` property indicates whether or not the toolbar adjusts its size automatically based on the size of the buttons and the dock style.

- **BorderStyle** Specifies the style of the border. This can be `BorderStyle.None`, `BorderStyle.FixedSingle`, or `BorderStyle.Fixed3D`.

- **Buttons** Contains the collection of `ToolBarButton` objects. Each such object represents a single button on a `ToolBar`.

- **ButtonSize** Specifies the size of the buttons as a `Size` object.

- **Divider** This `Boolean` property indicates whether or not the toolbar displays a divider.

- **DropDownArrows** This `Boolean` property indicates whether or not dropdown buttons on a toolbar display down arrows.

- **ImageList** Indicates the `ImageList` object that contains the collection of images for buttons.

- **ImageSize** Specifies the size of the images for the buttons.

- **ShowToolTips** If set, the button's `ToolTip` will be shown when the mouse passes over the button.

- **TextAlign** Specifies where the text will appear in relation to the image. This can be either `ToolbarTextAlign.Right` or `ToolbarTextAlign.Underneath`. The default value is `ToolbarTextAlign.Underneath`.

- **Wrappable** If set, the toolbar buttons will wrap to the next line if the toolbar becomes too small to display all the buttons on the same line.

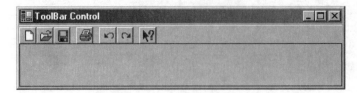

FIGURE 10.7 A toolbar with buttons with images on them

The ToolBarButton class represents one button on the ToolBar. Buttons can contain text (Text property) and images (ImageIndex property, which specifies an index of an image in the associated ImageList object). To specify the style of the button, we use the Style property, which may have the following values.

- **DropDownButton** Displays a menu or other window when clicked.
- **PushButton** A standard, three-dimensional button.
- **Separator** Used to separate other buttons with a space or line, depending on the value of the Appearance property.
- **ToggleButton** Appears sunken when clicked.

Other important properties of the ToolBarButton class are the following.

- **DropDownMenu** Specifies the menu (a Menu type) that will be displayed in the dropdown button.
- **Enabled** If set, the button is enabled.
- **Parent** Specifies the ToolBar control (a ToolBar type) that contains this button.
- **PartialPush** Indicates whether or not a toggle-style toolbar button is partially pushed.
- **Pushed** Indicates whether or not a toggle-style toolbar button is currently in the pushed state.
- **Visible** If set, the button is visible.

Let's look at how to create a ToolBar control programmatically with four buttons of different types (see also Figure 10.8):

```
Private Sub Button1_Click(ByVal sender As System.Object, _
ByVal e As System.EventArgs) Handles Button1.Click

Dim ToolBarButton1 As New ToolBarButton()
Dim ToolBarButton2 As New ToolBarButton()
Dim ToolBarButton3 As New ToolBarButton()
Dim ToolBarButton4 As New ToolBarButton()

Dim DropMenu As New MenuItem()
Dim Item As MenuItem
```

```
Dim ToolBar1 As New ToolBar()

ToolBar1.BorderStyle = System.Windows.Forms.BorderStyle.FixedSingle

ToolBarButton1.Text = "Btn1"
ToolBarButton1.Style = ToolBarButtonStyle.PushButton

ToolBarButton2.Text = "Btn2"
ToolBarButton2.Style = ToolBarButtonStyle.ToggleButton

ToolBarButton3.Text = "Btn3"
ToolBarButton3.Style = ToolBarButtonStyle.Separator

ToolBarButton4.Text = "Cmd"
ToolBarButton4.Style = ToolBarButtonStyle.DropDownButton

' Create menu

With DropMenu

  Item = New MenuItem("Cmd1")
  .MenuItems.Add(Item)
  Item = New MenuItem("Cmd2")
  .MenuItems.Add(Item)
  Item = New MenuItem("Cmd3")
  .MenuItems.Add(Item)

End With

ToolBarButton4.DropDownMenu = DropMenu

' Add the ToolBarButtons to the ToolBar

ToolBar1.Buttons.AddRange(New ToolBarButton() _
  {ToolBarButton1, ToolBarButton2, ToolBarButton3, ToolBarButton4})

' Add the ToolBar to the Form

Controls.Add(ToolBar1)

End Sub
```

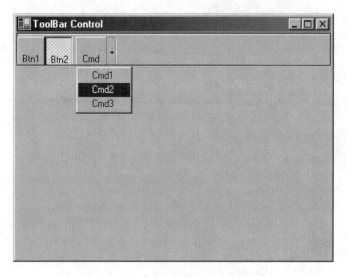

FIGURE 10.8   A ToolBar control with three buttons of different types

To create an event handler for the ToolBarButton, we implement the OnClick event handler for the Toolbar control and, within it, we check which of the buttons was clicked. In the case of the dropdown button, we create event handlers for the menu items.

StatusBar and StatusBarPanel classes

The StatusBar control is used to implement Windows status bars. The status bar is usually displayed at the bottom of the window and used by applications to display various information. By default, the ShowPanels property is set to "False". In this mode, we can use the Text property to display the text in the status bar.

The following example shows how to use the Text property to track the mouse position. We add the following code at the MouseMove event handler for the form (see also Figure 10.9):

```
Protected Overrides Sub OnMouseMove(ByVal e As _
  System.Windows.Forms.MouseEventArgs)
  StatusBar1.Text = e.X & ", " & e.Y
End Sub
```

To add panels to the status bar, we set the ShowPanels properties to "True" and use the Add method of the StatusBarPanelCollection class.

The following example shows how to dynamically add panels to the StatusBar control:

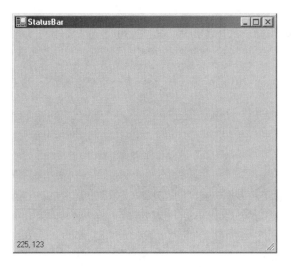

FIGURE 10.9   Using the Text property of the StatusBar control and MouseMove event handler to track the position of the mouse

```
Private Sub Button1_Click(ByVal sender As System.Object, _
  ByVal e As System.EventArgs) Handles Button1.Click
  With StatusBar1
    .ShowPanels = True
    .Panels.Add("Panel" & .Panels.Count)
  End With

End Sub
```

Each member of the Panels collection is of the StatusBarPanel type.

The SizingGrip Boolean property is used to specify if a sizing grip will be shown on the corner of the StatusBar control or not.

When one of the panels on the status bar is clicked, the PanelClick event occurs.

Earlier in this section we mentioned that the StatusBar control is usually used by applications to display various information. The following example shows how to use this control to display the status of the INS and CAPS keys (see also Figure 10.10):

```
Protected Overrides Sub OnKeyDown(ByVal e As _
  System.Windows.Forms.KeyEventArgs)

  Select Case e.KeyCode

  Case Keys.Insert
    If StatusBarPanel1.Text = "INS" Then
      StatusBarPanel1.Text = "OVR"
    Else
      StatusBarPanel1.Text = "INS"
    End If
```

```
        Case Keys.CapsLock
          If StatusBarPanel2.Text = "CAPS" Then
              StatusBarPanel2.Text = "caps"
          Else
              StatusBarPanel2.Text = "CAPS"
          End If
      End Select

      End Sub
```

FIGURE 10.10 The StatusBar control used to display the status of the INS and CAPS keys

ScrollBar class

The ScrollBar class serves as a base class for two derived classes that implement horizontal and vertical scroll bars – the HScrollBar and VScrollBar classes, respectively. The ScrollBar class provides common properties and events that are shared by its derived classes (see Figure 10.11).

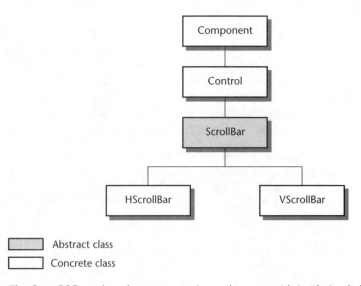

FIGURE 10.11 The ScrollBar class shares properties and events with its derived classes

The Minimum and Maximum properties of an Integer type are used to adjust the value range of the scroll bar. The default value of the Minimum property is 0. By changing this value, we can set the lower limit of values of the scrollable range. The Maximum property has the default value set to 100. By changing this value, we can set the upper limit of values of the scrollable range.

The SmallChange and LargeChange properties of an Integer type are used to adjust the distance the scroll box (thumb) moves. The default value of the SmallChange property is 0. This value is added to or subtracted from the Value property when the scroll box is moved a small distance. The LargeChange property is set to 10. By changing the value of this property, we change the value that is added to or subtracted from the Value property when the scroll box is moved a large distance.

When the Value property has changed – either programmatically or as a result of a Scroll event – the ValueChanged event occurs.

In most cases, we use scroll bars with container controls that do not have their own scroll bars to implement scrolling functionality. Another way to use scroll bars is to enter numeric data. The following example shows how to use the horizontal scroll bar to enter values in the 0–100 range. All we need to do is attach the following code to the Scroll event handler (see also Figure 10.12):

```
'----------------------------------------------------------
' Vertical Scroll Bar control demo
'----------------------------------------------------------


Private Sub HScrollBar1_Scroll(ByVal sender As System.Object, _
  ByVal e As System.Windows.Forms.ScrollEventArgs) _
  Handles HScrollBar1.Scroll

    TextBox1.Text = HScrollBar1.Value


End Sub
```

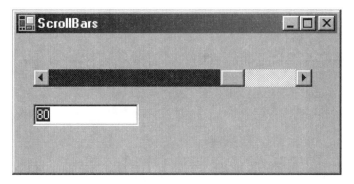

FIGURE 10.12 Using a horizontal scroll bar to enter numbers in a range

Note that, to enter numeric data, we can also use the `TrackBar` control discussed below.

MonthCalendar class

The `MonthCalendar` control allows users to visually select a date. This control is highly configurable and allows us to fine-tine it using several properties to suit our date and time input needs. Let's look at the properties and methods available in the `MonthCalendar` control.

● **AnnuallyBoldedDates** This array of `DateTime` objects indicates which annual days are shown in bold. The following example shows how to use this property to set bold dates for the first day of each month (see also Figure 10.13):

```
'---------------------------------------------------------
' MonthCalendar control demo
'---------------------------------------------------------

Dim BoldDates() As DateTime = _
  {New DateTime(2001,  1, 1), _
   New DateTime(2001,  2, 1), _
   New DateTime(2001,  3, 1), _
   New DateTime(2001,  4, 1), _
   New DateTime(2001,  5, 1), _
   New DateTime(2001,  6, 1), _
   New DateTime(2001,  7, 1), _
   New DateTime(2001,  8, 1), _
   New DateTime(2001,  9, 1), _
   New DateTime(2001, 10, 1), _
   New DateTime(2001, 11, 1), _
   New DateTime(2001, 12, 1)}

  ...


  Private Sub Button1_Click(ByVal sender As System.Object, _
    ByVal e As System.EventArgs) Handles Button1.Click

    MonthCalendar1.AnnuallyBoldedDates = BoldDates

  End Sub
```

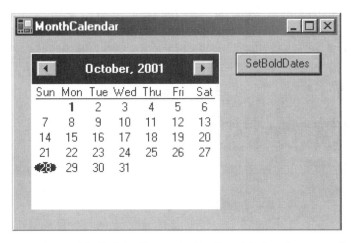

FIGURE 10.13 Using AnnuallyBoldedDates in the MonthCalendar control to highlight the first day of each month

- **BoldedDates** This property (the array of DateTime objects) allows us to find which dates are currently shown in bold.
- **CalendarDimensions** We use this property (of a Size type) to set or get the number of columns and rows of months displayed. The default value of this property is 1,1, meaning that only one month is displayed. To show a six-month calendar, we set this property to 3,2 or 2,3. The value of 2,1 shows two months in a row; 1,2 two months in a column. The example shown in Figure 10.14 shows a six-month calendar (the CalendarDimensions property is set to 3,2).

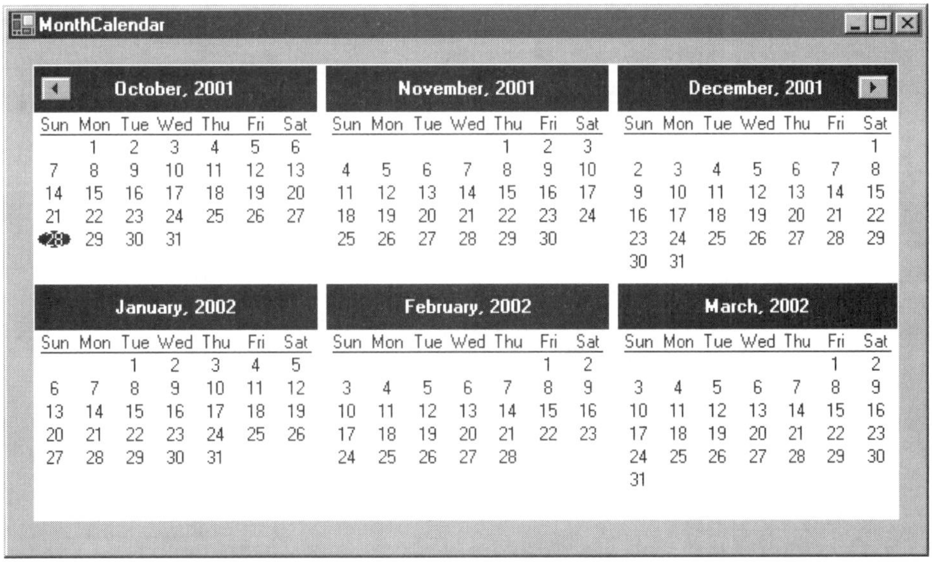

FIGURE 10.14 Using the CalendarDimensions property, this six-month calendar has been created

● **FirstDayOfWeek** Use this property (of a **Day** type) to get or set the first day of the week displayed in the control. By default, this is **Sunday** (for United States culture settings), but we can change this value to start the week from **Monday** (see Figure 10.15).

FIGURE 10.15 The FirstDayOfWeek property set to Monday

● **MinDate and MaxDate** We use these properties (of a **DateTime** type) to set the range of dates. For example, the following code will limit date selections to those within the year 2001:

```
Me.MonthCalendar1.MinDate = New Date(2001, 1, 1)
Me.MonthCalendar1.MaxDate = New Date(2001, 12, 31)
```

● **MaxSelectionCount** Use this **Integer** property to specify the maximum number of days that can be selected.

● **MonthlyBoldedDates** This property is an array of **DateTime** objects that specifies monthly days to be shown in bold. The following example shows how to make the first, fifteenth, and twenty-fifth of each month bold (see also Figure 10.16):

```
'----------------------------------------------------------
' MonthCalendar control demo
'----------------------------------------------------------

Dim BoldDates() As DateTime = _
  {New DateTime(2001, 1, 1), _
   New DateTime(2001, 1, 15), _
   New DateTime(2001, 1, 25)}

...

Me.MonthCalendar1.MonthlyBoldedDates = BoldDates
```

FIGURE 10.16 The `MonthlyBoldedDates` property has been used to highlight three days in each month

● **SelectionStart, SelectionEnd and SelectionRange** Use these properties to get or set the start and end date of the selected range of dates and to get a selected range of dates. The `SelectionStart` and `SelectionEnd` properties are of the `DateTime` type, while the `SelectionRange` property is of the `SelectionRange` type. The following example shows how to use the `SelectionStart` and `SelectionEnd` properties (see also Figure 10.17):

```
'-----------------------------------------------------------
' MonthCalendar control demo
'-----------------------------------------------------------

  Private Sub Button1_Click_1(ByVal sender As System.Object, _
    ByVal e As System.EventArgs) Handles Button1.Click

    With MonthCalendar1
      TextBox1.Text  = "Start : " & .SelectionStart & ControlChars.CrLf
      TextBox1.Text += "End    : " & .SelectionEnd
    End With

  End Sub
```

● **ShowToday** If set, the date specified by the `TodayDate` property is shown at the bottom of the control.

● **ShowTodayCircle** If set, the date specified by the `TodayDate` property is circled. Figure 10.18 shows how the different values of the `ShowToday` and `ShowTodayCircle` properties affect the display of the `MonthCalendar` control.

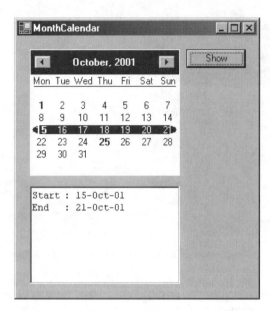

FIGURE 10.17 Using SelectionStart and SelectionEnd, a range of dates can be chosen

FIGURE 10.18 The effects of the different values of the ShowToday and ShowTodayCircle properties

● **ShowWeekNumbers** If set, week numbers (1–52) will be displayed to the left of each row of days, as shown in Figure 10.19. By default, week numbers are not shown.

FIGURE 10.19 With ShowWeekNumbers, the weeks of the year are numbered

● **SingleMonthSize** This property (of a Size type) returns the minimum size to display one month of the calendar.

● **TitleBackColor** Use this property (of a Color type) to specify the background color of the calendar's title.

● **TitleForeColor** Use this property (of a Color type) to specify the foreground color of the calendar's title.

● **TodayDate** Use this property (of a DateTime type) to get or set today's date.

● **TodayDateSet** This value indicates if the TodayDate value has been explicitly set.

● **TrailingForeColor** Use this property (of a Color type) to specify the color of days that are a part of months not fully displayed in the control. To hide such days – that is, make the MonthCalendar control display only full months – we can assign the value of this property to the value of the control's BackColor property, as shown in Figure 10.20.

The MonthCalendar control supports several methods that can be used to manipulate its contents. Here is a list of some of the important methods of this control.

● **AddAnuallyBoldedDate**(*DateTime*) **method** Adds a day that will be displayed in bold on an annual basis, such as your birthday.

● **AddBoldedDate**(*DateTime*) **method** Adds a day that will be displayed in bold in a month.

● **AddMonthlyBoldedDate**(*DateTime*) **method** Adds a day that will be displayed in bold on a monthly basis.

FIGURE 10.20 MonthCalendar displaying a full month only

- **RemoveXXX** methods Used to remove bolded days settings. There are methods to remove all annually bolded dates, all bolded dates, all monthly bolded dates, an annually bolded date, and a monthly bolded date.
- **GetDisplayRange(**Boolean**)** method Used to get date information for low and high limits of the displayed dates.
- **SetCalendarDimensions(**Integer, Integer**)** method Sets the number of columns and rows of months to display. This is the same as specifying a new value of the CalendarDimensions property.
- **SetDate(**DateTime**)** method Sets a date as the current selected date.
- **SetSelectionRange(**DateTime, DateTime**)** method Sets the selected dates for a month calendar to the specified date range. The following example shows how to use this method (see also Figure 10.20):

```
'---------------------------------------------------------
' MonthCalendar control demo
'---------------------------------------------------------

Private Sub Button1_Click_1(ByVal sender As System.Object, _
ByVal e As System.EventArgs) Handles Button1.Click
With MonthCalendar1

  .SelectionRange = New SelectionRange( _
  Convert.ToDateTime("2001/10/01"), _
  Convert.ToDateTime("2001/10/07"))

  TextBox1.Text  = "Start : " & .SelectionStart & ControlChars.CrLf
  TextBox1.Text += "End   : " & .SelectionEnd
End With

End Sub
```

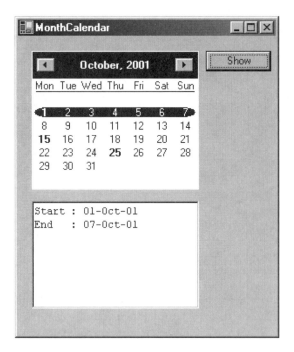

FIGURE 10.21 The SetSelectionRange (*DateTime*, *DateTime*) method in action

● **UpdateBoldedDates**() **method** Repaints the bolded dates after updates in the list of these.

When the date in the MonthCalendar control changes, the DateChanged event occurs and when a date is selected, the DateSelected event occurs.

Another way to provide users with the ability to select date and time is the DateTimePicker control, which is discussed in the next section.

DateTimePicker class

The DateTimePicker control can be used to allow users to select a date from a list of dates and times. To select dates, we should specify the value of the Format property (of the DateTimePickerFormat type) as either DateTimePickerFormat.Long or DateTimePickerFormat.Short. By setting the value of this property to DateTimePickerFormat.Time, we can select a time. Note that this also requires us to set the ShowUpDown property to "True" – otherwise the date picker will still be there when we click on the combo box down arrow. Figure 10.22 shows the DateTimePicker control in various formats – Long (this is the default format), Short, and Time.

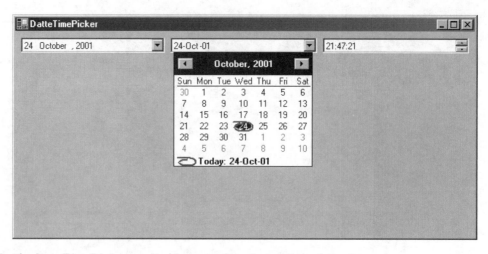

FIGURE 10.22 The DateTimePicker control in Long, Short, and Time formats

When we set the value of the Format property to DateTimePickerFormat.Custom, we can specify our own format. For example, to specify the date as day of the week, date, month, and year, we set the following value of the CustomFormat property:

```
Me.DateTimePicker1.CustomFormat = "dddd dd MMMM yyyy"
```

To set the range of dates and times, we use the MaxDate and MinDate properties (of the DateTime type). For example, the following code will limit possible date selections to within the year 2001:

```
Me.DateTimePicker1.MinDate = New Date(2001, 1, 1)
Me.DateTimePicker1.MaxDate = New Date(2001, 12, 31)
```

To get the selected date, we use the Value property (of the DateTime type). As you will remember from Chapter 5, this structure contains several properties to get parts of the date – Month, Day, Year, and DayOfWeek. For the time part, we can use the Hour, Minute, Second, and Millisecond properties. The following example shows how to use date-related properties of the DateTime structure. Add the following code to the ValueChanged event handler of the DateTimePicker control (see also Figure 10.23):

```
'--------------------------------------------------------
' DateTime control demo
'--------------------------------------------------------

Private Sub DateTimePicker1_ValueChanged(ByVal sender As _

  System.Object, ByVal e As System.EventArgs) _
  Handles DateTimePicker1.ValueChanged
  With (DateTimePicker1.Value)
```

```
     TextBox1.Text  = "Date  : " & .Day.ToString & ControlChars.CrLf
     TextBox1.Text += "Month : " & MonthName(.Month) & ControlChars.CrLf
     TextBox1.Text += "Year  : " & .Year.ToString & ControlChars.CrLf
     TextBox1.Text += .DayOfWeek.ToString
   End With

 End Sub
```

FIGURE 10.23 Selecting dates using the properties of the DateTime structure

Note that to get the entire value from the control we can also use the Text property.

UpDownBase controls

The UpDownBase class serves to provide a control that consists of a text box and a small vertical scroll bar, which is usually called a spinner control. The UpDownBase class allows us to limit the list of values a user may select, and provides more intuitive ways to select these values – either by clicking the up or down buttons or entering the appropriate type of value directly into the text box.

To allow users to select values with the arrow keys, we need to set the InterceptArrowKeys property to "True". Clicking the up and down buttons is handled by the UpButton() and DownButton() methods.

If we want to restrict users to the values contained in the list, we should set the ReadOnly property to "True". The vertical scroll bar can be placed either at the right or left side of the text box – this is controlled by the UpDownAlign property (of a LeftRightAlignment type).

The UpDownBase class serves as a base class for the two controls – the NumericUpDown control, which is used to display numerical values, and DomainUpDown control, used to display string values.

The NumericUpDown control displays the numerical values in the range, defined by the Minimum and Maximum properties (of a Decimal type). The Increment property (of a Decimal type) indicates how the Value property should be incremented or decremented with each click on an up or down button. To format the numerical display, we can use the DecimalPlaces, Hexadecimal, and ThousandsSeparator properties.

The DomainUpDown control displays values, stored in the Items collection. Its contents can be sorted – this is defined by the value of the Sorted property. The SelectedItem and SelectedIndex properties allow us to find the currently selected value.

ProgressBar class

The ProgressBar control is used to indicate the progress of an action. It does this by displaying an appropriate number of rectangles on a horizontal bar. The bar is filled when the action is complete. The Value property contains the current progress value – it can be within the Minimum and Maximum range.

The following example shows how to use the Timer control (discussed later in this chapter) to manipulate the values of the ProgressBar control, imitating an operation that takes some time to complete (see also Figure 10.24):

```
'----------------------------------------------------------
' ProgressBar control demo
'----------------------------------------------------------

Private Sub Button1_Click(ByVal sender As System.Object, _
  ByVal e As System.EventArgs) Handles Button1.Click

    Timer1.Start()

End Sub

Private Sub Timer1_Tick(ByVal sender As System.Object, _

  ByVal e As System.EventArgs) Handles Timer1.Tick
  With ProgressBar1
   .Value += 1
   If .Value = .Maximum Then
    Timer1.Stop()
   End If
  End With

End Sub
```

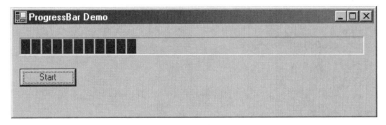

FIGURE 10.24 Using the `Timer` control with the `ProgressBar` control to show that an action is taking time to do

TrackBar class

The `TrackBar` control is used to provide a way to change the values visually. This control contains two parts – the thumb (which is the moving part of the control) and the tick marks. The position of the thumb corresponds to the `Value` property, which can hold values within the `Minimum` and `Maximum` range.

The `TickFrequency` property (of the `Integer` type) is used to specify the spacing of ticks. They can be placed above or below the control, at both sides or be made invisible – this is managed via the `TickStyle` property (of the `TickStyle` type). The possible values for this property are as follows.

- **Both** Indicates that tick marks are located on both sides of the control.
- **BottomRight** Indicates that tick marks are located at the bottom of a horizontal control or on the right side of a vertical control.
- **None** Indicates that no tick marks appear in the control.
- **TopLeft** Indicates that tick marks are located at the top of a horizontal control or on the left of a vertical control.

The `SmallChange` and the `LargeChange` properties (of the `Integer` type) are used to specify the number of positions the thumb moves in response to left or right arrow key presses (this is called a "small change", with the default value of 1) or page up or page down key presses (this is called a "large change" with the default value of 5).

When the `Value` property changes, the `ValueChanged` event occurs.

The following example shows how to use the `TrackBar` control to create a "color picker" application (see also Figure 10.25):

```
'-----------------------------------------------------------
' TrackBar control demo
'-----------------------------------------------------------

Imports System.Drawing
Public Class Form1
  Inherits System.Windows.Forms.Form
```

```
Public Sub New()
'Add any initialization after the InitializeComponent() call
  UpdateColorValue()
End Sub
...


Sub UpdateColorValue()
 Panel1.BackColor = Color.FromArgb(TrackBar1.Value, TrackBar2.Value, _
  TrackBar3.Value)
 Label1.Text = "RGB = " & TrackBar1.Value & "," & _
  TrackBar2.Value & "," & TrackBar3.Value
End Sub

Private Sub ValueChanged(ByVal sender As Object, _
 ByVal e As System.EventArgs) _
 Handles TrackBar1.ValueChanged, TrackBar2.ValueChanged, _
  TrackBar3.ValueChanged
 UpdateColorValue()
 End Sub
End Class
```

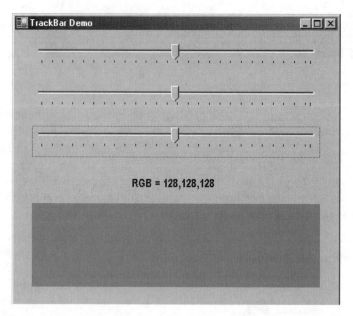

FIGURE 10.25 Using the TrackBar control to make a color picker application

In this application, we use three TrackBar controls (for the red, green, and blue parts of the color), the Panel control, to show the current code selection, and the Label control to show the values of the selected color. All updates are implemented in the UpdateColorValue method, which is called at the Form initialization phase, as well as from the event handler for each TrackBar control.

PictureBox class

The PictureBox class is used to display graphics in bitmap, GIF, JPEG, icon, or metafile formats. The Image property (of the Image type) specifies the picture, while the SizeMode property (of the PictureBoxSizeMode type) controls the appearance of the image – normal (the image is placed in the control's upper left corner), stretched (the size of the image is adjusted to the size of the control), autosized (the size of the control is adjusted to the size of the image), or centered (the image is centered within the control).

Figure 10.26 shows how various values of the SizeMode property affect the appearance and placement of the image within the PictureBox control.

The ClientSize property (of the Size type) controls the size of the PictureBox. The BorderStyle property (of the BorderStyle type) is used to specify the border around the control.

To load the image into the PictureBox control at runtime, use the following code:

```
PictureBox1.Image = Image.FromFile("c:\book\ch05\dotnet.gif")
```

To clear the contents of the PictureBox control, use the code below:

```
PictureBox1.Image = Nothing
```

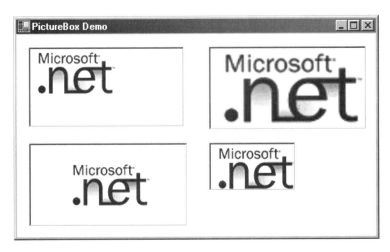

FIGURE 10.26 The various values of the SizeMode property can be used to change the appearance and placing of images

Timer class

The `Timer` control implements a timer. Its sole purpose is to raise an event at user-defined intervals. Note that this control is designed for single-threaded environments and requires that the user code has message processing operating at the same thread. Here is a brief description of the `Timer` control properties, methods, and events.

- **Enabled** This `Boolean` property indicates whether or not the timer is enabled.
- **Interval** Sets or gets the time between timer ticks in milliseconds as an `Integer` value.
- **Start()** **method** Starts the timer. The timer can also be started by setting the value of the `Enabled` property to "True".
- **Stop()** **method** Stops the timer. A timer can be also stopped by setting the value of the `Enabled` property to "False".
- **Tick** This event occurs when the time – specified by the `Interval` property – has elapsed.

The following example shows how to use the `Timer` control:

```
'--------------------------------------------------------
' Timer control demo
'--------------------------------------------------------

Public Class Form1
  Inherits System.Windows.Forms.Form

  Dim Count As Byte
  Private Sub Timer1_Tick(ByVal sender As System.Object, _
    ByVal e As System.EventArgs) Handles Timer1.Tick
    Count += 1
    Label1.Text = Count
  End Sub

  Private Sub Button1_Click(ByVal sender As System.Object, _
    ByVal e As System.EventArgs) Handles Button1.Click
    Timer1.Start()
  End Sub

  Private Sub Button2_Click(ByVal sender As System.Object, _
    ByVal e As System.EventArgs) Handles Button2.Click
    Timer1.Stop()
  End Sub
End Class
```

HelpProvider class

This class implements the HelpProvider control, which provides pop-up or online help for other controls. There are two ways to use this control in Windows forms applications.

The simplest way is to enable the Help button on the right side of the Window caption. To do this, we need to set the HelpButton property to "True" and the MinimizeBox and MaximizeBox properties to "False". Note that we can have either a help button or both "min" and "max" buttons, but never all three – or any other combination for that matter.

Next, we add the HelpProvider control to our application. This enables the HelpString or the HelpProvider property for each control, and we can specify the help text as the value of this property. For example:

```
Dim HelpProvider1 = New System.Windows.Forms.HelpProvider()

. . .


HelpProvider1.SetHelpString(Button1, "Main Application Button")
HelpProvider1.SetShowHelp(Button1, True)


. . .
```

Now if we run our application, we can click on the Help button, then on the control in question. Its Help string will be displayed just over it (see Figure 10.27).

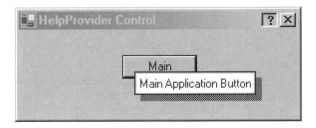

FIGURE 10.27 Using the HelpProvider control and Help button to display the button's Help string

A more complicated way is to use the separate help file. Currently, there is support for help files in the HTMLHelp 1.x, HTMLHelp 2.0, and HTML formats. In the example below, we use the help file named C:\WINNT\Help\nthelp.chm – it is a part of the Windows help system. We specify the name of the file in the HelpNamespace property of the HelpProvider control:

```
HelpProvider1.HelpNamespace = "C:\WINNT\Help\nthelp.chm"
```

Next, we specify either the HelpKeyword property or the HelpNavigator property. If we set the HelpKeyword property, we will get the exact help screen associated with this keyword. For example:

```
HelpProvider1.SetHelpKeyword(Form1, "overview")
HelpProvider1.SetShowHelp(Form1, True)
```

If we use the `HelpNavigator` property, we can specify one of the following values.

● **AssociatedIndex** Displays the topic for the specified index.

● **Find** Displays the search page.

● **Index** Displays an index.

● **KeywordIndex** displays the keyword for the specified index.

● **TableOfContents** Displays the table of contents of the HTML 1.0 help file.

● **Topic** Displays the topic.

If we want to use the help file, implemented as an HTML page, we should create topics as named links:

```
<H2><A NAME="ABOUT">About</A></H2>
```

and then specify the names as keywords (the name of the anchor corresponds to the string registered with the help provider).

Another way to provide help in Windows forms applications is to use the `ToolTip` class, described in the next section.

ToolTip class

This class is used to display short, descriptive text when the user points at other controls. The `ToolTip` class provides a `ToolTip` property for any other control on a Web form. We use the `SetToolTip` method to specify the `ToolTip` text for other controls. In order for the `ToolTip` to appear, the `Active` property should be set to "True". Other properties and methods of the `ToolTip` class include the following.

● **AutomaticDelay** Specifies the number of milliseconds before the `ToolTip` text appears as an `Integer` value.

● **AutoPopDelay** Specifies the number of milliseconds that the `ToolTip` text is visible after the mouse pointer is placed on the control as an `Integer` value.

● **InitialDelay** Specifies the initial delay for the `ToolTip` text as an `Integer` value.

● **ReshowDelay** Specifies the number of milliseconds that it takes to redisplay the `ToolTip` text as an `Integer` value when the mouse pointer moves from one region of the control to another.

● **ShowAlways** Indicates that the `ToolTip` text will be shown even if the control is not active.

● **GetToolTip(Control) method** Returns the `ToolTip` text for the specified control.

● **RemoveAll() method** Clears all `ToolTip` texts.

The following example shows how to specify the `ToolTip` text for the controls on the form programmatically (see also Figure 10.28):

```
With ToolTip1

  .SetToolTip(Button1, "Button1")
  .SetToolTip(TextBox1, "TextBox1")
  .SetToolTip(Label1, "Label1")

End With
```

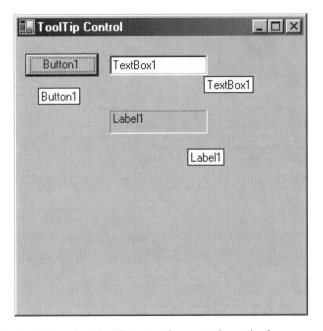

FIGURE 10.28 Specifying the ToolTip text for controls on the form

Another interesting possibility is using the ToolTip and StatusBar controls to display explanatory text. Here is an example for the Button control. To do this, we should intercept two events – MouseHover, which is fired when the mouse is over the control, and MouseLeave, which indicates that the mouse leaves the control (see also Figure 10.29):

```
Private Sub Button1_MouseHover(ByVal sender As Object, _
  ByVal e As System.EventArgs) Handles Button1.MouseHover

  ToolTip1.Active = False
  StatusBarPanel1.Text = ToolTip1.GetToolTip(sender)

End Sub
```

```
Private Sub Button1_MouseLeave(ByVal sender As Object, _
  ByVal e As System.EventArgs) Handles Button1.MouseLeave

  StatusBarPanel1.Text = ""
  ToolTip1.Active = True

End Sub
```

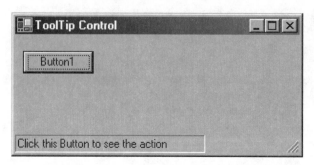

FIGURE 10.29 Using ToolTip and StatusBar controls to show explanatory text for a button

Note that in the example above, we have disabled the ToolTip text by setting the ToolTip1.Active property to "False". Remove this line, as well as the line that restored the ToolTip display, to show ToolTip text both for the control and in the StatusBar.

ErrorProvider class

This class provides a way to associate an error message with the control. To do so we add the ErrorProvider control to our form and create a Validating event handler for the control we want to validate. As soon as our control loses the focus, its Validating event handler will receive the control and, in its code, we call the SetError method of the ErrorProvider class. Here is an example (see also Figure 10.30):

```
Private Sub TextBox1_Validating(ByVal sender As Object, _
  ByVal e As System.ComponentModel.CancelEventArgs) _
  Handles TextBox1.Validating

  If TextBox1.Text.ToUpper = "JOHN DOE" Then
   ErrorProvider1.SetError(TextBox1, "Please use real names")
  Else
   ErrorProvider1.SetError(TextBox1, "")
  End If

End Sub
```

FIGURE 10.30 Using the `ErrorProvider` class to associate an error message with a control

By changing the properties of the `ErrorProvider` control we can make it more suitable for our tasks. Here is the list of the main properties of the `ErrorProvider` control.

- **`BlinkRate`** Specifies the rate at which the error icon flashes as an `Integer` value.
- **`BlinkStyle`** Indicates when the error icon should blink. Possible values of this property (of an `ErrorBlinkStyle` type) are `AlwaysBlink` (the error message will also blink), `NeverBlink`, and `BlinkIfDifferentError`. The last value specifies that the icon blinks when the icon is already displayed and a new error string is set for the control.
- **`ContainerControl`** Specifies the parent control (of a `ContainerControl` type) for the `ErrorProvider` control. This property is used to specify where the error message will be shown.
- **`Icon`** Specifies the icon to be displayed.

To specify the error description string for the particular control, we use the `SetError` method. Using this method with the empty string clears the error message. To align the icon relative to the control, we use the `SetIconAlignment(Control, ErrorIconAlignment)` method. Possible arrangements are `BottomLeft`, `BottomRight`, `MiddleLeft`, `MiddleRight`, `TopLeft`, and `TopRight`. To set the amount of extra space to leave between the specified control and the error icon, we use the `SetIconPadding(Control, Integer)` method. To show an icon directly in the field, use the following code (see also Figure 10.31):

```
ErrorProvider1.SetIconAlignment(TextBox1, _
  ErrorIconAlignment.MiddleRight)
ErrorProvider1.SetIconPadding(TextBox1, _
  ErrorProvider1.Icon.Size.Width-4)
```

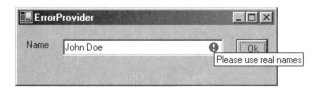

FIGURE 10.31 Visual aspects, such as alignment of the error icon and space between it and text, can be set

The value `ErrorProvider1.Icon.Size.Width-4` in the code above moves an icon four pixels "inside" the text box.

NotifyIcon class

This class implements the Windows forms `NotifyIcon` control, which displays an icon in the status area of the Windows taskbar (it used to be called Windows system tray) for the processes that run in the background and do not have user interfaces. The `NotifyIcon` class has a small set of properties.

- **ContextMenu** Specifies the context menu for the tray icon as a `ContextMenu` object.
- **Icon** Specifies the icon as an `Icon` object.
- **Text** Specifies the `ToolTip` text displayed when the mouse hovers over a system tray icon.
- **Visible** If set, the icon is visible in the Windows system tray.

After we have initialized the `NotifyIcon` class and executed our application, its icon will be visible in the Windows system tray (see Figure 10.32).

FIGURE 10.32 The `NotifyIcon` control's icon appears once it has been initialized and the application has been executed

When we right-click on the tray icon, its context menu appears and we can execute commands implemented in the main application (see Figure 10.33).

FIGURE 10.33 Right-clicking on the tray icon makes its context menu appear

As the context menu is implemented with the `ContextMenu` class, we can create the following event handlers for it:

```
Private Sub MenuItem1_Click(ByVal sender As System.Object, _
  ByVal e As System.EventArgs) Handles MenuItem1.Click

  MsgBox("General Info Requested", MsgBoxStyle.Information)

End Sub

Private Sub MenuItem3_Click(ByVal sender As System.Object, _
  ByVal e As System.EventArgs) Handles MenuItem3.Click

  MsgBox("Video Info Requested", MsgBoxStyle.Information)

End Sub

Private Sub MenuItem4_Click(ByVal sender As System.Object, _
  ByVal e As System.EventArgs) Handles MenuItem4.Click

  MsgBox("Memory Info Requested", MsgBoxStyle.Information)

End Sub

Private Sub MenuItem5_Click(ByVal sender As System.Object, _
  ByVal e As System.EventArgs) Handles MenuItem5.Click

  MsgBox("Storage Info Requested", MsgBoxStyle.Information)

End Sub
```

This ends our discussion of Windows forms controls. The next topic in this chapter is common dialog boxes.

10.3 Common dialog boxes

The System.Windows.Forms namespace contains controls that implement common dialog boxes, which are built-in dialog boxes used to select colors, fonts, open and save files, as well as perform printing, print preview, and printer setup. The following is a list of controls that represent standard dialog boxes.

- **ColorDialog** Used to select color from a palette or add customized colors to this palette.
- **FontDialog** Used to select fonts from ones currently installed on the system.
- **OpenFileDialog** Used to open files.

- **SaveFileDialog** Used to save files.
- **PrintDialog** Used to select a printer, pages to print, and other printer-related settings.
- **PageSetupDialog** Used to set page details for printing.
- **PrintPreviewDialog** Used to preview the document as it will appear when it is printed.

Several common dialog controls are based on the CommonDialog class, as shown in Figure 10.34.

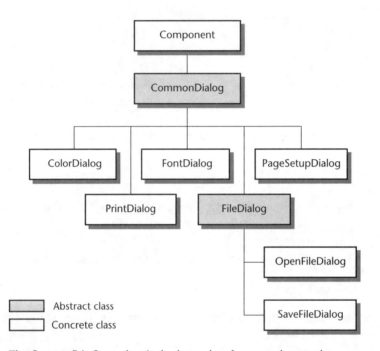

FIGURE 10.34 The CommonDialog class is the base class for several controls

The CommonDialog abstract class defines the basic functionality of its derived classes. For example, all derived classes should implement the ShowDialog() method to run a common dialog box via a call to the RunDialog() method. It also provides the HelpRequest event, which occurs when the user clicks on the help button, and the OnHelpRequest method, which raises this event.

In the following sections, we will look at each of the standard dialog box controls in more detail.

ColorDialog class

The `ColorDialog` control is used to select colors from a palette or add customized colors to it. The following example shows the minimal code required to use the `ColorDialog` control (see also Figure 10.35):

```
'----------------------------------------------------------
' ColorDialog demo
'----------------------------------------------------------

Private Sub Button1_Click(ByVal sender As System.Object, _
  ByVal e As System.EventArgs) Handles Button1.Click

  If ColorDialog1.ShowDialog() = DialogResult.Ok Then
      Panel1.BackColor = ColorDialog1.Color
  End If

End Sub
```

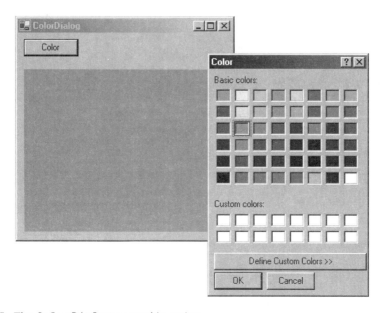

FIGURE 10.35 The `ColorDialog` control in action

Note that, in this case, users have access to customized colors. If we set the `AllowFullOpen` property to "`False`", the "`Define Custom Colors`" button is disabled and the user is restricted to the predefined colors in the palette. By setting the `SolidColorOnly` property to "`True`" we disable selection of dithered colors. Setting the `AnyColor` property to "`True`" shows all available colors. To set the initial selected color, assign an appropriate value to the `Color` property (of the `Color` type).

FontDialog class

The FontDialog control is used to select fonts that are currently installed on the system. The following example shows the minimal code required to use the FontDialog control (see Figure 10.36):

```
'-------------------------------------------------------
' FontDialog demo
'-------------------------------------------------------

Private Sub Button1_Click(ByVal sender As System.Object, _
  ByVal e As System.EventArgs) Handles Button1.Click

With FontDialog1
  If .ShowDialog() <> DialogResult.Cancel then
    Label1.Font = .Font
  End If

End With
```

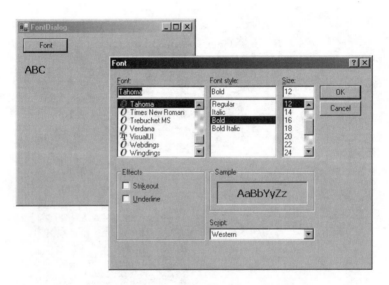

FIGURE 10.36 The FontDialog control up and running

The default dialog box contains list boxes for font, font style, size, check boxes for strikeout and underline effects, a selection box for scripts, and a sample preview. The following list shows Boolean properties of the FontDialog control, which can be used to change its appearance.

- **AllowScriptChange** If set to "True", users can change the character set specified in the script combo box.
- **AllowSimulations** If set to "True", the GDI font simulations are allowed.
- **AllowVectorFonts** If set to "True", vector font selections are allowed.
- **AllowVerticalFonts** If set to "True", vertical fonts are shown.
- **FixedPitchOnly** If set to "True", only fixed-pitch fonts can be selected.
- **MaxSize** Specifies the maximum point size that can be selected.
- **MinSize** Specifies the minimum point size that can be selected.
- **ScriptsOnly** If set to "True", only ANSI character sets can be selected.
- **ShowApply** If set to "True", the apply button will be shown.
- **ShowColor** If set to "True", the color choice will be displayed.
- **ShowEffects** If set to "True", users can select strikethrough, underline, and text color options.
- **ShowHelp** If set to "True", the help button will be shown.

The following example shows a customized FontDialog control that allows only the selection of specified font sizes, no vector fonts or script change, allows font color selection, and contains an apply button to preview the selected font (see Figure 10.37):

```
'-------------------------------------------------------
' FontDialog demo
'-------------------------------------------------------


Private Sub Button1_Click(ByVal sender As System.Object, _
  ByVal e As System.EventArgs) Handles Button1.Click

  With FontDialog1
    .MinSize = 10
    .MaxSize = 18
    .AllowVectorFonts = False
    .AllowScriptChange = False
    .ShowApply = True
    .ShowColor = True
    If .ShowDialog() <> DialogResult.Cancel Then
      Label1.Font = .Font
      Label1.ForeColor = .Color
    End If
  End With


End Sub
```

```
Private Sub FontDialog1_Apply(ByVal sender As Object, _
 ByVal e As System.EventArgs) Handles FontDialog1.Apply

  Label1.Font = FontDialog1.Font
  Label1.ForeColor = FontDialog1.Color


End Sub
```

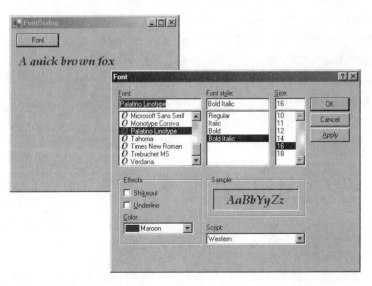

FIGURE 10.37 This customized FontDialog control gives a choice of specific font sizes and, color, and has an apply button

The Font property of the FontDialog control contains various characteristics of the font. This can be seen if we change our code to this:

```
Private Sub Button1_Click(ByVal sender As System.Object, _
 ByVal e As System.EventArgs) Handles Button1.Click

 With FontDialog1
 If .ShowDialog() <> DialogResult.Cancel then
   Label1.Text = .Font.ToString
 End If

 End With
End Sub
```

If we run this code, we will see something like:

```
[Font: Name=Tahoma, Size=12, Units=3, GdiCharSet=0,
 GdiVerticalFont=False]
```

displayed in the Label control.

FileDialog controls

FileDialog controls are based on the FileDialog class, which provides the basic functionality for the OpenFileDialog and SaveFileDialog controls. This class contains the following properties, which are common to both dialog boxes.

- **AddExtension** If set to "True", the dialog box automatically adds an extension to a file name if no extension is given.
- **CheckFileExists** If set to "True", the dialog box shows a warning message if the file specified by a user does not exist.
- **CheckPathExists** If set to "True", the dialog box shows a warning message if the path specified by a user does not exist.
- **DefaultExt** Specifies the default file extension.
- **DereferenceLinks** If set to "True", the dialog box returns the file location for the selected shortcut (.LNK) file. Setting this property to "False" returns the shortcut file itself.
- **FileName** Specifies the selected file name.
- **FileNames** Specifies the selected file names.
- **Filter** Sets the current file name filter string.
- **FilterIndex** Specifies which filter should be selected.
- **InitialDirectory** Specifies the initial directory for the dialog box.
- **RestoreDirectory** If set to "True", the dialog box restores the current directory before closing.
- **ShowHelp** If set to "True", the help button is shown in the dialog box.
- **Title** Specifies the dialog box title.
- **ValidateNames** If set to "True", the dialog box will accept only valid Win32 file names.

The FileOk event occurs when the user presses the open or save button.

OpenFileDialog class

The OpenFileDialog control is used to select files to open. The following example shows the minimal code required to use the OpenFileDialog control:

```
Private Sub Button1_Click(ByVal sender As System.Object, _
 ByVal e As System.EventArgs) Handles Button1.Click

 With OpenFileDialog1
  If .ShowDialog <> DialogResult.Cancel Then
   Label1.Text = .FileName
  End If
 End With

End Sub
```

If, for example, we want to allow users to select multiple text files, we need to extend our code as is shown below (see also Figure 10.38):

```
Private Sub Button1_Click(ByVal sender As System.Object, _
 ByVal e As System.EventArgs) Handles Button1.Click

  With OpenFileDialog1
   .Multiselect = True
   .Filter = "Text files (*.txt)|*.txt"
   If .ShowDialog <> DialogResult.Cancel Then
    ListBox1.Items.AddRange(.FileNames)
   End If
  End With

End Sub
```

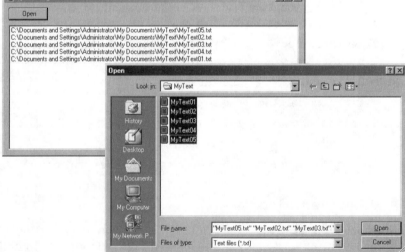

FIGURE 10.38 Selecting several files

The SaveFileDialog control is used to select the file name under which to save your data. We will look at this class next.

SaveFileDialog class

The SaveFileDialog control, implemented by the SaveFileDialog class, is used to select files to save. The CreatePrompt property indicates whether or not the dialog box prompts the user for permission to create a file if the user specifies a file that does not exist. The OverwritePrompt property indicates whether or not the Save As dialog box displays a warning if the user specifies a file name that already exists.

To open the file in read/write mode, we use the OpenFile() method, which returns a Stream object that represents a file.

The following example shows how to use the SaveFileDialog control to save the contents of the TextBox control in a file (see also Figure 10.39):

```
Private Sub Button1_Click(ByVal sender As System.Object, _
ByVal e As System.EventArgs) Handles Button1.Click

Dim FileToSave As FileStream
Dim Writer As StreamWriter

SaveFileDialog1.Filter = _
  "txt files (*.txt)|*.txt|All files (*.*)|*.*"
SaveFileDialog1.FilterIndex = 1
SaveFileDialog1.RestoreDirectory = True
SaveFileDialog1.CreatePrompt = True
SaveFileDialog1.DefaultExt = "txt"
SaveFileDialog1.FileName = "MyText"
SaveFileDialog1.InitialDirectory = "c:\"

If SaveFileDialog1.ShowDialog() = DialogResult.OK Then

  FileToSave = SaveFileDialog1.OpenFile()
  If Not (FileToSave Is Nothing) Then

  Writer = New StreamWriter(FileToSave)
  Writer.WriteLine(TextBox1.Text)
  Writer.Close()
  FileToSave.Close()

  End If
 End If


 End Sub
```

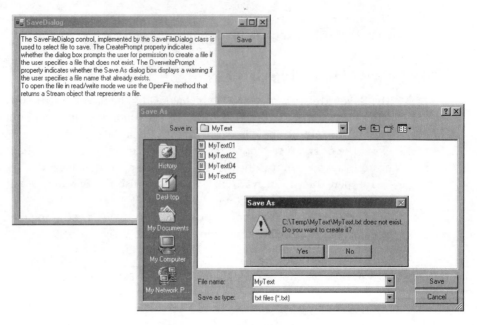

FIGURE 10.39 The SaveFileDialog control can contain helpful prompts

The last three dialog box-related classes we will cover in this section are used to help us print files.

PrintDialog class

This class implements the PrintDialog control that is used to select a printer, choose the pages to print, and specify other print-related settings. In order to use the PrintDialog control, we should create either a print job (PrintDocument class) or the settings for an individual printer (PrinterSettings class).

Here is a list of the PrintDialog class properties (see Figure 10.40).

- **AllowPrintToFile** Indicates whether or not the Print to file check box is enabled. The default value for this property is "True".

- **AllowSelection** Indicates whether or not the From... To... Page option button is enabled. The default value for this property is "False".

- **AllowSomePages** Indicates whether or not the page option button is enabled. The default value for this property is "False".

- **Document** Specifies the PrintDocument object used to obtain the PrinterSettings.

- **PrinterSettings** Specifies the PrinterSettings that will be modified by this dialog box.

- **PrintToFile** Indicates whether or not the Print to file check box is checked. The default value for this property is "False".

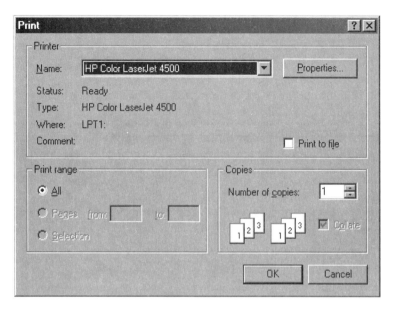

FIGURE 10.40 The PrintDialog box with various properties enabled

- **ShowHelp** Indicates whether or not the help button is displayed. The default value for this property is "False".
- **ShowNetwork** Indicates whether or not the network button is displayed. The default value for this property is "True".

The following example shows the minimal code required to launch the PrintDialog control.

```
Private Sub Button1_Click (ByVal sender As System.Object, _
    ByVal e As System.EventArgs) Handles Button1.Click

    Dim PrintDoc As New PrintDocument()
    Dim PrintDialog As New PrintDialog()

    PrintDialog.Document = PrintDoc
    PrintDoc.DefaultPageSettings.Landscape = True

    If PrintDialog.ShowDialog() = DialogResult.OK Then
        '
        ' Print here
        '
    End If

End Sub
```

PageSetupDialog **class**

This class implements the PageSetupDialog control that is used to set page preferences, such as border and margin adjustments, headers and footers, as well as orientation – portrait or landscape.

Here is a list of the PageSetupDialog class properties (see Figure 10.41).

- **AllowMargins** Indicates whether or not the margins section of the dialog box is enabled. The default value for this property is "True".
- **AllowOrientation** Indicates whether or not the orientation section of the dialog box (landscape v. portrait) is enabled. The default value for this property is "True".
- **AllowPaper** Indicates whether or not the paper section of the dialog box (paper size and paper source) is enabled. The default value for this property is "True".
- **AllowPrinter** Indicates whether or not the printer button is enabled. The default value for this property is "True".
- **Document** Specifies the PrintDocument object to get page settings from.
- **MinMargins** Indicates the minimum margins the user is allowed to select, in hundredths of an inch.
- **PageSettings** Specifies the PageSettings object that will be modified by this dialog box.
- **PrinterSettings** Indicates the printer settings the dialog box will modify when the user clicks the print button.
- **ShowHelp** Indicates whether or not the help button is displayed. The default value for this property is "True".
- **ShowNetwork** Indicates whether or not the network button is displayed. The default value for this property is "True".

The following example shows the minimal code required to launch the PageSetupDialog control.

```
Private Sub Button2_Click(ByVal sender As System.Object, _
    ByVal e As System.EventArgs) Handles Button2.Click

    Dim PageSetup As New PageSetupDialog()
    Dim PageSettings As New PageSettings()

    PageSetup.PageSettings = PageSettings
    PageSetup.ShowDialog()

End Sub
```

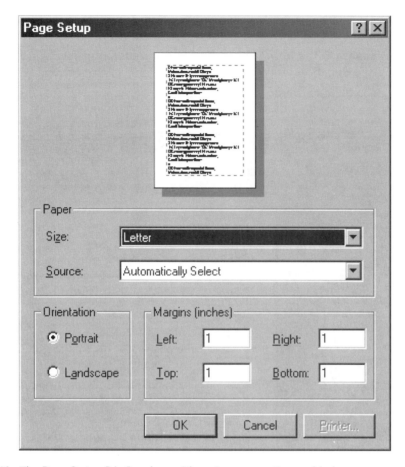

FIGURE 10.41 The PageSetupDialog box with various properties enabled

PrintPreviewDialog class

This class implements the PrintPreviewDialog control that is used to display how a PrintDocument will appear when printed.

Here is a list of the PrintPreviewDialog class properties (see Figure 10.42).

- **AutoZoom** If set to "True", resizing the control or changing the number of pages shown will automatically adjust the Zoom to make everything visible. The default value for this property is "True".

- **Columns** Specifies the number of pages displayed horizontally across the screen. The default value for this property is 1.

- **Document** Indicates the document to preview.

- **Rows** Specifies the number of pages displayed vertically down the screen. The default value for this property is 0.

- **StartPage** Specifies the page number of the upper left page. The default value for this property is 0.
- **UseAntiAlias** Indicates whether or not to use anti-aliasing (smoothing) when displaying the print preview.
- **Zoom** Indicates the zoom factor of the page preview.

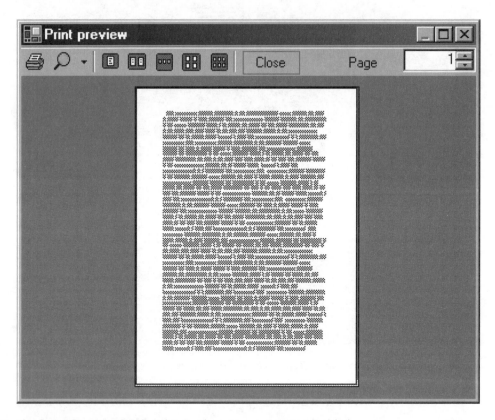

FIGURE 10.42 The PrintPreviewDialog box with various properties enabled

For more information about printing in Windows forms applications, see under Printing in the next chapter.

This ends our tour around Windows forms controls. In the next section, we will learn how to use ActiveX controls in Windows forms.

10.3 Using ActiveX controls

ActiveX controls are COM components. Such components support interfaces as well as properties, events, and methods. All this information is stored in the type library that is part of the ActiveX control, or contained in a separate .TLB file. This makes ActiveX controls very good candidates to be used within Windows forms. But Windows forms can host only Windows forms controls that are derived from the `System.Windows.Forms.Control` class. The ActiveX control importer utility (`Aximp.exe`) which comes with the Microsoft .NET framework SDK is the tool that converts type definitions in a COM type library for an ActiveX control into a Windows forms control. To do this, the ActiveX control importer generates a wrapper control that derives from the special class `System.Windows.Forms.AxHost`. This control contains an instance of the underlying ActiveX control and knows everything about this control, but for Windows forms it acts as just another Windows forms control. This wrapper hosts the ActiveX control and exposes its properties, methods, and events.

The command line for the ActiveX Control Importer is:

```
AXIMP [options]{activex.dll|activex.ocx}
```

Table 10.1 shows a list of the options for the ActiveX control importer.

Table 10.1   The options for the ActiveX control importer and what they mean

Option	Meaning
/delaysign	Forces strong name delay signing (the assembly will not be signed on creation). Used with the /keyfile or /keycontainer options.
/keycontainer:containername	Indicates the key container holding the strong name key pair.
/keyfile:filename	Indicates the file containing the strong name key pair.
/publickey:filename	Indicates the file containing the strong name public key.
/source	Generates C# source code for the Windows forms wrapper.
/?	Displays the command line syntax.

The ActiveX control importer produces an assembly that contains the common language runtime metadata and control implementation for the types defined in the original type library. Generated files are named as follows:

- CLR proxy for COM types – `<progid>.dll`;
- Windows forms proxy for ActiveX controls – `Ax<progid>.dll`.

Let's look at the following example. Suppose we would like to use Microsoft Internet Explorer in our Windows forms application. Microsoft Internet Explorer is implemented as an ActiveX control, so this makes it possible to host it in our form. First, we use the AXIMP utility to generate the required assemblies (see Figure 10.43):

```
>AXIMP c:\winnt\system32\shdocvw.dll
```

Next, we install generated assemblies in the global assembly cache (using the GACUTIL tool) or use them in a single Windows forms project.

FIGURE 10.43 Using the AXIMP utility to generate the assemblies required to host Internet Explorer in a form

As soon as our ActiveX control is wrapped with the required Windows forms code, we can use it in our code. The following code shows how to use the Microsoft Internet Explorer ActiveX control in a Windows forms application (see Figure 10.44):

```
Imports AxSHDocVw


...


Dim AxWebBrowser As AxSHDocVw.AxWebBrowser
AxWebBrowser = New AxSHDocVw.AxWebBrowser()

CType(AxWebBrowser1, _
 System.ComponentModel.ISupportInitialize).BeginInit()

  AxWebBrowser1.Enabled = True
  AxWebBrowser1.Location = New System.Drawing.Point(8, 48)
   AxWebBrowser1.Size = New System.Drawing.Size(424, 304)

CType(Me.AxWebBrowser1, _
 System.ComponentModel.ISupportInitialize).EndInit()


...


  Private Sub Button1_Click(ByVal sender As System.Object, _
   ByVal e As System.EventArgs) Handles Button1.Click


  AxWebBrowser1.Navigate("http://www.awl.com")


  End Sub
```

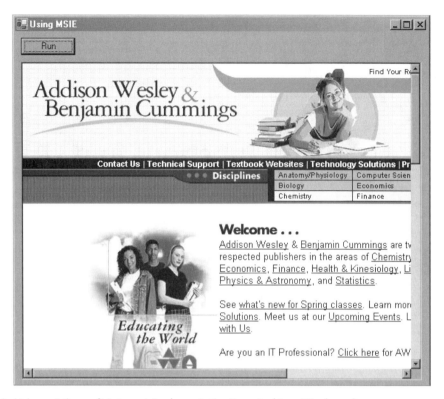

FIGURE 10.44 Using a Microsoft Internet Explorer ActiveX control in a Windows form

Note that in the initialization phase we can access properties of the ActiveX controls only inside the `BeginInit` and `EndInit` blocks. These provide safe places to perform user initialization. Before `BeginInit` we can't touch the control; afterwards, the "system" can use it. The initialization occurs at runtime.

10.4 Conclusion

In this chapter, we learned about additional Windows forms controls, common dialog boxes, and how we can use ActiveX controls in Windows forms applications. These controls can be used to provide extended user interface features. We discussed several groups of controls – panels, splitters, tab controls and tab pages, status bars, scroll bars, and so on. For each group, we provided a list of classes that comprise it, detailed descriptions of each class, its properties and methods, and usage examples.

We will continue to learn about Windows forms in the next chapter where we will talk about graphical functions available in the `System.Drawing` namespace and its secondary namespaces.

chapter 11

Graphical functions and GDI+

- The graphics device interface

- The graphics device interface plus (GDI+)

- Graphics in Microsoft .NET

- `System.Drawing` namespace

- `System.Drawing.Drawing2D` namespace

- `System.Drawing.Imaging` namespace

- Practice

- `System.Drawing.Text` namespace

- Printing

- Graphics in ASP.NET applications

In this chapter, we will explore the graphical functions available in the `System.Drawing` namespace and its secondary namespaces. Clearly such a huge topic deserves more than one chapter – possibly a book on its own – so in this chapter we will only cover the essentials of the graphical functions and provide several examples that will help you start to use graphics functionality in .NET applications.

We start this chapter with an overview of the graphics device interface (GDI) and its advanced version – the graphics device interface plus (GDI+) – then move on to discuss the `System.Drawing` namespace and its secondary namespaces.

The second part of this chapter is dedicated to printing in .NET applications, and the third part looks at using graphics functionality in ASP.NET applications.

Before we jump into details, it should be said that programmers familiar with graphics programming in Visual Basic and those who use C or C++ will find that a lot of new features are provided by GDI+ and the `System.Drawing` namespace. Also note that, under .NET, we use a unified programming model to access graphics functions so there are no differences in graphics programming for Visual Basic or C or C++ or C# (or any other .NET language) programmers.

11.1 The graphics device interface

Programmers experienced with Windows development should be familiar with the concept of the graphics device interface (GDI). It is part of Windows OS and provides functions and structures to generate graphical output for such devices as screens and printers. The GDI contains functions to draw lines, curves, closed figures, paths, text, and bitmaps. To specify colors and styles when drawing, the GDI provides pens, brushes, and fonts. Pens are used to draw lines and curves, brushes to fill the inner spaces of closed figures such as rectangles and ellipses, while fonts are used to write text, naturally.

To be able to utilize graphics, programs should obtain a device context for the particular device used, whether it be a screen or printer. A device context is a GDI-managed structure that contains various information about the device. Using a device context, we can not only utilize various drawing functions, but also retrieve information about the capabilities of the device – its type, dimensions, resolution, and so on.

Besides physical devices, the GDI supports logical devices – memory or metafiles. We can use the same set of graphics fuctions to output to logical devices. For example, once all the application output is stored as a metafile it can be played later any number of times or sent to various physical devices.

11.2 The graphics device interface plus (GDI+)

The graphics device interface plus (GDI+) is a portion of the current version of the Microsoft Windows XP operating system. It provides two-dimensional vector graphics, imaging, and typography. GDI+ also adds several new features and optimizes existing ones found in the GDI.

Among the new features in GDI+, we can find alpha blending support for all graphics primitives, gradient, and texture fills, scalable regions, native support for image file formats, such as .jpeg, .png, .gif, .bmp, .tiff, .exif, and .icon, extensible architecture for dynamically adding new image file formats, color management support for sRGB, ICM2, and sRGB64, native ClearType support, full Unicode support on all platforms, and texture- and gradient-filled text. GDI+ functionality can be used with Windows and web forms.

Figure 11.1 shows the main components of the GDI+ as well as the position of this graphics interface in the graphics support available for Win32 and .NET applications.

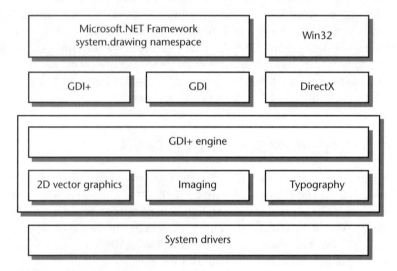

FIGURE 11.1   The main parts of the GDI+ and where it fits in with graphics support for Win32 and .NET applications

GDI+ programming model

Instead of the device context (DC) that was used in GDI applications, in GDI+ we use the Graphics object. It plays a similar role to the DC, but allows us to utilize an object-oriented model of GDI+. The difference between the DC and the Graphics object lies in the fact that the Graphics object is not tied to a pen, brush, font, or other object as the DC is. This means that we do not need to select (with a SelectObject method) those objects into the DC before starting graphics operations – we specify them as arguments when we call graphics fuctions.

The other difference lies in the object-oriented nature of GDI+. Many of the GDI+ methods are overloaded. Such methods share the same name, but have different argument lists. This provides us with more flexibility – we can select the method that fits our needs without needing to supply extra parameters that are not significant for our graphics operation.

There are several other changes in GDI +. For example there is no notion of a current position, drawing and filling methods are now separated, and there are more functions to work with regions.

After this brief overview of GDI and GDI+, let's look at how we can use the graphics functionality provided by these interfaces in Microsoft .NET applications.

11.3   Graphics in Microsoft .NET

All graphical functions provided by the Microsoft .NET Framework are available via the `System.Drawing` namespace (which can be found in the `System.Drawing.dll` assembly). It provides access to the rich functionality of GDI+, which is also available via the secondary namespaces shown in Figure 11.2.

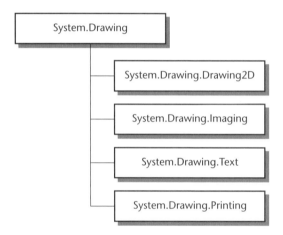

FIGURE 11.2   The `System.Drawing` namespace and the secondary namespaces are the route to GDI+'s functionality

In this chapter, we will look at the major functionality available via the aforementioned namespaces and provide some examples of how to use graphics functions in Windows and ASP.NET applications. We will start with the `System.Drawing` namespace.

11.4   System.Drawing namespace

The main class in this namespace is `Graphics`. It provides the device context for drawing. We can create device contexts from handles by using the `FromHDC(IntPtr)` method, Windows handles by using the `FromHWnd(IntPtr)` method, and images by using the `FromImage(Image)` method. After we get the device context, we can manipulate regions, perform rendering and transformation, work with metafiles, and draw various geometric figures – arcs, Bezier curves, ellipses, lines, and so on – on the device surface. This is supported by the set of DrawXXX methods shown below:

- DrawArc;
- DrawBezier;
- DrawClosedCurve;
- DrawCurve;
- DrawEllipse;
- DrawIcon;
- DrawImage;
- DrawImageUnscaled;
- DrawLine;
- DrawLines;
- DrawPath;
- DrawPie;
- DrawPolygon;
- DrawRectangle;
- DrawRectangles;
- DrawString.

All closed shapes (ellipses, polygons, rectangles, and so on) can be filled with the specified Brush. To do so, the following FillXXX methods can be used:

- FillClosedCurve;
- FillEllipse;
- FillPath;
- FillPie;
- FillPolygon;
- FillRectangle;
- FillRectangles;
- FillRegion.

To draw on the device's surface, we can also use such classes as Brush, Pen, Font, and Color.

Brush class

The Brush class is used to fill enclosed surfaces with patterns, colors, or bitmaps. This class is used as an abstract base class for various other classes, such as HatchBrush, LinearGradientBrush, PathGradientBrush, SolidBrush, and TextureBrush.

Pen class

The Pen class is used to draw lines, polygons, rectangles, arcs, and pies. The Brush and Pen classes include a set of standard solid pens and brushes for all of the known (predefined) colors – available via the System.Pens and System.Brushes classes respectively. For example, instead of creating a red pen, we can use the one that is already defined in the system:

```
Pens.Red
```

Font class

To describe the font used to render text, we use the Font class. This class supports such attributes as typeface, size, and style. Fonts can be created from device contexts, handles to fonts, or logical fonts. Fonts are parts of font families (we will see an example of this later in the chapter). Fonts can have regular, italic, bold, strikeout, and underline styles. If the required style is not available as a physical font, the GDI+ can simulate it.

Color class

To describe the color, we use the Color structure. The System.Drawing.Color structure represents an alpha, red, green, and blue (ARGB) color and contains definitions for all system-defined colors – from AliceBlue to YellowGreen – as well as methods and properties to get components (the A, R, G, B) of the color.

While red, green, and blue components should be familiar to most programmers, the alpha component can be confusing. It is used in alpha blending and its value specifies how transparent a color is. The default value – 255 – produces an opaque color. A value of 0 mean the color is completely transparent.

To create a color, use the FromARGB(*Integer, Integer, Integer, Integer*) method, which allows you to specify the RGB color (Color.Green, for example) and integer alpha value. For example, to define a semi-transparent green color we use the following call:

```
SemiTransGreen = Color.FromARGB(128, Color.Green)
```

Besides the methods of the System.Drawing.Color structure, we can find ones that return brightness, hue, and saturation of the color, as well as those that convert the color to ARGB, KnownColor, or String.

Bitmap class

The Bitmap class, as with the Metafile class, is based on the abstract Image class, which is responsible for loading and saving images. The Bitmap class encapsulates the physical bitmap – the pixel data for an image and its attributes. Bitmaps can be created from handles to icons or loaded from files and resources. Using the methods of the `Bitmap` class, we can not only retrieve the attributes of an image – width, height, resolution – but also manipulate it on the pixel level using `GetPixel` (*Integer*, *Integer*) and `SetPixel`(*Integer*, *Integer*, *Color*) methods. The `Bitmap` class also provides methods to make transparent bitmaps, set or get an image palette, rotate and flip images, and save images to files using different graphics formats and codes. Table 11.1 shows formats, supported by GDI+.

TABLE 11.1 Graphics formats supported by GDI+ and what they mean

Graphics format	Description
BMP	Bitmap image format
GIF	Graphics interchange format
JPEG	Joint photographic experts group format
EXIF	Exchangeable image file format
PNG	Portable network graphics format
TIFF	Tag image file format

Later in this chapter we will see several examples of image manipulation.

Icon class

The `Icon` class represents a Windows icon – a small, transparent bitmap that has its the size determined by the operating system. Icons can be created from handles or loaded from files, their attributes – height, width, size – can be manipulated by code, and they can be converted into bitmaps or saved in files.

Region class

Earlier we mentioned that there is extended support for regions in the GDI+. Regions are used to define drawing areas. The `Brush` object is used to fill a region. Regions are scalable – their coordinates are specified in world coordinates (a Cartesian coordinate system that is linear along both axes). The `Region` class allows us to create regions from graphics paths and rectangles. We can intersect, exclude, and unite regions, and perform transformations, translations, and XOR operations on them. The `Union`(*GraphicsPath*) and `Intersect`(*GraphicsPath*) methods are new in GDI+ and allow us to form complex regions easily by combining shapes and paths.

Conversions

To support conversion from one data type to another, the `System.Drawing` namespace contains several converters, which are based on the `TypeConverter` Class, available via the `System.ComponentModel` namespace.

- **ColorConverter** Used to convert colors from one data type to another (see the ConvertFromString and ConvertToString methods).
- **FontConverter** Used to convert Font objects from one data type to another.
- **IconConverter** Used to convert Icon objects from one data type to another.
- **ImageConverter** Used to convert Image objects from one data type to another.
- **ImageFormatConverter** Used to convert Image objects from one format to another.
- **PointConverter** Used to convert Point objects from one data type to another
- **RectangleConverter** Used to convert Rectangle objects from one data type to another.
- **SizeConverter** Used to convert Size objects from one data type to another.

Overall, the System.Drawing namespace provides a lot of graphics functionality for our .NET applications. Programmers familiar with graphics support in Visual Basic or C or C++ will find the object-oriented model easier to use, while those who have just moved to development should find the concepts of GDI+ very intuitive.

Now let's look at other System.Drawing namespaces.

11.5 System.Drawing.Drawing2D namespace

The System.Drawing.Drawing2D namespace contains classes and enumerations that provide advanced two-dimensional and vector graphics functionality. Using this namespace we can utilize gradient brushes, perform geometric transformations with the Matrix class, and create paths by using the GraphicsPath class.

Gradient brushes

The System.Drawing.Drawing2D namespace defines two classes that represent gradient brushes – the LinearGradientBrush and PathGradientBrush classes. Both are based on the abstract Brush class and extend it with gradient-filling functionality. The LinearGradientBrush class provides two-color gradients, as well as customized multicolor gradients. To specify the blend pattern, we should use the Blend class or the SetBlendTriangularShape and SetSigmaBellShape methods of the Linear GradientBrush class.

The PathGradientBrush class is used to fill the interior area of a path with a gradient. The Blend class, as well as several methods of the PathGradientBrush class, itself affects the resulting image.

Geometric transformations

The Matrix class (based on the abstract base class Image) presents a three-by-three matrix used in geometric transformations. This class contains various transformation methods, such as Invert, Multiply, Reset, Rotate, RotateAt, Scale, Shear, TransformPoints, TransformVectors, Translate, and VectorTransformPoints.

GraphicsPath class

Paths are used to draw outlines of shapes, fill the interiors of shapes, and create clipping regions. The `GraphicsPath` class provides methods to create figures that are included in a path. Each figure is either a sequence of connected lines or a graphics primitive. To add a new figure to a path, we use the `StartFigure()` method, then one of these `AddXXX()` methods:

- `AddArc`;
- `AddBezier`;
- `AddBeziers`;
- `AddClosedCurve`;
- `AddCurve`;
- `AddEllipse`;
- `AddLine`;
- `AddLines`;
- `AddPath`;
- `AddPie`;
- `AddPolygon`;
- `AddRectangle`;
- `AddRectangles`;
- `AddString`.

The figure is closed using the `CloseFigure()` method.

Later in this chaper we will see an example of how to use paths in .NET applications.

11.6 System.Drawing.Imaging namespace

The `System.Drawing.Imaging` namespace provides imaging functionality based on advanced GDI+ functions. In this namespace we will find the `Metafile` class, used for recording and saving metafiles, the `Encoder` and `Decoder` classes, for working with images in different formats, and the `PropertyItem` class, for storing and retrieving metadata in image files.

Metafiles

Metafiles are used to record a sequence of graphics operations that later can be played back on any device supported by GDI+. A metafile consists of a header and information about the graphics operations. Metafiles can contain vector graphics, raster images, and text.

In GDI+, the enhanced Windows metafile image format (EMF+) is used, but the `Metafile` class also supports the original WMF and EMF formats. The format of a metafile impacts on the commands it may contain. EMF files can contain only GDI commands, while EMF+ files can contain both GDI and GDI+ commands.

To create a metafile, we use one of the `Metafile` class constructors. After this we use a `Metafile` object to perform all graphics operations as we do with some physical device. Having done this, we save the metafile on disk and can play it later. To do so, we create a `Metafile` object from the file and use the `DrawImage()` method of the `Graphics` class to "draw" it.

11.7 Practice

Now that we have had an overview of the main functionality provided by the `System.Drawing` namespace and secondary namespaces, such as `System.Drawing.Drawing2D` and `System.Drawing.Imaging`, let's have some examples that illustrate how to use this functionality.

OnPaint method

To be able to use graphical functions, we need to get a reference to a graphics object – the `Graphics` class, which provides the device context for drawing. We can do this in the `OnPaint` event handler, which is called every time the form must be redrawn, such as, when it is created, resized, or moved.

The `OnPaint` event handler receives a `PaintEventArgs` object supplied by the system. This object contains various members that specify the `Graphics` object used to paint and the rectangle in which to paint it. We use the `Graphics` member to access the drawing surface, as shown below:

```
Protected Overrides Sub OnPaint(ByVal e As
  System.Windows.Forms.PaintEventArgs)
  '
  ' Get drawing surface
  '
  Dim Graph As Graphics
  Graph = e.Graphics
  '
  ' All graphics manipulations goes here
  '

  End Sub
```

After this, we can use the `Graphics` object and its methods to draw graphics in our applications. Below we will look at several examples that utilize the GDI+ functionality provided by the `System.Drawing` namespace.

Drawing lines

To draw a line, we use the DrawLine(*Pen*, *Point*, *Point*) method of the Graphics object. Before we can call this method, we should create a Pen object that will define the color and width of our line. We also need to create two Point objects that will define the starting and ending points for our line. We place all of the code in the OnPaint event handler, as shown below (see also Figure 11.3):

```
Protected Overrides Sub OnPaint(ByVal e As
 System.Windows.Forms.PaintEventArgs)

  Dim Graph As Graphics
  Graph = e.Graphics
'
' Create black pen that is 3 pixels wide
'
    Dim blackPen As New Pen(Color.Black, 3)

    Dim startPoint As New Point(50, 50)

    Dim endPoint As New Point(150, 150)

    Graph.DrawLine(blackPen, startPoint, endPoint)

End Sub
```

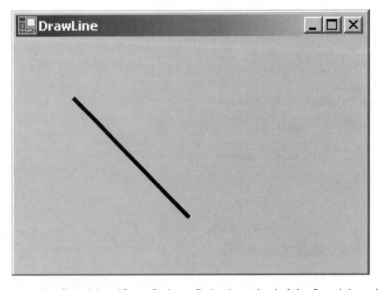

FIGURE 11.3   Using the DrawLine(*Pen*, *Point*, *Point*) method of the Graphics object to draw a line

Drawing strings

To draw a string, we use the DrawString(*String*, *Font*, *Brush*, *PointF*) method of the Graphics object. Before we can call this method, we should create several objects that will be used as parameters of this method.

We start with the Brush object, which will specify the color of the string – opaque black in our example:

```
Dim Brush As New SolidBrush(Color.Black)
```

Next, we create a font, specifying the font family, size, style, and unit of size measurement (pixels in our example):

```
Dim familyName As New FontFamily("Arial Narrow")
Dim myFont As New Font(familyName, 24, FontStyle.Regular,
 GraphicsUnit.Pixel)
```

Having done this, we create a PointF object that is used to specify the starting point of our string:

```
Dim startPoint As New PointF(10, 20)
```

Now we are ready to call the DrawString() method:

```
Graph.DrawString("Graphics in .NET", myFont, Brush, startPoint)
```

All of the above code should be placed in the OnPaint event handler, as shown below (see also Figure 11.4):

```
Protected Overrides Sub OnPaint(ByVal e As
 System.Windows.Forms.PaintEventArgs)

  Dim Graph As Graphics
  Graph = e.Graphics
 '
 ' Brush is used to specify the color of the string (opaque black)
 '
  Dim Brush As New SolidBrush(Color.Black)
 '
 ' We will use Arial Narrow font 24-pixels, Normal
 '
  Dim familyName As New FontFamily("Arial Narrow")
  Dim myFont As New Font(familyName, 24, FontStyle.Regular,
   GraphicsUnit.Pixel)

  Dim startPoint As New PointF(10, 20)

  Graph.DrawString("Graphics in .NET", myFont, Brush, startPoint)

End Sub
```

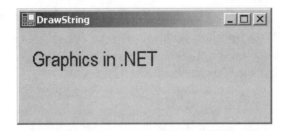

FIGURE 11.4 Drawing a string in the OnPaint event handler

We can also specify the rectangle to draw text in – in this case our string will wrap to fit this rectangle. The following example shows how to do this (see also Figure 11.5):

```
Protected Overrides Sub OnPaint(ByVal e As
  System.Windows.Forms.PaintEventArgs)

  Dim Graph As Graphics
  Graph = e.Graphics
'
' Define a rectangle and fill it with white brush
'
  Dim Rect As RectangleF
  Rect = New RectangleF(50, 50, 150, 150)
  Graph.FillRectangle(New SolidBrush(Color.White), Rect)
'
' Brush is used to specify the color of the string (opaque black)
'
  Dim Brush As New SolidBrush(Color.Black)
'
' We will use Arial Narrow font 24-pixels, Normal
'
  Dim familyName As New FontFamily("Arial Narrow")
  Dim myFont As New Font(familyName, 24, FontStyle.Regular, _
    GraphicsUnit.Pixel)

  Graph.DrawString("Graphics in .NET is based on GDI+", myFont, _
    Brush, Rect)
End Sub
```

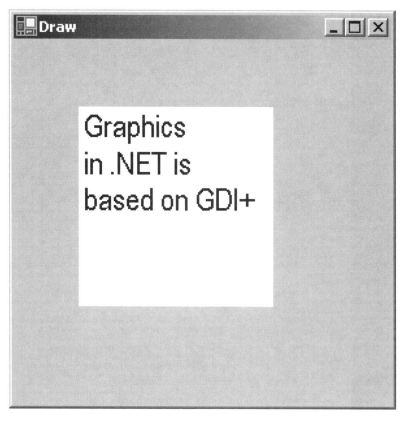

FIGURE 11.5 OnPaint can also be used to specify which rectangle to draw the text in

If we want to center our text within the rectangle, we use the StringFormat object. Here is an example (see also Figure 11.6):

```
'

' Specify centered text
'
Dim StrFmt As New StringFormat()
StrFmt.Alignment = StringAlignment.Center


...


'

' And use this string format
'
Graph.DrawString("Graphics in .NET is based on GDI+", myFont, _
  Brush, Rect, StrFmt)
```

FIGURE 11.6   The text has been centered using the `StringFormat` object

Drawing shapes

To draw a shape, we use one of the DrawXXX() methods, where XXX specifies the shape to draw. To draw filled shapes, we use the FillXXX() methods and specify the Brush object.

For example, to draw a rectangle, we create a Brush object, which will specify the color of the inner area of the rectangle – red in our example (see Figure 11.7):

```
Protected Overrides Sub OnPaint(ByVal e As
  System.Windows.Forms.PaintEventArgs)

  Dim Graph As Graphics
  Graph = e.Graphics
'
' Brush is used to specify the inner color (red)
'
  Dim Brush As New SolidBrush(Color.Red)

  Graph.FillRectangle(Brush, 50, 50, 150, 150)

End Sub
```

FIGURE 11.7   Using the DrawXXX() method and the Brush object, it is possible to create a red rectangle (which is shown as dark gray in the figure)

Note that instead of creating an instance of the Brush class directly, we can call its constructor in the FillRectangle method call:

```
Graph.FillRectangle(New SolidBrush(Color.Red), 50, 50, 150, 150)
```

In the previous example, we used a solid brush. The following examples show how to specify hatched and gradient brushes (see also Figures 11.8 and 11.9):

```
Imports System.Drawing.Drawing2D
...


'
' Use diamond-shaped hatched brush
'
Dim Brush As New HatchBrush(HatchStyle.DottedDiamond, Color.Red,
 Color.Black)
Graph.FillRectangle(Brush, 50, 50, 150, 150)
```

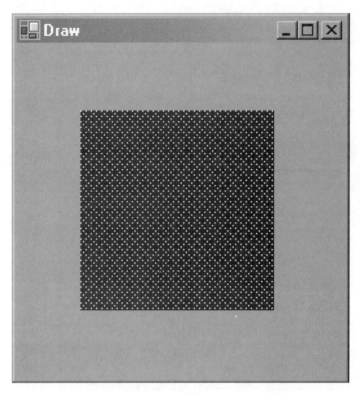

FIGURE 11.8   Using the `FillRectangle` method, a hatched brush can be specified

To specify a gradient brush, we should define a rectangle to fill (see Figure 11.9):

```
Imports System.Drawing.Drawing2D

...


 Dim Rect As Rectangle
 Rect = New Rectangle(50, 50, 150, 150)
 '
 ' Use forward-diagonal gradient brush
 '
 Dim Brush As New LinearGradientBrush(Rect, _
   Color.White, Color.LightGray, LinearGradientMode.ForwardDiagonal)
 Graph.FillRectangle(Brush, Rect)
```

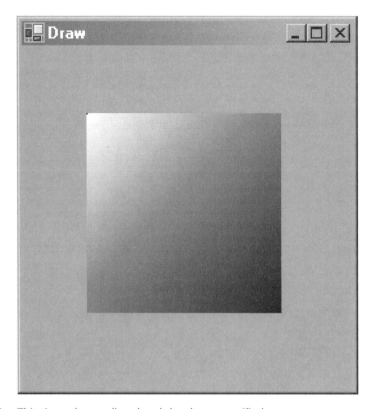

FIGURE 11.9   This time, the gradient brush has been specified

Using a `PathGradient` brush, we can create more complex filling effects.

When brushes are used to fill the inner area of a closed shape, pens are used to draw the shape itself. We have already seen how to create a simple pen (under the heading Drawing lines earlier in the chapter). To change the pen's appearance, we can use such properties as `PenType`, `DashStyle`, `Width`, `Color`, `StartCap`, and `EndCap`. The following example takes our line drawing code and specifies round ends, as well as a wider pen (see also Figure 11.10):

```
Protected Overrides Sub OnPaint(ByVal e As
  System.Windows.Forms.PaintEventArgs)

  Dim Graph As Graphics
  Graph = e.Graphics
  '
  ' Create black pen that is 30 pixels wide
  '
```

```
Dim blackPen As New Pen(Color.Black, 30)
blackPen.StartCap = LineCap.Round
blackPen.EndCap   = LineCap.Round

Dim startPoint As New Point(50, 50)

Dim endPoint As New Point(150, 150)

Graph.DrawLine(blackPen, startPoint, endPoint)

End Sub
```

FIGURE 11.10   Round ends and a wider pen than usual have been specified in the `OnPaint` event handler

To specify a textured brush, we create a `TextureBrush` object and give the graphics file that will be used as a texture a name.

Let's draw some more shapes. To draw an arc, we use the `DrawArc(Pen, Rectangle, Single, Single)` function, which takes four arguments. The first one specifies the `Pen`, the second the rectangle, and the third and fourth are used to specify the start and sweep angles. Here is an example of an arc (see also Figure 11.11):

```
Protected Overrides Sub OnPaint(ByVal e As
  System.Windows.Forms.PaintEventArgs)

  Dim Graph As Graphics
  Graph = e.Graphics

  Dim Rect As Rectangle
  Rect = New Rectangle(50, 50, 150, 150)
  Graph.DrawArc(Pens.Black, Rect, 0, 180)


End Sub
```

FIGURE 11.11 An arc, created with the DrawArc(*Pen*, *Rectangle*, *Single*, *Single*) function

Now, let's draw an ellipse. To do so we use the DrawEllipse(*Pen*, *Rectangle*) method, which takes two arguments. The first one specifies the **Pen**, the second the rectangle. Here is an example (see also Figure 11.12):

```
Protected Overrides Sub OnPaint(ByVal e As
 System.Windows.Forms.PaintEventArgs)
  Dim Graph As Graphics
  Graph = e.Graphics

  Dim Rect As Rectangle
  Rect = New Rectangle(50, 50, 150, 150)
  Graph.DrawEllipse(Pens.Black, Rect)

End Sub
```

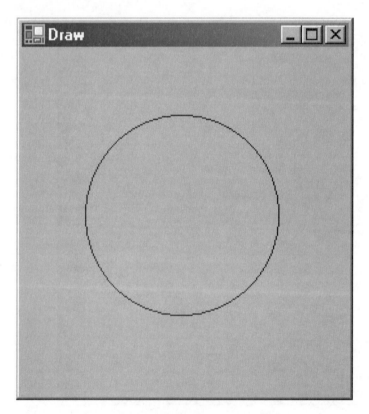

FIGURE 11.12 A circle can be created with the help of the DrawEllipse function (*Pen*, *Rectangle*) if the height and width of the "rectangle" specified are the same

Note that in the previous example we have used a rectangle with the same width and height (100 pixels) and we have ended up with a circle. If we change the rectangle, as in the example below, we will get an ellipse (see Figure 11.13):

```
Dim Rect As Rectangle
Rect = New Rectangle(50, 50, 250, 150)

Graph.DrawEllipse(Pens.Black, Rect)
```

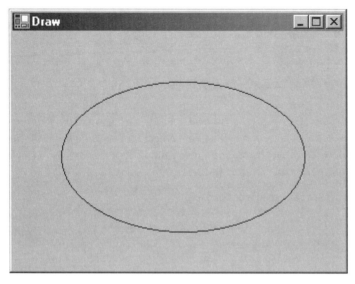

FIGURE 11.13 Changing the dimensions of the rectangle produces an ecllipse

Working with images

GDI+ provides full support for images stored in various formats, such as `.jpeg`, `.gif`, `.bmp`, `.icon`, and so on. To render an image on screen, we need to create a `Bitmap` object and specify it as one of the parameters of the `DrawImage()` method. In the following example, we create a `Bitmap` object based on a `.gif` file and show it on screen (see Figure 11.14):

```
Protected Overrides Sub OnPaint(ByVal e As
  System.Windows.Forms.PaintEventArgs)

  Dim Graph As Graphics
  Graph = e.Graphics
  Dim Bitmap As Bitmap
'
' Load .gif image from file
'
  Bitmap = New Bitmap("c:\book\ch11\dotnet.gif")

  Graph.DrawImage(Bitmap, 10, 10, Bitmap.Width, Bitmap.Height)

  End Sub
```

FIGURE 11.14 Creating a `Bitmap` object from a `.gif` file and showing it on screen

Using the `System.Drawing` namespace, we can also create graphical images on the fly. To do so, we create a new `Bitmap` object, get its drawing surface, draw on it, and then save this bitmap in one of the formats supported by `System.Drawing`. Here is an example of how to create a BMP file:

```
Imports System.Drawing.Imaging


...



Dim Graph As Graphics
Dim G As Graphics
'
' The pixel format is 32 bits per pixel
'
Dim Bitmap As New Bitmap(800, 600, PixelFormat.Format32bppArgb)
'
' Get drawing surface
'
Graph = Graphics.FromImage(Bitmap)
'
' Set white backgroud
'
Graph.FillRectangle(New SolidBrush(Color.White), _
  New Rectangle(0, 0, 800, 600))
'
' Specify font for string
'
Dim Font As New Font("Arial Narrow", 24)
Dim startPoint As New PointF(10, 20)
```

```
'
' Draw string
'
Graph.DrawString(".NET Can Do Graphis!", Font, _
  New SolidBrush(Color.Red), startPoint)
'
' Save as a .bmp file
'
Bitmap.Save("c:\book\ch11\demo.bmp", ImageFormat.Bmp)
```

Using the RotateFlip method of the Bitmap object, we can rotate and flip images. The RotateFlipType parameter specifies how an image should be flipped or rotated. The following is a list of possible values of this parameter:

- Rotate180FlipNone;
- Rotate180FlipX;
- Rotate180FlipXY;
- Rotate180FlipY;
- Rotate270FlipNone;
- Rotate270FlipX;
- Rotate270FlipXY;
- Rotate270FlipY;
- Rotate90FlipNone;
- Rotate90FlipX;
- Rotate90FlipXY;
- Rotate90FlipY;
- RotateNoneFlipNone;
- RotateNoneFlipX;
- RotateNoneFlipXY;
- RotateNoneFlipY.

The following example shows how to use the RotateFlip method (see also Figure 11.15):

```
...

Dim Bitmap As Bitmap

'
' Load .gif image from file
'
Bitmap = New Bitmap("c:\book\ch11\dotnet.gif")
```

```
'
' Perform a 180-degree rotation without flipping
'
Bitmap.RotateFlip(RotateFlipType.Rotate180FlipNone)
Graph.DrawImage(Bitmap, 10, 10, Bitmap.Width, Bitmap.Height)
'
' Perform a 180-degree rotation without flipping — restore image
'
Bitmap.RotateFlip(RotateFlipType.Rotate180FlipNone)
Graph.DrawImage(Bitmap, 20 + Bitmap.Width, 10, Bitmap.Width, _
  Bitmap.Height)
'
' Perform only a horizontal flip
'
Bitmap.RotateFlip(RotateFlipType.RotateNoneFlipX)
Graph.DrawImage(Bitmap, 10, 20 + Bitmap.Height, Bitmap.Width, _
  Bitmap.Height)
'
' Perform a horizontal and vertical flip without rotation
'
Bitmap.RotateFlip(RotateFlipType.RotateNoneFlipXY)
Graph.DrawImage(Bitmap, 20 + Bitmap.Width, 20 + Bitmap.Height, _
  Bitmap.Width, Bitmap.Height)
```

FIGURE 11.15 The RotateFlip method produces interesting effects

Drawing paths

As you will remember from our discussion of the GraphicsPath class (see under System.Drawing.Drawing2D namespace earlier in this chapter), it can be used to draw outlines of shapes, fill the interiors of shapes, and create clipping regions. The following example shows how to use the GraphicsPath class and some of its methods (see also Figure 11.16):

```
Protected Overrides Sub OnPaint(ByVal e As
  System.Windows.Forms.PaintEventArgs)
  Dim Graph As Graphics
  Graph = e.Graphics
    '
    ' Create a GraphicsPath object
    '
  Dim Path As GraphicsPath
  Path = New GraphicsPath()
    '
    ' First figure
    '
  Path.StartFigure()

  Path.AddRectangle(New RectangleF(50, 0, 100, 100))
  Path.AddLine(New Point(50, 0), New Point(150, 100))
  Path.AddLine(New Point(150, 0), New Point(50, 100))

  Path.CloseFigure()
    '
    ' Second figure
    '
  Path.StartFigure()

  Path.AddEllipse(New RectangleF(50, 0, 100, 100))
  Path.AddLine(New Point(100, 50), New Point(100, 200))
  Path.AddEllipse(New RectangleF(50, 100, 100, 100))
  Path.CloseFigure()
    '
    ' Now, draw it!
    '
  Graph.DrawPath(New Pen(Color.Black), Path)

End Sub
```

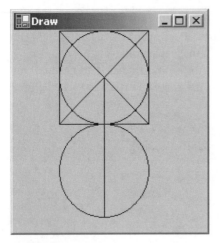

FIGURE 11.16 Effects created using the `GraphicsPath` class and some of its methods

The `Invalidate` method

In case we need to force redrawing of our window, we can call the `Invalidate` method – part of the `Control` class, which is defined in the `System.Windows.Forms` namespace. This method has no parameters. Consider the following example. Suppose we have an application that allows us to draw various graphics primitives by selecting them from a menu (see Figure 11.17).

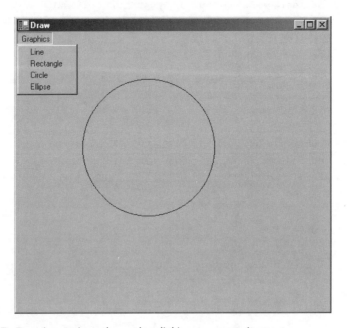

FIGURE 11.17 Drawing various shapes by clicking on menu items

We start by adding the following declaration in the Form1 class declaration:

```
Dim GraphType As Integer = 0
```

Next, we create event handlers for each menu item:

```
Private Sub MenuItem1_Click(ByVal sender As System.Object,
  ByVal e As System.EventArgs) Handles MenuItem1.Click
    GraphType = 1
    Invalidate()
End Sub

Private Sub MenuItem2_Click(ByVal sender As System.Object,
  ByVal e As System.EventArgs) Handles MenuItem2.Click
    GraphType = 2
    Invalidate()
End Sub

Private Sub MenuItem3_Click(ByVal sender As System.Object,
  ByVal e As System.EventArgs) Handles MenuItem3.Click
    GraphType = 3
    Invalidate()
End Sub

Private Sub MenuItem4_Click(ByVal sender As System.Object,
  ByVal e As System.EventArgs) Handles MenuItem4.Click
    GraphType = 4
    Invalidate()
End Sub
```

In each menu handler, we specify the types of graphics primitives we want to draw and call the Invalidate() method, which fires the Paint event. Note that if we remove the Invalidate() method call, and run the program, the shapes will not redraw when the menu is changed unless a redraw is forced by some other mechanism, such as iconizing and restoring the application. In the OnPaint event handler, we check the type of the graphics primitive and perform the appropriate actions. Here is the code for the OnPaint event handler:

```
Protected Overrides Sub OnPaint(ByVal e As
  System.Windows.Forms.PaintEventArgs)

  Dim Graph As Graphics
  Graph = e.Graphics

  Dim startPoint As New Point(100, 50)
  Dim endPoint As New Point(200, 200)
```

```
Dim Rect As Rectangle = New Rectangle(startPoint.X, startPoint.Y, _
                                      endPoint.X, endPoint.Y)

    Select Case GraphType
    Case 1  ' Draw Line

      Graph.DrawLine(Pens.Black, startPoint, endPoint)

    Case 2  ' Draw Rectangle

      Graph.FillRectangle(Brushes.Red, Rect)

    Case 3  ' Draw Circle

      Graph.DrawEllipse(Pens.Black, Rect)

    Case 4  ' Draw Ellipse

      Rect.Width = Rect.Width + 100
      Graph.DrawEllipse(Pens.Black, Rect)

    End Select
End Sub
```

Drawing without the OnPaint method

So far, we have seen various graphics examples that were created around the OnPaint event handler. While this is the most widely used technique to draw graphics, sometimes we may need a more immediate screen update and not want to wait for the paint message to get round the system. For example, suppose we need to draw different shapes depending on the button pressed. In this case, we can implement all of the drawing in the event handler for the particular button. Here is an example – we draw a rectangle as a reaction to a button click:

```
Private Sub Button1_Click(ByVal sender As System.Object,
  ByVal e As System.EventArgs) Handles Button1.Click
  Dim Graph As Graphics
  Dim Brush As New SolidBrush(Color.Beige)
  Dim Rect As New Rectangle(10, 50, 150, 150)
  Dim Pen As New Pen(Color.Beige, 2)

  Graph = Graphics.FromHwnd(Me.Handle)
  Graph.DrawRectangle(Pen, Rect)

End Sub
```

In this example we use the `FromHwnd` call of the `Graphics` object, which allows us to create a new `Graphics` object from the handle to a window. We obtain this handle from the value stored in the `Me.Handle` property of the Windows form.

The other way to display graphics is to do this at startup. In this case, we insert all of the graphics code into either the `New` method that constructs our form or the `InitializeComponent` method. Note that in both cases there is no redrawing of graphics – in other words, all of the graphics will be lost when we resize, minimize, or reopen our window or part of the window is covered by another window. To support redrawing, always add your graphics code to the `OnPaint` event handler in the ways we have seen in the examples in this chapter.

11.8 System.Drawing.Text namespace

The last namespace in the `System.Drawing` namespace is `System.Drawing.Text`, which provides advanced GDI+ typography functionality. It contains one base class, `FontCollection`, from which the `InstalledFontCollection` and `PrivateFontCollection` classes are derived. The `InstalledFontCollection` class is a collection of fonts currently installed on the system. The `PrivateFontCollection` class is a collection of fonts that are used by the application currently running. This last collection contains private versions of existing fonts, which can be manipulated by our application without affecting the whole system, as well as fonts temporarily installed by the application.

The following example shows how to get the names of all installed fonts (see also Figure 11.18):

```
Imports System.Drawing.Text

...

    Dim FC As FontCollection
    Dim FF As Array
    Dim I  As Integer

'
' Create a new instance of the InstalledFontCollection class
'
    FC = New InstalledFontCollection()
'
' Get font families
'
    FF = FC.Families
'
' Iterate the array
'
    For I = 0 To UBound(FF) - 1
     TextBox1.AppendText(FF(I).Name & vbCrLf)
    Next
```

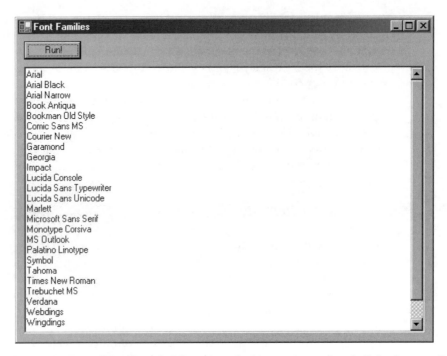

FIGURE 11.18 Using the `InstalledFontCollection` class to produce a list of all the fonts available

The following example presents the graphic version of this list (see Figure 11.19):

```
Protected Overrides Sub OnPaint(ByVal e As
 System.Windows.Forms.PaintEventArgs)
  Dim FC = New InstalledFontCollection()
  Dim FF As FontFamily()
  Dim I As Integer
  Dim F As Font
  Dim Y = 10

  FF = FC.Families

  e.Graphics.TranslateTransform(AutoScrollPosition.X, _
   AutoScrollPosition.Y)
  For I = 0 To UBound(FF) - 1
   If FF(I).IsStyleAvailable(FontStyle.Regular) Then
    F = New Font(FF(I).Name, 10)
    e.Graphics.DrawString(FF(I).Name, F, Brushes.Black, 10, Y)
    Y = Y + F.Height
    F.Dispose()
   End If
  Next
End Sub
```

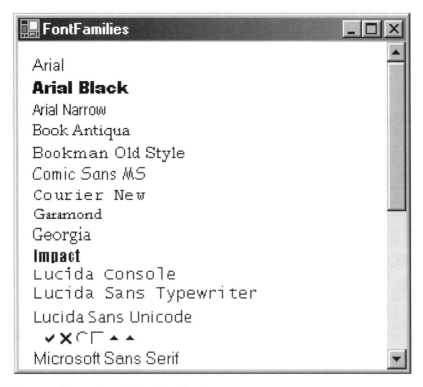

FIGURE 11.19 The graphic version of the list of fonts

Note that in order to add scroll bars to our main window, we have added the following line to the `InitializeComponent` method:

```
Me.AutoScrollMinSize = New Size(200, 400)
```

As in the previous example, we get the `FontFamilies` collection and iterate it. At each step we check if the currently selected font supports regular (that is, not italic nor bold) style and, if this is true, we create a 10-pixel font based on the name of the currently selected one. Next, we draw a string with the name of this font and increase the next drawing position by the height of the current font. In order to support scrolling, we use the `TranslateTransform` method of the `Graphics` object. We pass two parameters to this method, which contain the position of the autoscroll in the scrollable control, which is the main application window in our example.

To manipulate a `PrivateFontCollection` class, we create a new instance of this class, then add fonts stored in the files or in memory using the `AddFontFile` or `AddMemoryFont` methods. After this, we use fonts stored in the `PrivateFont Collection` to create `Font` objects and pass them to methods that accept fonts as parameters.

In this chaper we have covered a lot of the functionality provided by the System.Drawing namespace. We have learned about the main classes included in this namespace, and its purpose. Also, we have created several examples that illustrate usage of these classes. The rest of this chapter is dedicated to printing support in .NET applications and using graphics in web applications built with Microsoft ASP.NET technology.

11.9 Printing

The System.Drawing.Printing namespace contains nearly all of the classes that are used to print text and graphics. Note that print preview functionality is provided by PrintPreviewControl, which is part of the System.Windows. Forms namespace. Table 11.2 shows some of the main classes found in the System.Drawing.Printing namespace.

TABLE 11.2   The main classes in the System.Drawing.Printing namespace and what they do

Class	Description
PageSettings	Specifies settings for one printed page.
PaperSize	Specifies the characteristics (width, height, type) of a piece of paper.
PreviewPageInfo	Specifies the print preview information for one printed page.
PrintController	Controls the document printing process.
PrintDocument	Main printing object that sends output to a printer.
PrinterResolution	Represents the resolution supported by a printer.
PrinterSettings	Specifies various printer settings, including available paper sizes, paper sources, printer resolution, and so on.

We will look at these classes in the following sections.

PrintDocument class

Basic printing functionality is implemented by the PrintDocument class. We use this instance of the class to specify properties such as DefaultPageSettings and PrinterSettings, and then call the Print method that prints the document. The name of the printer set in the PrinterSettings object can be taken from the Printers folder in the control panel (see Figure 11.20).

To get the name of the printer to be used in your code, right-click on the appropriate icon in the Printers folder and select the Properties command in the menu (see Figure 11.21).

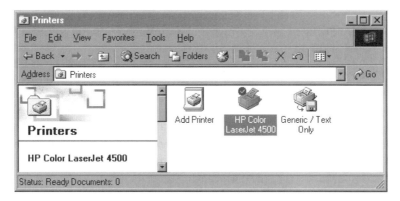

FIGURE 11.20 The `Printers` folder in the control panel is the source of your printer names, which you need to know to change settings

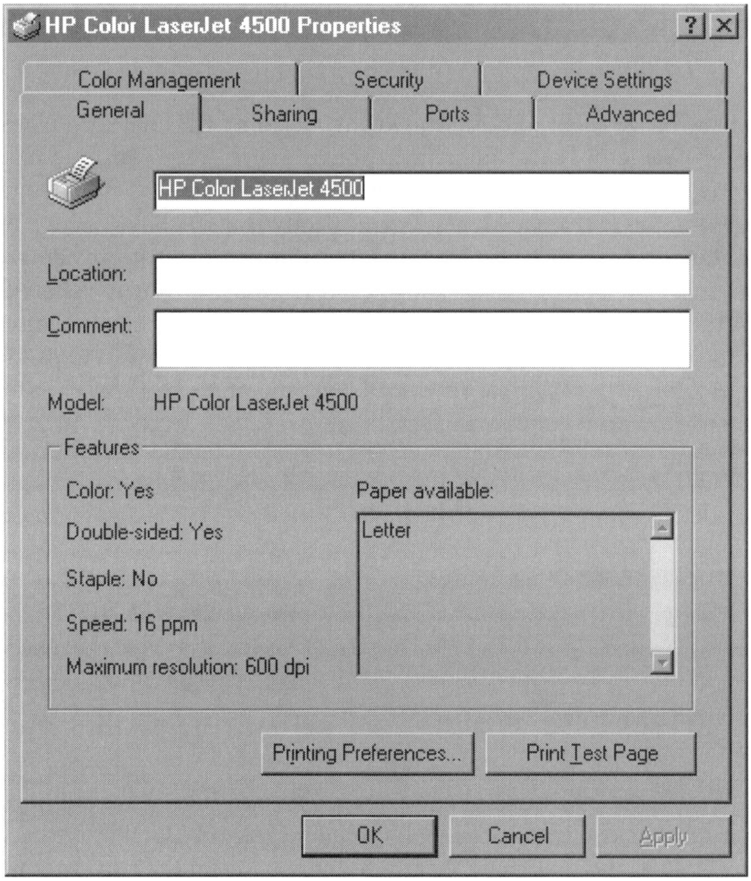

FIGURE 11.21 Information found in the `Properties` part of the `Printers` folder

Then you can copy the name of the printer and paste it directly into your code.

The following example shows how to implement basic printing functionality by means of the `PrintDocument` class.

```
Dim PrintDoc As New PrintDocument()
'
' Specify printer we will use
'
PrintDoc.PrinterSettings.PrinterName = "HP Color LaserJet 4500"
'
' Set Orientation to landscape
'
PrintDoc.DefaultPageSettings.Landscape = True


'
' We are ready to print
'
PrintDoc.Print()
```

For each page about to print, the `PrintDocument` class raises a `PrintPage` event. The event handler we must implement for this event receives arguments packed within the `PrintPageEventArgs` class instance. Members of this class allow us to cancel the printing job (the `Cancel` property), specify that we have more pages to print (the `HasMorePages` property), get the portion of the page inside the margins (the `MarginBounds` property), get the total area of the page (the `PageBounds` property), and get the page settings for the current page (the `PageSettings` property). The `Graphics` property provides access to the `Graphics` object, which is used to paint the page.

The following example shows the implementation of the `PrintPage` event handler used to print graphics images:

```
Private Sub PrintDoc_PrintPage(sender As Object,
  ev As PrintPageEventArgs)

 Dim ImgToPrint As Image()
 ImgToPrint = Image.FromFile("c:\book\ch11\dotnet.gif")
 ev.Graphics.DrawImage(Image, ev.Graphics.VisibleClipBounds)

 ev.HasMorePages = False


 End Sub
```

To print a text file, we need to do some more work, such as create a font, read files line by line, and make sure that each line fits within the page width. We also need to calculate how many lines will fit on the page and call the `DrawString` method to send our document to the printer. All of this should be placed in the `PrintPage` event handler.

PrintController class

This class controls the document printing process. When we call the Print method of the PrintDocument class, it invokes the OnStartPrint, OnEndPrint, OnStartPage, and OnEndPage methods of the PrintController-derived class StandardPrintController, for instance. These methods specify how to print the document. Figure 11.22 shows how the methods of the PrintController class relate to the methods and events of the PrintDocument class.

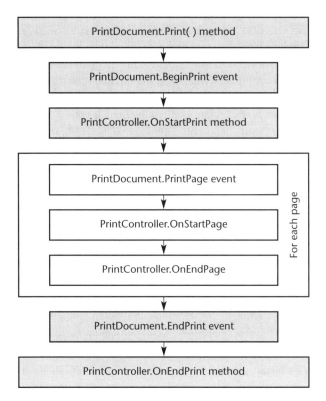

FIGURE 11.22 The methods of the PrintController class relate to the methods and events of the PrintDocument class

The System.Drawing.Printing namespace provides two classes that are based on the PrintController class. The StandardPrintController class is used to print a document, while the PreviewPrintController class is used to display a print preview on the screen. Usually a document to be printed is presented as a series of images that are stored in an array of PreviewPageInfo type.

PreviewPageInfo class

Each element of this type represents the print preview information for a single page. This class is used by the `PrintController` class. The `Image` property contains an image of the printed page, while the `PhysicalSize` property specifies the size of the printed page, to 1/100ths of an inch.

PageSettings class

This class is used to specify the settings for one printed page. The `Bounds` property finds the bounds of the page, which depend on the orientation. The `Color` property defines whether or not the page should be printed in color. The `Landscape` property specifies the orientation of the page – either portrait or landscape. To define the margins of the page, we use the `Margins` property. The `PaperSize` property specifies the paper size of the page, while the paper source (upper tray, lower tray, automatic feed, manual feed, and so on) is specified by the `PaperSource` property. To define the printer resolution (high, medium, low, draft, or customized), we use the `PrinterResolution` property (see the description of the `PrinterResolution` class below) and to specify the printer settings for this page, we use the `PrinterSettings` property, which provides access to the `PrinterSettings` object described below.

PageSize class

This class is used to specify the size of the piece of paper used to print the document. There are the `Height` and `Width` properties, which define the size, as well as the `Kind` property, which allows us to specify one of the standard paper sizes (A3, A4, letter, and so on), and the `Name` property, which allows us to get or set the name of the type of paper.

PrinterResolution class

The `PrinterResolution` class represents the resolution supported by a printer. It can be either one of the predefined levels (high, medium, low, draft) or customized. In the latter case, the X and Y properties contain the horizontal and vertical directions of the printer resolution.

PrinterSettings class

The `PrinterSettings` class is used to get various printer settings – list the installed printers, available paper sizes, paper sources, printer resolutions, and so on. The `Copies` property is used to specify the number of copies we want to print, the `PrinterName` property sets or gets the name of the printer in use, and the `PrintRange` property is used to specify the range of pages we want to print.

The following example shows how to use the `PrinterSettings` class to get a list of all the printers accessible by the computer:

```
Private Sub Button1_Click(ByVal sender As System.Object,
  ByVal e As System.EventArgs) Handles Button1.Click

    Dim PS As PrinterSettings = New PrinterSettings()
    Dim Printers As PrinterSettings.StringCollection
    Dim I As Integer
  '
  ' Get InstalledPrinters collection
  '
    Printers = PS.InstalledPrinters
  '
  ' ... and iterate it
  '
    For I = 0 To Printers.Count - 1
      TextBox1.Text = TextBox1.Text & Printers.Item(I) & vbCrLf
    Next
  End Sub
```

To summarize what we have learned in this section, let's look at the steps required to print a document.

1 Create an instance of the `PrintDocument` class.
2 Specify the printer settings or allow users to do so via the `PrinterSettings` dialog box.
3 Implement the `PrintPage` event handler and printing logic within it.
4 If needed, allow users to change the page settings.
5 Call the `PrintDocument.Print()` method to start printing.

Using the same logic, we can implement `PrintPreview` – the only difference in this case will be that the `PrintController` will output to the print preview screen instead of to the printing device.

11.10 Graphics in ASP.NET applications

So far we have seen how to use classes defined in the `System.Drawing` namespace to draw graphics in Windows applications. In this section, we will learn how to perform graphics manipulations in web applications built with Microsoft ASP.NET technology.

When dealing with graphics in ASP.NET applications, we synthesize off-screen images on the server using the drawing code seen so far and send them to the client. This means that we have two options – to store or not to store our dynamically created images. If we decide to store them, we need to create a temporary file on a per session basis and implement the code that deletes it when the session ends. Once our graphics are stored in the file, we can specify its name as a value of the `ImageUrl` property of the `Image` server control. The other option is to create an ASPX file that generates an image and sends it as a stream by specifying the content type as, for example, an `"image/jpeg"`. This approach has two advantages – we do not need to deal with temporary file management and we can use the ASPX file as an SRC property (this indicates the location (a URL) of the graphics file that should be displayed on the HTML page) of an HTML `IMG` tag, thus extending our solution to HTML and ASP pages, not only ASPX pages as in the first case.

Let's look at an example of how to use graphics in ASP.NET applications. The following code, stored as GRAPH.ASPX, generates a yellow rectangle with navy text within it. Note that most of the code (except the bold lines at the end of the listing) is the same as that used to create graphics in Windows applications, which we saw earlier in this chapter:

```
<%@ Import Namespace="System.Drawing" %>
<%@ Import Namespace="System.Drawing.Imaging" %>


<%@ Page Language="VB" %>
<script runat="server">


    '/////////////////////////////////////////////////////
    '
    ' Page_Load : All code that should be processed
    ' as soon as the page is loaded goes here
    '
    '/////////////////////////////////////////////////////


    Sub Page_Load(ByVal sender As Object, ByVal e As EventArgs)

    Dim Bmp As New Bitmap(200, 60, PixelFormat.Format24bppRgb)
    Dim Graph As Graphics = Graphics.FromImage(Bmp)

    Dim Rect As RectangleF
    Rect = New RectangleF(0, 0, 200, 60)
    Graph.FillRectangle(New SolidBrush(Color.Yellow), Rect)

    Dim Brush As New SolidBrush(Color.Navy)
    Dim familyName As New FontFamily("Arial Narrow")
    Dim myFont As New Font(familyName, 24, FontStyle.Bold, _
     GraphicsUnit.Pixel)
```

```
        Dim StrFmt As New StringFormat()
        StrFmt.Alignment = StringAlignment.Center

        Graph.DrawString("Graphics in ASP.NET", myFont, Brush, _
        Rect, StrFmt)

        Response.ContentType = "image/jpeg"
        BMP.Save(Response.OutputStream, ImageFormat.JPEG)

        End Sub

    </script>
```

Here is the HTML file that shows how to use our newly created graphics "generator" (see also Figure 11.23):

```
    <html>
    <head>
     <title>ASP.NET Graphics Demo</title>
    </head>

    <body>
     <center>

     <h2>ASP.NET Graphics Demo</h2>
     <img src="graph.aspx" border="2">

     </center>
    </body>
    </html>
```

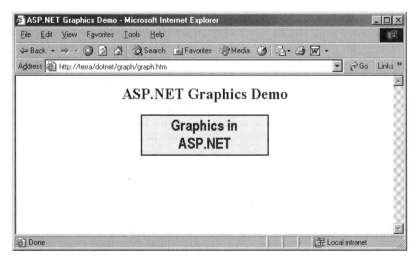

FIGURE 11.23 Using graphics in an ASP.NET application

In this section, we have seen how to use classes defined in the System.Drawing namespace to create graphics in ASP.NET applications. As the example above shows, using classes defined in the System.Drawing namespace in ASP.NET applications is as easy as it is in Windows forms applications – the changes in the code are minimal. This gives developers an opportunity to create a whole new class of web applications, which was not possible with standard ASP.

11.11 Conclusion

In this chapter, we have covered the graphics functionality that is available by using the classes defined in the System.Drawing namespace. We started with a discussion of the basic principles of the GDI, new features found in the GDI+, then moved on to a more detailed study of the System.Drawing namespace.

After the overview of the main classes in the System.Drawing namespace and its secondary namespaces, we saw various examples of how to generate graphics in Windows forms applications.

The second part of this chapter was dedicated to printing. We learned about the main classes that comprise the System.Drawing.Printing namespace and outlined the steps required to implement printing functionality in our applications.

At the end of the chapter, we learned how to use graphics in ASP.NET applications. This feature simplifies the creation of graphics in web applications and opens the door to a whole new class of such applications.

In the next chapter, we will continue to learn about classes of the Microsoft .NET Framework. We will discuss how we can work with data using classes that come as part of ADO.NET.

chapter 12

Working with data – ADO.NET

- ADO.NET and its namespaces

- Managed providers

- Connections

- Commands

- DataReader class

- DataAdapter class

- Tables, rows, and columns

- Using transactions

- Processing errors

In this chapter we will explore ADO.NET – the data access component of the Microsoft .NET Framework. As with ASP.NET, ADO.NET is not just a new version of Microsoft ADO, but a completely new data access architecture based on managed providers and a set of classes that we will discuss in this chapter.

ADO.NET is built from the ground up for distributed applications used in today's disconnected scenarios. It is built around the disconnected model based on the DataSet class (an in-memory XML database that stores related tables, relationships, and constraints).

In this chapter, we will cover the namespaces that contain classes used in ADO.NET, will learn about managed providers to access OLE DB data sources and SQL Server databases, we will talk about the four main components of a managed provider – connections, commands, data readers, and data adapters – discuss tables, rows, and columns exposed via the object model provided by the DataSet class, and learn how to use actions and process errors that may occur during operations with databases. As before, we will provide examples to illustrate the topics discussed.

12.1 ADO.NET and its namespaces

All data-related classes reside in the System.Data namespace, which can be found in the System.Data.dll assembly and its secondary namespaces:

- System.Data.Common;
- System.Data.OleDb;
- System.Data.SqlClient;
- System.Data.SqlTypes.

Let's look at the purpose and contents of the System.Data namespace and, after this, at the purpose and contents of its secondary namespaces.

The System.Data namespace consists of classes, interfaces, delegates, and enumerations. The central class of ADO.NET is the DataSet class. This is the disconnected data container that serves as an in-memory cache of data. The DataSet, together with managed providers, supports reading from and writing modified data back to a data source.

The DataSet contains a DataTableCollection – a collection of one or more DataTable objects where each DataTable object holds data from a single data source. The DataRelationCollection contains DataRelation objects that describe the parent–child relationships between two tables. This is shown in Figure 12.1.

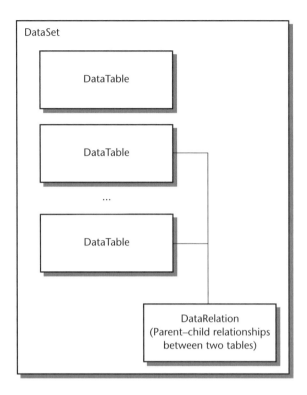

FIGURE 12.1   The DataSet, its DataTable objects and DataRelation object, which describes the relationship between two tables

When we create a relationship between two tables, the UniqueConstraint (the object that ensures column values are unique) and the ForeignKeyConstraint (the object that specifies what action should be taken when a primary key value is changed or deleted) are created automatically.

Each DataTable object contains a DataColumnCollection that includes one or more DataColumn objects, which define the schema of a table. The type of data stored by the columns is specified by the DataType property. The ReadOnly and AllowNull properties can be used to ensure data integrity, while the Expression property can be used to create calculated columns.

The DataRowCollection contains one or more DataRow objects that each represent a single row in a table. The DataView object represents a view of a table and can be used for sorting, searching, editing, and navigation.

The Constraint property of a DataTable object contains a Constraint Collection of constraints that can be enforced on columns in a table – each constraint is of the Constraint type. The ExtendedProperties property is a collection of user-defined name/value pairs associated with a table or a column. The ChildRelations property of a DataTable object contains the child relations for the table, while the ParentRelations property contains the parent relations for it.

Figure 12.2 shows how the objects mentioned above relate to each other.

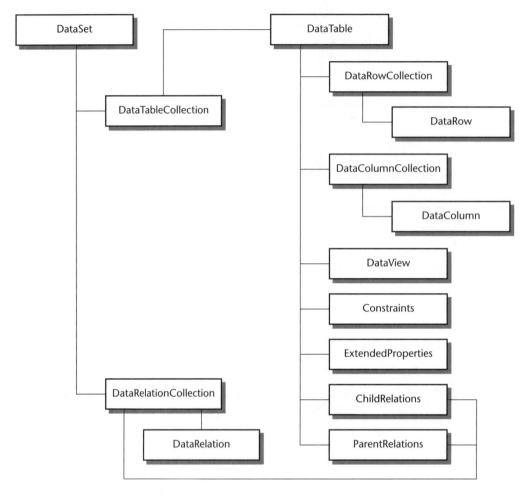

FIGURE 12.2 The DataSet, all the objects within it, and how they work together

System.Data.Common namespace

This namespace contains several classes that are used by .NET data providers. Here we can find the following classes.

- **DataAdapter** Acts as a mapping layer between the data source and the DataSet object. It retrieves data from the data source, populates the DataSet object, and sends changes back to the data source.

- **DataColumnMappingCollection**. A collection of one or more DataColumn Mapping objects containing a description of a column mapping.

- **DataTableMappingCollection** A collection of one or more DataTable Mapping objects containing a description of a mapped relationship between this table and a source table.

- **DBDataPermission** Provides support for secured data access. This helps a .NET data provider to ensure that a user has a security level adequate for accessing data.

- **DBDataPermissionAttribute** Supports customized security attributes and associates security actions with them.

- **RowUpdatingEventArgs and RowUpdatedEventArgs** Provide data for events. RowUpdating and RowUpdate respectively are fired when the row is updating and updated.

System.Data.OleDb namespace

This namespace contains classes that implement the OLE DB data provider (a COM-based application programming interface (API) for accessing data in any format – spreadsheets, text files and soon – by means of an OLE DB provider, the provider exposing data from a particular type of data source – SQL Server databases, Microsoft Access databases, or Microsoft Excel spreadsheets). The basic classes are OleDbDataAdapter (which represents a set of data commands and a connection to a database), OleDbCommand (which represents a SQL statement or stored procedure that will be executed against a data source), OleDbConnection (which represents an open connection to a data source), and OleDbDataReader (which supports reading a forward-only stream of data rows from a data source). Other classes in this namespace include the following.

- **OleDbCommandBuilder** Used to automatically generate SQL statements for single-table updates. It generates INSERT, UPDATE, and DELETE statements based on the SELECT statement we provide.

- **OleDbErrorCollection** A collection of OleDbError objects that contain information for a warning or error returned by the data source.

- **OleDbParameterCollection** A collection of OleDbParameter objects that represent parameters for an OleDbCommand.

- **OleDbPermission** Provides support for secured data access to an OLE DB data source.

- **OleDbPermissionAttribute** Supports customized security attributes.

- **OleDbRowUpdatingEventArgs and OleDbRowUpdatedEventArgs** Provide data for events fired when the row is updating (RowUpdating event) and row is updated (RowUpdated event).

- **OleDbSchemaGuid** Contains the properties that map to an OLE DB schema row set.

- **OleDbTransaction** Represents a SQL transaction to be executed at an OLE DB data source.

System.Data.SqlClient namespace

This namespace contains classes that implement the SQL Server's data provider. The basic classes are SqlClientDataAdapter (which represents a set of data commands and a connection to a database), SqlClientCommand (which represents a SQL statement or stored procedure that will be executed against a data source), `SqlClientConnection` (which represents an open connection to a data source), and `SqlClientDataReader` (which supports reading a forward-only stream of data rows from a data source). Other classes in this namespace include the following:

- **`SqlClientPermission`** Provides support for secured data access to the SQL Server's data source.
- **`SqlClientPermissionAttribute`** Supports customized security attributes.
- **`SqlCommandBuilder`** Used to automatically generate SQL statements for single-table updates. It generates `INSERT`, `UPDATE`, and `DELETE` statements based on the `SELECT` statement we provide.
- **`SqlErrorCollection`** A collection of `SqlError` objects that contain information for a warning or error returned by the data source.
- **`SqlParameterCollection`** A collection of `SqlParameter` objects that represent parameters for an `SqlClientCommand`.
- **`SqlDbRowUpdatingEventArgs`** and **`SqlDbRowUpdatedEventArgs`** Provide data for events fired when the row is updating (`RowUpdating` event) and row is updated (`RowUpdated` event).
- **`SqlTransaction`** Represents a SQL transaction to be executed at a SQL Server's data source.

System.Data.SqlTypes namespace

This namespace contains classes that represent the SQL Server's native data types. These classes can be used in all situations where type conversions can cause loss of precision.

12.2 Managed providers

Earlier in this chapter we saw two namespaces that implement OLE DB and SQL Server managed providers (.NET providers) – `System.Data.OleDb` and `System.Data.SqlClient` respectively. A managed provider is a group of .NET components that implement a set of core and additional objects that serve as a bridge between a `DataSet` object and a data source. Managed providers are based on the `DBDataAdapter` class and implement interfaces like `IDbCommand`, `IDbConnection`, and `IDataReader`. The core objects of a managed provider are:

- `Connection` Represents a unique session to a data store;
- `Command` Represents a SQL statement to be executed on a data store;
- `DataReader` Represents a forward-only, read-only stream of data records from a data store;
- `DataAdapter` Represents a set of `Commands` and a `Connection` that are used to get data from a data store and put it in a `DataSet`.

Currently, Microsoft provides two managed providers – OLE DB and SQL – directly. The third managed provider – ODBC.NET – is available as a free download from Microsoft's website.

The ODBC.NET data provider is an add-on component for the .NET Framework. The provider accesses native ODBC drivers in the same way that the OLE DB.NET data provider accesses native OLE DB providers. The following drivers are compatible with the ODBC.NET data provider:

● Microsoft SQL ODBC driver;
● Microsoft ODBC driver for Oracle;
● Microsoft Jet ODBC driver.

The ODBC.NET data provider requires the installation of MDAC 2.7 or later. Tracing and connection pooling are handled by the ODBC driver manager utility, which is installed as part of MDAC 2.7. At the time of writing, the ODBC.NET provider is available as a separate free download from Microsoft's website.

OLE DB managed provider

This provider uses native OLE DB and COM interop to access the data. This provider can be used to work with data stores that are not Microsoft SQL Server 7.0 or higher. Currently, the OLE DB managed provider supports the following OLE DB providers that are compatible with ADO.NET:

● MSDAORA – Microsoft OLE DB provider for Oracle;
● Microsoft.Jet.OLEDB.4.0 – Microsoft OLE DB provider for Microsoft Jet 4.0.

We can also use the SQLOLEDB provider to work with the Microsoft SQL Server, but we will get a better performance if we use the native SQL Server's managed provider described in the next section.

Note that the OLE DB managed provider does not support OLE DB 2.5 interfaces, and existing OLE DB providers that require support for such interfaces (Exchange, Internet Publishing) will not work properly with the OLE DB managed provider. Also, the OLE DB managed provider does not work with the OLE DB provider for ODBC (MSDASQL). To use ODBC connectivity, we can relate it to the ODBC.NET managed provider.

SQL Server managed provider

The SQL Server managed provider is designed to work directly with the Microsoft SQL Server 7.0 or later. It uses the tabular data stream (TDS) protocol to communicate directly with the SQL Server without adding an OLE DB or ODBC layer.

Now that we have learned about managed providers and providers available in ADO.NET, let's look in more detail at their core components – namely connections, commands, a data reader, and data adapter.

12.3   Connections

A connection is the first thing we need to access a data store. Both managed providers implement the `IDbConnection` interface and inherit the following properties and methods.

- **ConnectionString** This property (of a `String` type) specifies the string used to open a connection to a data store.
- **ConnectionTimeout** This property (of an `Integer` type) specifies the time to wait while trying to establish a connection before terminating the attempt and generating an error. The default value is 15 seconds.
- **Database** This property (of a `String` type) specifies the name of the current database or the database to be used once a connection is open.
- **State** This property returns the current state of the connection. It is of the `ConnectionState` type and may have the values `Broken`, `Closed`, `Connecting`, `Executing`, `Fetching`, and `Open`. The `OleDbConnection` and `SqlConnection` classes support only `Open` and `Closed` values of this property.

The `OleDbConnection` class implements the following properties.

- **DataSource** This property (of a `String` type) gets the location and file name of the data source.
- **Provider** This property (of a `String` type) gets the name of the OLE DB provider that is specified in the `"Provider= "` part of the connection string.
- **ServerVersion** This property (of a `String` type) returns the version of the connected server in the form ##.##.####, where the first two digits are the major version, the next two digits are the minor version, and the last four digits are the release version.

The `SqlConnection` class implements the following properties.

- **PacketSize** This property (of an `Integer` type) returns the size in bytes of network packets used to communicate with an instance of the SQL Server. The default value is 8192.
- **ServerVersion** This property (of a `String` type) returns the version of the SQL Server in the form `major.minor.build`, where major and minor are exactly two digits and build is exactly four digits.
- **WorkstationID** This property (of a `String` type) returns the network name of the database client.

Here are the methods of the `IDbConnection` interface.

- **BeginTransaction() method** Used to begin a database transaction. The overloaded version of this method can take an argument of an `IsolationLevel` type, which specifies the transaction locking behavior for the connection.

- **ChangeDatabase(*String*) method** Used to change the current database to the one specified as an argument of this method.
- **Close() method** Used to close the currently opened connection to a data store. It rolls back any pending transactions, then releases the connection to the connection pool or closes the connection if connection pooling is disabled.
- **CreateCommand() method** Used to create a command associated with this connection. It returns an **IDbCommand** object (this object will be discussed below).
- **Open() method** Used to open a new connection to a data store with the settings specified in the **ConnectionString** property.

The OleDbConnection class also implements the GetOleDbSchemaTable(*Guid*, *Object*) method that returns the schema table (OleDbSchemaGuid type) and associated restriction columns of the specified schema.

Let's have an example of how to use the SqlConnection object to establish connections with the Microsoft SQL Server 2000:

```
'----------------------------------------
' ADO.NET Connection Example. SQL Server
'----------------------------------------


Imports System
Imports System.Data.SqlClient


Module Cons

 Sub Main()

  Dim Conn As SqlConnection
  Conn = New SqlConnection("server=localhost;" & _
    "database=Northwind;uid=sa;pwd=;")
  Conn.Open
  Console.WriteLine(Conn.State.ToString)
  Console.WriteLine(Conn.PacketSize.ToString)
  Console.WriteLine(Conn.ServerVersion.ToString)
  Console.WriteLine(Conn.WorkstationID.ToString)
  Conn.Close

 End Sub


End Module
```

To establish an OleDbConnection with a Microsoft access database we may use the following code:

```
'-----------------------------------------
' ADO.NET Connection Example. MS Access
'-----------------------------------------


Imports System
Imports System.Data.OleDb

Module Cons

  Sub Main()

    Dim Conn As OleDbConnection
    Dim DBPath As String = "C:\Program Files\Microsoft Office\" & _
      "Office\Samples"
    Dim ConnStr As String = "Provider=Microsoft.Jet.OLEDB.4.0;" & _
      "DataSource=" & _
      DBPath & "Authors.mdb"
    Conn = New OleDbConnection(ConnStr)
    Conn.Open
    Console.WriteLine(Conn.State.ToString)
    Console.WriteLine(Conn.DataSource.ToString)
    Console.WriteLine(Conn.Provider.ToString)
    Console.WriteLine(Conn.ServerVersion.ToString)

    Conn.Close

  End Sub


End Module
```

Note that the only differences between the two examples above are in the namespaces we use – System.Data.SqlClient for the SQL Server managed provider and System.Data.OleDb for the OLE DB managed provider – and the format of the connection string – in the case of the SQL Server, we do not specify a name of the provider as the SqlClient namespace contains classes designed to work with the Microsoft SQL Server only. The rest of the code is nearly identical for both SqlClient and OleDb.

After we have established a connection to a data source, we can work with it by sending one or more commands. We will discuss these in the next section.

12.4 Commands

Commands – implemented as `OleDbCommand` and `SqlCommand` classes – are the only way to execute SQL statements and stored procedures in ADO.NET. Both managed providers implement the `IDbCommand` interface and inherit the following properties.

- **CommandText** This property (of a `String` type) specifies the SQL statement, name of the stored procedure or table (for the OLE DB managed provider only) to be executed against the data store. The meaning of the contents of this property depends on the value set for the `CommandType` property.

- **CommandTimeout** This property (of an `Integer` type) specifies the number of seconds to wait before terminating the attempt to execute a command and generating an error. The default value is 30 seconds.

- **CommandType** Specifies the type of the command in the `CommandText` property. The `CommandType` property is of the `CommandType` type and can have the values of `StoredProcedure` (indicates that the `CommandText` property contains the name of the stored procedure to execute), `TableDirect` (indicates that the `CommandText` property contains the name of a table the columns of which are all returned), or `Text` (indicates that the `CommandText` property contains a SQL statement to execute). The default value of this property is `Text`.

- **Connection** Specifies the `Connection` object (of an `IDbConnection` type) used to execute this command.

- **Parameters** Specifies the collection of parameters for this command (of a `IDataParameterCollection` type) – that is, arguments of parameterized stored procedures or parameter queries.

- **Transaction** Specifies the transaction in which this command executes as an `IDbTransaction` object.

- **UpdatedRowSource** Specifies how query command results are applied to the row (`DataRow`) being updated by the `DataAdapter.Update` method. This property is of the `UpdateRowSource` type and can have the values of `Both` (indicates that both the output parameters and the first returned row are mapped to the changed row in the `DataSet`), `FirstReturnedRecord` (indicates that the data in the first returned row is mapped to the changed row in the `DataSet`), `None` (indicates that any returned parameters or rows are ignored), or `OutputParameters` (indicates that output parameters are mapped to the changed row in the `DataSet`).

The following are methods of the `IDbCommand` interface.

- **Cancel() method** Cancels the execution of the current command.

- **CreateParameter() method** Creates a new instance of a `DataParameter` object (of a `IDbDataParamater` type).

- **ExecuteNonQuery() method** Executes a command against the `Connection` and returns the number of rows affected (for `INSERT`, `UPDATE`, and `DELETE` SQL statements) or –1 for all other types of statements. This method must be used for queries that do not return rows. Note that any output parameters or return values mapped to parameters of the **Command** object come populated with data.

- **ExecuteReader() method** Executes a command (specified by the **CommandText** property) against the connection (specified by the **Connection** property) and creates a new **DataReader** object (of an **IDataReader** type). The overloaded version of this method allows us to specify a combination of one or more **CommandBehaviour** values that indicate the results of the query and its effect on the database.

- **ExecuteScalar() method** Executes a command (specified by the **CommandText** property) against the connection (specified by the **Connection** property) and returns only the first column of the first row in the result set returned by the query. The result set may contain multiple rows, which are ignored by **ExecuteScalar**.

- **Prepare() method** Creates a compiled version of the command on the data store.

Let's look at some examples of how to use the **Command** object with the SQL Server database:

```
'----------------------------------------
' ADO.NET Connection Example. SQL Server
'----------------------------------------


Imports System
Imports System.Data.SqlClient

Module Cons

 Sub Main()

  Dim Conn As SqlConnection
  Dim Cmd  As SqlCommand

  Conn = New SqlConnection("server=localhost;" & _
    "database=Northwind;uid=sa;pwd=;")
  Conn.Open
  Cmd = New SqlCommand("SELECT * FROM Employees", Conn)

  Conn.Close

 End Sub

End Module
```

The code above creates a new `SqlCommand` object with the transact SQL statement and associates it with the `SqlConnection` object.

Using the `SqlCommand` object, we can also execute stored procedures. For example, we can execute the `SalesByCategory` stored procedure in the `Northwind` database to find the total purchases for the products in a given category for a given year.

As we already know, it is necessary to put the name of the stored procedure into the `CommandText` property and set the `CommandType` property to `CommandType.StoredProcedure`. We also need to supply the parameters in the `Parameters` collection of the `Command` object. The following example shows how to do this:

```
'----------------------------------------
' ADO.NET Connection Example. SQL Server
'----------------------------------------


Imports System
Imports System.Data.SqlClient


Module Cons

 Sub Main()

  Dim Conn  As SqlConnection
  Dim Cmd   As SqlCommand
  Dim Param As SqlParameter

  Conn = New SqlConnection("server=localhost;" & _
    "database=Northwind;uid=sa;pwd=;")
  Conn.Open

  Cmd = New SqlCommand("SalesByCategory", Conn)
  Cmd.CommandType = CommandType.StoredProcedure

 '
 ' CategoryName parameter
 '

  Param = New SqlParameter("@CategoryName", SqlDbType.VarChar, 15)
  Param.Direction = ParameterDirection.Input
  Param.Value = "Beverages"
  Cmd.Parameters.Add(Param)

 '
 ' OrdYear parameter
 '
```

```
    Param = New SqlParameter("@OrdYear", SqlDbType.VarChar, 4)
    Param.Direction = ParameterDirection.Input ' not necessary!
    Param.Value = "1998"
    Cmd.Parameters.Add(Param)

    Conn.Close
  End Sub


End Module
```

In the example above, we have used the stored procedure that accepts two parameters. We have created two `SqlParameter` objects – one for each stored procedure's parameters – and, after setting its names, data types, sizes, directions (`Input` is the default value for the `Direction` property – we can skip this step), and values, we add them to the `Parameters` collection of the `SqlCommand` object.

The SQL Server managed provider also implements the `ExecuteXmlReader()` method, which allows us to take advantage of the SQL Server's XML features (`FOR XML` clause in the `SELECT` statement) to create an XML representation of the result set. This method creates an `XmlReader` object. Here is an example of how to use this functionality (see Figure 12.3):

```
    '----------------------------------------
    ' ADO.NET Connection Example. SQL Server
    '----------------------------------------


    Imports System
    Imports System.Data.SqlClient
    Imports System.XML


    Module Cons


     Sub Main()


      Dim Conn As SqlConnection
      Dim Cmd  As SqlCommand
      Dim XmlRdr As XmlReader


      Conn = New SqlConnection("server=localhost;" & _
        "database=Northwind;uid=sa;pwd=;")
      Conn.Open
      Cmd = New SqlCommand("SELECT * FROM Orders WHERE OrderId=10270" & _
        " FOR XML Auto", Conn)


      XmlRdr = Cmd.ExecuteXmlReader
      xmlRdr.MoveToContent
```

```
        Console.WriteLine(xmlRdr.ReadOuterXml)

     Conn.Close

   End Sub

 End Module
```

FIGURE 12.3   An XML representation of a result set, created using the ExecuteXMLReader() method

Note that in the example above we have used the FOR XML AUTO clause in the SELECT statement to retrieve results directly as XML from the SQL Server 2000. We also used the ExecuteXmlReader() method of the Command object to create an XMLReader object containing XML returned from the SQL Server 2000.

Now we know how to open a connection and execute a SQL statement or stored procedure. In the next section, we will learn how to get the data returned as a result of executing Command. We will do this with the help of the DataReader class.

12.5 DataReader class

Earlier in this chapter we defined a DataReader class as one that supports reading a forward-only stream of data rows from a data source. Both managed providers implement the IDataReader interface and inherit the following properties.

- **Depth** Returns the level of nesting for the current row as an Integer value.
- **IsClosed** This Boolean property indicates whether or not the data reader is closed.

- **RecordsAffected** Returns the number of rows (as an `Integer` value) changed, inserted, or deleted by the execution of the SQL statement. If no rows are affected or the statement fails, this property will be set to 0, and for **SELECT** statements this property will be set to –1.

`OleDbDataReader` and `SqlDataReader` classes also have the following properties.

- **FieldCount** Returns the number of columns in the current row as an `Integer` value.

- **Item** Returns the value of a column in its native format (of an `IDataRecord.Item` type). This property can be used either with the column name – `Item(String)` – or with the column ordinal – `Item(Integer)`.

Following are the methods of the `IDataReader` interface.

- **Close() method** Closes the current `DataReader` object.

- **GetSchemaTable() method** Returns a `DataTable` with the column metadata.

- **NextResult() method** Moves the data reader to the next result, when reading the results of batch SQL statements, and returns a `Boolean` value that indicates if there are more rows to read.

- **Read() method** Moves the data reader to the next record and returns a `Boolean` value that indicates if there are more rows to read.

Managed providers also implement the following methods.

- **GetBoolean(Integer) method** Returns the value of the specified column as a `Boolean` value.

- **GetByte(Integer) method** Returns the value of the specified column as a byte.

- **GetBytes(Integer, Long, Byte, Integer, Integer) method** Reads a stream of bytes from the specified column offset into the buffer as an array starting at the given buffer offset.

- **GetChar(Integer) method** Returns the value of the specified column as a character.

- **GetChars(Integer, Long, Char, Integer, Integer) method** Reads a stream of characters from the specified column offset into the buffer as an array starting at the given buffer offset.

- **GetDataTypeName(Integer) method** Returns the name of the source data type for the specified column.

- **GetDateTime(Integer) method** Returns the value of the specified column as a `DateTime` object.

- **GetDecimal(Integer) method** Returns the value of the specified column as a `Decimal` object.

- **GetDouble(Integer) method** Returns the value of the specified column as a double precision floating point number.

- **GetFieldType(*Integer*) method** Returns the data type for the specified column.
- **GetFloat(*Integer*) method** Returns the value of the specified column as a single-precision floating point number.
- **GetGuid(*Integer*) method** Returns the value of the specified column as a GUID.
- **GetInt16(*Integer*) method** Returns the value of the specified column as a 16-bit signed integer.
- **GetInt32(*Integer*) method** Returns the value of the specified column as a 32-bit signed integer.
- **GetInt64(*Integer*) method** Returns the value of the specified column as a 64-bit signed integer.
- **GetName(*Integer*) method** Returns the name of the specified column.
- **GetOrdinal(*String*) method** Returns the column ordinal for the name of the column.
- **GetString(*Integer*) method** Returns the value of the specified column as a string.
- **GetTimeSpan(*Integer*) method** Returns the value of the specified column as a TimeSpan object.
- **GetTimeSpan(*Integer*) method** Returns the value of the specified column in its native format.
- **GetValues(*Object*()) method** Returns all the attribute columns in the current row.
- **IsDBNull(*Integer*) method** Returns a value indicating whether or not the column contains non-existent or missing values.

The managed provider for the SQL Server also contains a set of GetSqlXXX(*Integer*) methods for each data type defined in the System.Data.SqlTypes namespace – SqlBoolean, SqlDateTime, SqlMoney, and so on.

To create a DataReader object, we must use the ExecuteReader() method of the OleDbCommand or SqlCommand objects. The following example shows how to create an SqlDataReader object:

```
'----------------------------------------
' ADO.NET Connection Example. SQL Server
'----------------------------------------

Imports System
Imports System.Data.SqlClient

Module Cons

 Sub Main()

  Dim Conn  As SqlConnection
  Dim Cmd   As SqlCommand
```

```
Conn = New SqlConnection("server=localhost;" & _
  "database=Northwind;uid=sa;pwd=;")
Conn.Open
Cmd = New SqlCommand("SELECT * FROM Employees", Conn)

Dim DR As SqlDataReader = Cmd.ExecuteReader()

Conn.Close

End Sub


End Module
```

After we have created a **DataReader** object, we have two options. We can use the
Read method to iterate through the result set, or we can use this object with the data-
aware controls in the ASP.NET web forms or Windows forms applications.

The following example shows how to use the Read() method of the
SqlDataReader object (see also Figure 12.4):

```
'-----------------------------------------
' ADO.NET Connection Example. SQL Server
'-----------------------------------------


Imports System
Imports System.Data.SqlClient


Module Cons

Sub Main()

  Dim Conn  As SqlConnection
  Dim Cmd    As SqlCommand

  Conn = New SqlConnection("server=localhost;" & _
    "database=Northwind;uid=sa;pwd=;")
  Conn.Open
  Cmd = New SqlCommand("SELECT * FROM Employees", Conn)

  Dim DR As SqlDataReader = Cmd.ExecuteReader()

   While DR.Read()

    Console.WriteLine(DR("FirstName") & " " & DR("LastName"))
```

```
        End While

        Conn.Close

      End Sub

    End Module
```

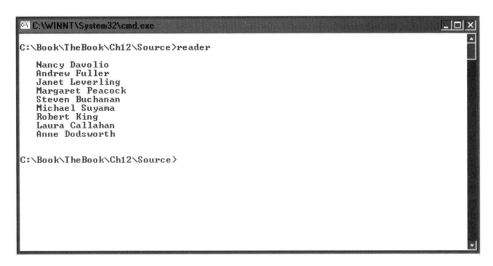

FIGURE 12.4   Using the Read() method of the DataReader object

Note how we have accessed columns in the previous example. We have used the default Item property that returns the value of a column in its native format. The same result can be achieved with the following code, which uses the GetValue(*Integer*) method or the DataReader object to get the value of the specified column:

```
While DR.Read()

  Console.WriteLine(DR.GetValue(DR.GetOrdinal("FirstName")) & _
    " " & DR.GetValue(DR.GetOrdinal("LastName")))

End While
```

To use the DataReader object with data-aware controls in an ASP.NET web forms page – the DataGrid server-side control, for example – we need to specify its DataSource property and call its DataBind() method. Here is how to do this (see also Figure 12.5):

```
<%@ Import Namespace=System.Data %>
<%@ Import Namespace=System.Data.SqlClient %>

<script runat="server">

 Sub Page_Load()

  Dim Conn  As SqlConnection
  Dim Cmd   As SqlCommand
  Dim Param As SqlParameter

  Conn = New SqlConnection("server=localhost;" & _
   "database=Northwind;uid=sa;pwd=;")
  Conn.Open

  Cmd = New SqlCommand("SalesByCategory", Conn)
  Cmd.CommandType = CommandType.StoredProcedure

  Param = New SqlParameter("@CategoryName", SqlDbType.VarChar, 15)
  Param.Direction = ParameterDirection.Input
  Param.Value = "Beverages"
  Cmd.Parameters.Add(Param)

  Param = New SqlParameter("@OrdYear", SqlDbType.VarChar, 4)
  Param.Direction = ParameterDirection.Input
  Param.Value = "1998"
  Cmd.Parameters.Add(Param)

  Dim DR As SqlDataReader = Cmd.ExecuteReader()

  Grid.DataSource = DR
  Grid.DataBind()

  Conn.Close

 End Sub

</script>

<asp:DataGrid
 id="Grid"
 BorderColor="black"
 BorderWidth="1"
 CellPadding="3"
 AutoGenerateColumns="true"
 runat="server">

</asp:DataGrid>
```

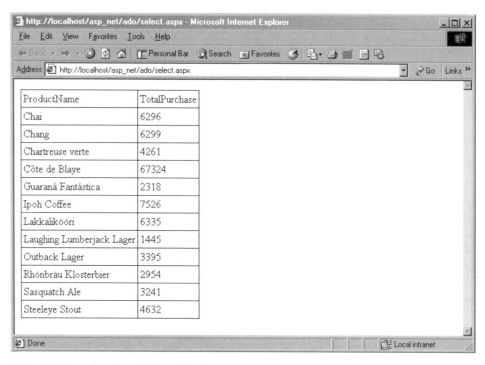

FIGURE 12.5   Using the `DataReader` object with data-aware controls in an ASP.NET

We will learn about data-aware controls in the next chapter. In the meantime, let's discuss the fourth component of managed providers – the `DataAdapter` class.

12.6 DataAdapter class

Earlier in this chapter, we defined the data adapter as a set of `Commands` and a `Connection` that are used to get data from a data store and put it in a `DataSet`. Data adapters implement the `IDataAdapter` interface that defines the following properties.

- `MissingMappingAction` This property specifies whether unmapped source tables or columns are passed with their source names in order to be filtered or to raise an error. This property is of the `MissingMappingAction` type and it can have the values `Error` (which indicates that a `SystemException` should be generated), `Ignore` (which indicates that a column or table without a mapping is ignored), and `Passthrough` (which indicates that the source column or source table has been created and added to the `DataSet` using its original name). The default value for this property is `Passthrough`.

- **MissingSchemaAction** This property specifies whether or not missing source tables, columns, and their relationships are added to the data set schema, ignored or cause an error message to be raised. This property is of the MissingSchemaAction type and it can have the values Add (the necessary columns are added to complete the schema), AddWithKey (the necessary columns and primary key information are added to complete the schema), Error (which indicates that a SystemException should be generated), and Ignore (extra columns will be ignored). The default value for this property is Add.

- **TableMappings** This property indicates how a source table is mapped to a data set table. It is of the ITableMappingCollection type.

An IDataAdapter interface defines the following methods.

- **Fill(*DataSet*) method** Adds or refreshes rows in the DataSet to match those in the data source using the DataSet name, and creates a DataTable named "Table".

- **FillSchema(*DataSet*, *SchemaType*) method** Adds a DataTable named "Table" to the specified DataSet and configures the schema to match that in the data source based on the specified SchemaType.

- **GetFillParameters() method** Returns the parameters set by the user when executing an SQL SELECT statement as an IDataParameter array.

- **Update(*DataSet*) method** Calls the respective INSERT, UPDATE or DELETE statements for each inserted, updated, or deleted row in the specified DataSet from a DataTable named "Table".

Two data adapters implemented in ADO.NET – OleDbDataAdapter and SqlDataAdapter – inherit from the DBDataAdapter class, as shown in Figure 12.6 below.

The DataAdapter class serves as a base class for data adapters. It defines one additional property – AcceptChangesDuringFill. This indicates whether or not the AcceptChanges() method of a DataRow object is called after this object is added to the DataTable.

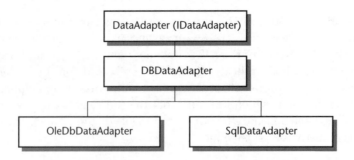

FIGURE 12.6   OleDbDataAdapter and SqlDataAdapter inherit from the DBDataAdapter class

The DBDataAdapter class is based on the DataAdapter class and is used as a starting point to create a DataAdapter designed for use with a relational database. Each managed provider has its own implementation of the DBDataAdapter class – the OLE DB managed provider has the OleDbDataAdapter, while the SQL Server managed provider has the SqlDataAdapter. Both adapters implement the following properties for loading and updating data.

- **SelectCommand** This property (of an SqlCommand type) specifies an SQL statement used by the Fill method to select records in the data source and place them in the DataSet.

- **InsertCommand** This property (of an SqlCommand type) specifies an SQL statement used by the Update method to insert new records into the data source that corresponds to new rows in the DataSet.

- **UpdateCommand** This property (of an SqlCommand type) specifies an SQL statement used by the Update method to update records in the data source that corresponds to modified rows in the DataSet.

- **DeleteCommand** This property (of an SqlCommand type) specifies an SQL statement used by the Update method for deleting records from the data source that corresponds to deleted rows in the DataSet.

Note that only the SelectCommand property is required, as other properties – InsertCommand, UpdateCommand, and DeleteCommand – can be generated automatically by ADO.NET. To do so, we need to create the CommandBuilder object for this DataAdapter. This object will autogenerate the INSERT, UPDATE, and DELETE commands based on the value in the SelectCommand property.

Let's look at an example of how we can use the DataAdapter:

```
'----------------------------------------
' ADO.NET Connection Example. SQL Server
'----------------------------------------


Imports System
Imports System.Data
Imports System.Data.SqlClient
Imports System.XML


 Module Cons

 Sub Main()

   Dim DA  As SqlDataAdapter
   Dim DS  As New DataSet
```

```
    DA = New SqlDataAdapter("SELECT * FROM Employees", _
      "server=localhost;database=Northwind;uid=sa;pwd=;")

    DA.Fill(DS, "Employees")

  End Sub


End Module
```

Here we create a new SqlDataAdapter that extracts data from the Employees table in the Northwind database. We use the Fill() method to place the extracted data in the DataSet.

As you will recall, the DataSet is a collection of DataTable objects and relationships between tables. This means that we can have more than one table in our DataSet:

```
'----------------------------------------
' ADO.NET Connection Example. SQL Server
'----------------------------------------

Imports System
Imports System.Data
Imports System.Data.SqlClient
Imports System.XML

 Module Cons

 Sub Main()

   Dim Emp_DA  As SqlDataAdapter
   Dim Cust_DA As SqlDataAdapter
   Dim DS      As New DataSet

 '
 ' Get data from Employees table
 '
   Emp_DA = New SqlDataAdapter("SELECT * FROM Employees", _
     "server=localhost;database=Northwind;uid=sa;pwd=;")
   Emp_DA.Fill(DS, "Employees")

 '
 ' Get data from Customers table
 '
```

```
        Cust_DA = New SqlDataAdapter("SELECT * FROM Customers", _
          "server=localhost;database=Northwind;uid=sa;pwd=;")
        Cust_DA.Fill(DS, "Customers")

    End Sub

End Module
```

After running the code above, we will have our `DataSet` filled with the data from two tables – `Employees` and `Customers`. To access one of the tables, we use the following syntax:

```
DS.Tables.Item("Employees")
```

or

```
DS.Tables.Item("Customers")
```

The `Fill()` method of the `DataAdapter` performs all of the actions – it establishes a connection with a data store, executes a SQL statement, and fills the results from the execution into a `DataSet` specified as a parameter of this method. It also creates a new `DataTable` object in the `DataSet`. There are several overloaded `Fill()` methods that we can choose to better fit our needs.

- **Fill(*DataSet*) method** Adds or refreshes rows in the `DataSet` to match those in the data source using the `DataSet` name, and creates a `DataTable` named `"Table"`.

- **Fill(*DataTable*) method** Adds or refreshes rows in the `DataTable` to match those in the data source, using the `DataTable` name.

- **Fill(*DataSet*, *String*) method** Adds or refreshes rows in the `DataSet` to match those in the data source, using the `DataSet` name and `DataTable` names.

- **Fill(*DataTable*, *IDataReader*) method** Adds or refreshes rows in the `DataTable` to match those in the data source, using the specified `DataTable` and `IDataReader`.

- **Fill (*DataTable*, *IDbCommand*, *CommandBehavior*) method** Adds or refreshes rows in the `DataTable` to match those in the data source, using the `DataTable` name, the specified SQL SELECT statement, and `CommandBehavior`.

- **Fill (*DataSet*, *Integer*, *Integer*, *String*) method** Adds or refreshes rows in a specified range (`StartRecord` and `MaxRecords`) in the `DataSet` to match those in the data source, using the `DataSet` name and `DataTable` names.

- **Fill (*DataSet*, *String*, *IDataReader*, *Integer*, *Integer*) method** Adds or refreshes rows in a specified range (`StartRecord` and `MaxRecords`) in the `DataSet` to match those in the data source, using the `DataSet` name, `DataTable`, and `IDataReader` names.

● **Fill (*DataSet*, *Integer*, *Integer*, *String*, *IDbCommand*, *CommandBehavior*) method** Adds or refreshes rows in a specified range (StartRecord and MaxRecords) in the DataSet to match those in the data source, using the DataSet name, source table name, command string, and command behavior.

The CommandBehavior argument (of the CommandBehavior type) specifies a description of the results and the effect of the query command on the database. This argument can be a combination of the values CloseConnection (which indicates that after command execution the associated Connection object is closed when the associated DataReader is closed), KeyInfo (which indicates that the query returns column and primary key information), SchemaOnly (which indicates that the query returns column information only and does not affect the database state), SequentialAccess (which indicates that the results of the query are read sequentially to the column level), SingleResult (which indicates that the query returns a single result), and SingleRow (which indicates that the query is expected to return a single row).

When we call the Fill() method, it retrieves data from the data store and brings it back in the form of an XML file. This XML file ends up in the DataTable object created in the DataSet we specify as a parameter of the Fill() method. The following example shows how to save the DataSet as an XML file:

```
'---------------------------------------
' ADO.NET Connection Example. SQL Server
'---------------------------------------

Imports System
Imports System.Data
Imports System.Data.SqlClient
Imports System.XML

 Module Cons

 Sub Main()

    Dim Emp_DA  As SqlDataAdapter
    Dim DS      As New DataSet

    Cust_DA = New SqlDataAdapter("SELECT * FROM Customers", _
      "server=localhost;database=Northwind;uid=sa;pwd=;")
    Cust_DA.Fill(DS, "Customers")

    DS.WriteXML("Customers.XML", XmlWriteMode.WriteSchema)

 End Sub

 End Module
```

The content of `Customers.XML` (with some omissions) is as follows:

```xml
<?xml version="1.0" standalone="yes"?>
<NewDataSet>
 <xsd:schema id="NewDataSet" targetNamespace=""
 xmlns="" xmlns:xsd="http://www.w3.org/2001/XMLSchema"
 xmlns:msdata="urn:schemas-microsoft-com:xml-msdata">
 <xsd:element name="NewDataSet" msdata:IsDataSet="true">
 <xsd:complexType>
 <xsd:choice maxOccurs="unbounded">

 <xsd:element name="Customers">
 <xsd:complexType>
 <xsd:sequence>

 <xsd:element name="CustomerID" type="xsd:string" minOccurs="0" />
 <xsd:element name="CompanyName" type="xsd:string" minOccurs="0" />
 <xsd:element name="ContactName" type="xsd:string" minOccurs="0" />
 <xsd:element name="ContactTitle" type="xsd:string" minOccurs="0" />
 <xsd:element name="Address" type="xsd:string" minOccurs="0" />
 <xsd:element name="City" type="xsd:string" minOccurs="0" />
 <xsd:element name="Region" type="xsd:string" minOccurs="0" />
 <xsd:element name="PostalCode" type="xsd:string" minOccurs="0" />
 <xsd:element name="Country" type="xsd:string" minOccurs="0" />
 <xsd:element name="Phone" type="xsd:string" minOccurs="0" />
 <xsd:element name="Fax" type="xsd:string" minOccurs="0" />

 </xsd:sequence>
 </xsd:complexType>
 </xsd:element>
 </xsd:choice>
 </xsd:complexType>
 </xsd:element>
 </xsd:schema>

  <Customers>
    <CustomerID>ALFKI</CustomerID>
    <CompanyName>Alfreds Futterkiste</CompanyName>
    <ContactName>Maria Anders</ContactName>
    <ContactTitle>Sales Representative</ContactTitle>
    <Address>Obere Str. 57</Address>
    <City>Berlin</City>
    <PostalCode>12209</PostalCode>
```

```
    <Country>Germany</Country>
    <Phone>030-0074321</Phone>
    <Fax>030-0076545</Fax>
  </Customers>
  <Customers>
    <CustomerID>ANATR</CustomerID>
    <CompanyName>Ana Trujillo Emparedados y helados</CompanyName>
    <ContactName>Ana Trujillo</ContactName>
    <ContactTitle>Owner</ContactTitle>
    <Address>Avda. de la Constitución 2222</Address>
    <City>México D.F.</City>
    <PostalCode>05021</PostalCode>
    <Country>Mexico</Country>
    <Phone>(5) 555-4729</Phone>
    <Fax>(5) 555-3745</Fax>
  </Customers>
  <Customers>
    <CustomerID>ANTON</CustomerID>
    <CompanyName>Antonio Moreno Taquería</CompanyName>
    <ContactName>Antonio Moreno</ContactName>
    <ContactTitle>Owner</ContactTitle>
    <Address>Mataderos  2312</Address>
    <City>México D.F.</City>
    <PostalCode>05023</PostalCode>
    <Country>Mexico</Country>
    <Phone>(5) 555-3932</Phone>
  </Customers>

<!- Most of the data is removed for brevity ->

  <Customers>
    <CustomerID>WOLZA</CustomerID>
    <CompanyName>Wolski  Zajazd</CompanyName>
    <ContactName>Zbyszek Piestrzeniewicz</ContactName>
    <ContactTitle>Owner</ContactTitle>
    <Address>ul. Filtrowa 68</Address>
    <City>Warszawa</City>
    <PostalCode>01-012</PostalCode>
    <Country>Poland</Country>
    <Phone>(26) 642-7012</Phone>
    <Fax>(26) 642-7012</Fax>
  </Customers>
</NewDataSet>
```

The XML document above consists of two parts – the schema definition part and the data itself. In the schema definition part (which starts with the <xsd:schema> element), we will find the description of all the fields, in the table, along with its names and data types. Each field corresponds to one <xsd:element> of the XML document.

In the example above, we have used the WriteXml method of the DataSet object to produce the XML document that represents the contents of the DataSet. We have specified the XmlWriteMode argument as WriteSchema to get the contents of the DataSet with the metadata. Another type of XmlWriteMode argument is IgnoreSchema. With this we will get only data and DiffGram – a DataSet including original and current values. The DiffGram is a subset of an UpdateGram used in the Microsoft SQL Server. We will talk about diffgrams later in this chapter.

The DataSet object also supports the WriteXmlSchema(), ReadXml(), and ReadXmlSchema() methods. The WriteXmlSchema() method writes the DataSet as an XML schema. For example:

```
'----------------------------------------
' ADO.NET Connection Example. SQL Server
'----------------------------------------


Imports System
Imports System.Data
Imports System.Data.SqlClient
Imports System.XML


 Module Cons

 Sub Main()

   Dim Emp_DA  As SqlDataAdapter
   Dim Cust_DA As SqlDataAdapter
   Dim DS      As New DataSet

   Cust_DA = New SqlDataAdapter("SELECT * FROM Customers", _
     "server=localhost;database=Northwind;uid=sa;pwd=;")
   Cust_DA.Fill(DS, "Customers")

   DS.WriteXMLSchema("Customers_SC.XML")

 End Sub

 End Module
```

will produce the following XML document:

```
<?xml version="1.0" standalone="yes"?>
<xsd:schema id="NewDataSet" targetNamespace=""
 xmlns="" xmlns:xsd="http://www.w3.org/2001/XMLSchema"
 xmlns:msdata="urn:schemas-microsoft-com:xml-msdata">
<xsd:element name="NewDataSet" msdata:IsDataSet="true">
<xsd:complexType>
<xsd:choice maxOccurs="unbounded">

<xsd:element name="Customers">
<xsd:complexType>
<xsd:sequence>

 <xsd:element name="CustomerID" type="xsd:string" minOccurs="0" />
 <xsd:element name="CompanyName" type="xsd:string" minOccurs="0" />
 <xsd:element name="ContactName" type="xsd:string" minOccurs="0" />
 <xsd:element name="ContactTitle" type="xsd:string" minOccurs="0" />
 <xsd:element name="Address" type="xsd:string" minOccurs="0" />
 <xsd:element name="City" type="xsd:string" minOccurs="0" />
 <xsd:element name="Region" type="xsd:string" minOccurs="0" />
 <xsd:element name="PostalCode" type="xsd:string" minOccurs="0" />
 <xsd:element name="Country" type="xsd:string" minOccurs="0" />
 <xsd:element name="Phone" type="xsd:string" minOccurs="0" />
 <xsd:element name="Fax" type="xsd:string" minOccurs="0" />

</xsd:sequence>
</xsd:complexType>
</xsd:element>
</xsd:choice>
</xsd:complexType>
</xsd:element>
</xsd:schema>
```

The ReadXml() and ReadXmlSchema() methods can be used to read XML schema
and data or XML schema only in the DataSet.

Earlier in this section we talked about four properties of the DataAdapter –
SelectCommand, InsertCommand, UpdateCommand, and DeleteCommand. We said
that only the SelectCommand property is required and that the CommandBuilder
object can generate other properties for this DataAdapter. The following example
shows that the DataAdapter object fills the SelectCommand property automatically
(see also Figure 12.7):

```
'-----------------------------------------
' ADO.NET Connection Example. SQL Server
'-----------------------------------------

Imports System
Imports System.Data
Imports System.Data.SqlClient
Imports System.XML

Module Cons

Sub Main()

   Dim DA  As SqlDataAdapter
   Dim DS  As New DataSet

   DA = New SqlDataAdapter("SELECT * FROM Employees", _
     "server=localhost;database=Northwind;uid=sa;pwd=;")

   DA.Fill(DS, "Employees")

   Console.WriteLine(DA.SelectCommand.CommandText)

 End Sub

End Module
```

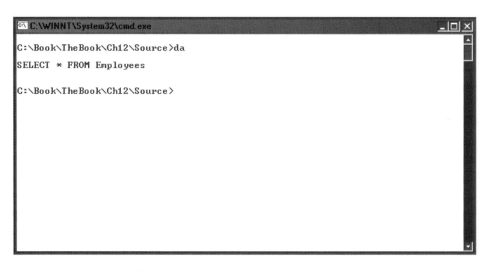

FIGURE 12.7   The DataAdapter has filled the SelectCommand property automatically

Other properties – `InsertCommand`, `UpdateCommand`, and `DeleteCommand` – are null, and an attempt to read from them causes an exception. To fill them, we need to create a new `CommandBuilder` object and use its `GetInsertCommand()`, `GetUpdateCommand()`, and `GetDeleteCommand()` methods as shown below:

```
'----------------------------------------
' ADO.NET Connection Example. SQL Server
'----------------------------------------


Imports System
Imports System.Data
Imports System.Data.SqlClient
Imports System.XML


Module Cons

Sub Main()

   Dim DA   As SqlDataAdapter
   Dim DS   As New DataSet
   Dim CmdBld As SqlCommandBuilder

   DA = New SqlDataAdapter("SELECT * FROM Employees", _
     "server=localhost;database=Northwind;uid=sa;pwd=;")

   DA.Fill(DS, "Employees")

   CmdBld = New SqlCommandBuilder(DA)

   Console.WriteLine(DA.SelectCommand.CommandText)
   Console.WriteLine(CmdBld.GetInsertCommand.CommandText)
   Console.WriteLine(CmdBld.GetUpdateCommand.CommandText)
   Console.WriteLine(CmdBld.GetDeleteCommand.CommandText)

  End Sub


 End Module
```

For our example, the `CommandBuilder` object will generate the following SQL statements:

```
INSERT INTO Employees(
 LastName , FirstName , Title , TitleOfCourtesy , BirthDate ,
 HireDate , Address , City , Region , PostalCode , Country ,
 HomePhone , Extension , Photo , Notes , ReportsTo ,
 PhotoPath )
VALUES (
 @p1 , @p2 , @p3 , @p4 , @p5 , @p6 , @p7 , @p8 , @p9 , @p10 ,
 @p11 , @p12 , @p13 , @p14 , @p15 , @p16 , @p17 )

UPDATE Employees
 SET LastName = @p1 , FirstName = @p2 , Title = @p3 ,
 TitleOfCourtesy = @p4 , BirthDate = @p5 , HireDate = @p6 ,
 Address = @p7 , City = @p8 , Region = @p9 ,
 PostalCode = @p10 , Country = @p11 , HomePhone = @p12 ,
 Extension = @p13 , Photo = @p14 , Notes = @p15 ,
 ReportsTo = @p16 , PhotoPath = @p17
 WHERE ( EmployeeID = @p18 AND LastName = @p19 AND FirstName = @p20
  AND Title = @p21 AND TitleOfCourtesy = @p22 AND BirthDate = @p23
  AND HireDate = @p24 AND Address = @p25 AND City = @p26
  AND Region = @p27 AND PostalCode = @p28 AND Country = @p29
  AND HomePhone = @p30 AND Extension = @p31 AND ReportsTo = @p32
  AND PhotoPath = @p33 )

DELETE FROM  Employees
 WHERE ( EmployeeID = @p1 AND LastName = @p2 AND FirstName = @p3
  AND Title = @p4 AND TitleOfCourtesy = @p5 AND BirthDate = @p6
  AND HireDate = @p7 AND Address = @p8 AND City = @p9
  AND Region = @p10 AND PostalCode = @p11 AND Country = @p12
  AND HomePhone = @p13 AND Extension = @p14 AND ReportsTo = @p15
  AND PhotoPath = @p16 )
```

Note that when we call the Update() method of the DataAdapter object, the appropriate values for the InsertCommand, UpdateCommand, and DeleteCommand properties are generated automatically depending on the SELECT command we have specified. If the values for these properties have been set already, the DataAdapter object will use them.

While this approach works in most cases, the preferred way is to specify our own InsertCommand, UpdateCommand, and DeleteCommand values. In this way we will be able to explicitly control how the update is done and ensure that it has better performance than does the autogenerated case.

Each xxxCommand property of the DataAdapter object is of the OleDbCommand or SqlCommand type (depending on the DataAdapter and managed provider we use). For more information on these objects see the Commands section earlier in this chapter. The following code snippet shows how to create the UPDATE command manually and associate it with the UpdateCommand property:

```
Dim UpdateCmd As SqlCommand

...

'
' Initialize the SqlCommand object
'
UpdateCmd = New SqlCommand("UPDATE Customers " & _
 "SET CustomerName=@pCustName WHERE CustomerID=@pCustID", _
 DA.SelectCommand.Connection)

'
' Create and append parameters for the UPDATE command
'
UpdateCmd.Parameters.Add(New SqlParameter("@pCustName", _
 SqlDbType.VarChar))
UpdateCmd.Parameters.Add("@pCustName").SourceColumn = "CustomerName"

UpdateCmd.Parameters.Add(New SqlParameter("@pCustID", _
 SqlDbType.Int))
UpdateCmd.Parameters.Add("@pCustName").SourceColumn = "CustomerID"

'
' Assign the SqlCommand to the UpdateCommand property
'
DA.UpdateCommand = UpdateCmd

'
' Manipulate the DataSet
'

...

'
' Update DataSet using our UPDATE command
'
DA.Update(DS, "Customers")
```

The same steps are used to associate the **INSERT** and **DELETE** commands with the **InsertCommand** and **DeleteCommand** properties of the **DataAdapter** object.

12.7 Tables, rows, and columns

We already know that the `DataSet` contains a collection of tables. To access the tables in the `DataSet` we use the following syntax:

```
DS.Tables.Item("Employees")
```

or

```
DS.Tables.Item("Customers")
```

For example, to find the figure returned for the query about how many rows a table has, we can use the following code:

```
Cust_DA = New SqlDataAdapter("SELECT * FROM Customers", _
  "server=localhost;database=Northwind;uid=sa;pwd=;")
Cust_DA.Fill(DS, "Customers")

Cust = DS.Tables.Item("Customers")
Console.WriteLine(Cust.TableName & " contains " & _
  Cust.Rows.Count & " record(s)")
```

Each item in the `Tables` collection is of a `DataTable` type. In the previous example, we used the `Rows` collection of the `DataTable` to find out how many rows the table contains. To iterate rows and columns, we can use the following code (see also Figure 12.8):

```
'----------------------------------------
' ADO.NET Connection Example. SQL Server
'----------------------------------------

Imports System
Imports System.Data
Imports System.Data.SqlClient
Imports System.XML

Module Cons

Sub Main()

    Dim Cust_DA As SqlDataAdapter
    Dim DS      As New DataSet
    Dim Cust    As DataTable
    Dim Row     As DataRow
    Dim Col     As DataColumn
```

```
    Cust_DA = New SqlDataAdapter("SELECT * FROM Customers", _
      "server=localhost;database=Northwind;uid=sa;pwd=;")
    Cust_DA.Fill(DS, "Customers")

    Cust = DS.Tables.Item("Customers")

    For Each Row In Cust.Rows
     For Each Col In Cust.Columns
      Console.WriteLine(Col.ColumnName & "=" & Row(Col))
     Next
     Console.WriteLine("──────────")
    Next


  End Sub


End Module
```

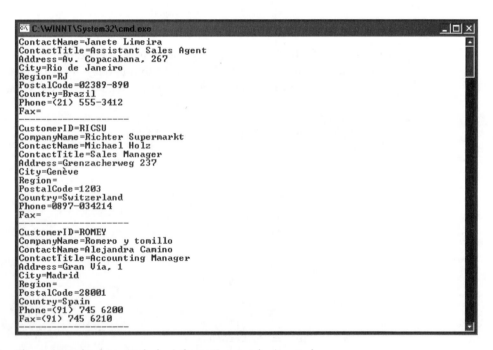

FIGURE 12.8   The rows and columns tabular information can be iterated

The examples given above look pretty simple – we have just used collections of the
DataSet filled for us by the DataAdapter. If, however, we want to add a new record,
for example, we have several choices:

- use a Command object to execute an appropriate SQL INSERT statement;
- use a Command object to execute an appropriate stored procedure;
- use appropriate methods of the collections of the DataSet object and then call its Update() method.

Let's look at an example of how we can use this last option:

```vbnet
'----------------------------------------
' ADO.NET Connection Example. SQL Server
'----------------------------------------


Imports System
Imports System.Data
Imports System.Data.SqlClient
Imports System.XML


 Module Cons


 Sub Main()


    Dim Cust_DA As SqlDataAdapter
    Dim DS       As New DataSet
    Dim Cust     As DataTable
    Dim Row      As DataRow
    Dim Col      As DataColumn


    Cust_DA = New SqlDataAdapter("SELECT * FROM Customers", _
      "server=localhost;database=Northwind;uid=sa;pwd=;")
    Cust_DA.Fill(DS, "Customers")


    Cust = DS.Tables.Item("Customers")


    Row = Cust.NewRow
    Row(0) = "AFED"
    Row(1) = "Alex's Minimart"
    Row(2) = "Alexei Fedorov"
    Row(3) = "Ocean Drive 345"
    Row(4) = "Spenserville"
    Row(5) = ""
    Row(6) = "95432"
    Row(7) = "USA"
    Row(8) = "717 256-0173"


    Cust.Rows.Add(Row)
```

```
For Each Row In Cust.Rows
  For Each Col In Cust.Columns
    Console.WriteLine(Col.ColumnName & "=" & Row(Col))
  Next
  Console.WriteLine("————————")
Next

End Sub

End Module
```

If we run this code, we can see that the new Row has been added to our table (see Figure 12.9).

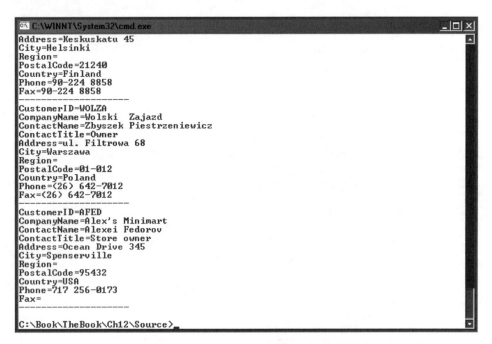

FIGURE 12.9   Using methods of the DataSet object a new row can be added to a table

As we have not called the Update() method, no data changes were posted to the data store. After we have changed our DataSet, we can look at its diffgram by using the following call to the WriteXml() method:

```
DS.WriteXML("Customers.XML", XmlWriteMode.DiffGram)
```

Here is the diffgram for our changed DataSet:

```xml
<?xml version="1.0" standalone="yes"?>
<diffgr:diffgram xmlns:msdata="urn:schemas-microsoft-com:xml-msdata"
 xmlns:diffgr="urn:schemas-microsoft-com:xml-diffgram-v1">
  <NewDataSet>
    <Customers diffgr:id="Customers1" msdata:rowOrder="0">
      <CustomerID>ALFKI</CustomerID>
      <CompanyName>Alfreds Futterkiste</CompanyName>
      <ContactName>Maria Anders</ContactName>
      <ContactTitle>Sales Representative</ContactTitle>
      <Address>Obere Str. 57</Address>
      <City>Berlin</City>
      <PostalCode>12209</PostalCode>
      <Country>Germany</Country>
      <Phone>030-0074321</Phone>
      <Fax>030-0076545</Fax>
    </Customers>
    <Customers diffgr:id="Customers2" msdata:rowOrder="1">
      <CustomerID>ANATR</CustomerID>
      <CompanyName>Ana Trujillo Emparedados y helados</CompanyName>
      <ContactName>Ana Trujillo</ContactName>
      <ContactTitle>Owner</ContactTitle>
      <Address>Avda. de la Constitución 2222</Address>
      <City>México D.F.</City>
      <PostalCode>05021</PostalCode>
      <Country>Mexico</Country>
      <Phone>(5) 555-4729</Phone>
      <Fax>(5) 555-3745</Fax>
    </Customers>

<!- Most of the data is removed for brevity ->

    <Customers diffgr:id="Customers91" msdata:rowOrder="90">
      <CustomerID>WOLZA</CustomerID>
      <CompanyName>Wolski  Zajazd</CompanyName>
      <ContactName>Zbyszek Piestrzeniewicz</ContactName>
      <ContactTitle>Owner</ContactTitle>
      <Address>ul. Filtrowa 68</Address>
      <City>Warszawa</City>
      <PostalCode>01-012</PostalCode>
      <Country>Poland</Country>
      <Phone>(26) 642-7012</Phone>
      <Fax>(26) 642-7012</Fax>
    </Customers>
```

```
    <Customers diffgr:id="Customers1" msdata:rowOrder="91"
     diffgr:hasChanges="inserted">
      <CustomerID>AFED</CustomerID>
      <CompanyName>Alex's Minimart</CompanyName>
      <ContactName>Alexei Fedorov</ContactName>
      <ContactTitle>Store owner</ContactTitle>
      <Address>Ocean Drive 345</Address>
      <City>Spenserville</City>
      <Region />
      <PostalCode>95432</PostalCode>
      <Country>USA</Country>
      <Phone>717 256-0173</Phone>
    </Customers>
  </NewDataSet>
</diffgr:diffgram>
```

Note that the last `<Customer>` node has a `diffgr:hasChanges` attribute set to
`"inserted"`. This indicates that we have a new record. We can get a more simplified
diffgram if we use the `GetChanges()` method of the `DataSet`, which returns a copy
of the `DataSet` containing all changes made to it since it was last loaded or since the
`AcceptChanges()` method was called:

```
DS.GetChanges.WriteXML("Customers.XML", XmlWriteMode.DiffGram)
```

To remove a record, we use the `Remove()` method of the `Rows` collection, and to perform an "update", we simply change a value of an appropriate `Column`.

Once we have done with our modifications, we call the `Update()` method, which
posts all updates to the data store:

```
Cust_DA.Update(DS, "Customers")
```

We will end our discussion of tables, rows, and columns with a brief reference section.

DataTable class

The `DataTable` class represents one table of in-memory data in the `DataSet`. To
manipulate data in the `DataTable`, we can use the following properties.

- **CaseSensitive** This `Boolean` property indicates whether or not string comparisons within the table are case-sensitive.
- **ChildRelations** Returns the `DataRelationCollection`, which defines the
  child relations for this table.
- **Columns** Returns the `DataColumnCollection` of columns (`DataColumn` object)
  for this table.
- **Constraints** Returns the `ConstraintCollection` of constraints (`Constraint`
  object) maintained by this table.

- **DataSet** Returns the DataSet object associated with this table.
- **DefaultView** Returns the DataView object associated with this table. This customized view may include a filtered view or a cursor position.
- **ExtendedProperties** Returns the PropertyCollection of customized user information.
- **HasErrors** This Boolean property indicates whether or not there are errors in any of the rows in any of the tables of the associated DataSet.
- **Locale** Specifies the locale (CultureInfo class) information used to compare strings within the table.
- **MinimumCapacity** Specifies the initial starting size for the table. The default value is 25 rows.
- **Namespace** Specifies the namespace for the XML representation of the data stored in the table as a String value.
- **ParentRelations** Returns the DataRelationCollection that defines the parent relations for this table.
- **Prefix** Specifies the namespace for the XML representation of the data stored in the table as a String value.
- **PrimaryKey** Specifies an array of columns (DataColumn()) that function as primary keys for the data table.
- **Rows** Returns the DataRowCollection of rows that belong to this table.
- **TableName** Specifies the name of this table as a String value.

We can use the following methods of the DataTable class.

- **AcceptChanges() method** Commits all changes made to this table since the last time the AcceptChanges method was called. When this method is called, any DataRow object still in the edit mode successfully ends its edits. The DataRowState also changes – all Added and Modified rows become Unchanged, Deleted rows are removed. This method must be called before we attempt to update the DataSet with the Update() method.
- **BeginLoadData() method** Used in conjunction with LoadDataRow and EndLoadData methods, this method turns off notifications, index maintenance, and constraints while loading data.
- **Clear() method** Clears the data in the DataTable by removing all rows.
- **Clone() method** Creates a new DataTable object with the same structure as the current table – all schemas, relations, and constraints.
- **Compute(*String*, *String*) method** Computes the given expression on the current rows that pass the filter criteria.
- **Copy() method** Creates a new DataTable object with the same structure (table schemas, relations, and constraints) and data as the current table.

- **EndLoadData() method** Ends data loading started with the `BeginLoadData()` method.

- **GetChanges() method** Returns a copy of the `DataTable` which contains all changes made to it since it was last loaded or since the `AcceptChanges()` method was called. The overloaded version of this method takes a `DataRowState` type parameter that acts as a filter for the data.

- **GetErrors() method** Returns an array of `DataRow` objects that contain errors.

- **ImportRow(*DataRow*) method** Copies a `DataRow` object into this table. The copy includes the original and current values, `DataRowState` values, and errors.

- **LoadDataRow(*Object*(), *Boolean*) method** Finds and updates a specified row. If no matching row is found, a new row is created using the given values.

- **NewRow() method** Creates a new `DataRow` object with the same schema as the table.

- **RejectChanges() method** Rolls back all changes that have been made to the table since it was loaded or the last time the `AcceptChanges()` method was called.

- **Select() method** Gets an array of `DataRow` objects. When selecting rows, we can specify filter criteria in order of primary key, the specified sort order, or specified state.

DataRow class

The `DataRow` class represents a row of data in a `DataTable`. Rows in the `DataTable` object are accessible via the `Rows` collection. To create a new `DataRow` object with the same schema as the table, we use the `NewRow()` method of the `DataTable`.

The `DataRow` class provides the following properties.

- **HasErrors** This `Boolean` property indicates whether or not there are errors in a columns collection.

- **Item(*String*)** Provides access to the data stored in a specified column.

- **ItemArray** Allows us to get or set the values for this row via an array of an `Object` type.

- **RowError** Specifies the custom error description for a row as a `String` value.

- **RowState** Returns the current state of the row with regard to its relationship to the `DataRowCollection`. This property is used in conjunction with the `GetChanges()` and `HasChanges()` methods of the `DataSet`. Possible values of the `RowState` property (defined by the `DataRowState` type) include `Added` (which shows that the row has been added to a `DataRowCollection` and the `AcceptChanges()` method has not been called), `Deleted` (which shows that the row was deleted by the `Delete()` method), `Detached` (which shows that the row has been created but not yet added to a `DataRowCollection`, or it has been removed from a collection), `Modified` (which shows that the row has been modified and the `AcceptChanges()` method has not been called), and `Unchanged` (which shows that the row has not changed since the `AcceptChanges()` method was last called).

- **Table** Specifies the `DataTable` associated with this `DataRow`.

We can use the following methods of the `DataRow` class:

- **AcceptChanges() method** Commits all changes made to this row since the last time `AcceptChanges` method was called.
- **BeginEdit() method** Begins an edit operation on a `DataRow` object. Calling this method puts the `DataRow` into edit mode.
- **CancelEdit() method** Cancels the current edit on the row.
- **ClearErrors() method** Clears any errors in the row, including the `RowError` property and errors set with `SetColumnError()` method.
- **Delete() method** Deletes the row. To undelete a deleted row, use the `RejectChanges()` method.
- **EndEdit() method** Ends the edit on a `DataRow` object started with the `BeginEdit()` method. This method is called automatically when we call the `AcceptChanges()` method.
- **GetChildRows(*DataRelation*) method** Returns the child rows of a `DataRow` as an array of `DataRow` objects.
- **GetColumnError(*DataColumn*) method** Returns the error description for a column. Overloaded versions of this method can accept a `String` name of the column or an `Integer` ordinal.
- **GetColumnsInError() method** Gets an array of columns that have errors as an array of `DataColumn` objects.
- **GetParentRow(*DataRelation*) method** Gets the parent row of a `DataRow`.
- **GetParentRows(*DataRelation*) method** Gets the parent rows of a `DataRow` as an array of `DataRow` objects.
- **HasVersion(*DataRowVersion*) method** Indicates whether or not a specified version exists. We call this method with an argument of the `DataRowVersion` type – it may contain the values `Default` (the row contains its default values), `Original` (the row contains its original values), `Current` (the row contains current values), or `Proposed` (the row contains a proposed value).
- **IsNull(DataColumn) method** Indicates whether or not the specified column contains a null value. Overloaded versions of this method can accept a `String` name of the column or an `Integer` ordinal.
- **RejectChanges() method** Rejects all changes made to the row since the last time the `AcceptChanges()` method was called. When this method is called, the `CancelMethod()` is implicitly called to cancel any edits. If the `RowState` property

is `Deleted` or `Modified`, the row reverts to its previous values and the `RowState` becomes `Unchanged`. If the `RowState` is `Added`, the row is removed.

- **SetColumnError(*DataColumn*, String) method** Sets the error description for a column. Overloaded versions of this method can accept a `String` name of the column or an `Integer` ordinal.

- **SetParentRow(*DataRow*) method** Sets the parent row of a DataRow.

DataColumn class

This class represents the schema of a column in a `DataTable`. We can access the columns of the `DataTable` object via the `Columns` property.

The `DataColumn` class provides the following properties.

- **AllowDBNull** This `Boolean` property indicates whether or not null values are allowed in this column for rows belonging to the table.

- **AutoIncrement** This `Boolean` property indicates whether or not the column automatically increments the value of the column for new rows added to the table.

- **AutoIncrementSeed** Specifies the starting value for a column that has its `AutoIncrement` property set to "True" as a `Long` value.

- **AutoIncrementStep** Specifies the increment used by a column with its `AutoIncrement` property set to "True" as a `Long` value. The default value is 1.

- **ColumnMapping** Specifies the `MappingType` of the column. This property determines how a `DataColumn` is mapped when a `DataSet` is saved as an XML document using the `WriteXml()` method. The `ColumnMapping` is of the `MappingType` type and it may have one of the values `Attribute` (the column is mapped to an XML attribute), `Element` (the column is mapped to an XML element), `Hidden` (the column is mapped to an internal structure), or `SimpleContent` (the column is mapped to an `XmlText` node).

- **ColumnName** Specifies the name of the column as a `String`.

- **DataType** Specifies the type of data stored in the column as a `Type`.

- **DefaultValue** Specifies the default value (of an `Object` type) for the column when creating new rows. The type of the `DefaultValue` is specified in the `DataType` property.

- **Expression** Specifies the expression (of a `String` value) used to filter rows, calculate the values in a column, or create an aggregate column.

- **ExtendedProperties** Returns the collection (of a `PropertyCollection` type) of customized user information.

- **MaxLength** Specifies the maximum length of a text column as an `Integer` value. The default value for this property is –1 (the column has no maximum length).

- **Namespace** Specifies the namespace for the XML representation of this column as a `String` value.

- **Ordinal** Specifies the index of the column in the `DataColumnCollection` as an `Integer` value.

- **Prefix** Specifies an XML prefix that aliases the namespace of the `DataTable` as a `String` value.

- **ReadOnly** This `Boolean` property indicates whether or not the column allows changes once a row has been added to the table.

- **Table** Specifies the `DataTable` to which the column belongs.

- **Unique** This `Boolean` property indicates whether or not the values in each row of the column must be unique.

12.8 Using transactions

A transaction is a series of operations performed as single unit of work. All operations in a transaction must be completed successfully in order to make the transaction successful. The transaction has a beginning and an end that specify the boundary of the transaction. Usually we use transactions in a stored procedure with the help of `BEGIN TRANSACTION` and `COMMIT/ROLLBACK TRANSACTION` statements – these allow us to run the transaction in a single round trip to the database server.

ADO.NET supports manual transactions – we can control the transaction boundary and explicitly start and end transactions. To perform operations within a single transaction, we need to create an `SqlTransaction` or `OleDbTransaction` object and associate it with the `Connection` object. We will use the `SqlTransaction` object for our examples.

This object provides several properties and methods that can be used to control a transaction. We can commit changes made to the database using the `Commit()` method if every operation in the transaction has been completed successfully. To roll back changes we use the `Rollback()` method. Let's look at an example of how to use the `SqlTransaction` object:

```
Dim Conn  As SqlConnection
Dim Cmd   As SqlCommand
Dim Trans As SqlTransaction

Conn = New SqlConnection("ConnectionString")
Cmd  = New SqlCommand

Conn.Open

'
' Begin transaction
'
```

```
Trans = Conn.BeginTransaction

'

' Associate Command with Transaction

'

Cmd.Transaction = Trans

Try

'

' Perform data operations here

'

 Trans.Commit

Catch

'

' Rollback the Transaction

'

 Trans.Rollback

Finally

 Conn.Close

End Try
```

Wrapping the code in a try/catch/finally block ensures that our transaction executes correctly. The transaction is committed in the end of the try block when all the data operations have been executed successfully. Any exception thrown is caught in the catch block where the transaction is rolled back to undo changes made within the transaction.

12.9 Processing errors

The DataAdapter class throws generic exceptions when problems occur. To obtain a descriptive error message for each fault in a row and column in any table in a DataSet, we use the following technique.

● Check the HasError property to see if any of the tables in the DataSet contain errors.

● If no errors are detected in the DataSet, we can safely proceed with the Update.

- If errors are detected in the `DataSet`, we use the `GetErrors` method to obtain the rows that contain the errors.
- Once we have determined which rows contain the errors, we use the `GetColumnError(DataColumn)` method to determine the incorrect columns for each row with errors.

The following example illustrates the technique described above:

```
If (Not DS.HasErrors) Then
'
' Proceed with Update
'

Else

For Each Table In DS.Tables

 If Table.HasErrors Then

  ErrRows = Table.GetErrors
  For I=0 to ErrRows.Length

   For Each Col In Table.Columns

    Console.WriteLine(Col.ColumnName & " " & _
    ErrRows(I).GetColumnError(Col))

   Next
    ErrRows(I).ClearErrors
  Next

 End If

Next

 End If
```

To catch the errors raised by managed providers, we can access provider-specific information. To do so, we need to process the `Errors` collection from the `OleDbException` or `SqlException` class. The following example shows how to do this:

```
Try
    '
    ' Open a connecton
    '
    Conn.Open

Catch Ex

    Dim I As Integer

    For I = 0 to Ex.Errors.Count-1

        Console.WriteLine("Message  : " & Ex.Errors(I).Message)
        Console.WriteLine("Source   : " & Ex.Errors(I).Source)

    Next

End Try
```

The Message and Source properties exist for both OleDbError and SqlError classes. Additional properties of the OleDbError class provide the following information:

- **NativeError** Returns the database-specific error information as an Integer code.
- **SQLState** Returns the five-character error code following the ANSI SQL standard for the database.

The SqlError class provides the following properties.

- **Class** Returns the severity level of the error returned from the SQL Server.
- **LineNumber** Returns the line number within the Transact-SQL command batch or stored procedure that contains the error.
- **Number** Returns a number that identifies the type of error.
- **Procedure** Returns the name of the stored procedure or remote procedure call (RPC) that generated the error.
- **Server** Returns the name of the instance of the SQL Server that generated the error.
- **State** Returns the number modifying the error to provide additional information.

12.10 Conclusion

In this chapter we learned about ADO.NET – the data access component of the Microsoft .NET Framework.

We started this chapter with a discussion of cover namespaces that contain classes used in the ADO.NET – the System.Data namespace, which can be found in the

`System.Data.dll` assembly, and its secondary namespaces `System.Data.Common`, `System.Data.OleDb`, `System.Data.SqlClient`, and `System.Data.SqlTypes`.

After this we learned about managed providers to access OLE DB data sources and SQL Server databases. We also talked about the four main components of a managed provider – connections, commands, data readers, and data adapters.

We also discussed tables, rows, and columns exposed via the object model provided by the `DataSet` class.

We ended this chapter by learning how to use transactions and process errors that may occur with databases during operations.

The material covered here provides a solid foundation for the topic of our next chapter – using data-aware controls to present and manipulate data.

chapter 13

Using data binding controls

- Working with data in web forms applications

- Working with data in Windows forms applications

In the previous chapter, we discussed ADO.NET and its major components – the `DataAdapter` and `DataSet` classes and managed providers for the OLE DB data sources and Microsoft SQL Server. While ADO.NET classes do a perfect job of accessing data providing us with all the functionality to select, insert, update, and delete data, for our applications we also need a presentation layer that will give our users a friendly interface with which to reach the functionality of ADO.NET.

In this chapter, we will learn about the data binding controls available in ASP.NET and Windows forms. Data binding is the process of automatically setting properties of one or more controls at runtime from a structure that contains data. While in this chapter we will mostly talk about binding to ADO.NET, ASP.NET and Windows forms can also be bound to other data sources. For example, we can use the following collections as a source of data for our applications:

- `Array;`
- `ArrayList;`
- `HashTable;`
- `Queue;`
- `SortedList;`
- `Stack;`
- `StringCollection.`

Database-related structures that can serve as a source of data include:

- `DataView;`
- `DataTable;`
- `DataSet;`
- `SqlDataReader;`
- `OleDbDataReader.`

In general, any object – either standard or customized – that implements the `IList` interface can be used as a source of data for the data-bound control.

This chapter is divided into two parts. In the first part, we will discuss the data-binding controls available in ASP.NET and how to use them in Windows forms applications. In the second part of this chapter, we will learn about the data-binding features of Windows forms controls.

13.1 Working with data in web forms applications

Data binding in web forms is supported by the very flexible declarative syntax that permits us to specify the source of data. Here is an example:

```
<%# CustomerID %>
```

Such a declaration can be placed anywhere on a page and will be evaluated when the `Page.DataBind()` method is called. Note that this is similar to ASP's:

```
<% =CustomerÏID %>
```

but the difference here is when the declaration is evaluated – in ASP it will be evaluated when the page is processed.

In this chapter, we will discuss how to use the following data-bound ASP.NET controls:

- `Repeater`;
- `DataList`;
- `DataGrid`;

as well as how to use data binding with other ASP.NET controls.

Repeater control

The `Repeater` control is the simplest data binding control available in ASP.NET. We use this control to display a list of records from a database table and can specify a template to be applied to each item displayed in the list. The following example shows how to display all records from the `Categories` table in the `Northwind` database (see also Figure 13.1).

```
<%@ Import Namespace="System.Data" %>
<%@ Import Namespace="System.Data.SqlClient" %>

<script runat="server">

 Sub Page_Load()

  Dim Conn As SqlConnection
  Dim Cmd  As SqlCommand

  Conn = New SqlConnection("server=localhost;" & _
    "database=Northwind;uid=sa;pwd=;")
  Cmd = New SqlCommand("SELECT CategoryName, Description " & _
    "FROM Categories", Conn)

  Conn.Open
  Rpt.DataSource = Cmd.ExecuteReader
  Rpt.DataBind
  Conn.Close

  End Sub
```

```
 </script>

<html>
 <head>
  <title>Repeater</title>
 </head>
<body>
 <form runat="server">
 <asp:Repeater
  id = "Rpt"
  runat="server">

  <ItemTemplate>

     <li> <%# Container.DataItem("CategoryName") %>
     (<%# Container.DataItem("Description" ) %>)
     </li>

  </ItemTemplate>

 </asp:Repeater>
 </form>
</body>
</html>
```

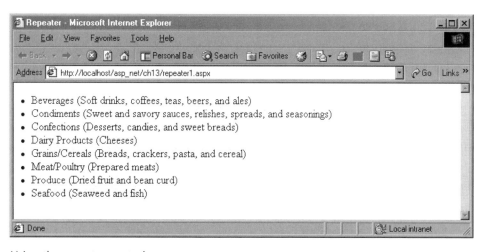

FIGURE 13.1   Using the repeater control

In the example above, we use the code in the Page_Load event handler to associate the Categories table with the Repeater web server control. We use the SqlConnection object to establish a connection with the SQL Server database and the SqlCommand object to specify the SELECT statement used to extract data from the database. Then we open the connection and get the SqlDataReader object by calling the ExecuteReader method of the SqlCommand object. After this we associate the SqlDataReader object with the Repeater control using its DataSource property. The DataBind method loads records from the SqlDataReader into the control.

Note that the Repeater control serves as a container for other tags. In the example above we have used the <ItemTemplate> tag, but there are others – more about this later. The <ItemTemplate> tag is used to specify how the database records should be displayed in the Repeater control. In our example we used the bulleted list to show each category with the category description in brackets on the same line as the category name. Within the <ItemTemplate> tag we can use any HTML tags, controls, text, and so on. To display a field from a record we use the following syntax:

```
<%# Container.DataItem("CategoryName") %>
```

The # character indicates that we are going to display data. The Container.DataItem("CategoryName") part specifies that we are interested in the value of the CategoryName field that is stored in the DataItem (items from the SqlDataReader) within the control that contains this statement. In our example, the Container control is an instance of the RepeaterItem class.

The <ItemTemplate> tag we have used in the example above is the only one that is required in the Repeater control for it to work. Other optional template tags include the following.

- **AlternatingItemTemplate** If defined, this template determines the content and layout of alternating (odd-indexed) items. Otherwise the ItemTemplate is used.
- **SeparatorTemplate** If defined, this template specifies the content to be rendered between items.
- **HeaderTemplate** If defined, this template determines the content and layout of the list header.
- **FooterTemplate** If defined, this template determines the content and layout of the list footer.

The templates listed above can be useful if we need to perform more complex formatting. For example, we can use the HeaderTemplate and FooterTemplate to show our data in tabular format (see also Figure 13.2):

```
<asp:Repeater
  id = "Rpt"
  runat="server">

  <HeaderTemplate>
   <table border=1>
    <tr>
```

```
        <td><b>Category</b></td>
        <td><b>Description</b></td>
      </tr>
    </HeaderTemplate>

    <ItemTemplate>

      <tr>
        <td> <%# Container.DataItem("CategoryName") %> </td>
        <td> <%# Container.DataItem("Description" ) %> </td>
      </tr>

    </ItemTemplate>

    <FooterTemplate>
      </table>
    </FooterTemplate>

  </asp:Repeater>
```

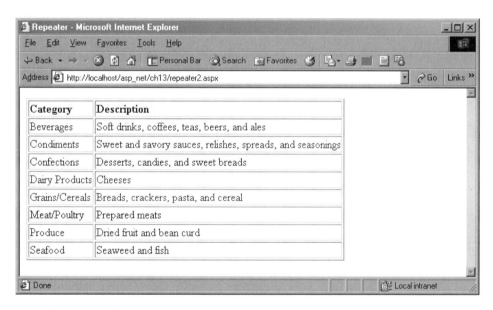

FIGURE 13.2 Using the HeaderTemplate and FooterTemplate, we can display data as a table

To display odd and even items with different backgrounds, we can use `AlternatingItemTemplate`, as shown in the example below (see also Figure 13.3):

```
<asp:Repeater
  id = "Rpt"
  runat="server">

  <HeaderTemplate>
   <table border=1>
    <tr>
     <td><b>Category</b></td>
     <td><b>Description</b></td>
    </tr>
  </HeaderTemplate>

  <ItemTemplate>

   <tr>
     <td> <%# Container.DataItem("CategoryName") %> </td>
     <td> <%# Container.DataItem("Description" ) %> </td>
   </tr>

  </ItemTemplate>

  <AlternatingItemTemplate>

   <tr bgcolor="#c0c0c0">
     <td> <%# Container.DataItem("CategoryName") %> </td>
     <td> <%# Container.DataItem("Description" ) %> </td>
   </tr>

  </AlternatingItemTemplate>

  <FooterTemplate>
   </table>
  </FooterTemplate>

</asp:Repeater>
```

Category	Description
Beverages	Soft drinks, coffees, teas, beers, and ales
Condiments	Sweet and savory sauces, relishes, spreads, and seasonings
Confections	Desserts, candies, and sweet breads
Dairy Products	Cheeses
Grains/Cereals	Breads, crackers, pasta, and cereal
Meat/Poultry	Prepared meats
Produce	Dried fruit and bean curd
Seafood	Seaweed and fish

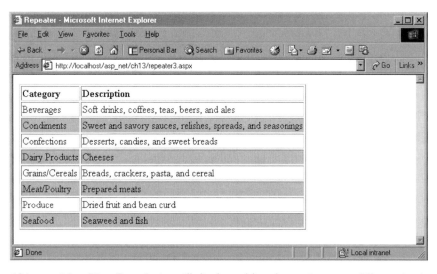

FIGURE 13.3 `AlternatingItemTemplate` will display odd and even items on different backgrounds

Suppose we want to display our data in a tabular format, but some of the fields contain a `NULL` value. What will happen? Figure 13.4 shows the results of displaying data returned by the following query:

```
SELECT CompanyName, ContactName, Region FROM Customers
```

Company	Contact	Region
Alfreds Futterkiste	Maria Anders	
Ana Trujillo Emparedados y helados	Ana Trujillo	
Antonio Moreno Taquería	Antonio Moreno	
Around the Horn	Thomas Hardy	
Berglunds snabbköp	Christina Berglund	
Blauer See Delikatessen	Hanna Moos	
Blondesddsl père et fils	Frédérique Citeaux	
Bólido Comidas preparadas	Martín Sommer	
Bon app'	Laurence Lebihan	
Bottom-Dollar Markets	Elizabeth Lincoln	BC
B's Beverages	Victoria Ashworth	
Cactus Comidas para llevar	Patricio Simpson	
Centro comercial Moctezuma	Francisco Chang	
Chop-suey Chinese	Yang Wang	

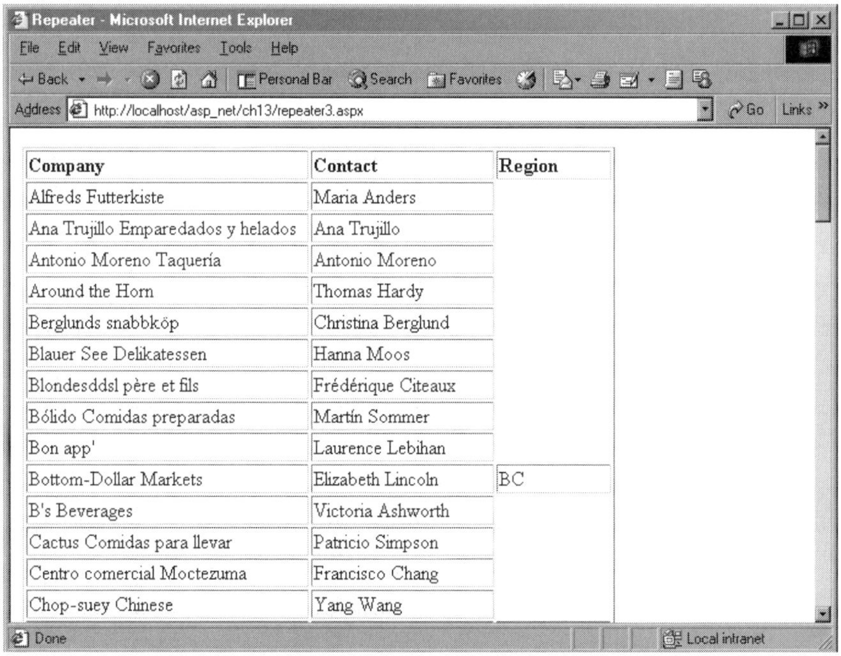

FIGURE 13.4 The formatting of a table is affected by cells having a `NULL` value

Note that when a `Region` field contains the `NULL` value, the table cell is not properly formatted. To avoid this, we can change our `SELECT` query to the following:

```
SELECT CompanyName, ContactName,
IsNull(Region, 'Not Specified') As Region FROM Customers
```

Instead of `"Not Specified"`, we can use any literal text, even a `"NULL"`. Figure 13.5 shows how the output will look after we have changed our `SELECT` query.

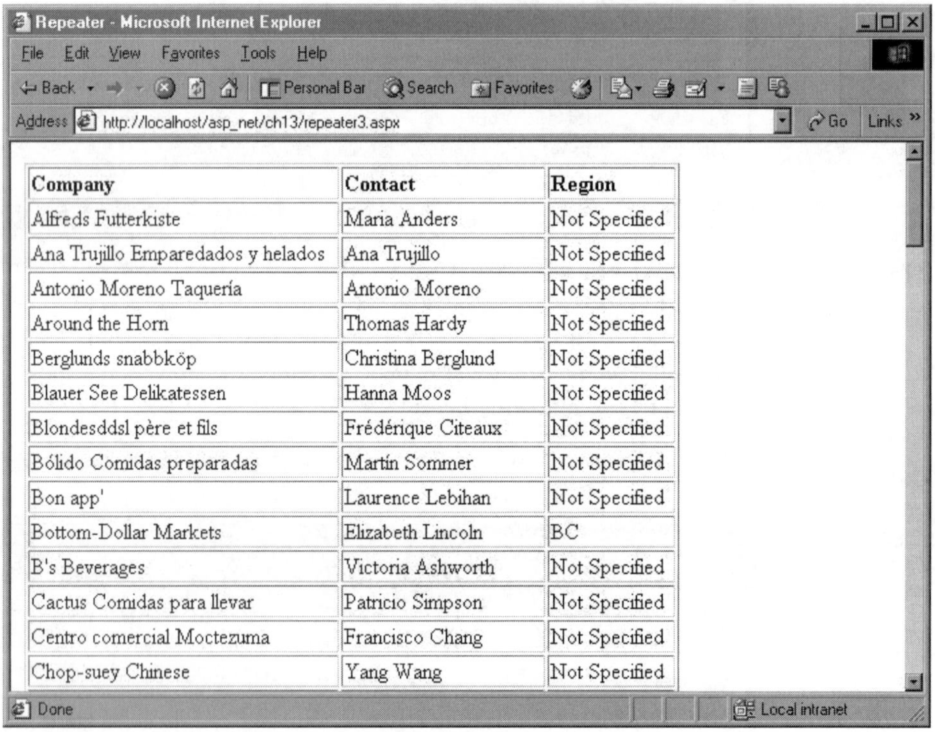

Company	Contact	Region
Alfreds Futterkiste	Maria Anders	Not Specified
Ana Trujillo Emparedados y helados	Ana Trujillo	Not Specified
Antonio Moreno Taquería	Antonio Moreno	Not Specified
Around the Horn	Thomas Hardy	Not Specified
Berglunds snabbköp	Christina Berglund	Not Specified
Blauer See Delikatessen	Hanna Moos	Not Specified
Blondesddsl père et fils	Frédérique Citeaux	Not Specified
Bólido Comidas preparadas	Martín Sommer	Not Specified
Bon app'	Laurence Lebihan	Not Specified
Bottom-Dollar Markets	Elizabeth Lincoln	BC
B's Beverages	Victoria Ashworth	Not Specified
Cactus Comidas para llevar	Patricio Simpson	Not Specified
Centro comercial Moctezuma	Francisco Chang	Not Specified
Chop-suey Chinese	Yang Wang	Not Specified

FIGURE 13.5 Changing the SELECT query helps resolve the formatting of NULL value cells

If we want to display just an empty cell, we may use `" "` as the text for the `NULL` value.

As an alternative to this approach, we can use our own text and place it in the `<script>` block:

```
<script>

...

Function CheckForNull(S As String) As String
  If S = "" Then
   IsNull = "Not Specified"
```

```
   Else
     IsNull = S
   End If
 End Function

 ...
 </script>
```

Then we use the following function when we display a field:

```
   <ItemTemplate>

    <tr>
      <td> <%# Container.DataItem("CompanyName") %> </td>
      <td> <%# Container.DataItem("ContactName") %> </td>
      <td>
       <%# CheckForNull(Container.DataItem("Region").ToString()) %>
      </td>
    </tr>

   </ItemTemplate>
```

As our <%# ... %> tag defines just the content of the HTML table cell, we can use HTML formatting in our IsNull function. For example:

```
 IsNull = "<span style='background:red;color:white'>Empty</span>"
```

DataList control

The DataList control is a ASP.NET web server control that is a template-defined data-bound list. This control provides more functionality when, for example, selecting and editing than the Repeater control, discussed in the previous section.

Here is an example of how to use the DataList control (see also Figure 13.6):

```
<%@ Import Namespace="System.Data" %>
<%@ Import Namespace="System.Data.SqlClient" %>

<script runat="server">

 Sub Page_Load()

  Dim Conn As SqlConnection
  Dim Cmd  As SqlCommand
```

```vbnet
  Conn = New SqlConnection("server=localhost;" & _
    "database=Northwind;uid=sa;pwd=;")
  Cmd = New SqlCommand("SELECT CategoryName, Description " & _
    "FROM Categories", Conn)

  Conn.Open
  DList.DataSource = Cmd.ExecuteReader
  DList.DataBind
  Conn.Close

 End Sub

</script>

<html>
 <head>
  <title>DataList</title>
 </head>
<body>
 <form runat="server">

<asp:DataList
  id = "DList"
  runat="server">

  <ItemTemplate>

    <%# Container.DataItem("CategoryName") %>
    (<%# Container.DataItem("Description" ) %>)

  </ItemTemplate>

 </asp:DataList>

 </form>
</body>
</html>
```

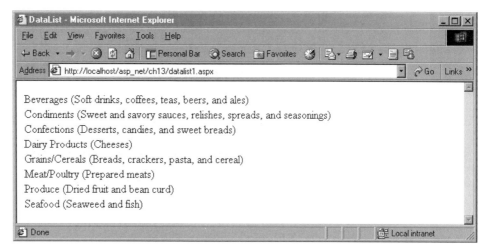

FIGURE 13.6   The DataList control in action

The DataList control displays information in the HTML table that can be fine-tuned using the CellPadding, CellSpacing, and GridLines properties of the control. For example (see also Figure 13.7):

```
<asp:DataList
   id = "DList"
   CellPadding=10
   CellSpacing=10
   GridLines="Both"
   runat="server">

   <ItemTemplate>

      <%# Container.DataItem("CategoryName") %>
      (<%# Container.DataItem("Description" ) %>)

   </ItemTemplate>

</asp:DataList>
```

To display data in multiple columns, we use the RepeatDirection and RepeatColumns properties of the control. For example, here is how to display data in three columns (see Figure 13.8):

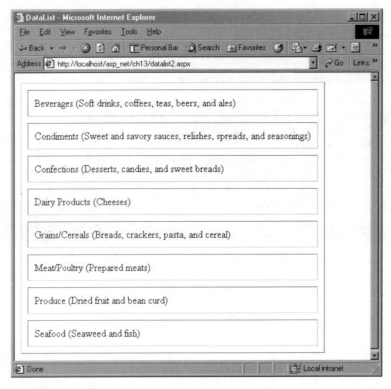

FIGURE 13.7   Using the `CellPadding`, `CellSpacing`, and `GridLines` properties to fine-tune the layout

```
<asp:DataList
  id = "DList"
  CellPadding=10
  CellSpacing=10
  GridLines="Both"
  RepeatColumns = 3
  RepeatDirection="Vertical"

  runat="server">

  <ItemTemplate>

    <%# Container.DataItem("CategoryName") %>
    (<%# Container.DataItem("Description" ) %>)

  </ItemTemplate>

</asp:DataList>
```

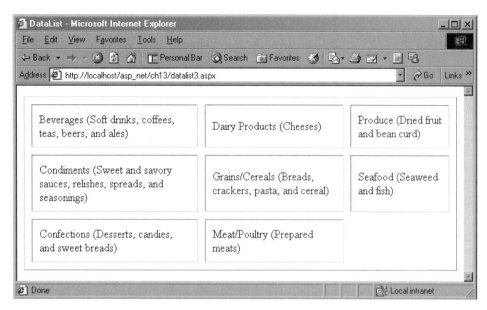

FIGURE 13.8   Using the RepeatDirection and RepeatColumns properties, data can be displayed in columns

The RepeatLayout property controls the layout of items in a list. The default value for this property is a Table – data is displayed within an HTML table. If we set this property to Flow, items will be displayed without a table structure, each item being displayed inside a <SPAN> tag.

The DataList control supports several events.

● **CancelCommand** This event occurs when the control with the Command property set to Cancel is clicked in the DataList control.

● **DeleteCommand** This event occurs when the control with the Command property set to Delete is clicked in the DataList control.

● **EditCommand** This event occurs when the control with the Command property set to Edit is clicked in the DataList control.

● **ItemCommand** This event occurs when the control is clicked in the DataList control.

● **UpdateCommand** This event occurs when the control with the Command property set to Update is clicked in the DataList control.

● **SelectedIndexChanged** This event occurs when an item on the list is selected.

To be able to generate events, we need to use ASP.NET server controls. For example, we can use the LinkButton control to create a menu of product categories, as shown in the example below (see also Figure 13.9):

```
<asp:DataList
  id = "DList"
  CellPadding=10
  CellSpacing=10
  GridLines="Both"
  RepeatColumns = 4
  RepeatDirection="Vertical"

  runat="server">

  <ItemTemplate>

    <asp:LinkButton
     id="Btn1"
     Text = '<%# Container.DataItem("CategoryName") %>'
     runat="server"
    />

  </ItemTemplate>

</asp:DataList>
```

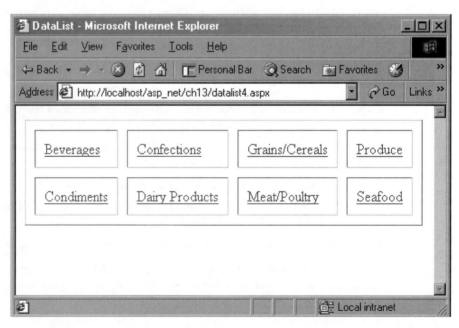

FIGURE 13.9   The LinkButton control can be used to generate a menu of product categories

To find which items in the "menu" were clicked, we should add the event handler for the ItemCommand event, as shown below (see also Figure 13.10):

```
<%@ Import Namespace="System.Data" %>
<%@ Import Namespace="System.Data.SqlClient" %>

<script runat="server">

 Sub Page_Load()

  Dim Conn As SqlConnection
  Dim Cmd  As SqlCommand

  If Not IsPostBack Then

   Conn = New SqlConnection("server=localhost;" & _
    "database=Northwind;uid=sa;pwd=;")
   Cmd = New SqlCommand("SELECT CategoryName, Description " & _
    "FROM Categories", Conn)

   Conn.Open
   DList.DataSource = Cmd.ExecuteReader
   DList.DataBind
   Conn.Close

  End If

 End Sub

 Sub ShowCategory(sender As Object, e As DataListCommandEventArgs)

  Response.Write("Selected Index : " & e.Item.ItemIndex.ToString())

 End Sub

</script>

<html>
 <head>
  <title>DataList</title>
 </head>
<body>
 <form runat="server">
```

```
<asp:DataList
  id = "DList"
  CellPadding=10
  CellSpacing=10
  GridLines="Both"
  RepeatColumns = 4
  RepeatDirection="Vertical"
  OnItemCommand = "ShowCategory"
  runat="server">

  <ItemTemplate>
    <asp:LinkButton
      id="Btn1"
      Text = '<%# Container.DataItem("CategoryName") %>'
      runat="server"
    />

  </ItemTemplate>

 </asp:DataList>
 </form>
</body>
</html>
```

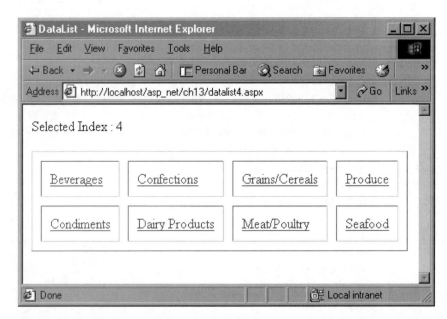

FIGURE 13.10   The event handler for the ItemCommand event will produce a list of items that have been clicked

To display the name of the selected category instead of the index, we can use the object model of the `DataList` control or simply assign the name of the category to the `CommandArgument` property of the `LinkButton` control (see also Figure 13.11):

```
Sub ShowCategory(sender As Object, e As DataListCommandEventArgs)

    Response.Write ("Selected Category : " & e.CommandArgument)

End Sub

...

    <ItemTemplate>
      <asp:LinkButton
       id="Btn1"
       Text = '<%# Container.DataItem("CategoryName") %>'
       CommandArgument = '<%# Container.DataItem("CategoryName") %>'
       runat="server"
      />

    </ItemTemplate>
```

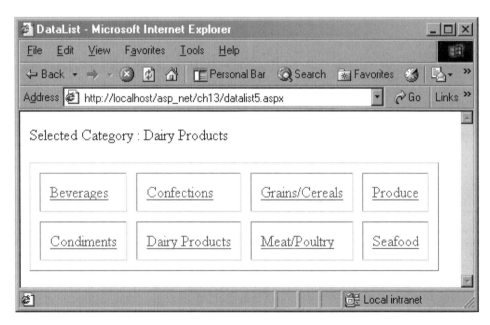

FIGURE 13.11 Giving the name of the category to the CommandArgument property of the LinkButton control enables it to be displayed

We can use the `SelectedItemTemplate` template of the `DataList` control to specify the display option for the selected item. The following example shows how to use the `SelectedItemTemplate` to display the currently selected item with white font on a black background (see also Figure 13.12):

```
<%@ Import Namespace="System.Data" %>
<%@ Import Namespace="System.Data.SqlClient" %>


<script runat="server">

 Sub Page_Load()

  If Not IsPostBack Then
   LoadData()
  End If

 End Sub

 Sub LoadData

  Dim Conn As SqlConnection
  Dim Cmd  As SqlCommand

  Conn = New SqlConnection("server=localhost;" & _
   "database=Northwind;uid=sa;pwd=;")
   Cmd = New SqlCommand("SELECT CategoryName, Description " & _
    "FROM Categories", Conn)

  Conn.Open
  DList.DataSource = Cmd.ExecuteReader
  DList.DataBind
  Conn.Close

 End Sub

 Sub ShowCategory(sender As Object, e As DataListCommandEventArgs)

  DList.SelectedIndex = e.Item.ItemIndex
  LoadData()

 End Sub

</script>
```

```
<html>
 <head>
  <title>DataList</title>
 </head>
<body>
 <form runat="server">
<asp:DataList
   id = "DList"
   CellPadding=10
   CellSpacing=10
   GridLines="Both"
   RepeatColumns = 4
   RepeatDirection="Vertical"

   OnItemCommand = "ShowCategory"

   runat="server">

   <ItemTemplate>
     <asp:LinkButton
       id="Btn1"
       Text = '<%# Container.DataItem("CategoryName") %>'
       runat="server"
     />

   </ItemTemplate>

   <SelectedItemTemplate>

     <span style='background:black;color:white;'>
      <%# Container.DataItem("CategoryName") %>
     </span>

   </SelectedItemTemplate>

 </asp:DataList>
 </form>
</body>
</html>
```

So far, we have seen how to use the DataList control to display a menu of product categories from the Categories table in the Northwind database. In order to make

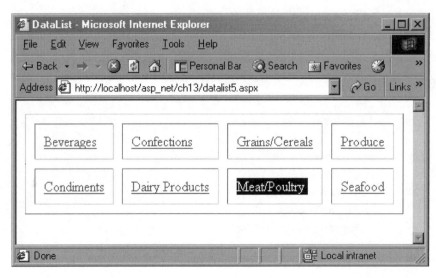

FIGURE 13.12 Using the `SelectedItemTemplate`, we can display the selected item in white text on a black background

our example more interesting, let's allow users to see a list of products in each selected category. To do this we need a second `DataList` control that will display data from the `Products` category, selected using the following SQL statement:

```
SELECT ProductName, QuantityPerUnit FROM Products WHERE CategoryID=n
```

where **n** is the category identifier for a given category. This is stored in the `Categories` table as a primary key for this table. The first thing we need to do is change the `SELECT` query for our list of categories:

```
SELECT CategoryID, CategoryName FROM Categories
```

Next, we use the `DataKeyField` property of the first `DataList` control to specify the name of the primary key. Then we can access the value of the primary key by means of the `DataKeys` collection of the `DataList` control with the following assignment:

```
DList.DataKeys.Item(e.Item.ItemIndex)
```

The `DataKeys` collection contains the values of the primary keys for the table specified in the `DataSource` property. The following example illustrates this (see also Figure 13.13):

```
<%@Page Debug="True" %>
<%@ Import Namespace="System.Data" %>
<%@ Import Namespace="System.Data.SqlClient" %>


<script runat="server">

  Sub Page_Load()
```

```
 If Not IsPostBack Then
  LoadData()
 End If

End Sub

Sub LoadData

 Dim Conn As SqlConnection
 Dim Cmd  As SqlCommand

 Conn = New SqlConnection("server=localhost;" & _
  "database=Northwind;uid=sa;pwd=;")
 Cmd = New SqlCommand("SELECT CategoryID, CategoryName " & _
  "FROM Categories", Conn)

 Conn.Open
 DList.DataSource = Cmd.ExecuteReader
 DList.DataBind
 Conn.Close

End Sub

Sub LoadProds(ID as Integer)

 Dim Conn As SqlConnection
 Dim Cmd  As SqlCommand

 Conn = New SqlConnection("server=localhost;" & _
  "database=Northwind;uid=sa;pwd=;")
 Cmd = New SqlCommand("SELECT ProductName, QuantityPerUnit " & _
  "FROM Products WHERE CategoryID=" & ID, Conn)

 Conn.Open
 ProdList.DataSource = Cmd.ExecuteReader
 ProdList.DataBind
 Conn.Close

End Sub

Sub ShowCategory(sender As Object, e As DataListCommandEventArgs)
```

```
   DList.SelectedIndex = e.Item.ItemIndex
   LoadData()
   LoadProds(DList.DataKeys.Item(e.Item.ItemIndex))


 End Sub


</script>


<html>
 <head>
  <title>DataList</title>
 </head>
<body>
 <form runat="server">
<asp:DataList
   id = "DList"
   CellPadding=10
   CellSpacing=10
   GridLines="Both"
   RepeatColumns = 4
   RepeatDirection="Vertical"
   DataKeyField="CategoryID"
   OnItemCommand = "ShowCategory"

   runat="server">

   <ItemTemplate>
     <asp:LinkButton
      id="Btn1"
      Text = '<%# Container.DataItem("CategoryName") %>'
      runat="server"
     />

   </ItemTemplate>

  <SelectedItemTemplate>

    <span style='background:black;color:white;'>
     <%# Container.DataItem("CategoryName") %>
    </span>

   </SelectedItemTemplate>
```

```
    </asp:DataList>
    <asp:DataList
     id="ProdList"
     GridLines="Both"
     CellPadding=10
     CellSpacing=10
     RepeatColumns = 2
     RepeatDirection="Horizontal"
     runat="server">

      <ItemTemplate>

        <%# Container.DataItem("ProductName") %>
        (<%# Container.DataItem("QuantityPerUnit") %>)
      </ItemTemplate>

    </asp:DataList>
    </form>
  </body>
</html>
```

FIGURE 13.13 DataKeys has the values of the primary keys for the table specified in the DataSource property

To support editing of the items in the `DataList` control, we use the `EditItemTemplate` template. Let's add the editing functionality to the `Products` table extracted from the `Northwind` database. We will allow users to update and delete selected items from this table. The following example shows how to do this (see also Figure 13.14):

```
<%@Page Debug="True" %>
<%@ Import Namespace="System.Data" %>
<%@ Import Namespace="System.Data.SqlClient" %>


<script runat="server">

 Sub Page_Load()

  If Not IsPostBack Then
   LoadData()
  End If

 End Sub

 Sub LoadData

  Dim Conn As SqlConnection
  Dim Cmd  As SqlCommand

  Conn = New SqlConnection("server=localhost;" & _
   "database=Northwind;uid=sa;pwd=;")
  Cmd = New SqlCommand("SELECT * FROM Products", Conn)

  Conn.Open
  ProdList.DataSource = Cmd.ExecuteReader
  ProdList.DataBind
  Conn.Close

 End Sub

 Sub EditProduct(sender As Object, e As DataListCommandEventArgs)

  ProdList.EditItemIndex = e.Item.ItemIndex
  LoadData

 End Sub
```

```
Sub DeleteProduct(sender As Object, e As DataListCommandEventArgs)

  Dim Conn As SqlConnection
  Dim Cmd  As SqlCommand

  Conn = New SqlConnection("server=localhost;" & _
   "database=Northwind;uid=sa;pwd=;")
  Cmd = New SqlCommand("DELETE Products WHERE " & _
   "ProductID=@ProdID", Conn)

  Cmd.Parameters.Add(New SqlParameter("@ProdID", SqlDbType.Int))
  Cmd.Parameters("@ProdID").Value = _
   ProdList.DataKeys.Item(e.Item.ItemIndex)

  Conn.Open
  Cmd.ExecuteNonQuery
  ProdList.DataBind()
  ProdList.EditItemIndex = -1
  Conn.Close
  LoadData

End Sub

Sub UpdateProduct(sender As Object, e As DataListCommandEventArgs)

  Dim Conn As SqlConnection
  Dim Cmd  As SqlCommand

  Conn = New SqlConnection("server=localhost;" & _
   "database=Northwind;uid=sa;pwd=;")
  Cmd = New SqlCommand("UPDATE Products SET ProductName=@ProdName" & _
   _  " WHERE ProductID=@ProdID", Conn)

  Cmd.Parameters.Add(New SqlParameter("@ProdName", _
   SqlDbType.VarChar, 40))
  Cmd.Parameters("@ProdName").Value = _
   CType(e.Item.FindControl("ProdName"), TextBox).Text

  Cmd.Parameters.Add(New SqlParameter("@ProdID", SqlDbType.Int))
  Cmd.Parameters("@ProdID").Value = _
   ProdList.DataKeys.Item(e.Item.ItemIndex)
```

```
     Conn.Open
     Cmd.ExecuteNonQuery
     ProdList.DataBind()
     ProdList.EditItemIndex = -1
     Conn.Close
     LoadData


  End Sub

  Sub CancelEdit(sender As Object, e As DataListCommandEventArgs)

    ProdList.EditItemIndex = -1
    LoadData


  End Sub

</script>
<html>
 <head>
  <title>DataList</title>
 </head>
<body>
 <form runat="server">
<asp:DataList
   id = "ProdList"
   CellPadding=10
   CellSpacing=10
   GridLines="Both"
   RepeatColumns = 2
   RepeatDirection="Vertical"
   DataKeyField="ProductID"

   OnEditCommand   ="EditProduct"
   OnDeleteCommand="DeleteProduct"
   OnUpdateCommand="UpdateProduct"
   OnCancelCommand="CancelEdit"

   runat="server">

   <ItemTemplate>
```

```
  <asp:LinkButton
   Text="Edit"
   CommandName="edit"
   runat="server"
  />

  <%# Container.DataItem("ProductName") %>
 </ItemTemplate>

 <EditItemTemplate>

  <b>Product Name:</b><br>
  <asp:TextBox
   id="ProdName"
   Text='<%# Container.DataItem("ProductName") %>'
   runat="server"
  />
 <br>
 <center>
 <asp:LinkButton
  id="button2"
  Text="Update"
  CommandName="update"
  runat="server"
 />

  <asp:LinkButton
   id="button3"
   Text="Delete"
   CommandName="delete"
   runat="server"
  />

  <asp:LinkButton
   id="button4"
   Text="Cancel"
   CommandName="cancel"
   runat="server"
 />
  </center>
  </EditItemTemplate>

 </asp:DataList>
 </form>
</body>
</html>
```

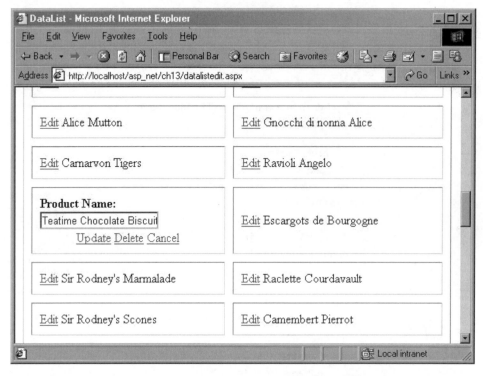

FIGURE 13.14 Editing functions have been added with the `EditItemTemplate` so updates and deletions can be achieved

Let's dissect our example to find out how it works. We started with the basic `DataList` control, which displays a list of products in two columns. Then we added the `LinkButton` for each item in the list – in the `ItemTemplate` template. When we press them the `LinkButton` fires the `EditCommand` event, which is directed to the `OnEditCommand` event handler of the `DataList` control. The code in the event handler sets the `EditItemIndex` property to the index of the selected item. This causes the `EditItemTemplate` template to take an action. It shows the `TextBox` control with the contents of the field and three buttons – `Update`, `Delete`, and `Cancel`. Each button has an appropriate event handler specified by `OnUpdateCommand`, `OnDeleteCommand`, and `OnCancelCommand` of the `DataList` control.

To cancel a current operation, we simply set the `EditItemIndex` property to –1, which means that none of the items in the `DataList` control is currently selected for editing.

The event handler for the `Update` command executes the UPDATE SQL statement to change the contents of the appropriate field in the `Products` table. This is done by means of the parameterized `SqlCommand` object, which takes two parameters – the new name of the product and the product identifier.

We use the same approach to create the DELETE SQL statement. In this case, it is done by using the parameterized `SqlCommand` object, which takes one parameter – the product identifier.

One final note for this example. For update and delete operations, we have used the UPDATE and DELETE SQL statements. This was done for illustrative purposes. In real-life applications, it is preferable to use stored procedures that may implement more advanced functionality, support for transactions, checking for referential integrity, and so on.

Earlier in this section we saw how to use two templates of the DataList control – the SelectedItemTemplate and the EditItemTemplate. This control also supports all of the templates of the Repeater control – AlternatingItemTemplate, SeparatorTemplate, HeaderTemplate, and FooterTemplate, as well as sets of styles that allow us to customize the appearance of the DataList control and its different parts. These styles include:

- AlternatingItemStyle;
- EditItemStyle;
- FooterStyle;
- HeaderStyle;
- ItemStyle;
- SelectedItemStyle;
- SeparatorStyle.

Each property is of the TableItemStyle type and, by using it, we can define such attributes as the background color, style of the border, font, vertical alignment, and so on. The following example shows how to define styles for the header, item, and alternating item in the DataList control (see also Figure 13.15):

```
<%@ Import Namespace="System.Data" %>
<%@ Import Namespace="System.Data.SqlClient" %>

<script runat="server">

 Sub Page_Load()

  Dim Conn As SqlConnection
  Dim Cmd  As SqlCommand

  Conn = New SqlConnection("server=localhost;" & _
   "database=Northwind;uid=sa;pwd=;")
  Cmd = New SqlCommand("SELECT ProductName FROM Products", Conn)

  Conn.Open
  DList.DataSource = Cmd.ExecuteReader
  DList.DataBind
  Conn.Close

 End Sub

</script>
```

```html
<html>
 <head>
  <title>DataList</title>
 </head>
<body>
 <form runat="server">
<asp:DataList
  id = "DList"
  CellPadding=10
  CellSpacing=10
  GridLines="Both"
  RepeatColumns = 3
  RepeatDirection="Horizontal"
  runat="server">

  <HeaderStyle
   BackColor="#a7c7b7"
   HorizontalAlign="Center"
   Font-Size="Large"
  />

  <ItemStyle
   BackColor="#d0d0d0"
  />

  <AlternatingItemStyle
   BackColor="#000000"
   ForeColor="#ffffff"
  />

  <HeaderTemplate>Products</HeaderTemplate>

  <ItemTemplate>

    <%# Container.DataItem("ProductName") %>

  </ItemTemplate>

  <AlternatingItemTemplate>

    <%# Container.DataItem("ProductName") %>

  </AlternatingItemTemplate>

 </asp:DataList>
 </form>
</body>
</html>
```

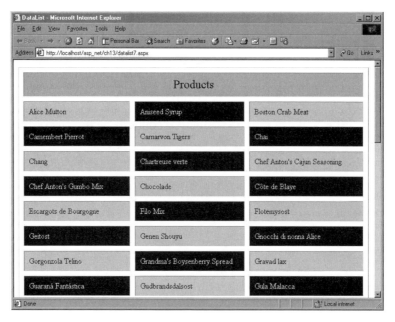

FIGURE 13.15 Styles can be defined in the DataList control

Styles can be also specified as part of the <asp:DataList> tag, as shown below:

```
<asp:DataList
   id = "DList"
   CellPadding=10
   CellSpacing=10
   GridLines="Both"
   RepeatColumns = 3
   RepeatDirection="Horizontal"

   HeaderStyle-BackColor="#a7c7b7"
   HeaderStyle-HorizontalAlign="Center"
   HeaderStyle-Font-Size="Large"

   ItemStyle-BackColor="#d0d0d0"

   AlternatingItemStyle-BackColor="#000000"
   AlternatingItemStyle-ForeColor="#ffffff"

   runat="server">
```

To show or hide different parts of the control, we can use the ShowFooter and ShowHeader properties.

DataGrid control

The DataGrid control is the advanced version of the DataList control and it allows us to select, sort, and edit items from the data source. The DataGrid control also supports paging via the database data, as well as the ability to specify the column type – bound column, button column, hyperlink column, and so on.

The following example shows the DataGrid control that displays an HTML table, with all the records from the Products table in the Northwind database in it (see also Figure 13.16):

```
<%@ Import Namespace="System.Data" %>
<%@ Import Namespace="System.Data.SqlClient" %>

<script runat="server">

 Sub Page_Load()

  Dim Conn As SqlConnection
  Dim Cmd  As SqlCommand

  Conn = New SqlConnection("server=localhost;" & _
    "database=Northwind;uid=sa;pwd=;")
  Cmd = New SqlCommand("SELECT * FROM Products", Conn)

  Conn.Open
  Grid.DataSource = Cmd.ExecuteReader
  Grid.DataBind
  Conn.Close

 End Sub

</script>

<html>
 <head>
  <title>DataGrid</title>
 </head>
<body>
 <form runat="server">

 <asp:DataGrid
  id = "Grid"
  runat="server"
 />

 </form>
</body>
</html>
```

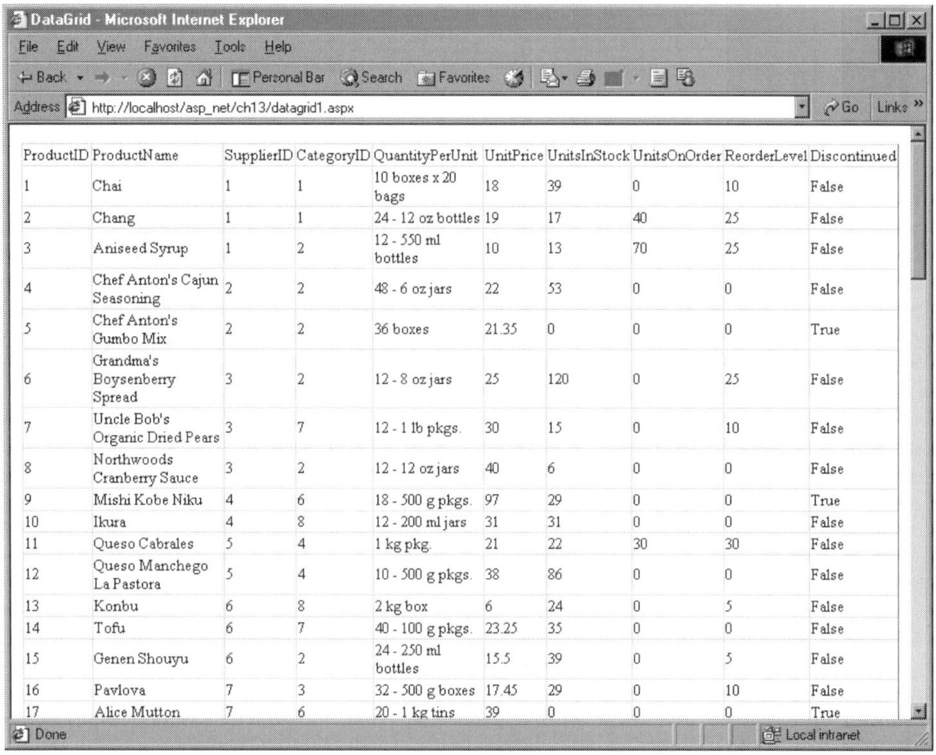

ProductID	ProductName	SupplierID	CategoryID	QuantityPerUnit	UnitPrice	UnitsInStock	UnitsOnOrder	ReorderLevel	Discontinued
1	Chai	1	1	10 boxes x 20 bags	18	39	0	10	False
2	Chang	1	1	24 - 12 oz bottles	19	17	40	25	False
3	Aniseed Syrup	1	2	12 - 550 ml bottles	10	13	70	25	False
4	Chef Anton's Cajun Seasoning	2	2	48 - 6 oz jars	22	53	0	0	False
5	Chef Anton's Gumbo Mix	2	2	36 boxes	21.35	0	0	0	True
6	Grandma's Boysenberry Spread	3	2	12 - 8 oz jars	25	120	0	25	False
7	Uncle Bob's Organic Dried Pears	3	7	12 - 1 lb pkgs.	30	15	0	10	False
8	Northwoods Cranberry Sauce	3	2	12 - 12 oz jars	40	6	0	0	False
9	Mishi Kobe Niku	4	6	18 - 500 g pkgs.	97	29	0	0	True
10	Ikura	4	8	12 - 200 ml jars	31	31	0	0	False
11	Queso Cabrales	5	4	1 kg pkg.	21	22	30	30	False
12	Queso Manchego La Pastora	5	4	10 - 500 g pkgs.	38	86	0	0	False
13	Konbu	6	8	2 kg box	6	24	0	5	False
14	Tofu	6	7	40 - 100 g pkgs.	23.25	35	0	0	False
15	Genen Shouyu	6	2	24 - 250 ml bottles	15.5	39	0	5	False
16	Pavlova	7	3	32 - 500 g boxes	17.45	29	0	10	False
17	Alice Mutton	7	6	20 - 1 kg tins	39	0	0	0	True

FIGURE 13.16 The `DataGrid` control has been used to display all the products in the database

To reduce the number of columns the `DataGrid` control displays, we should set the `AutoGenerateColumns` property to `"False"` and manually specify which columns we would like to display. This can be done in the `<Columns>` element within the `<asp:DataGrid>` tag (see also Figure 13.17):

```
<%@ Import Namespace="System.Data" %>
<%@ Import Namespace="System.Data.SqlClient" %>

<script runat="server">

 Sub Page_Load()

  Dim Conn As SqlConnection
  Dim Cmd  As SqlCommand

  Conn = New SqlConnection("server=localhost;" & _
   "database=Northwind;uid=sa;pwd=;")
  Cmd = New SqlCommand("SELECT * FROM Products", Conn)
```

```
      Conn.Open
      Grid.DataSource = Cmd.ExecuteReader
      Grid.DataBind
      Conn.Close

    End Sub

</script>

<html>
 <head>
  <title>DataGrid</title>
 </head>
<body>
 <form runat="server">

 <asp:DataGrid
  id = "Grid"
  AutoGenerateColumns = "False"
  runat="server">

  <Columns>

   <asp:BoundColumn
    HeaderText="Product"
    DataField="ProductName"
   />
   <asp:BoundColumn
    HeaderText="Quantity"
    DataField="QuantityPerUnit"
   />
   <asp:BoundColumn
    HeaderText="Price"
    DataField="UnitPrice"
    DataFormatString="{0:c}"
   />

  </Columns>

 </asp:DataGrid>

 </form>
</body>
</html>
```

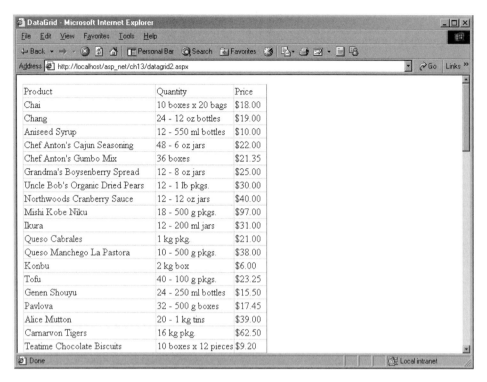

FIGURE 13.17 The desired number of columns has been set in the `<Columns>` element in the `<asp:DataGrid>` tag

Each `<asp:BoundColumn>` element inside the `<Columns>` element is used to specify one data-bound column. In our example, we have defined three such columns by using the `HeaderText` property to specify the label for the column heading and the `DataField` property to associate this column with the database field. In the third column definition, we have also used the `DataFormatString` property to specify that the column values should be displayed as a currency.

Each column defined in the `<Columns>` element has a `Visible` property which can be set to "`True`" or "`False`" to show or hide the column. This can be done either manually or using code.

Earlier in this chapter we saw how to add editing capabilities to the `DataList` control. To do this, we used the `EditItemTemplate` template and described the `TextBox` control that provides the editing functionality. The `DataGrid` control automatically creates the `TextBox` control when an item is selected for editing. Suppose we have the following example (see also Figure 13.18):

```
<%@ Import Namespace="System.Data" %>
<%@ Import Namespace="System.Data.SqlClient" %>

<script runat="server">

 Sub Page_Load()

  If Not IsPostBack Then
   LoadData
  End If

 End Sub

 Sub LoadData()

  Dim Conn As SqlConnection
  Dim Cmd  As SqlCommand

  Conn = New SqlConnection("server=localhost;" & _
   "database=Northwind;uid=sa;pwd=;")
  Cmd = New SqlCommand("SELECT * FROM Products", Conn)

  Conn.Open
  Grid.DataSource = Cmd.ExecuteReader
  Grid.DataBind
  Conn.Close

 End Sub

 Sub EditProduct(sender As Object, e As DataGridCommandEventArgs)

  Grid.EditItemIndex = e.Item.ItemIndex
  LoadData

 End Sub

 Sub CancelEdit(sender As Object, e As DataGridCommandEventArgs)

  Grid.EditItemIndex = -1
  LoadData

 End Sub
```

```
   Sub UpdateProducts(sender As Object, e As DataGridCommandEventArgs)

   '
   ' Update data code goes here
   '

     Grid.EditItemIndex = -1
     LoadData

   End Sub

</script>

<html>
 <head>
  <title>DataGrid</title>
 </head>
<body>
 <form runat="server">

 <asp:DataGrid
  id = "Grid"
  AutoGenerateColumns = "False"

  DataKeyField="ProductID"
  OnEditCommand="EditProduct"
  OnCancelCommand="CancelEdit"
  OnUpdateProduct="UpdateProduct"

  runat="server">

  <Columns>

   <asp:EditCommandColumn
    EditText="Edit"
    CancelText="Cancel"
    UpdateText="Update"
    ButtonType="PushButton"
   />
```

```
<asp:BoundColumn
 HeaderText="Product"
 DataField="ProductName"
/>
<asp:BoundColumn
 HeaderText="Quantity"
 DataField="QuantityPerUnit"
/>
<asp:BoundColumn
 HeaderText="Price"
 DataField="UnitPrice"
 DataFormatString="{0:c}"
/>

</Columns>

</asp:DataGrid>

</form>
</body>
</html>
```

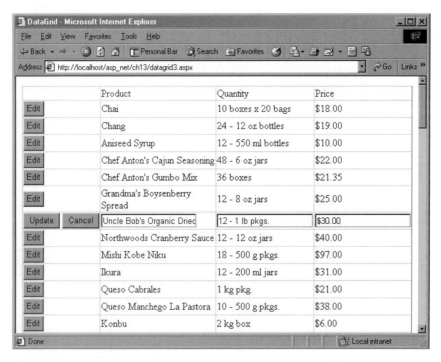

FIGURE 13.18 The EditCommandColumn element allows users to edit the table

In the example above, we have added the `EditCommandColumn` element and specified names for the edit, update, and cancel commands. This column is added automatically for each row in the `DataGrid` control. When the row is not selected for editing, the `EditCommandColumn` element displays the `Edit` button. When we click on this button, the `EditCommandColumn` element displays `Update` and `Cancel` buttons.

We associate the event handlers for all three buttons in the `OnEditCommand`, `OnCancelCommand`, and `OnUpdateCommand` properties of the `DataGrid` control. The code for these event handlers is nearly identical to the code we used in the editing example for the `DataList` control.

To extend the editing functionality of the `DataGrid` control we can use `EditItemTemplate`. To do so, we create a number of `<asp:TemplateColumn>` elements and place `EditItemTemplate` and other controls – validators, for example – inside it.

The sorting capabilities of the `DataGrid` control are supported by the `AllowSorting` property. Let's take the following example (see also Figure 13.19):

```
<%@ Import Namespace="System.Data" %>
<%@ Import Namespace="System.Data.SqlClient" %>

<script runat="server">

 Dim SortExpression As String = "ProductID"

 Sub Page_Load()

  If Not IsPostBack Then
   LoadData
  End If

 End Sub

 Sub LoadData()

  Dim Conn As SqlConnection
  Dim Cmd  As SqlCommand

  Conn = New SqlConnection("server=localhost;" & _
   "database=Northwind;uid=sa;pwd=;")
  Cmd = New SqlCommand("SELECT * FROM Products ORDER BY " & _
   SortExpression, Conn)
```

```
    Conn.Open
    Grid.DataSource = Cmd.ExecuteReader
    Grid.DataBind
    Conn.Close

  End Sub

  Sub SortProducts(sender As Object, e As DataGridSortCommandEventArgs)

    SortExpression = e.SortExpression
    LoadData()

  End Sub


</script>

<html>
 <head>
  <title>DataGrid</title>
 </head>
<body>
 <form runat="server">

 <asp:DataGrid
  id = "Grid"
  HeaderStyle-BackColor="#c0c0c0"

  AutoGenerateColumns = "False"
  AllowSorting="True"
  OnSortCommand="SortProducts"
  runat="server">

  <Columns>
   <asp:BoundColumn
    HeaderText="Product"
    DataField="ProductName"
    SortExpression="ProductName"
   />
```

```
  <asp:BoundColumn
   HeaderText="Quantity"
   DataField="QuantityPerUnit"
   SortExpression="QuantityPerUnit"
  />
  <asp:BoundColumn
   HeaderText="Price"
   DataField="UnitPrice"
   DataFormatString="{0:c}"
   SortExpression="UnitPrice"
  />
  </Columns>

 </asp:DataGrid>

 </form>
 </body>
 </html>
```

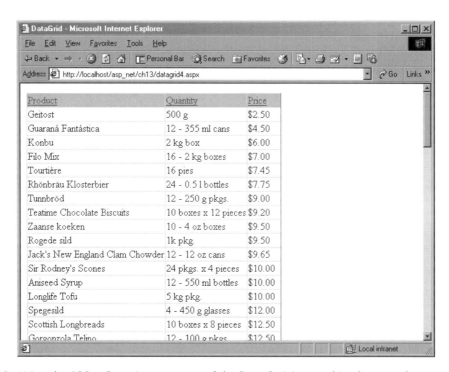

FIGURE 13.19 Using the AllowSorting property of the DataGrid control implements the sorting functionality

In the example above, we implemented the sorting functionality for the `DataGrid` control. To do so, we set the `AllowSorting` property to `"True"` and attached the event handler for the `SortCommand` event via the `OnSortCommand` property. We have also specified the `SortExpression` property for each `<asp:BoundColumn>` element in our grid. The `DataGrid` control does not perform sorting of the data itself – we must do this in our code. In this example, we use the `SortCommand` event handler to execute a `SELECT` SQL query with the `ORDER BY` clause set to the name of the column header the user clicked. This executes the query and returns the data sorted by the selected column.

The paging capabilities of the `DataGrid` control are supported by the `AllowPaging` property. Consider the following example (see also Figure 13.20):

```
<%@ Import Namespace="System.Data" %>
<%@ Import Namespace="System.Data.SqlClient" %>

<script runat="server">

 Sub Page_Load()

  If Not IsPostBack Then
   LoadData
  End If

 End Sub

 Sub LoadData()

  Dim Conn As SqlConnection
  Dim Cmd  As SqlCommand
  Dim DA   As SqlDataAdapter
  Dim DS   As DataSet

  Conn = New SqlConnection("server=localhost;" & _
   "database=Northwind;uid=sa;pwd=;")

  DA = New SqlDataAdapter("SELECT * FROM Products", Conn)
  DS = New DataSet
  DA.Fill(DS, "Products")

  Grid.DataSource = DS
  Grid.DataBind

 End Sub
```

```
Sub PageProducts(sender As Object, e As DataGridPageChangedEventArgs)

  Grid.CurrentPageIndex = e.NewPageIndex
  LoadData()

End Sub


</script>

<html>
 <head>
  <title>DataGrid</title>
 </head>
<body>
 <form runat="server">

 <asp:DataGrid
  id = "Grid"
  AutoGenerateColumns = "False"

  AllowPaging="True"
  OnPageIndexChanged="PageProducts"

  runat="server">

  <Columns>
   <asp:BoundColumn
    HeaderText="Product"
    DataField="ProductName"
   />
   <asp:BoundColumn
    HeaderText="Quantity"
    DataField="QuantityPerUnit"
   />
   <asp:BoundColumn
    HeaderText="Price"
    DataField="UnitPrice"
    DataFormatString="{0:c}"
   />
  </Columns>

 </asp:DataGrid>

 </form>
</body>
</html>
```

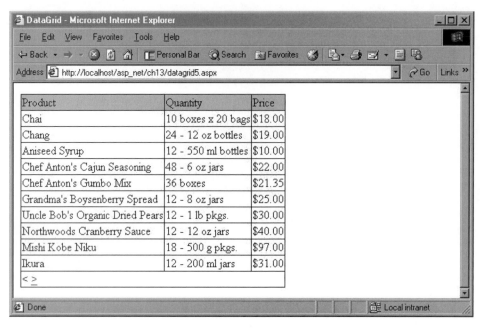

FIGURE 13.20 In the `DataGrid` control, setting the `AllowPaging` property to `"True"` enables us to page a table

In the example above, we set the `AllowPaging` property to `"True"` and specified the event handler for the `PageIndexChanged` event in the `OnPageIndexChanged` property. In the event handler, we assigned the new value for the `CurrentPageIndex` property of the `DataGrid` control.

Currently, the `DataGrid` control supports paging only with data sources that implement the `ICollection` interface. This means that we cannot use the `DataReader` as a source of data. Instead, all data should be loaded into the memory before the `DataGrid` control can page through it. Also, for each new page, the data must be reloaded from the source. This can be done when we use the `DataSet` object instead of the `DataReader` object.

If we have a lot of records, storing everything in the memory will not be appropriate. In this case, we can implement our own paging logic.

To change the appearance of the `Pager` control that navigates through the pages (by default this is < and > links), we can use the `PagerStyle` element and its `Mode` attribute. For example, setting the `Mode` attribute to `"NumericPages"` will display links to the pages (see also Figure 13.21):

```
<asp:DataGrid
  id = "Grid"
  HeaderStyle-BackColor="#c0c0c0"
  BorderColor="black"
```

```
AutoGenerateColumns = "False"
AllowPaging="True"
OnPageIndexChanged="PageProducts"
runat="server">

<PagerStyle
 Mode="NumericPages"
 HorizontalAlign="Center"
 />


<Columns>

  . . .

</Columns>

</asp:DataGrid>
```

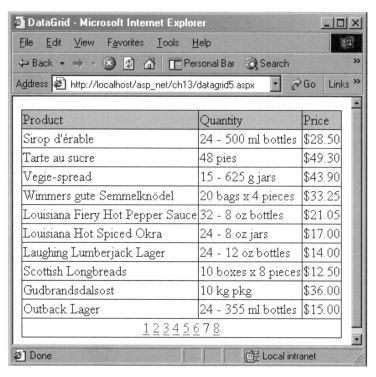

FIGURE 13.21 The appearance of the Pager control can be altered to show links to pages using the Mode attribute of the PagerStyle element

To reduce the number of page links displayed, we can use the `PageButtonCount` property, the default value of which is 10. If there are additional pages, this fact will be displayed as an ellipsis (...) (see also Figure 13.22).

$$\underline{1} \quad \underline{2} \quad \underline{3} \quad 4 \quad \underline{5} \ldots$$

FIGURE 13.22 The number of page links has been reduced by the PageButtonCount property

The `Pager` control can be placed at the top, bottom, or top and bottom of the DataGrid. This is specified by the `Bottom`, `Top`, and `TopAndBottom` values of the `Position` property.

If we don't use page numbers, we can specify the text for the previous and next page buttons. The default values are "<" and ">", but we can change this by setting new values for the `PrevPageText` and `NextPageText` properties.

Data binding with other ASP.NET controls

Earlier in this chapter we saw how to use the `Repeater`, `DataList`, and `DataGrid` web server controls to display and edit data loaded from the database. Several other ASP.NET web controls also support data binding:

- `CheckBoxList`;
- `DropDownList`;
- `HTMLSelect`;
- `ListBox`;
- `RadioButtonList`.

These controls have a `DataSource` property that allows us to associate them directly with the database data. For other controls, such as the `LinkButton`, we can indirectly specify the data via the `Text` value when we use such controls in the `Repeater` control. We saw an example of this earlier in this chapter when we implemented a menu of a product's categories.

The following example shows how to bind data to the `DropDownList` control (see also Figure 13.23):

```
<%@ Import Namespace="System.Data" %>
<%@ Import Namespace="System.Data.SqlClient" %>


<script runat="server">

 Sub Page_Load()
```

```
  If Not IsPostBack Then
   LoadData
  End If

End Sub

Sub LoadData()

  Dim Conn As SqlConnection
  Dim Cmd  As SqlCommand

  Conn = New SqlConnection("server=localhost;" & _
   "database=Northwind;uid=sa;pwd=;")
  Cmd = New SqlCommand("SELECT * FROM Products", Conn)

  Conn.Open

  Product.DataSource = Cmd.ExecuteReader
  Product.DataTextField="ProductName"
  Product.DataBind

  Conn.Close

End Sub

Sub SelectProduct(sender As Object, e As EventArgs)

  Selection.Text = Product.SelectedItem.Text

End Sub

</script>

<html>
 <head>
  <title>DropDownList</title>
 </head>
<body>
 <form runat="server">

 <asp:DropDownList
  id = "Product"
  runat="server"
 />
```

```
<asp:Button
  id = "Btn1"
  Text = "Select"
  OnClick="SelectProduct"
  runat="server"
/>
<asp:TextBox
  id="Selection"
  runat="server"/>

</form>
</body>
</html>
```

This ends our discussion of ASP.NET data-aware controls. In the second part of this chapter, we will see how to use the Windows forms `DataGrid` control to manipulate data in Windows forms applications.

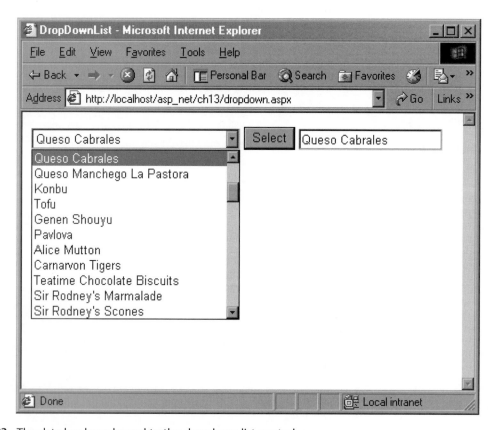

FIGURE 13.23 The data has been bound to the dropdown list control

13.2 Working with data in Windows forms applications

When creating Windows forms applications, we can take advantage of the data binding capabilities of nearly all Windows controls. Here is a list of controls that are often bound to data sources:

- `TextBox`;
- `ComboBox`;
- `ListBox`;
- `CheckedListBox`;
- `ErrorProvider`.

Each control supports the `DataBindings` property (of a `Binding` type), which allows us to specify the source of the data and the data member to bind to the control. For example, to bind the `TextBox` control to the `CustID` field from the `Customers` table, accessible via the `DataSet`, we use the following code:

```
Text2.DataBindings.Add(New Binding("Text", ds, "Customers.CustID"))
```

Let's take the following example (some of the code has been omitted for the sake of brevity – the final result is shown in Figure 13.24):

```
Public Class Form1
    Inherits System.Windows.Forms.Form

    Dim BMCustomers As BindingManagerBase

    Public Sub New()
        MyBase.New()

        'This call is required by the Windows Form Designer.
        InitializeComponent()

        'Add any initialization after the InitializeComponent() call

        BMCustomers = Me.BindingContext(Cust_DS, "Customers")

    End Sub

    Private Sub InitializeComponent()

        . . .
```

```
Me.TextBox1 = New System.Windows.Forms.TextBox()
Me.TextBox2 = New System.Windows.Forms.TextBox()
Me.TextBox3 = New System.Windows.Forms.TextBox()
Me.TextBox4 = New System.Windows.Forms.TextBox()

Me.Button1 = New System.Windows.Forms.Button()
Me.Button2 = New System.Windows.Forms.Button()

Me.SqlDataAdapter1 = New System.Data.SqlClient.SqlDataAdapter()
Me.SqlSelectCommand1 = New System.Data.SqlClient.SqlCommand()

'
'SqlConnection1
'
Me.SqlConnection1.ConnectionString = _
 "data source=(local);initial catalog=Northwind;" & _
 "persist security info=False;user id" & _
 "=sa;workstation id=THERION;packet size=4096"
'
'TextBox1
'
Me.TextBox1.DataBindings.Add(New _
 System.Windows.Forms.Binding("Text", Me.Cust_DS1, _
 "Customers.CustomerID"))
Me.TextBox1.Location = New System.Drawing.Point(112, 16)
Me.TextBox1.Name = "TextBox1"
Me.TextBox1.Size = New System.Drawing.Size(184, 20)
Me.TextBox1.TabIndex = 0
'
'TextBox2
'
Me.TextBox2.DataBindings.Add(New _
 System.Windows.Forms.Binding("Text", Me.Cust_DS1, _
 "Customers.CompanyName"))
Me.TextBox2.Location = New System.Drawing.Point(112, 48)
Me.TextBox2.Name = "TextBox2"
Me.TextBox2.Size = New System.Drawing.Size(184, 20)
Me.TextBox2.TabIndex = 1
'
'TextBox3
'
Me.TextBox3.DataBindings.Add(New _
```

```
    System.Windows.Forms.Binding("Text", Me.Cust_DS1, _
     "Customers.ContactName"))
    Me.TextBox3.Location = New System.Drawing.Point(112, 80)
    Me.TextBox3.Name = "TextBox3"
    Me.TextBox3.Size = New System.Drawing.Size(184, 20)
    Me.TextBox3.TabIndex = 2
    '
    'TextBox4
    '
    Me.TextBox4.DataBindings.Add(New _
     System.Windows.Forms.Binding("Text", Me.Cust_DS1, _
     "Customers.ContactTitle"))
    Me.TextBox4.Location = New System.Drawing.Point(112, 112)
    Me.TextBox4.Name = "TextBox4"
    Me.TextBox4.Size = New System.Drawing.Size(184, 20)
    Me.TextBox4.TabIndex = 3
    '
    'Button1
    '
    Me.Button1.BackColor = System.Drawing.Color.Silver
    Me.Button1.Location = New System.Drawing.Point(144, 168)
    Me.Button1.Name = "Button1"
    Me.Button1.TabIndex = 8
    Me.Button1.Text = "<"
    '
    'Button2
    '
    Me.Button2.BackColor = System.Drawing.Color.Silver
    Me.Button2.Location = New System.Drawing.Point(224, 168)
    Me.Button2.Name = "Button2"
    Me.Button2.TabIndex = 9
    Me.Button2.Text = ">"
    '
    'SqlDataAdapter1
    '
    Me.SqlDataAdapter1.SelectCommand = Me.SqlSelectCommand1
    '
    'SqlSelectCommand1
    '
    Me.SqlSelectCommand1.CommandText = "SELECT CustomerID,   " & _
     "CompanyName, ContactName, ContactTitle, Address, City, " & _
     "Region, PostalCode, Country, Phone, Fax FROM Customers "
    Me.SqlSelectCommand1.Connection = Me.SqlConnection1

End Sub
```

```
Private Sub Form1_Load(ByVal sender As Object, _
  ByVal e As System.EventArgs) Handles MyBase.Load
    SqlDataAdapter1.Fill(Cust_DS, "Customers")
End Sub

Private Sub Button1_Click(ByVal sender As System.Object, _
  ByVal e As System.EventArgs) Handles Button1.Click
    BMCustomers.Position -= 1
End Sub

Private Sub Button2_Click(ByVal sender As System.Object, _
  ByVal e As System.EventArgs) Handles Button2.Click
    BMCustomers.Position += 1
End Sub
End Class
```

In the example above, we use four TextBox controls that are bound to the CustomerID, CompanyName, ContactName, and ContactTitle fields from the Customers table in the Northwind database. We extract the data from the database using the SqlConnection and SqlDataAdapter objects. When our application loads for the first time, we use the Fill method of the SqlDataAdapter object to extract the data and place it in the DataSet – this is done in the Form1_Load event handler. Each TextBox control is bound to an appropriate field with the following code:

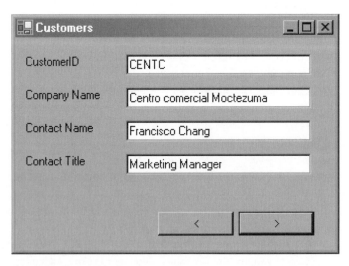

FIGURE 13.24 The TextBox control has been bound to the CustID field

```
Me.TextBox1.DataBindings.Add(New _
    System.Windows.Forms.Binding("Text", Me.Cust_DS1, _
    "Customers.CustomerID"))
```

We also use two buttons to navigate through our `DataSet` – the button marked with the `"<"` character navigates to the previous record; the button marked with the `">"` character to the next record. At the application initialization phase, we create an instance of the `BindingManagerBase` class:

```
Dim BMCustomers As BindingManagerBase


    . . .


BMCustomers = Me.BindingContext(Cust_DS, "Customers")
```

and use this object in the event handlers of our navigation buttons.

The `BindingManagerBase` class enables the synchronization of data-bound controls on a Windows form that are bound to the same data source. It assures us that controls are bound to the current item so they display the information for the same row.

The `BindingContext` property of the form is responsible for managing the collections of data that controls are bound to.

The data binding we have seen in the example above is called "simple data binding". This means that for each `TextBox` control, we have used the `DataBindings` collection to associate a `Text` property with the field in a `DataSet`.

Complex data binding allows us to bind a control to a collection (not to a single item within the collection). For example, the `DataGrid` control has a `DataSource` property that can be set to an entire `DataSet`.

DataGrid control

The `DataGrid` control displays all the information in a `DataSet` as a series of rows. Each row can be edited in place. Changes are automatically moved back into the underlying collection of objects as the user moves from row to row. To use a `DataGrid` control in a Windows application, we set the `DataSource` property to a `DataSet`, and a `DataMember` property to the name of an appropriate table in a `DataSet`. Here is an example (see also Figure 13.25):

```
Private Sub Form1_Load(ByVal sender As Object, _
    ByVal e As System.EventArgs) Handles MyBase.Load

    SqlDataAdapter1.Fill(Cust_DS, "Customers")
    DataGrid1.DataSource = Cust_DS
    DataGrid1.DataMember = "Customers"

End Sub
```

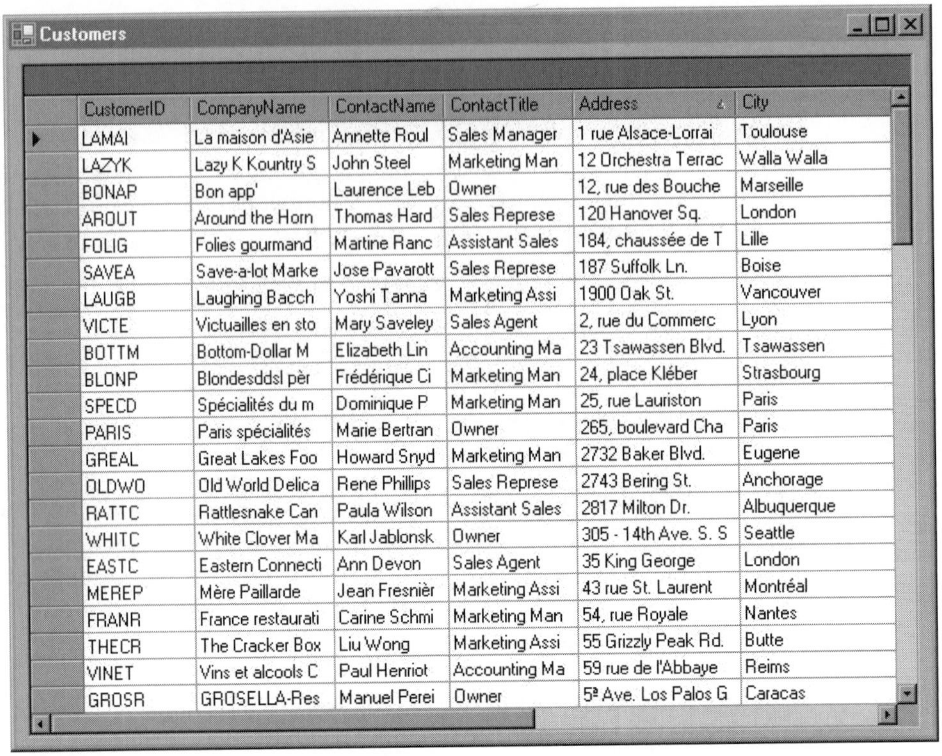

Customers

CustomerID	CompanyName	ContactName	ContactTitle	Address	City
LAMAI	La maison d'Asie	Annette Roul	Sales Manager	1 rue Alsace-Lorrai	Toulouse
LAZYK	Lazy K Kountry S	John Steel	Marketing Man	12 Orchestra Terrac	Walla Walla
BONAP	Bon app'	Laurence Leb	Owner	12, rue des Bouche	Marseille
AROUT	Around the Horn	Thomas Hard	Sales Represe	120 Hanover Sq.	London
FOLIG	Folies gourmand	Martine Ranc	Assistant Sales	184, chaussée de T	Lille
SAVEA	Save-a-lot Marke	Jose Pavarott	Sales Represe	187 Suffolk Ln.	Boise
LAUGB	Laughing Bacch	Yoshi Tanna	Marketing Assi	1900 Oak St.	Vancouver
VICTE	Victuailles en sto	Mary Saveley	Sales Agent	2, rue du Commerc	Lyon
BOTTM	Bottom-Dollar M	Elizabeth Lin	Accounting Ma	23 Tsawassen Blvd.	Tsawassen
BLONP	Blondesddsl pèr	Frédérique Ci	Marketing Man	24, place Kléber	Strasbourg
SPECD	Spécialités du m	Dominique P	Marketing Man	25, rue Lauriston	Paris
PARIS	Paris spécialités	Marie Bertran	Owner	265, boulevard Cha	Paris
GREAL	Great Lakes Foo	Howard Snyd	Marketing Man	2732 Baker Blvd.	Eugene
OLDWO	Old World Delica	Rene Phillips	Sales Represe	2743 Bering St.	Anchorage
RATTC	Rattlesnake Can	Paula Wilson	Assistant Sales	2817 Milton Dr.	Albuquerque
WHITC	White Clover Ma	Karl Jablonsk	Owner	305 - 14th Ave. S. S	Seattle
EASTC	Eastern Connecti	Ann Devon	Sales Agent	35 King George	London
MEREP	Mère Paillarde	Jean Fresnièr	Marketing Assi	43 rue St. Laurent	Montréal
FRANR	France restaurati	Carine Schmi	Marketing Man	54, rue Royale	Nantes
THECR	The Cracker Box	Liu Wong	Marketing Assi	55 Grizzly Peak Rd.	Butte
VINET	Vins et alcools C	Paul Henriot	Accounting Ma	59 rue de l'Abbaye	Reims
GROSR	GROSELLA-Res	Manuel Perei	Owner	5ª Ave. Los Palos G	Caracas

FIGURE 13.25 The `DataGrid` control displays all the information in a `DataSet` as rows

To change the attributes of a grid's caption, we can use the `CaptionForeColor`, `CaptionBackColor`, and `CaptionFont` properties. The text of the grid's caption can be set by the `CaptionText` property.

We can use a set of properties of the `DataGrid` control to change the way it displays data. For example, to display alternate rows in a different color, we can use the `AlternateBackColor` property. The `ForeColor` and `BackColor` properties specify the foreground and background colors of the `DataGrid` control itself. The `TableStyles` property holds a collection of `DataGridTableStyle` objects that can be used to further customize the appearance of the grid. This object allows us to specify the following properties.

- **`AllowSorting`** This `Boolean` property indicates whether or not the grid can be resorted by clicking on a column header.
- **`AlternatingBackColor`** This property (of a `Color` type) specifies the background color of alternating rows.
- **`BackColor`** This property (of a `Color` type) specifies the background color of the grid.
- **`ColumnHeadersVisible`** This `Boolean` property indicates whether or not the column headers of a table are visible.

- **ForeColor** This property (of a `Color` type) specifies the foreground color of the grid.
- **GridLineColor** This property (of a `Color` type) specifies the color of grid lines.
- **GridLineStyle** This property (of a `DataGridLineStyle`) specifies the line style of the grid. Possible values are `No` (no gridlines between cells) and `Solid` (solid gridlines between cells).
- **HeaderBackColor** This property (of a `Color` type) specifies the background color of all row and column headers.
- **HeaderForeColor** This property (of a `Color` type) specifies the foreground color of headers.
- **LinkColor** This property (of a `Color` type) specifies the color of the text that the user can click to navigate to a child table.
- **PreferredColumnWidth** This `Integer` property specifies the default width of the grid columns in pixels.
- **PreferredRowHeight** This `Integer` property specifies the preferred row height for the grid rows in pixels.
- **ReadOnly** This `Boolean` property indicates if the grid's contents can be modified.
- **RowHeadersVisible** This `Boolean` property indicates whether or not row headers are visible.
- **RowHeaderWidth** This `Integer` property specifies the width of row headers.
- **SelectionBackColor** This property (of a `Color` type) specifies the background color of selected rows.
- **SelectionForeColor** This property (of a `Color` type) specifies the foreground color of selected rows.

We can also customize the appearance of individual columns. The `GridColumnStyles` property holds a collection of `DataGridColumnStyle` objects. This object allows us to specify the following properties.

- **Alignment** This property (of a `HorizontalAlignment` type) specifies the alignment of text in a column. The default value is `"Left"`. Possible values also include `"Center"` and `"Right"`
- **HeaderText** This `String` property specifies the text of the column header.
- **MappingName** This `String` property specifies the name used to map the column style to a data member.
- **NullText** This `String` property specifies the text to be displayed in a column that contains a `DbNull` value.
- **ReadOnly** This `Boolean` property indicates whether the data in the column can be edited.
- **Width** This `Integer` property specifies the width of the column.

The AutoColumnSize property is a constant. It specifies that the grid automatically size columns to the maximum width of the first ten rows.

To find the cell that has the focus, we use the CurrentCell property. The CurrentRowIndex property returns the index of the selected row and the Item property is used to value a specified cell.

Several events allow us to monitor activity in the DataGrid. For example, to detect when the user selects another cell, we can use the CurrentCellChanged event. For example, to display the current row, add the following event handler:

```
Private Sub DataGrid1_CurrentCellChanged(ByVal sender As Object, _
ByVal e As System.EventArgs) Handles DataGrid1.CurrentCellChanged

Label1.Text = String.Format("Row : {0}", DataGrid1.CurrentRowIndex)


End Sub
```

To find which part of the control the user has clicked, we can use the HitTest method in the MouseDown event. The HitTest method returns a DataGrid.HitTestInfo object, which contains the row and column of a clicked area.

To validate data, we must use the underlying objects that represent data and their events. For example, we may use the ColumnChanging and RowChanging events of the DataTable object in a DataSet or the RowUpdating event of the DataAdapter object.

Let's extend our example and add a ComboBox control that will allow us to select a country and then display a list of customers for this selected country. We will start with adding a new SqlDataAdapter object that will fill another DataSet. This SqlDataAdapter will use the following SQL query to select a list of countries:

```
SELECT DISTINCT Country FROM Customers
```

Our new DataSet will be filled at the form load event:

```
Protected Overrides Sub OnLoad(ByVal e As System.EventArgs)
SqlDataAdapter2.Fill(Country1, "Customers")
End Sub
```

We attach this DataSet to the ComboBox control with the following code:

```
ComboBox1.DataSource = Me.Country1
ComboBox1.DisplayMember = "Customers.Country"
```

We also need to change the SELECT query for our DataGrid – now it should include one parameter that will specify the country to get a list of customers from:

```
SqlSelectCommand1.CommandText = _
 "SELECT CustomerID, CompanyName, ContactName, ContactTitle, " & _
 "Address, City, Region, PostalCode, Country, Phone, Fax "      & _
 "FROM Customers WHERE (Country = @Country)"
```

We specify the value for this parameter in the event handler for the SelectedIndexChanged event of the ComboBox control (see also Figure 13.26):

```
Private Sub ComboBox1_SelectedIndexChanged(ByVal sender As Object, _
    ByVal e As System.EventArgs) Handles ComboBox1.SelectedIndexChanged

With SqlDataAdapter1.SelectCommand.Parameters

    .Item("@Country").Value = ComboBox1.SelectedValue

End With

Cust1.Clear()
SqlDataAdapter1.Fill(Cust1, "Customers")

End Sub
```

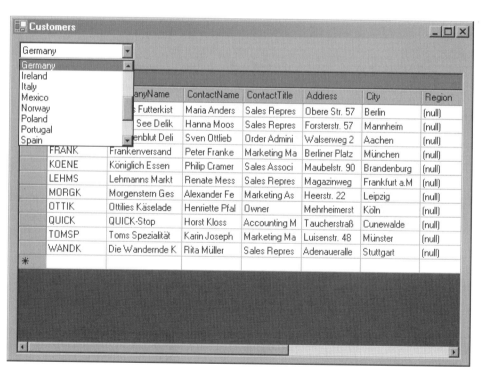

FIGURE 13.26 Allowing users to select a country

13.3 Conclusion

In this chapter, we discussed data binding controls available in ASP.NET and how to use them in web forms applications. We have seen how to use the `Repeater`, `DataList`, and `DataGrid` controls. For each control we have discussed its usage, customization, and provided many examples of how to use its features. We have also seen how to data-bind other ASP.NET controls, such as `DropDownListBox`, and provided a list of controls that can be data-bound.

Then we learned about the data binding features of Windows forms controls. We briefly covered the basics of data binding and discussed two types of binding – simple, which allows us to bind a control to a single field, and complex, which supports data binding to a whole data structure. We have seen how to use the `TextBox` controls to implement simple data binding and the `DataGrid` control to bind to an entire `DataSet`.

In the next chapter, we will learn about the Microsoft .NET Framework classes that can be used to work with XML data.

chapter **14**

Working with XML

- `System.Xml namespace`

In this chapter we will learn about XML support in the Microsoft .NET Framework. XML is the universal format for data on the web. It allows developers to easily describe and deliver rich, structured data from any application in a standard, consistent way. XML is at the core of many features of the Microsoft .NET Framework – configuration management, object serialization, remoting, web services, database access, and file storage are just a few.

In this chapter we will discuss the following topics:

● the System.Xml namespace and its secondary namespaces – System.Xml.Xsl, System.Xml.XPath, System.Xml.Schema, and System.Xml.Serialization;

● reading and writing XML documents;

● working with the XML DOM;

● querying XML with XPath;

● transformations using XSLT.

14.1 System.Xml namespace

XML support in the Microsoft .NET Framework is implemented in the System.Xml namespace (which can be found in the System.XML.dll assembly) and its secondary namespaces. The System.Xml namespace contains the core XML classes necessary to read and write XML documents and map the documents to the document object model (DOM). The most important classes found in the System.Xml namespace are the following.

● **XmlTextReader** This class represents a reader that provides fast, non-cached forward-only access to XML data.

● **XmlTextWriter** This class represents a writer that provides a fast non-cached forward-only way of generating streams or files containing XML data that conforms to the W3C XML 1.0 specification.

● **XmlDocument** This class represents an XML document.

● **XmlNodeList** This class represents an ordered collection of nodes.

● **XmlNamedNodeMap** This class represents a collection of nodes that can be accessed by name or index.

● **XmlNodeReader** This class represents a reader that provides fast, non-cached forward-only access to XML data in an XmlNode.

● **XmlNode** This class represents a single node in the document.

Secondary namespaces provide additional functionality.

● **System.Xml.Xsl** Contains classes that allow us to transform documents using XSL stylesheets. The most important class in this namespace is the XslTransform class, which transforms XML data using an XSLT stylesheet.

- **System.Xml.XPath** Contains classes that allow us to navigate XML documents using XPath. The most important classes in this namespace are XPathDocument, which provides a fast cache for XML document processing using XSLT, XPathNavigator, used to read data from any data store using a cursor model, and XPathNodeIterator, which provides an iterator over a set of selected nodes.

- **System.Xml.Schema** Contains classes to work with XSD schemas and validate documents. The key classes in this namespace are XmlSchema, which contains the definition of a schema in XSD format, and XmlSchemaObject, which represents a schema.

- **System.Xml.Serialization** Contains objects that enable classes to be serialized to XML. The key class in this namespace is XmlSerializer, which provides the Serialize method to convert objects into XML documents.

The classes mentioned above, as well as other classes implemented in the System.Xml namespace and its secondary namespaces, provide standards-based support for processing XML. The supported standards are as follows.

- **XML 1.0** This includes document type definition (DTD) support (XmlTextReader class). For more information on XML 1.0, see the specification available on the World Wide Web Consortium website at:
www.w3.org/TR/1998/REC-xml-19980210

- **XML namespaces** Both at stream level and DOM. For more information on XML namespaces, see the specification available on the World Wide Web Consortium website at:
www.w3.org/TR/REC-xml-names/

- **XML Schemas** These include schema mapping and serialization, but there is not yet one for validation. For more information on XML schemas, see the specification available on the World Wide Web Consortium website at:
www.w3.org/TR/xmlschema-1/

- **XPath expressions** These are of the XmlNavigator class. For more information see the specification available on the World Wide Web Consortium website at:
www.w3.org/TR/xpath

- **XSL/T transformations** These are of the XslTransform class. For more information on XSL/T, see the specification on the World Wide Web Consortium website at:
www.w3.org/TR/xslt

- **DOM Level 2 Core** This is of the XmlDocument class. For more information on DOM, see the specification available on the World Wide Web Consortium website at:
www.w3.org/TR/DOM-Level-2/

- **SOAP 1.1** This includes the Soap contract language and Soap discovery used in XML object serialization. For more information on XSL/T, see the specification available at:
msdn.microsoft.com/xml/general/soapspec.asp

Figure 14.1 shows the architecture of XML support in Microsoft .NET Framework.

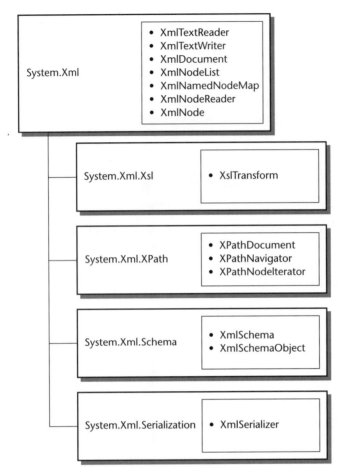

FIGURE 14.1 The support architecture for XML in the Microsoft .NET Framework

Reading and writing XML documents

The System.Xml namespace provides an abstract class called XmlReader. This class represents a reader that provides fast, non-cached forward-only access to XML data and serves as a base for the following classes.

- **XmlNodeReader** This is an implementation of XmlReader that reads XML data from an XmlNode.
- **XmlTextReader** This class is the fastest implementation of XmlReader. It checks for well-formed XML, but does not support data validation. This reader cannot expand general entities and does not support default attributes.
- **XmlValidatingReader** This is an implementation of XmlReader that can validate data using DTDs or schemas. This reader can also expand general entities and supports default attributes.

Figure 14.2 shows how these classes relate to each other.

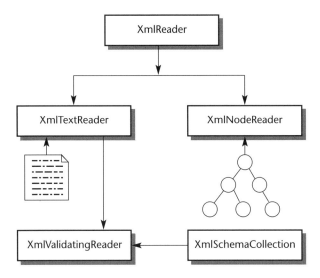

FIGURE 14.2   The relationships between the XMLReader class and related classes

The XmlReader class defines the following properties.

- **AttributeCount** Returns the number of attributes on the current node as an Integer value.
- **BaseURI** Returns the base URI of the current node as a String.
- **CanResolveEntity** This Boolean property indicates whether or not this reader can parse and resolve entities.
- **Depth** Returns the depth of the current node in the XML document as an Integer value.
- **EOF** This Boolean property indicates whether or not the XmlReader is positioned at the end of the stream.
- **HasAttributes** This Boolean property indicates whether or not the current node has any attributes.
- **HasValue** This Boolean property indicates whether or not the node can have a Value.
- **IsDefault** This Boolean property indicates whether or not the current node is an attribute that was generated from the default value defined in the DTD or schema.
- **IsEmptyElement** This Boolean property indicates whether or not the current node is an empty element.
- **Item** Returns the value of the attribute as a String. The attribute can be specified either by index – Item(*Integer*), by name – Item(*String*), or by local name and namespace URI – Item(*String, String*).
- **LocalName** Returns the name of the current node without the namespace prefix as a String.

- **Name** Returns the name of the current node, including the namespace prefix, as a String.

- **NamespaceURI** Returns the namespace URI of the current node as a String.

- **NameTable** Returns the XmlNameTable object associated with the string within the node.

- **NodeType** Returns the type of the current node as an XMLNodeType object.

- **Prefix** Returns the namespace prefix for the current node as a String.

- **QuoteChar** Returns the quotation mark character used to enclose the value of an attribute node.

- **ReadState** Returns the current state of the reader as a ReadState object.

- **Value** Returns the text value of the current node as a String.

- **XmlLang** Returns the current xml:lang scope as a String within which the current node resides.

- **XmlSpace** Returns the current xml:space scope as a String.

Here are the methods of the XmlReader class.

- **Close() method** Closes the stream and sets the ReadState property to Closed.

- **GetAttribute(*Integer*) method** Returns the value of an attribute with the specified index. Overloaded versions of this can return the value of an attribute specified by name – GetAttribute (*String*) – or by local name and namespace URI – GetAttribute(*String*, *String*).

- **IsName(*String*) method** Gets a Boolean value indicating whether or not the string argument is a valid XML name.

- **IsNameToken(*String*) method** Gets a Boolean value indicating whether or not the string argument is a valid XML name token.

- **IsStartElement(*String*) method** Tests if the current content node is a start tag. The overloaded version of this method allows us to specify a node by its local name and namespace URI – IsStartElement(*String*, *String*).

- **LookupNamespace(*String*) method** Resolves a namespace prefix in the current element's scope.

- **MoveToAttribute(*Integer*) method** Moves to the specified attribute with the specified index. Overloaded versions of this method allow us to specify the name of the attribute – MoveToAttribute(*String*), or its local name and namespace URI – MoveToAttribute (*String*, *String*).

- **MoveToContent() method** Moves to the first or next content node.

- **MoveToElement() method** Moves to the element that contains the current attribute node.

- **MoveToFirstAttribute() method** Moves to the first attribute within the node.

- **MoveToNextAttribute() method** Moves to the next attribute within the node.

- **Read()** **method** Reads the next node from the stream.
- **ReadAttributeValue()** **method** Parses the attribute value into one or more text and/or EntityReference node types.
- **ReadElementString()** **method** Can be used for reading simple text-only elements.
- **ReadEndElement()** **method** Checks that the current content node is an end tag and advances the reader to the next node.
- **ReadInnerXml()** **method** Reads all the content, including markup, as a string.
- **ReadOuterXml()** **method** Reads the content, including markup, representing this node and all its children.
- **ReadStartElement()** **method** Checks that the current node is an element and advances the reader to the next node.
- **ReadString()** **method** Reads the contents of an element or text node as a string.
- **ResolveEntity()** **method** When overriden in a derived class, it resolves the entity reference for EntityReference nodes.
- **Skip()** **method** Skips the current element.

The XmlReader class supports the pull model (a client pulls the data from the XmlReader), based on the Read() method:

```
Do While (Reader.Read())

    '

    ' Process XML document here

    '


    Loop
```

The XmlTextReader class implements the XmlReader class and provides the following additional properties:

- **Encoding** Returns the encoding attribute for the XML document as an Encoding object.
- **LineNumber** Returns the current line number as an Integer value.
- **LinePosition** Returns the current line position as an Integer value.
- **Normalization** This Boolean property indicates whether or not to do whitespace normalization.
- **WhitespaceHandling** Indicates how whitespace is handled. This property is of the WhitespaceHandling type and its default value is WhitespaceHandling.All.
- **XmlResolver** Specifies the XmlResolver object used for resolving DTD references.

The additional methods of the XmlTextReader class are:

- **GetRemainder() method** Reads the remainder of the buffered XML.
- **ReadBase64(*Byte()*, *Integer*, *Integer*) method** Decodes Base64 and returns the decoded binary bytes.
- **ReadBinHex(*Byte()*, *Integer*, *Integer*) method** Decodes BinHex and returns the decoded binary bytes.
- **ReadChars(*Char()*, *Integer*, *Integer*) method** Reads the text contents of an element into a character buffer.

Let's look at how we can use the XmlTextReader to access XML data. Suppose we have the following XML document, which contains data about employees (this document will be referred in our code as nw_elements.xml):

```
<?xml version="1.0" encoding="utf-8" ?>
<Northwind>
 <employees>
  <FirstName>Nancy</FirstName>
  <LastName>Davolio</LastName>
  <Title>Sales Representative</Title>
  <BirthDate>1948-12-08T00:00:00</BirthDate>
  <HireDate>1992-05-01T00:00:00</HireDate>
  <Address>507 – 20th Ave. E. Apt. 2A</Address>
  <City>Seattle</City>
  <Region>WA</Region>
  <PostalCode>98122</PostalCode>
 </employees>


 <!–Data removed for brevity –>

 <employees>
  <FirstName>Anne</FirstName>
  <LastName>Dodsworth</LastName>
  <Title>Sales Representative</Title>
  <BirthDate>1966-01-27T00:00:00</BirthDate>
  <HireDate>1994-11-15T00:00:00</HireDate>
  <Address>7 Houndstooth Rd.</Address>
  <City>London</City>
  <PostalCode>WG2 7LT</PostalCode>
 </employees>
</Northwind>
```

The following example shows how to use the XmlTextReader object to navigate through all the element nodes in the document:

```
'----------------------------------------
' XML.NET Example. XmlTextReader
'----------------------------------------

Imports System
Imports System.XML

 Module Cons

 Sub Main()

  Dim Reader As XmlTextReader = New XmlTextReader("nw_elements.xml")
  Dim Str As String
  Str = " "

  Do While (Reader.Read())

  Console.Write(Str.PadLeft(Reader.Depth))

  Console.WriteLine(String.Format("Name : {0} Type : {1} " & _
    "Value : {2}", Reader.Name, Reader.NodeType, Reader.Value))

  Loop

 End Sub

 End Module
```

The resulting output (just for the portion of the XML document provided above) is:

```
Name : xml Type : XmlDeclaration Value : version="1.0" encoding="utf-8"
 Name : Northwind Type : Element Value :
 Name : employees Type : Element Value :
  Name : FirstName Type : Element Value :
   Name :  Type : Text Value : Nancy
  Name : FirstName Type : EndElement Value :
  Name : LastName Type : Element Value :
   Name :  Type : Text Value : Davolio
  Name : LastName Type : EndElement Value :
  Name : Title Type : Element Value :
   Name :  Type : Text Value : Sales Representative
  Name : Title Type : EndElement Value :
  Name : BirthDate Type : Element Value :
```

```
Name :  Type : Text Value : 1948-12-08T00:00:00
Name : BirthDate Type : EndElement Value :
Name : HireDate Type : Element Value :
 Name :  Type : Text Value : 1992-05-01T00:00:00
Name : HireDate Type : EndElement Value :
Name : Address Type : Element Value :
 Name :  Type : Text Value : 507 — 20th Ave. E. Apt. 2A
Name : Address Type : EndElement Value :
Name : City Type : Element Value :
 Name :  Type : Text Value : Seattle
Name : City Type : EndElement Value :
Name : Region Type : Element Value :
 Name :  Type : Text Value : WA
Name : Region Type : EndElement Value :
Name : PostalCode Type : Element Value :
 Name :  Type : Text Value : 98122
Name : PostalCode Type : EndElement Value :
Name : employees Type : EndElement Value :


 ...


Name : employees Type : Element Value :
 Name : FirstName Type : Element Value :
  Name :  Type : Text Value : Anne
 Name : FirstName Type : EndElement Value :
 Name : LastName Type : Element Value :
  Name :  Type : Text Value : Dodsworth
 Name : LastName Type : EndElement Value :
 Name : Title Type : Element Value :
  Name :  Type : Text Value : Sales Representative
 Name : Title Type : EndElement Value :
 Name : BirthDate Type : Element Value :
  Name :  Type : Text Value : 1966-01-27T00:00:00
 Name : BirthDate Type : EndElement Value :
 Name : HireDate Type : Element Value :
  Name :  Type : Text Value : 1994-11-15T00:00:00
 Name : HireDate Type : EndElement Value :
 Name : Address Type : Element Value :
  Name :  Type : Text Value : 7 Houndstooth Rd.
 Name : Address Type : EndElement Value :
 Name : City Type : Element Value :
  Name :  Type : Text Value : London
```

```
 Name : City Type : EndElement Value :
 Name : PostalCode Type : Element Value :
  Name :  Type : Text Value : WG2 7LT
 Name : PostalCode Type : EndElement Value :
Name : employees Type : EndElement Value :
Name : Northwind Type : EndElement Value :
```

That was an XML document without attributes – all the information about the employees was stored in the subnodes of the `<employees>` node. Now let's change our XML document and place all the employee-related information in the attributes of the `<employees>` node. The new version of our XML document is shown below (this document will be referred in our code as nw.xml):

```xml
<?xml version="1.0" encoding="utf-8" ?>
 <Northwind>
  <employees
   FirstName="Nancy"
   LastName="Davolio"
   Title="Sales  Representative"
   BirthDate="1948-12-08T00:00:00"
   HireDate="1992-05-01T00:00:00"
   Address="507 – 20th Ave. E. Apt. 2A"
   City="Seattle"
   Region="WA"
   PostalCode="98122"
  />

<!–Data removed for brevity –>

  <employees
   FirstName="Anne"
   LastName="Dodsworth"
   Title="Sales Representative"
   BirthDate="1966-01-27T00:00:00"
   HireDate="1994-11-15T00:00:00"
   Address="7 Houndstooth Rd."
   City="London"
   PostalCode="WG2 7LT"
  />

</Northwind>
```

In order to read the attributes of a node, we first need to check if it has any. We can do this using the `HasAttributes` property. To access attributes without knowing any of their names, we can use an indexed access or enumeration method to list them all.

Indexed access is based on the `AttributeCount` property, which returns the size of the attributes collection and a loop through this collection using the `GetAttribute()` method:

```
Dim Count As Integer
Dim I     As Integer

  ...

Count = Reader.AttributeCount
For I=0 to Count-1
  Console.WriteLine(Reader.GetAttribute(I))
Next
```

The enumeration method is based on the `MoveToFirstAttribute()` and `MoveToNextAttribute()` methods:

```
Reader.MoveToFirstAttribute()
Do While (Reader.MoveToNextAttribute())

  Console.WriteLine(Reader.Value)

Loop
```

The following example shows how to read the XML document that contains attributes:

```
'----------------------------------------
' XML.NET Example. XmlTextReader
'----------------------------------------

Imports System
Imports System.XML

 Module Cons

 Sub Main()

  Dim Reader As XmlTextReader = New XmlTextReader("nw.xml")
  Dim Str As String
  Str = " "

  Do While (Reader.Read())

  Console.Write(Str.PadLeft(Reader.Depth))
```

```
Console.WriteLine(String.Format("Name : {0} Type : {1} " & _
 "Value : {2}", Reader.Name, Reader.NodeType, Reader.Value))


If Reader.HasAttributes

 Reader.MoveToFirstAttribute()

  Console.Write(Str.PadLeft(Reader.Depth+1))
  Console.WriteLine(String.Format("Name : {0} Type : {1} " & _
    "Value : {2}", Reader.Name, Reader.NodeType, Reader.Value))

  Do While (Reader.MoveToNextAttribute())

  Console.Write(Str.PadLeft(Reader.Depth+1))
  Console.WriteLine(String.Format("Name : {0} Type : {1} " & _
    "Value : {2}", Reader.Name, Reader.NodeType, Reader.Value))

  Loop

 End If

 Loop

 End Sub

 End Module
```

The resulting output (just for the portion of the XML document provided above) is:

```
Name : xml Type : XmlDeclaration Value : version="1.0" encoding="utf-8"
 Name : encoding Type : Attribute Value : utf-8
 Name : Northwind Type : Element Value :
 Name : employees Type : Element Value :
  Name : FirstName Type : Attribute Value : Nancy
  Name : LastName Type : Attribute Value : Davolio
  Name : Title Type : Attribute Value : Sales Representative
  Name : BirthDate Type : Attribute Value : 1948-12-08T00:00:00
  Name : HireDate Type : Attribute Value : 1992-05-01T00:00:00
  Name : Address Type : Attribute Value : 507 – 20th Ave. E. Apt. 2A
  Name : City Type : Attribute Value : Seattle
  Name : Region Type : Attribute Value : WA
  Name : PostalCode Type : Attribute Value : 98122

 ...
```

```
Name : employees Type : Element Value :
  Name : FirstName Type : Attribute Value : Anne
  Name : LastName Type : Attribute Value : Dodsworth
  Name : Title Type : Attribute Value : Sales Representative
  Name : BirthDate Type : Attribute Value : 1966-01-27T00:00:00
  Name : HireDate Type : Attribute Value : 1994-11-15T00:00:00
  Name : Address Type : Attribute Value : 7 Houndstooth Rd.
  Name : City Type : Attribute Value : London
  Name : PostalCode Type : Attribute Value : WG2 7LT
Name : Northwind Type : EndElement Value :
```

When we discussed methods of the XmlReader class, we listed several that allow us to navigate through the document. For example, we can use the MoveToContent() method to skip certain parts of the document – nodes of the ProcessingInstruction, DocumentType, Comment, Whitespace, or SignificantWhitespace types. This method seeks the next content node – non-whitespace text – CDATA, Element, EndElement, EntityReference, or EndEntity nodes.

To skip a single node, we can use the Skip() method. Other movement methods include those already discussed – MoveToFirstAttribute() and MoveToNextAttribute() – as well as the MoveToAttribute() and MoveToElement() methods.

The XmlReader class provides several Read methods that can be used to extract data from an XML document. For example, if we are positioned on an element with the text content, we can use the ReadStartElement(), ReadString(), and ReadEndElement() methods to read each portion of the element. To extract just the text part of an element node, we can use the ReadElementString() method. To get the text value of the attribute, we use the ReadAttributeValue() method.

The ReadInnerXml() and ReadOuterXml() methods can be useful if we want to get the textual form of the nodes without parsing its content.

The XmlNodeReader class can be used to access data in an XmlNode. The following example shows how to use the XmlNodeReader:

```
'---------------------------------------
' XML.NET Example. XmlNodeReader
'---------------------------------------

Imports System
Imports System.XML

Module Cons

Sub Main()

  Dim XmlDoc As New XmlDocument
  XmlDoc.Load("nw_elements.xml")
  Dim Reader As XmlNodeReader = New XmlNodeReader(XmlDoc)
```

```
Do While (Reader.Read)

  Console.WriteLine(String.Format("Name : {0} Type : {1} " & _
    "Value : {2}", Reader.Name, Reader.NodeType, Reader.Value))

Loop

End Sub

End Module
```

The third type of XmlReader-derived class is XmlValidatingReader – this is used to validate an XML file against a DTD or a schema (either XDR or XSD). We perform validation by associating an XmlValidatingReader object with an XmlTextReader. The XmlValidatingReader exposes a Schemas collection of an XmlSchema Collection type that contains one or more schemas (DTD, XDR, XSD) represented as XmlSchema objects that can be used to validate the document.

If there are validation errors, they will be reported through a Validation EventHandler. This is a procedure where an args argument contains information about the error. The args.ErrorCode and args.Message properties return a numerical code and text description of the error. To get information about the location of the error in the XML file, we can use the LineNumber and LinePosition properties of the XmlTextReader object. If a handler for validation errors is not specified, the XmlValidatingReader will throw an exception when a validation error occurs.

The ValidationType property specifies the type of validation to be performed. The possible values of this property are the following.

- **Auto** Performs validation if DTD or schema information is found in the XML document.
- **DTD** Validates according to DTD.
- **None** Does not validate – the XmlValidatingReader acts as a non-validating parser.
- **Schema** Validates according to XSD schemas.
- **XDR** Validates according to XDR schemas.

The following example outlines the usage of the XmlValidatingReader object:

```
'-----------------------------------------------
' XML.NET Example. XmlValidatingReader example
'-----------------------------------------------

Dim Reader    As XmlTextReader
Dim VReader   As XmlValidatingReader
Dim Validated As Boolean

...
```

```
Sub ValidateDocument

 Reader    = New XmlTextReader("document.xml")
 VReader   = New XmlValidatingReader(Reader)
 Validated = True

 AddHandler VReader.ValidationEventHandler, _
  New ValidationEventHandler(AddresOf ValidationError)

 VReader.ValidationType = ValidationType.DTD

 Do While (VReader.Read())
  '
  ' Reader performs validation
  '
 Loop

 If Validated Then
  Console.WriteLine("Validation succeeded")
 Else
  Console.WriteLine("Validation failed")
 End If

End Sub

Sub ValidationError(ByVal o As Object, _
 ByVal args As ValidationEventArgs)

 Validated = False
 Console.Write ("Validation Error : " & args.Message)
 Console.Write (" Line : " & Reader.LineNumber & _
  " Position : " & Reader.LinePosition)
 Console.WriteLine

 End Sub
```

Using the XmlReader or its derived classes as a base class, we can create our own customized readers to implement application-specific logic. Typically, we override the Read method to handle reading of a specific node type differently. We may do this if we want to perfom stream processing, implement specific business rules without requiring the complexity of XSLT, or build a DOM tree simply to edit the document. For example, we can use customized readers to convert attributes into elements (that is a change from being attributecentric to elementcentric) and vice versa, remove specific nodes from the stream, change specific information about a node or change the structure of the document.

To write XML documents, we use the `XmlTextWriter` class, which implements properties and methods found in the `XmlWriter` class. The `XmlTextWriter` class represents a writer that provides a fast, non-cached forward-only way of generating streams or files containing XML data that conforms to the W3C extensible markup language (XML) 1.0 specification and the namespaces in the XML specification.

The `XmlTextWriter` class provides a set of properties, the most commonly used of which are shown below.

- **Formatting** Specifies the formatting of the output. This property can be set either to `Formatting.Indented`, to indent child elements with respect to their parents, or `Formatting.None`, for no indentation (this is the default value for this property).

- **Indentation** Specifies how many `IndentChars` to write for each level in the hierarchy when `Formatting` property is set to `Formatting.Indented`. The default value is 2.

- **IndentChar** Specifies which character to use for indenting when the `Formatting` property is set to `Formatting.Indented`. The default value is the space character.

- **Namespaces** This `Boolean` property indicates whether or not to implement name-space support.

- **QuoteChar** Specifies the character to use to quote attribute values. This can be either a single quote character (') or a double quote character ("). The default value is the double quote.

The following is a list of the most commonly used methods of the `XmlTextWriter` class.

- **Close()** method Closes the output stream or file.
- **Flush()** method Flushes the buffer to the output stream or file.
- **WriteAttributeString(_String_, _String_)** method Writes an attribute with the specified value.
- **WriteCData(_String_)** method Writes a `<![CDATA[...]]>` section containing the specified text.
- **WriteComment(_String_)** method Writes an XML comment `<!-...->` containing the specified text.
- **WriteDocType(_String_, _String_, _String_, _String_)** method Writes the DOC-TYPE declaration with the specified name and optional attributes.
- **WriteElementString(_String_, _String_)** method Writes an element containing a string value.
- **WriteEndAttbite()** method Completes an attribute started with the `WriteStartAttribute`.
- **WriteEndDocument()** method Closes any open elements or attributes.
- **WriteEndElement()** method Completes an element started with `WriteStartElement`.

- **WriteFullEndElement()** **method** Completes an element started with WriteStartElement.

- **WriteNode(*XmlReader, Boolean*)** **method** Copies everything from the reader to the writer.

- **WriteProcessingInstruction(*String, String*)** **method** Writes a processing instruction with a space between the name and text in the form <?name text?>.

- **WriteRaw(*String*)** **method** Writes raw text to the output.

- **WriteStartAttribute(*String, String, String*)** **method** Writes the start of an attribute.

- **WriteStartDocument()** **method** Writes the XML declaration with the version "1.0".

- **WriteStartElement(*String, String, String*)** **method** Writes the specified start tag.

- **WriteWhitespace(*String*)** **method** Writes whitespace to the output.

The following example shows how to use the XmlTextReader and XmlTextWriter objects to copy the contents of an XML file to the console (see also Figure 14.3):

```
'---------------------------------------
' XML.NET Example. XmlTextWriter
'---------------------------------------


Imports System
Imports System.XML

 Module Cons

 Sub Main()

  Dim Reader As XmlTextReader = New XmlTextReader("nw_elements.xml")
  Dim Writer As XmlTextWriter = New XmlTextWriter(Console.Out)

  Writer.Formatting  = Formatting.Indented
  Writer.Indentation = 2

  Writer.WriteNode(Reader, False)

 End Sub

 End Module
```

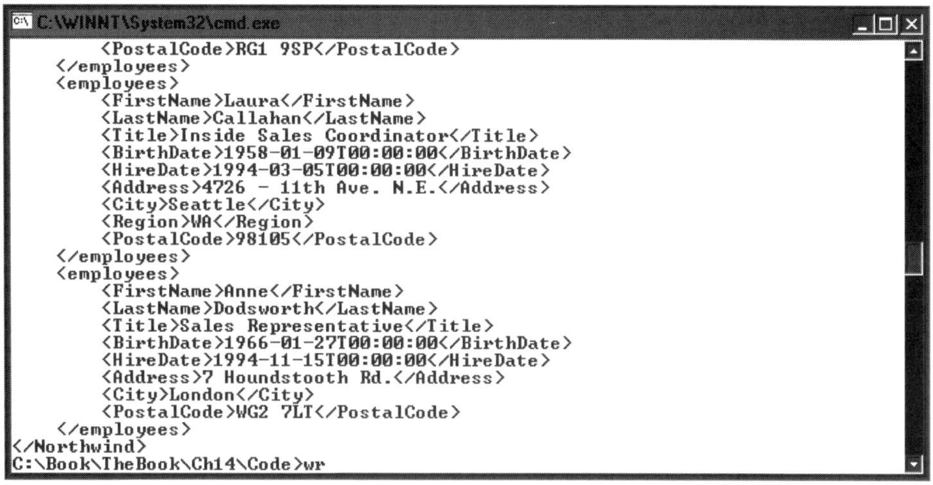

```
C:\WINNT\System32\cmd.exe                                        _ □ ×
        <PostalCode>RG1 9SP</PostalCode>
      </employees>
      <employees>
        <FirstName>Laura</FirstName>
        <LastName>Callahan</LastName>
        <Title>Inside Sales Coordinator</Title>
        <BirthDate>1958-01-09T00:00:00</BirthDate>
        <HireDate>1994-03-05T00:00:00</HireDate>
        <Address>4726 - 11th Ave. N.E.</Address>
        <City>Seattle</City>
        <Region>WA</Region>
        <PostalCode>98105</PostalCode>
      </employees>
      <employees>
        <FirstName>Anne</FirstName>
        <LastName>Dodsworth</LastName>
        <Title>Sales Representative</Title>
        <BirthDate>1966-01-27T00:00:00</BirthDate>
        <HireDate>1994-11-15T00:00:00</HireDate>
        <Address>7 Houndstooth Rd.</Address>
        <City>London</City>
        <PostalCode>WG2 7LT</PostalCode>
      </employees>
</Northwind>
C:\Book\TheBook\Ch14\Code>wr
```

FIGURE 14.3   Using XmlTextReader and XmlTextWriter to copy file contents to a console

The following example shows how to use the XmlTextWriter object to create an
XML document with the structure shown in Figure 14.3 (see also Figure 14.4):

```
'--------------------------------------
' XML.NET Example. XmlTextWriter
'--------------------------------------


Imports System
Imports System.IO
Imports System.XML

 Module Cons

 Sub Main()

   Dim OutFile As String = "employees.xml"
   Dim Writer As XmlTextWriter = New XmlTextWriter(OutFile, Nothing)

   Writer.Formatting  = Formatting.Indented
   Writer.Indentation = 2


 '
 ' Start the document
 '

   Writer.WriteStartDocument()
```

```
'
' Place a comment
'
  Writer.WriteComment("XmlTextWriter Demo")


'
' Start the root node
'
  Writer.WriteStartElement("Northwind")


'
' Start the employees node
'
    Writer.WriteStartElement("employees")


'
' Write subnodes
'
    Writer.WriteElementString("FirstName" , "Peter")
    Writer.WriteElementString("LastName"  , "Pan")
    Writer.WriteElementString("Title"     , "Accounting Manager")
    Writer.WriteElementString("BirthDate" , "1974-02-03T00:00:00")
    Writer.WriteElementString("HireDate"  , "1996-01-15T00:00:00")
    Writer.WriteElementString("Address"   , "1274 Pacific Drive")
    Writer.WriteElementString("City"      , "Santa Monica")
    Writer.WriteElementString("Region"    , "CA")
    Writer.WriteElementString("PostalCode", "95149")


'
' End the employees node
'
    Writer.WriteEndElement()


'
' End the root node
'
  Writer.WriteEndElement()


'
' End the document
'
  Writer.WriteEndDocument()
```

```
'
' Flush buffer to stream and clode writer
'

  Writer.Flush()
  Writer.Close()


'
' Load the file into an XmlTextReader to ensure well formed XML
'

  Dim Reader As XmlTextReader = New XmlTextReader(OutFile)
  Writer = New XmlTextWriter(Console.Out)
  Writer.Formatting  = Formatting.Indented
  Writer.Indentation = 2

  Writer.WriteNode(Reader, False)

End Sub

End Module
```

Earlier in this chapter we saw an XML document where the employees' data is stored as attributes of the <employees> node. To change our document so it is attribute centric, we need to replace all the WriteElementString() method calls with WriteAttributeString() method calls, as shown below (see also Figure 14.5):

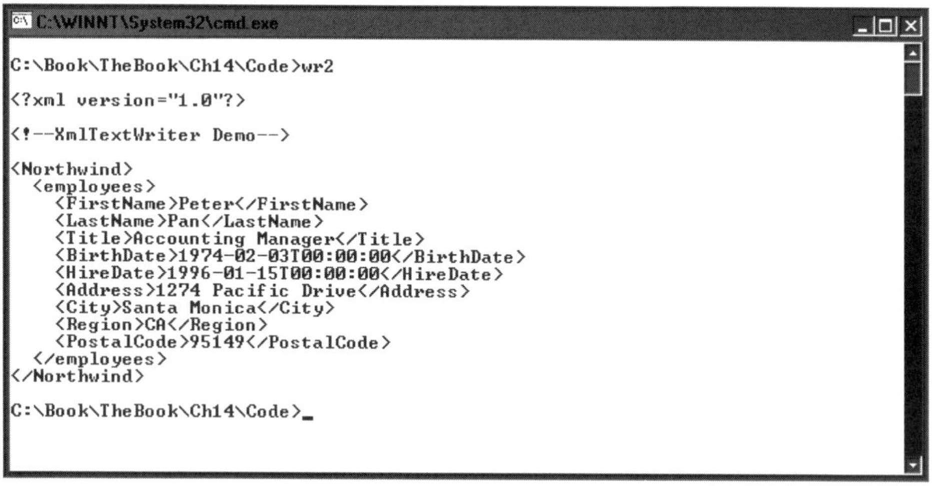

```
C:\WINNT\System32\cmd.exe                                      _|□|×

C:\Book\TheBook\Ch14\Code>wr2

<?xml version="1.0"?>

<!--XmlTextWriter Demo-->

<Northwind>
  <employees>
    <FirstName>Peter</FirstName>
    <LastName>Pan</LastName>
    <Title>Accounting Manager</Title>
    <BirthDate>1974-02-03T00:00:00</BirthDate>
    <HireDate>1996-01-15T00:00:00</HireDate>
    <Address>1274 Pacific Drive</Address>
    <City>Santa Monica</City>
    <Region>CA</Region>
    <PostalCode>95149</PostalCode>
  </employees>
</Northwind>

C:\Book\TheBook\Ch14\Code>_
```

FIGURE 14.4   Using the XmlTextWriter to create an XML document

```
'----------------------------------------
' XML.NET Example. XmlTextWriter
'----------------------------------------

Imports System
Imports System.IO
Imports System.XML

 Module Cons

 Sub Main()

  Console.WriteLine

  Dim OutFile As String = "employees.xml"
  Dim Writer As XmlTextWriter = New XmlTextWriter(OutFile, Nothing)

  Writer.Formatting  = Formatting.Indented
  Writer.Indentation = 2

'
' Start the document
'
  Writer.WriteStartDocument()

'
' Place a comment
'
  Writer.WriteComment("XmlTextWriter Demo")

'
' Start the root node
'
  Writer.WriteStartElement("Northwind")

'
' Start the employees node
'
   Writer.WriteStartElement("employees")

'
' Write attributes of the employees node
'
```

```
        Writer.WriteAttributeString("FirstName" , "Peter")
        Writer.WriteAttributeString("LastName"  , "Pan")
        Writer.WriteAttributeString("Title"      , "Accounting Manager")
        Writer.WriteAttributeString("BirthDate" , "1974-02-03T00:00:00")
        Writer.WriteAttributeString("HireDate"  , "1996-01-15T00:00:00")
        Writer.WriteAttributeString("Address"    , "1274 Pacific Drive")
        Writer.WriteAttributeString("City"       , "Santa Monica")
        Writer.WriteAttributeString("Region"     , "CA")
        Writer.WriteAttributeString("PostalCode", "95149")

    '
    ' End the employees node
    '
      Writer.WriteEndElement()

    '
    ' End the root node
    '
      Writer.WriteEndElement()

    '
    ' End the document
    '
      Writer.WriteEndDocument()

    '
    ' Flush buffer to stream and clode writer
    '

      '
      ' Load the file into an XmlTextReader to ensure well formed XML
      '

      Dim Reader As XmlTextReader = New XmlTextReader(OutFile)
      Writer = New XmlTextWriter(Console.Out)
      Writer.Formatting  = Formatting.Indented
      Writer.Indentation = 2

      Writer.WriteNode(Reader, False)

      Console.WriteLine

    End Sub

    End Module
```

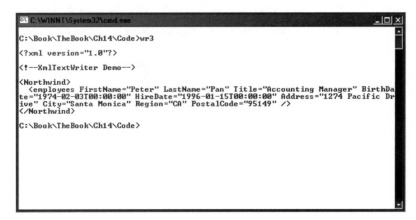

FIGURE 14.5 The document has been changed so it is attribute-centric using the
`WriteAttributeString()` method

Working with XML DOM

The `XmlDocument` class provides support for the W3C document object model
(DOM) level 1 core and the core DOM level 2. This class represents the entire XML
document as an in-memory node tree and allows us to navigate and edit the document. The `XmlDocument` class provides properties and methods that should be
familiar to those who have used the MSXML parser.

We use `XmlDocument` instead of `XmlTextReader` when we need random access to
all of a document's contents, to modify the document structure, to perform XSL/T
transformations, or perform complex XPath filtering.

Figure 14.6 shows the `XmlDocument` architecture.

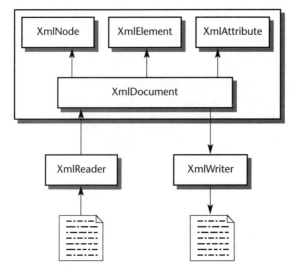

FIGURE 14.6 XML document architecture

The XmlDocument class provides the following properties.

- **Attributes** Returns an XmlAttributeCollection that contains the attributes for this node.
- **ChildNodes** Returns the XmlNodeList that contains all the child nodes for this node.
- **DocumentElement** Returns the root XmlElement for the document.
- **FirstChild** Returns the first child node of the node as an XmlNode object.
- **HasChildNodes** This Boolean property indicates whether or not this node has child nodes.
- **InnerText** Specifies the concatenated values of the node and all its children as a String.
- **InnerXml** Specifies the markup, representing the children of the current node as a String.
- **Item(*String*)** Returns the child element with the specified name. Overloaded versions of this property – Item(*String*, *String*) – may be used to get the child element specified by its local name and namespace URI.
- **LastChild** Returns the last child node of the node as an XmlNode object.
- **Name** Returns the name of the node as a String.
- **NodeType** Returns the type of the current node. Each XmlNodeType value maps to a specific class – the XmlNodeType.Attribute maps to the XmlAttribute class, the XmlNodeType.Element to XmlElement, and the XmlNodeType.Text to XmlText, and so on.
- **OuterXml** Returns the markup representing this node and all its children as a String.
- **ParentNode** Returns the parent of this node as an XmlNode object.
- **PreserveWhitespace** This Boolean property indicates whether or not to preserve whitespace.
- **Value** Gets or sets the value of the node. The value returned depends on the type of node (specified by the NodeType property).

Here is a list of the commonly used methods of the XmlDocument class.

- **AppendChild(*XmlNode*) method** Adds the specified node to the end of the list of children of this node.
- **CreateAttribute(*String*) method** Creates an XmlAttribute object with the specified name. Overloaded versions of this method can create an attribute node with the specified name and namespace URI, as well as with the specified prefix, local name, and namespace URI.
- **CreateElement(*String*) method** Creates an XmlElement object with the specified name. Overloaded versions of this method can create an element with the specified name and namespace URI, as well as with the specified prefix, local name, and namespace URI.

- **CreateNavigator()** method Creates an XPathNavigator object, used to navigate this object.

- **CreateNode(*String*, *String*, *String*)** method Creates an XmlNode object with the specified node type, name, and namespace URI. The overloaded version of this method can create a node with the specified node type, prefix, name, and namespace URI.

- **CreateTextNode(*String*)** method Creates an XmlText object with the specified text.

- **GetElementByID(*String*)** method Returns the XmlElement with the specified ID.

- **GetElementsByTagName(*String*)** method Returns an XmlNodeList with a list of all descendant elements that match the specified name.

- **InsertAfter(*XmlNode*, *XmlNode*)** method Inserts the specified node immediately after the specified reference node.

- **InsertBefore(*XmlNode*, *XmlNode*)** method Inserts the specified node immediately before the specified reference node.

- **Load(*Stream*)** method Loads the specified XML data from a stream, specifies the URL – Load(*String*), TextReader object – Load(*TextReader*), or XmlReader object – Load(*XmlReader*).

- **LoadXml(*String*)** method Loads the XML document from the specified string.

- **ReadNode(*XmlReader*)** method Creates an XmlNode object from the XmlReader.

- **RemoveAll()** method Removes all child nodes and/or attributes from the current node.

- **RemoveChild(*XmlNode*)** method Removes the specified child node of the current node.

- **ReplaceChild(*XmlNode*, *XmlNode*)** method Replaces the specified child node with the specified node.

- **Save(*Stream*)** method Saves the XML document to the specified location, which can be a Stream object, file – Save(String), TextWriter object – Save(*TextWriter*), or XmlWriter object – Save(XmlWriter).

- **SelectNodes(*String*)** method Selects a list of nodes matching the XPath expression.

- **SelectSingleNode(*String*)** method Selects the first XmlNode that matches the XPath expression.

- **WriteContentTo** method Saves all child nodes of the XmlDocument node to the specified XmlWriter object. This method is the functional equivalent of the InnerXml property.

- **WriteTo** method Saves the XmlDocument node to the specified XmlWriter object. This method is the functional equivalent of the OuterXml property.

The following example shows how to use an XmlDocument object to iterate an XML document.

```
'----------------------------------------
' XML.NET Example. XmlDocument object
'----------------------------------------

Imports System
Imports System.XML

  Module Cons

    Sub Main()

      Dim XmlDoc    As New XmlDocument
      Dim Root      As XmlNode
      Dim Node      As XmlNode
      Dim ChildNode As XmlNode

      XmlDoc.Load("nw_elements.xml")
      Root = XmlDoc.DocumentElement

      For Each Node In Root.ChildNodes

        Console.WriteLine(Node.Name)

        For Each ChildNode in Node.ChildNodes

        Console.WriteLine(" " & ChildNode.Name & _
            " = " & ChildNode.InnerText)
        Next

      Next

    End Sub

  End Module
```

In the example above, we used the Load() method to load an XML document from a file. Then we took the root element by using the DocumentElement property and used the ChildNodes collection to iterate through all the child nodes of the root element. For each child node, we once again used the ChildNodes collection to iterate through its child nodes. For each child node of the root element, we print its name, and for each child subnode, we print its name and value. The resulting output will look like this (only the portion concerned is shown):

```
employees
 FirstName = Nancy
 LastName = Davolio
 Title = Sales Representative
 BirthDate = 1948-12-08T00:00:00
 HireDate = 1992-05-01T00:00:00
 Address = 507 - 20th Ave. E. Apt. 2A
 City = Seattle
 Region = WA
 PostalCode = 98122

 ...

employees
 FirstName = Anne
 LastName = Dodsworth
 Title = Sales Representative
 BirthDate = 1966-01-27T00:00:00
 HireDate = 1994-11-15T00:00:00
 Address = 7 Houndstooth Rd.
 City = London
 PostalCode = WG2 7LT
```

To iterate the XML document that contains the attributes within the nodes, we use the Attributes collection of the Node, as shown in the example below:

```
'----------------------------------------
' XML.NET Example. XmlDocument object
'----------------------------------------

Imports System
Imports System.XML

Module Cons

 Sub Main()

   Dim XmlDoc    As New XmlDocument
   Dim Root      As XmlNode
   Dim Node      As XmlNode
   Dim Attrib    As XmlNode

   XmlDoc.Load("nw.xml")
   Root = XmlDoc.DocumentElement
```

```
  For Each Node In Root.ChildNodes

    Console.WriteLine(Node.Name)

    For Each Attrib in Node.Attributes

    Console.WriteLine(" " & Attrib.Name & _
        " = " & Attrib.Value)
    Next

  Next

  End Sub

End Module
```

Using the XmlDocument object, we can modify the existing document or create a new document from scratch. The following example shows how to add a new <employees> node and subnodes to the existing document:

```
'----------------------------------------
' XML.NET Example. XmlDocument object
'----------------------------------------

Imports System
Imports System.XML

 Module Cons

  Sub Main()

    Dim XmlDoc      As New XmlDocument
    Dim Root        As XmlNode
    Dim Node        As XmlNode
    Dim ChildNode   As XmlNode
    Dim Element     As XmlElement
    Dim SubElement  As XmlElement
    Dim Text        As XmlText

    XmlDoc.Load("nw_elements.xml")
    Root = XmlDoc.DocumentElement
```

```vb
'
' Create a new node
'

  Element = XmlDoc.CreateElement("employees")


'
' FirstName
'

  SubElement = XmlDoc.CreateElement("FirstName")
  Text = XmlDoc.CreateTextNode("Peter")
  SubElement.AppendChild(Text)
  Element.AppendChild(SubElement)
  Root.AppendChild(Element)


'
' LastName
'

  SubElement = XmlDoc.CreateElement("LastName")
  Text = XmlDoc.CreateTextNode("Pan")
  SubElement.AppendChild(Text)
  Element.AppendChild(SubElement)
  Root.AppendChild(Element)


'
' Title
'

  SubElement = XmlDoc.CreateElement("Title")
  Text = XmlDoc.CreateTextNode("Accounting Manager")
  SubElement.AppendChild(Text)
  Element.AppendChild(SubElement)
  Root.AppendChild(Element)


'
' Show modified document
'
  For Each Node In Root.ChildNodes

   Console.WriteLine(Node.Name)
```

```
   For Each ChildNode in Node.ChildNodes

     Console.WriteLine(" " & ChildNode.Name & _
       " = " & ChildNode.InnerText)
   Next

  Next

 End Sub

End Module
```

To create a new node, we use the `CreateElement()` method of the `XmlDocument` object. Then we use the same method to create subelements. For each subelement, we also create an `XmlText` object that specifies the contents of the node, then we use the `AppendChild()` methods to add the `XmlText` object to the subnode, add this subnode to the new node, and add the new node to the root of the XML document. Figure 14.7 shows the new `<employees>` entry added to the existing document.

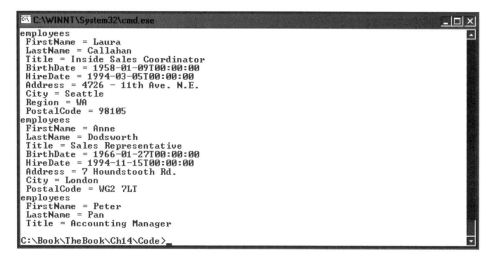

FIGURE 14.7   A new `<employees>` entry has been created using the `CreateElement()` and `AppendChild()` methods

We can also use the `InnerXml` property to assign the whole set of subnodes to the new node in one operation. The following example shows how to do this:

```
'----------------------------------------
' XML.NET Example. XmlDocument object
'----------------------------------------

Imports System
Imports System.XML

 Module Cons

  Sub Main()

    Dim XmlDoc    As New XmlDocument
    Dim Root      As XmlNode
    Dim Node      As XmlNode
    Dim ChildNode As XmlNode
    Dim Element   As XmlElement
    Dim Str       As String

    XmlDoc.Load("nw_elements.xml")
    Root = XmlDoc.DocumentElement

 '
' Create a new node
 '

    Element = XmlDoc.CreateElement("employees")

    Str = "<FirstName>Peter</FirstName>" & _
     "<LastName>Pan</LastName>" & "<Title>Accounting Manager</Title>"

    Element.InnerXml = Str
    Root.AppendChild(Element)


    For Each Node In Root.ChildNodes

     Console.WriteLine(Node.Name)

     For Each ChildNode in Node.ChildNodes

      Console.WriteLine(" " & ChildNode.Name & _
       " = " & ChildNode.InnerText)
     Next

    Next

  End Sub

 End Module
```

This simplifies the creation of subnodes, but now we are responsible for the XML text assigned to the `InnerXml` property.

To create attributes of the node, we use the `SetAttribute()` method of the `XmlElement` object. We specify the name of the attribute and its value as an argument for this method. For example:

```
Element = XmlDoc.CreateElement("employees")

Element.SetAttribute("FirstName", "Peter")
Element.SetAttribute("LastName" , "Pan")
Element.SetAttribute("Title"    , "Accounting Manager")

Root.AppendChild(Element)
```

To remove an XML element, we use the `RemoveChild()` method. For example, to remove the employee we have added to our document, we may use the following call to this method:

```
Root.RemoveChild(Root.LastChild)
```

Querying XML with XPath

There are several ways in which we can query an XML document with XPath syntax. We can use the `SelectNodes()` and `SelectSingleNode()` methods to get a list of nodes matching the XPath expression or we can create the `XPathNavigator` object, which will allow us to navigate through the XML in an `XmlDocument` object. The following example shows how to use the `SelectSingleNode()` method to select a node that matches the specified criterion (first name is Anne):

```
'----------------------------------------
' XML.NET Example. XmlNode object
'----------------------------------------

Imports System
Imports System.XML

 Module Cons

  Sub Main()

    Dim XmlDoc    As New XmlDocument
    Dim Root      As XmlNode
    Dim Node      As XmlNode
    Dim Attrib    As XmlNode
```

```
XmlDoc.Load("nw.xml")
Root = XmlDoc.DocumentElement

Node = root.SelectSingleNode("employees[@FirstName='Anne']")

  For Each Attrib in Node.Attributes

  Console.WriteLine(" " & Attrib.Name & _
      " = " & Attrib.Value)
  Next


End Sub

End Module
```

The following example shows how to use the `SelectNodes()` method to select all employees who are based in a specified region:

```
'-----------------------------------------
' XML.NET Example. XmlNode object
'-----------------------------------------

Imports System
Imports System.XML

Module Cons

Sub Main()

    Dim XmlDoc    As New XmlDocument
    Dim Root      As XmlNode
    Dim Nodes     As XmlNodeList
    Dim Node      As XmlNode
    Dim Attrib    As XmlNode

    XmlDoc.Load("nw.xml")
    Root = XmlDoc.DocumentElement

    Nodes = root.SelectNodes("employees[@Region='WA']")

    Console.WriteLine("Found " & Nodes.Count & _
      " employees in WA region")
```

```
For Each Node In Nodes
 For Each Attrib in Node.Attributes

 Console.WriteLine(" " & Attrib.Name & _
    " = " & Attrib.Value)
 Next

 Next

End Sub

End Module
```

The XPathNavigator object provides a cursor-style model for navigating over a store, along with XPath query support. It does not provide editing of the underlying store. An XPathNavigator object can be created with the help of the CreateNavigator() method of the XmlDocument object. An XPathNavigator object contains the following commonly used properties:

- **HasAttributes** This Boolean property indicates whether or not the element node has any attributes.
- **HasChildren** This Boolean property indicates whether or not the current node has child nodes.
- **Name** Returns the qualified name of the current node as a String.
- **NodeType** Returns the type of the current node as an XPathNodeType object.
- **Value** Returns the text value of the current node as a String.

Here is a list of commonly used methods of the XPathNavigator object.

- **GetAttribute(*String*, *String*) method** Returns the value of the attribute with the specified name and namespace URI.
- **Matches(*String*) method** Returns "True" if the current node matches the specified XPath expression. The overloaded version of this method accepts the XPath expression as an XPathExpression object.
- **MoveTo(*XPathNavigator*) method** Moves to the same position as the specified XPathNavigator.
- **MoveToAttribute(*String*, *String*) method** Moves to the attribute with the matching local name and namespace URI.
- **MoveToFirstChild() method** Moves to the first child of the current node.
- **MoveToId(*String*) method** Moves to the node that has a type ID attribute with the specified value.
- **MoveToNext() method** Moves to the next sibling of the current node.
- **MoveToNextAttribute() method** Moves to the next attribute node.

- **MoveToParent()** method Moves to the parent of the current node.
- **MoveToPrevious()** method Moves to the previous sibling node.
- **MoveToRoot()** method Moves to the root node.
- **Select(*String*)** method Selects a node set using the specified XPath expression. The overloaded version of this method accepts the XPath expression as an XPathExpression object.
- **SelectChildren(*XPathNodeType*)** method Selects all the child element nodes of the current node matching the selection criteria.

The following example uses the XPathNavigator object to navigate through the XML document:

```vb
'----------------------------------------
' XML.NET Example. XPathNavigator object
'----------------------------------------


Imports System
Imports System.XML
Imports System.XML.XPath


 Module Cons

  Sub Main()

    Dim XmlDoc    As New XmlDocument
    Dim XPathNav  As XPathNavigator

    XmlDoc.Load("nw.xml")
    XPathNav = XmlDoc.CreateNavigator()


  '
  ' Go to root of the document
  '

    XPathNav.MoveToRoot()
  '
  ' Go to first child node - <Northwind>
  '

    XPathNav.MoveToFirstChild()

    Console.WriteLine(XPathNav.Name)

    XPathNav.MoveToNext()
```

```
'
' Go to first <employee> node
'

  XPathNav.MoveToFirstChild()

  Console.WriteLine(" " & XPathNav.Name)


'
' Show attributes if any
'

    If XPathNav.HasAttributes Then
      ShowAttributes(XPathNav)
    End If

    XPathNav.MoveToParent()


'
' Iterate through <employee> nodes
'

  While (XPathNav.MoveToNext())

    Console.WriteLine(XPathNav.Name)


'
' Show attributes if any
'

    If XPathNav.HasAttributes Then
      ShowAttributes(XPathNav)
    End If

    XPathNav.MoveToParent()

  End While

  End Sub

  Sub ShowAttributes(Nav as XPathNavigator)

    Nav.MoveToFirstAttribute()
    Console.WriteLine("   " & Nav.Name & "=" & Nav.Value)
```

```
   While (Nav.MoveToNextAttribute)
    Console.WriteLine("  " & Nav.Name & "=" & Nav.Value)
   End While


  End Sub
End Module
```

Here is an example of how to use the `Select()` method of the `XPathNavigator`
object to create a collection of selected nodes and iterate through them with the
`XmlPathNodeIterator` object:

```
'----------------------------------------
' XML.NET Example. XPathNavigator object
'----------------------------------------

Imports System
Imports System.XML
Imports System.XML.XPath

 Module Cons

  Sub Main()

    Dim XmlDoc    As New XmlDocument
    Dim XPathNav  As XPathNavigator

    XmlDoc.Load("nw_elements.xml")
    XPathNav = XmlDoc.CreateNavigator()

  '
  ' Go to root of the document
  '

    XPathNav.MoveToRoot()

   Dim Iterator as XPathNodeIterator  = _
    XPathNav.Select("descendant::employees")

   While(Iterator.MoveNext())
    Console.WriteLine(Iterator.Current.Name & _
      "=" & Iterator.Current.Value)
   End While


   End Sub
End Module
```

In our last example, we shall use the **XPathNavigator** object to create a collection of nodes that match the specified XPath expression:

```
'----------------------------------------
' XML.NET Example. XPathNavigator object
'----------------------------------------

Imports System
Imports System.XML
Imports System.XML.XPath

 Module Cons

  Sub Main()

    Dim XmlDoc    As New XmlDocument
    Dim XPathNav  As XPathNavigator

    XmlDoc.Load("nw.xml")
    XPathNav = XmlDoc.CreateNavigator()

    Dim Iterator as XPathNodeIterator  = _
      XPathNav.Select("Northwind/employees[@Region='WA']")

   While(Iterator.MoveNext())
     Console.WriteLine(Iterator.Current.Name)
   End While

  End Sub
End Module
```

Transformations using XSLT

Extensible stylesheet language transformation (XSLT) is used to transform an XML document into another XML document, an HTML document or text. XSLT offers tremendous flexibility for presenting and exchanging data between dissimilar devices and business systems. This transformation process is specified by the W3C XSLT Version 1.0 recommendation. In the .NET Framework, the **XslTransform** class, found in the **System.Xml.Xsl** namespace, is an XSLT processor that implements the functionality of this specification.

Figure 14.8 shows **XslTransform** architecture.

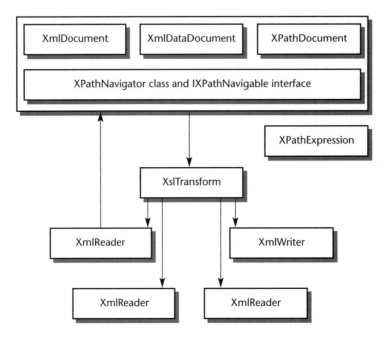

FIGURE 14.8   The architecture of the XslTransform class

Each of the three XML sources shown above – the XmlDocument object, XmlDataDocument object, and XPathDocument object – expose the XPathNavigator in the IXPathNavigable interface and can be passed to an XslTransform object to perform the XSL transformation. The XslTransform object can transform to different outputs and is based on a pull streaming model. The XmlWriter output allows for creation of XML documents. The stream and TextWriter outputs allow for the creation of non-XML streams. The XPathExpression class allows for the creation of compiled XPath expressions to be reused in queries. If you have an often used query, then there is a performance gain in using compiled expressions. This class also provides the interface for namespace-prefixed queries in XPath. The XslTransform class performs XML data transformation using an XSLT stylesheet. It provides the Load() method that is used to load the XSLT stylesheet, including any xsl:include and xsl:import references, and the Transform() method, which transforms the specified XML data using the loaded XSLT stylesheet and outputs the results.

Suppose we have an XML document with the following attributecentric structure:

```
<?xml version="1.0" encoding="utf-8" ?>
 <Northwind>
  <employees
    EmployeeID="1"
    LastName="Davolio"
    FirstName="Nancy"
    Title="Sales Representative"
    TitleOfCourtesy="Ms."
    BirthDate="1948-12-08T00:00:00"
    HireDate="1992-05-01T00:00:00"
    Address="507 - 20th Ave. E.Apt. 2A"
    City="Seattle"
    Region="WA"
    PostalCode="98122"
    Country="USA"
    HomePhone="(206) 555-9857"
    Extension="5467"
  />


  ...


</Northwind>
```

and we want to transform it into an HTML table where one row shows employee data – the first and last names in their own cells, then titles and addresses in the adjoining cells. To do this, we can use the following XSLT stylesheet:

```
<?xml version="1.0"?>
<xsl:stylesheet xmlns:xsl="http://www.w3.org/1999/XSL/Transform"
 version="1.0">
<xsl:template match="/">
<HTML>
<BODY>
<TABLE BORDER="2">
 <TR>
  <TD>First Name</TD>
  <TD>Last Name</TD>
  <TD>Title</TD>
  <TD>Address</TD>
 </TR>
 <xsl:for-each select="Northwind/employees">
 <TR>
```

```
  <TD>
   <xsl:value-of select="@FirstName"/>
  </TD>
  <TD>
   <xsl:value-of select="@LastName"/>
  </TD>
  <TD><xsl:value-of select="@Title"/></TD>
  <TD><xsl:value-of select="@Address"/></TD>
 </TR>
</xsl:for-each>
</TABLE>
</BODY>
</HTML>
</xsl:template>
</xsl:stylesheet>
```

The following code shows how to use the **XslTransform** object to perform the transformation:

```
'----------------------------------------
' XML.NET Example. XslTransform object
'----------------------------------------

Imports System
Imports System.XML
Imports System.XML.XSL

 Module Cons

  Sub Main()

   Dim XmlDoc     As New XmlDocument
   Dim XSlDoc     As New XslTransform
   Dim Writer     As New XmlTextWriter(Console.Out)

   XmlDoc.Load("nw.xml")
   XslDoc.Load("nw.xsl")
   XslDoc.Transform(XmlDoc, Nothing, Writer)

  End Sub
 End Module
```

The result of this transformation is shown in Figure 14.9.

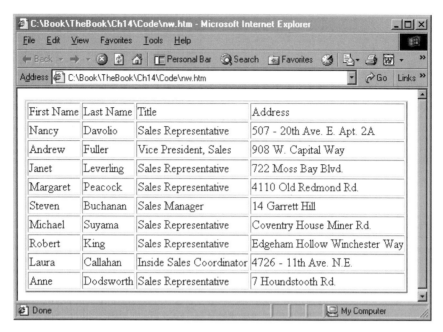

FIGURE 14.9   Transforming an XML document to HTML using XSLT template

For an element-centric XML document like the one shown below:

```
<?xml version="1.0" encoding="utf-8" ?>
 <Northwind>
  <employees>
<EmployeeID>1</EmployeeID>
<LastName>Davolio</LastName>
<FirstName>Nancy</FirstName>
<Title>Sales Representative</Title>
<TitleOfCourtesy>Ms.</TitleOfCourtesy>
<BirthDate>1948-12-08T00:00:00</BirthDate>
<HireDate>1992-05-01T00:00:00</HireDate>
<Address>507 – 20th Ave. E.Apt. 2A</Address>
<City>Seattle</City>
<Region>WA</Region>
<PostalCode>98122</PostalCode>
<Country>USA</Country>
<HomePhone>(206) 555-9857</HomePhone>
<Extension>5467</Extension>
  ...
  </employees>

</Northwind>
```

we may use a slightly different XSLT stylesheet, as shown below:

```
<?xml version="1.0"?>
<xsl:stylesheet xmlns:xsl="http://www.w3.org/1999/XSL/Transform"
 version="1.0">
<xsl:template match="/">
<HTML>
<BODY>
<TABLE BORDER="2">
 <TR>
  <TD>First Name</TD>
  <TD>Last Name</TD>
  <TD>Title</TD>
  <TD>Address</TD>
 </TR>
 <xsl:for-each select="Northwind/employees">
 <TR>
  <TD><xsl:value-of select="FirstName"/></TD>
  <TD><xsl:value-of select="LastName"/></TD>
  <TD><xsl:value-of select="Title"/></TD>
  <TD><xsl:value-of select="Address"/></TD>
 </TR>
</xsl:for-each>
</TABLE>
</BODY>
</HTML>
</xsl:template>
</xsl:stylesheet>
```

If we want to pass parameters to our XSLT stylesheet – for example, to select employees in a specified region – we must change our template like this:

```
<?xml version="1.0"?>
<xsl:stylesheet xmlns:xsl="http://www.w3.org/1999/XSL/Transform"
 version="1.0">
<xsl:param name="region" />
<xsl:template match="/">
<HTML>
<BODY>
<TABLE BORDER="2">
 <TR>
  <TD>First Name</TD>
  <TD>Last Name</TD>
  <TD>Title</TD>
  <TD>Address</TD>
```

```
</TR>
<xsl:for-each select="Northwind/employees[@Region=$region]">
<TR>
 <TD>
  <xsl:value-of select="@FirstName"/>
 </TD>
 <TD>
  <xsl:value-of select="@LastName"/>
 </TD>
 <TD><xsl:value-of select="@Title"/></TD>
 <TD><xsl:value-of select="@Address"/></TD>
 </TR>
</xsl:for-each>
</TABLE>
</BODY>
</HTML>
</xsl:template>
</xsl:stylesheet>
```

Then, to pass the value to the xsl:param element named region, we create the XsltArgumentList class, add our parameter and required value, and use an instance of this class in the call to the Transform() method:

```
'----------------------------------------
' XML.NET Example. XslTransform object
'----------------------------------------

Imports System
Imports System.XML
Imports System.XML.XSL

 Module Cons

  Sub Main()

    Dim XmlDoc    As New XmlDocument
    Dim XSlDoc    As New XslTransform
    Dim Writer    As New XmlTextWriter(Console.Out)
    Dim Args      As New XsltArgumentList

    XmlDoc.Load("nw.xml")
    XslDoc.Load("nw.xsl")

    Args.AddParam("region", "", "WA")
    XslDoc.Transform(XmlDoc, Args, Writer)

  End Sub
End Module
```

14.2 Conclusion

In this chapter, we discussed XML support in the Microsoft .NET Framework. We learned about the `System.Xml` namespace and its secondary namespaces – `System.Xml.Xsl`, `System.Xml.XPath`, `System.Xml.Schema`, and `System.Xml.Serialization`. We also discussed the basic classes implemented in the `System.Xml` namespace and saw examples of how to use classes such as an `XmlReader`, `XmlNodeReader`, `XmlValidatingReader`, and `XmlTextWriter` to read, validate, and write XML files. Then we discussed XML document object model (DOM) support in .NET and saw how to use the `XmlDocument` object and its properties and methods to navigate through the XML document tree. Next, we learned about XPath support in .NET and saw how to use the `XPathNavigator` and `XPathNodeIterator` objects. We finished this chapter by discussing XML transformations using XSLT and saw how to use the `XslTransform` object to transform XML documents using XSLT stylesheets and the `XsltArgumentList` object to supply parameters to XSLT stylesheets.

XML plays an essential role in web services – reusable web components that can be invoked from any platform capable of communicating over the internet. We will discuss web services in the next chapter.

chapter 15

Building and consuming web services

- Web service protocols

- Service description language

- Discovery

- `System.Web.Services` namespace

- Creating a web service

- Consuming a web service

- Microsoft.NET My Services

In this chapter, we will learn about web services – reusable web components that can be invoked from any platform capable of communicating over the internet. Web services expose their functionality via standard web protocols, such as HTTP and XML, and enable us to interconnect web applications. We can say that web services are URL-addressable resources that return requested information to a client or manipulate the data model behind the web service.

Figure 15.1 shows the main steps in an interaction between a web service consumer and the web service.

Step 1 is called discovery. In this step, the web service consumer arrives at the web server that hosts one or more web services, and receives an HTML or XML document that contains a link to the WSDL file.

In step 2, the web service consumer requests the WSDL file that describes the web services available and how to communicate with them. After finding out which service will be used, the web service consumer proceeds to step 3.

In step 3, the web service consumer invokes the required web service using the protocol definitions described in the WSDL file. Depending on the protocol of communication – SOAP, HTTP-GET or HTTP-POST – the consumer receives a SOAP or XML document that contains the response from the web service.

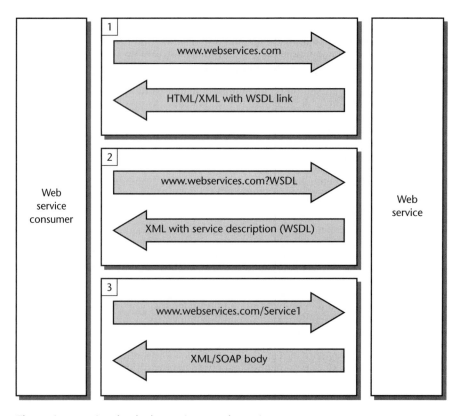

FIGURE 15.1 The main steps involved when using a web service

Now let's look at the main building blocks of web services in turn – protocols, sevice description language, and discovery.

15.1 Web service protocols

To communicate with web services, we can use HTTP-GET, HTTP-POST or SOAP protocols. HTTP-GET and HTTP-POST use HTTP as an underlying protocol and encode parameters as name/value pairs in the HTTP request. The GET method appends data to the URL of the server-side script, while POST methods encode name/value pairs in the body of the HTTP request message. The following examples show HTTP-GET and HTTP-POST requests and responses for the web service (for a description of this service see under Creating a web service later in this chapter). First is HTTP-GET:

```
GET /WebServices/wsdemo.asmx/GreetUser?Name=string HTTP/1.1
Host: localhost
HTTP/1.1 200 OK
Content-Type: text/xml; charset=utf-8
Content-Length: length


<?xml version="1.0" encoding="utf-8"?>
<string xmlns="http://www.abc.com">string</string>
```

Here is an example of HTTP-POST:

```
POST /WebServices/wsdemo.asmx/GreetUser HTTP/1.1
Host: localhost
Content-Type: application/x-www-form-urlencoded
Content-Length: length

Name=string
HTTP/1.1 200 OK
Content-Type: text/xml; charset=utf-8
Content-Length: length


<?xml version="1.0" encoding="utf-8"?>
<string xmlns="http://www.abc.com">string</string>
```

The Simple Object Access Protocol (SOAP) is a standard that allows clients and servers to exchange data in XML format. Unlike HTTP protocols such as POST and GET, SOAP relies solely on XML to store information instead of an HTTP request message. This gives us the ability to not only send name/value pairs, but also more complex objects, such as images, classes, data sets, and so on.

The SOAP specification defines the SOAP message format, how to send messages, receive messages, and encode data. The following example shows a SOAP request and response:

```
POST /WebServices/wsdemo.asmx HTTP/1.1
Host: localhost
Content-Type: text/xml; charset=utf-8
Content-Length: length
SOAPAction: "http://www.abc.com/GreetUser"

<?xml version="1.0" encoding="utf-8"?>
<soap:Envelope
 xmlns:xsi="http://www.w3.org/2001/XMLSchema-instance"
 xmlns:xsd="http://www.w3.org/2001/XMLSchema"
 xmlns:soap="http://schemas.xmlsoap.org/soap/envelope/">

  <soap:Body>
    <GreetUser xmlns="http://www.abc.com">
      <Name>string</Name>
    </GreetUser>
  </soap:Body>

</soap:Envelope>



HTTP/1.1 200 OK
Content-Type: text/xml; charset=utf-8
Content-Length: length

<?xml version="1.0" encoding="utf-8"?>
<soap:Envelope
 xmlns:xsi="http://www.w3.org/2001/XMLSchema-instance"
 xmlns:xsd="http://www.w3.org/2001/XMLSchema"
 xmlns:soap="http://schemas.xmlsoap.org/soap/envelope/">

  <soap:Body>
    <GreetUserResponse xmlns="http://www.abc.com">
      <GreetUserResult>string</GreetUserResult>
    </GreetUserResponse>
  </soap:Body>

</soap:Envelope>
```

In Microsoft .NET, SOAP implementation is based on HTTP-POST protocol.

15.2 Service description language

The web services description language (WSDL) defines an XML document that describes a set of SOAP messages and how the messages are exchanged. It also defines how to communicate with the web service using HTTP-GET and HTTP-POST protocols.

Here is an example of a WSDL file for a web service:

```
<?xml version="1.0" encoding="utf-8"?>
<definitions xmlns:s="http://www.w3.org/2001/XMLSchema"
xmlns:http="http://schemas.xmlsoap.org/wsdl/http/"
xmlns:mime="http://schemas.xmlsoap.org/wsdl/mime/"
xmlns:tm="http://microsoft.com/wsdl/mime/textMatching/"
xmlns:soap="http://schemas.xmlsoap.org/wsdl/soap/"
xmlns:soapenc="http://schemas.xmlsoap.org/soap/encoding/"
xmlns:s0="http://www.abc.com" targetNamespace="http://www.abc.com"
xmlns="http://schemas.xmlsoap.org/wsdl/">

  <types>
    <s:schema attributeFormDefault="qualified"
     elementFormDefault="qualified"
     targetNamespace="http://www.abc.com">
     <s:element name="GreetUser">
       <s:complexType>
         <s:sequence>
           <s:element minOccurs="1" maxOccurs="1" name="Name"
            nillable="true" type="s:string" />
         </s:sequence>
       </s:complexType>
     </s:element>
     <s:element name="GreetUserResponse">
       <s:complexType>
         <s:sequence>
           <s:element minOccurs="1" maxOccurs="1"
            name="GreetUserResult" nillable="true"
            type="s:string" />
         </s:sequence>
       </s:complexType>
     </s:element>
     <s:element name="string" nillable="true" type="s:string" />
    </s:schema>
  </types>
```

```xml
<message name="GreetUserSoapIn">
  <part name="parameters" element="s0:GreetUser" />
</message>
<message name="GreetUserSoapOut">
  <part name="parameters" element="s0:GreetUserResponse" />
</message>

<message name="GreetUserHttpGetIn">
  <part name="Name" type="s:string" />
</message>
<message name="GreetUserHttpGetOut">
  <part name="Body" element="s0:string" />
</message>

<message name="GreetUserHttpPostIn">
  <part name="Name" type="s:string" />
</message>
<message name="GreetUserHttpPostOut">
  <part name="Body" element="s0:string" />
</message>

<portType name="Greeting ServiceSoap">
  <operation name="SayHello">
    <documentation>Greets the user</documentation>
    <input name="GreetUser" message="s0:GreetUserSoapIn" />
    <output name="GreetUser" message="s0:GreetUserSoapOut" />
  </operation>
</portType>

<portType name="Greeting ServiceHttpGet">
  <operation name="SayHello">
    <documentation>Greets the user</documentation>
    <input name="GreetUser" message="s0:GreetUserHttpGetIn" />
    <output name="GreetUser" message="s0:GreetUserHttpGetOut" />
  </operation>
</portType>

<portType name="Greeting ServiceHttpPost">
  <operation name="SayHello">
    <documentation>Greets the user</documentation>
    <input name="GreetUser" message="s0:GreetUserHttpPostIn" />
    <output name="GreetUser" message="s0:GreetUserHttpPostOut" />
  </operation>
</portType>
```

```
<binding name="Greeting ServiceSoap" type="s0:Greeting ServiceSoap">
  <soap:binding transport="http://schemas.xmlsoap.org/soap/http"
   style="document" />
  <operation name="SayHello">
    <soap:operation soapAction="http://www.abc.com/GreetUser"
     style="document" />
    <input name="GreetUser">
      <soap:body use="literal" />
    </input>
    <output name="GreetUser">
      <soap:body use="literal" />
    </output>
  </operation>
</binding>

<binding name="Greeting ServiceHttpGet" type="s0:Greeting
ServiceHttpGet">
  <http:binding verb="GET" />
  <operation name="SayHello">
    <http:operation location="/GreetUser" />
    <input name="GreetUser">
      <http:urlEncoded />
    </input>
    <output name="GreetUser">
      <mime:mimeXml part="Body" />
    </output>
  </operation>
</binding>

<binding name="Greeting ServiceHttpPost" type="s0:Greeting
ServiceHttpPost">
  <http:binding verb="POST" />
  <operation name="SayHello">
    <http:operation location="/GreetUser" />
    <input name="GreetUser">
      <mime:content type="application/x-www-form-urlencoded" />
    </input>
    <output name="GreetUser">
      <mime:mimeXml part="Body" />
    </output>
  </operation>
</binding>
```

```
    <service name="Greeting Service">
      <documentation>Basic Web Service Example</documentation>
      <port name="Greeting ServiceSoap"
       binding="s0:Greeting ServiceSoap">
        <soap:address
         location="http://localhost/WebServices/wsdemo.asmx" />
      </port>
      <port name="Greeting ServiceHttpGet"
         binding="s0:Greeting ServiceHttpGet">
        <http:address
         location="http://localhost/WebServices/wsdemo.asmx" />
      </port>
      <port name="Greeting ServiceHttpPost"
       binding="s0:Greeting ServiceHttpPost">
        <http:address location="http://localhost/WebServices/wsdemo.asmx"
  />
      </port>
    </service>
  </definitions>
```

A WSDL document starts with the <definitions> element. This element contains other elements that describe the web service. They include the following.

- **Types** A container for data type definitions. It contains physical type descriptions as XML Schema (XSD).

- **Message** Format of an individual transmission. Each web method has two messages – input and output. The input specifies the parameters of the web method, while the output describes the return data from the web method. Microsoft .NET autogenerated WSDL files use the name convention MethodName + Protocol + In/Out – for example, GreetUserSoapIn defines the input method GreetUser for the SOAP protocol.

- **PortType** Groups messages into logical operations. There is one PortType element for each protocol supported by a web service. All operations are defined by the <operation> elements within the PortType element.

- **Operation** Description of an action supported by a service.

- **Binding** Connects PortType to an implementation. There is one Binding element for each protocol supported by a web service.

- **Service** Defines the physical location of an end point. This element contains one Port element for each protocol supported by a web service.

- **Port** Describes the protocol and data format for a single end point.

- **Data Schema** Low-level typing for message parameters.

Later in this chapter we will see how to use the web services description language utility (WSDL.EXE) to generate a web service proxy DLL class.

For more information on WSDL, visit the following websites:
www.w3.org/TR/wsdl
http://msdn.microsoft.com/xml/general/wsdl.asp

15.3   Discovery

Discovery (Disco) makes it possible for clients to discover web services. The special
XML document that usually takes the form of a file with a .disco extension contains
references to such resources as WSDL, documents, and links for a particular web service. A .disco file (also called "a discovery file") is placed at the root of a virtual
directory that contains other web service-related files. Figure 15.2 shows the directory
structure for web services.

```
\Inetpub
 \wwwroot
  \MyWebService
    WSDemo.asmx
    web.config
    WSDemo.disco
    \bin
```

FIGURE 15.2   The directory structure for web services

A .disco file has the following structure:

```
<?xml version="1.0" ?>

<disco:discovery xmlns:disco="http://schemas.xmlsoap.org/disco/">

<!-   References ->

</disco:discovery>
```

Between the <discovery> elements, we can add reference information that contains
the location of the service contract (WSDL file). To do so, we use the <contractRef>
tag with the ref attribute, as shown below:

```
<scl:contractRef ref="http://localhost/WebServices/wsdemo.asmx?WSDL" />
```

A complete `.disco` file is shown below:

```
<?xml version="1.0" ?>

<disco:discovery xmlns:disco="http://schemas.xmlsoap.org/disco/"
 xmlns:scl=" http://schemas.xmlsoap.org/disco/scl">

<scl:contractRef ref="http://localhost/WebServices/wsdemo.asmx?WSDL"/>

</disco:discovery>
```

A `.disco` file is usually called a static discovery file. We can also create dynamic discovery files – `.vsdisco` files – which have the following structure:

```
<dynamicDiscovery
   xmlns="urn:schemas-dynamicdiscovery:disco.2000-03-17">
</dynamicDiscovery>
```

We can optionally specify exclude paths – where the dynamic discovery mechanism should not look for web services. The following example shows a `.vsdisco` file with exclude paths:

```
<?xml version="1.0" ?>
<dynamicDiscovery
 xmlns="urn:schemas-dynamicdiscovery:disco.2000-03-17">
<exclude path="_vti_cnf" />
<exclude path="_vti_pvt" />
<exclude path="_vti_log" />
<exclude path="_vti_script" />
<exclude path="_vti_txt" />
</dynamicDiscovery>
```

We can use a combination of static and dynamic discovery to provide the best results for clients looking for web services implemented at our web server.

UDDI

Universal discovery, description and integration (UDDI) is the Yellow Pages of web services. It extends Disco by defining how to interact with a rich web service information repository. UDDI allows companies to publish their services and find web services published by other companies. UDDI itself is a SOAP-based web service which supports an API that consists of SOAP request/response messages. A UDDI registry consists of four main types of information:

● business information, such as name, contact infomation, services, and so on;

● service information, i.e. business and a technical description of a service;

● binding template, which specifies how to connect to and communicate with a service;

● tModel, which provides technical information for interfaces.

An UDDI programmer's API is divided into two groups of operations – namely enquiry and publishing.

- The enquiry API retrieves information from a registry and does not require authentication. Some examples of an enquiry include `find_business` (which locates information about one or more businesses), `find_service` (which locates services within a registered business), `find_binding` (which locates bindings within a registered service), `get_businessDetail` (which gets information about the registered business), `get_serviceDetail` (which gets extended information about the registered service), and so on.

- The publishing API inserts/updates information to the registry and requires authentication and encryption. Some examples include `delete_business` (which deletes a business from the registry), `delete_service` (which deletes a service from the registry), `save_business` (which registers/updates a business), `save_service` (which registers/updates a service), and so on.

The UDDI specification was jointly developed by Microsoft, IBM, and Ariba. For more information on UDDI, visit the following website: www.uddi.org/

15.4 System.Web.Services namespace

The `System.Web.Services` namespace, which can be found in the `System.Web.Services.dll` assembly, contains classes that are used to create and consume web services. The classes in this namespace are `WebService` (which provides access to the common ASP.NET objects), `WebServiceAttribute` (which can be used to add additional information to a web service), `WebMethodAttribute` (which defines a method as a web method exposed by a web service), and `WebService BindingAttribute` (which declares the binding that one or more web service methods are implementing within the class implementing the web service).

The `System.Web.Services` namespace also contains the three secondary namespaces shown in Figure 15.3.

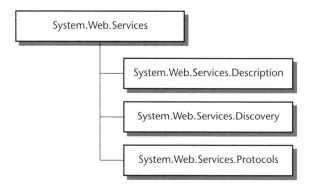

FIGURE 15.3   The secondary namespaces in the `System.Web.Services` namespace

The `System.Web.Services.Description` namespace contains classes that can be used to publicly describe a web service in the web service description language (WSDL). Classes included in this namespace correspond to the elements of the WSDL file, which are as follows.

- **Binding** Specifies the concrete data format and protocols used in a web service.
- **Message** In the abstract, the content – either document-oriented or procedure-oriented – of data passed by a web service.
- **Operation** Provides an abstract definition of an action supported by a web service.
- **Port** Defines an individual end point contained in a web service.
- **PortType** Represents the collection of all **Port** objects contained in a web service.
- **Service** Groups together a set of related ports associated with a web service.
- **Types** Describes data type definitions relevant to exchanged messages.

Several other classes defined in this namespace are used by the basic classes listed above.

The `System.Web.Services.Discovery` namespace contains classes that allow web service consumers to locate available web services on a web server via a process called discovery. Classes in this namespace include `ContractReference`, `DiscoveryClientProtocol`, `DiscoveryDocument`, `DiscoveryReference`, `SchemaReference`, `SoapBinding`, and several other secondary classes.

The `System.Web.Services.Protocols` namespace contains classes that implement protocols used to exchange data between web services and clients. Some of the classes included in this namespace are the following.

- **HttpGetClientProtocol** Specifies the class for ASP.NET web service client proxies that use the HTTP-GET protocol.
- **HttpPostClientProtocol** Specifies the class for ASP.NET web service client proxies that use the HTTP-POST protocol.
- **HttpWebClientProtocol** Specifies the class for ASP.NET web service client proxies that use HTTP.
- **SoapClientMessage** Represents a SOAP request sent by a client or a SOAP response received by client.
- **SoapHeader** Represents the contents of a SOAP header.
- **SoapHttpClientProtocol** Specifies the basic class for ASP.NET web service client proxies when using SOAP.
- **SoapMessage** Represents the data in a SOAP request or SOAP response.
- **SoapServerMessage** Represents the data in a SOAP request received or a SOAP response sent by a web service method.

15.5 Creating a web service

ASP.NET web services can be created with any tool you prefer – from "traditional" Notepad to Microsoft Visual Studio.NET or other third-party tools. The only required file to create a web service is an .asmx file – it tells the web server that this is a web service and it will interpret it accordingly. Here is the code for a very simple web service that accepts a user's name and returns a greeting which includes the supplied name:

```
<%@ WebService Language="VB" Class="WSDemo" %>
Imports System
Imports System.Web.Services


Public Class WSDemo : Inherits WebService

<WebMethod(Description:= "Greets the user")> _
    Public Function SayHello(Name As String) As String

    Dim Greeting As String
    If Name <> "" Then
     Return "Hello from Web Service, " & Name
    Else
     Return "Hello from Web Service, Stranger"
    End If

   End Function

   End Class
```

The first line contains a WebService directive which tells us that this is a web service implementation, and the class name (WSDemo in this example) of the class that implements the web service.

Our class – WSDemo – derives from the WebService class. This is not requiresd, but it gives us access to the common ASP.NET objects, such as Application, Session, User, and Context. We can use the User.Identity property, for example, to determine whether or not the user is authorized to call the web service. This requires the authentication for the web service to be turned on. Note that our class is declared as Public – to be a web service, the class must be declared as public.

Our class contains one public method – SayHello – that accepts a user name and returns a string that is composed from the static text ("Hello from Web Service,") and, depending on the input, either the supplied user name or static text "Stranger". Note that the <WebMethod> attribute is in the method definition. This attribute identifies our method as a web method that will be exposed in the web service. Only public methods will be exposed in the web service, though it can have private methods as well.

Now we can save our code in the directory on the web server and test it. If we open up a web browser and type the URL of the web service we have just created, we will see a screen, which may look like that shown in Figure 15.4.

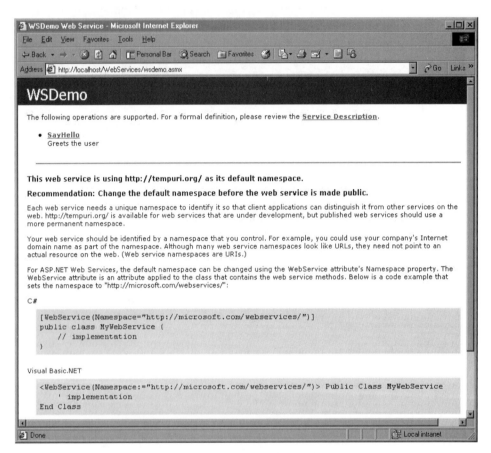

FIGURE 15.4   Typing the URL of our web service in the web browser calls up this screen

At the top of the screen, we have the name of our web service – WSDemo – and a description of the method it supports – SayHello. The rest of the screen provides some helpful information about changing the default namespace. Note that we have simply written the code for the web service, saved it with an .asmx extension and browsed to its location. The rest is done by ASP.NET. However, this is not all of the power of ASP.NET – if we click on the SayHello link, we will get a screen that may look like Figure 15.5.

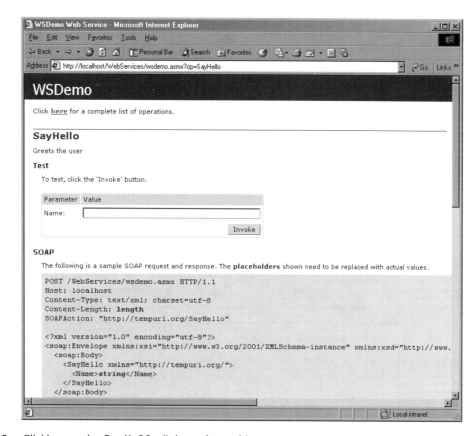

FIGURE 15.5 Clicking on the SayHello link produces this screen

In the top part of the screen we have a TextBox that allows us to test our service. All we need to do is supply the Name parameter and press the Invoke button to call our web service.

The rest of the screen provides examples of how to invoke this web service using SOAP, HTTP-GET, and HTTP-POST protocols.

Now let's enter a name in the TextBox – Peter Pan, for example – and click the Invoke button. The screen shown in Figure 15.6 will appear.

This is the response from our web service – an XML document generated by our code. What we have seen above is how ASP.NET allows us to test our web services as well as web services created by other companies and get information about the methods it provides, as well as how to invoke them.

We can also use this tool to view the web services contract – the WSDL document associated with this web service – and get more details about how to communicate with it. To get the WSDL document for our web service, we must append the ?WSDL parameter at the end of the web service URL:

```
http://localhost/WebServices/wsdemo.asmx?WSDL
```

FIGURE 15.6   When we enter a name in the TextBox and click Invoke, this screen appears

This will produce a screen like the one shown in Figure 15.7.

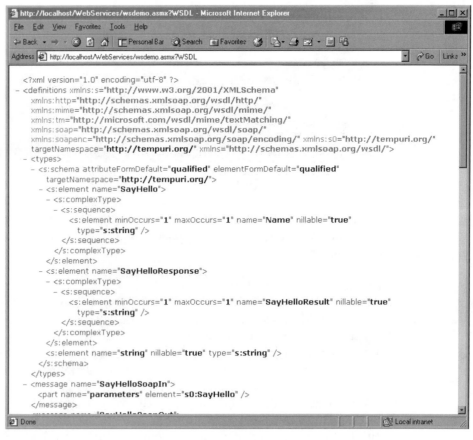

FIGURE 15.7   We get the WSDL contract for our web service by adding ?WSDL to the URL

In our example of a web service, we have used the `WebService` directive to specify that our code implements a web service. To specify additional information about our web service, we can use the `WebService` attribute with the class declaration. This attribute is supported by the `WebServiceAttribute` class, which supports the following properties that may appear in the `WebService` attribute.

- **Description** Gives a descriptive message for the web service.
- **Name** Specifies the name of the web service. By default, this is the name of the class implementing the web service.
- **Namespace** Specifies the default XML namespace to use for the web service. Namespaces are used to distinguish our web service from other services on the web. The default value for this property is `http://tempuri.org/`. It should be changed before the web service is made public.

The following example shows how to use the `WebService` attribute:

```
<WebService(Description := "Basic Web Service Example", _
    Name := "Greeting Service", Namespace := "http://www.abc.com")> _
Public Class WSDemo : Inherits WebService


    . . .


    End Class
```

Now, if we navigate to our web service URL, we will see the screen shown in Figure 15.8.

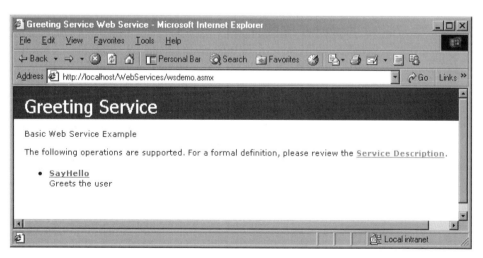

FIGURE 15.8   Using our web service URL, we will see this screen

Note that the `Name` attribute is used to create a web service header and the `Description` attribute is used to provide a texttual description of the web service.

The `WebMethod` attribute we used to describe our web method is based on the `WebMethodAttribute` class and supports the following properties.

- **BufferResponse** Specifies whether or not the response for this request is buffered. The default value is `"True"` – the request is buffered.

- **CacheDuration** Specifies the number of seconds the response should be held in the cache. The default value for this property is 0 – the response is not cached.

- **Description** Gives a descriptive message for the web method.

- **EnableSession** Specifies whether or not a session state is enabled for a web service method. The default value is `"False"` – session state is disabled.

- **MessageName** Specifies the alias for this method. The default value is the name of the web method.

- **TransactionOption** Specifies the type of automatic transaction support a web service method will have. The default value is `Disabled`. Other possible values for this property include `NotSupported` (the web service method does not run within the scope of a transaction), `Required` (the web service method requires a transaction – a new transaction will be created for the web service method), and `RequiresNew` (the web service method requires a new transaction – the web service will be created within a new transaction).

The following example shows how to use the `WebMethod` attribute:

```
<WebMethod(Description:= "Greets the user", _
    CacheDuration := 60, _
    EnableSession := True, _
    MessageName := "GreetUser")> _
  Public Function SayHello(Name As String) As String


    ...


    End Function
```

Using data in web services

Let's create a web service that returns data stored in a database. For our example, we will choose the `Employees` table in the `Northwind` database. Here is the code for our web service:

```
'----------------------------------------
' Northwind Web Service
'----------------------------------------
<%@ WebService Class="Northwind" %>
Imports System
Imports System.Web.Services
Imports System.Data
Imports System.Data.SqlClient
Imports System.XML

<WebService(Description := "Northwind Web Service Example", _
  Name := "Data Services", Namespace := "http://www.abc.com")> _
Public Class Northwind : Inherits WebService

 <WebMethod(Description:= "Returns a list of employees")> _
   Public Function GetEmployees() As DataSet

    Dim Emp_DA  As SqlDataAdapter
    Dim DS      As New DataSet

    Emp_DA = New SqlDataAdapter("SELECT FirstName, LastName, " & _
      "Title, Address, City, PostalCode, Country FROM Employees", _
      "server=localhost;database=Northwind;uid=sa;pwd=;")
    Emp_DA.Fill(DS, "Customers")

    Return DS

   End Function

  End Class
```

In our GetEmployees web method, we create an SqlDataAdapter object with the SELECT statement to extract data from the database table and then use its Fill method to store the extracted data in the DataSet object. This object is returned to the calling application.

If we call the GetEmployees web method, we will receive an XML document that represents a DataSet – this is done automatically by .NET (see Figure 15.9).

All we need to do is apply an appropriate XSL stylesheet to display the received data or use one of the navigation methods discussed in the previous chapter to navigate the XML document and extract the required data.

Now we know how to create web services, let's look at how to implement web service consumers.

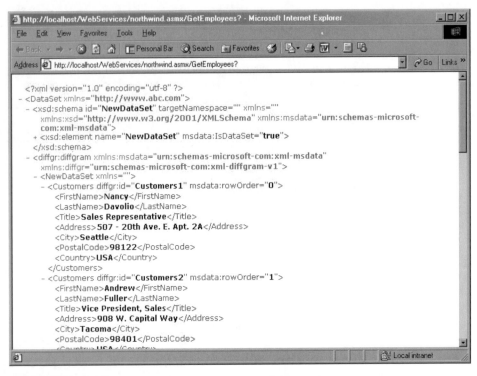

FIGURE 15.9   Calling the `GetEmployees` method, an XML document of a `DataSet` will appear automatically

15.6   Consuming a web service

As with web services, we can create web service consumers with any tool we like. Consumers communicate with web services via standard protocols – SOAP, HTTP-GET, and HTTP-POST – and exchange XML-encoded messages.

Using the HTTP-GET protocol

Let's start with the simplest type of web service client – one who uses the HTTP-GET protocol to communicate with the service. If we navigate to the URL of our web service – `http://localhost/WebServices/wsdemo.asmx` in our example – then click on the method name in the first screen (see Figure 15.4 earlier in this chapter), we will get the default web service consumer autogenerated for us by .NET. It uses HTTP-GET protocol to communicate with the web service. Here is the GET request and response which describes the interaction between the service and a consumer:

```
GET /WebServices/wsdemo.asmx/GreetUser?Name=string HTTP/1.1
Host: localhost
HTTP/1.1 200 OK
Content-Type: text/xml; charset=utf-8
Content-Length: length

<?xml version="1.0" encoding="utf-8"?>
<string xmlns="http://www.abc.com">string</string>
```

Using the HTTP-GET protocol, we can navigate to the following URL to invoke the Web method:

```
http://localhost/WebServices/wsdemo.asmx/GreetUser?Name=Alexei+Fedorov
```

Here is the response from the invoked web method:

```
<?xml version="1.0" encoding="utf-8" ?>
 <string xmlns="http://www.abc.com">
  Hello from Web Service, Alexei Fedorov
 </string>
```

Using the HTTP-POST protocol

Using the HTTP-POST protocol is a little bit more complex than the HTTP-GET-based consumer we have seen above. To do so, we need to generate a web service proxy DLL class. We do this by using the WSDL.EXE utility, which generates source code for the proxies to the web services (type the entire command on one line):

```
wsdl /l:VB /protocol:HttpPost
 http://localhost/WebServices/WSDemo.asmx?WSDL
```

This will create a proxy for the WSDemo web service from the web services description language (WSDL) document specified in the command line:

```
http://localhost/WebServices/WSDemo.asmx?WSDL
```

We have specified that this proxy should use the HTTP-POST protocol to communicate with the web service and the source file should be generated for Visual Basic.NET language.

Here is the result generated by the WSDL.EXE utility:

```
'-------------------------------------------------------------------
' <autogenerated>
'     This code was generated by a tool.
'     Runtime Version: 1.0.2914.16
'
'     Changes to this file may cause incorrect behavior and will
'     be lost if the code is regenerated.
' </autogenerated>
'-------------------------------------------------------------------
```

```vbnet
Option Strict Off
Option Explicit On

Imports System
Imports System.Diagnostics
Imports System.Web.Services
Imports System.Web.Services.Protocols
Imports System.Xml.Serialization


'
'This source code was auto-generated by wsdl, Version=1.0.2914.16.
'


Public Class GreetingService
 Inherits System.Web.Services.Protocols.HttpPostClientProtocol

 <System.Diagnostics.DebuggerStepThroughAttribute()>  _
 Public Sub New()
   MyBase.New
   Me.Url = "http://localhost/WebServices/WSDemo.asmx"
 End Sub

 <System.Diagnostics.DebuggerStepThroughAttribute(),  _
  System.Web.Services.Protocols.HttpMethodAttribute(_
  GetType(System.Web.Services.Protocols.XmlReturnReader),  _
  GetType(System.Web.Services.Protocols.HtmlFormParameterWriter))>  _
 Public Function SayHello(ByVal Name As String) As  _
   <System.Xml.Serialization.XmlRootAttribute("string",  _
   [Namespace]:="http://www.abc.com", IsNullable:=true)> String

   Return CType(Me.Invoke("SayHello", (Me.Url + "/GreetUser"),  _

   New Object() {Name}),String)
 End Function

 <System.Diagnostics.DebuggerStepThroughAttribute()>  _
 Public Function BeginSayHello(ByVal Name As String, ByVal callback _
   As System.AsyncCallback, ByVal asyncState As Object) As  _
   System.IAsyncResult

   Return Me.BeginInvoke("SayHello", (Me.Url + "/GreetUser"),  _
   New Object() {Name}, callback, asyncState)

 End Function
```

```
<System.Diagnostics.DebuggerStepThroughAttribute()>  _
Public Function EndSayHello(ByVal asyncResult As _
 System.IAsyncResult) As String

  Return CType(Me.EndInvoke(asyncResult),String)

End Function
End Class
```

Next, we need to compile this code into a dynamic link library that can be used in our consumer code. We do this with the following command line (type the entire command on one line):

```
vbc /t:library /r:system.web.services.dll /r:system.xml.dll
 /r:system.dll greeting_service.vb
```

Now we can use this DLL. Here is an example of a console application that uses our web service:

```
Imports System
Imports System.XML

Module Cons

Sub Main()

 Dim Greeting As New GreetingService
 Console.WriteLine(Greeting.SayHello("Alexei Fedorov"))

End Sub

End Module
```

We compile this application with the following command line (type the entire command on one line):

```
vbc wsclient.vb /r:system.dll /r:system.xml.dll
 /r:system.web.services.dll /r:greeting_service.dll
```

Now we can run our application and receive the result (shown in Figure 15.10).

So far, we have seen how to create web service consumers who use the HTTP-GET and HTTP-POST protocols to invoke web service methods. Now let's create an active server pages (ASP) consumer who will invoke the web service via a SOAP protocol.

The first thing we need to find out is the format of the SOAP message we should send to the web service. Here is a SOAP request and response that describes an interaction between the service and consumer (this can be found on the start page for our web service):

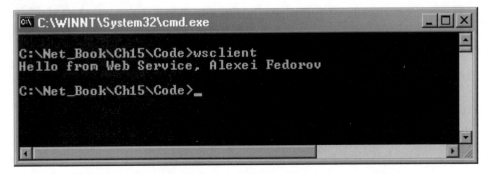

FIGURE 15.10 This is the result of running our application

```
POST /WebServices/wsdemo.asmx HTTP/1.1
Host: localhost
Content-Type: text/xml; charset=utf-8
Content-Length: length
SOAPAction: "http://www.abc.com/GreetUser"

<?xml version="1.0" encoding="utf-8"?>
<soap:Envelope xmlns:xsi="http://www.w3.org/2001/XMLSchema-instance"
xmlns:xsd="http://www.w3.org/2001/XMLSchema"
xmlns:soap="http://schemas.xmlsoap.org/soap/envelope/">
  <soap:Body>
    <GreetUser xmlns="http://www.abc.com">
      <Name>string</Name>
    </GreetUser>
  </soap:Body>
</soap:Envelope>

HTTP/1.1 200 OK
Content-Type: text/xml; charset=utf-8
Content-Length: length

<?xml version="1.0" encoding="utf-8"?>
<soap:Envelope xmlns:xsi="http://www.w3.org/2001/XMLSchema-instance"
xmlns:xsd="http://www.w3.org/2001/XMLSchema"
xmlns:soap="http://schemas.xmlsoap.org/soap/envelope/">
  <soap:Body>
    <GreetUserResponse xmlns="http://www.abc.com">
      <GreetUserResult>string</GreetUserResult>
    </GreetUserResponse>
  </soap:Body>
</soap:Envelope>
```

As we can see from the SOAP request above, we need to send the POST request to the web server with the specially formatted XML document in its body. This document will contain the SOAP envelope, which will be parsed and executed by the web server. The following example shows how to send this SOAP envelope to invoke our web service:

```
<%
'----------------------------------------
' ASP Web Services Consumer
'----------------------------------------

 XMLDoc = "<?xml version='1.0' encoding='utf-8'?>" & vbCRLF & _
 "<soap:Envelope xmlns:xsi='http://www.w3.org/2001/" & _
 "XMLSchema-instance' " & _
 "xmlns:xsd='http://www.w3.org/2001/XMLSchema' " & _
 "xmlns:soap='http://schemas.xmlsoap.org/soap/envelope/'>" & vbCRLF & _
 "<soap:Body>" & vbCRLF & _
 "<GreetUser xmlns='http://www.abc.com'>" & vbCRLF & _
 "<Name>Peter Pan</Name>" & vbCRLF & _
 "</GreetUser>" & vbCRLF & _
 "</soap:Body>" & vbCRLF & _
 "</soap:Envelope>"

 Set XMLHttp = Server.CreateObject("MSXML2.XMLHttp")

 XMLHttp.Open "POST", "http://localhost/WebServices/wsdemo.asmx", false
 XMLHttp.SetRequestHeader "Content-type", "text/xml;charset=utf-8"
 XMLHttp.SetRequestHeader "SOAPAction", "http://www.abc.com/GreetUser"

 XMLHttp.Send XMLDoc

 Response.Write XMLHttp.ResponseText

%>
```

In the code above, we have created an XML document and then used the **XMLHttp** object (part of the Microsoft XMLDOM parser) to send the POST request to the web service. We will receive a response in the format shown in Figure 15.11.

In this and previous sections we have seen how to create and consume our own web services using ASP.NET. In the next section, we will briefly discuss a set of commercial web services implemented by Microsoft – Microsoft .NET My Services.

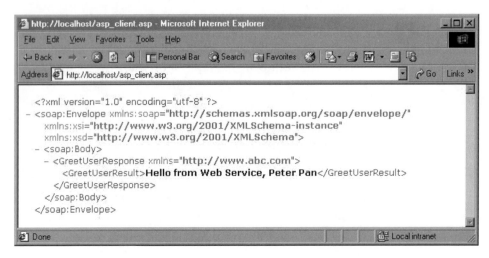

FIGURE 15.11 The response to our POST request to the web service

15.7 Microsoft .NET My Services

Microsoft .NET My Services (formerly codenamed "HailStorm") is a set of core XML web services that store information for users – information such as their personal profile, contacts, lists, calendar, electronic wallet, physical location, document stores, application settings, and favorite websites, to name but a few. Applications call on .NET My Services, with the explicit permission of the user, to access these key pieces of personal data in order to customize or personalize service to that user.

From the programmer's point of view, Microsoft .NET My Services is a collection of XML web services that are invoked over the internet using industry standard protocols, including simple object access protocol (SOAP), extensible markup language (XML), and UDDI.

Microsoft .NET My Services is based on the passport authentication system (or .NET identity) that provides a passport unique ID and initially included the following services.

- **.NET Alerts** This service provides a single point from which short XML messages can be sent to one or more users. Although alerts are posted to a single location, the messages are transparently routed to one or more of the user's applications or devices. The logic for deciding how, where, and when a message is delivered can be customized to meet the needs of a particular user, device or application. Microsoft .NET Alerts uses two mechanisms to deliver alerts. The basic model provides the baseline functionality of sending and receiving alerts. The streams model includes more robust features, such as filtering, buffering, and persistence, as well as more refined control over the routing of alerts.

- **.NET ApplicationSettings** This service provides a repository in which a user can store settings for applications and groups of applications. By maintaining a user's preferred application settings in a centralized web service, `Microsoft .NET ApplicationSettings` allows the user to enjoy customized application settings regardless of the device on which he is working.

- **.NET Calendar** This service stores and manages the scheduling of individual and group events and appointments that are associated with an identity. This service supplies scheduling information on demand to other Microsoft .NET services, applications, and devices. The .NET calendar service can be used for regular scheduling or group collaboration. Group collaborative features include meeting delegates and role-based access to another identity's calendar. The .NET calendar service is integrated with the Microsoft .NET alerts service to perform reminder alerts and meeting acceptance/decline alerts with the Microsoft .NET contacts service for service distribution lists and the Microsoft .NET inbox service to send and retrieve meeting requests. The .NET inbox service will forward meeting invitations to be directly booked (tentatively) on attendees' calendars that have the correct permissions for this behavior and will forward meeting responses that attendees send back to the organizer to update the organizer's calendar.

- **.NET Categories** This service supports a classification model for data within Microsoft .NET My Services. This classification model is very abstract and makes few assumptions about the ways in which applications use the categories maintained by this service. The design is simple and open, allowing this model of categorization to be used by a wide spectrum of applications for a diverse range of purposes. The `.NET Categories` service manages a list of category definitions such as child, anniversary, and employee. Each category definition has a human-readable name and a description. A given category implies a more general category, while "friends" implies "acquaintances". A category may be classified by using other categories. For example, anniversaries and birthdays are categorized as `specialDates`.

- **.NET Contacts** This service is a repository for users to store and track contact information and relationships for all the people and organizations in their lives. Each Microsoft .NET My Services user has one `Contacts` document that can contain multiple contact records. The `.NET Contacts` schema mirrors the `Microsoft .NET Profile` service for information including, but not limited to, name, addresses, phone numbers, and e-mail addresses, as well as allowing the owner to control how the contacts are categorized. The user can control visibility of individual contacts and grant various levels access to their list of contacts, applications, and other users based on the role templates. With the user's consent, an application could populate a form with the user's contacts. The user could then select a contact and the application could fill out the `"Ship To:"` fields (name, address, city, state) automatically for the contact as part of a gift purchase.

- **.NET Devices** This service stores characteristics of a user's devices. It is designed primarily to be used in conjunction with the other Microsoft .NET services, allowing data such as alerts or documents to be delivered to devices on various transports in a customized manner.

- **.NET Documents** This service stores and manages online files and folders for Microsoft .NET My Services users. Files are provided on demand to .NET-based services, applications, and devices. The `.NET Documents` service can be used for roaming through personal files or sharing files with other Microsoft .NET Passport users.

- **.NET FavoriteWebSites** This service stores and organizes the addresses of Microsoft .NET My Services users' favorite websites. In many ways, this service is similar to the Internet Explorer Favorites menu or the Favorites button in Microsoft MSN Explorer. Both of these applications maintain favorite websites and track usage. Favorite websites and their categorization can be retrieved and maintained from different applications and computers.

- **.NET Inbox** This service is designed to store and manage e-mails for the associated identity. Its primary purpose is to supply this information on demand to applications operating on the identity's behalf. Using this service, an identity can manage e-mail from a variety of devices and even manage multiple accounts from the same application.

- **.NET Lists** This service supports a list model for data within Microsoft .NET My Services. The list and list item models are very abstract and make few assumptions about the ways in which applications use the lists maintained by this service. The design is simple and open, allowing the `.NET Lists` service to be used by a wide spectrum of applications for a diverse range of purposes. As with all services in .NET My Services, the `.NET Lists` service allows freeform, namespace qualified extensions to be added to a list or an item within a list. This mechanism is useful for adding semistructured information to the service. However, the service is unable to validate the schema of these extensions.

- **.NET Locations** This service provides a repository of location reports on the current location of the user bound to the service. This service is not designed to provide real-time streamed location reporting. For such an application, a location stream should be connected via the Microsoft .NET Presence service.

- **.NET Presence** This service provides information about the location of a user associated with the service. Unlike the Microsoft .NET Locations service, which describes the user's physical location or address, the `.NET Presence` service only maintains records of the user's electronic or virtual location. This service can be used in conjunction with the other services in Microsoft .NET My Services to intelligently filter, buffer, and route data to the user based on the data provided by the `.NET Presence` service.

- **.NET Profile** This service is designed to store and manage a user's personal profile information, including, but not limited to, name, addresses, phone numbers, and e-mail addresses. Each Microsoft .NET My Services user has one `Profile` service document and maintains complete control over read and write access to the information contained within it. The user can control the visibility of nodes and grant various levels access to applications and other users based on the role templates. Users can grant one-time or continued access. Applications can use profile data to complete a form as part of a transaction.

- **.NET Services** This is a central "metaservice" that maintains and enforces the relationships between users and the other .NET My Services services. Provisioning – the process of registering a user with a service – is conducted via the .NET services service. The .NET services service is also a directory for all the other .NET services. A client application does not need to know the location of each and every service; it simply requests the location of a particular service from .NET services. The location of the chosen service is then returned to the client dynamically.

- **.NET Wallet** This service is designed to store and manage information for the associated identity, including payment method information, such as card-based payment information using credit and debit cards, and account-based payment information. The .NET wallet service supplies this information on demand to Microsoft .NET-based services, applications or devices. The .NET wallet service uses Microsoft .NET My Services to support a rich sharing model based on the access control list, role map, and identity header.

The latest information about .NET My Services can be found at:
www.microsoft.com/myservices

15.8 Conclusion

In this chapter, we discussed web services – reusable web components that can be invoked from any platform capable of communicating over the internet. We started with an overview of the main building blocks of web services, then discussed the `System.Web.Services` namespace and its secondary namespaces, as well as the main classes included in these namespaces and their purpose.

Then we learned how to create our own web services and how to use the testing facilities provided by ASP.NET, as well as creating web services that return data stored in a database.

Next, we discussed how to create web service consumers and saw how to create consumers that use different web protocols to communicate with a web service – HTTP-GET, HTTP-POST, and SOAP. We have also seen how to use ASP to create a web service consumer.

In the last part of this chapter, we briefly discussed a set of commercial web services implemented by Microsoft – Microsoft .NET My Services.

We have now come to the end of our journey through the Microsoft .NET platform and its major technologies. Let's just pause for a moment and see how far we've come.

We started with a broad overview of the platform itself and its main components – development tools and .NET languages, .NET Enterprise servers, as well as a brief discussion of the .NET Framework class library, common language runtime (CLR), and the "core" web services. Then we spent a whole chapter learning about the main components of the .NET Framework – CLR, which is the infrastructure that .NET uses to execute all its applications, from simple console applications to web forms (ASP.NET applications) and Windows forms-based applications. We learned about the main components of CLR and its purpose, discussed Microsoft's intermediate language, Just-In-Time compiler, assemblies, and global assembly cache, and provided an introduction to the common type system (CTS), which is the component of the CLR that specifies the types supported by the CLR.

Next, we started our discovery of the .NET Framework class library and learned about types, arrays, collections, and strings, as well as the classes and namespaces that allow us to use streams and perform I/O operations and network communications.

With this knowledge as our foundation, we moved deeper into the .NET Framework class library and discussed active server pages .NET (ASP.NET) and web forms – two technologies used to create web applications and web forms controls – and the ASP.NET server controls used to create the ASP.NET applications user interface.

Traditional Windows applications are now based on Windows forms and we covered this technology, Windows forms controls, and graphical functions and GDI+.

Next, we learned about ADO.NET – the data access component of the .NET Framework, which is a completely new data access architecture based on managed providers. We also learned about the data binding controls available in ASP.NET and Windows forms.

XML is the universal format for data on the web. We discussed XML support in the .NET Framework. We also learned about web services – reusable web components that can be invoked from any platform capable of communicating over the internet. Both XML and web services allow us to create a new class of applications.

I hope that you now have a clear picture of what Microsoft .NET is, of its main components, technologies, and capabilities, and that you have enough practical examples to start to create great applications for the Microsoft .NET platform. Happy programming!

Appendix: Selected .NET web resources

- www.microsoft.com/net

  Part of Microsoft's site dedicated to .NET.

- msdn.microsoft.com/net

  Part of Microsoft's developers' network site dedicated to .NET.

- msdn.microsoft.com/vstudio/nextgen/default.asp

  Part of Microsoft's developers' network site dedicated to Visual Studio.NET.

- www.gotdotnet.com

  The Microsoft .NET Framework team's own developer community website.

- www.asp.net

  The Microsoft .NET Framework team's own site dedicated entirely to ASP.NET technology.

- www.aspnextgen.com/MobileQuickStart

  The .NET mobile web SDK QuickStart is a series of samples and supporting commentary designed to quickly acquaint you with the .NET mobile web SDK.

- www.ibuyspy.com

  The IBuySpy ASP.NET sample application was built to show how you can use the new Microsoft .NET Framework and ASP.NET development framework to build a fully featured e-commerce application.

- www.aspnextgen.com

  ASP.NET tutorials, labs, and general news about ASP.NET technologies.

- www.andymcm.com/dotnetfaq.htm

  This FAQ tries to answer some commonly asked questions about the fundamentals of the .NET Framework – the nuts and bolts of how the .NET Framework works at a low level. Topics include assemblies, garbage collection, security, interoperability with COM, and remoting.

- www.dotnetwire.com

  The prime source for Microsoft .NET news.

- www.123aspx.com

  The largest single ASP.NET directory. There are currently over 400 links to related ASP.NET sites grouped into sections such as applications and tools, references and white papers, tutorials, examples, and many, many more.

- www.4guysfromrolla.com

  ASP.NET tutorials, articles, and general news about ASP.NET technologies.

- www.aspfree.com

  Free ASP live demos, source code, and more.

Index